Death and Dying, Life and Living

Death and Dying, Life and Living

Fourth Edition

Charles A. Corr
Southern Illinois University
Edwardsville

Clyde M. Nabe
Southern Illinois University
Edwardsville

Donna M. Corr
St. Louis Community College
at Forest Park

Australia • Canada • Mexico • Singapore • Spain
United Kingdom • United States

Sponsoring Editor: *Vicki Knight*
Assistant Editor: *Dan Moneypenny*
Marketing Manager: *Lori Grebe*
Marketing Assistant: *Laurel Anderson*
Project Manager, Editorial Production: *Janet Hill*
Print/Media Buyer: *Vena Dyer*
Permissions Editor: *Sue Ewing*

Printed in the United States of America

1 2 3 4 5 6 7 06 05 04 03 02

For more information about our products, contact us at:
Thomson Learning Academic Resource Center
1-800-423-0563
For permission to use material from this text, contact us by: **Phone:** 1-800-730-2214
Fax: 1-800-730-2215
Web: http://www.thomsonrights.com

Library of Congress Control Number: 2002105824

ISBN 0-534-558194

Production Service: *Helen Walden*
Photo Editor: *Sue Howard*
Text Designer: *Cloyce Wall*
Cover Designer: *Roger Knox*
Cover Photo: *Garry Black/Masterfile*
Compositor: *Parkwood Composition*
Cover and Interior Printer: *Phoenix Color Corp. (BTP)*

Wadsworth/Thomson Learning
10 Davis Drive
Belmont, CA 94002-3098
USA

Asia
Thomson Learning
5 Shenton Way #01-01
UIC Building
Singapore 068808

Australia
Nelson Thomson Learning
102 Dodds Street
South Melbourne, Victoria 3205
Australia

Canada
Nelson Thomson Learning
1120 Birchmount Road
Toronto, Ontario M1K 5G4
Canada

Europe/Middle East/Africa
Thomson Learning
High Holborn House
50/51 Bedford Row
London WC1R 4LR
United Kingdom

Latin America
Thomson Learning
Seneca, 53
Colonia Polanco
11560 Mexico D.F.
Mexico

Spain
Paraninfo Thomson Learning
Calle/Magallanes, 25
28015 Madrid, Spain

We dedicate this fourth edition of *Death and Dying, Life and Living* to all victims of violence, especially those who were affected by the events of September 11, 2001

Death is no enemy of life; it restores our sense of the value of living. Illness restores the sense of proportion that is lost when we take life for granted. To learn about value and proportion, we need to honor illness, and ultimately to honor death.

A. W. Frank, *At the Will of the Body* (1991, p. 120)

How should one die?

We live in a world which dreads the question and which turns away from it. Earlier civilizations looked death straight in the face. . . . Never perhaps has our relationship with death been so poor as in these times of spiritual barrenness, where human beings, in their haste to exist, seem to sidestep the mystery. They do not realize that in so doing they rob the love of life of an essential source.

F. Mitterand, Preface, in M. de Hennezel, *La mort intime: Ceux qui vont mourir nous apprennent a vivre* (1995, p. 9)

About the Authors

Charles A. Corr, Ph.D., has taught courses on death and dying, children and death, and related subjects at Southern Illinois University Edwardsville since 1975. Since 1978, he has been a member of the Association for Death Education and Counseling (Board of Directors, 1980–1983) and the National Hospice and Palliative Care Organization. Dr. Corr is a long-time member and former chairperson (1989–1993) of the International Work Group on Death, Dying, and Bereavement. Currently, he is also a member of the Board of Directors of the Hospice Institute of the Florida Suncoast, a member of the Executive Committee of Children's International Project on Palliative/Hospice Services, and a member of the Executive Committee of the National Kidney Foundation's transAction Council. His publications include *Helping Children Cope with Death: Guidelines and Resources* (2nd ed., 1984); *Childhood and Death* (1984); *Adolescence and Death* (1986); *Handbook of Adolescent Death and Bereavement* (1996); five additional books co-edited with Donna Corr; and approximately 70 book chapters and articles in professional journals. Dr. Corr's work has been recognized by the Association for Death Education and Counseling (ADEC) in an award for Outstanding Personal Contributions to the Advancement of Knowledge in the Field of Death, Dying, and Bereavement (1988) and in its Death Educator Award (1996); by Children's Hospice International (CHI) in an award for Outstanding Contribution to the World of Hospice Support for Children (1989) and in the establishment of its Charles A. Corr Award for Lifetime Achievement (Literature) (1995); and by Southern Illinois University Edwardsville in Research Scholar (1990), Outstanding Scholar (1991), and Kimmel Community Services (1994) awards.

The Reverend Clyde M. Nabe, Ph.D., has taught courses on death and dying since 1976 at Southern Illinois University Edwardsville. He is an Episcopal priest and has been priest-in-charge in several missions and parishes. Dr. Nabe's research and publications have focused on issues in medical ethics, philosophy of religion, and comparative religion.

Donna M. Corr, R.N., M.S. in Nursing, has worked as a nurse with open heart, kidney transplant, oncology, and hospice patients. She was for 17 years a faculty member (rising from instructor to professor) in the Nursing Faculty of St. Louis Community College at Forest Park, St. Louis, Missouri, and then a Lecturer for two semesters at Southern Illinois University Edwardsville. Her publications include five books co-edited with Charles Corr: *Hospice Care: Principles and Practice* (1983); *Hospice Approaches to Pediatric Care* (1985); *Nursing Care in an Aging Society* (1990); *Sudden Infant Death Syndrome: Who Can Help and How* (1991); and *Handbook of Childhood Death and Bereavement* (1996). Books edited by Donna and/or Charles Corr have received five Book of the Year Awards from the *American Journal of Nursing.*

Brief Contents

Contents

Part Five DEVELOPMENTAL PERSPECTIVES 297

Preface

We offer the fourth edition of *Death and Dying, Life and Living* as a contribution to ongoing human conversations about death, dying, and bereavement. In his allegory, "The Horse on the Dining-Room Table" (our Prologue in this book), Richard Kalish wrote that we cannot magically make death disappear from our lives nor erase completely the sadness and other forms of distress associated with it. However, we can talk, share insights and attitudes, learn from each other, and strive together to cope more effectively with dying, death, and bereavement. Constructive interactions like these help us lead more productive lives in the face of death.

In the interval since the third edition of this book was published, new encounters with death have occurred, new issues have come to the fore, new insights and attitudes have emerged, and much that is of enduring value has evolved and matured. One of the most powerful of these new encounters took the form of the terrorist attacks on America that occurred on September 11, 2001. We have worked diligently to incorporate these and other death-related developments in this new edition.

Features

This book can be used as a primary textbook for undergraduate and graduate courses in death, dying, and bereavement; as a supplementary text in related courses; and as a general resource in this field. Individual instructors and other readers can easily adapt the contents of this book to their own needs and preferences. In particular, different parts of the book can be studied in any order, and most chapters within a specific section can be read on their own. Instructors can request a copy of the *Instructor's Manual with Test Bank* (ISBN 0534-57569-2) and/or computerized test bank (ExamView: ISBN 0534-57570-6) from their local sales representative, or by calling the Academic Resource Center at 1-800-423-0563. The *Instructor's Manual with Test Bank* provides suggestions on how to use this book, resources for courses (from organizations, printed materials, guest speakers, and audiovisuals), detailed guides for each individual chapter, and an extensive test bank.

Each of the seven parts in this book opens with a short introduction, and every chapter begins with an introductory paragraph and a representative vignette or case study. Each chapter closes with a brief summary, questions for review and discussion, a list of suggested readings, and a list of search terms for InfoTrac. (InfoTrac is available free from the publisher when bundled with this book; it provides access to the full texts of thousands of publications that enable the user to search for in-depth information on specific topics.) New or updated tables and figures, along with more than 100 pieces of artwork (photos, drawings, and other images) illustrate the content of this edition. In addition, two appendices identify and describe 164 books on death-related topics for children and adolescents, along with three sources for ongoing information about such publications.

The following features distinguish our work in this book:

1. An emphasis on *coping*—instead of merely reporting how individuals *react* to death-related encounters, we strive for an appreciation of the *efforts made to manage* those encounters and to integrate their implications into ongoing living.
2. The use of a *task-based approach* to explain coping by individuals and by communities with life-threatening illness and dying, with loss and grief, with funeral and memorial rituals, and as a bereaved child or adolescent.
3. Sensitivity to a *developmental perspective* which considers death-related issues in ways that emphasize experiences of individuals at different points in the human life course.
4. An emphasis on *cultural differences* within American society that recognizes distinctive modes of death-related encounters, attitudes, and practices typically found in Americans of Hispanic, African, Asian or Pacific Island, and Native American backgrounds.
5. A practical orientation that highlights *helping with death-related experiences*—helping others, helping oneself, and helping through families, social groups, institutions, and communities.
6. An appreciation of *moral, ethical, religious, and spiritual values* not only in debates about controversial issues like assisted suicide and euthanasia, but also throughout the book as undergirding for such topics as care of the dying, support for the bereaved, and helping children and adolescents.
7. Recognition of *important lessons about life and living*—lessons about limitation and control; individuality and community; vulnerability and resilience; and quality in living and the search for meaning—that can be learned from the study of death, dying, and bereavement.

New to This Edition

Four major changes stand out in the structure and content of this fourth edition. First, wherever appropriate we have made a special effort to incorporate references to *the September 11, 2001, attack on America*, along with some of their implications. Four examples of this are the new vignette in Chapter 4 that describes some of the events of September 11, the new section in the same Chapter that discusses how the death system in our society initially responded to those events, the new section in Chapter 9 on "Traumatic Loss and Death," and the revised vignette and subsequent discussions in Chapter 17 of those aspects of the September 11 events that relate to suicide.

Second, following a suggestion from reviewers we have included *a description of funeral practices in Chapter 4* as part of our larger discussion of death-related practices within the contemporary American death system.

Third, we have *shifted the focus of Chapter 11*. Previously, that chapter had been confined to funeral and other memorial practices. Now it examines more broadly *community support and assistance* in helping persons who are coping with loss and grief.

Fourth, we have *almost entirely rewritten Chapter 20, "HIV Infection and AIDS,"* in order to stay current with important changes involving this disease, while also making the text more readable and relevant for readers.

Beyond these four changes, in Part Two we have made more explicit our three-part approach to analyzing death-related *experiences* through analyses of *encounters* with death (in Chapter 2), *attitudes* toward death (in Chapter 3), and *practices* associated with death (in Chapter 4). This three-part strategy is reinforced in Chapter 5 where we describe cultural differences in the death-related encounters, attitudes, and practices of four broad cultural groups within American society.

The three chapters in Part Three are now even more closely parallel in their structure than they were previously to the three chapters in Part Four (and thus their titles have been revised, where necessary). In each case,

- *The first of these three chapters addresses issues involved in coping*—with dying in Chapter 6, with loss and grief in Chapter 9.
- *The second of these chapters explores what individuals can do to help persons who are coping*—helping in coping with dying in Chapter 7 and helping in coping with loss and grief in Chapter 10.
- *The third of these chapters discusses what communities have done or can do to help persons who are coping*—with life-threatening illnesses and dying in Chapter 8 and with loss and grief in Chapter 11.

Among many other distinctive features in this fourth edition of *Death and Dying, Life and Living,* there are 12 new or revised vignettes, 35 new or significantly revised boxes, 25 new tables or tables with new data, 7 new or revised figures, nearly 300 new references, 40 new photographs and images, and 14 new or substantially revised sections in the text. We have also again worked diligently to simplify and clarify the text of this fourth edition, to make its tone even more personal, and to update its factual base.

Throughout this fourth edition, we report the most recent statistical data currently available from the National Center for Health Statistics. That includes 1999 data on: numbers of deaths, death rates, and causes of death for the population as a whole in Chapter 2; for four selected cultural groups in Chapter 5; and for children, adolescents, adults, and the elderly in Chapters 12–15. We also provide new data on: average life expectancy and location of death in Chapter 2; accidental deaths and homicide in Chapter 4; hospitals, long-term care facilities, home health care programs, and hospice programs in Chapter 8; organ donation and transplantation in Chapter 16; overall patterns in suicide (Chapter 17), suicide and homicide among adolescents (Chapter 13), and suicide among the elderly (Chapter 15); assisted suicide in Oregon in Chapter 18; and HIV/AIDS in Chapter 20. New data from the 2000 census have led us to reorganize Chapter 5 to reflect the fact that Hispanic Americans are now the largest minority group in our society and enable us to describe projected growth between 2000 and 2050 among Americans who are 100 years of age or older in Chapter 15.

In addition, we present new or substantially revised sections in this edition on: what readers might learn about life and living from the study of death, dying, and bereavement (Chapter 1); ways in which the American death system initially responded to the events of September 11, 2001 (Chapter 4); accidents, homicide, war, and genocide (Chapter 4); similarities and differences between hospice care and palliative care (Chapter 8); traumatic loss and death (Chapter 9); pet loss (Chapter 10); aftercare programs in the funeral industry (Chapter 11); SIDS deaths in our society and their reduction by more than half from 1988 through 1999 (Chapter 12); organ donation and transplantation (Chapter 16); recent legislative changes in U.S. estate taxes (also Chapter 16); recent changes in euthanasia legislation and practices in the Netherlands, together with developments during the first four years in which assisted suicide has been legal in Oregon (Chapter 18); and near-death experiences (Chapter 19).

One important feature of our distinctive effort to devote four full chapters to developmental perspectives on death, dying, and bereavement involves the identification and description of literature on these topics for young readers. Accordingly, we revised Box 12.4 to identify 60 selected books on death-related topics for children. Annotated descriptions and complete bibliographical information for these and 45 other titles—many new to this edition—are provided in

Appendix A. Similarly, Box 13.5 now identifies 36 books on death-related topics for adolescents, with annotated descriptions and complete bibliographical information for these and 23 other titles in Appendix B. We believe these two boxes and their related appendices are the most thorough and helpful sources of information about death-related literature for young readers available from any textbook in our field. Finally, we also rewrote and restructured Box 12.5 to identify 9 useful books to help adults talk about death with children. Here and in Box 13.5 we provide information about three sources from which additional book-related information in our field can be obtained and from which many of the titles we mention can be purchased.

Acknowledgments

We are grateful to all who have shared their personal and/or professional life experiences with us and who have helped us learn many of the important lessons about death, dying, and bereavement that we seek to share in this fourth edition. We especially want to thank all who helped in the preparation of this fourth edition. Louise Cleary, Dan Lanneau, and Cathy Lasky of Hospice of the Florida Suncoast were extraordinarily generous in helping us with photographs. LeAnn Isaly of the Pinellas Care Center, Patricia Sawyer of AIDS Service Association of Pinellas, Inc., Joseph Lennox-Smith of Positive Education, Inc., and Kathy Robinson and her colleagues at Friends-Together, Inc., shared their expertise on matters involving HIV and AIDS. Kate Tallent explained to us the work of the Doorways program in St. Louis. Our thanks also go to many others who are credited in the text for the boxes, photos, and images that they helped us to obtain and that are such important features of this book.

We are indebted to all of the reviewers who worked on the previous editions of this book: David Balk, now of Oklahoma State University; Kenneth Curl, University of Central Oklahoma; Kenneth Doka, The College of New Rochelle; Nancy Falvo, Clarion University of Pennsylvania; Mal Goldsmith, Southern Illinois University Edwardsville; Nancy Goodloe, Baylor University; Elizabeth Kennedy Hart, University of Akron; Joseph Heller, California State University, Sacramento; Clayton Hewitt, Middlesex Community Technical College; Dean Holt, Pennsylvania State University; Patricia LaFollette, Florida State University; Daniel Leviton, University of Maryland; Jean G. Lewis, Austin Peay State University; Martha Loustaunau, New Mexico State University; Sarah O'Dowd, Community College of Rhode Island; Thomas Paxson, Southern Illinois University Edwardsville; Velma Pomrenke, University of Akron; Constance Pratt, Rhode Island College; James Rothenburger, University of Minnesota; Rita Santanello, Belleville Area College; Raymond L. Schmitt, Illinois State University; Dorothy Smith, State University of New York, Plattsburgh; James Thorson, University of Nebraska, Omaha; Mirrless Underwood, Greenfield Community College; and Robert Wrenn, University of Arizona.

We owe a particular debt of gratitude to those who took part in the review processes for this edition (although their names were unknown to us until our work on this project was nearly completed): Bryan Bolea, Grand Valley State University; Sandra Brackenridge, Idaho State University; Brookes Cowan, University of Vermont; Bert Hayslip, University of North Texas; Elizabeth Kennedy Hart, University of Akron; Susan Lamanna, Onondaga Community College; Debra Mattison, University of Michigan; Jude Molnar, Fairmont State College; Randy Russac, University of North Florida; James Thorson, University of Nebraska, Omaha; J. B. Watson, Stephen F. Austin State University; and Richard Yinger of Palm Beach

Community College. It is extremely helpful to receive insightful and constructive comments from so many experienced instructors who teach courses in this field in a variety of institutions across the United States and who were willing to share their ideas to help make this book stronger.

At our publisher, we have received consistently valuable help and guidance from Vicki Knight, Janet Hill, Sue Ewing, Bob Western, and Jennifer Wilkinson. Helen Walden combined unusual efficiency and cooperation as our production service manager.

Although we have worked hard to provide accurate, up-to-date knowledge about death, dying, and bereavement, neither we nor anyone else could claim to have covered every aspect of this extraordinarily broad field of study. For that reason, we encourage readers to pursue additional opportunities that are available to them for further study and research on these subjects. We welcome comments and suggestions for improvements that we might make in this book, because we know that imperfections are inevitable in as large and sweeping an enterprise as this project and in a field that often changes rapidly and has many ramifications. Such comments or suggestions—along with outlines or syllabi of courses in which this book has been used, as well as references and other supplementary materials—can be sent to us by e-mail at charlescorr@mindspring.com or nabec@earthlink.net.

Charles A. Corr
Clyde M. Nabe
Donna M. Corr

Prologue

The Horse on the Dining-Room Table

by Richard A. Kalish

I STRUGGLED UP THE SLOPE OF MOUNT Evmandu to meet the famous guru of Nepsim, an ancient sage whose name I was forbidden to place in print. I was much younger then, but the long and arduous hike exhausted me, and, despite the cold, I was perspiring heavily when I reached the plateau where he made his home. He viewed me with a patient, almost amused, look, and I smiled wanly at him between attempts to gulp the thin air into my lungs. I made my way across the remaining hundred meters and slowly sat down on the ground—propping myself up against a large rock just outside his abode. We were both silent for several minutes, and I felt the tension in me rise, then subside until I was calm. Perspiration prickled my skin, but the slight breeze was pleasantly cool, and soon I was relaxed. Finally I turned my head to look directly into the clear brown eyes, which were bright within his lined face. I realized that I would need to speak.

"Father," I said, "I need to understand something about what it means to die, before I can continue my studies." He continued to gaze at me with his open, bemused expression. "Father," I went on, "I want to know what a dying person feels when no one will speak with him, nor be open enough to permit him to speak, about his dying."

He was silent for three, perhaps four, minutes. I felt at peace because I knew he would answer. Finally, as though in the middle of a sentence, he said, "It is the horse on the dining-room table." We continued to gaze at each other for several minutes. I began to feel sleepy after my long journey, and I must have dozed off. When I woke up, he was gone, and the only activity was my own breathing.

I retraced my steps down the mountain—still feeling calm, knowing that his answer made me feel good, but not knowing why. I returned to my studies and gave no further thought to the event, not wishing to dwell upon it, yet secure that someday I should understand.

Many years later I was invited to the home of a casual friend for dinner. It was a modest house in a typical California development. The eight or ten other guests, people I did not know well, and I sat in the living room—drinking Safeway Scotch and bourbon and dipping celery sticks and raw cauliflower into a watery cheese dip. The conversation, initially halting, became more animated as we got to know each other and developed points of contact. The drinks undoubtedly also affected us.

Eventually the hostess appeared and invited us into the dining room for a buffet dinner. As I entered the room, I noticed with astonishment that a brown horse was sitting quietly on the dining-room table. Although it was small for a horse, it filled much of the large table. I caught my breath, but didn't say anything. I was the first one to enter, so I was able to turn to watch the other guests. They responded much as I did—they entered, saw the horse, gasped or stared, but said nothing.

The host was the last to enter. He let out a silent shriek—looking rapidly from the horse to each of his guests with a wild stare. His mouth formed soundless words. Then in a voice choked with confusion he invited us to fill our plates from the buffet. His wife, equally disconcerted by what was clearly an unexpected horse, pointed to the name cards, which indicated where each of us was to sit.

The hostess led me to the buffet and handed me a plate. Others lined up behind me—each of us quiet. I filled my plate with rice and chicken and sat in my place. The others followed suit.

It was cramped, sitting there, trying to avoid getting too close to the horse, while pretending that no horse was there. My dish overlapped the edge of the table. Others found other ways to avoid physical contact with the horse. The host and hostess seemed as ill at ease as the rest of us. The conversation lagged. Every once in a while, someone would say something in an attempt to revive the earlier pleasant and innocuous discussion, but the overwhelming presence of the horse so filled our thoughts that talk of taxes or politics or the lack of rain seemed inconsequential.

Dinner ended, and the hostess brought coffee. I can recall everything on my plate and yet have no memory of having eaten. We drank in silence—all of us trying not to look at the horse, yet unable to keep our eyes or thoughts anywhere else.

I thought several times of saying, "Hey, there's a horse on the dining-room table." But I hardly knew the host, and I didn't wish to embarrass him by mentioning something that obviously discomforted him at least as much as it discomforted me. After all, it was his house. And what do you say to a man with a horse on his dining-room table? I could have said that I did not mind, but that was not true—its presence upset me so much that I enjoyed neither the dinner nor the company. I could have said that I knew how difficult it was to have a horse on one's dining-room table, but that wasn't true either; I had no idea. I could have said something like, "How do you feel about having a horse on your dining-room table?", but I didn't want to sound like a psychologist. Perhaps, I thought, if I ignore it, it will go away. Of course I knew that it wouldn't. It didn't.

I later learned that the host and hostess were hoping the dinner would be a success in spite of the horse. They felt that to mention it would make us so uncomfortable that we wouldn't enjoy our visit—of course we didn't enjoy the evening anyway. They were fearful that we would try to offer them sympathy, which they didn't want, or understanding, which they needed but could not accept. They wanted the party to be a success, so they decided to try to make the evening as enjoyable as possible. But it was apparent that they—like their guests—could think of little else than the horse.

I excused myself shortly after dinner and went home. The evening had been terrible. I never wanted to see the host and hostess again, although I was eager to seek out the other guests and learn what they felt about the occasion. I felt confused about what had happened and extremely tense. The evening had been grotesque. I was careful to avoid the host and hostess after that, and I did my best to stay away altogether from the neighborhood.

Recently I visited Nepsim again. I decided to seek out the guru once more. He was still alive, although nearing death, and he would speak only to a few. I repeated my journey and eventually found myself sitting across from him.

Once again I asked, "Father, I want to know what a dying person feels when no one will speak with him, nor be open enough to permit him to speak, about his dying."

The old man was quiet, and we sat without speaking for nearly an hour. Since he did not bid me leave, I remained. Although I was content, I feared he would not share his wisdom, but he finally spoke. The words came slowly.

"My son, it is the horse on the dining-room table. It is a horse that visits every house and sits on every dining-room table—the tables of the rich and of the poor, of the simple and of the wise. This horse just sits there, but its presence makes you wish to leave without speaking of it. If you leave, you will always fear the presence of the horse. When it sits on your table, you will wish to speak of it, but you may not be able to.

"However, if you speak about the horse, then you will find that others can also speak about the horse—most others, at least, if you are gentle and kind as you speak. The horse will remain on the dining-room table, but you will not be so distraught. You will enjoy your repast, and you will enjoy the company of the host and hostess. Or, if it is your table, you will enjoy the presence of your guests. You cannot make magic to have the horse disappear, but you can speak of the horse and thereby render it less powerful."

The old man then rose and, motioning me to follow, walked slowly to his hut. "Now we shall eat," he said quietly. I entered the hut and had difficulty adjusting to the dark. The guru walked to a cupboard in the corner and took out some bread and some cheese, which he placed on a mat. He motioned to me to sit and share his food. I saw a small horse sitting quietly in the center of the mat. He noticed this and said, "That horse need not disturb us." I thoroughly enjoyed the meal. Our discussion lasted far into the night, while the horse sat there quietly throughout our time together. ■

Part One

Learning about Death, Dying, and Bereavement

LIFE AND DEATH ARE TWO ASPECTS OF THE same reality. To see this fact represented in graphic form, look at the image on page 2 of this book. You can decipher its meaning by rotating the image one quarter turn clockwise and then one quarter turn counterclockwise. Clearly, one could not properly understand one aspect of this image ("life") without also grasping something about its second aspect ("death"). Similarly, we believe that learning about death, dying, and bereavement is an important way of learning about life and living, and the reverse is equally true. Just as every human being is inevitably involved in learning about life and living, we suggest that each person is also engaged in a process of learning about death, dying, and bereavement. In this book, we pursue that process in a deliberate and explicit way.

Our Prologue, Richard Kalish's allegory, "The Horse on the Dining-Room Table," teaches us that it is desirable to talk about death together, to share insights and attitudes, to try to learn from each other, and to strive to cope more effectively in the face of death. But how do we begin?

One good place to start is with some preliminary remarks about education in the field of death, dying, and bereavement. Thus, in Chapter 1 we examine the nature and role of this type of education, its development in recent years, its principal dimensions, and its central goals. These introductory remarks are a kind of warmup for the main event, which follows in the remainder of this book. Some readers might prefer to bypass this warmup by jumping directly to the central work of this book and returning later to Chapter 1. Others will benefit from some preparatory comments about certain aspects of the project ahead. ■

Chapter One

EDUCATION ABOUT DEATH, DYING, AND BEREAVEMENT

IN THIS CHAPTER, WE EXPLORE THE NATURE and role of education about death, dying, and bereavement. Sometimes called *death education*, this really is education about life and living as seen from a death-related perspective. We begin our exploration with the experiences of a college student who is examining death-related literature for children in a course on death and dying. Then we look at the emergence of death education in the last half of the 20th century. We also consider some concerns that might have led you or someone like you to read this book or to become interested in this type of education. Next, we examine how this kind of

Death and life: two dimensions of the same reality. To interpret the drawing, rotate the image one quarter turn clockwise, then one quarter counterclockwise.

education might be conducted, which leads us to a discussion of four main dimensions of death education and some of its principal goals. We conclude this chapter by asking what we can learn about life and living by studying death, dying, and bereavement. ■

A College Class on Death and Dying, and Death-Related Literature for Young Children

At first, Ellen Johns' friends began to tease her when they learned that she was reading children's books for a college class. But they stopped their teasing and didn't seem to have much more to say when she challenged them by asking: "Exactly how would you explain death to a 7-year-old child? And how would you help a child cope with a family death or a death among his or her friends?"

Ellen was an education major in college who had seized the chance to take an elective course on death and dying. At first, she had only been thinking about getting some practical help about what she should say or do if she ever had a bereaved child in one of her classes. But as she thought further about it, she realized that some of her special education students might themselves be in precarious health or even be seriously hurt in an accident. And then there were those shootings and other violent events taking place in some schools that the media had reported recently.

So Ellen was glad when her college course gave her a chance to read some books about death-related topics that had been written for young children. She was surprised that there were so many of these books (see Box 12.3). Ellen especially liked the simplest stories, like *The Dead Bird* (M. W. Brown, 1958) in which some children find a dead bird while they are playing, touch its cold, stiff body, and bury it in their own little ceremony. Ellen also found several books about the death of a grandparent or a pet. Two books—*Dusty Was My Friend* (Clardy, 1984) and *I Had a Friend Named Peter* (Cohn, 1987)—told about children whose friends were killed in automobile accidents. *Rudi's Pond* (Bunting, 1999) described an elementary school class in which the children wrote poems and constructed a memorial for a classmate who died from a congenital heart condition. *We Remember Philip* (N. Simon, 1979) even explained how some young students in his class helped their teacher mourn the death of his adult son who had died in a mountain climbing accident and commemorate his life.

Ellen was glad there were resources like these to which she and others could turn when she encountered loss and death in one of her classrooms. Doing this project also helped her think about what her professor called "death education." As she did so, Ellen was impressed by the many ways in which educators could work cooperatively with parents, religious leaders, and others to prepare children for sad situations or to help them when they had to cope with any type of loss and grief.

The Emergence of Death Education

During the 1960s and early 1970s, people often said that death was a *taboo* topic in American society, a subject that was somehow not acceptable for scholarly research and education (for example, Feifel, 1963). Research and writing on death, dying, and bereavement were quite limited. In effect, a fundamental and defining aspect of human life had largely been removed from sustained investigation and critical study. It was as if death needed to be quarantined in order not to infect the way in which people wished to think about and live out their lives.

A reaction to prohibitions like this was almost inevitable. New initiatives by modern pioneers like Herman Feifel (1959), Elisabeth Kübler-Ross (1969, 1997), and Cicely Saunders (DuBoulay, 1984) encouraged behavioral scientists, clinicians, and humanists to turn their attention to these topics. Thoughtful people began to study death-related behavior, develop new programs of care for the dying and the bereaved, and conduct research on attitudes toward death. This was the beginning of the development of what has been called *thanatology* (from *thanatos*, the Greek word for "death," + "*-ology*" = a science or organized body of knowledge).

These beginnings were soon followed by a desire to share the results of the new "death awareness" movement (Pine, 1977, 1986). This desire expressed itself in a wide range of articles, books, and literature of all sorts (many of which are cited and reflected in this book), in the establishment of organizations and journals in this field, and eventually in countless programs of different types of what we have called death education. This new movement recognized that

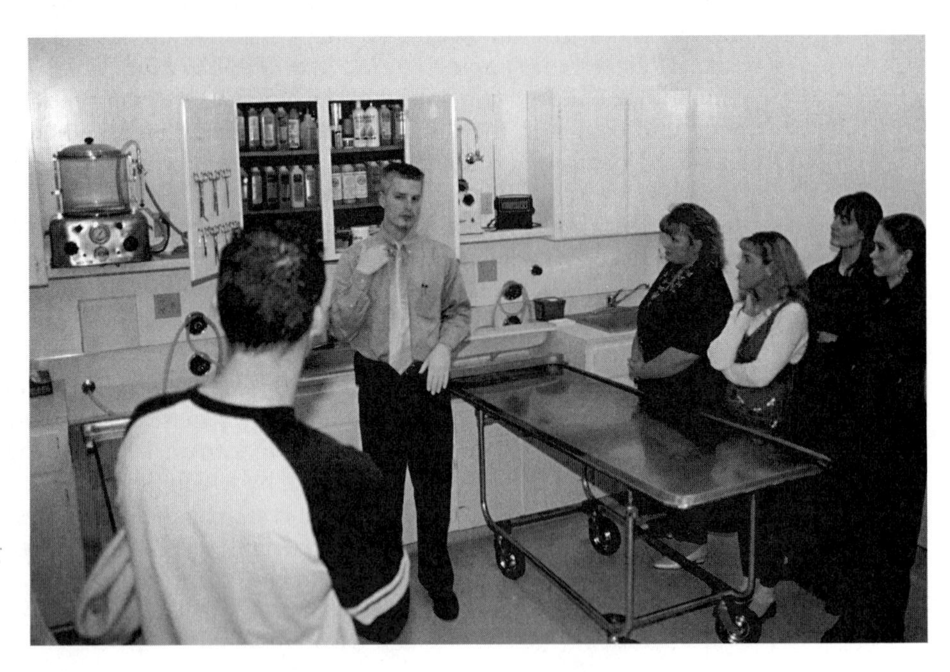

High school students learn about embalming during a visit to a funeral home.

throughout human life everyone receives messages about death, dying, and bereavement in a variety of informal and formal ways. The critical issue is the validity and value of those messages.

For example, Bertman (1974) once asked: "Whatever really happened to 'Little Red Riding Hood'?" In Box 1.1 we provide three different examples of how publishers have answered that question. Do you recognize any of them?

The first example is the original ending by the author, Charles Perrault (1628–1703). In this version, at the conclusion of the story the wolf *eats* Little Red Riding Hood (as he had previously eaten her grandmother). Do you remember the story ending that way when you first read it? Or perhaps you recall the woodsman in the second example who intervened with his ax (low technology) *after* the wolf had gobbled up Little Red Riding Hood? Or maybe you remember how a hunter came on the scene with his gun (high technology) in the third example *before* the wolf could eat our heroine?

These different endings teach different lessons to young readers about what can happen when a child does not listen to his or her parents. In the first example, Little Red Riding Hood is eaten by the wolf (she dies); in the second example, Little Red Riding Hood is swallowed up but then brought back to life (at the expense of the wolf's life); in the third example, Little Red Riding Hood is in grave peril but is saved from death (while the wolf dies). Why do you think some publishers changed the ending of this well-known tale?

Why Did You Become Involved in Death Education?

We might ask why people come to read a book like this one, why they enroll in a course on death and dying, or why an instructor happens to teach such a course (Kalish, 1989). For example, did you enter into this study for reasons like those of Ellen Johns in the vignette near the beginning of this chapter? Did you come to this field *because of the work you are doing*, perhaps as a teacher, a nurse, or a counselor? Or was it *because you are preparing to enter some profession or vocation in which you may be asked to help people who are coping with death, dying, or bereavement* like medicine, social work, the ministry, or volunteer service through a hospice organization?

For example, when nurses enroll in educational offerings in this field they may be recognizing or remembering times when they might find themselves alone in the middle of the night with a dying person or a grieving family. Such nurses are striving to prepare themselves to respond more effectively to the persons who turn to them for assistance. Many nurses also realize that death education applies not only to their clients but to themselves as well. As Shneidman (1978) once noted, death-related interactions are unique in that the problems being faced by the client are always problems that have been or will at some point also be faced by the helper. As a result, death education always has implications for both vocational and personal concerns.

Box 1.1 What Really Happened to Little Red Riding Hood?

Example 1:

The Wolf, seeing her come in, said to her, hiding himself under the bedclothes:

"Put the custard and the little pot of butter upon the stool, and come and lie down with me."

Little Red Riding-Hood undressed herself and went into bed, where, being greatly amazed to see how her grandmother looked in her night-clothes, she said to her:

"Grandmamma, what great arms you have got!"

"That is the better to hug thee, my dear."...

"Grandmamma, what great teeth you have got!"

"That is to eat thee up."

And, saying these words, this wicked wolf fell upon Little Red Riding-Hood, and ate her up.

SOURCE: From Lang, 1904, p. 66.

Example 2:

"The better to EAT you with," said the wolf. And he sprang from the bed and ate Little Red Riding Hood up.

A passing woodsman stepped into the house to see how Little Red Riding Hood's grandmother was feeling. And when he saw the wolf, he said, "Ah ha! I've found you at last, you wicked old rascal!" He lifted his ax, and with one blow, killed him. Then he cut the wolf open and out stepped Little Red Riding Hood and her grandmother.

They thanked the woodsman for what he had done. Then all three sat down and ate the cake and the butter and drank of the grape juice which Little Red Riding Hood had brought.

SOURCE: From Jones, 1948.

Example 3:

"THE BETTER TO EAT YOU WITH, MY DEAR," cried the wolf. He pushed back the covers, and jumped out of the bed. Then Little Red Riding Hood saw that it was the big wolf pretending to be her grandmother!

At that moment a hunter passed the house. He heard the wolf's wicked voice and Little Red Riding Hood's frightened scream. He burst open the door. Before the wolf could reach Little Red Riding Hood, the hunter lifted his gun to his shoulder, and killed the wicked wolf. Little Red Riding Hood was very happy and she thanked the kind hunter.

Grandmother unlocked the door and came out of the closet, where she had been hiding. She kissed Little Red Riding Hood again and again. And she thanked the hunter for saving them both from the big wolf. They were all so happy that they decided to have a party right then and there. Grandmother gave the hunter and Little Red Riding Hood a big glass of fresh milk, and took one herself. They ate up all the cake and fruit that Little Red Riding Hood had brought to her grandmother. And they all lived happily ever after.

SOURCE: From Anonymous, 1957.

Perhaps you came to the study of death education because your personal concerns were more direct or more pressing. Are you *dealing with the aftermath of an unresolved death-related experience in your own life?* Or are you *struggling to cope with a current death-related experience in your life?* Many people who have experienced the death of a loved one in the past or whose close relative or friend is presently striving to meet the challenges of a terminal illness turn to this type of education. Sometimes a student in a class is himself or herself living with a life-threatening condition. These people may want to use the information and other resources that death education provides in order to help them cope with their own experiences. If this is true for you, your feelings may be tender and you may be vulnerable to added pain. For this reason, death education needs to develop a special sensitivity to and compassion for its participants, to make a special effort to care for those who engage in this study (Attig, 1981).

Of course, education is different from counseling and a classroom is not really an appropriate place in which to expect to receive individual therapy. Certainly, educators in this field must be alert to individuals who are unable to cope with difficult personal experiences by themselves. For such people, education alone may not be sufficient to address their needs. If you are in this situation, it may be appropriate to seek a referral for personal counseling or therapy. Also, if you have recently experienced a major loss in your life and do not find comfort in a dispassionate, educational approach to death-related topics, you might choose to postpone enrolling in a course on death and dying until some later time. The point here is that the classroom environment may not meet all needs at all times.

Perhaps you are simply *curious about some subject or issue in the field of death, dying, and bereavement.* People become curious about this field as a result of publicity about social phenomena such as death reports in the media, stories about homicide committed by juveniles, or debates about physician-assisted suicide. Curiosity of this type may also be combined with *a desire to prepare for personal experiences that might arise in the future.* For example, some students have said to us: "No important person in my life has yet died. But my grandparents are getting pretty old." These are proactive individuals who are aware that life is fragile, who are not content simply to wait until events demand some response under pressure, and who prefer to seize the initiative ahead of time in order to prepare themselves (as much as possible) to cope with the death of loved ones and friends. Individuals such as this are sufficiently astute to realize that no human life is ever completely "death free."

What Is Death Education Like?

How Is Death Education Conducted?

Death education may be conducted in a formal or informal way, or it may arise from "teachable moments." *Formal or planned death education* is usually associated with programs of organized instruction of the kind that are found in schools,

A grandmother and her grandson discuss death and loss during a visit to a cemetery.

colleges, professional workshops, and volunteer training programs. One of the main goals of this book is to support programs of formal death education.

Informal or unplanned death education is more typical and more widespread, although it may not always be recognized for what it is. Most human beings first learn about loss, sadness, and coping in the arms of a parent or guardian and through interactions within a family or similar social group. They go on to learn other lessons about death, dying, and bereavement from their own experiences, from the people whom they meet throughout their lives, and from the events in which they take part. Travel, the media, and many other sources contribute raw materials and insights to a lifelong process of informal death education that may take place almost without one's notice. For many Americans, witnessing the horrific events of September 11, 2001, when terrorist attacks caused large-scale death and destruction, drove home unexpected lessons and stimulated new discussions of death, dying, and bereavement.

In particular, opportunities for informal death education emerge naturally from *teachable moments.* These are the unanticipated events in life that offer important occasions for developing useful educational insights and lessons, as well as for personal growth. For example, when Ellen Johns read the children's literature described in the vignette near the beginning of this chapter, she realized that these books and others like them (see Box 12.4) were describing many different situations in which children might encounter loss or death in one form or another. A natural disaster, an act of violence, barely avoiding an auto accident, the death of a pet, or the funeral of a loved one are only a few of the many instances in which teachable moments thrust themselves into the middle of life and offer important opportunities for informal death education for both children and adults.

Dimensions of Death Education

Our experiences in teaching courses on death and dying have led us to recognize four central *dimensions* of death education. These dimensions relate to what people know, how they feel, how they behave, and what they value (Corr, 1995c). They are the cognitive, affective, behavioral, and valuational dimensions of death education—distinguishable but interrelated aspects of this educational process.

Death education is most obviously a *cognitive* or intellectual enterprise because it provides factual information about death-related experiences and tries to help us understand or interpret those events. For example, we all know that how we live can put us at risk for death. But we may not realize that *nearly half of all deaths in the United States arise from or are associated with our behaviors*, such as the following: whether or not we use tobacco (cigarettes, cigars, or smokeless chewing tobacco); our diet and activity patterns; and how (if at all) we use alcohol, firearms, illegal drugs, and motor vehicles (Kessler, 2001; McGinnis & Foege, 1993).

In addition to providing information, the cognitive dimension of death education can also suggest new ways of organizing or interpreting the data of human experience. A good example of this kind of cognitive reorganization took place during the early 1980s, when some physicians recognized that they were diagnosing a relatively rare form of skin cancer (Kaposi's sarcoma, which had hitherto been confined largely to a specific group of elderly males) in an unusually high number of young adult men. This realization helped identify a new disease and cause of death, acquired immunodeficiency syndrome (AIDS) and human immunodeficiency virus (HIV) (see Chapter 20).

The *affective* dimension of death education has to do with feelings, emotions, and attitudes about death, dying, and bereavement. For example, a wide range of feelings are involved in experiences of loss and bereavement. Consequently, it is appropriate for education in this area to try to sensitize those who are not bereaved to the depth, intensity, duration, and complexities of grief following a death. Much of this awareness has not been communicated effectively to the public at large. As a result, many people still seem to think—wrongly—that a few days or weeks may be more than adequate to "forget" or "get over" the death of an important person in one's life. In fact, mourning a significant death in one's life is far more like an ongoing process of learning to live with one's loss than it is like solving a problem once and for all (see Chapter 9). Sharing and discussing grief responses is an important part of the affective dimension of education in the field of death, dying, and bereavement.

In another aspect of its affective dimension, death education seeks to appreciate the feelings of those who have not yet encountered death in any personal form. For example, many bereaved persons have told us how it appears insensitive and arrogant to them when someone who is not bereaved says, "I know how you feel." How could that be true of someone who has not experienced their loss? To the bereaved, such statements (however well intentioned they may be) seem to diminish the uniqueness and poignancy of their loss.

Death education also has a *behavioral* dimension as it explores why people act as they do in death-related situations, which of their behaviors are helpful or unhelpful, and how they could or should act in such situations. For example, in contemporary American society, much behavior, both public and private, seeks to avoid contact with death, dying, and bereavement. Often, that is because people do not know what to say or what to do in such situations. They pull back from contact with the dying or the bereaved, leaving people alone in very stressful circumstances, without support or companionship at a time when sharing and solace may be most needed.

By contrast, the modern hospice movement has shown that much can be done to help those who are coping with dying (see Chapter 8). Similarly, research on funeral rituals and on support groups for the bereaved has shown ways in which individuals and society can assist those who are coping with bereavement (see Chapter 11). This behavioral education points out the great value that is found simply in the *presence* of a caring person (see Chapter 10). It advises potential helpers not so much to talk to grieving persons as to *listen* to them. It can help individuals develop skills in interacting with persons who are experiencing or who have experienced a significant loss. One basic behavioral lesson from death education is this: "Be comfortable with your discomfort" when you are in the presence of someone confronting a death-related challenge. It may be sufficient simply to be present, sit quietly, and do nothing else when that is really all that can be done.

The *valuational* dimension has to do with how death education can help to identify, articulate, and affirm the basic values that govern human lives. Life as we know it is inextricably bound up with death. We would not have *this life* if death were not one of its essential parts. Life and death, living and dying, attachments and loss, happiness and sadness—neither alternative in these and many other similar pairings stands alone in human experience. Death provides an essential (and inescapable) perspective from which humans can try to achieve an adequate understanding of their own lives (see Chapter 19).

Much of what we have already said directs attention to that which is valued: courage, endurance, resilience, concern for others, love, and community. But values often come sharply into focus when adults are asked what they will tell children about death and how they will respond to the moral problems of our time. Most grief experts recommend that death should not be hidden from children, that life should not be portrayed as an unending journey without shadows or tears (see Chapter 12). Hiding death from children, even if we really could do that, will not prepare them to cope effectively with future losses, a pervasive aspect of the human experience. Death education encourages adults to introduce children to the realities of life and death in ways that are appropriate to their developmental level and capacities, and with the support of mature values that will enable them to live wisely and cope with death constructively.

Reflecting on values is also closely related to many of the death-related challenges that confront us at the beginning of the 21st century: nuclear warfare and terrorism, epidemics and their prevention, famine and malnutrition, dislocation of populations, capital punishment, abortion, assisted suicide, euthanasia, and all of the quandaries posed by modern medicine and its complex technologies.

See Box 1.2 for a poignant example that addresses all four of the dimensions of death education.

Goals of Death Education

Education that is well planned always has in mind some general goals and specific objectives that it hopes to accomplish for and with those who are engaged in the activity. For example, college courses are commonly designed to encourage critical thinking in order to help individuals judge for themselves the value, meaning, and validity of subjects they address. Education about death, dying, and bereavement incorporates these broad aims and typically links them to more limited purposes (Corr, 1995c).

We were challenged to think about our own goals shortly after we first began teaching a course on death and dying. With no advance notice, we received the letter reproduced in Box 1.3 from a person who had not been in our course and whom we did not know. We appreciated Mrs. Koerner's kind words about our course, but we were also a bit perplexed: How should we evaluate her comments? Should we really take credit for teaching people how to die, as Mrs. Koerner seemed to think we were doing? That letter challenged us to say exactly what it is that we want to accomplish in our courses. As we return to this issue from time to time, we now think there are several basic goals in this type of education.

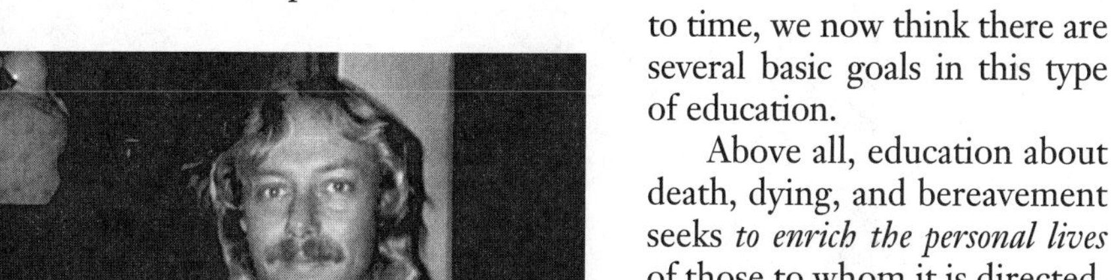

Bryan Lee Curtis and his son about one week before Bryan was diagnosed with an aggressive form of lung cancer at age 34.

Above all, education about death, dying, and bereavement seeks *to enrich the personal lives* of those to whom it is directed. In the end, as the ancient Greek philosopher Socrates is reported to have said, "the really important thing is not to live, but to live well" (Plato, *Crito*, 48b). Death education contributes to this goal by helping individuals to understand themselves more fully and to appreciate both their strengths and their limitations

Box 1.2 Bryan Lee Curtis

Bryan Lee Curtis wanted to inform people about the dangers of smoking cigarettes. But his goals went beyond merely providing information. He also wanted to bring about a change in attitudes toward smoking, an alteration in individual behaviors, and a reflection on personal values. To achieve these goals, Curtis asked a local newspaper to publish two photographs: the first, taken just before his 34th birthday, showed him with his two-year-old son when both were apparently in good health; the second, *taken just nine weeks later*, showed him less than three hours before his death, with his wife and son at his bedside (Landry, 1999a).

Curtis's death was caused by advanced lung cancer that had spread to his liver and that resulted from his 20-year habit of smoking. Curtis had begun smoking at age 13, eventually building up to a habit of more than two packs of cigarettes a day. His addiction was so strong that he was unable to quit smoking until just a week before his death when the ravages of his illness made it impossible for him to continue.

At first, the newspaper had been concerned that readers would respond negatively to these poignant pictures. In fact, readers were overwhelmingly positive in their comments; they understood very well the message that Curtis was trying to communicate. As a result, the story of Bryan Lee Curtis and his pictures appeared on Web sites around the world and were widely reprinted (DeGregory, 2000; Landry, 1999b; Noack, 1999). ■

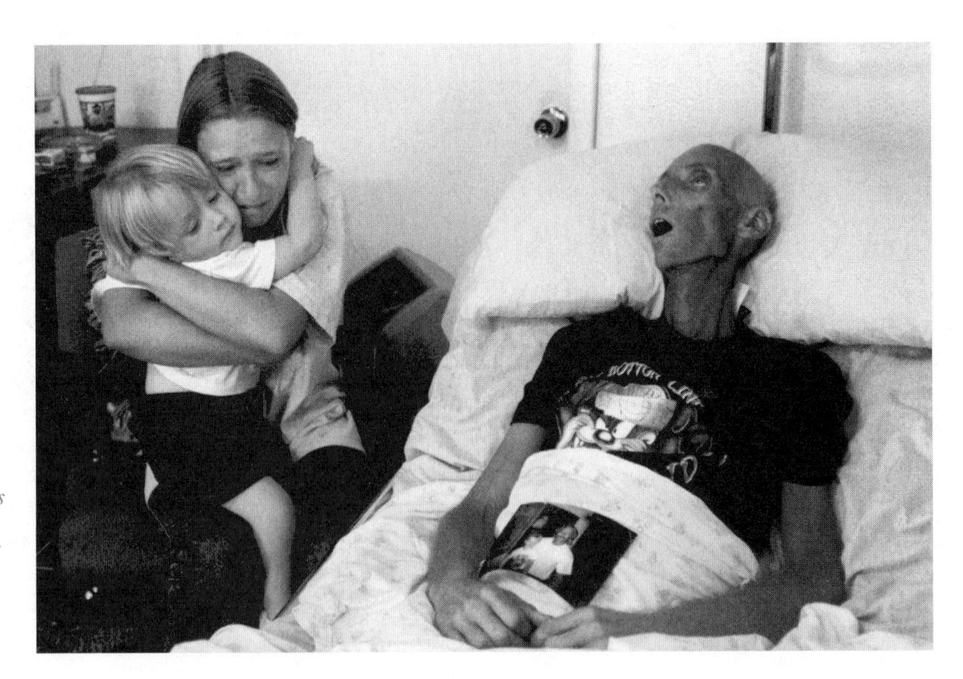

Bryan Lee Curtis and his wife and son on the day of his death about nine weeks after his diagnosis.

Box 1.3 A Letter to a Teacher in a Course on Death and Dying

October 16, 1975

Dear Dr. Corr,

Want to thank you for your course "Death and Dying."

Not having been in your classroom, you might wonder what prompts me to write this letter.

My mother was one of the most dedicated Christians we in our lives have ever known.

She became very ill and it took 54 days, in and out of an Intensive Care Unit, for her to die.

Doc and I spent as much time as humanly possible at her side.

One day she looked at me with her beautiful soft brown eyes and said, "Why didn't anyone teach me how to die? We are taught at our mother's knee how to live but not how to die."

Hope your course will help people through this experience because we will all have a turn unless the Rapture comes first.

God bless you,

Dr. and Mrs. S. Koerner ■

as finite human beings. A second goal of death education is *to inform and guide individuals in their personal transactions with society.* It does this by making them aware of services that are available to them and options that they might or might not select in such matters as end-of-life care or funeral practices and memorial rituals.

A third goal of death education is *to prepare individuals for their public roles as citizens.* It does this by clarifying important social issues that face society and its representatives, such as advance directives in health care, assisted suicide, euthanasia, and organ and tissue donation (see Chapters 16 and 18). A fourth goal of death education is *to support individuals in their professional and vocational roles.* Those whose work involves teaching young people about death, caring for the dying, or counseling the bereaved can benefit from the perspectives offered by a well-grounded death education.

A fifth goal of death education is *to enhance the ability of individuals to communicate effectively about death-related matters.* Effective communication is essential when one is addressing death-related topics that may be challenging for many people (Strickland & DeSpelder, 1995). A sixth goal of death education is *to assist individuals in appreciating how development across the human life course interacts with death-related issues.* Children and adolescents, as well as young, middle-aged, and older adults, face issues that are dissimilar in many ways and cope with them differently when they confront death, dying, and bereavement (see Chapters 12 through 15).

What Can We Learn about Life and Living by Studying Death, Dying, and Bereavement?

As you read this book, we suggest that you ask yourself what you are learning about death, dying, and bereavement, as well as what that is teaching you about life and living. For ourselves, we have come to see that life and death, living and dying, are inexorably intertwined. That explains the title of this book and our basic conviction that the study of death-related topics inevitably and simultaneously teaches us about life and living.

For example, studying death, dying, and bereavement quickly discloses that we are in fact finite, limited beings. This realization has clear impact on our living, for we learn that while there are many things in life that we can control, there are many others that we cannot. Death-related education reveals some specific things we can *control*, even as it shows many of the *limitations* that make our control less than complete.

Further, when studying death-related topics we recognize that in the end it is always an individual person who must deal with these particularized experiences: no one else can die our death or experience our grief. Death in this sense is marked out by its unique individuality. However, studying death, dying, and bereavement also teaches us that being human means being involved in community and being inescapably linked to other persons. Thus, we learn that life and death both involve *individuals* and *communities.*

Again, although we often act as if we were invulnerable and might wish to believe it, both life and death make our vulnerability to pain and suffering all too obvious. Still, we also learn from our studies of death, dying, and bereavement that this vulnerability is not the same as helplessness. We learn that most human beings have powerful coping capacities and are amazingly resilient. In fact, some persons respond to death-related challenges in ways that can be ennobling and even awesome. Thus, human beings find themselves located between *vulnerability* and *resilience.*

Beyond this, our studies of death-related topics reveal the importance of quality in living and the human search for meaning. One man who was facing his own imminent death founded an organization called "Make Today Count" (Kelly, 1975). In doing this, he implicitly recommended that we all should try to "make today count" by striving to maximize the quality of our own lives right now and by appreciating that even though life is transient it can be good. In addition, our studies show us that when death challenges the value of life, humans work hard to find sources of inspiration and religious or philosophical frameworks within which enduring meaning can be established. Thus, *quality in living* and the *search for meaning* are significant issues for those who are coping with death as well as for those who are simply living their day-to-day lives.

We mention these particular themes here because you will sometimes find them easily in the text, but at other times they will be below the surface of the studies to follow. In that sense, these four themes (control/ limitation; individual persons/community; vulnerability/resilience; quality in living/the search for meaning) are subtexts throughout this book. We also noted them to be prominent

A hospice teen volunteer discusses advance directives and end-of-life customs with community members at a town hall meeting.

aspects of the ways in which people experienced the events of September 11, 2001, and their aftermath. For these reasons, we believe you can enrich your studies of the subjects in this book if you will occasionally stop to dig below the surface of the text and bring to the surface these themes—as well as others that you find.

Summary

In this chapter, we examined education about death, dying, and bereavement. We noted some of the factors that led to the development of this form of education. We also considered some reasons why individuals might become interested in this type of education. We mentioned formal death education of the type represented by this book, as well as informal death education that is most evident in what we called "teachable moments." We explored four central dimensions of death education (cognitive, affective, behavioral, and valuational). We looked at six goals for this type of education, and we asked what we could learn about life and living through the study of death, dying, and bereavement. All of this reminds us again of the main lesson from the prologue to this book: human beings cannot magically make death, loss, and grief disappear from their lives, but they can study these subjects and share insights with each other as a way of learning to live richer, fuller, and more realistic lives.

Questions for Review and Discussion

1. This book is part of an effort to improve education about death, dying, and bereavement. In your judgment, is it useful for people to engage in this type of

education? Why or why not? Would you recommend this type of education to a friend or relative? Why or why not?

2. What is there in your own life that brought you to the study of death, dying, and bereavement? How do your concerns compare to those depicted in the vignette near the beginning of this chapter or to those described in the section in this chapter that asked "Why Did You Become Involved in Death Education?"

3. What do you think you might learn about death, dying, and bereavement from reading this book? About life and living?

4. If you are reading this book as part of a course on death, dying, and bereavement, what do you think you might learn from sharing what you are studying with others? (If you wish to share what you learn from such interactions with the authors of this book, please e-mail us at **charlescorr@mindspring.com** or at **nabec@earthlink.net**).

5. The Prologue to this book is "The Horse on the Dining-Room Table" by Richard A. Kalish. The Epilogue is "Calendar Date Gives Mom Reason to Contemplate Life" by Elizabeth Vega-Fowler. Read these pieces now if you have not already done so. What did you learn from each of them? What similarities and differences do you see in the lessons that these authors want to teach us?

Suggested Readings

This list and those at the end of other chapters in this book focus almost exclusively on book-length publications. Bibliographical data for these publications appear in the References at the end of this book. Journal articles and other literature can be accessed at the InfoTrac Web site, using the search terms provided at the end of each chapter.

The writings of two early leaders in this field are important and still worth consulting:

Feifel, H. (Ed.). (1959). *The Meaning of Death.*

Feifel, H. (Ed.). (1977b). *New Meanings of Death.*

Shneidman, E. S. (1973a). *Deaths of Man.*

Shneidman, E. S. (1980/1995). *Voices of Death.*

General resources in the field of death, dying, and bereavement include:

Howarth, G., & Leaman, O. (Eds.). (2001). *Encyclopedia of Death and Dying.*

Kastenbaum, R. (2000). *The Psychology of Death* (3rd ed.).

Kastenbaum, R. (Ed.). (2002). *Macmillan Encyclopedia of Death and Dying.*

Wass, H., Corr, C. A., Pacholski, R. A., & Forfar, C. S. (1985). *Death Education II: An Annotated Resource Guide.*

Wass, H., Corr, C. A., Pacholski, R. A., & Sanders, C. M. (1980). *Death Education: An Annotated Resource Guide.*

Zalaznik, P. H. (1992). *Dimensions of Loss and Death Education* (3rd ed.).

InfoTrac College Edition
For more information, explore the InfoTrac College Edition at **http://www.infotrac-college.com/Wadsworth**

Enter search terms: DEATH EDUCATION, FORMAL EDUCATION, INFORMAL EDUCATION, TEACHABLE MOMENTS

Part Two

Death

Gordon Allport once said that in some ways each of us is like *every* other human being, in other ways each of us is only like *some* other human beings, and in still other ways each of us is like *no* other human being (J. W. Worden, personal communication, April 22, 2001). In studying death, dying, and bereavement, it helps to sort out these various aspects: the universal, the particular, and the uniquely individual. This part examines the particular: contemporary experiences with death in the United States.

Human beings always live within particular *cultural* frameworks. Of course, not every individual and/or minority group shares every aspect of the experiences that characterize a society as a whole. Thus, specific individuals and members of distinct groups within the United States have their own unique experiences with life and death. This leads us, in the chapters that follow, to describe both the broad context of American society and representative examples of many cultural differences that can be found within that general framework.

Human beings also live within particular *historical* frameworks. Thus, the patterns of experience with death within contemporary American society differ from the experiences of individuals who lived in earlier periods in the United States. (And, of course, the death-related experiences of people living in other countries may be very different from those of most Americans.)

In the chapters that follow, we examine *death-related experiences* in terms of *encounters with death* in Chapter 2, *attitudes toward death* in Chapter 3, and *death-related practices* in Chapter 4. Encounters, attitudes, and practices are specific aspects of the totality of human experience, each shaping the others and each being shaped by the others. In everyday human experience, encounters, attitudes, and practices are so closely intertwined as to be almost indistinguishable. In Chapters 2, 3, and 4, we discuss them separately in order to facilitate individual analysis.

In Chapter 5 we sketch some specific *cultural differences* within our society. By contrast with the earlier portrait of mainstream American society in Chapters 2 through 4, this profile in Chapter 5 helps make us more sensitive to cultural and other differences between individuals and social groups in the United States. ■

Chapter Two

CHANGING ENCOUNTERS WITH DEATH

WE BEGIN OUR ANALYSIS OF DEATH-RELATED experiences in the United States by considering some typical ways in which Americans *encounter or meet up with death* near the beginning of the 21st century. Significant features of these encounters are not always obvious, nor are they the only possible ways in which humans have interacted or might interact with mortality. Earlier peoples did not encounter death as we do at the present, nor do many peoples in other parts of the world today. To clarify that point, our vignette for this chapter describes the death of a physician in Uganda caused by the Ebola virus.

We then take up our main work by briefly noting the total number of deaths in the United States in 1999 (the year for which most recent data are available as this chapter is written). Next, we identify five principal features of death-related encounters in our society: death rates, average life expectancy, causes of death, dying trajectories, and locations where death occurs. We also indicate throughout some of the ways in which these features have changed over time in the United States.

Because encounters with death, dying, and bereavement are always, to some degree, the product of a historical process and a social or cultural context, we examine some of the historical, social, and cultural factors that seem to be associated with changes in American patterns of encountering death. Here, we identify five variables—industrialization, public health measures, preventive health care for individuals, modern cure-oriented medicine, and the nature of contemporary families—that appear to be most closely related to changing encounters with death in our society. ■

The Death of an African Physician

On Tuesday, December 5, 2000, Dr. Matthew Lokwiya, a physician in his early 40s, died in the northern town of Gulu in Uganda (Rosenberg, 2000; *St. Petersburg Times*, 2000). He had recently praised the staff at his hospital for not running away when a new outbreak of Ebola virus was recognized in their area. Despite their courage, since the reappearance of the disease several nurses in the local hospital and 22 health care workers throughout the country had died by the time of Dr. Lokwiya's death.

There is no cure for those who contract the Ebola virus (although not all die). The virus is transmitted through body fluids and has dramatic symptoms: severe pain, high fever, bleeding from the eyes, and often-rapid death. Care is mainly limited to isolating those who are infected, treating them aggressively with fluids to fight dehydration, and practicing precautions against spreading the infection. Dr. Lokwiya's friends said that he probably contracted the virus while treating a nurse and friend who later died. He became a patient on November 30, just five days before his death.

According to news reports (*St. Petersburg Times*, 2000), the death toll from previous outbreaks of the Ebola virus had reached 90 percent of those infected, although the death rate in Uganda when Dr. Lokwiya died was "just 40 percent" (as the reports said).

Reading about these events, Americans may find it almost impossible to imagine a disease with a death rate of 40 percent—much less one whose death toll might go as high as 90 percent. So when we learn about these encounters with death, they may seem to be so different from the death-related encounters with which we are familiar that we are almost inclined to dismiss them as describing strange, incredible events in a far-off place that have little or no significance for us. After all, it certainly seems to be the case that communicable diseases are so much better managed in America than in Africa.

International health officials agree to some extent with this attitude. But they want Americans to understand exactly how and why their encounters with communicable diseases and death are so distinct from those reported in Uganda. They also note that although outbreaks of the Ebola infection have occurred only in Africa, the human immunodeficiency virus (HIV) is thought to have originated somewhere in that part of the world and has become a worldwide scourge. In addition, the same health officials remind us that nowadays a person who had recently been infected with a fatal, incurable virus could get on an airplane somewhere else in the world and land in the United States the same day—long before symptoms of the infection begin to show themselves.

As evidence that events like this do occur, on February 7, 2001, there was a report of a woman who flew from Congo to Newark International Airport in New Jersey and then on to Toronto's Pearson International Airport (*St. Petersburg Times*, 2001a). One day after she arrived at her final destination in Hamilton, Ontario, the woman became sick and was admitted to a local hospital with symptoms that resembled those attributed to the Ebola virus. All of those who took part in her treatment and were exposed to her blood and bodily fluids were concerned about the dangers they might now face.

Encountering Death in America Today

We can learn a lot about contemporary encounters with death in the United States from a study of relevant demographic statistics. For example, there were nearly 2.4 million deaths in the United States in 1999 (see Table 2.1), in a total population that the 2000 census estimates to be approximately 281.4 million (U.S. Bureau of the Census, 2001). These deaths, along with earlier ones that individuals may have experienced, are part of our death-related encounters. They help to shape our present and future attitudes toward death, as well as our death-related practices and our broader experiences with life and living.

However, we cannot understand a number as large as 2.4 million in the abstract, and we cannot study all aspects of our experiences at once—not even all aspects of death-related experiences. Thus we concentrate in this chapter on outlining five central features within the broad patterns of death-related encounters that are typically found in our society.

Death Rates

The first of these features is death rates, for the population as a whole and for selected subgroups (population cohorts) within our society. A death rate is determined by choosing some specific group of people and determining how many members of that group die during a particular time period. For instance, the overall death rate for males of all races in the United States in 1999 was determined by dividing the number of deaths among these males (1,175,460) by the total number of males in the entire population. Usually, a death rate is expressed as some number of deaths per 1,000 or 100,000 persons (Shryock et al., 1980). As shown in Table 2.1, the death rate for males in the United States

Table 2.1 Number of Deaths and Death Rates (per 100,000 Population) by Age and Sex: United States, 1999

Age (yrs)	All Races, Both Sexes		All Races, Male		All Races, Female	
	Number	Rate	Number	Rate	Number	Rate
All ages	2,391,399	877.0	1,175,460	882.0	1,215,939	872.2
Under 1	27,937	731.4[a]	15,646	801.5[a]	12,291	658.1[a]
1–4	5,249	34.7	2,975	38.5	2,274	30.8
5–9	3,474	17.4	1,964	19.2	1,510	15.5
10–14	4,121	21.1	2,528	25.3	1,593	16.7
15–19	13,778	69.8	9,780	96.3	3,998	41.7
20–24	16,878	93.6	12,634	137.6	4,244	48.0
25–29	17,703	97.2	12,542	138.5	5,161	56.4
30–34	23,363	118.4	15,734	161.0	7,629	76.6
35–39	36,804	163.2	23,681	211.1	13,123	115.8
40–44	52,452	235.5	33,437	302.9	19,015	169.3
45–49	68,120	351.9	43,303	455.8	24,817	251.8
50–54	84,854	516.0	52,356	654.6	32,498	384.7
55–59	104,884	814.6	63,441	1,026.1	41,443	619.2
60–64	134,095	1,275.4	79,283	1,595.9	54,812	988.3
65–69	186,695	1,976.2	107,529	2,479.5	79,166	1,549.1
70–74	265,905	3,031.6	147,391	3,816.5	118,514	2,414.2
75–79	338,349	4,616.3	174,853	5,719.8	163,496	3,826.7
80–84	360,241	7,478.2	166,117	9,156.8	194,124	6,464.2
85 and over	646,148	15,476.1	209,989	16,931.3	436,152	14,861.2
Not stated	356	—	277	—	79	—

[a]Death rates under 1 year (based on population estimates) differ from infant mortality rates (based on live births); see Table 12.1 for infant mortality rates.

SOURCE: Hoyert et al., 2001.

in 1999 was 882.0 per 100,000 (or 8.8 per 1,000) while the death rate for females was slightly less at 872.2 per 100,000 (or 8.7 per 1,000).

A death rate can only be determined if one has access to a fund of demographic data. These data derive from birth, death, and census records, which are familiar features of modern society. Where those records are absent or have not been maintained carefully, as in the past or in many poor and not well-organized societies today, statistical accuracy gives way to more or less imprecise estimates.

Changing Death Rates in the United States

Studies of international data on death rates have long shown that Americans—and, in general, those who reside in other developed societies around the world—have many advantages in their encounters with death (Preston, 1976). Although the total number of deaths in the United States in 1999 is impressive on its own, we can point out some notable advantages for those living in American society in the 21st century without going beyond our own borders simply by comparing current U.S. death rates with those at the beginning of the 20th century.

Just 100 years ago, death rates were considerably higher than they are today—in the United States and in most industrialized nations of the world, as is clear from the data in Table 2.2. In 1900, the death rate for the total American population of approximately 76 million people was 17.2 deaths per 1,000 in the population. By 1954, that rate had dropped to 9.2 per 1,000 (U.S. Bureau of the Census, 1975). That was a drop of nearly 47 percent in only 54 years—a stunning change unparalleled in any other period in human history. Nevertheless, as Table 2.2 and Figure 2.1 show, by 1999 the overall American death rate had dropped even lower, to just fewer than 8.8 per 1,000. (In fact, however, we should note that overall American death rates increased by about 1 percent from 1998 to 1999—the first time there has been such an increase since 1994.)

It is increasingly difficult to reduce overall death rates as they get lower and lower. We can see this just by contrasting a decline of nearly 47 percent from 1900 to 1954 with a decline of approximately 4.3 percent from 1954 to 1999. Thus, in recent years overall death rates in the United States have tended to level out and may be approaching a minimum level below which they are not likely to go.

Reductions in overall death rates have a significant impact on encounters with death. Above all, they mean that most living Americans are likely to have fewer encounters with natural death than did our great-grandparents. The typical American alive today will have lived through fewer deaths of family, friends, and neighbors than did his or her ancestors at the same time of life. It is not surprising then that when death actually does occur, it seems a stranger, an alien figure that has no natural or appropriate place in human life (see Box 2.1).

Differences in Changing Death Rates: Gender and Class

But this is not the whole story. Substantial declines in death rates throughout the 20th century are found in nearly every segment of the population in the

Table 2.2 Death Rates by Gender and Age, All Races, per 1,000 Population: United States, 1900 and 1999

	1900			1999		
Age (yrs)	Both Sexes	Males	Females	Both Sexes	Males	Females
All ages	17.2	17.9	16.5	8.8	8.8	8.7
Under 1	162.4	179.1	145.4	7.3	8.0	6.6
1–4	19.8	20.5	19.1	0.3	0.4	0.3
5–14	3.9	3.8	3.9	0.2	0.2	0.2
15–24	5.9	5.9	5.8	0.8	1.2	0.4
25–34	8.2	8.2	8.2	1.1	1.5	0.7
35–44	10.2	10.7	9.8	2.0	2.6	1.4
45–54	15.0	15.7	14.2	4.3	5.5	3.1
55–64	27.2	28.7	25.8	10.2	12.8	7.9
65–74	56.4	59.3	53.6	24.8	31.1	19.7
75–84	123.3	128.3	118.8	57.5	70.0	49.2
85+	260.9	268.8	255.2	154.8	169.3	148.6

SOURCE: U.S. Bureau of the Census, 1975; Hoyert et al., 2001.

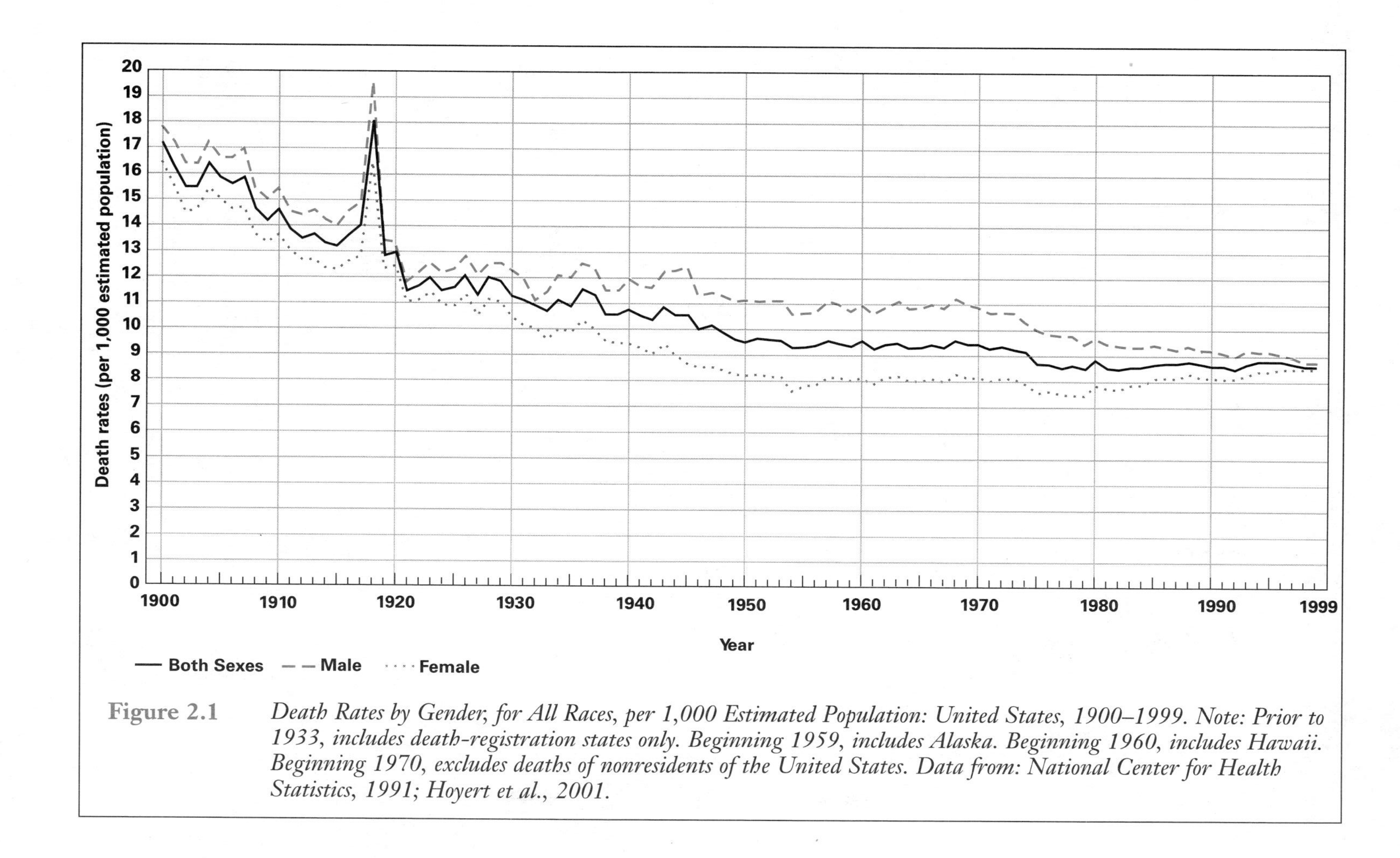

Figure 2.1 *Death Rates by Gender, for All Races, per 1,000 Estimated Population: United States, 1900–1999. Note: Prior to 1933, includes death-registration states only. Beginning 1959, includes Alaska. Beginning 1960, includes Hawaii. Beginning 1970, excludes deaths of nonresidents of the United States. Data from: National Center for Health Statistics, 1991; Hoyert et al., 2001.*

Box 2.1 On Being Notified of a Death in Our Society Today

This is all new to me. I know there are others like myself who have led semi-charmed lives and often find themselves saying, "No one close to me has ever died." Even the aunt you treasured when you were nine waits to die until you're thirty-one and haven't seen her in eleven years. It's a death cushion. The tragedy, the devastation, the dropping to your knees in anguish never comes. You are spared.

This story is about not being spared. It's about when the tragedy, the devastation, the dropping to your knees in anguish comes. It's about reaching the brink of acceptance and then being slammed by death in ways you couldn't possibly have fathomed.

I keep going back to that moment with the beeper cradled in my palm as if it were the present because I haven't accepted much since. I sometimes run it all backward, subtracting each thing that happened by the week, by the day, by the hour . . . but I can never seem to erase the first phone call. The one that comes with a ring of camouflage—could be the dry cleaners, could be the finance department trying to verify something on your expense report, could be the security guard downstairs notifying you that your lunch order has arrived.

Or it could be the trapdoor that drops you into your first hard lesson in death, American style. ■

SOURCE: Shine, 2000, p. 15.

United States. There are, however, differences among these declines that can be examined in terms of several significant variables, the most prominent of which are gender, race, and social class (Antonovsky, 1967; Gove, 1973; Hoyert et al., 1995; Kitagawa & Hauser, 1973; Retherford, 1975; Stillion, 1985). We will consider racial and cultural differences in Chapter 5. Here, we focus on gender and class differences.

In terms of gender differences, death rates for males in the United States declined from 17.9 per 1,000 population in 1900 to 8.8 per 1,000 in 1999, while similar rates for females declined from 16.5 to 8.7 (see Table 2.2 and Figure 2.1). That is, females began with a lower rate at the beginning of the century and achieved a slightly lower mortality rate than males at the end of the period.

In addition to gender differences, it is well recognized (Blane, 1995; Goldscheider, 1971) that a "social inequality of death" exists in the sense that members of the least advantaged socioeconomic classes tend on average to have higher death rates than members of middle and upper socioeconomic classes within the same society. The reason for this is that those who are better off economically are likely to have the advantages of better education, housing, nutrition, access to health care, and financial resources. This part of the story is perhaps obvious, although there may be some subtler differences within and between members of various socioeconomic classes. One of the most important factors producing this disparity is that in the United States a large segment of the population has inadequate or no health insurance. In fact, the United States (compared to other industrial nations) is the only one that does not provide health insurance to all of its citizens, a situation that typically (though not exclusively) most affects members of the lowest socioeconomic classes.

Differences in Changing Death Rates: Infants and Children

Another important difference concerning those who die in the United States has to do with infants and children. At the beginning of the 20th century, the very young in the United States were much more likely to die than they are today. Overall death rates for infants—newborns and children under 1 year of age—were nearly 23 times higher in 1900 than in 1999: 162.4 versus 7.1 infant deaths per 1,000 live births. This is a huge reduction—an "exponential decline" (Guyer et al., 2000, p. 1312)—in infant death rates in less than a century.

The United States was the richest country in the world at the beginning of the 20th century and remains so in the 21st century. However, in 1999 there still were 27,937 infant deaths in the United States. In fact, "the United States continues to rank poorly in international comparisons of infant mortality" (Guyer et al., 1998, p. 1333). More than 20 other countries with a population of at least 2.5 million currently have lower infant death rates than those in the United States, ranging from Singapore and Japan with rates of 3.8 per 1,000 live births to the United Kingdom and Portugal, with rates of 6.1 and 6.9, respectively (Guyer et al., 1998). Some (but not all) of these countries are comparatively small and have relatively homogeneous populations, but it appears that a variety of factors combine to influence infant mortality rates. (For additional information on infant death rates, see Table 2.3 in this chapter and Figure 5.2 in Chapter 5.)

Decreases in infant death rates immediately affect not only infants who would have died if past conditions had continued to prevail but other members of society as well. For example, parents in 1900 were far more likely to be confronted by the death of one of their children than were parents in the latter half of the century (Rosenblatt, 1983; Uhlenberg, 1980). Also, youngsters in 1900 were far more likely to encounter the death(s) of one or more of their brothers or sisters than are children today.

Further, pregnancy and birth are not only life threatening for babies; they are also life threatening for their mothers. Death rates among pregnant women and women in the process of giving birth or immediately after childbirth were much higher in the United States in 1900 than they are today. Maternal death rates of 608 per 100,000 live births in 1915 had been reduced to 7.1 by 1995 (U.S. Bureau of the Census, 1998) but rebounded to 9.9 in 1999 (Hoyert et al., 2001). This overall reduction is a substantial achievement, but the 1999 figures are more than twice the maternal death rate in countries like Norway and Switzerland, and are three times higher than the goal the United States had hoped to reach by the year 2000: not more than 3.3 maternal deaths per 100,000

Table 2.3 Number of Infant Deaths and Infant Mortality Rates by Age, Race, and Hispanic Origin: United States, 1999

	All Races		White		Black		Hispanic[a]	
Age	Number	Rate	Number	Rate	Number	Rate	Number	Rate
Under 1 year (= infant mortality)	27,937	7.1	18,067	5.8	8,822	14.6	4,416	5.8
Under 28 days (= neonatal mortality)	18,728	4.7	12,164	3.9	5,920	9.8	2,988	3.9
28 days–11 months (= postneonatal mortality)	9,209	2.3	5,903	1.9	2,902	4.8	1,428	1.9

[a]Persons of Hispanic origin may be of any race.

SOURCE: Hoyert et al., 2001; Kochanek et al., 2001.

live births (*St. Louis Post-Dispatch*, 1998, Nov. 28, p. A4). Moreover, although there were only 391 maternal deaths in the United States in 1999, experts estimate that about half of these deaths are preventable. In particular, young mothers and those who view pregnancy as risk free or whose pregnancy is unintended or unwanted may fail to seek proper care that might prevent or treat complications leading to death.

Of course, death is always a greater threat to vulnerable populations than to those who are healthy and well off. Death rates at the beginning of the 20th century were high for the sick, the weak, and the aged, and they continue to be high for similar groups today. Today, death rates for nearly every vulnerable group are much lower than they were in times past. Those who are most vulnerable to death today are not as fortunate as their less vulnerable contemporaries, but as a group they are far better off than their counterparts were in 1900. Many deaths are now avoided that would have taken place in our society in the past or that might still take place in other societies today.

Average Life Expectancy

Average life expectancy is closely related to death rates and is another significant feature in the changing pattern of encounters with death. Many have confused life span (the maximum length of life for individuals or the biological limit on length of life in a species) with life expectancy (an estimate of the average number of years a group of people will live) (Yin & Shine, 1985). Here, we speak only of life expectancy (not life span) and we always express that as an average figure.

One author (Thorson, 1995, p. 34) dramatized the fact that life expectancy figures are averages by imagining "a sample of ten people, six of whom died by age 1 and the rest of whom lived full lives of eighty years." In this group, the six babies lived less than a total of six years, whereas the other four people lived a total of 320 years. To say that 32.6 years (6 + 320 ÷ 10) was the average life expectancy for all ten individuals in this unusual group would misrepresent both the whole cohort and each of its subpopulations.

Projected average life expectancy for all individuals born in the United States in 1999 was 76.7 years, continuing the record high figure first reached in 1998 (see Table 2.4). In 1999, record high projected average life expectancies were reached for white and black males (74.6 years and 67.8 years, respectively), while average life expectancies decreased by 0.1 years for white and black females (to 79.9 years and 74.7 years, respectively). Also, the gender gap in average life expectancy for the population as a whole narrowed from 6.4 years in 1995 to 5.5 years in 1999, while the racial differential between the white and black populations narrowed from 6.9 years to 5.9 years.

Average life expectancy identifies the average remaining length of life that can be expected for individuals of a specific age. For example, as shown in

Table 2.4 Average Life Expectancy at Selected Ages, by Race and Sex: United States, 1999

	All Races*			White			Black		
Age (yrs)	Both Sexes	Male	Female	Both Sexes	Male	Female	Both Sexes	Male	Female
0	76.7	73.9	79.4	77.3	74.6	79.9	71.4	67.8	74.7
1	76.3	73.5	78.9	76.8	74.1	79.3	71.5	67.9	74.7
5	72.4	69.6	75.0	72.9	70.2	75.4	67.6	64.1	70.9
10	67.4	64.7	70.0	67.9	65.2	70.5	62.7	59.2	66.0
15	62.5	59.8	65.1	63.0	60.3	65.5	57.8	54.3	61.0
20	57.7	55.0	60.2	58.2	55.6	60.6	53.1	49.6	56.2
25	53.0	50.4	55.4	53.4	50.9	55.8	48.5	45.2	51.4
30	48.2	45.7	50.5	48.6	46.2	50.9	43.9	40.7	46.6
35	43.5	41.1	45.7	43.9	41.5	46.1	39.3	36.3	41.9
40	38.8	36.5	41.0	39.2	36.9	41.3	34.8	31.9	37.4
45	34.2	32.0	36.3	34.6	32.4	36.6	30.6	27.8	33.0
50	29.8	27.7	31.7	30.1	28.0	32.0	26.6	24.0	28.7
55	25.5	23.5	27.3	25.7	23.8	27.5	22.8	20.4	24.7
60	21.5	19.6	23.1	21.6	19.8	23.2	19.3	17.2	20.9
65	17.7	16.1	19.1	17.8	16.1	19.2	16.0	14.3	17.3
70	14.3	12.8	15.4	14.3	12.9	15.5	13.0	11.6	14.0
75	11.2	10.0	12.1	11.2	10.0	12.1	10.4	9.2	11.1
80	8.5	7.4	9.1	8.5	7.5	9.0	8.2	7.2	8.6
85	6.3	5.5	6.6	6.2	5.4	6.6	6.2	5.6	6.5
90	4.6	4.1	4.8	4.5	4.0	4.7	4.8	4.4	4.8
95	3.4	3.0	3.5	3.2	2.9	3.3	3.6	3.5	3.6
100	2.6	2.4	2.6	2.3	2.2	2.4	2.8	2.8	2.7

*Includes races other than white and black.

SOURCE: Hoyert et al., 2001.

Table 2.4 a person in the United States who was already 20 years of age in 1999 could expect to live an additional 57.7 years on average, whereas a 60-year-old person could expect to live an average of 21.5 additional years.

During the 20th century, overall average life expectancy in the United States increased from fewer than 50 years to 76.7 years. This is a gain of more than 50 percent in a period of only 100 years! To put this another way, not until the 20th century in the United States and in some other industrialized countries did the average human life expectancy exceed the biblical promise of "three score and ten" (that is, 70 years; see Figure 2.2). However, it is clearly not the case that no one in the United States lived beyond the estimated averages—many did (see, for example, Box 2.2). That is the whole point of averages: many individuals in a group exceed the average figure and many others do not reach it.

In general, average life expectancy increased rapidly in the United States during the 20th century because of a decrease in the number of deaths occurring during the early years of life. When more individuals survive birth, infancy, and childhood, average life expectancy for the population rises. As time passes, however, it becomes more and more difficult to reduce death rates (especially during infancy and childhood) and to extend average life expectancy. When it is increasingly difficult to lower death rates among the young, improvements in death rates among mature adults and the elderly have a more modest impact on increases in overall average life expectancy. Most of the early and relatively easy victories have already been won in the campaign to lower death rates and increase average life expectancy. The battles that lie ahead are much more difficult, and so the rate of increase in average life expectancy in the United States has slowed in recent years (Smith, 1995).

One last point to note is that as average life expectancy increases, it is the elderly who are more and more perceived by individuals in our society as the dying—so much so that in our society death is exclusively associated in many people's minds with the aged. Recall from Table 2.1 that just over 75 percent of all deaths in the United States in 1999 involved those who were 65 years of age or older.

Causes of Death: Communicable versus Degenerative Diseases

A third distinguishing factor in death-related experiences has to do with *causes of death*. Around 1900 in the United States, the largest number of deaths resulted from infectious or *communicable diseases* (see Table 2.5). These are acute diseases that can be transmitted or spread from person to person (Ewald, 1994; Morse, 1993). Among them are infections of the Ebola virus and other hemorrhagic fevers of the type described in our vignette about the death of Dr. Matthew Lokwiya near the beginning of this chapter.

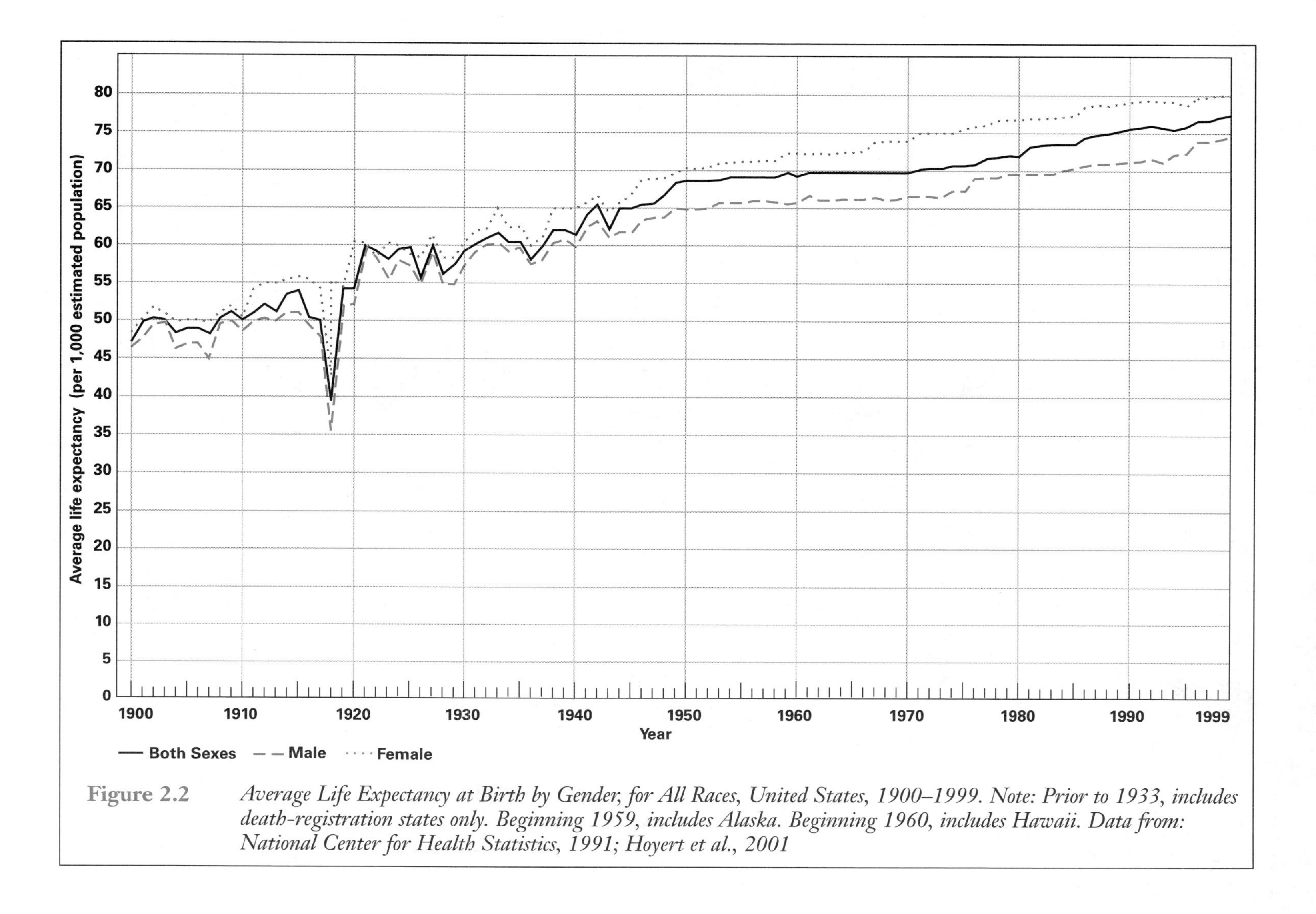

Figure 2.2 *Average Life Expectancy at Birth by Gender, for All Races, United States, 1900–1999. Note: Prior to 1933, includes death-registration states only. Beginning 1959, includes Alaska. Beginning 1960, includes Hawaii. Data from: National Center for Health Statistics, 1991; Hoyert et al., 2001*

Box 2.2 Two Epitaphs from New Hampshire

Sacred to the Memory of Amos Fortune
who was born free in Africa
a slave in America, he purchased
liberty, professed Christianity,
lived reputably, died hopefully
Nov. 17, 1801 Aet. 91.

Sacred to the Memory of Violate
by purchase the slave of Amos Fortune
by marriage his wife, by her
fidelity his companion and solace
She died his Widow
Sept. 13, 1802 Aet. 73. ■

SOURCE: From Mann & Greene, 1962, p. 37.

Earlier cultures experienced sporadic waves of these communicable diseases. From time to time, epidemics of such diseases as influenza, cholera, scarlet fever, measles, smallpox, and tuberculosis would run through human communities. Perhaps the most famous of these epidemics, at least for Europeans, was the black (bubonic) plague of the 14th century, which killed nearly 25 million people in a total European population much smaller than that of today (Gottfried, 1983).

Communicable diseases are often accompanied by observable symptoms like diarrhea, nausea, vomiting, headache, fever, and muscle ache. In cultures where vaccines and/or antibiotics were not or are not available—and in many undeveloped or poverty-stricken portions of the world today—those providing physical care for people with communicable diseases mainly dealt (or still deal) with these symptoms rather than with their underlying causes. In other words, they tried to isolate the ill person in order to minimize the likelihood of spreading the disease. They also offered or continue to offer such things as shelter from the elements, a warm fire, a place to rest, hot food (chicken soup!), and a cool cloth to wipe a feverish brow. We saw this approach taken to those infected by the Ebola virus in the vignette near the beginning of this chapter.

Today, relatively few people in developed countries die of communicable diseases—with the notable exception of deaths associated with infection by the human immunodeficiency virus (HIV) and acquired immunodeficiency syndrome (AIDS). In recent years, however, there has been growing concern about potential threats from other communicable diseases such as meningitis and West Nile virus (a form of encephalitis carried by birds and spread by mosquitoes that was first discovered in North America in the summer of 1999 when it killed nine people in the New York City area). Of special interest is a possible resurgence in the lethal potential of drug-resistant communicable diseases such as tuberculosis (for example, Platt, 1995), which might become particularly

Table 2.5 The Ten Leading Causes of Death, in Rank Order, All Races, Both Sexes: United States, 1900 and 1999

Rank	Cause of Death	Deaths per 100,000 Population	Percentage of All Deaths
	1900		
	All causes	1,719.1	100.0
1	Influenza and pneumonia	202.2	11.8
2	Tuberculosis (all forms)	194.4	11.3
3	Gastritis, duodenitis, enteritis, etc.	142.7	8.3
4	Diseases of the heart	137.4	8.0
5	Vascular lesions affecting the central nervous system	106.9	6.2
6	Chronic nephritis	81.0	4.7
7	All accidents	72.3	4.2
8	Cancer (malignant neoplasms)	64.0	3.7
9	Certain diseases of early infancy	62.6	3.6
10	Diphtheria	40.3	2.3
	1999		
	All causes	877.0	100.0
1	Diseases of the heart	265.9	30.3
2	Cancer (malignant neoplasms)	201.6	23.0
3	Cerebrovascular diseases	61.4	7.0
4	Chronic lower respiratory diseases	45.5	5.2
5	Accidents (unintentional injuries)	35.9	4.1
6	Diabetes mellitus	25.1	2.9
7	Influenza and pneumonia	23.4	2.7
8	Alzheimer's disease	16.3	1.9
9	Nephritis, nephrotic syndrome, and nephrosis	13.0	1.5
10	Septicemia	11.3	1.3

SOURCES: U.S. Bureau of the Census, 1975; Hoyert et al., 2001

dangerous in environments like hospitals and nursing homes where ill and potentially vulnerable people are together in close quarters. Following the terrorist attacks on America of September 11, 2001, there were several incidents involving anthrax-laden envelopes in the mail that caused some infections and deaths. There also has been much concern about the possibility that some terrorists might use smallpox as a bioweapon (Miller et al., 2001; Tucker, 2001).

In our society today, death typically results from the long-term wearing out of body organs, a deterioration associated with aging, lifestyle, and environment. That is, people in our society die mainly of a set of chronic conditions or causes called *degenerative diseases.* In fact, the four leading causes of death in the United States (diseases of the heart, malignant neoplasms [cancers], cerebrovascular diseases, and chronic lower respiratory diseases (formerly called chronic obstructive pulmonary diseases or COPD) all fall into the category of degenerative diseases. Two of these degenerative diseases (heart disease and cancer) alone accounted for more than 53 percent of all deaths in our society in 1999, despite the fact that death rates from both of these causes have been in gradual decline for some years.

Deaths produced by degenerative diseases have their own typical characteristics. For example, vascular diseases (coronary attacks, strokes, embolisms, aneurysms, and so on) sometimes cause quick, unanticipated deaths. Nevertheless, although the outcome or exposure of the underlying condition may be sudden (as is suggested by the term "stroke"), these diseases themselves usually develop slowly over time and generally produce a gradual (but often unnoticed) debilitation. When such debilitation does not occur, the first symptom may be a dramatic, unexpected, almost instantaneous death. Such a death may be relatively painless—in one's sleep or after a rapid onset of unconsciousness. Deaths resulting from degenerative diseases, however, are more often slower and may be quite painful—even heart attacks do not necessarily lead to "easy" or "quick" deaths.

Many people know something about leading causes of death in our society. Still, it is surprising to discover inadequacies in what is thought to be known. Consider the example of cancer, currently the second leading cause of death in our society. In fact, cancer is really a collection of diseases all involving malignant cells that reproduce aggressively, each with its own distinctive characteristics and mortality rate (see Figure 2.3). When we have asked students to identify the leading cancer cause of death for males and for females, they most often reply that it is prostate or colon cancer for males and breast cancer for females. In fact, since the early 1950s for males and the mid-1980s for females, the leading cancer cause of death for members of both genders has been lung cancer! This is an ironic outcome especially for women who are told by cigarette advertising, "You've come a long way, baby."

Dying Trajectories

Different causes of death are typically associated with different patterns of dying called *dying trajectories* (Glaser & Strauss, 1968). Their differences are marked primarily by duration and shape. *Duration* refers to the time involved between the onset of dying and the arrival of death. *Shape* designates the course of the dying process, whether one can predict how it will advance, and whether death is expected or unexpected. Some dying trajectories involve a swift or almost instantaneous onset of death, while others last a long time; some can be anticipated, others are ambiguous or unclear (perhaps involving a series of remissions and relapses), and still others give no advance warning at all (see Figure 2.4).

Most communicable diseases are characterized by a relatively brief dying trajectory. The period of time from the onset of the infection until its resolution, either in death or in recovery, is usually short—measured in days or weeks. A rapid dying trajectory like this was what happened to Dr. Matthew Lokwiya in the vignette near the beginning of this chapter. (HIV infection is a notable exception to this pattern; beginning as a communicable disease, it often develops into the chronic complications of AIDS, which in many ways resemble degenerative diseases in their overall pattern; see Chapter 20).

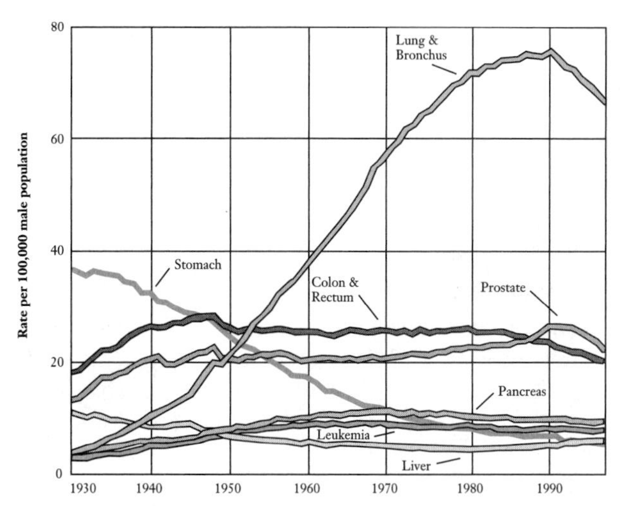

*Per 100,000, age-adjusted to the 1970 US standard population. **Note:** Due to changes in ICD coding, numerator information has changed over time. Rates for cancers of the liver, lung & bronchus, and colon & rectum are affected by these coding changes.
SOURCE: US Mortality Public Use Data Tapes 1960–1997, US Mortality Volumes 1930–1959, National Center for Health Statistics, Centers for Disease Control and Prevention, 2000. American Cancer Society, Surveillance Research, 2001

Females

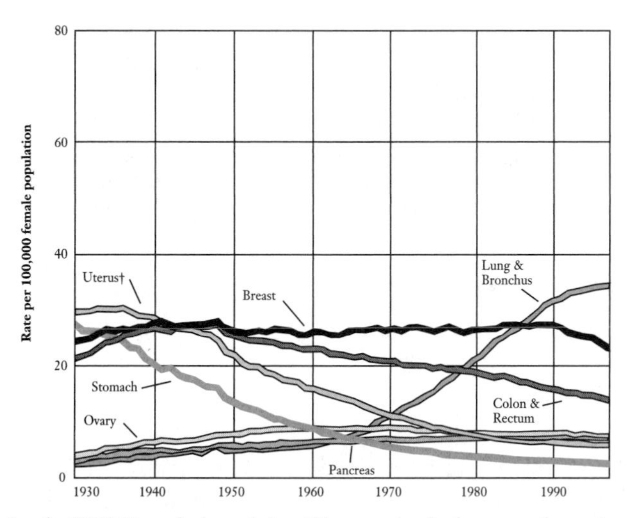

*Per 100,000, age-adjusted to the 1970 US standard population. †Uterus cancer death rates are for uterine cervix and uterine corpus combined. **Note:** Due to changes in ICD coding, numerator information has changed over time. Rates for cancers of the uterus, ovary, lung & bronchus, and colon & rectum are affected by these coding changes.
SOURCE: US Mortality Public Use Data Tapes 1960–1997, US Mortality Volumes 1930–1959, National Center for Health Statistics, Centers for Disease Control and Prevention, 2000. American Cancer Society, Surveillance Research, 2001

Figure 2.3 *Cancer Death Rates by Gender and Site, United States, 1930–1997 (per 100,000). SOURCE: From* Cancer Facts and Figures—2001, *by the American Cancer Society. Copyright © 2001, American Cancer Society, Inc. Reprinted with permission.*

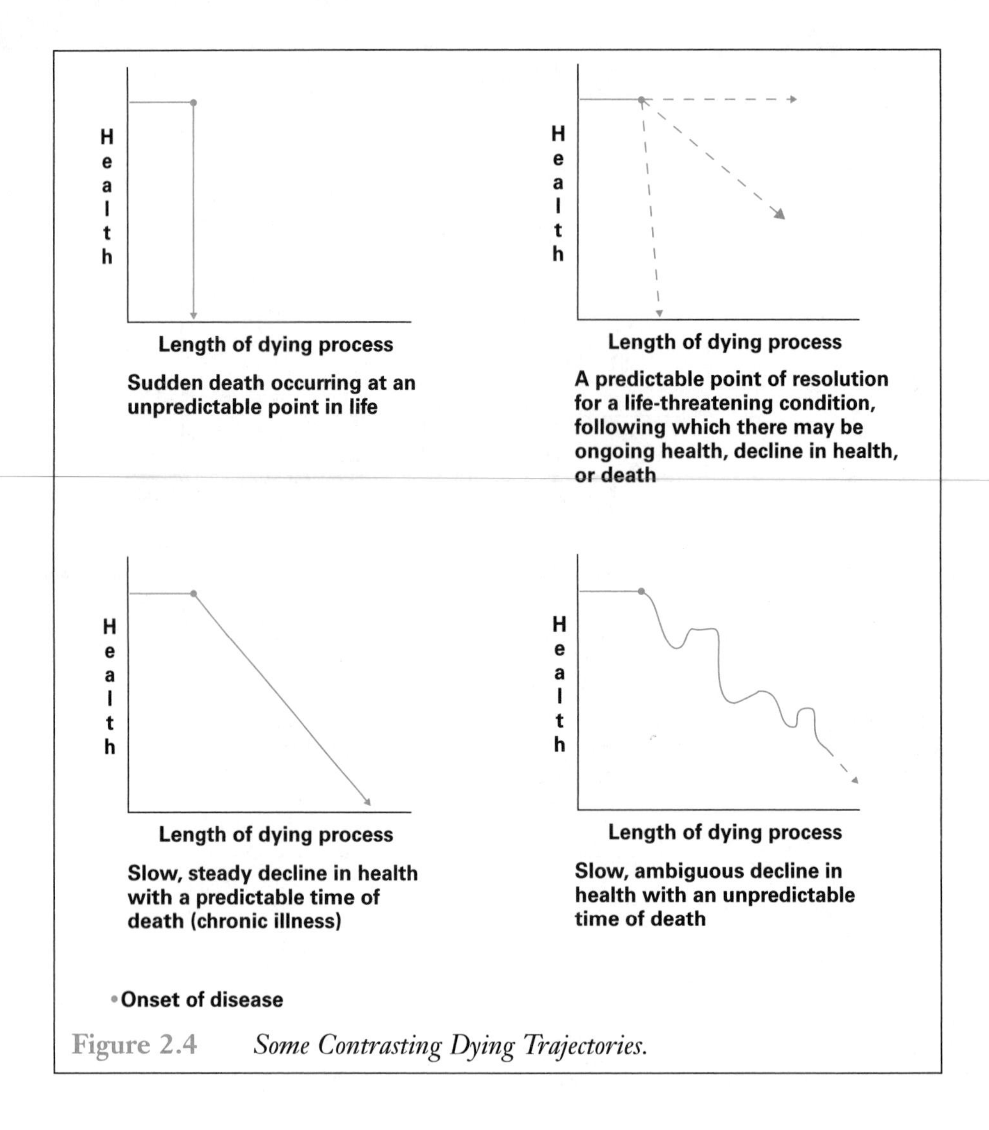

Figure 2.4 *Some Contrasting Dying Trajectories.*

Dying trajectories associated with degenerative diseases are likely to be considerably different from those linked to communicable diseases. In general, the former are lengthier, sometimes much lengthier; are often far less predictable; and may be linked with long-term pain and suffering, loss of physical control over one's body, or loss of one's mental faculties. Diseases with dying trajectories of this type include motor neuron disease (for example, amyotrophic lateral sclerosis, often called "ALS" or "Lou Gehrig's disease"), Alzheimer's disease, Parkinson's disease, muscular dystrophy, and multiple sclerosis.

Consider the case of cancer as an example of a degenerative disease often displaying a complicated dying trajectory. Cancer is one of the most dreaded diseases in our culture, despite the fact that it is much less often a fatal diagnosis or one with a prognosis of imminent death than it was 25 years ago. Perhaps much of the fear of cancer has to do with the dying processes that we associate with this disease. Familiar images of cancer usually involve suffering, pain, and discomfort for a long period of time. These images have been reinforced by the popular media and by the personal stories of a number of prominent individuals (see Box 6.1). Nevertheless, this is not an entirely appropriate depiction of cancer. Not all cancers are fatal, some do not involve much pain or discomfort, some can be "cured" either outright or at least in the sense that intervention leads to survival of five years or more, and much depends on family history and individual circumstances.

The effects of therapeutic interventions, such as those available to treat some degenerative diseases, may complicate differences in the duration of dying trajectories. When such interventions are successful, they may restore quality and longevity of life to persons with such diseases. Alternatively, an intervention may halt the advance of the disease and leave the affected individual to live out the balance of his or her life in a partially debilitated or handicapped condition. Some other interventions may only be able to slow (not halt or bring to a stop) the progress of a degenerative disease or prolong the dying of people with the disease. This prolongation of living or dying is characteristically measured in terms of months and even years.

The relative prominence of degenerative diseases in the United States today alters American experiences with dying and death. Although death is less frequently encountered in our society, when it does occur it is often associated with a protracted and ambiguous dying trajectory. On one hand, this may provide more time for individuals to say their goodbyes, get their affairs in order, and prepare for death. On the other hand, experiences with dying from degenerative diseases often drain physical, emotional, social, spiritual, and financial resources.

Location of Death

Imagine that it is the year 1900. You are at the bedside of a loved one who is dying. You are *in that person's home*, because that is where most people in the United States in 1900—perhaps as many as 80 percent—die: in their own beds (Lerner, 1970). You and your loved one are surrounded by sights, sounds, smells, and people that are familiar. Hospitals or other sorts of health care institutions are not the places where people living in 1900 encounter death. (This is also true of many encounters with death in most developing countries around the world in the early years of the 21st century). In 1900, only people who have no personal resources or no family and friends to care for them are likely to be found in public hospitals as they approach death. In 1900, those who have the personal and/or economic resources certainly would not want to leave the comforts of home—their own bed, their own friends and family—to go somewhere else to die. By contrast, more than 72 percent of people in today's United States die *in a public institution* of some sort (usually a hospital or long-term care facility)—in a strange place, in a strange bed, and surrounded mostly by strangers (see Table 2.6).

In 1900, you and other members of the family would have been the primary health care providers. What you provide to the dying person is largely palliative care—that is, care for distressing symptoms. If there is fever, you apply a cool cloth along with frequent washings. If the dying person is hungry, you prepare familiar, favorite foods. If the dying person grows frightened, you hold his or her hand, sit with him or her, read or recite words of comfort, and share your love.

When death is near, you also are near, in the same or next room. After death, you clean and clothe the body—the last act of love in a lifelong drama. The body might well be left in the bed while friends and neighbors "visit." Or perhaps the body is placed in a coffin (sometimes handmade by you and other family members—another last action for the deceased) and laid out in the parlor for a wake or visitation. After the funeral, the body is lowered by the family into a grave that you have helped to dig in a nearby family plot or churchyard. As a mark of special honor, the family fills in the grave. The struggles of one family to do this are well depicted in William Faulkner's novel *As I Lay Dying* (1930).

In this situation, death is familiar. Most members of a family have seen, heard, and been touched by the death of a family member. Children also are included in these situations. If grandmother is dying in her bed in the same house, children participate by talking with her, sitting with her, or helping with small chores. Children are present during the wake (since it is held in the home) and the funeral. Death is not a stranger in these children's lives.

All these customs have changed for most (but not all) Americans. In 1949, 49.5 percent of all deaths in our society occurred in some sort of health care institution (mainly in a hospital). By 1999, more than 72 percent of all deaths in the United States took place in an institution; 50.1 percent in a hospital or medical center and 22.0 percent in some sort of long-term care facility (see Table 2.6). In recent years, there has been a modest shift away from hospitals into nursing homes and private residences, but still the vast majority of deaths in our society now occur in public institutions. In general, what happened in our society during the last half of the 20th century is that death for many has gradually

Table 2.6 Location of Death: United States, 1999

	Number	Percentage
Total	2,394,871[a]	100.0
Hospital or medical center	1,218,853	50.9
Nursing home	527,390	22.0
Residence	533,616	22.3
Other places	114,297	4.8
Place unknown	715	0.03

[a]NOTE: This total includes 3,472 deaths in the United States in 1999 of nonresidents. All published reports from NCHS are confined to deaths of residents and are the basis for all other tables and death-related statistical data in this book.

SOURCE: National Center for Health Statistics. (2001). National Vital Statistics System. Unpublished tabulations.

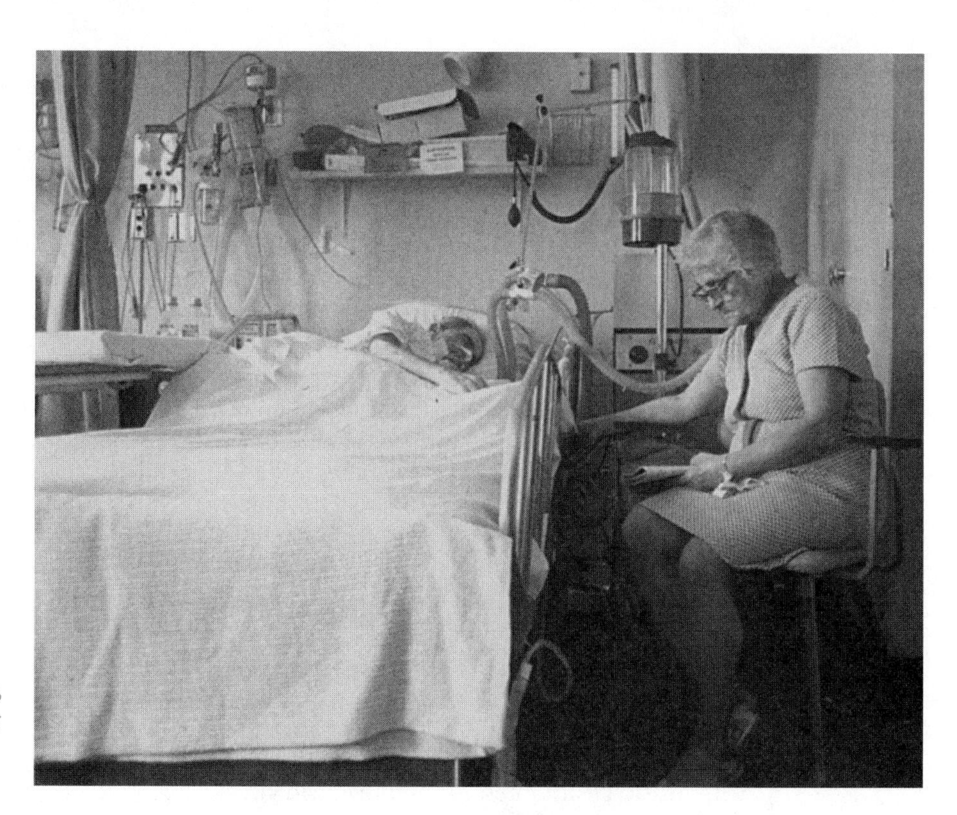

Sitting, waiting, and anticipating in a high-tech medical setting.

been moved out of the mainstream of life. In turn, families have more and more become spectators at a family member's death, rather than participants or primary caregivers. When many Americans die today, they are away from the people they know best and with whom they have shared personal, long-term histories. This is not a criticism of professional caregivers; our point is only to note that they are not the same people who would have provided care in the past. When there is an absence of long-term relationships with the person who is dying, those who are providing care may be unaware of his or her personal interests, values, needs, and preferences. This is one reason that many contemporary Americans report that they fear dying more than death. It is also one reason that there has been so much recent interest in advance directives as an effort to ensure that one's voice will be heard and respected when critical decisions are made in end-of-life care (see Chapter 16).

Because dying now often occurs outside the home, death is unknown, or at least not well known, to many of us. In these circumstances, family members may not be present at the moment of death in our society. Except among certain groups (for example, some Mormons, Orthodox Jews, and Amish), the last loving actions—cleaning and dressing the body—for most persons who die in our society are performed by strangers: nurses, nurse's aides, funeral directors. The body is most likely taken from the place where death occurred to a funeral home. There, after preparation, the family may see the body dressed, arranged, made up. In many ways, the actual event of death is hidden or removed from the lives of most people. Often at many cemeteries today, families are removed from the grave site before the casket is lowered into the grave, or the last separation may take place at a chapel near the cemetery entrance and at a distance from the grave site. All of these customs can force family members into the helpless, empty inertia of bystanders.

In short, direct, personal encounters with all facets of natural human death have been diminished in our society. Care for the dying and of the dead has been moved away from the family and out of the home for many in our society (although the situation is changing somewhat with the support of programs like hospice). Thus, few may experience the moments immediately before, at the time of, or directly after the death of someone they love. For all others, death is increasingly distanced—some would say estranged or made alien—from the mainstream of life's events.

What Factors Helped Bring about These New Mortality Patterns?

There are five factors to consider when we think about changing encounters with death. Death rates, for example, had already begun to decrease in a noticeable way in the middle to latter half of the 19th century. What was happening that could account for this decrease?

The earliest and most important factor was *industrialization* in the late 18th and 19th centuries. This historical and social phenomenon had several immediate consequences. Among them were increased production of food, better clothing, and better housing, all of which supported a healthier population. That is, industrialization led to improvements in the environment and in our general standard of living; in turn, that meant death became a less familiar visitor in human lives.

Industrialization also brought about the development of more effective means of communication (for example, telegraph and telephone) and more effective means of transportation (for example, rail systems, better highways, more efficient trucking)—which, in turn, changed patterns of encounters with death. For instance, now when crops fail in one place, that fact can be made known to people in other areas, surpluses from elsewhere can be moved to that place, and malnutrition and starvation can be alleviated or eliminated. High death rates from hunger and malnutrition in some poor societies in recent years have exposed deficiencies in these aspects of those societies. Food shipped from other parts of the world has gone to waste when bottled up by inadequate port or distribution facilities.

The second major factor in reducing death rates involved *public health measures* that first achieved significance in the 19th and early 20th centuries. For example, threats posed by many communicable diseases (such as cholera, typhoid, encephalitis, malaria) were reduced by a better understanding of their vectors or how they were transmitted (for example, by mosquitoes or rats) and the subsequent control of those vectors. In addition, Pasteur's discovery in the late 19th century that communicable diseases are caused by microbial agents led to isolation of those with communicable diseases (quarantine), separation of drinking water sources from sewage, and other improvements in basic sanitation. These actions contributed to declining death rates and helped in the prevention of morbidity and mortality in the society as a whole.

When industrialization and public health measures first led to a decline in death rates in the United States, fewer people died, but young people—infants in particular—continued to die at high rates. Nutrition and preventive health measures for individuals had to be better understood before overall death rates, and particularly deaths in infancy, could be reduced further. When such measures were pursued in increasingly effective ways, there were significant gains in average life expectancy during the late 1930s and 1940s.

The third major factor working to reduce death rates in our society is *preventive health care for individuals.* This is most evident in techniques like vaccination, whereby an individual can be inoculated or infected in a controlled way with an illness. The purpose of the vaccination procedure is to permit the individual's own immune system to build up defenses to future attacks by the illness. These preventive measures originated in 1798, when Jenner introduced a vaccination for smallpox. However, it took nearly a century for another such advance: the introduction by Louis Pasteur in 1881 of a vaccination for anthrax (Wehrle & Top, 1981). Beginning around the end of the 19th century, the number of available vaccines increased rapidly, although advances occurred at irregular intervals. These vaccines protected more and more persons from deadly—often childhood—diseases, thus quickly helping to increase average length of life. Other methods of preventive health care for individuals include the use of media to circulate advice on healthy diet and exercise, warnings against the health-related dangers of tobacco use, and efforts to persuade pregnant women not to drink alcoholic beverages or use illegal drugs.

All of these factors were influential in changing encounters with death before the fourth major variable, *the rise of modern cure-oriented medicine*, which first gained significance in the second quarter of the 20th century. By this time, the hospital had begun to be a major contributor to health care. The biomedical model of disease had become dominant with its tendencies to emphasize cure over prevention. Physicians were now important in providing health care, and health care had become curative in many important ways. To provide this sort of health care, special technologies were developed, many of which are quite expensive. Thus, they are localized in particular places, mainly hospitals. Health care is usually not delivered to where the sick person is; rather, the person with disease is delivered to the place where health care is provided.

Medicine had now become an important factor in reducing death rates and in accelerating changes that had begun much earlier. Especially since the introduction of successful antibiotics (that is, antimicrobial agents such as penicillin)—largely a post–World War II (after 1945) phenomenon—modern medicine contributed to improvements in death rates and average life expectancy of

contemporary peoples, at least in the industrialized nations. Along with earlier factors, modern cure-oriented medicine has affected both overall death rates and infant death rates, although the latter have not improved (declined) as quickly as the former and only approached their current levels in the late 1950s and 1960s.

A fifth factor that is also significant in how death is encountered and experienced in our society has to do with *the nature of contemporary families.* When families were large, extended social groups who generally lived near each other and had members (especially women) who stayed at home, many members could be counted on to take part in caring for the ill, the dying, the bodies of the dead, and the bereaved. When families are smaller, more obliged to have all of their adult members work out of the home, more scattered throughout the country or the world, and with members who are generally less connected to each other—and especially when family and other kinship groups are shattered or nonexistent, as is the case for many single and homeless individuals in our society—then encounters with dying, death, and bereavement occur in quite a different way. Religious communities and friendly neighbors might have taken up some of this slack, but for many in our mobile, secular, and impersonal society those ties are also less typical, less strong, and less available.

And so we arrive at our world: for many people in our society, death is removed in numerous important ways from the home and from the mainstream of contemporary living, or is encountered without some of the community supports that might have been in place in the natural or informal familial and other social networks of times past. Of course, this does not mean that death no longer comes into our world in any form; the issue is *the form its takes* when it does come into our world. For example, when death rates (especially those associated with birth and infants) are as low as they now are in the United States, potential parents can decide to have fewer offspring and to delay first pregnancies since they are less fearful than parents in earlier times that death will disrupt their plans. The form that death takes in our society depends on certain variables, such as the causes of death; the dying trajectories we encounter; the location in which death occurs; and how our family, our ethnic group, and our local community are or are not able to rally to support individuals experiencing dying, death, and bereavement.

We will all die, sooner or later. And we will all have encounters with death, dying, and bereavement in the course of our lives. What we have seen in this chapter is that those encounters will typically be different for us than in times past in our own country or currently in some other parts of the world. Our encounters with death in the United States today are an important component in a special set of experiences. In many ways, these experiences represent desirable improvements over the lot of other human beings; in other ways, they have less favorable implications. We will explore further aspects of those changing experiences with death in subsequent chapters.

Summary

In this chapter, we learned about *contemporary encounters with death*, especially those found in the United States and in other developed countries. We examined those encounters both in themselves and as they differ from mortality patterns in our society in the past or in developing countries in other parts of the world at present. In the United States today, death rates are lower overall, average life expectancy is longer, people die mainly of degenerative rather than communicable diseases, typical dying trajectories are quite different from what they once were, and more people die in institutions than at home. In addition, we examined five variables or principal factors that are correlated with these changes in death-related encounters: industrialization, public health measures, preventive health care for individuals, modern cure-oriented medicine, and the nature of contemporary families.

Questions for Review and Discussion

1. What was it like for you to be part of American society in September and October of 2001 when we first encountered deaths caused by anthrax spores sent through the mails? Did those encounters change your attitudes or practices in any way?

2. Two types of statistical data can be used to illustrate changes in encounters with death in American society: death rates and average life expectancy. How have these sets of data changed over the last hundred years in the United States? How have these changes affected your encounters with death, dying, and bereavement?

3. People in American society a hundred years ago often died of communicable diseases; today they often die of degenerative diseases. How do we distinguish these two types of causes of death, and what are the patterns of dying that are associated with them typically like? How might these different causes of death affect your encounters with death, dying, and bereavement?

4. This chapter noted changes in the locations that people typically die in American society. Think about how encounters with death are likely to be different when a person dies at home and when a person dies away from home (for example, in an institution like a hospital or nursing home). How will these changes in location affect the encounters with death of the person who is dying and of those who are his or her survivors?

Suggested Readings

The basic materials and principles of demography are described in the following:

Centers for Disease Control and Prevention (CDC). *Morbidity and Mortality Weekly Report.* Provides current information and statistics about disease. See **www.cdc.gov.**

National Center for Health Statistics (NCHS). This agency of the CDC offers various publications containing preliminary, provisional, and final mortality data. See also the NCHS home page at **www.cdc.gov/nchs.**

National Safety Council. *Accident Facts.* Published annually. See **www.nsc.org**.

Shryock, H. S., Siegel, J. S., & Associates. (1980). *The Methods and Materials of Demography.*

U.S. Bureau of the Census. (1975). *Historical Statistics of the United States, Colonial Times to 1970, Bicentennial Edition.*

U.S. Bureau of the Census. *Statistical Abstract of the United States.* Published annually; reflects data from a year or two earlier. See also the census bureau's Web page at **www.census.gov**.

Connections between mortality rates and socioeconomic factors are examined in:

Benjamin, B. (1965). *Social and Economic Factors Affecting Mortality.*

Cohen, M. N. (1989). *Health and the Rise of Civilization.*

Goldscheider, C. (1971). *Population, Modernization, and Social Structure.*
Kitagawa, E. M., & Hauser, P. M. (1973). *Differential Mortality in the United States: A Study in Socioeconomic Epidemiology.*
Preston, S. H. (1976). *Mortality Patterns in National Populations: With Special Reference to Recorded Causes of Death.*

Differences in mortality rates arising from age or gender are considered in:

Preston, S. H., & Haines, M. R. (1991). *Fatal Years: Child Mortality in Late Nineteenth-Century America.*
Retherford, R. D. (1975). *The Changing Sex Differential in Mortality.*
Stillion, J. M. (1985). *Death and the Sexes: An Examination of Differential Longevity, Attitudes, Behaviors, and Coping Skills.*

InfoTrac College Edition
For more information, explore the InfoTrac College Edition at **http://www.infotrac-college.com/Wadsworth**

Enter search terms: AVERAGE LIFE EXPECTANCY, COMMUNICABLE DISEASES, DEATH ENCOUNTERS (OR DEATH-RELATED ENCOUNTERS OR ENCOUNTERS WITH DEATH), DEATH RATES (OR MORTALITY RATES), DEGENERATIVE DISEASES, DYING TRAJECTORIES, PLACE OF DEATH (OR LOCATION OF DEATH)

Chapter Three

CHANGING ATTITUDES TOWARD DEATH

IN THIS CHAPTER, WE EXAMINE ATTITUDES associated with death held by individuals and societies. According to the *Oxford English Dictionary*, the term *attitude* arose in art. Originally it meant the disposition or posture of a figure in statuary or painting. That definition led to the notion that a posture of the body could be related to a particular mental state. From there, the term "attitude" came to be associated with some "settled behaviour or manner of acting, as representative of feeling or opinion" (*Oxford English Dictionary*, 1989, I, p. 771).

These definitions show that an attitude is a way of presenting oneself to or being in the world. If one's bodily posture (one's attitude) includes an upraised fist, a general tenseness, and a facial grimace as one leans toward another person, that posture itself will affect how that particular encounter develops. Compare such an attitude with one that includes open arms, a smile, and a generally relaxed body. Good examples of attitudes expressed in everyday behavior include offering to shake hands when one meets another person or spreading one's arms wide and hugging or kissing the cheek of an individual as a form of greeting. Both of these behavioral patterns indicate friendliness, lack of hostility, and the absence of a weapon in one's grasp. Attitudes like these influence one's encounters by predisposing the person who is being greeted to a friendly or cordial response. The point we want to emphasize is that one's way of being in the world, or how one meets the world, often influences the kinds of encounters one has and how those encounters are likely to develop. It also works the other way around; one's encounters influence one's own bodily postures and habits of mind.

Here we illustrate the role that attitudes play in death-related experiences through an example taken from Amish life in the United States and an analysis of ways in which encounters and attitudes interact in death-related experiences. Then we turn to the main work of the chapter: an outline of four basic categories of death-related attitudes and a description of five dominant patterns in Western attitudes toward death. We conclude with a case study of death-related attitudes among the New England Puritans during the 17th century. ■

The Death of an Amish Man

John Stolzfus bore one of the most common names in the Old Order Amish community in eastern Pennsylvania where he had lived all of his life. The Stolzfus family traced its roots through 18th-century immigrants from Alsace and then back to Swiss origins in the 16th-century Anabaptist movement. The Anabaptists were persecuted in Europe for their rejection of infant baptism (on the grounds that children come into the world without a knowledge of good and evil and thus do not need to be baptized as infants in order to remove sin). The Amish (named after their founder, Jacob Ammann) are one of the few groups that survive today from the Anabaptist movement. No Amish remain in Europe, but some 90,000–100,000 can be found in parts of the United States and Canada (Bryer, 1979; Hostetler, 1994; Zielinski, 1975, 1993).

As a member of a close-knit Amish community, John Stolzfus centered his life on religious beliefs and practice, a large extended family, and work on a farm. The Old Order Amish are known for their distinctive dress. The men wear plain, dark clothes fastened with hooks and eyes, broad-brimmed hats, and full beards without mustaches, and the women dress in bonnets and long, full dresses. Members of this community use horse-drawn buggies instead of automobiles, espouse pacifism, and reject many modern devices (such as telephones, high-line electricity, and tractors with pneumatic tires).

These are the outward expressions of a slow-changing culture that is determined to follow biblical injunctions as it understands them. Their central guidelines include: "Be not conformed to this world" (Rom. 12:2) and "Be ye not unequally yoked together with unbelievers" (2 Cor. 6:14). Amish society essentially turns inward to community in order to worship God, moderate the influences of humanity's evil circumstances, and preserve values in ethical relationships through obedience and conformity. The community blends religion and culture: an emphasis on oral tradition, shared practical knowledge, closeness to nature, respect for elders, striving for self-sufficiency, and smallness in social scale. Usually, 30 to 40 households in geographical proximity take turns in hosting biweekly religious services in their homes.

The Stolzfus family rose with the sun and went to bed shortly after nightfall. As a child, John was assigned chores that contributed to meeting the needs of his family. This sort of work continued during his school years, with different responsibilities appropriate to his age, growth, and maturity. John's schooling did not extend beyond the eighth grade, since members of the community judged that this was sufficient for the lives they had chosen to lead. They were wary that additional formal education might only tend to subvert their traditional beliefs and values. Like most of his peers, John was baptized at the age of 18 into his local church district, and one November day soon after, he married a young woman from the same community.

At first, the young couple lived with John's family and he continued to work on their farm. Eventually, through a small inheritance from a relative and with some financial help from their families, John and his wife bought a small piece of land to farm on their own. The birth of their first three children, building their own house, and the great communal activity of raising a large barn on their farm all marked a productive period in John's life.

Shortly after the birth of their fifth child, John's first wife died. Relatives helped with the care of the children and with work on the expanding farm until John found one of his wife's unmarried cousins who was willing to marry him and take on the role of mother for his existing children and for the additional children they would have together. After that, life went on for many years in a quiet and steady way. Eventually, the offspring from both of John's marriages grew up and were themselves married. John and his second wife became respected members of their community, he as a deacon or minister to the poor in the church, and she for her work in church groups and for her quiet presence at community gatherings.

Eventually, after what he thought of as a good life, John began to decline in vigor and in his ability to get around. In accordance with Amish custom, a small house (called a "grandfather house") was built next to the main farmhouse, and John retired there. After his retirement, John concentrated on reading his beloved Bible, whittling simple wooden toys, and spending time with his second wife, their children, and their grandchildren. When he could no longer get out of bed, both John and other members of his community realized that his death was not far off. Gradually, Amish neighbors of all ages began to come by in order to pray together and say goodbye one last time. John spoke openly of his coming death and used these visits to encourage others to prepare for and calmly accept their own deaths. At the age of 82, John Stolzfus died peacefully one night in his own bed, as one of his daughters sat quietly in a nearby rocking chair and two of his grandchildren slept in their own beds in the same room.

The family cleaned and dressed John's body in traditional white garments. Then the body was placed in a six-sided wooden coffin that had been made ready a few weeks before, and the coffin was laid out in the central room of the house on top of several planks and two sawhorses covered by a plain sheet. Friends helped with many of these arrangements and made sure that those who had known John were notified of his death. That evening, the next day, and the following evening, other members of the community came to the house to bring gifts of food and to offer practical, emotional, and spiritual support to John's family. Several people took turns sitting with the body through the night until the grave could be dug and other preparations made for the funeral. In keeping with the whole of his life, John Stolzfus's funeral was a simple event, a familiar ritual that involved members of the community in the services, the burial, a communal meal afterward, and a recognized pattern of consolation activities during the following weeks and months. No one was shocked or surprised by this death or by its surrounding events. Experience, tradition, and shared attitudes had prepared individuals and the community as a whole to support each other and to contend with the cycles of life and death in their midst.

The Interplay of Death-Related Encounters and Attitudes

In Chapter 2, we examined how death-related events thrust themselves into human life. The *encounters* that we have with these events constitute one important component of our death-related experiences. In the present chapter, we explore a second important aspect of those experiences: our *attitudes* toward death. When events in the world come to our attention, we are usually already in a particular posture. That is, our beliefs, feelings, and habits of thought lead us to receive information and process encounters in selective ways. For instance, we pay attention to what one person is saying even while we ignore other communications going on in the background—or vice versa. Similarly, we are favorably disposed to some types of encounters, but not so favorably disposed—or even negatively disposed and actively hostile—to others. In these ways, death-related attitudes are both products and determinants of many of our encounters with the world. Thus, a central issue relating to attitudes concerns the ways in which patterns of belief and feeling enter into what we think and do, especially as our attitudes become dispositions or habitual ways of thinking about and acting in the world.

What this means is that we human beings *contribute* to our experiences. We are not merely passive receivers of information. We shape and form our knowledge of what is happening, depending on our prior beliefs and feelings. We meet the world from a particular stance, in specific ways. The Amish do this in their special ways and the Puritans (whom we will discuss at the end of this chapter) did it in theirs; everyone does it in some way or other.

At the same time, events around us help to shape in their own ways our knowledge and understanding of the world. Death-related encounters certainly play an important role in shaping death-related attitudes. As we learned in Chapter 2 for instance, unlike the example of John Stolzfus, most people in the United States today die in a hospital or other institution. As a result, their deaths may be physically removed from the presence of family members and friends. That makes such deaths remote from their survivors. Most Americans today do not often confront death directly, a circumstance that can contribute to and support a belief that death is, or should be, invisible. But think of this situation also the other way round. If one's habitual way of behaving in the face of someone else's stress is to withdraw because it creates discomfort, then one is likely to stay away from the hospital where someone is dying. In this way, *attitudes* toward death (for example, "death is stressful—stay away from stressful situations") influence encounters. The attitudes that one holds may tend to encourage one to withdraw or become remote from encounters with death.

Death-Related Attitudes

Death Anxiety

In recent years, much research on death-related attitudes has focused on matters related to death anxiety (Neimeyer, 1994; Neimeyer & Van Brunt, 1995). Results of these studies are interesting, especially when repeated reports confirm the plausibility of their conclusions. For example, in many studies women report higher death anxiety than men. It is not clear precisely whether women really are more anxious than men about death or whether women are simply more open than men in discussing their attitudes toward emotionally intense subjects. Many studies also note that older adults appear to report less death anxiety than some younger persons, such as adolescents, and individuals with strong religious convictions report less death anxiety than those who do not share such a value framework. Death anxiety has also been examined in terms of other demographic (e.g., occupation, health status, and experience with death) and personality (e.g., psychopathology) factors, but results are more mixed. Death anxiety may not be linear (that is, increasing or decreasing steadily as life goes on) but may vary with life accomplishments and past or future regrets (Tomer & Eliason, 1996). It also may not be easy to change people's anxieties about death.

It seems evident that death anxiety is a complex and still not fully understood subject. Moreover, the efforts of researchers to measure various forms of death anxiety, to determine the variables that do or do not influence such anxiety, and to compare different population groups in terms of their death anxieties are not without difficulties. For example, many of these studies seem to have assumed that: (1) death anxiety does exist (in all humans and all respects, or just in some?); (2) individuals will be both willing and able to disclose their death anxieties; and (3) adequate instruments and methodologies are available to identify and measure death anxieties. In fact, whereas Becker (1973) argued that awareness of individual mortality is the most basic source of anxiety, Freud (1913/1954, p. 304) seemed to think that we could not really be anxious about death since "our own death is indeed quite unimaginable . . . at bottom nobody believes in his own death . . . [and] in the unconscious everyone of us is convinced of his own immortality." Further, however much or little an individual may be anxious about death, most of the research on this subject depends upon self-reports (in response to questionnaires, interviews, projective tests), usually taken on a one-time basis from conveniently accessible groups like college students (for example, Thorson et al., 1998). Researchers conducting these studies are sensitive to questions of interpretation, such as: How valid or reliable are such reports? Are they representative or out of context? In particular, if one's score on a death anxiety scale is low, does that indicate low death anxiety or high denial and active repression of scary feelings? Note that the familiar distinction between fears (attitudes or concerns directed to some specific focus) and anxieties (attitudes that are more generalized and diffuse or less particularized in their objects) is set aside in most of this research.

Still, instruments for studying death anxiety have improved since the early Death Anxiety Scale (Templer, 1970; see also Lonetto & Templer, 1986) involving 15 short statements that one endorses as true or false to a number of more recent measures described in the *Death Anxiety Handbook* (Neimeyer, 1994). There also have been efforts (for example, Neimeyer & Van Brunt, 1995) to encourage greater sophistication and effectiveness in this field.

Death-Related Concerns and Responses

One way to move forward in our thinking about death-related attitudes might be to focus not merely on aversive attitudes (such as anxiety, denial, distancing, fear) but on more accepting attitudes as well. It is also useful to sort out death-related attitudes in terms of the specific focus of their concern. For example, the word *death* is often used to designate, not the situation or state of being dead, but the *process of dying* or coming to be dead. Thus, when we say, "John had a very difficult death," we are likely to be referring not to John's death but to the manner of his dying. Alternatively, the word death sometimes refers primarily to the *aftermath of a death.* Thus, one might say, "Mary is finding John's death to be quite hard." These different ways of speaking reveal that death-related attitudes can focus on one or more of the following: (1) attitudes about one's own dying; (2) attitudes about the death of one's self; (3) attitudes about what will happen to the self after death; and (4) attitudes related to the dying, death, or bereavement of someone else (Choron, 1964; Collett & Lester, 1969).

One's Own Dying Attitudes (which include beliefs, feelings, values, postures, and dispositions to action) are frequently directed to *one's own dying.* Such attitudes among contemporary Americans commonly reflect fears and anxiety about the possibility of experiencing a long, difficult, painful, or undignified dying process, especially in an alien institution under the care of strangers who might not respect one's personal needs or wishes. People who hold these attitudes often express a preference that their dying might occur without any form of distress, without prior knowledge, and in their sleep. One outcome of such a preference may be to prepare a living will or to designate someone as an agent for one's durable power of attorney in health matters (see Chapter 16) to ensure that the dying process will not be unduly and painfully prolonged.

In other societies or among individuals who are guided by a different set of concerns, many people hold attitudes that lead them to fear a sudden, unanticipated death. For such individuals, it is important to have time to address what some have called "unfinished business" by expressing to their loved ones such sentiments as "Thank you," "I love you," "I am sorry for anything I might have done to hurt you," "I forgive you for anything you might have done to hurt me," or simply, "Goodbye." Others may wish to have enough time and awareness to "get ready to meet their Maker" or otherwise prepare themselves for death through meditation and a special positioning of the body (see Box 3.1). Even in our society, many want to satisfy personal concerns about how their goods will be distributed after their deaths. Some individuals who find value in setting an example for others or bearing suffering for some altruistic or religious motive may even look forward to their dying with courage and some degree of anticipation. Attitudes toward dying are at the heart of each of these examples.

The Death of One's Self A second category of death-related attitudes is primarily concerned with death itself, specifically the *death of one's self.* Here the focus is on what death means and what will happen to the self at the moment of death. For example, one's attitude might principally be focused on a concern that death means nothingness, the complete evacuation or erasure of the personal self. One way this concern might be acted out is to resist death with all possible means available. Then again, those who find life difficult or filled with hardships might look forward to its ending, to the simple cessation of the tribulations they are now experiencing. Such persons might reject difficult, painful, or expensive interventions along with those perceived as likely to be ineffective. In either case, the main focus of concern is death itself and the nonexistence, nonbeing, loss of self, or loss of personal identity thought to be associated with death.

What Will Happen to the Self after Death A third category of death-related attitudes concerns *what will happen to the self after death.* Here the central concerns have to do with what the consequences or aftereffects of death will mean for the self. For some, that might involve anxiety about the unknown. For others, it might include a fear of judgment and/or punishment after death. For still others, it might depend upon anticipation of a heavenly reward for a lifetime of hard work, upright living, or faithfulness. In a similar way, many see death itself as merely a bridge or passage to another life in which, for example, the conditions of their existence might be improved over this present life or in which a reunion might be achieved with a loved person who had died earlier. The focus in all of these attitudes is on some outcome or result for the self that is thought to follow one's own death.

The Dying, Death, or Bereavement of Another The death-related attitudes we have examined thus far all have to do with attitudes held by an individual about his or her experiences prior to, at the time of, and after his or her own death. A fourth set of death-related attitudes is principally concerned not with the self, but with the *dying, death, or bereavement of another.* For example, I might be mainly concerned about the implications for me of someone else's dying or death. I

Box 3.1 The Death of a Tibetan Buddhist Teacher

In . . . 1983, Kyabje Ling Rinpoche, senior tutor to His Holiness the Dalai Lama . . . suffered the first in a series of small (strokes). On Christmas Day of that year, four of the disciples spontaneously gathered together at Ling Rinpoche's house in the foothills of the Himalayas. While sitting in his downstairs room rejoicing over their chance meeting, they were informed that he had just passed away . . . He was eighty-one years old.

In death, Ling Rinpoche's exceptional spiritual attainment was made quite evident. He died . . . in a special meditation posture modeled on the posture the Buddha assumed at *parinirvana* [his passage from this world]. In the Tibetan tradition, the body of a dead person is left on the deathbed for at least three days in order to allow the stream of consciousness to leave the body peacefully. Several techniques can be utilized during the death experience if one is an accomplished meditator. With these techniques, the body does not show any signs of deterioration as long as the consciousness remains in it. . . . Ling Rinpoche maintained a technique called the Meditation on the Clear Light of Death for a total of thirteen days. The Swiss disciple who cared for him during the last weeks of his life visited his room daily to make sure everything was satisfactory. She confirmed that during this entire time Ling Rinpoche's face remained beautiful and flesh-toned, and his body showed none of the normal signs of death.

His Holiness the Dalai Lama was so moved by the spirituality of his personal teacher that he decided to have Ling Rinpoche's body embalmed instead of cremated. Today the statue holding the remains of Kyabje Ling Rinpoche may be viewed at the palace of the Dalai Lama in Dharamsala. ■

SOURCE: From Blackman, 1997, pp. 73, 75.

might worry that I will not be sufficiently strong and resourceful to see an ill and dying person whom I love through the challenges and losses that he or she faces. Or perhaps I look forward to taking care of someone who so frequently cared for me in the past. If so, I might make arrangements to keep that person at home with me, rather than permitting him or her to enter some institutional care setting. Equally, I might be concerned about impending separation from someone whom I love. If the dying individual is a disagreeable person or is experiencing great difficulty in his or her struggles, I might anticipate the relief that will be associated with that person's death. Or I might be fearful about how I will be able to go on with living after someone else is gone.

Alternatively, it might be the implications for someone else of my own dying or death that are of primary concern to me. For example, I might be concerned about the burdens that my illness and dying are placing upon those whom I love. Or I might be worried about what will happen to loved ones after I am gone or how my death will affect plans and projects that I had previously pursued. With these concerns in mind, some individuals strive to remain alert as long as they can so that they can spend more time with those they love. Others make provisions to support their survivors-to-be. Still others redouble efforts to complete their prized projects or at least to take them as far as they can.

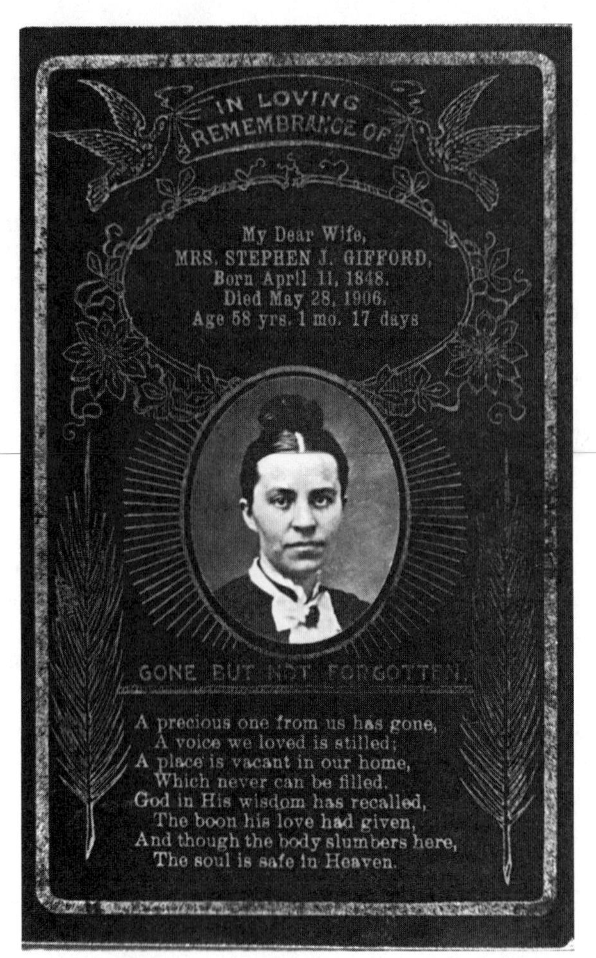

Fond sentiments in an early 20th century memorial card.

Some Implications of Death-Related Attitudes

Two major implications of our discussion of death-related attitudes are that such attitudes vary greatly and that humans can exert some influence over their own death-related attitudes. In terms of *variation in death-related attitudes*, it is common to hear talk of fears and anxieties in attitudes about death. Certainly, these are familiar elements or aspects of death-related attitudes, perhaps because dying, death, and bereavement represent something sharply different from or even opposed to the life we now know. Thus, if we ask ourselves what most bothers or frightens us about the implications of death, or what are some of the ways in which we would most like *not* to die, it is not surprising that fears and anxieties should quickly rise to the surface.

However, death-related attitudes need not always center on fear or anxiety. In general, humans may adopt a broad range of attitudes, feelings, and emotions concerning death and its implications, just as they can have many different attitudes about various aspects of life and living.

In terms of the *influence that humans can exert over death-related attitudes*, it is notable that humans are able to reflect upon their own and other possible attitudes, select with some degree of freedom the attitudes that they wish to hold, and change their attitudes in the light of new encounters or additional reflection on matters related to death (see Box 3.2). Two knowledgeable commentators have offered these remarks on the human condition: "Appreciation

Box 3.2 A Colonial Epitaph from Wolfpits, Connecticut (1830)

Remember me as you draw nigh
As you are now, so once was I.
As I am now, so must you be,
Prepare for death and follow me.

SOURCE: From Jones, 1967, p. 148.

of finiteness can serve not only to enrich self-knowledge but to provide the impulse to propel us forward toward achievement and creativity" (Feifel, 1977a, p. 11); "Everything can be taken from a man but one thing: the last of the human freedoms—to choose one's attitude in any given set of circumstances, to choose one's own way" (Frankl, 1984, p. 86). Although attitudes are fundamental to human life and behavior, they can be changed—even though such changes may not be easy to make.

Five Dominant Patterns in Western Attitudes toward Death

Other ways to understand the richness and complexity of death-related attitudes can be found in the work of historians, sociologists, psychologists, and anthropologists. In this section, we turn to one account of such attitudes offered by a French cultural historian, Philippe Ariès (1974b, 1981). Ariès described five dominant patterns in the attitudes of Western societies toward death and tried to identify their historical underpinnings. Because the historical dimension of Ariès's work is not central to our interests in this book, we focus here on his portrait of five basic patterns in attitudes related to death. These five attitudinal patterns are tame death, death of the self, remote and imminent death, death of the other, and death denied (see Table 3.1). Throughout this section, we follow Ariès's description of two primary components in each attitudinal pattern: *attitudes toward death itself* and *attitudes toward the dead.*

Ariès believed that different death-related attitudes can coexist in any society and in any individual. Not surprisingly, attitudes are likely to be complex when concerned with any subject that is as central to human life as is death. Without denying this complexity, we set out here to disentangle these attitudes so that each can be studied more clearly. Holding each of these strands apart for analysis helps to clarify their individual roles within the overall fabric of human experience, although in everyday life they run together and intertwine.

Table 3.1 Death-Related Attitudes in Western Thought: Five Patterns and Two Themes According to Philippe Ariès

Tame Death	Death of the Self	Remote and Imminent Death	Death of the Other	Death Denied; Forbidden Death
Theme 1: Attitudes Toward Death				
The moment of death is familiar, simple, public	The moment of death is a final ordeal; it affects God's Last Judgment of the person			The moment of death is banished from view
Focus is on the community	Focus is on the dying person		Focus is on survivors	Focus is on survivors (or bureaucrats?)
Death is a sleep, until the Second Coming of Christ Afterlife is nonthreatening	Death leads to heaven or hell Afterlife may involve suffering	Death is a natural event but it is also frightening; ambivalence is the main feature	Death is an intolerable separation from the beloved; it is a sleep awaiting a reunion. Death is also a release into nature; there is little mention of God or hell.	Death is dirty and indecent
Theme 2: Attitudes Toward the Dead				
Bodies are buried in common graves in cemeteries near churches; the powerful are buried in the churches themselves Cemeteries are public squares	For upper classes, coffins are used and the grave site is marked; others are still buried in common graves	Cemeteries move away from churches; they serve *only* as burial grounds Fascination with the cadaver; dissection becomes a "fashionable art" Survivors keep some part of the dead loved one (heart or hair); the "eroticization" of death	Private graves are common; cult of the dead (visiting graves, etc.) The dead are disembodied spirits that may continue to be in this world; rise of "spiritualism"	Coffins are "caskets" Emphasis is on visitation and the attempt to make the dead appear "alive" ("sleeping")

SOURCE: Based on Ariès, 1981.

Tame Death

Ariès (1981) used the phrase *tame death* to describe a pattern of death-related attitudes in which death is regarded as the opposite of a wild force—that is, the opposite of something that is beyond our control and not subject to human domination. He held that within this attitude death has two essential characteristics: it has a familiar simplicity, and it is a public event.

The end of life does not come as a surprise to people who view *death as familiar and simple*. The dying person knows that he or she is dying. No attempt is made to evade death. Although dying persons who view death as tame may feel some regret for the loss of their lives, basically they calmly accept the inevitable. They may also review things they had owned and friends they had loved. Such dying persons may ask forgiveness of friends and commend first the friends and then themselves to God. Then communication ceases and the person waits calmly for death. Routine, simple, easeful: this is how these persons view death. We saw this attitude in the death of John Stolzfus in the vignette near the beginning of this chapter.

This calm simplicity is typically also related to a belief about what death is. For example, many people in Christian Europe once thought of death primarily as a kind of sleep. Among such believers, those who died were thought to sleep until the Second Coming of Christ. At that moment, the saints would enter a heavenly home; those who were not saints would remain forever asleep. In either case, death would be peaceful and nonthreatening—that is, "tame."

The second characteristic of this pattern of death-related attitudes is that *death is a public event.* People who share this attitude think a vile and ugly death is one that is sudden and solitary. Dying persons who hold this attitude prefer to be surrounded by friends, family, neighbors, and other members of the community who choose to be present. According to Ariès, this is partly because the individual is not believed to be of greatest importance in this scene; the community matters most. Death is a social event that affects the entire community, and the whole community, not only the individual who is dying, has to deal with it. Thus, death is not to be accomplished alone.

Tame death is also characterized by a particular attitude toward the dead. Some people fear the dead and see the corpse as a source of pollution. Under these circumstances, cemeteries are likely to be located outside of the human community. However, when death is viewed as a tame feature of human experience, the dead do not inspire fear. When this is the dominant attitude, living people move around near the dead with no anxiety, and cemeteries may be located within the human community. Historically, cemeteries even became centers of social life; marketing, judicial proceedings, and social gatherings occurred in them. They were the public squares of their time.

Death and the dead are familiar in these circumstances. For Ariès, tame death is the most basic pattern because it is the most pervasive and the most persistent. Thus, Ariès believed that this pattern is not completely absent from society today. For instance, he argued that many working-class people in the West and many people in rural areas display some of these attitudes.

Death of the Self

Ariès (1985) dramatized another dominant pattern of death-related attitudes by describing sculptures found in medieval cathedrals. Before the 11th century, when reference was made to the next world, an image of the Second Coming of Christ was dominant. In this image, Christ was portrayed in glory, surrounded by the saints (including the dead members of the church). However, in the 12th century another image began to play a larger and larger role: the image of the Last Judgment, where the just are separated from the damned. This change in imagery reveals that people no longer felt unthreatened by what might follow after their death or felt assured of their own salvation. What is important in these changing attitudes is an emerging focus on the *death of the self.*

For anxiety to arise about personal salvation, individuals must have a strong sense of self. According to Ariès, recognition of the significance of the individual is a key ingredient in this second attitudinal pattern. Biography—the history of a life, my life—is thought to be important. An attitude of this type is often associated with the belief that God or some other heavenly figure maintains a "book of life," a record or register of what each individual has done. According to this notion, the deeds that made up a life are weighed after death. This type of idea also sometimes includes the view that the moment of death is the final ordeal for an individual. At that moment—just preceding the actual event of death—the dying individual supposedly witnesses a struggle between a patron saint and the devil for his or her soul. The patron saint points to good deeds performed, the devil points to bad deeds, and a judgment is rendered. How one behaves at this moment is believed to be crucial because the manner in which one dies determines the outcome and decides the meaning of the person's whole life.

Similar beliefs focusing on the moment of death are present in many current religious traditions. Some Jews hold that it is important at that moment to try to recite the Shema ("Hear, O Israel: the LORD is our God, the LORD alone, You shall love the LORD your God with all your heart, and with all your soul, and with all your might"—Deuteronomy 6:4,5). Muslims are taught that invoking the Divine Name at the moment of death can be salvific (Jonker, 1997; Kassis, 1997). Some Buddhists hold that chanting the name of Amitabha Buddha assures that one will find oneself in the Pure Land after death (Yeung, 1995). Needless to say, these sorts of beliefs can burden the moment of death with great anxiety. In the West, this anxiety contributed to the development of the practice of the *ars moriendi*, the art of dying well (Beaty, 1970; Kastenbaum, 1989a, 1989c; O'Connor, 1942).

The second central theme in Ariès's analysis involves attitudes toward the dead. An emphasis on death of the self includes in part a revulsion at the dead body. That revulsion shows up in several ways: the face of the corpse might be covered; one might hide the body from view, either by sewing it into a shroud or placing it in a coffin. Sometimes even this is not enough and the coffin itself has to be covered by a cloth (the pall). This attitude toward the dead is different from the one encountered in tame death, which views the dead without revulsion.

Remote and Imminent Death

According to Ariès (1981), when society is not dominated by religious modes of thinking, changes occur that alter how people think about, feel about, and react to death.

Ariès reported that in the human community two invaders from nature have always been feared: sex and death. The ancient world and medieval Europe kept at bay these invaders of the social community by carefully controlling what people believed and how they behaved with regard to sex and death. In the modern world, these ancient (largely, religious) controls have lost much of their force and as the cultural reins on nature—especially on death—

that appeared to tame death became looser, death came to be viewed as untamed, wild, invasive.

This outlook involves a paradox. On one hand, death is proclaimed to be a natural event, not a supernatural one. Calm acceptance of one's mortality is expected. On the other hand, much effort is expended to keep death at a distance because death is seen as frightening. In other words, death is both nearby (natural, beautiful) and at a distance (untamed, dangerous, something to be feared)—both *remote and imminent.* In this single, oxymoronic phrase, Ariès captured the tone of an attitude toward death that is primarily one of ambivalence.

Attitudes toward the dead are also different and distinctive. The body (like death) is seen as purely natural. At death, the soul is thought to leave the body and the body decomposes back into the natural ingredients from which it originated. However, the ambivalence in this pattern of death-related attitudes shows up in how the dead are thought of, too. For example, concerns about what to do with dead bodies are expressed. In this view, cemeteries should be situated outside of towns, and these modern cemeteries are seen as specialized places for burial. They serve only one purpose and are not viewed as places for social life. Of course, one effect of relocating cemeteries in this way is to make the dead more remote from the living.

For Ariès, attitudes involving remote and imminent death are associated with a struggle to keep death-related feelings and behavior under tight control, but that control is very fragile. Anxiety, fear, and fascination with death are common in a posture that is basically ambivalent about death.

Death of the Other

Another pattern of feelings, beliefs, and behaviors places emphasis on *the death of the other*—that is, on relationships broken by death. In this view, death is seen as an intolerable separation of those bound together by human affections. Ariès called this attitude a view of *death untamed.* Feelings, beliefs, and behaviors are perceived as nearly out of control in this attitude. Part of this perception may result when human affection is typically limited to a smaller number of family members, rather than being distributed among a larger number of individuals, as in other societal contexts. So much feeling concentrated on so few persons (as in contemporary nuclear families) helps to make the death of those persons intolerable.

In this attitude, death itself is often seen as a peaceful, waiting sleep. Thus, the sleeping dead are waiting for reunion with loved ones in the next life. This notion of a reunion is distinctive. An attitude like this is quite pervasive in much of modern Western society. For example, a young girl once described to one of us how she and her mother had baptized their new dog. Their aim in doing this seems to have been to ensure that when they reached the next life, not only would they be reunited with loved persons, but the household pet would also be there!

We can note several other aspects of this type of attitude. Death is not expected to involve suffering. Hell has virtually disappeared in descriptions of the afterlife that are linked to this outlook. Daily life in the afterlife (often called heaven) is often described as remarkably like life in this world. Thus, one child observed in an interview that "when you die, God takes care of you like your mother did when you were alive—only God doesn't yell at you all the time" (Adler, 1979, p. 46).

The "death of the other" attitude also generates particular ways to deal with the dead. Cemeteries are viewed as unsanitary places. Thus, whenever possible they are located outside of towns. Burial is most commonly a function of the civil government (rather than of the church) under this pattern. The ideas that the resting place of the dead should be granted in perpetuity and that there should be hereditary ownership of cemetery plots are also associated with this pattern. The cemetery becomes the focus of all piety for the dead and there is an emphasis on making visits to the cemetery. This pattern Ariès called a new cult of the dead. It is well represented by Mount Auburn Cemetery outside Boston (dedicated in September 1831), which is a model of the American "rural" or "garden" cemetery whose art and architecture were intended to instruct the living, inculcate morality, and cultivate the finer emotions (French, 1975; Zanger, 1980).

Death Denied or Forbidden Death

Ariès (1981) claimed that an absolutely new attitude toward dying appeared in the 20th century, virtually reversing earlier customs surrounding death. He called this new attitudinal pattern *death denied* or *forbidden death* and was sympathetic to Gorer's (1965a) description of "the pornography of death." Death is "denied" or "forbidden" because it is seen as dirty and indecent. Accordingly, it is thought to be somehow offensive or unacceptable to die in public. Thus, death is made into a solitary, private action. Some appear to believe that dying persons prefer to be left alone to die, even though there is good, longstanding research to demonstrate precisely the opposite (for example, Hinton, 1967).

A social emphasis on denying or forbidding death arises from many sources, but perhaps especially from a shift in attention away from the dying person and toward others. Continuing the process begun in "the death of the other," an emphasis deepens on *our response* to the other person's death. The feelings and sensibilities of those around the dying person take precedence. If we as others are made uncomfortable by a death, then that feeling must be accommodated.

The simplest way to protect others from the odors, sights, sounds, and feelings associated with death is to remove death from their presence, so contemporary society often banishes death. According to Ariès, when a death occurs in much of today's society, one can hardly tell that anything has happened. Society no longer observes a pause in its ongoing rhythms of working and playing. Except for a brief funeral period—which usually involves only the closest associates of the dead person and only those who choose to participate—the surface of societal life is unmarked by the death of one of its members. The message seems to be that nothing—or at least nothing very important—has happened.

To achieve this goal, one must hide not only the facts about the expected outcome; one must also hide the emotional response to those facts. Thus, many Americans avoid situations in which feelings might be shown, both before and after a death. As a result, many in contemporary society have adopted an attitude toward mourning that is historically quite unusual. In this attitude, mourning is thought to be morbid, even pathological. Thus, there is often a refusal to share in the suffering of the bereaved. As a result, the bereaved are often more or less isolated, just as the dying person is frequently isolated. Except in very controlled circumstances (for example, during the funeral and the visitation) and ways of expression, it is thought that grief should be experienced and expressed in private.

Ariès (1981) also pointed to another way in which death has been forbidden or banished in our society by describing the "medicalization" of Western society. Recall from Chapter 2 that prior to the 1880s physicians played little or no role in deathbed scenes. However, late in the 19th century visits to physicians became important, even necessary, steps when illness entered one's life. Death began to be viewed less and less as a natural, necessary phenomenon. Instead, the belief arose that technology can and should achieve almost anything, including the prevention of death. When death occurs, it is viewed as an "accident" or "failure" in medical practice. To prevent this lapse from occurring, more and more people turn to technological centers of treatment—hospitals and other similar institutions. Death is thus largely banished from the home. The result is that death can be kept hidden much more effectively. After all, whereas neighbors and relatives might drop into the home, they are much less likely to drop into the hospital, especially given that institution's rules about visiting hours.

Perhaps the ultimate banishment of death occurs when no one is present at the moment of death: the dying person is alone in a room and is unconscious. Here the dying person has lost all control over and any say in his or her death. Death no longer belongs to the dying person, or even to the family. It now, as Ariès said, belongs to bureaucrats.

Attitudes toward the dead show a similar pattern of denial in this outlook. According to Ariès, one characteristic effect of this denial is that coffins no longer look like coffins. They become "caskets." The term casket originated as a diminutive form of cask, a small box or chest for jewels, letters, or other things of value; caskets themselves were works of art, as tombs used to be. The use of this term also seems to imply that what is contained in the casket is something valuable (not something to fear). Indeed, in this attitude, almost all memorial activities are now focused on the visit to the deceased, and when people go to a visitation, what they experience is the illusion of life. Morticians carefully work to erase signs of death. After the Civil War in the United States, embalming became an important part of the care of the dead. One main point of embalming appears to be not so much to preserve the dead body as to keep it from showing signs of death at a viewing. Thus, dead bodies are indeed not thought of as frightening; in part that may because they are "not dead"! (Think of how often people at a visitation remark how "he looks like he's just sleeping.")

By adopting attitudes of forbidden death, Ariès (1974a) concluded that Western societies had brought about a "reversal of death," which has three central characteristics: (1) the dying person is deprived of his or her own death; (2) mourning is denied; and (3) new funerary rites such as embalming are invented in the United States.

The Puritans of Seventeenth-Century New England

The critical role of attitudes in shaping the character of experiences with death can be illustrated in one final example: that of the Puritans of 17th-century New England. We selected this example because it draws upon a historical group in the United States and because it differs in so many ways from contemporary death-related attitudes. It also reminds us once again that the patterns that Ariès has described are not strictly sequential; one pattern does not simply replace another, and different groups may emphasize different attitudinal patterns (or different aspects of a pattern).

The Puritans originated as a reformist group within the Church of England. Those Puritans who came to America found a new land in which they were free to uphold their beliefs and practice their religion as they wished. The New England Puritans established thriving settlements in various colonies, but their presence was particularly notable in Massachusetts during the middle and latter portions of the 17th century. Here, they emphasized the importance of preaching and conversion through an intense personal experience.

For the Puritans, everything that existed or happened was part of a divine purpose. At the same time, they viewed human history since the betrayal of Adam and Eve as one long descent into ever-deepening depravity. In this situation, no human being could be truly worthy of salvation, nor could any good works earn the favor of God's grace. Nevertheless, the Puritans believed that God, in His infinite mercy and love, had chosen a select and predetermined few for salvation.

The great question for each individual Puritan was whether or not he or she was a member of God's holy elect. No one could ever have confident knowledge concerning the answer to that question. To think that one did have such knowledge would be to think that one understood the all-knowing mind of God. More likely, to believe that one was assured of salvation was good evidence that one had actually succumbed to the seductive falsehoods of Satan. Confidence in the "sure and certain hope of resurrection to eternal life" was simply not open to the Puritans.

Nevertheless, the question of personal salvation preoccupied individual Puritans. Each Puritan struggled continuously with his or her conscience to discern, in the midst of innumerable signs of personal depravity, at least some indicators or "marks" that he or she might be among the chosen few. Thus, Puritanism was "a faith marked by a never-ending, excruciating uncertainty . . . [in which] the Puritans were gripped individually and collectively by an intense and unremitting fear of death, while simultaneously clinging to the traditional Christian rhetoric of viewing death as a release and relief for the earth-bound soul" (Stannard, 1977, pp. 75, 79). For the Puritans, one must constantly recognize one's own utter and total depravity, while at the same time praying earnestly for a salvation that one is helpless to secure.

Puritan preachers dwelt vividly on the contrast between the potential terrors and bliss of the afterlife. Those who were not among the elect were subject to the eternal torment of the damned. Those who actually were among the elect were themselves troubled by lack of certainty even up to the very moment of death. Thus, as Stannard (1977, p. 89) has argued, "The New England Puritans, despite their traditional optimistic rhetoric, were possessed of an intense, overt fear of death—the natural consequence of what to them were three patently true and quite rational beliefs: that of their own utter and unalterable depravity; that of the omnipotence, justness, and inscrutability of God; and that of the unspeakable terrors of Hell."

These attitudes toward death among the New England Puritans had implications not only for individual adults but also for children and for society as a whole. The Puritan worldview combined a deep love of children with a strong sense of their depravity and sinful pollution (so different, in this latter regard, from the Amish). Also, the era of the Puritans in New England was a time when infants and children were actually at great risk of dying, and when parents gave birth to many children in the expectation that few would remain alive to care for them in the hour of their own deaths. Perhaps for both these reasons, in their personal relationships with their children Puritan parents were advised to maintain an attitude of "restraint and even aloofness, mixed with . . . an intense parental effort to impose discipline and encourage spiritual precocity" (Stannard, 1977, p. 57).

Puritan children were constantly reminded of the likelihood that they might die at any moment. They were threatened with the dangers of personal judgment and damnation in which even their own parents might testify against them. The expectation of reunion with parents after death was denied to them. They were also reminded of the guilt they would bear if through sinfulness they should bring harm to their parents. In this vein, books for children, including even the *New England Primer* (1727/1962) from which they learned the alphabet, were designed to remind young readers of the imminence and possible consequences of death. How different this attitude is from those of today, or even from 19th-century emphases, such as that expressed in one of the famous McGuffey's readers (1866), which stressed eternal reunion of children and parents after death for a new life in heaven (see Box 3.3; also Minnich, 1936a, 1936b; Westerhoff, 1978).

Burial practices are a particularly good indicator of death-related attitudes among the New England Puritans. At first, absence of ceremony and restraint of emotion reflected the Puritan reaction to the excesses of "papist" practices. That is, the corpse was regarded as a meaningless husk, burial was swift and simple, and excessive displays of sadness or grief were discouraged. Funeral sermons were not delivered at the time of burial and were not very different from other forms of preaching.

Box 3.3 What Is Death?

Child.

1. Mother, how still the baby lies!
   I can not hear his breath;
   I can not see his laughing eyes;
   They tell me this is death.

2. My little work I thought to bring,
   And sit down by his bed,
   And pleasantly I tried to sing;
   They hushed me: he is dead!

3. They say that he again will rise,
   More beautiful than now;
   That God will bless him in the skies;
   O mother, tell me how!

Mother.

4. Daughter, do you remember, dear,
   The cold, dark thing you brought,
   And laid upon the casement here?
   A withered worm, you thought.

5. I told you, that Almighty power
   Could break that withered shell;
   And show you, in a future hour,
   Something would please you well.

6. Look at that chrysalis, my love;
   An empty shell it lies;
   Now raise your wondering glance above,
   To where yon insect flies!

Child.

7. O yes, mamma! how very gay
   Its wings of starry gold!
   And see! it lightly flies away
   Beyond my gentle hold.

8. O mother! now I know full well,
   If God that worm can change,
   And draw it from this broken cell,
   On golden wings to range;

9. How beautiful will brother be
   When God shall give him wings,
   Above this dying world to flee,
   And live with heavenly things!

(continues)

10. Our life is like a summer's day,
    It seems so quickly past:
    Youth is the morning, bright and gay,
    And if 'tis spent in wisdom's way,
    We meet old age without dismay,
    And death is sweet at last. ■

SOURCE: From McGuffey, 1866, pp. 109–110.

In the latter half of the 17th century, however, Puritan society in New England experienced many changes that threatened the prospects for its holy mission. Several important early leaders died (for example, John Winthrop, Thomas Shepard, John Cotton, and Thomas Hooker), a civil war in England and an ensuing official doctrine of religious toleration isolated the New England Puritans in their emphasis on doctrinal righteousness, and growing immigration and mercantilism in America produced an increasingly complex society in which the Puritan community declined in numbers and significance (Stannard, 1977).

In reaction, the embattled New England Puritans developed more and more elaborate funeral practices. Gloves were sent to friends and acquaintances as a form of invitation to the funeral, church bells were rung on the day of the funeral, a funeral procession conducted the coffin to the burial ground, and those who returned to the church or home of the deceased after the burial were given food and distinctively designed, costly funeral rings as tokens of attendance. As the deaths of Puritan leaders and community pillars were experienced, prayer was conducted at the funeral and funeral sermons took on the form of eulogies. Gravestones carved with elaborate verses praising the

YOU are desired to Accompany the Corps of Sir *William Phipps*, Knight, from *Salters-Hall* in *Swithins Lane*, to the Parish-Church of St. *Mary Woolnoth*, in *Lumbard-street* : On Thursday the 21st. of *February*, 1694/5. At Five of the Clock in the Afternoon precisely : And bring this Ticket with you.

A Puritan view of death: An invitation to the funeral of Sir William Phipps (1651–1695).

moral and religious character of the deceased began to mark the sites of burial. Clearly, a special set of attitudes toward death existed in Puritan New England, shaped by deeply held beliefs and implemented in earnest practice.

Summary

In this chapter, we examined attitudes toward death—clusters of beliefs, feelings, habits of thought, behaviors, and underlying values. In so doing, we learned that the dominant pattern of death-related attitudes in the United States today is only one among many possible patterns. Our distinctive attitudes are not the eternal essence of how human beings everywhere and throughout all time think about, feel about, or behave in the face of death. We saw this in our analysis of four different categories or focal clusters of death-related attitudes (one's own dying, the death of one's self, what will happen to the self after death, and the dying, death, or bereavement of another), in Ariès's survey of five dominant patterns of Western social attitudes toward death (tame death, death of the self, remote and imminent death, death of the other, and death denied), and in two specific examples (the Amish in America today and the New England Puritans of the 17th century). Patterns of death-related attitudes can be strikingly different and diverse. Such patterns have changed before; they can, and will, change again.

Questions for Review and Discussion

1. This chapter discussed attitudes toward death, dying, and bereavement. Think about how the chapter described attitudes. How do attitudes differ from encounters (as discussed in Chapter 2)? How were your attitudes affected by your encounters (either directly or through the media) with the terrorist attacks on America of September 11, 2001?

2. This chapter described in some detail two specific sets or patterns of attitudes regarding death: those of the present-day Amish and those of the Puritans in 17th-century New England. Note similarities and differences in these sets of attitudes. How did or do the attitudes of these two groups affect their encounters with death, dying, and bereavement?

3. Think about the four categories of death-related attitudes described in this chapter: attitudes about your own dying, your death, what will happen to you after death, and the dying, death, or bereavement of someone you love. Which of these categories is most important to you at this point in your life? What in particular is happening in your life that leads you to focus on this specific category of death-related attitudes? What are your chief concerns within this category?

4. Philippe Ariès described five dominant patterns of attitudes toward death found in Western societies. Which of the five patterns seems most familiar to you? Which aspects of each of the five patterns can you find in your own experience?

Suggested Readings

Concerning death-related attitudes and their interpretation, see:

Becker, E. (1973). *The Denial of Death.*

Lonetto, R., & Templer, D. I. (1986). *Death Anxiety.*

Neimeyer, R. A. (Ed.). (1994). *Death Anxiety Handbook: Research, Instrumentation, and Application.*

The views of Philippe Ariès are set forth in three books:

Ariès, P. (1974b). *Western Attitudes toward Death: From the Middle Ages to the Present.*

Ariès, P. (1981). *The Hour of Our Death.*

Ariès, P. (1985). *Images of Man and Death.*

Along with these works, the following celebrated and often-reprinted essay, which influenced Ariès's analysis of attitudes in today's society, should be read:

Gorer, G. (1965a). "The Pornography of Death." In G. Gorer, *Death, Grief, and Mourning.*

On the art of dying *(ars moriendi)*, see:

Beaty, N. L. (1970). *The Craft of Dying.*

Boase, T. S. R. (1972). *Death in the Middle Ages: Mortality, Judgment and Remembrance.*

O'Connor, M. C. (1942). *The Art of Dying Well: The Development of the Ars Moriendi.*

Depictions of various attitudes toward death in Western art, literature, and popular culture can be found in:

Bertman, S. L. (1991). *Facing Death: Images, Insights, and Interventions.*

Enright, D. J. (Ed.). (1983). *The Oxford Book of Death.*

Weir, R. F. (Ed.). (1980). *Death in Literature.*

Consult the following for death-related attitudes in America:

Crissman, J. K. (1994). *Death and Dying in Central Appalachia: Changing Attitudes and Practices.*

Dumont, R., & Foss, D. (1972). *The American View of Death: Acceptance or Denial?*

Farrell, J. J. (1980). *Inventing the American Way of Death: 1830–1920.*

Geddes, G. E. (1981). *Welcome Joy: Death in Puritan New England.*

Hostetler, J. A. (1994). *Amish Society* (4th ed.).

Jackson, C. O. (Ed.). (1977). *Passing: The Vision of Death in America.*

Mack, A. (Ed.). (1974). *Death in American Experience.*

Siegel, M. (Ed.). (1997). *The Last Word: The New York Times Book of Obituaries and Farewells—A Celebration of Unusual Lives.*

Stannard, D. E. (1977). *The Puritan Way of Death: A Study in Religion, Culture, and Social Change.*

Zielinski, J. M. (1993). *The Amish across America* (rev. ed.).

InfoTrac College Edition
For more information, explore the InfoTrac College Edition at **http://www.infotrac-college.com/Wadsworth**

Enter search terms: DEATH ANXIETY, DEATH ATTITUDES (OR DEATH-RELATED ATTITUDES), DEATH DENIAL, FORBIDDEN DEATH, TAME DEATH

Chapter Four

DEATH-RELATED PRACTICES AND THE AMERICAN DEATH SYSTEM

IN THIS CHAPTER, WE TURN TO *DEATH-related practices* as the third key element in the general portrait that we are describing of experiences with death in our society. Our goal is to supplement what we have already learned about *death-related encounters* in Chapter 2 and *death-related attitudes* in Chapter 3, and to show how encounters and attitudes affect practices. To do this we begin with an encounter with death that could hardly have been imagined before it took place and that has drastically affected American attitudes and practices: the events of September 11, 2001. To provide context for these events, we then introduce the concept of a "death system" in our society and illustrate how it has been mobilized to respond to the events of September 11.

Next, we turn to accidents and homicide, two other forms of human-induced death that are all too common in our society, and to examples of socially sanctioned death involving war and genocide, the Holocaust, and the beginning of the nuclear era. Each of these subjects provides an example of how encounters with death shape death-related attitudes and practices. Finally, we examine death-related practices found in three distinctive examples: the interplay between death and language (language about death versus death-related language), media news reports and entertainment programs, and contemporary American funeral practices.

There are, of course, a bewildering variety of death-related practices in the United States, too many to explore adequately in a single chapter. We also cannot fully separate practices from encounters and attitudes. However, we believe the practices selected for discussion in this chapter are distinctive and important. Above all, we believe that these practices show that it is not correct to conclude as some (such as Gorer, 1965a; Kübler-Ross, 1969) have done that ours is a "death-denying society," one from which death has largely been exiled as a social or public presence. The evidence presented in this chapter suggests that it is more defensible to argue (as do Dumont & Foss, 1972; Weisman, 1972) that death-related practices in the United States are neither simply death-denying nor death-accepting. These practices and the American death system express both types of attitudes—sometimes separately, sometimes simultaneously—along with other attitudes as well. ■

September 11, 2001: Terrorism, Violence, and Death

September 11, 2001, was a clear, fall day on the East Coast of the United States of America. It was also a day that was to be filled with horror, large-scale death and injury, and massive destruction of property.

On that Tuesday morning, many people went to work at the 110-story towers of the World Trade Center in New York City and at the Pentagon in Arlington, Virginia. About the same time, crews and passengers boarded commercial airliners in Boston, suburban Washington, D.C., and Newark for flights to California.

Shortly after takeoff, hijackers commandeered four commercial airliners, each with a full load of fuel for a transcontinental flight. The hijackers took over these flights, removed their pilots, and diverted the planes to their own ends.

At 8:45 A.M., one plane was flown directly into the north tower of the World Trade Center about 20 stories below the top of the building. Eighteen minutes later, a second plane crashed into the south tower in a similar way. Shortly thereafter, about 9:30 A.M., a third plane crashed into the southwest side of the Pentagon. On the fourth plane, apparently some of the passengers joined together to resist the terrorists, fought with them, and prevented them from carrying out their intended plans (to crash into the White House or the Capitol in Washington, D.C., or perhaps Camp David in Maryland). As a result of that

Ongoing rescue and recovery activities at the site where the World Trade Center once stood.

struggle, this last plane crashed in western Pennsylvania, southeast of Pittsburgh, shortly after 10:00 A.M.

About 10:00 A.M., the south tower of the World Trade Center collapsed as a result of the structural damage that it had suffered from being hit by the airliner and especially from the intensity of the subsequent fire fed by jet fuel. Approximately 29 minutes later, the north tower also collapsed. Later, four other buildings in the World Trade Center complex and a nearby Marriott hotel also collapsed.

Some 248 passengers and crewmembers aboard the four airliners (including 19 terrorists) died in these events, along with 126 killed at the Pentagon. As this is written, it is estimated that several thousand people died at the scene of the World Trade Center disaster, including workers at the offices, restaurants, and shops in the complex, visitors, and more than 340 firefighters and police officers who rushed into the buildings or set up nearby command posts in their efforts to save lives and help out. A final count of those who died in New York City will be difficult to obtain, since many bodies may have been consumed by the fires or buried under massive rubble that is only gradually being removed from this crime scene. DNA testing will be required to identify some bodies; many families may never recover the bodies of their loved ones.

The Death System in Every Society

The concept of a *death system* is a way of understanding death-related practices and how a society interacts with death-related experiences (Kastenbaum, 1972). We use that concept in this chapter to examine American responses to the events of September 11, along with other death-related encounters, attitudes, and practices in contemporary American society. Kastenbaum defined a death

Postal stamp designs draw public attention to life-threatening illnesses.

system as the "sociophysical network by which we mediate and express our relationship to mortality" (p. 310). He meant that every society works out, more or less formally and explicitly, a system that it interposes between death and its citizens, one that interprets the former to the latter. The presence of such systems—which are easily recognizable by most members of a society when their attention is drawn to them—reflects the existence and importance of social infrastructures and processes of socialization in human interactions with death, dying, and bereavement (Fulton & Bendiksen, 1994; Parsons, 1951). According to Kastenbaum (1972), each societal death system has its own constitutive elements and characteristic functions (see Box 4.1).

Some type of death system is found *in every society.* It may be formal, explicit, and widely acknowledged in some of its aspects, even while it is largely hidden and often unspoken in other aspects. As Blauner (1966) has shown, many small, primitive, tribal societies must organize many of their activities around death's recurrent presence. In large, modern, impersonal societies such as in the developed countries of North America and Western Europe, the social implications of death are often less disruptive, less prominent, and more contained—at least until shocking events highlight them. Thus, the death system in contemporary American society appears to act in many important ways to keep death at a distance from the mainstream of life and to gloss over many of its harsh aspects. That is, our death system often acts to support death denial. The problem with this is that we may have "created systems which protect us in the aggregate from facing up to the very things that as individuals we most need to know" (Evans, 1971, p. 83). However, other aspects of our death system draw attention to death and respond to its appearances. For example, note the concern for three leading causes of death expressed by the U.S. Postal System in the design of the three stamps

Box 4.1 Elements and Functions of a Societal Death System

Elements of a death system include:

- *People*—individuals whose more or less permanent or stable social roles are somehow related to death, such as life insurance agents, medical examiners and coroners, funeral directors, lawyers, and florists
- *Places*—specific locations that have a death-related character, such as cemeteries, funeral homes, health care institutions, and the "hallowed ground" of a battlefield or disaster
- *Times*—occasions that are associated with death, such as Memorial Day, Good Friday, or the anniversary of a death
- *Objects*—things linked to death, such as death certificates, hearses, obituaries and death notices in newspapers, weapons, tombstones, and a hangman's gallows or electric chair
- *Symbols*—objects and actions that signify death, such as a black armband, a skull and crossbones, certain solemn organ music, and certain words or phrases ("Ashes to ashes, dust to dust . . . ")

Functions of a death system are:

- *To give warnings and predictions*, as in sirens or flashing lights on emergency vehicles or media alerts concerning the potential for violent weather or an earthquake
- *To prevent death*, as in the presence of police or security officers and systems of emergency medical care
- *To care for the dying*, as in modern hospice programs and some aspects of hospital services
- *To dispose of the dead*, as in the work of the funeral industry, along with cemeteries and crematories
- *To work toward social consolidation after death*, as in funeral rituals or self-help groups for the bereaved
- *To help make sense of death*, as in the case of many religious or philosophical systems
- *To bring about socially sanctioned killing* of either humans or animals, as in training for war, capital punishment, and the slaughtering of livestock for food ■

SOURCE: Based on Kastenbaum, 1972.

reproduced on page 69. The key point here is that every society has some system for coping with the fundamental challenges that death presents to human existence. Thus, it is helpful to the study of death, dying, and bereavement to examine the nature of a society's death system and the ways in which it functions.

The American Death System and the Events of September 11, 2001

The September 11, 2001, attack occurred within the continental United States and struck at some of the most prominent symbols of American economic and military power in the form of the World Trade Center towers and the Pentagon (The Editors of *New York* Magazine, 2001). Like terrorist attacks throughout the world with which many people have had to learn to cope and to live with for a long time (for example, Lifton, 1999), this one killed and injured innocent men, women, and children. Included were individuals of many ethnic backgrounds, cultures, races, and religions, as well as citizens from more than 80 countries around the world, as diverse as Australia, Bangladesh, Germany, Great Britain, India, Israel, Mexico, Pakistan, and South Korea (Bumiller, 2001; *St. Petersburg Times*, 2001f). The attack also raised homicidal terrorism to a new level within the United States, exceeding in its scope the effects of the bomb that exploded on February 26, 1993, in a parking garage beneath the World Trade Center, killing six persons and injuring over 1,000 more, or the truck bombing of the Alfred P. Murrah Federal Building in Oklahoma City on April 19, 1995, in an attack that killed 168 people and injured more than 500 others (Linenthal, 2001; Michel & Herbeck, 2001).

On September 11, many Americans seemed surprised that terrorists would or could attack the United States. In fact, during the 1990s alone Americans and American interests abroad were attacked on numerous occasions. For example, in 1995 a car bomb was detonated at a U.S. military headquarters in Riyadh, Saudi Arabia, killing five military personnel. In 1996 a truck bomb exploded outside the Khobar Towers barracks in Dharan, Saudi Arabia, killing 19 American service personnel and wounding hundreds. In 1998 car bombs were exploded outside American embassies in Kenya and Tanzania within minutes of each other, killing over 224 people and injuring thousands (some of whom were Americans, but the vast majority were Kenyans and Tanzanians). And in 2000, an American destroyer, the USS *Cole*, was attacked in the harbor at Aden, Yemen, killing 17 and injuring 39 more.

It would have been highly desirable if elements of the American death system in one of its designated functions could have provided specific *warnings and predictions* that might have prevented any or all of these events. For whatever reasons, that did not happen.

Still, on September 11 itself other elements of American society and its death system did spring into almost immediate action. Acting to create informal networks, some passengers on one of the planes joined together to try to overcome their hijackers and frustrate the goals of the terrorists, while others used cell phones to warn outsiders about what was happening or to leave messages for loved ones (see Box 4.2). Others, including many firefighters and police officers, rushed to the scenes of the tragedy and ran into burning buildings in an attempt to *prevent death* and save lives—only to lose their own lives when the buildings collapsed.

Box 4.2 Brian Sweeney's Message from a Hijacked Plane

This is the reported message that Brian Sweeney, a 38-year-old passenger on United Airlines Flight 175 that crashed into the World Trade Center's South Tower, left for his wife, Julie, on their answering machine shortly before 9 A.M. on September 11, 2001:

> "Hey, Jules, it's Brian. I'm on a plane and it's hijacked and it doesn't look good. I just wanted to let you know that I love you and I hope to see you again. If I don't, please have fun in life and live your life the best you can. Know that I love you and no matter what, I'll see you again." ■

SOURCE: *St. Petersburg Times*, 2001e.

The Federal Aviation Administration immediately grounded all airplanes in the United States to forestall a further attack from the air and to make it difficult for co-conspirators to leave the country. The FBI began to scrutinize selected telephone conversations for congratulatory calls, sought out material witnesses and others who might have been involved in this terrorist conspiracy, and began to trace the sources of funding that it required. Hospitals and rescue workers prepared to *care for the injured and the dying*, while pathologists and funeral directors set out to *dispose of the dead* in appropriate ways by removing bodies from the scene, identifying them, and preparing them for funeral services.

In the days that followed, Mayor Rudy Giuliani of New York and other political and religious leaders moved to extend and coordinate many of these efforts, sought to *work toward social consolidation*, and tried to *help make sense of death* in these circumstances. Many Americans came together in memorial services and around rallying symbols, such as the phrase "United We Stand" or the song "God Bless America." Counselors advised how adults should speak to children about these events, and President George W. Bush spoke to the nation and to the world about American perceptions of these events as an attack not only on the United States but also on the civilized world. The President appointed a new Director of Homeland Security, and also mobilized American military power and the international political community to root out and bring to justice those who were behind the conspiracy that culminated on September 11. It became clear that this goal might require some *socially sanctioned killing*—for instance, through war actions.

The September 11 attack, coupled with the subsequent sending of anthrax spores through the mail by unknown persons in September and October 2001, resulted in many types of challenges to personal safety and security for Americans at home and abroad. These challenges may not have overwhelmed the American death system, but they have impacted it in significant ways. Above all, these events have mobilized American society in many ways and at many different levels—local, state, national, and international—and their consequences cannot be fully seen or appreciated at the time of this writing.

Human-Induced Death Brought about by Individuals

During the 20th century American society witnessed an enormous increase in the numbers of deaths that human beings visited upon themselves and others, going far beyond isolated incidents of terrorist behavior. In part, this is the consequence of a simple increase in the number of people who are alive. A population explosion such as the last century witnessed inevitably results in more deaths no matter what else happens. However, it may also lead to more tension and stress that may increase interpersonal violence in response. In many instances, such violence results in premature death. In this section, we examine human-induced death resulting from individual behaviors in the form of accidents and homicide. (Other examples of human-induced death resulting from the actions of individuals, like suicide, assisted suicide, and euthanasia, will be examined in Chapters 17 and 18.)

Accidents

Accidents are the fifth leading cause of death in the United States for the population as a whole, and the leading cause of death among all persons age 1 to 44 (Hoyert et al., 2001; National Safety Council, 2000). In 1999, 97,860 Americans died in accidents, representing 4.1 percent of all deaths that year. In addition, 9 million people suffered disabling injuries. Among the fatalities, 42,401 of the deaths or 43.3 percent involved motor vehicles.

Accident-related deaths declined in absolute numbers from 1990 to 1993, but have increased since that time and currently exceed 1990 levels. The decline seems to have resulted from educational efforts that have urged Americans to become more safety conscious in their driving practices—for example, by driving more carefully, wearing seatbelts, and not driving after consuming alcoholic beverages. Along with this new awareness, accidents have moved from the fourth to the fifth leading cause of death in our society, largely as a result of shifts in the relative importance of other causes of death. In recent years, increases in numbers of accidental deaths in our society appear to be related to an expanding population and an upsurge in fast-paced, stress-filled lifestyles in our highly developed technological society. Still, if one assumes that each accidental death affects an average of 10 survivors, nearly 1 million persons were affected by such deaths in the United States in 1999.

Members of every societal subgroup—males and females, young and old, Caucasian Americans and African Americans, Hispanic Americans and Asian Americans—can be killed in automobile accidents, but the behaviors of some groups make them more susceptible to this form of death than are others. For example, individuals 15 to 24 years of age consistently have the highest death rates from motor vehicle accidents (26.8 deaths per 100,000 in 1999; see Kochanek et al., 2001), and mortality rates from vehicular accidents remain historically much higher for males than for females.

Mothers Against Drunk Driving (MADD) sponsor a billboard in an effort to reduce injuries and death from motor vehicle accidents.

These deaths contrast with some basic assumptions about mortality patterns in contemporary society. For example, in automobile accidents it is adolescents and young adults who are most likely to die, not the elderly. Also, these deaths are most often sudden, unexpected, and violent. Often the person killed is badly disfigured in the accident, perhaps even burned. The scenario may go like this: a knock on the door (or a telephone call) by a police officer leads to the announcement that someone is dead (Iserson & Iserson, 1999). Disbelief and denial may follow; he (or she) had just driven to a movie! How could death have intervened? If the body is disfigured, survivors may never see it again. If not and if the person is delivered to a hospital for stabilization, then attempts at emergency intervention and/or determination of death—sometimes followed by requests to authorize organ, tissue, and/or eye donation—may pose unexpected challenges to shocked family members. An air of unreality may pervade the experience. Grief and mourning following such a death are often complicated.

Homicide

The good news about deaths from homicide (now termed "assault" in the new international system of classifying and coding causes of death) in the United States is that although "from 1987 to 1991 homicide mortality rose at an average rate of more than 6 percent per year" (Murphy, 2000, p. 7), since that time homicide as a cause of death in our society has been in a downward trend. For example, homicides declined by 8.8 percent from 1997 to 1998 alone, and by a further 4.6 percent in 1999. There were 16,889 homicide deaths in the United States in 1999 with an overall death rate in that year of 6.2 per 100,000 (Hoyert et al., 2001). Homicide has declined from eleventh in rank among leading causes of death for the population as a whole in 1990 to only fourteenth in 1999.

The bad news is that the numbers and rates of homicide death in the United States are extraordinarily high for a developed society in the 21st century. In fact, contemporary American society has the dubious distinction of leading the industrial West in both the number and rates of homicide (Seltzer, 1994).

The distribution of this sort of human-induced death varies widely across the population. Perhaps the most disturbing features of the demography of homicide are its prominence as a cause of death among the young and among males. (See Chapter 5 for comments on homicide in selected racial and cultural groups.) For at least the last decade, the highest rates of homicide deaths have been found among Americans who are 15 to 24 years old, followed directly by those 25 to 34 years of age. In 15- to 24-year-olds, homicide is currently the second leading cause of death (exceeded only by accidents and followed closely by suicide). After young adulthood, homicide generally declines with increasing age as a leading cause of death.

In terms of gender, males in the United States are far more likely than females to be both the perpetrators and the victims of homicide. In particular, homicide is especially prominent as a cause of death among males in American society with approximately 3.5 male deaths from homicide to each female death from the same cause in recent years. Further, nearly 60 percent of all homicide deaths in the United States involve males between the ages of 15 and 44.

Two features that stand out in any analysis of American homicide deaths can lead to better understanding of this subject. First, approximately 50 percent of all homicides occur between family members or acquaintances (Seltzer, 1994). A corollary of this is that in 90 percent of all homicides the victims and the assailants are of the same race. A second prominent feature of homicide in our society is that it is heavily correlated with the use of firearms.

What we learn from the data on homicide is that it is a significant component—even though it has been declining in overall importance—in American behaviors and American encounters with death. Increasingly, homicide is the cause of deaths in groups that have not typically been thought of as vulnerable to death—notably adolescents and young adults. In addition, some homicide deaths appear utterly capricious and therefore meaningless, as in the case where a stray bullet from a drive-by shooting or carjacking strikes someone uninvolved in that activity. All of these factors help to explain why homicide intrudes in a forceful way on many contemporary Americans' thinking about death.

Nevertheless, in a sense homicidal behavior is overplayed in its significance in discussions of death in the American death system. For example, the popular media have tended to seize on and give disproportionate attention to selected examples of violence and homicide, such as those involving school shootings. Thus, all Americans are familiar with the shootings at Columbine High School in Littleton, Colorado, in April of 1999, in which ten students, one teacher, and the two perpetrators lost their lives and many others were wounded. But these are very atypical experiences. For example, one commentator (Twomey, 2001, p. 14A) noted that "the news media report crime, particularly violent crime, far out of proportion to its actual occurrence." Another expert (Males, 2001, p. 14A) declared that "the only rage killings that win sustained national attention are school shootings with white victims" and white youths as perpetrators.

The basic facts to keep in mind about homicide in the American death system are that it has been declining as a leading cause of death in the broad American population since 1992, but that a significant number of homicide deaths still do occur in our society. Homicide is far too often a cause of death in the United States for its present levels to be regarded as acceptable. Americans must strive to prevent or minimize instances of homicidal violence in our society. To do so, we need to set aside erroneous and misleading perceptions of homicide in the United States and come to understand this important death-related phenomenon and its causes in accurate, factual terms.

Beyond the fact that some instances of homicidal violence are particularly shocking and traumatic, nearly all homicides result in sudden and unexpected death with only a short transition from the act of violence to the death. Consequently, this type of death presents special problems for survivors: they are faced with an unexpected death in circumstances that might be unclear, traumatic, and often involve some social stigma. Even if the agent is identified, this may not help. In fact, it may further complicate the grief of survivors when the agent is a family member, friend, or peer, and when the homicide has been deliberately perpetrated on innocent people. Also, legal proceedings against the agent may be complex and families of victims are often deliberately shut out of or kept at a distance from such proceedings. A sense of outrage, fed by impressions of injustice and lack of control, may complicate their mourning (Magee, 1983; Redmond, 1989).

Socially Sanctioned Death

Socially sanctioned death is another form of human-induced death. It reflects societal death systems in very public ways because this form of death commonly involves large numbers of people, both as perpetrators and as victims. To arrange for and bring about large numbers of deaths requires extensive systematic organization. Legal, economic, military, and political structures, sometimes along with educational and scientific research structures, are typically involved in these actions. Here, we consider war and genocide, the Holocaust, and the beginning of the nuclear era, with special attention to what they mean for death-related encounters, attitudes, and practices in the contemporary American death system.

War and Genocide

Death involving large numbers of people has resulted in recent years from war and genocide. For example, the Chinese have killed more than 1 million Tibetans since 1950 (Ingram, 1992) and repressive regimes have killed at least thousands and sometimes millions of citizens in countries like Cambodia and Myanmar (Burma). Similarly, certain regions of the Balkans have witnessed an "ethnic cleansing" that killed or dispossessed large numbers of people. And in 1994, the Rwandan government even called on everyone in the Hutu majority population to murder everyone in the Tutsi minority. During this horrific experience, Christian pastors in one Tutsi community sent a letter to their church president, a Hutu, that included a phrase which is now the title of a book: *We Wish to Inform You that Tomorrow We Will Be Killed with Our Families* (Gourevitch, 1998)!

The number of deaths arising from these violent conflicts is astonishing. For example, World War I (1914–1919) saw at least 9 million soldiers killed in combat or dead from combat injuries (Elliot, 1972), the Korean War (1950–1953) produced 1 million deaths among combatants, and it has been estimated that nearly 62 million people were killed by the Soviet regime in the 70 years after 1917 (Glover, 1999). In the Balkans during the 1990s, not only were many people killed, but rape, torture, and enslavement of men and women were used as systematic instruments of terror. Three Bosnian Serbs were found guilty by a United Nations war crimes tribunal in February, 2001, of crimes against humanity for such acts committed during 1992 and 1993 (*St. Petersburg Times*, 2001b). Numbers of people killed in wars often do not include civilian deaths, which are notoriously difficult to identify. Generals count dead combatants on both sides because that is important for them to know or at least to estimate accurately. The number of civilians killed (sometimes called "collateral damage") is of lesser interest—unless, of course, one is among or somehow connected to those civilians. In addition, figures on civilian deaths may even be hidden for a variety of reasons—for instance, to avoid evidence of war crimes.

By 1972, Elliot estimated that 110 million people had already died during the 20th century at the hands of other human beings in massacres, wars, and other forms of societal conflict. Since that time, conflicts have occurred in Vietnam, Cambodia, Afghanistan, Lebanon, Ethiopia, Somalia, the Balkans, Rwanda, and many other places. Elliot's figure is now clearly much too low for the 20th century as a whole.

Even if we could obtain accurate figures for deaths of this sort, how could we possibly make sense of them? How can we grasp the deaths of huge numbers of people often in far-off locations? Many individuals have found the death of a single beloved person to be incomprehensible and unintelligible; how to make sense of the deaths of thousands or millions may well elude our imaginations (Elliot, 1972). An important danger here is that we may become accustomed or desensitized to the numbers of these sorts of deaths. They are so unimaginable that we may stop trying to comprehend them or to cope with them at all. But that may make us even more vulnerable to accepting them as tolerable.

The Holocaust

During World War II, what became under the Nazis a systematic program to eliminate whole classes of people from the face of the earth can still be regarded as unique for its scope and political or ideological basis (Bauer, 1982; Dawidowicz,

1975; Pawelczynska, 1979; Reitlinger, 1968). The Nazis slaughtered 6 million European Jews and millions of others during the late 1930s and early 1940s.

The Nazi program of genocide was fueled by a particular ideology (not only politics or economics or even military considerations). According to the Nazis' perverted philosophy, members of the Jewish "race"—along with whole categories of other people, such as gypsies, Jehovah's Witnesses, and homosexuals—were classified as *Untermensch* or subhuman. At first, this led to outbursts of anti-Semitism, loss of civil and human rights, relocation and ghettoization, and shipment to "concentration camps." Inhabitants in many of these camps soon became a slave labor force working on behalf of the German war effort, although this did not protect them from extremely harsh living and working conditions, inadequate rations, and brutal pressures of all sorts that led to large numbers of deaths. At the same time, random violence, terror, and crude forms of systematic killing were implemented both within and outside the camps in areas that fell under Nazi control. Ample and adequate documentation of these horrors is available from both firsthand witnesses (for example, Kulka, 1986; Langbein, 1994; Levi, 1986) and later historians (Gilbert, 1993).

In 1941, a decision was made to go further: the "final solution" was to eradicate the Jews from all areas within Nazi control. In search of efficiency, relatively crude methods of killing—bludgeoning, hanging, and shooting people to death, machine gunning and burying them in mass graves, and using engine exhaust gasses to suffocate those who were being transported in closed vans to locations where their bodies were burned or interred—were replaced by the infamous gas chambers and crematories of the "extermination camps" *(Vernichtungslager)*. The term itself is significant: one kills a human being, but one exterminates a less-than-human pest.

This final stage of the Holocaust reached its peak of depravity in southwestern Poland at a former military barracks on the edge of the city of Auschwitz (Oswiecim)—whose gate still today proclaims the infamous and cruelly ironic motto "*Arbeit macht frei*" ("Work makes one free")—and its newly constructed satellite about two miles away in the countryside at Birkenau (Brzezinka). Here, in the words of the camp commander (Hoess, 1959, p. 160), was developed "the greatest human extermination center of all time." And here (but elsewhere also), cruel and hideous experiments were undertaken under the guise of medical research (Lifton, 1986; Michalczyk, 1994).

According to the most authoritative calculations currently available, at Auschwitz/Birkenau alone "the number of victims was at least 1.1 million, about 90 percent of whom were Jews from almost every country in Europe," although with slightly different data and assumptions "the number of Jewish victims killed in the camp would rise to about 1.35 million, with the total number of Auschwitz victims reaching about 1.5 million" (Piper, 1994, pp. 62, 72). All of these deaths took place from the time when the first prisoners arrived (June 14, 1940)—and especially after September 1941, when the use of cyanide gas was first tested—until January 27, 1945, when the Soviet army liberated the camp and freed some 7,000 remaining prisoners. Toward the end, it is reported that some 80 percent of the people (mainly women, children, and the elderly) who arrived at Auschwitz/Birkenau in the daily transports (which tied up railroad

The entrance to a total death environment at Auschwitz.

equipment desperately needed by the German military for the war effort) went directly to their deaths from the notorious "selections" held at railside as they arrived at the camp.

Nothing like this had been seen in the world previously. To visit Auschwitz many years after the Holocaust is to confront an enormous incongruity between what is in many ways an ordinary, even banal, setting, and innumerable images of horror that endure as a reminder of the dark side of human capacity (Corr, 1993b; Czarnecki, 1989). Perhaps that is why some writers (such as Czech, 1990; Gilbert, 1993) have employed the techniques of chronology and cartography to depict the horrors of the Holocaust in impersonal, dispassionate ways, while others (such as MacMillan, 1991; Wiesel, 1960) have used literary forms to convey in imaginative and evocative ways messages about the Holocaust that are not effectively transmitted in other forms. And there have been impressive accounts of what was involved in survival and resistance within the death camps of the Holocaust (DesPres, 1976; Langbein, 1994).

The basic lesson for all to draw from these horrible events—like many fundamental morals—is simple: "We have the choice between the Holocaust as a warning and the Holocaust as a precedent" (Bauer, 1986, xvii). Although some have sought to deny the facts of the Holocaust (Lipstadt, 1993), its reality and implications continue to resonate within the North American death system (Novick, 1999). Consider just a few examples: the book *Schindler's List* (Keneally, 1982) and Steven Spielberg's Oscar-winning movie (1993) of the same title; the dedication in 1993 of the U.S. Holocaust Memorial Museum in Washington, D.C.; the founding in 1994 of the Survivors of the Shoah Visual History

Foundation in Los Angeles (800-661-2092); and the many institutions listed in the directory of the Association of Holocaust Organizations (Shulman, 2001).

The Beginning of the Nuclear Era

The beginning of the nuclear era introduced a form of socially sanctioned death and an ongoing death-related threat for which there is no adequate historical precedent. Nuclear power was first unleashed on July 16, 1945, at the Trinity test site in New Mexico. It became a new force for death at Hiroshima on August 6, 1945, when an estimated 100,000 people died in a single flash of light and, again, three days later at Nagasaki, when 50,000 more died in the second atomic bombing. In both Japanese cities, mass death from the blast and heat of the bomb was joined for the first time to the lingering effects of radiation, secondary effects that are believed to have caused deaths equal in number to those killed outright.

What was unique at Hiroshima was the instantaneous quality of the first large-scale wave of deaths and the fact that they resulted from a single nuclear "device." Also distinctive were the lingering effects of radiation and the unparalleled destructive potential of nuclear weapons. The scope and character of this new way of encountering death have challenged the best efforts of reporters (such as Hersey, 1948; Lustig, 1977) and scholars (such as Lifton, 1964, 1967) to understand and articulate their implications. The unique features of Hiroshima have also led to debates about the moral, political, and other aspects of using such weapons (such as Alperovitz, 1995; Lifton, 1982; Lifton & Mitchell, 1995; Maddox, 1995).

In both the Holocaust and Hiroshima, as well as in various terrorist assaults, women, children, and the elderly were killed as readily as men in the military. During World War II in particular, saturation bombing and other methods of waging war intentionally blurred the distinction between combatants and noncombatants. These techniques were employed as much to destroy civilian morale as to damage specific military targets. At Hiroshima, that strategy was carried further in such a way that life itself seemed to come under a threat against which there was no adequate defense.

Since 1945, the lethal potential of nuclear weapons has been magnified many times over, along with their accuracy and modes of delivery (Arkin & Fieldhouse, 1985). Death and destruction can now be brought down on humankind in a degree and form that is far beyond the wildest dreams—or nightmares—of human beings over nearly the whole of recorded history.

The level of tension associated with nuclear weapons declined somewhat with the dissolution of the Soviet Union in 1991 and subsequent efforts to destroy some warheads and their delivery systems. However, there are new worries that economic difficulties in Russia may lead to problems with remaining nuclear weapons. Furthermore, many are now concerned about nuclear threats from terrorist groups or rogue governments who might construct suitcase bombs or crash planes into nuclear reactors. Also, nuclear tensions rose in May 1998 when India and Pakistan conducted independent underground tests of nuclear devices that they could employ in warfare against each other or against China. In fact, in February 2001 Pakistan announced that it was ready to deploy nuclear weapons on its submarines (*St. Petersburg Times*, 2001c). Additionally, in 2001 President Bush gave new impetus to plans for a ballistic missile defense system, and the movie *Thirteen Days* helped to stimulate new discussions of the dangers of nuclear attacks by dramatizing the 1963 Cuban missile crisis, in which the United States and the Soviet Union came to the brink of nuclear warfare over the stationing of nuclear missiles in Cuba.

The nuclear era has also revealed another face as nuclear power has become a source of much-needed energy supplies. Here, the initial appearance is benign and welcome; and in many ways it has remained so. However, accidents in nuclear reactors at Three Mile Island in Pennsylvania in 1979 and at Chernobyl in Ukraine in 1986 have shown that even a peaceful source of nuclear energy can pose a real threat to humankind. Explosion, fire, and local irradiation, however lethal they may be to the surrounding territory, are nothing compared to the airborne radiation and long-term contamination of land, water, food supplies, and people of the type that followed the 1986 events at Chernobyl. (The last reactor at Chernobyl was finally and completely shut down as an active power plant in 2000.)

How are these dangers associated with nuclear weaponry and nuclear power to be kept in check? How should they be balanced against legitimate needs for self-defense and sources of energy to sustain quality in living? More broadly, what does it mean to live under the nuclear shadow? For some, it seems the subject does not bear thinking about; they simply put it out of their minds through techniques of dissociation and denial. For others, the power of the threat and the difficulty of doing anything about it diminish their joy in living and their sense of promise for the future. For all, it is a new and unprecedented dimension of death-related experiences in the early years of the 21st century.

Looking back, Lifton and Mitchell (1995, p. xi) wrote, "you cannot understand the twentieth century without Hiroshima." We would say that death-related experiences in the 20th century cannot be understood without considering war and genocide, the Holocaust, and the beginning of the nuclear era. All of these involved mass death. War and genocide most often had to do with ideological, ethnic, and economic conflict. The Holocaust resulted from a perverted ideology, and the nuclear era reflected a new technology. In each case, the results involved what Leviton (1991a, 1991b) called "horrendous death," a transformation in both the quantity and the quality of human encounters with death that remains momentous and without parallel even now in the 21st century.

Death and Language

One way in which a society and its death system try to control and influence how death is experienced is evident in language patterns and practices. Both *language about death* and *death-related language*—which may seem to point to the same thing, but are in fact quite distinct—reflect strong social messages concerning appropriate emotions and behaviors regarding death.

Language about Death

In the contemporary American death system (and in the death systems of some other societies as well), many people often go to great lengths to avoid saying words like *dead* and *dying.* In place of this direct language, individuals commonly employ *euphemisms*—that is, they substitute a word or expression with comparatively pleasant or inoffensive associations for language that they view as harsher or more offensive, even though the latter ways of speaking might more precisely designate what is intended. Thus, people don't die; they merely "pass away." In principle, euphemisms are pleasing ways of speaking; in practice, they usually involve underlying attitudes that seek to "prettify" language to make it appear more delicate, "nice," or socially acceptable and to avoid seeming disagreeable, impolite, or nasty. Using euphemisms is not necessarily undesirable in itself, but it can come to be so when it becomes excessive or when it reflects an unwillingness to confront the realities of life and death directly. A brief survey of "sympathy cards" ("She's not dead, she's just sleeping") can illustrate this point.

Euphemisms that relate to death are familiar to most users and students of language (Neaman & Silver, 1983; Rawson, 1981). They arise in many contexts. Long before recent interest in "thanatology" (itself a euphemism for death-related studies), these figures of speech were recognized by scholars (for example, Pound, 1936). Terms like "kicked the bucket" (originally, a graphic description of one way of committing suicide by hanging) or "bought the farm" are euphemistic descriptions of death. The "dearly departed" have been "called home," "laid to rest," or "gone to their reward." Much the same is true for those who "conk out," who are "cut down," or whose "number is up." Anyone who is "on his last legs" has "run the good race," "is down for the long count," and "it's curtains." The precise status of those who are "no longer with us" is not quite clear.

Professional caregivers sometimes say that they "lost" Mr. Smith last night or that he "expired." Such language always has some original foundation. One has lost the company of a spouse or friend who has died; the spirit or last breath has gone out of the person. But those who use such expressions today are usually not thinking of such linguistic justifications. They are most often simply unwilling to speak directly. Hence the hyperbole of bureaucratic health care, which twists death into the contortions of "negative patient care outcome," or the ways in which counterespionage agencies talk about "terminating with extreme prejudice" instead of speaking about killing.

The change in labels from "undertaker" (a word that the *Oxford English Dictionary* traces back to 1698 in England) to "mortician" (a term originating in America in 1895 with roots in the Latin word *mors* or death) to "funeral director" or "funeral services practitioner" reflects both a euphemistic tendency and a broadened vocational scope.

Language may be more effective as a vehicle for accurate communication when people speak directly in ways that are neither excessively camouflaged nor brutal. Consider the state to which our society has come in trying to express in ordinary language what veterinarians do to very sick, old, or infirm cats and dogs. Among many of the people who speak to the authors of this book, such animals are not simply "killed" or "euthanized." Rather, they are "put to sleep." What meaning does that convey to young children—who may then be urged to stop asking annoying questions and take a nap? It is very challenging to try to express the same point in some other way in colloquial but effective English. Some say that animals are "put out of their misery" or "put down." Does that help to explain things?

Euphemisms are not solely linked to death. On the contrary, they are ways to stand back from or cover over all sorts of taboo topics. Consider, for example, common expressions for genital organs or excretory functions. Both the New England Puritans of the 17th century and adherents of the romantic movement in the United States during the 19th century firmly suppressed talk about sexuality even as they readily spoke of death (usually for moral or religious purposes). In the 21st century, it often seems that people have simply inverted these attitudes and practices so as to be tongue-tied about death but all too unconstrained and loquacious about sex.

Direct speech and candor are not always desirable. Frankness can be admirable or out of place; the same is true for avoidance. Both overemphasis and underemphasis, whether on sexuality or on death, are equally unbalanced postures. Both distort and demean central realities of life. Still, as Neaman and Silver (1983, pp. 144–145) have noted, contemporary American society is special:

> At no other time in history has a culture created a more elaborate system of words and customs to disguise death so pleasantly that it seems a consummation devoutly to be wished. . . .
>
> The motives for euphemizing death are in many ways similar to those for disguising our references to pregnancy and birth. Great superstition surrounded these events, as did great distaste and a sense of social impropriety. Propelled by these feelings, we have attempted to strip death of both its sting and its pride—in fact to kill death by robbing it of its direct and threatening name. The terms change and the euphemisms grow, but the evasion of the word "death" survives.

Linguistic attempts to avoid talking about death are more than detours around the unpleasant. Euphemisms become problematic whenever they are not held in check or counterbalanced by personal experience. Most euphemisms originated in a rich soil of experiential contact with death. As death-related encounters have become increasingly less frequent and more limited in much of American society (see Chapter 2), these essential roots of language have dried up. The problem with an overabundance of euphemisms in recent American talk about death is that they reveal and themselves contribute to a kind of distancing or dissociation from important and fundamental events of life itself.

Death-Related Language

One might conclude from the preceding that death-related language is simply absent from most ordinary speech. Such a conclusion would be "dead wrong." In talk about actual events pertaining to death and dying, it is quite common for language about death to be avoided. But in a curious and paradoxical reversal, *death language* is frequently employed in talk about events that have nothing to do with actual death and dying (see, for example, Partridge, 1966; Wentworth & Flexner, 1967; Weseen, 1934).

Most people in contemporary American society speak quite openly about dead batteries, dead letters, a deadpan expression, a dead giveaway, deadlines, and being dead drunk. Everyone knows people who are dead tired, dead on their feet, dead certain, dead beat or dead broke, deadly dull, deadlocked, dead to the world in sleep, or scared to death. Marksmen who hit the target dead center have a dead eye or are dead shots. Gamblers recognize a "dead man's hand" (aces and eights, all black cards; the hand that Wild Bill Hickok was holding when he was shot dead), while truckers "deadhead" back home with an empty vehicle. Parents may be "worried to death" about children who "will be the death" of them. Those who are embarrassed may "wish they were dead" or that they "could just die." Orville Kelly (1977, p. 186), a man with a life-threatening illness, reported encountering a friend who said, "I'm just dying to see you again."

Similarly, in today's society when one has nothing else to do one may be said to be killing time. There is quite a difference between a lady killer who is dressed "fit to kill" and a killjoy. And most contemporary Americans know what it means to "die on base," "flog a dead horse," or "kill the lights." To "kill a bottle of whiskey" leaves us with a "dead soldier." To be "dead as a doornail" is to be as hammered into insensitivity as was the nail head driven into the center of doors against which knockers were once struck before doorbells came into prominence. Good comedians "slay" their audiences, who "die of laughter"; poor comedians "die on their feet."

In these and many other similar phrases, death-related language emphasizes and exaggerates what is said. To be dead right is to be very right, completely right, absolutely right, the rightest one can be. Death-related language dramatizes or intensifies a word or phrase that might have seemed insufficiently forceful on its own or too weak to convey the intended meaning or depth of feeling. It trades on the ultimacy and finality of death to heighten in the manner of the superlative.

Placing this familiar use of death-related language alongside common euphemisms teaches interesting lessons about linguistic practices in the contemporary American death system. Death language is frequently avoided when Americans speak of death itself, but it is often employed (sometimes with enthusiasm) when they are not speaking directly about death. In fact, language is powerful; naming can influence the reality we experience. Perhaps that is why death-related language is easily employed in "safe situations" that have nothing to do with death itself, while just the reverse is the case when one uses euphemisms that seek to soften death or allude to it obliquely.

Death and the Media

The media play an important role in the contemporary American death system, as is evident in news reports and entertainment programs. As we saw in Chapter 2, many Americans have limited personal experience with natural human death. However, most people in the United States have experienced in a vicarious or secondhand way thousands of violent or traumatic deaths. One estimate is that "by the time the average child graduates from elementary school, she or he will have witnessed at least 8,000 murders and more than 100,000 other assorted acts of violence. Depending on the amount of television viewed, our youngsters could see more than 200,000 violent acts before they hit the schools and streets of our nation as teenagers" (Huston et al., 1992, pp. 53–54). These vicarious experiences come to us through news and entertainment services provided by newspapers and magazines or on the radio, but it is television and other electronic media that appear to be most influential.

Vicarious Death Experiences: News Reports in the Media

On September 11, 2001, and in the days immediately following, television was perhaps at its best in informing the American public about a horrific, death-related event. It had hard news to report and graphic images to share. However, that was a high point that is not always typical of the media in general and television in particular. For example, human-induced deaths are pervasive on televised evening news reports. In such reports, homicide, accidents, war, and other forms of traumatic death and violence are staple "newsworthy" events. Hence the slogan, "If it bleeds, it leads" (Kerbel, 2000).

In fact, routine televised accounts of violence and war often generate a kind of psychological immunity in the general public to the impact of death. Experiencing violent death in these vicarious ways often does not seem to have the same impact as being there in person. Watching someone being shot to death on a smaller-than-life-size television screen is quite different from direct participation in the event. These media deaths are distant or remote for most people, and death itself may remain outside our actual experience despite frequent vicarious encounters with its surrogates (see Box 4.3).

One reason for the remote or distanced quality of these newsworthy events is that they are *a highly selective portrait of death and life* in today's society and around the world. That which is "newsworthy" is by definition out of the ordinary. We know this and can recognize the truth in the words of one knowledgeable commentator (Krugman, 2001, p. 16A) who observed that "the media, and especially news channels that have to keep people watching all day, thrive on hype." As a result, the news media are preoccupied with the deaths of special persons or with special sorts of death. They depict death in a selective, distorted, and sensationalized way to individuals in a society that has less and less contact with natural human death. Ordinary people who die in ordinary ways are not newsworthy; they are tucked away in death announcements on the back pages

Box 4.3 Electronic Representations of Violence and Death

Nothing is more common in the postmodern world than the replication of the violence of interactive video games and Internet images. In a world of semblances, people die by violence but their deaths are and are not understood as real. Violence is envisaged as simultaneously actualizing and derealizing death. If all is semblance, a game, death's finality is fictive, undecidable. . . . When school children kill their teachers and classmates we are convinced that they have been overcome by the images in which they are immersed, that they reenact the virtual murders they witness hour after hour on video and TV monitors. How real for them is the difference between pulling a trigger on a gun and clicking a mouse? They learn afterward—in the flesh, so to speak, and always too late—that these dead and wounded bodies are not only images, that the images are surfaces of vulnerable flesh. ■

SOURCE: Wyschogrod and Caputo, 1998, p. 303.

of a newspaper or silently omitted from the television news. Television in particular is heavily focused on stories that can be accompanied by dramatic visual images.

One exception to the rules of newsworthiness are the brief notices that report the fact of an individual's death, names of survivors, and plans (if any) for funeral or burial services. Typically, these *death announcements* (sometimes called *obituaries*) appear in small type (a source of complaint among some elderly or visually impaired readers), in alphabetized columns, near the classified advertisement section in newspapers. This location is not surprising, since death announcements are essentially public notices paid for by survivors and usually arranged through funeral directors. Like the classified ads, which they resemble, death announcements record ordinary events of everyday life. They differ greatly from the news stories that the media run without charge to mark the deaths of prominent persons.

The selectivity implicit in what is thought to be newsworthy carries with it a curious kind of reassurance. It encourages people to comfort themselves with thoughts like these: since I am not a very special person and since I do not expect to die in any very special way, I can distance myself from the staple fare of death in newspapers and on television, and thus from unpleasant associations with death. The specialized and highly selective drama of death in media news reports is abstract and insubstantial; it lacks the definite shape, feelings, texture, and concreteness of one's own life. Having been shocked by so many out-of-the-ordinary, newsworthy events, people often become thick-skinned, passive spectators, hardened against the personal import of death. It becomes just one more among many distant and unusual phenomena paraded before us in a regular, unending, and not always very interesting series.

Moreover, the unusual modes of death reported so selectively in the media may themselves come to be seen as ordinary or typical. For example, extensive and highly dramatized coverage of tragic school shootings in our society has led many to believe death is common in our high schools when, in fact, the schools are among the safest places for children in America. By contrast with these dreadful events in which a small number of deaths have been blown out of proportion, one's own death—which is not perceived as anything like these secondhand events—may come to appear less likely and less proximate.

Fantasized Death and Violence: Entertainment

The distortion of death in news reports is compounded in many entertainment programs in the media. Death and violence are ever present in American entertainment media—on television and in movies, video games, and music lyrics (Wass, 2002). But this is typically a very unrealistic presence. Think of cowboy, war, or gangster movies, police or military shows and science fiction fantasies on television, battles with alien invaders in video games, and the language of much "gangsta rap."

What is most remarkable about the typical portrayal of death in these media is that it is usually very unrealistic or fantasized. Those who die are unimportant people or "bad guys." Heroes and heroines repeatedly survive extreme peril, whereas actors die one week only to reappear unharmed the next. Violent fantasies of a very graphic nature are acted out—but suffering, grief, and other consequences of this violence and death are mostly noticeable for their absence. Murders take place, but audiences are chiefly interested in whether or not their perpetrator can be identified. Killings occur, but they usually satisfy a sense of poetic justice and their consequences are not of much interest. The realities of death, dying, and bereavement are rarely apparent. Thus, as a result of their research on American film, Schultz and Huet (2000, p. 137) concluded: "In American film, death is distorted into a sensational stream of violent attacks by males, with fear, injury, further aggression, and the absence of normal grief reactions as the most common responses."

A committee of the American Academy of Pediatrics (AAP, 1995) studied this matter and related research. It concluded that "American media are the most violent in the world, and American society is now paying a high price in terms of real-life violence" (p. 949). Some reject a cause-effect link between media violence and violence in real life, but the AAP has noted that a majority of researchers in the field (for example, Comstock & Paik, 1991; Eron, 1993; Strasburger, 1993) are convinced that such a link has been firmly established. Thus, the AAP (1995, p. 949) concluded that "although media violence is not the only cause of violence in American society, it is the single most easily remediable contributing factor."

Children's cartoons on television are sharp examples of this very special vision of death, although they may often be more benign than many of the examples just cited. These cartoons illustrate our point by simplifying the complexities of other entertainment forms. Since it is assumed that attention spans in an audience of children are short and distraction is always likely, the plot must be gripping and it must continually reassert its hold over viewers (Minow & LaMay, 1995). Thus, television cartoons frequently emphasize lively action, as in cats chasing mice or dogs chasing cats, which may improperly reinforce a perception in some children that death is temporary.

In the well-known Roadrunner cartoon series, Wile E. Coyote relentlessly pursues the flightless bird only to be caught over and over again in his own traps. He is repeatedly the apparent victim of horrible death experiences, but he usually enjoys an instant resurrection and in the end he always survives. In other words, *he never dies; he just keeps getting killed.* Destruction is followed so rapidly by delight, joy, and renewed activity that there is no time for grief. The cartoon is about the ongoing action of an endless chase. It is not really about death, although inevitably it communicates many messages about that subject.

In the latter part of the 20th century, death became an even more vivid presence in adult entertainment. Earlier, no one ever bled when shot or stabbed in a movie. Fistfights erupted in saloons, six-guns blazed away, actors staggered against walls and crumpled in death—but all the while their clothes were clean and their hats usually remained firmly on their heads. By contrast, the movie *Saving Private Ryan* (1988) was widely praised as an accurate portrait of the real horrors of war because it showed lost limbs and ghastly wounds. Of course, shock and horror in the media are often excessive. Graphic representations of blood, gore, and crashing automobiles are now standard fare in much that passes for contemporary entertainment. So much artificial blood and apparent mayhem can make today's movie and television viewers jaded. It is no longer easy to surprise or impress them, or even to catch and hold their attention.

Again, death has been distorted through a process of selectivity and fantasization. Clearly, selectivity is unavoidable in reporting the news or telling a story, and fantasy is neither unhealthy nor undesirable in itself. The games, songs, and fairy tales of childhood have long been full of fantasy and death, and children have coped with it without major difficulty. Two factors have been central: (1) the way in which the violence and death—and their real-life consequences—are (or are not) presented; and (2) a firm grasp by the audience on the essential distinction between fantasy and reality. The problem in our society is a looser grip on the realities of life and death, coupled with increasing violence and gore. Selectivity, distortion, and fantasy become dangerous in media representations of death when they substitute for or supplant a balanced appreciation of life.

Contemporary American Funeral Practices

Funeral practices in the American death system may take many forms. In this section, we describe these practices in a general way, while remaining aware that they may differ depending on religious, cultural, and ethnic perspectives, or simply because of local customs. Typical elements usually found in many contemporary American funeral practices are:

- Removal of the body from the place of death
- Preparing the body for viewing and/or final disposition
- A viewing of the body
- A funeral service
- Delivery of the body for final disposition
- In-ground burial or above-ground entombment in a mausoleum or crypt

An increasing number of Americans choose to cremate the body of a deceased person, either as an alternative to viewing, a funeral, and disposition of the body as a whole, or as a supplement coming after a funeral and primarily affecting only the ultimate mode of disposition. Other Americans prefer immediate disposition of the body or donating the body for medical research and education. Some of these alternatives may be combined with a memorial service in which the body is not present. Additional information on American funeral practices can be obtained from local sources (such as funeral homes, memorial societies, cemeteries, crematories) and from the national resources listed in Box 4.4.

As we learned in Chapter 2, most people in the United States today die in some type of public institution. When that occurs, staff members typically notify the family if they are not already present, help make arrangements to clean and care for the body until those who need to do so can arrive, assist in making contact with a local funeral director, and organize the removal of the body from the place of death. Members of a hospice or home care team often do much the same when a death occurs at home.

It has been noted that many Americans are not very familiar with the work of funeral service personnel (see Box 4.5). In fact, their role is fairly straightforward. To begin with, they usually transport the body to a funeral home, while arranging for a death certificate to be properly completed and exchanged for a permit to bury the body or otherwise dispose of it. In some cases involving "direct disposition," the funeral director may simply transport the body to a crematorium or to an appropriate destination (such as the anatomy department of a local medical school) for donation to medical research and education. In all of these cases, efforts will be made to show respect for the body as the remains of someone valued as a human being and to act in accordance with the religious or philosophical beliefs that an individual and his or her social group hold about life and death (Ball, 1995; Habenstein & Lamers, 1974; Kephart, 1950).

Most bodies in the American death system are washed, embalmed, dressed, and prepared by funeral service personnel for a "viewing," "visitation," or "wake" as it may variously be described. In some cultural groups family members or representatives of the group may carry out or take part in this work. *Embalming* grew in popularity in the United States after the Civil War as a practice that made it possible to ship dead bodies back home for burial from distant battlefields (Mayer, 1996). The most celebrated example of this occurred in the case of Abraham Lincoln, whose body was shipped by rail from Washington, D.C., where he was assassinated, to Springfield, Illinois, for burial. This journey took place during a warm part of the year when rapid decomposition of the body was likely, especially as the funeral train made many stops along the way to serve

Box 4.4 Selected National Resources for Information on Funerals and Related Matters

Cremation Association
of North America
401 N. Michigan Avenue, Suite 2200
Chicago, IL 60611
312-644-6610
www.cremationassociation.org

Funeral and Memorial Societies
of America (Funeral Consumers
Alliance)
P.O. Box 10
Hinesburg, VT 05461
802-482-3437
www.funerals.org

International Association
of Pet Cemeteries
5055 Route 11, P.O. Box 163
Ellenburg Depot, NY 12935
518-594-3000
www.iaopc.com

International Cemetery
and Funeral Association
1895 Preston White Drive, Suite 220
Reston, VA 20191
800-645-7700; 703-391-8400
www.icfa.org

International Order
of the Golden Rule
13523 Lakefront Drive
St. Louis, MO 63045
800-637-8030; 314-209-7142
www.ogr.org

Jewish Funeral Directors of America
Seaport Landing
150 Lynnway, Suite 506
Lynn, MA 01902
781-477-9300
www.jfda.org

Monument Builders
of North America
3158 S. River Road, Suite 224
Des Plaines, IL 60018
800-233-4472; 847-803-8800
www.monumentbuilders.org

National Catholic Cemetery
Conference
710 N. River Road
Des Plaines, IL 60016
847-824-8131
www.ntriplec.org

National Funeral Directors
Association
13625 Bishop's Drive
Brookfield, WI 53005-6607
800-228-6332; 414-789-1880
www.ndfa.org

National Funeral Directors
and Morticians Association
3951 Snapfinger Parkway, Suite 570
Decatur, GA 30035
800-434-0958; 404-286-6680
www.nfdma.com

National Selected Morticians
5 Revere Drive, Suite 340
Northbrook, IL 60062
800-323-4219; 847-559-9569
www.nsm.org

Neptune Society
Local contacts in CA, FL, NY,
OR, WA
www.neptunesociety.com ■

Box 4.5 Comments on the Work of Funeral Directors from the President of the National Funeral Directors Association (1997–1998)

If you are one of those people who thinks funeral directors are a slightly mysterious lot, I am here to tell you that you are absolutely correct. The very nature of our work helps to perpetuate this public image, which reveals little if anything about us personally or about the true nature of our work.

Funeral directors move unobtrusively behind the scenes, performing hundreds of separate tasks in preparation for each funeral service they arrange. Planning a funeral is as complicated as planning a wedding, although funeral directors generally have only 72 hours to get the job done. When the ceremonies actually begin, we do our best to become invisible. It is this image of funeral directors, parking cars, opening doors, and standing quietly off to the side, blending into the wallpaper with their hands folded in front of them, that captures the public eye. It is no wonder most people don't really understand what we do or why we do it. (p. vii) ■

SOURCE: Harley, 1999.

the needs of grief-stricken Americans. If normal biological processes of decomposition had not been delayed, Mr. Lincoln's body would have become an object of social repugnance long before the train reached its destination.

Embalming today involves the removal of blood and other bodily fluids from a corpse and their replacement with artificial preservatives that may help to retard decomposition and to color the skin. Embalming may or may not be accompanied by efforts to restore the cosmetic appearance of the corpse. No state law or federal regulation requires embalming to be done, unless certain conditions are present. For instance, embalming may be required if the body is to be transported on a common carrier, such as a train or airplane.

In the contemporary American death system, embalming is mainly practiced to permit viewing of the body during a wake or visitation in some public gathering (for example, at a funeral home) or in cases of a funeral with an open casket (Iserson, 1994; Raether, 1989). Advocates of embalming argue that it prevents the spread of disease by disinfecting the corpse and neutralizing contaminants in discarded blood and bodily fluids. Of course, much the same could be achieved by direct cremation, immediate burial in a sealed container, or refrigerating the body. In fact, it appears that embalming is most often undertaken to slow decay in the bodily tissues of the corpse. It provides time for relatives and friends of the deceased to gather from a distance in a large and dispersed society, and it makes possible viewing of the body once they have come together.

During a *visitation* or *viewing* in our society, the casket containing the body is often open, either fully or at least so as to reveal the upper half of the body. In

Taking part in funeral ritual can help oneself and others in coping with loss and grief.

some instances, the casket may be closed—sometimes as a matter of preference, at other times because of the condition of the corpse. Typically, mourners approach the casket, sometimes to say a brief prayer or for a moment of reflection. Often, they return again and again to the casket to stare at, touch, or kiss the dead body. They seem to be saying final farewells and impressing a last image into their minds, even as the cold, rigid, and nonlifelike features of the corpse convey to them in a silent but forceful way the realities of its differences from a living body. As they come together for a visitation or funeral, participants often find themselves sharing stories about the deceased in ways that help locate and secure that person (and themselves) in the history and memory of the community of those who were touched by the deceased person.

Following a funeral or religious service, *disposal of bodies* in the United States is typically carried out in one of the following ways: burial in the ground; entombment in some sort of crypt, vault, or mausoleum above the ground; cremation and subsequent disposition of the cremains; or donation to a medical or other institution for dissection or other similar purposes, such as scientific research or professional education (Habenstein & Lamers, 1962; Iserson, 1994).

In-ground burial is still the most common form of body disposal in the United States. Generally, the body is buried within several days of the death, although some groups such as Orthodox Jews and Muslims seek to bury prior to sundown on the day of the death or at least within 24 hours. The amount of time between death and burial in our society is usually related to the time needed to prepare the body, make necessary arrangements, and—above all—

gather together family members and other important persons from distant parts of the country. *Entombment* in some type of above-ground structure is essentially a variant on in-ground burial.

In the case of burial, the classic picture of this phase of disposition of the body in America would describe a formal procession of vehicles from a funeral home or place of worship to a cemetery, followed by a gathering of mourners around the casket at the burial site, brief prayers or last words about the deceased, lowering of the casket into a grave, individual tossing of symbolic shovelfulls of dirt over the casket, and filling in of the grave. In recent years, formal processions of vehicles have diminished and mourners are likely to be encouraged to leave the grave site before the casket is lowered into a vault or grave liner within the grave (which are designed to protect the casket and prevent settling of the ground), the vault is sealed closed, and the grave is filled in. Sometimes, cemeteries have built chapels and prefer that the last rite be performed there, rather than at the grave site. These practices mainly have to do with allocation of workload among the cemetery's personnel and a desire not to risk upsetting mourners as workers go about such activities as enclosing the casket within a vault or grave liner, lowering it into the grave, and refilling the grave.

Cremation involves placing the body in some sort of container and reducing its size through the application of intense heat (Irion, 1968). The container need not be a casket; crematories typically only require that the body be turned over to them in an enclosed, rigid, combustible container, which can be handled easily and safely. The body and its container are then heated to 1600–1800 degrees Fahrenheit for a period of 2 to 2½ hours. Because most of the human body is water, the water evaporates. At the high temperatures reached during cremation, the rest of the soft tissues are consumed by spontaneous combustion. The effect of this process is to reduce the size of bodily remains in a rapid and significant fashion. The residue is primarily ash and those fragments of dense bone that have not been vaporized by heat. When these remains have cooled, they are collected and then usually ground up or pulverized into a coarse powder. Subsequently, the person responsible for the "cremains" may choose what to do with this residue. For example, they may be scattered over water (as practiced by the Neptune Society in coastal parts of the country) or enclosed in an urn or permanent container. The urn may then be kept by survivors, buried in the ground, or placed in a niche (a small compartment) in a mausoleum-like columbarium. Cremation is often popularly thought of as an alternative to embalming, viewing, and a funeral, but it may also follow those activities as a step between them and final disposition.

Sloane (1991, p. 220) observed that "the most remarkable changes in the American cemetery industry in the last forty years have been the resurgence of entombment as an important method of disposal and the steady, recently spectacular, rise of cremation." Entombment in an above-ground space may reflect such variables as soil conditions (e.g., a high water table as in some parts of New Orleans) which make in-ground burial difficult or impossible, a desire to save land space, or a preference for final disposition in a structure that is enclosed, dry, heated, and air conditioned.

In the United States in 1999, 1,468 crematories conducted 595,617 cremations. That figure represented approximately 25 percent of the nearly 2.4 million deaths in our society in 1999. The proportion of deaths involving cremation increased by almost 5 percent from 1994 to 1999 and is projected to increase by an additional 10 percent by the year 2010 (Cremation Association of North America, 2000; www.cremationassociation.org). The largest numbers of cremations took place in the states of California, Florida, and New York.

Some contemporary Americans prefer to *donate their bodies for teaching or research purposes.* If so, arrangements must be made well ahead of time with the receiving institution, because there has not been a shortage of such donations in our society in recent years. Also, careful preservation of the body is important for this purpose, and the techniques required to prevent decay are considerably more stringent than those used in a typical embalming procedure. Thus, the receiving institution will usually have a formal protocol for body donation and will typically require access to the body shortly after death. Following use of the body for scientific or educational purposes, the elements that remain may be cremated or buried by the institution or returned to next of kin for like disposition.

An alternative to a traditional funeral is a *memorial service.* Essentially, memorial services incorporate many of the practices that have already been described, but without the presence of a body. Memorial services might be held when a body has been lost at sea or is otherwise unavailable, when the body has been immediately cremated and the cremains scattered, when the body has been donated for medical research or education, or in other similar situations. Memorial societies in North America encourage memorial services as a way to reduce costs and to turn away from what they regard as an unhealthy emphasis on the corpse (Morgan & Morgan, 2001). They do not favor embalming, caskets, and all of the other elements needed to prepare a body for viewing. Instead, they prefer memorial services that focus on commemorating the life of the person through music, poetry, readings, and personal testimonials.

Although the Federal Trade Commission regulates the funeral industry, we cannot provide a single list of accurate prices for funeral services and associated merchandise because costs vary greatly across the country and by individual funeral home. The simplest way to determine cost is to ask a local funeral home for its price list or to draw up with a funeral director a "pre-need" plan (Bern-Klug et al., 2000). Preplanning is offered by almost all funeral homes in the United States as a way to design a specific plan that suits an individual and to determine what it will cost. In Box 4.6, we identify some of the main cost elements that enter into the price of funeral services in the United States. (Also, in Chapter 11 we describe some of the principal tasks that a funeral ritual should serve.)

One last point about the work of American funeral directors concerns the roles that some of them assume in responses to mass disasters as members of a Disaster Mortuary Operational Response Team (DMORT, 1988). As temporary federal employees in this capacity, DMORT team members establish temporary morgue facilities, assist with victim identification using latent fingerprints, forensic dental pathology, or forensic anthropology methods, and conduct processing, preparation, and disposition of human remains. The importance of this

Box 4.6 Typical Cost Items for Funeral Services and Merchandise

Service:	Includes:
Basic services of funeral director and staff, and overhead costs	Having personnel available 24 hours a day, 365 days a year to respond to respond to initial call; conducting arrangements conference; planning the funeral; consulting with family and clergy; shelter of remains; preparing and filing necessary notices; obtaining necessary authorizations and permits; coordinating with cemetery, crematory, and other third parties; plus a proportionate share of basic overhead costs (e.g., facility maintenance, equipment and inventory costs, insurance and administration expenses)
Embalming	Usually not required by law, but may be necessary if certain funeral arrangements (e.g., viewing, delay before funeral, transportation of the body over a long distance, and with certain diseases) are selected
Other preparation of the body	For example: restoration, cosmetology, washing and disinfection, manicuring
Transfer of deceased to the funeral home	Usually based on a stipulated distance, with added charges beyond that distance
Use of facilities and staff for viewing	At the funeral home first day; each added day
Use of facilities and staff for funeral ceremony	At the funeral home; at another location or facility
Use of facilities and staff for memorial service	At the funeral home, including folders, book, and acknowledgment cards; at another location; not including these printed materials
Use of equipment and staff graveside services	
Use of vehicles	Hearse; service/utility car; limousine
Pastoral services; music	
Cemetery plot and/or other charges	
Forwarding/receiving of remains to/from another funeral home	

Merchandise:	Includes:
	Casket, outer burial container (vault or grave liner), cremation urn, register books, acknowledgment cards, memorial folders, flowers, clothing

Some Alternatives:

Direct cremation (basic services of funeral director and staff, proportionate share of overhead costs, removal of remains, transportation to crematory, necessary authorizations, and cremation). Also, alternative containers made of materials like fiberboard or composition materials.

Immediate burial plus casket (basic services of funeral director and staff, proportionate share of overhead costs, removal of remains, transportation to cemetery). With or without casket provided by purchaser.

SOURCE: Based on Canine, 1999, and general price list (effective January 1, 2001) from Moss-Feaster Funeral Homes, Pinellas County, Florida.

work was evident in the work of a DMORT team following the events of September 11 (Hazell, 2001).

Summary

In this chapter, we focused on selected examples of death-related practices in the United States, which complemented our discussions of death-related encounters and attitudes in Chapters 2 and 3. We also introduced in this chapter the concept of a societal "death system" and the example of the terrorist attacks in the United States on September 11 to show how the American death system has recently mobilized itself in response to a particularly difficult challenge. We then examined a series of examples that showed the contemporary American death system in operation. For example, we offered an account of deaths resulting from both individual behaviors (as seen in accidents and homicides) and socially sanctioned practices (as illustrated in war and genocide, the Holocaust, and the beginning of the nuclear era) in an effort to demonstrate how these events changed human encounters with death and have had important ongoing implications up to the present time. Next, we considered American linguistic practices, noting that many individuals use euphemistic language to avoid talking about death as such, even as they use death-related language to discuss topics that are not at all related to death. We also identified highly selective and fantasized portraits of death and violence in the media (in both news reports and entertainment), and we described typical features of funeral practices in our society.

Questions for Review and Discussion

1. This chapter described selected examples of death-related practices in the United States in recent years. On a theoretical level, how do death-related *practices* join with death-related *encounters* and *attitudes* to make up a mosaic of death-related *experiences* in our society? Did you find our description of death-related practices in our society to be representative of your experiences within that society?

2. This chapter introduced the concept of a *death system* and its five elements: people, places, times, objects, and symbols. Think about the death system you live within. What elements (that is, what people, places, and so on) of this system have you encountered?

3. In the 20th century, violence has become an ever-larger factor in encounters with death. What role (if any) have accidents, homicide, or terrorism played in your encounters with death? Think about a specific example of an

accidental death, a homicide, or the terrorist assault of September 11, 2001. How, if at all, did this event affect your attitudes and behaviors?

4. Can you think of additional examples of pertinent speech patterns as you read or discussed the sections on language about death and death-related language in this chapter?

5. What have your experiences of funeral practices in contemporary American society been like? If you have not had any such experiences, what reasons can you give for that fact? How do those reasons reflect your attitudes toward death, dying, and bereavement?

Suggested Readings

On 20th-century experiences with death and some of the ways in which they have been influenced by societal institutions and practices, see:

Charmaz, K. (1980). *The Social Reality of Death: Death in Contemporary America.*

Elliot, G. (1972). *The Twentieth Century Book of the Dead.*

Seale, C. (1998). *Constructing Death: The Sociology of Dying and Bereavement.*

Sontag, S. (1978). *Illness as Metaphor.*

Among the many historical, biographical, and literary accounts related to the Holocaust, see:

Bauer, Y. (1982). *A History of the Holocaust.*

Camus, A. (1947/1972). *The Plague.*

Czarnecki, J. P. (1989). *Last Traces: The Lost Art of Auschwitz.*

Czech, D. (1990). *Auschwitz Chronicle, 1939–1945.*

Dawidowicz, L. S. (1975). *The War against the Jews 1933–1945.*

Gilbert, M. (1993). *Atlas of the Holocaust* (2nd rev. printing).

Gutman, I., & Berenbaum, M. (Eds.). (1994). *Anatomy of the Auschwitz Death Camp.*

Kulka, E. (1986). *Escape from Auschwitz.*

Levi, P. (1986). *Survival in Auschwitz and The Reawakening: Two Memoirs.*

MacMillan, I. (1991). *Orbit of Darkness.*

Pawelczynska, A. (1979). *Values and Violence in Auschwitz: A Sociological Analysis.*

Reitlinger, G. (1968). *The Final Solution: The Attempt to Exterminate the Jews of Europe 1939–1945* (2nd rev. ed.).

Wiesel, E. (1960). *Night.*

On the beginning of the nuclear era and some of its implications, see:

Alperovitz, G. (1995). *The Decision to Use the Atomic Bomb and the Architecture of an American Myth.*

Arkin, W., & Fieldhouse, R. (1985). *Nuclear Battlefields.*

Hersey, J. (1948). *Hiroshima.*

Lifton, R. J. (1967). *Death in Life: Survivors of Hiroshima.*

Lifton, R. J. (1979). *The Broken Connection.*

Lifton, R. J., & Mitchell, G. (1995). *Hiroshima in America: Fifty Years of Denial.*

Maddox, R. J. (1995). *Weapons for Victory: The Hiroshima Decision Fifty Years Later.*

For broader analyses of "horrendous death," see:

Leviton, D. (Ed.). (1991a). *Horrendous Death, Health, and Well-Being.*

Leviton, D. (Ed.). (1991b). *Horrendous Death and Health: Toward Action.*

For euphemisms and death-related language, consult:

Neaman, J. S., & Silver, C. G. (1983). *Kind Words: A Thesaurus of Euphemisms.*

Partridge, E. (1966). *A Dictionary of Slang and Unconventional English.*

Rawson, H. (1981). *A Dictionary of Euphemisms and Other Doubletalk.*

Wentworth, H., & Flexner, S. B. (Eds.). (1967). *Dictionary of American Slang (with Supplement).*

Information about American and worldwide funeral practices can be found in:

Canine, J. D. (1999). *What Am I Going to Do with Myself When I Die?*

Habenstein, R. W., & Lamers, W. M. (1962). *The History of American Funeral Directing* (rev. ed.).

Habenstein, R. W., & Lamers, W. M. (1974). *Funeral Customs the World Over* (rev. ed.).

Mayer, R. A. (1996). *Embalming: History, Theory, and Practice* (2nd ed.).

Morgan, E., & Morgan, J. (2001). *Dealing Creatively with Death: A Manual of Death Education and Simple Burial* (14th rev. ed.).

Raether, H. C. (Ed.). (1989). *The Funeral Director's Practice Management Handbook.*

InfoTrac College Edition
For more information, explore the InfoTrac College Edition at **http://www.infotrac-college.com/Wadsworth**

Enter search terms: CREMATION, DEATH PRACTICES (OR DEATH-RELATED PRACTICES), DEATH-RELATED LANGUAGE, DEATH SYSTEM, EMBALMING, EUPHEMISMS, GENOCIDE, THE HOLOCAUST, THE NUCLEAR ERA (ALSO CHERNOBYL, HIROSHIMA, NAGASAKI, THREE MILE ISLAND), SOCIALLY SANCTIONED DEATH, TERRORISM.

Chapter Five

CULTURAL DIFFERENCES AND DEATH

THUS FAR IN PART TWO WE HAVE GIVEN A broad account of experiences with death, dying, and bereavement—describing death-related encounters, attitudes, and practices, along with prominent features of the contemporary death system in the United States. But this is not the whole story. The United States of America is not a single, homogeneous entity with only one death system and one universal set of death-related encounters and attitudes. On the contrary, our society embraces within its boundaries a kaleidoscope of cultural, social, racial, ethnic, and religious groupings, each of which may have important differences in some aspects of their death-related experiences.

Most of what we have discussed thus far is a background shared by all individuals in American society. Everyone living in the United States today is compelled, to one extent or another, to interact with our society's death system. For example, some official designated by the larger society must declare a person to be dead—no matter who that person may be. Nevertheless, members of different social groups interact with our society's situations and values in different ways.

For that reason, we pay special attention in this chapter—and elsewhere throughout this book—to some of the many ways in which cultural differences affect death-related experiences. Following a short vignette, we consider some of the cautions that need to be observed in making claims about cultural differences in the field of death, dying, and bereavement. Then we describe what is known about the three principal topics of Chapters 2, 3, and 4 (death-related encounters, attitudes, and practices) in relationship to four selected cultural groups in America (Hispanic Americans, African Americans, Americans who trace their backgrounds to Asian countries or the Pacific Islands, and Native Americans). Throughout, our analysis draws on the general social and cultural background provided in Chapters 2 through 4 and points forward both to the issue-oriented chapters that follow and to broader studies of cultural differences outside the borders of the United States. ■

A Happy Funeral

A charming picture book for young readers entitled *The Happy Funeral* (Bunting, 1982) describes two young Chinese-American sisters who are preparing to take part in their grandfather's funeral. When their mother first tells May-May and Laura about their grandfather's death, she says that he is going to have a happy funeral. The girls are puzzled by that concept. "It's like saying a sad party. Or hot snow. It doesn't make sense" (p. 1).

May-May and Laura are perplexed and they are unclear about many of the events that follow. Although they loved their grandfather and are clearly expected to be participants in this community event, the girls have not had much experience with death and funerals. They are insiders to the community, but outsiders in many ways to what is about to happen. Above all, they do not expect to be happy at their grandfather's funeral.

At the funeral home, bunches of flowers are everywhere and incense sticks burn in front of Grandfather's casket. There are many gifts for Grandfather's "journey to the other side," such as a map of the spirit world, some food, and half a comb (Grandmother keeps the other half, to be rejoined when she is reunited with her husband after her own death). A cardboard house, play money, and pictures of various objects (for example, a drawing of Chang, the big black dog that Grandfather had when he was a boy, and a picture of a red car with a silver stripe of the kind that Grandfather never was able to have in this life) are burned, with the idea that they will become real when they turn into smoke and rise to the spirit world.

At the funeral service in the Chinese Gospel Church, there are more flowers and a big photograph of Grandfather framed in roses. The adults talk about Grandfather's fine qualities and the many good things that he did. Some of the adults cry and Laura feels a big lump in her throat when she realizes how tiny Grandmother is and that she is even older than Grandfather. After the ceremony, a woman gives a small candy to each of the mourners "to sweeten your sorrow" (p. 22). Then Grandfather's casket is put in a glass-sided car and his photograph is propped on the roof of one of the two flower cars. With a marching band playing spirited music, the cars parade throughout the streets of Chinatown. That part is a happy funeral.

At the cemetery, Grandfather's casket is placed on a wooden table next to a big hole in the ground. The minister says that Grandfather is going to his spiritual reward, but Laura tries to think of him flying the wonderful kites that he used to make. During all of these events, Laura alternates between warm memories and feelings of sadness, between smiles and tears. Eventually, she realizes that although she and May-May were not happy to have their grandfather die, his funeral really was a happy one because he was ready for his death and he left a good legacy through his well-lived life and everyone's fond memories of him. Mom "never said it was happy for us to have him go" (p. 38).

What Can Be Said about Cultural Differences: Some Cautions and Opportunities

We must keep firmly in mind three primary cautions concerning whatever we can say about cultural differences in relationship to death, dying, and bereavement. First, to open a door to the many cultural groups within the broad panorama of American society is immediately to confront *a dazzling multiplicity of population clusters*. We have chosen in this chapter to indicate in brief sketches some qualities of death-related experiences often found in four groups—Hispanic Americans (properly called "persons of Hispanic origin" for statistical purposes), African Americans, Americans who trace their backgrounds to Asian countries or the Pacific Islands, and Native Americans. These are important cultural groups in our society, but obviously they are just four of many cultural groups that could be selected for study.

In addition to the perplexing variety of groups within American society, there also are many differences within the four groups that are to be considered here. None of these groups is a single, undifferentiated entity. Among Americans of Hispanic origin, there are Puerto Ricans, Mexican Americans, Cuban Americans, and immigrants from Central and South America. In fact, there is a debate among these groups as to whether and for whom terms like *Hispanic*, *Latino*, or *Chicano* are the best descriptors. Among African Americans, there are rural and urban, rich and poor, and Christian and Muslim. Among Asian Americans, there are people who trace their ancestries to the very different societies of Cambodia, China, Japan, Korea, Thailand, Vietnam, other Asian countries, or to the Pacific Islands. And among Native Americans (termed "American Indians" by the National Center for Health Statistics and sometimes called "First Nation Peoples" in Canada), there are literally hundreds of distinct groupings (for example, Navajo, Zuni, Dakota, Seminole) that can trace their ancestral homes to nearly every part of the North American continent. It is both naive and prejudicial to think of these many subgroups within our four primary ones as essentially interchangeable or wholly like the others within the primary group.

The second caution to keep in mind is *the state of our current knowledge about issues related to death, dying, and bereavement.* This caution refers to knowledge of these subjects in general and especially to issues associated with cultural differences. Research, teaching, and publication in the field of death, dying, and bereavement is mainly a phenomenon that began in the second half of the 20th century. Prior to that time, there were scattered scholarly reports on these topics, especially in selected fields such as anthropology and history. But research from a wide range of perspectives really only began to appear during the 1950s and 1960s. Such research could not be said to have reached an acceptable degree of depth, breadth, and maturity until the 1970s and thereafter.

When we wrote the first edition of this text in the early 1990s, we noted how little research had been done to that point on cross-cultural themes. A decade later, little has changed. Most of what is known in the field of death, dying, and bereavement about various cultural groups is based on a few studies in various locales throughout the United States. However, what might be true of some African Americans in New York City might not be equally valid for African Americans living in rural Alabama. Among Hispanic Americans, Mexican Americans in Texas are a different community from Mexican Americans living in California, and Mexican Americans in any part of the United States are a different cultural group from Puerto Ricans in New York City. Thus, existing literature on cultural differences in death-related experiences repeatedly notes that there is a dearth of data—much less analysis—about how ethnic minorities in America deal with these issues.

Together, these first two cautions mean that at present there is much that remains unknown about death, dying, and bereavement. Limitations are especially evident in the specialized cultural aspects of those topics. Some data and some analyses are available, but they are limited in many respects and often require that conclusions be carefully qualified. That is why we are able here only to offer sketches of cultural differences, the beginnings of the fuller portraits that will emerge if researchers seize the opportunities now available to set forth richer materials and more detailed analyses in these important subject areas.

A third caution to keep in mind is *the need to avoid the danger of stereotypes.* Everyone discussed in this chapter is simultaneously an American, a member of some particular cultural group, and an individual person. No one of them in any aspect of his or her death-related experiences is completely identical to any other individual—even to other members of his or her own cultural group.

Japanese Americans reflect this distinction in some very precise distinctions made between generations. *Issei* are members of the older, first generation who were born in Japan, came to live in the United States between 1890 and 1924, often spoke English only poorly if at all, lived much of their lives in Japanese enclaves, and usually had strong ties to the attitudes and practices of their ancestors. *Nisei* (some of whom became famous as members of the American military in World War II) are members of the intermediate or second generation who were born in America between 1910 and 1940, attended American schools, and spoke English as their main language, but who wished to maintain some links to the attitudes and practices of their ancestors. *Sansei* are members of a third generation, born after World War II in America to American parents of Japanese ancestry, and who in many ways are indistinguishable in their education, attitudes, and practices from American peers who have no cultural or ethnic links to Japan (Kitano, 1976). These distinctions illustrate quite plainly the need to avoid lumping people (such as all Japanese Americans) together in stereotypical ways and the value of respect for individuality in any multicultural account of death, dying, and bereavement.

Still, even given these caveats, we believe that it is important to say something about the sort of differences one is likely to encounter among various subcultures in the American death system. To pay attention to these differences is to seize the opportunity to overcome two dangers. The first of these dangers arises from the assumption that everyone is like us or like the dominant culture in beliefs, values, and practices. This chapter should help to make clear just how inaccurate that view is. When we ignore the relevant differences, we are likely to misunderstand and provide poorer care for those in need because of that misunderstanding. When we strive to appreciate cultural differences, our encounters, attitudes, and practices are likely to be enriched. Similarly, through efforts like those made in this chapter, we gain the possibility of overcoming a second, perhaps even more important danger. That danger lies in assuming that everyone who belongs to a subculture shares the values, beliefs, and practices of the subculture and is therefore unlike those in the dominant culture. This is to make such persons into the "other," someone strange whom we cannot understand. This too points in the direction of our failing to provide appropriate care for those in need. The opportunity that lies before us is to become more informed by and more sensitive to the individuality of our fellow Americans.

With these cautions, dangers, and opportunities in mind, we can turn once again to the three primary topics of Chapters 2, 3, and 4—encounters with death, attitudes toward death, and death-related practices—in order to apply them here in turn to each of the four cultural groups we have chosen to discuss (Hispanic Americans, African Americans, Americans who trace their backgrounds to Asian countries or the Pacific Islands, and Native Americans). In general, we will find ourselves on firmest ground in our discussion of encounters with death, since there are statistical data available that have been gathered by various governmental agencies about such matters as death rates, causes of death, and the immediate implications of death in these cultural groups and in some of their subgroups. By contrast, for attitudes toward death and death-related practices, there is little careful research to support any broad generalizations. In fact, many of the available studies conclude with a warning that the sample in the study was too limited in size or makeup to draw any general conclusions. Thus, our reports that follow on death-related attitudes and practices must be seen as little more than a sampling of some members of each of our groups, one that illustrates how diverse each of these groups really is.

People of different backgrounds and cultures may turn to each other for information and support in coping with death-related issues.

Encounters with Dying, Death, and Bereavement

Hispanic Americans

According to the 2000 census, Hispanics are now the largest minority group in the United States, consisting of more than 35.3 million persons or 12.5 percent of the total population (see Table 5.1). This is an increase of nearly 58 percent from the 1990 census count of 22.4 million Hispanic Americans (Guzman, 2001). However, this needs careful qualification. Population counts in the 2000 census describe the resident population of the 50 United States (residents of the Commonwealth of Puerto Rico and the U.S. Island Areas [the U.S. Virgin Islands, Guam, American Samoa, and the Commonwealth of the Northern Mariana Islands] are counted separately and are not included in totals given in Table 5.1). These U.S. resident figures for 2000 reflected both real changes (increases and decreases) in the population, as well as important changes in the census process. Real changes in the Hispanic-American population during the 1990s resulted from high immigration (especially among people of Mexican ori-

Table 5.1 Resident Population: United States, 1900 and 2000

	1900[a]		2000[b]	
	Number	Percentage	Number	Percentage
Total population	75,994,000	100.0	281,421,906	100.0
Male	38,816,000	51.1	138,053,563	49.1
Female	37,178,000	48.9	143,368,343	50.9
Hispanic or Latino (of any race)[c]	(NA)		35,305,818	12.5
Not Hispanic or Latino	(NA)		246,116,088	87.5
One race only:	(NA)		274,595,678	97.6
Caucasian Americans	66,809,000	87.9	211,460,626	75.1
African Americans	8,834,000	11.6	34,658,190	12.3
Asian Americans and Pacific Islanders	(NA)		10,641,833	3.9
Native Americans[d]	(NA)		2,475,956	0.9
Some other race	(NA)		15,359,073	5.5
Two or more races	(NA)		6,826,228	2.4

[a] Excludes Alaska and Hawaii
[b] Excludes individuals living in the Commonwealth of Puerto and the U.S. Island Areas who are counted separately. Note also that in the 2000 census individuals could report more than one race, as well as "Hispanic"; as a result, numbers within categories for 2000 may add to more or less than the total population given above.
[c] Persons of Hispanic origin may be of any race; not included in data for the total population.
[d] Includes Aleuts and Eskimos.

SOURCE: U.S. Bureau of the Census, 2000.

gin) and high birth rates. Changes in the census process have to do with census coverage and the census questionnaire itself (for example, the new questionnaire asked "Is this person Spanish/Hispanic/Latino?"). Perhaps more importantly, individuals responding to the 2000 census were permitted to classify themselves in more than one racial or cultural category—reflecting the so-called "Tiger Woods description," whereby this famous, young golfer insists on describing himself as "Cablinasian" to reflect the ethnic blend in his ancestry of Caucasian, Black, American Indian, and Asian. Further, to speak of a "Hispanic" American is to point to a cultural category, not a racial one. In fact, Hispanic Americans may be of any race. Therefore, in the 2000 census (for example) some individuals (e.g., those with parents of different races) who were formerly classified solely in a particular racial category (e.g., solely as Caucasian Americans, African Americans, etc.) may have chosen to add a second such category or to also classify themselves as Hispanic.

Nevertheless, although the present figures may be in part an artifact of the new processes and classification system used in the 2000 census, the Hispanic portion of the American population has clearly been growing over the past decades. For some time, Hispanics had been predicted to become the largest minority group in our society not later than the year 2010. Note also that these figures on Hispanic Americans who reside in the 50 states do not include 3.8 million Hispanics who were counted separately in the Commonwealth of Puerto Rico. For all of these reasons, we believe there is a sufficient basis to regard Hispanic Americans as currently being the largest minority group in American society.

Within the Hispanic-American population, approximately 58.5 percent are of Mexican origin, 9.6 percent originated in Puerto Rico, 3.5 percent are Cuban Americans, and some 28.4 percent have other origins (mostly in Central America, South America, and the Dominican Republic) (U.S. Bureau of the Census, 2000). Some people of Hispanic origin are recent immigrants, others have lived in the continental United States for generations, and all Puerto Ricans have been U.S. citizens since 1917.

Efforts to study death rates among Hispanic Americans face special difficulties. In the United States, most of the data collected on death rates come from records in county offices. Such records depend upon death certificates, which provide space to record both the race and the specific Hispanic origin of the individual who has died (see Figure 16.1). Much depends, therefore, on the accuracy of the person who fills out the death certificate and on reliable information from his or her sources. Nevertheless, these are the best data available and the foundation for all that follows here.

Within the United States, there were 103,740 deaths of Hispanic Americans in 1999 (see Table 5.2). This figure is strikingly low—it amounts to 4.3 percent of all deaths in the United States in 1999 within a group that is well over 12 percent of the total population. As a result, the Hispanic-American death rate of 331.0 per 100,000 in 1999 is only about one-third that of the non-Hispanic white ("Anglo") death rate of 944.4. The principal reason for these low numbers of deaths and death rates among Hispanic Americans seems to be the fact that "the Hispanic population has a greater proportion of young persons" than do other groups within our society (Kochanek & Hudson, 1994, p. 9).

This picture is likely to change as the Hispanic-American population ages, as more of its members are born within the United States, and as it increasingly

Table 5.2 Deaths by Specified Race or National Origin and Gender: United States, 1999

	Both Sexes	Percentage of Total	Male	Percentage of Race Total	Female	Percentage of Race Total
All races	2,391,399	100.0	1,175,460	49.2	1,215,939	50.8
Caucasian Americans, Non-Hispanic	1,953,197	81.7	944,913	48.4	1,008,284	51.6
African Americans, Non-Hispanic	281,979	11.8	143,883	51.0	138,096	49.0
Hispanic origin[a]	103,740	4.3	57,991	55.9	45,749	44.1
Asian Americans and Pacific Islanders	33,675	1.4	18,330	54.4	15,345	45.6
Native Americans[b]	11,312	0.5	6,092	53.9	5,220	46.1

[a]Includes persons of Hispanic origin of any race.
[b]Includes Aleuts and Eskimos.

SOURCE: Hoyert et al., 2001.

Hispanic Americans tend to the grave of a family member.

integrates itself into mainstream American society. For example, infant mortality rates among Hispanic Americans in 1999 were already 5.8 per 1,000 live births, the same as the rate for non-Hispanic white ("Anglo") infants (Kochanek et al., 2001). Also, like members of many other cultural groups, especially those dominated by immigrants, as Hispanic Americans adjust to their surrounding culture in the United States, they often take on many of the characteristics of that culture, further confounding claims about that which is distinctive in Hispanic-American experiences with death, dying, and bereavement (Rosenwaike & Bradshaw, 1988, 1989; Salcido, 1990; Soto & Villa, 1990).

Among causes of death, there are significant differences between the Hispanic and non-Hispanic populations in the United States. For example, two leading causes of death—heart disease and cancer—accounted for 59 percent of all deaths in 1992 for the non-Hispanic white population, but only 43 percent of deaths in the Hispanic population (Kochanek & Hudson, 1994). Similarly, two leading causes of death for the non-Hispanic white population—chronic lower respiratory diseases and suicide—do not have similar prominence among Hispanic Americans.

By contrast, deaths from HIV infection and homicide rank much higher (fourth and fifth, respectively) among Hispanic Americans than they do for the non-Hispanic white population (Plepys & Klein, 1995). As a general rule, this is particularly true for young Hispanic-American males. Not surprisingly, in a population with a large proportion of young persons one is likely to find "a larger proportion of deaths due to causes that are more prevalent at younger ages" (Kochanek & Hudson, 1994, p. 9). Nevertheless, differences in homicide rates among different Hispanic-American communities suggest that other factors are also at work, such as poverty and other socioeconomic variables.

African Americans

African Americans are the second largest minority group among residents of the United States, consisting of almost 34.7 million persons or 12.3 percent of the total population (see Table 5.1). In 1999, non-Hispanic African Americans experienced 281,979 deaths or about 11.8 percent of all deaths in the United States in that year (see Table 5.2). African Americans are linked in many ways by origins on the African continent, the history of slavery and slave trading, and experiences of discrimination. Slavery itself was a practice with many death-related implications. These included the killings involved in taking individuals prisoner and removing them from their tribal homes, suffering and death during transport to the New World, harsh living and working conditions on this side of the Atlantic, and all that is entailed in being treated as objects who could become the property of others. That background influences many aspects of contemporary African-American experiences with death in America. As Kalish and Reynolds (1981) wrote more than 20 years ago, "To be Black in America is to be part of a history told in terms of contact with death and coping with death" (p. 103).

As we noted in Chapter 2, substantial declines in death rates during the 20th century are found in nearly every segment of the population in the United States. There are, however, differences among these declines. During the period from 1900 to 1974 death rates for African Americans as a group consistently exceeded those for Caucasian Americans (see Figure 5.1; Kitagawa & Hauser, 1973). Nevertheless, in 1974 overall death rates for African Americans for the first time were lower than those for Caucasian Americans, and this new pattern of African-American statistical advantage continued through 1999, when African Americans had overall death rates of 817.7 per 100,000 versus 917.7 for Caucasian Americans (Hoyert et al., 2001). In addition, in 1999 African-American males had lower death rates than their Caucasian-American counterparts (880.0 versus 911.2 per 100,000), and African-American females had significantly lower death rates than their Caucasian-American counterparts (761.3 versus 924.1 per 100,000) (Hoyert et al., 2001).

These figures suggest that relative disadvantages in death rates for African Americans during much of the last century, as well as relative advantages in recent years, may not have resulted simply from ethnicity. Many minority groups in American society are disadvantaged in their socioeconomic standing and such disadvantages almost always reveal themselves in higher death rates (Benjamin, 1965; Blane, 1995). One decade-long study of 530,000 individuals confirmed that employment status, income, education, occupation, and marital status—as well as race—all have "substantial net associations with mortality" (Sorlie et al., 1995, p. 949). Poverty, inadequate access to health care, and higher incidences of life-threatening behavior have immediate and unhappy implications for death rates. Because racial, cultural, and socioeconomic factors of this sort are so complex and closely intertwined, it is difficult to identify or rank

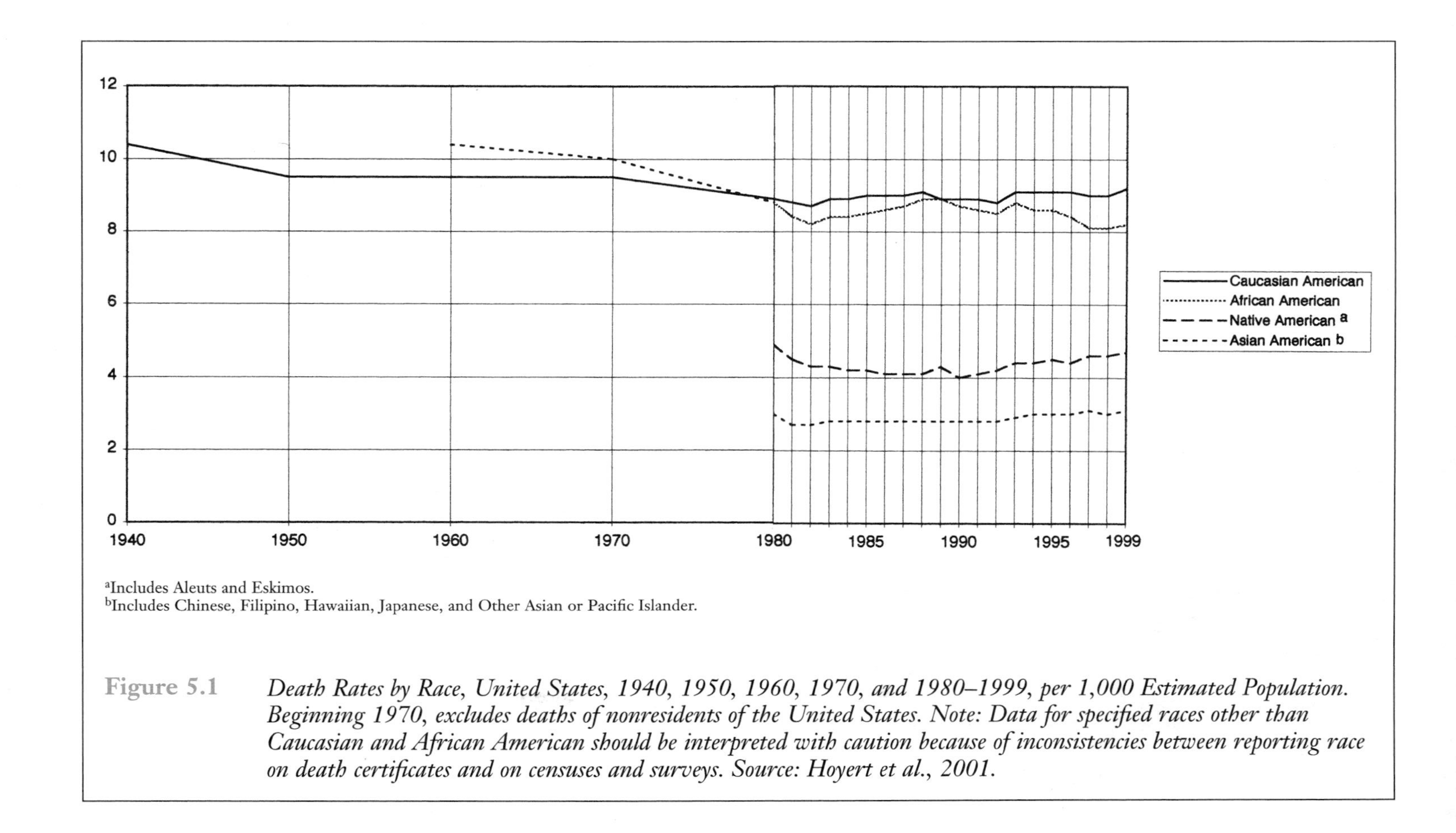

[a]Includes Aleuts and Eskimos.
[b]Includes Chinese, Filipino, Hawaiian, Japanese, and Other Asian or Pacific Islander.

Figure 5.1 *Death Rates by Race, United States, 1940, 1950, 1960, 1970, and 1980–1999, per 1,000 Estimated Population. Beginning 1970, excludes deaths of nonresidents of the United States. Note: Data for specified races other than Caucasian and African American should be interpreted with caution because of inconsistencies between reporting race on death certificates and on censuses and surveys. Source: Hoyert et al., 2001.*

causal factors influencing death rates for African-Americans as a group. However, correlations between membership in some subgroups within this population and the statistical likelihood of dying at an earlier or later age than some members of other subgroups or than Caucasian Americans are evident.

One can describe the situation facing African Americans today in various ways. For example, estimated average life expectancy for an African-American infant born in 1999 is nearly six years lower than for a Caucasian-American infant (71.4 years versus 77.3 years) (see Table 2.4). In fact, until old age, African Americans have higher death rates than their Caucasian counterparts and are at greater risk of dying from most causes. In terms of some African-American subgroups, however, things may be much different. For example, McCord and Freeman (1990) demonstrated that African-American males living in Harlem are less likely to reach the age of 65 than men living in Bangladesh, one of the poorest countries in the world. According to these authors, the "situation in Harlem is extreme, but it is not an isolated phenomenon. . . . Similar pockets of high mortality have been described in other U.S. cities" (p. 176).

Further, death rates due to homicide are much higher among African Americans than among Caucasian Americans. There are, for example, approximately 5.7 deaths of African Americans from homicide for each death of a Caucasian American from the same cause. Further, homicide is the leading cause of death among African-American males between the ages of 15 and 24. To be young, African-American, and male in our society is to find oneself at unusual risk for death by homicide in comparison with all other Americans. African Americans can find some comfort in the fact that their death rates from suicide are lower than those of Caucasian Americans, although suicide is increasing among young, African-American males.

Infant mortality rates were two and a half times higher among African Americans in 1999 than among Caucasian Americans—14.6 versus 5.8 deaths per 1,000 live births (Hoyert et al., 2001). Although infant mortality rates have declined significantly for both African Americans and Caucasian Americans during the past 40 years, differences in infant mortality rates between these two groups have actually increased (for many, complex reasons), and the present disparity between them is projected to continue through the first decade of the 21st century (Singh & Yu, 1995).

On a related point, although maternal death rates at the time of childbirth have decreased dramatically for all Americans over the past 100 years, in 1999 they were nearly four times higher among African Americans than among Caucasian Americans (25.4 vs. 6.8 per 100,000 live births). Also, there is a higher incidence of and lower survival rates with cancer among African Americans (Polednak, 1990). Finally, according to federal reports, whereas mortality from breast cancer fell among Caucasian-American women between 1989 and 1992, it actually rose among African-American women (*St. Louis Post-Dispatch*, 1995a).

These differences do not themselves directly reveal the underlying factors from which they result. Still, in studies in which other factors were held constant, some aspects of these higher death rates and lowered life expectancies were found to be more directly related to education and socioeconomic status than to race or ethnicity (Polednak, 1990). This finding is not surprising. For instance, Powell-Griner (1988) reported that higher risks of infant mortality are associated with illegitimacy, blue-collar families, inadequate prenatal care, and low birth weight. In many instances, these factors are not unrelated to each other; where they are added together, they are likely to converge in a way that puts an infant at higher risk of premature death (Plepys & Klein, 1995).

Last, as early as 1986 it was noted that "Blacks and Hispanics comprise a disproportionately high percentage of AIDS cases" (Institute of Medicine, 1986, p. 102). Despite the fact that HIV disease was no longer ranked among the 15 leading causes of death in 1999 for the American population as a whole, it remained the leading cause of death for African-American males and the third-leading cause of death for African-American females in the same year (Kochanek et al., 2001). Thus, deaths associated with HIV infection represent a major disequity related to racial and cultural differences in American society.

Asian and Pacific Island Americans

Asian and Pacific Island Americans are individuals who trace their origins back to the various countries in Asia or to the Pacific islands. Together, they are the third largest minority group among residents of the United States, consisting of over 10.6 million persons or 3.9 percent of the total population (see Table 5.1). The largest of the Asian-American communities are Chinese Americans (constituting approximately 24 percent of the total), followed by Filipino Americans (18 percent), Asian Americans from India (16.4 percent), Vietnamese Americans (11 percent), and Korean Americans (10.5 percent).

Deaths among Asian Americans and Pacific Islanders in the United States in 1999 are outlined in Table 5.2. Taken together, these add up to 33,675 deaths, representing 1.4 percent of all deaths for that year in a population that now totals almost three times that share of the U.S. resident population.

Death rates in the Asian-American and Pacific-Island-American community as a whole were 311.2 per 100,000, dramatically lower than the overall Caucasian-American death rate of 917.7 (see Figure 5.1). Causes of death among Asian Americans can be illustrated through Yu's (1986) report of similarities among Chinese Americans and Caucasian Americans: the three leading causes in both groups are heart disease, cancer, and cerebrovascular disease. Moreover, for each of the six leading causes of death, death rates are higher among foreign-born Chinese than among Chinese Americans born in the United States. One curiosity is that cancer rates for the buccal (mouth) cavity and pharynx are higher for Chinese Americans than for Caucasian Americans. It is uncertain whether this high incidence is the result of a genetic susceptibility to this form of cancer or some other (perhaps dietary) factor.

Infant mortality rates for Asian Americans vary slightly among subgroups, with the lowest rates found among Chinese Americans and the highest rates among Filipino Americans. Nevertheless, infant mortality rates of 4.0 per 1,000 for Asian Americans as a whole are and have been significantly lower than those for Caucasian Americans, Hispanic Americans, African Americans, and Native Americans (Ventura et al., 1997; Yu, 1982).

Korean-American mourners at the casket of their teenage son in Los Angeles.

Native Americans

Readily available information about death-related encounters among Native Americans (or American Indians, a population group that includes Aleuts and Eskimos for statistical purposes) is limited, not always reliable, and not easily subject to generalization. There are hundreds of Native American tribal groups in the United States and Canada, varying in size from fewer than 100 members (for example, Picuris Pueblo in New Mexico) to more than 100,000 members (for example, the Navajo) (Marquis, 1974). Each Native American group has its own set of death-related encounters, attitudes, and patterns of behavior.

Official estimates place the total population of Native Americans who reside in the United States at approximately 2.5 million persons or less than 1 percent of the total population (see Table 5.1). However, not all Native Americans live within a tribal group or on tribal lands, where data about their death-related experiences can easily be located and identified. In fact, an estimated 55–60 percent of Native Americans now live in urban areas in North America, where they may be invisible in many ways to an external observer (Thompson & Walker, 1990). Furthermore, it has been reported that there are some 6.7 million additional individuals who claim partial Native American ancestry (U.S. Congress, 1986). For all of these reasons, generalizations about death, dying, and bereavement may be particularly inappropriate or hazardous for this relatively small but very heterogeneous portion of American society.

There were 11,312 Native-American deaths in 1999 (see Table 5.2), just half of one percent of all deaths in the U.S. that year. That results in an overall death rate of 471.8 per 100,000 (see Figure 5.1). However, these are aggregate figures, subject to all of the limitations just noted. Death is likely to be encountered in quite different ways in different Native American groups.

Typically, Native Americans have died most frequently from infectious diseases, tuberculosis, diabetes mellitus, cirrhosis, and accidents. As some of these causes have become less significant and the average life expectancy of most Native Americans has increased, cancer has become more important as a cause of death in these groups, although its incidence among Native Americans has not been well studied (Michalek & Mahoney, 1990). Available research indicates that both Native-American males and females have lower rates than other groups for all disease sites combined; however, females have increased rates of cervical cancer. Overall, Native Americans also have the least favorable survival rates from cancer.

Native-American infant mortality rates of 8.0 per 1,000 are substantially higher than those for Caucasian Americans, Hispanic Americans, and Asian Americans although not as high as those for African Americans (Ventura et al., 1997). Trends in these rates for all American cultural groups appear to be affected mainly by maternal education and family income. Among all cultural groups, Native-American infants are at highest risk of dying of sudden infant death syndrome (Campbell, 1989; Singh & Yu, 1995).

Mahoney (1991) found high death rates from automobile accidents among Native-American populations in New York State, nearly double the overall rate in the United States. The largest portion (73.7 percent) of these deaths occurred among males (Mahoney, 1991). Carr and Lee (1978) found motor vehicle accidents to be the leading cause of death among Navajo males and the second leading cause among females on the reservation. Campbell (1989) made a similar report concerning Native-Americans in Montana. Olson and colleagues (1990) also reported that deaths due to motor vehicle crashes were exceptionally high among Native-American children in New Mexico.

However, high vehicular death rates among Native-American populations may in part be attributed to their living in areas where people live far apart from one another and where roads are often in poor condition. In these circumstances, increased motor vehicle use is necessary, but it is also more dangerous, given the condition of the roads. All this is compounded when poverty and alcoholism are additional contributing factors. This viewpoint is supported by Bachman (1992), who argued that what appear to be high homicide rates in some Native-American communities are influenced by such factors as the historical experience of a kind of internal colonialism, social disorganization, cultural conflicts, a subculture of violence, economic deprivation, and abuse of alcohol and drugs. Thus, when socioeconomic status and other cultural factors are controlled, it appears that "racial differences in homicide rates decrease substantially" (Holinger et al., 1994, p. 20).

Attitudes toward Death

Hispanic Americans

Among many Hispanic Americans, family and religion appear to play influential roles in shaping attitudes related to death, dying, and bereavement. For example, Kalish and Reynolds (1981) described the Mexican-American families in their study as tightly knit and as maintaining a strong locus of emotional support in the family unit. Accordingly, when a member is dying in a hospital, the family typically arranges shifts of visitors and may "camp in." Garcia-Preto (1986) also reported this for Puerto Ricans in New York. In addition, she wrote that "Puerto Ricans place great value on seeing a dying relative, resolving whatever conflicts may exist, and saying a final good-bye. . . . Not being able to be present during the illness or time of death of someone close to them makes the loss more difficult to accept" (pp. 33–34).

However, the nature of the Mexican-American family may be changing in important ways. For example, Salcido (1990) reported a rise in the number of single-family households among Mexican Americans. These families may not behave exactly as did others studied previously.

Kalish and Reynolds (1981) also reported that 90 percent of the Mexican Americans whom they studied in Los Angeles were Roman Catholic. That religious background may be one reason why Mexican Americans in this study were opposed to allowing someone to die even if that person wished to do so. Thus, it is not surprising that a study of Mexican Americans in Michigan and Arizona reported that their attitudes toward palliative care "are intertwined with culturally based beliefs about the role of the family in caregiving and religious or spiritual beliefs" (Gelfand et al., 2001, p. 395).

Additional generalizations have been made about other attitudes of Hispanic Americans in relationship to dying. Eisenbruch (1984) reported on conflicts between the expectations of health care providers and the attitudes and behaviors of many Puerto Ricans living in New York City. For example, an accepted grief reaction in this population group (but one often not looked on favorably by health care providers) includes *el ataque*, consisting of "seizure-like patterns, with a hyperkinetic episode, a display of histrionics or aggression, and sometimes the climax of stupor" (Eisenbruch, 1984, p. 335). This response is regarded in the Puerto Rican community as normal for women; following a code of *machismo*, the men show no grief. Campos (1990) reported that Puerto Ricans regard death as an adversity that should be met with fatalism and pessimism, and they seem to try to protect dying persons from knowing their prognoses. Garcia-Preto (1986) suggested that Puerto Ricans typically care for the ill at home, choosing hospitalization only when there is no other alternative.

Kalish and Reynolds (1981) found Mexican Americans more likely than other groups to call for a priest when a person is dying; indeed, the so-called "last rites" may be performed several times. They also found this group to express intense feelings of grief and to believe that it takes time to express such feelings property. The grieving process for Mexican Americans involves the gathering together of a large support group, which includes people from the community, friends, and family members (Salcido, 1990).

Memorials for those who have died are framed by culture: A cemetery in San Juan, Puerto Rico.

African Americans

Systematic study of attitudes associated with death, dying, and bereavement among African Americans has hardly begun. Kalish and Reynolds (1981) published one early report about such attitudes among African Americans in Los Angeles in 1976. They found that individuals in the study relied on friends, church associates, and neighbors for support when dealing with these issues. That is, Kalish and Reynolds found that family relationships were not as important among African Americans as they were among other groups in their study. However, this may have been related to the population studied: these African Americans reported the shortest average residence in California, so they may simply have had fewer family members upon whom they could rely.

Brown (1990) described the role of the family in African-American society quite differently. He reported that family is central to the care provided for the terminally ill among African Americans. The African Americans in Brown's study saw this care as a "public" rather than a "private" matter, meaning that the extended family, friends, and neighbors may all get involved. Brown suggested that African Americans are reluctant to place terminally ill persons in a hospital or nursing home, preferring instead to keep them at home. This seems to

An elderly man with a life-threatening illness is supported at home by his extended family.

reinforce Brown's claim that for African Americans there is a "strong sense of family loyalty" (p. 76) and to signal the need for professional health care workers to be sensitive to cultural differences among those whom they serve (Leininger, 1988, 1991, 1995).

We must reiterate our warning to be wary of overgeneralizations and stereotypes here. As Brown (1990) reported, *middle-class* African Americans may have taken over attitudes and behaviors that are closer to those of the dominant society than are the attitudes and behaviors of other African Americans. In other words, African Americans are as influenced by socioeconomic class, geographical location, and historical heritage as are members of other groups, so their reactions are varied and personal.

Asian and Pacific Island Americans

Kalish and Reynolds (1981) found members of the Japanese-American community in Los Angeles to insist on an attitude of careful control over communication. Accordingly, even when members of this community are dying and in distress, such persons are often quite restrained in communicating what they are feeling to health care providers. Similarly, Eisenbruch (1984) reported that Chinese Americans are "stoic" in the face of death (see also Tong & Spicer, 1994); death may be a taboo subject among some Chinese Americans (Tanner, 1995). Further, the strong tendency displayed by many Asian Americans not to question authority is an attitude that carries through to interactions with health care providers (Manio & Hall, 1987). This custom can lead to miscommunication; for example, the health care provider may fail to perceive a patient's pain because that person chooses to "save face" in front of a stranger.

Asian-American families also often assume the major role of decision maker on behalf of their patient-member (Blackhall et al. 1995; Tong & Spicer, 1994). Various studies among Japanese Americans (Hirayama, 1990), Cambodian Americans (Lang, 1990), and Chinese Canadians (Tong & Spicer, 1994) have also reported that families may be unlikely to tell seriously ill persons that they are dying. In general, Asian Americans prefer to die at home (Kalish & Reynolds, 1981; Tanner, 1995) and try to keep their elderly family members at home (Manio & Hall, 1987).

For many Asian Americans, death does not prevent a continued relationship between the deceased and the survivors (Eisenbruch, 1984). Thus, Kalish and Reynolds (1981) reported that all of their Japanese-American respondents believed that those who had died watch over those who remain alive on earth. Accordingly, funerals and other memorialization activities are likely to be regarded as important social events, because by taking care of the ancestors in this way, one ensures that the ancestors will contribute to the well-being of surviving descendants.

Native Americans

Many commentators (such as Brown, 1987; Hultkrantz, 1979) have suggested that Native Americans tend to view life and death not in a linear but in a circular or interwoven fashion in which death is regarded as part of life (see Box 5.1). This belief is well illustrated in *Annie and the Old One* (Miles, 1971), an award-winning book for children. When Annie is told that her grandmother (the Old One) will die ("go to Mother Earth") when her mother finishes weaving a rug, she misbehaves at school, lets the family's sheep loose one night, and tries in various ways to delay the weaving or distract her mother. Eventually, the adults realize what is happening and explain to Annie that death is a part of the natural cycle of life. In the end, Annie joins in the activity of weaving.

Nevertheless, death-related attitudes of specific Native American groups may range from acceptance without anxiety to a high level of fear. For example, Carr and Lee (1978) reported that among Navajos, death taboos "favor bringing the sick into the hospital to die rather than permitting them to die at home" (p. 280) so that the home will not be polluted by the experience of death. Perhaps we can only say here that each Native-American group and even each individual Native American may have a distinctive set of attitudes toward death—to which others must be sensitive and respectful.

Box 5.1 Why Do People Die? A Navajo Legend

When they [the Navajo people as the "Origin Legend" describes early events in their emergence into this world] reached the mainland they sought to divine their fate. To do this some one threw a hide-scraper into the water, saying: "If it sinks we perish, if it floats, we live." It floated and all rejoiced. But Coyote said: "Let me divine your fate." He picked up a stone, and saying, "If it sinks we perish; if it floats we live," he threw it into the water. It sank, of course, and all were angry with him and reviled him; but he answered them saying: "If we all live, and continue to increase as we have done, the earth will soon be too small to hold us, and there will be no room for the cornfields. It is better that each of us should live but a time on this earth and then leave and make room for our children." They saw the wisdom of his words and were silent. ■

SOURCE: From Matthews, 1897, p. 77.

Death-Related Practices

Hispanic Americans

In terms of funeral practices, Moore (1980) reported that Mexican Americans originally had voluntary self-help associations. When a member of such an association died, other members would be assessed for the costs of the funeral. Moore concluded that the funeral is the single most important family ceremony for this population group; members come from remote points, as they are expected to do. To have a socially effective funeral in this group, a certain level of expense and a certain number of people must be present. In such funerals, children are present and "women rather than men are the focus of interest and emotion" (Moore, 1980, p. 85; see also Box 5.2).

Eisenbruch (1984) noted that among Puerto Ricans in New York City the wake might continue for several days. This custom reinforces the finding noted earlier by Kalish and Reynolds (1981) that Hispanic Americans believe that it takes time to express properly one's feelings of grief. According to Campos (1990), during the wake and funeral Puerto Ricans strongly prohibit any speaking ill of the person who has died.

Kalish and Reynolds (1981) also reported that the Mexican Americans in their study wore black for the longest time by comparison with other groups whom they studied, visited graves more frequently, and wanted to spend more time during the burial at the grave site than some cemetery officials found desirable. This behavior sometimes led to conflict with professionals in the funeral and cemetery industries when they were unfamiliar with the practices of the group or uninformed about their rationale.

These descriptions of Hispanic-American mourning and funeral practices have been reinforced by Campos (1990), who found that Puerto Ricans prefer

Box 5.2 A Description of a Mexican-American Funeral

After the death and its certification, the body is moved to the funeral home. . . . There is greater participation by all ages and degrees of involvement with the dead person than in the normal [sic] American funeral.

The rosary is said in Spanish. . . . The old women wail. . . . We progress to the viewing—and touching, and kissing—of the body. . . . Condolences are then shifted from the dead person to his family and the wake moves to the home, for talking, eating and drinking.

The funeral mass the next day begins to shift the focus to the whole family and community. . . . Novenas, grave visits . . . punctuate the family's life for several months after the death. . . . For a period after the burial the family lives quietly; social activities are sharply reduced. In some families, radio and television are turned off. Girls are kept from dating. . . . For several months after the death of an old person, family controls are reasserted over all members. . . . Family reintegration at the funeral depends on the sacrifices made by the large family to be present at the ceremony.

Just as the family must rally, so must the community rally. . . . The family's link to the past—its historical status in the community—is reaffirmed. . . . The funeral helps maintain ethnic cohesiveness. ■

SOURCE: "The Death Culture of Mexico and Mexican Americans," by J. Moore. In R. A. Kalish (Ed.), *Death and Dying: Views from Many Cultures*, pp. 72–91, extracts from pp. 80–83.

lengthy formal mourning periods. Another report described a family of Mexican Americans in which adults and children at the wake touched the body and made the sign of the cross on it (Soto & Villa, 1990). These individuals also stayed at the grave site until the body was lowered into the grave. Last, it has been noted that a typical expression of sympathy in Spanish is "*Siento mucho su perdida*" (Soto & Villa, 1990, p. 123), which they translate as "I feel your loss very much." This is different from merely expressing regrets to another over his or her pain as a bereaved person.

African Americans

In times of grief, African Americans in the Kalish and Reynolds study (1981) saw themselves as freely expressive and regarded funerals as important (see also Hines, 1986). Similarly, the study group held funeral directors in high regard. Another author (Jackson, 1980) argued that African Americans view death as a moment in which recognition can be provided for the deceased person's ability to stand up to others and (in the case of males) for the individual's masculinity (see Box 5.3). Thus, what happens at the funeral (how many persons are present, the appearance of the casket, and so on) can be quite important. Kalish and

Box 5.3 Langston Hughes: As Befits a Man

I don't mind dying—
But I'd hate to die all alone!
I want a dozen pretty women
To holler, cry, and moan.

I don't mind dying
But I want my funeral to be fine:
A row of long tall mamas
Fainting, fanning, and crying.

I want a fish-tail hearse
And sixteen fish-tail cars,
A big brass band
And a whole truck load of flowers.

When they let me down,
Down into the clay,
I want the women to holler:
Please don't take him away!
Ow-ooo-oo-o!
Don't take daddy away!

Reynolds (1981) reported that their informants were likely at the funeral to touch but not kiss the body of the deceased. They were also unlikely to visit the grave.

This might be compared to Devore's (1990) report that African Americans "revert" (sic) to the ways of their African ancestors at the time of mourning. This means in part that anyone from the community closely associated with the family who wants to can come to the home of the survivors to offer condolences and any help that might be needed. Devore also described a typical African-American funeral as including "singing by choirs, soloists, and the congregation, testimony of friends, resolutions from church and community organizations, as well as acknowledgement of telegrams from those who could not attend, flowers and sympathy cards" (p. 57). The obituary (which tells the life story of the deceased) is read and a minister presents a eulogy. Devore also reported that African Americans exhibit their emotions openly in response to the eulogy; in fact, a funeral among African Americans "allows for unrestrained grief" (p. 60).

Distrust of the medical community on the part of many African Americans has been identified (Brown, 1990; Davidson & Devney, 1991). If accurate, this attitude might be responsible for other findings. For instance, Davidson and Devney (1991) linked such mistrust to the fact that African Americans have relatively low organ donor rates, with only 8.8 percent of donated organs coming from the African-American community. Such distrust may also help to account for poor prenatal care leading to higher infant mortality rates or for the fact that many African Americans prefer to care for dying persons at home.

Asian and Pacific Island Americans

Funerals are very important to Japanese Americans (Hirayama, 1990; Kalish & Reynolds, 1981). A funeral director (preferably Japanese American) determines what is appropriate at a funeral. Strict rituals are preferred, so that everyone knows his or her role. Many who take part in Japanese-American funerals attend as representatives of various groups to which the deceased was related rather than in a private or individual capacity. Thus, Japanese Americans are likely to have large, well-attended funeral ceremonies because of the large numbers of persons who are expected to attend.

When people attend such funerals, they bring gifts *(koden)* that have the effect of serving as a sort of group insurance. This is similar to practices in Samoan-American funerals (which carefully blend Samoan tradition, elaborate Christian ceremony, and the realities of a new environment), which include the giving of both money and fine mats (Ablon, 1970; King, 1990).

According to Kalish and Reynolds (1981), in Japanese-American society the wake and funeral are often held in the evening as a combined event; on the next day, a private service will likely be held at the grave site or crematorium. Japanese Americans are not likely to touch the body of the deceased person. They typically cremate the body of the deceased and some may also send the remains (or part of the remains) back to Japan to be buried near ancestors.

Chinese Americans care for the grave of a relative in suburban New York.

Concerning other Asian-American customs, Lee (1986) reported that people in large Chinatown communities tried to retain some traditional funeral practices, such as burning paper money, "funeral marches around the community, and a funeral dinner for relatives and friends" (p. 35)—as we saw in the vignette about a "happy funeral" near the beginning of this chapter. Manio and Hall (1987) found that many Asian Americans often make extensive photographic records of the funeral.

In light of beliefs in a continued interaction between the living and the deceased, within which the well-being of living descendants is at least partly related to the care taken by deceased ancestors, it is not surprising that Japanese Americans visit grave sites on a frequent basis to express their ongoing concern and care for their ancestors.

Japanese Americans in the Kalish and Reynolds (1981) study were reported to have very conservative mourning traditions. Few members of these groups believed that remarriage, or even dating after the death of a spouse, was appropriate, but they also held that wearing black was not necessary.

Native Americans

As an example of Native-American practices associated with mourning, there is a striking case of one Hopi man in San Francisco (Hanson, 1978). A death of a family member was followed by his having "auditory hallucinations." Officials at a local psychiatric authority judged this to represent psychosis. However, Hanson's agency returned the young man to his reservation, where he could participate in tribal rituals related to the burial of the dead. His hallucinations stopped. As Hanson remarked, "Practices that are difficult to understand are usually interpreted as indicators of psychopathology by the dominant society" (p. 20).

That Hopi man was not unique. Hopi women frequently report hallucinations as part of the mourning process (Matchett, 1972). In cases described by Matchett, the experiences were apparently neither like a séance nor like a dream, but allowed the beholder to converse with, describe in visual detail, and even struggle with the figure that appeared to her or him.

In Canada, people from remote areas who have acute life-threatening illnesses or long-term chronic illnesses are normally referred for treatment in urban tertiary-care hospitals. For First Nation peoples, one effect of this practice is to remove them from their home communities and to locate death in the alien cultural environment of an urban hospital. A report from Winnipeg described ways in which trained native interpreters acted as mediators for Cree, Ojibway, and Inuit patients who were terminally ill: (1) as language translators; (2) as cultural informants who could describe native health practices, community health issues, and cultural perspectives on terminal illness and postmortem rituals to clinical staff; (3) as interpreters of biomedical concepts to native peoples; and (4) as patient and community advocates—for instance, by enabling patients to return to their communities to spend their final days with their families (Kaufert & O'Neil, 1991).

Grilling salmon in preparation for a Native-American funeral feast in British Columbia.

With respect to grief and its expression, two reports are helpful. The first concerns Cree people living east of James Bay in the province of Quebec (Preston & Preston, 1991). For the Cree, death is regarded as "at once a commonplace event and one with much significance" (p. 137). Because they place great value on personal autonomy and competence, they strive not to interfere in the lives of others. "The ideal for Cree grieving is an immediate, shared, emotional release, with mutual support for those most at loss and perhaps at risk. But the release of crying and support is soon followed by a return to outward self-reliance and composure, though the inward, private feelings may still be strong" (Preston & Preston, 1991, p. 155).

A second report concerns the Tanacross Athabaskans of east central Alaska (Simeone, 1991). For these people, activities after death involve both a funeral and a memorial potlatch. The funeral has to do with preparing the corpse, building a coffin and grave fence, and conducting a Christian religious service. Nonrelatives assume the work of preparing the body and building the funeral structures because the spirit of the dead person is thought to be dangerous to relatives. However, it is relatives who prepare a three-day ceremony involving feasting, dancing, singing, oratory, and a distribution of gifts (such as guns, beads, and blankets) on the last night to those who have fulfilled their obligations. This ceremony is the memorial potlatch, which "marks the separation of the deceased from society and is the last public expression of grief" (Simeone, 1991, p. 159). One reason to distribute gifts is to objectify and personalize the grief of the hosts. Through the whole potlatch ceremony, social support is provided and strong emotions of grief are given legitimate expression in the Tanacross Athabaskan community, but the larger social context is one that contains grief in a culture that values emotional reserve.

Summary

In this chapter, we examined death-related encounters, attitudes, and practices among Hispanic Americans, African Americans, Americans who trace their backgrounds to Asian countries or the Pacific Islands, and Native Americans. In so doing, we tried to be careful to respect differences between and within these groups, to reflect the present state of our knowledge about these groups, and to avoid stereotypes. Without going beyond the four groups selected for analysis in this chapter, we noticed the rich diversity of death-related experiences within American society. Each of these groups is both a part of the larger society in which we all share and a distinct entity with its own unique death system. Normally, membership in such a cultural group is a matter of birth and socialization; individuals do not usually have an opportunity to choose such membership. Also, it can be difficult to overcome ethnocentric tendencies in which one is inclined to draw on long-standing experiences of one's own group as the norm and other groups as outsiders who vary from that norm. However, everyone can learn from the various cultural groups that exist in the United States. Taking part in the death-related practices of such groups (when outsiders are permitted to do so), reading about their attitudes and rituals, and sharing personal experiences (for example, through discussions in a course on death and dying) can enrich us, both as individuals and as citizens in a multicultural society. In the list of suggested readings that follows, we identify some resources for additional cultural research in the field of death, dying, and bereavement both within and beyond North America, and we occasionally cite examples of such work throughout this book.

Questions for Review and Discussion

1. In this chapter we focused attention on cultural differences in encounters with, attitudes toward, and practices in the face of death, dying, and bereavement. From this, we might say that this chapter showed us at least four different, more particularized death systems operating within the overarching American death system. What major factors do you note as unique to each of the four groups described? What major factors do you note as similar among each of the four groups described?

2. How would you describe the relationship between death-related encounters and attitudes, on one hand, and death-related practices, on the other hand, in any one or more of the four population groups discussed in this chapter?

3. Focusing on your own ethnic, religious, familial, or economic background, can you identify a particular death-related encounter, attitude, or practice that you have had to explain or defend to someone who does not share your background? What was it about the death-related encounter, attitude, or practice that seemed unusual to the person who did not share your background? Why did it seem unusual to that person? How did you explain the origins of the encounter, attitude, or practice?

Suggested Readings

Book-length studies of cultural differences and of different cultural experiences with death within American society include:

Braun, K., Pietsch, J., & Blanchette, P. (Eds.). (2000). *Cultural Issues in End-of-Life Decision Making.*

Coffin, M. M. (1976). *Death in Early America: The History and Folklore of Customs and Superstitions of Early Medicine, Burial and Mourning.*

Irish, D. P., Lundquist, K. F., & Nelson, V. J. (Eds.). (1993). *Ethnic Variations in Dying, Death, and Grief: Diversity in Universality.*

Kalish, R. A., & Reynolds, D. K. (1981). *Death and Ethnicity: A Psychocultural Study.*

Leininger, M. (1995). *Transcultural Nursing: Concepts, Theories, and Practices* (2nd ed.).

McGoldrick, M., Pearce, J. K., & Giordano, J. (Eds.). (1982). *Ethnicity and Family Therapy.*

Mindel, C. H., Habenstein, R. W., & Wright, R. (1988). *Ethnic Families in America: Patterns and Variations* (3rd ed.).

Parry, J. K. (Ed.). (1990). *Social Work Practice with the Terminally Ill: A Transcultural Perspective.*

Parry, J. K., & Ryan, A. S. (Eds.). (1995). *A Cross-Cultural Look at Death, Dying, and Religion.*

Radin, P. (1973). *The Road of Life and Death: A Ritual Drama of the American Indians.*

Stannard, D. E. (Ed.). (1975). *Death in America.*

For examples of reports on death-related experiences outside American society, see:

Abrahamson, H. (1977). *The Origin of Death: Studies in African Mythology.*

Brodman, B. (1976). *The Mexican Cult of Death in Myth and Literature.*

Counts, D. R., & Counts, D. A. (Eds.). (1991). *Coping with the Final Tragedy: Cultural Variation in Dying and Grieving.*

Danforth, L. M. (1982). *The Death Rituals of Rural Greece.*

Goody, J. (1962). *Death, Property, and the Ancestors: A Study of the Mortuary Customs of the LoDagaa of West Africa.*

Kalish, R. A. (Ed.). (1980). *Death and Dying: Views from Many Cultures.*

Kurtz, D. C., & Boardman, J. (1971). *Greek Burial Customs.*

Lewis, O. (1970). *A Death in the Sanchez Family.*

Rosenblatt, P. C., Walsh, P. R., & Jackson, D. A. (1976). *Grief and Mourning in Cross-Cultural Perspectives.*

Scheper-Hughes, N. (1992). *Death without Weeping: The Violence of Everyday Life in Brazil.*

InfoTrac College Edition
For more information, explore the InfoTrac College Edition at **http://www.infotrac-college.com/Wadsworth**

Enter search terms: AFRICAN AMERICANS AND DEATH, ASIAN AMERICANS AND DEATH, ETHNICITY AND DEATH, HISPANIC AMERICANS AND DEATH, NATIVE AMERICANS AND DEATH.

Part Three

Dying

IN AN EXTENDED SENSE OF THE WORD, every living thing can be said to be *dying* or moving toward death from the moment of its conception. However, this meaning of the word "dying" stretches it so far as to make it useless for most customary purposes. Even if we are all dying in some generic sense, some of us are more actively dying than others. In the three chapters that follow, we examine the special situation of those living persons who are closely approaching death—the situation more properly designated as *dying*.

Some people act as if those who are dying are already dead or are as good as dead. This is incorrect, unhelpful, and often hurtful. *Dying persons are living human beings*, and they continue to be living persons as long as they are dying. Thus, we emphasize two points here: (1) dying is a special situation in living, not the whole of life; and (2) death is the outcome of dying, not its equivalent.

Some ask, when does dying begin: when a fatal condition develops, when that condition is recognized by a physician, when knowledge of that condition is communicated to the person involved, when that person realizes and accepts the facts of his or her condition, or when nothing more can be done to reverse the condition and to preserve life (Kastenbaum, 2001)? It is not clear whether any or all of these elements are sufficient to define the state of dying. The situation reminds us of a remark attributed to the English statesman Edmund Burke (1729–1797) that it is difficult to determine the precise point at which afternoon becomes evening, even though everyone can easily distinguish between day and night.

For that reason, it is more helpful to focus not on *when dying begins*, but on *what is involved in dying*. Thus, in Chapter 6, we explore *coping with dying*, together with two types of theoretical models designed to help us understand such coping. In Chapter 7, we investigate *ways in which individuals can help persons who are coping with dying*. And in Chapter 8, we look at *how our society has tried to respond to the needs of dying persons*, including the ways in which our society has organized formal programs to care for those who are coping with dying. Here we give special attention to hospice programs and what they offer for end-of-life care. ■

Chapter Six

COPING WITH DYING

AN INDIVIDUAL WITH A LIFE-THREATENING illness or someone who is in the process of dying is first of all *a person, a living human being.* We emphasize this fact because it is fundamental to all that follows: *people who are dying are living human beings.* There may be much that is distinctive or special about individuals with life-limiting conditions or life-threatening illnesses, and particularly about those who are actively dying. That is because the *pressures of dying* often underscore the *preciousness of living.* However, like all other living persons, those who are dying have a broad range of needs and desires, plans and projects, joys and sufferings, hopes, fears, and anxieties.

Dying is a part (but only one part) of our experiences of life and living; death does not take place until life, living, and dying have ended (McCue, 1995). One cannot already be dead and yet still be dying. To be dead is to be through with dying; to be dying is still to be alive.

Dying persons are not merely individuals within whom biochemical systems are malfunctioning. That is important, but it is not the whole story. Dying is a human experience, and human beings are more than mere objects of anatomy and physiology. If they were merely those sorts of objects, we would have no need to pay attention to the other dimensions of dying persons.

However, in fact, each person who is dying is a complex and unique entity, intermixing physical, psychological, social, and spiritual dimensions (Saunders, 1967). Psychological difficulties, social discomfort, and spiritual suffering may be just as powerful, pressing, and significant for a dying person as physical distress. To focus on any one of these dimensions alone is to be in danger of ignoring the totality of the person and overlooking what matters most to him or her.

In this chapter, we investigate a series of issues that relate to dying persons and those who are involved with such persons. We begin with a short, concrete example of one couple and the issues that they faced in coping with life-threatening illness and dying. After that, we offer a definition of coping and an analysis of some key elements in coping. We next focus on coping with dying, keeping in mind that coping with dying typically involves more than one person. Then, we address two related concepts that have contributed in important ways to improved understanding of coping with dying—dying trajectories and awareness contexts. Finally, we offer an analysis of two types of models—one based on stages, the other on tasks—that have been proposed to explain what is involved in coping with dying. ■

Matt and Josephina Ryan: Coping with Life-Threatening Illness and Dying

Josephina Ryan was 63 when she first felt a small lump in her right breast. Until that terrible moment in the shower, Jo thought she had been very fortunate in the life that she had been given to live. She and Matt had met when he was stationed in her native Philippines. After their marriage and return to the States, the Ryans had five sons and a daughter, now all well established in their own lives and careers. Three of the boys and Christy were married, and they had given their parents six grandchildren between them. Jo had enjoyed raising her children and then returning to her career as a third-grade teacher. Matt was coming up to retirement now as a high school principal. He had been very fortunate five years ago when an early diagnosis and surgery had cured him of prostate cancer. After Matt's retirement, they were anticipating spending more time visiting their children and grandchildren, while also traveling to various places with Elderhostel.

When Matt was diagnosed with prostate cancer, it was like he had been hit over the head with a club. He was stunned and just didn't seem to know what to do. Jo was the strong one throughout that ordeal. She took a brief leave of absence from teaching, coordinated the medical care, kept in touch with all the kids, and was a gentle rock on which Matt could lean. Still, it did help that the testing and the surgery went by pretty fast, and Matt experienced no postoperative complications.

Jo had always feared breast cancer, since it had taken her mother and her aunt several years ago. So Jo had been relieved when her family physician had given her a clean bill of health six months ago after her annual physical exam. But now it seemed like maybe it really was her turn.

Still, her first thoughts were about Matt and the kids, not herself. Cindy was a strong personality, but Jake and Patrick still turned to Mom when times were tough for them. And, except for Tom and his wife, they all lived so far away. There were just so many things to think about!

Jo's biopsy shocked the Ryans. They had to decide quickly about treatment. A partial mastectomy and what the physicians called a "prophylactic" combination of radiation and chemotherapy seemed to kill all the malignant cells, but the nausea, hair loss, and other side effects were really hard to bear. Matt looked just like a lost child during this time, as if he were wandering through life but not recognizing any familiar landmarks.

Afterward, Jo and Matt did have some good time together. They sincerely hoped "the terrors" (as they called them) were all gone. But not many months later (or so it seemed), it looked as if the cancer had only gone into hiding temporarily and was roaring back with a vengeance. Her physicians were unsure whether this was a new disease or a recurrence of the old one. In any event, it must have lurked silently for a while to account for its rapid development and spread. There were more tests, new diagnoses, and several rounds of treatment, but the cancer kept spreading.

Toward the end Jo could hardly leave her bed. Prayer was comforting for the Ryan family, but it was truly a difficult time for Jo and Matt and all those who loved them.

Coping

The American humorist Josh Billings (1818–1885) is reported to have observed that "life consists not in holding good cards but in playing those you do hold well." How we play our cards, particularly in response to life's major challenges, is a metaphor for how we cope, as Matt and Josephina Ryan learned during their own struggles. In order to understand issues related to coping with dying, it will help us first to clarify what coping means and what it involves.

A Definition of Coping and Its Central Elements

The term *coping* has been defined as "constantly changing cognitive and behavioral efforts to manage specific external and/or internal demands that are appraised as taxing or exceeding the resources of the person" (Lazarus & Folkman, 1984, p. 141; compare Monat & Lazarus, 1991).

This definition can help us to understand both coping with living and coping with dying by:

- Focusing on *processes* of coping, with special reference to their changing character—thus emphasizing that coping involves activity and is not static
- Directing attention to *efforts* that are central to coping, whatever one is thinking or doing in order to cope—not only as traits that characterize internal feeling states—and reminding us that these efforts may take many forms (cognitive, behavioral, or others)
- Underlining efforts *to manage* a situation, to live or get along with it as best one can
- Linking coping to efforts addressing *specific demands* (wherever or however they originate) *that are perceived as stressful* (Note two corollaries: unperceived demands are usually not stressful; also because perceptions may change, coping processes may adjust to new perceptions.)
- Referring to efforts undertaken in response to *demands that are appraised as taxing or exceeding the resources of the person*, and thus distinguishing coping from routine, automatized, adaptive behaviors that do not involve an effortful response
- Taking care *not to confuse coping with outcome*

In short, coping includes any efforts to manage stressful demands, however successful or unsuccessful such efforts might be. Coping does not necessarily seek to *master* stressful demands. A coping person may try—more or less successfully—to master a particular situation but often is content to accept, endure, minimize, or avoid stressful demands.

Moos and Schaefer (1986) extended our understanding of coping by grouping coping skills into three separate categories (see Table 6.1): (1) *appraisal-focused coping* centers on how one understands or appraises a stressful situation; (2) *problem-focused coping* relates to what one does about the problem or stressor itself; and (3) *emotion-focused coping* involves what one does about one's reactions to the perceived problem. We prefer to call this last type of coping *reaction-focused coping* in order not to limit it to feelings alone (see Chapter 9, p. 210). In any event, a person's coping may emphasize any one or all of these focal perspectives, and, as Moos and Schaefer (1986, p. 13) observed, "the word *skill* underscores the positive aspects of coping and depicts coping as an ability that can be taught and used flexibly as the situation requires."

Coping as Learned and Dynamic Behavior

Coping is central to the response one makes to any situation that is perceived as stressful. Such situations might involve almost any aspect of life or death: a death or a significant loss of any type (the ending of a relationship, failing to succeed in some endeavor, being fired from a job, a divorce, and so forth), as well as happier events, such as winning the lottery, taking up a new challenge in life,

Table 6.1 Coping: Three Focal Domains and Nine Types of Skills

Appraisal-Focused Coping

1. *Logical analysis and mental preparation:* Paying attention to one aspect of the crisis at a time, breaking a seemingly overwhelming problem into small, potentially manageable bits, drawing on past experiences, and mentally rehearsing alternative actions and their probable consequences
2. *Cognitive redefinition:* Using cognitive strategies to accept the basic reality of a situation but restructure it to find something favorable
3. *Cognitive avoidance or denial:* Denying or minimizing the seriousness of a crisis

Problem-Focused Coping

4. *Seeking information and support:* Obtaining information about the crisis and alternate courses of action and their probable outcome
5. *Taking problem-solving action:* Taking concrete action to deal directly with a crisis or its aftermath
6. *Identifying alternative rewards:* Attempting to replace the losses involved in certain transitions and crises by changing one's activities and creating new sources of satisfaction

Emotion-Focused Coping

7. *Affective regulation:* Trying to maintain hope and control one's emotions when dealing with a distressing situation
8. *Emotional discharge:* Openly venting one's feelings and using jokes and gallows humor to help allay constant strain
9. *Resigned acceptance:* Coming to terms with a situation and accepting it as it is, deciding that the basic circumstances cannot be altered and submitting to "certain" fate

SOURCE: From "Life Transitions and Crises: A Conceptual Overview," by R. H. Moos and J. A. Schaefer. In R. H. Moos and J. A. Schaefer (Eds.), *Coping with Life Crises: An Integrated Approach*, pp. 3–28. Copyright 1986 Plenum Publishing Corporation. Reprinted with permission.

getting married, or having a baby. Any situations like these might be perceived as stressful. How they are perceived depends upon the individual. How the individual responds to such situations will have much to do with how he or she has learned to respond.

In thinking about coping with loss, Davidson (1975, p. 28) wrote: "We are born with the *ability* to adapt to change, but we all must *learn* how to cope with loss." As individuals move through life, they observe how others around them cope with separation, loss, and endings—the "necessary losses" (Viorst, 1986) that none of us can avoid, such as a child's discovery that his or her parents are not superhuman or an adult's observations of elderly parents who are becoming less able to care for themselves. Often, we try out in our own lives strategies we have watched others use in coping, or we simply rely on methods that have proved satisfactory to us in the past. Some of us have little choice in the ways in which we are able to cope: the situation does not present us with many alternatives. Sometimes we can do little about the source of the stress and must focus mainly on our reactions to that situation. In any case, each individual tries to acquire a repertoire of skills that facilitate coping with challenges in life, responding to needs, and helping that person to adapt in satisfactory ways.

In seeking to understand coping, it is important to know *how individuals who are coping perceive their situation and what they are actually thinking or doing in specific contexts of stressful demands* (Hinton, 1984; Silver & Wortman, 1980). One must ask what this particular person is actually thinking or doing as the stressful encounter unfolds, not what people in general do in similar situations, and not even what that individual might do, should do, or usually does in such circumstances. As we observed in the vignette near the beginning of this chapter, Matt and Jo Ryan each reacted to and coped with their spouse's life-threatening illness in different ways. Also, because coping involves shifting processes as the relationship between the person and his or her environment changes, different forms of coping may be undertaken at different times. For example, defensive responses may give way to problem-solving strategies. Thus what is critical is the actual focus of the individual's coping at any given time.

All of the ways in which one learns to cope are not likely to be of equal value. Some ways of coping are useful in most situations. Some have value in certain situations but not in others. Some merely seem to be effective even though they actually are counterproductive. Some ways of coping may be satisfactory to one person but hurtful to others. The better we learn to cope with past and present losses, the more likely we are to be able to cope successfully with losses in the future.

In each particular situation, we can ask: What does the individual perceive as stressful? How is the individual coping with that stress? Why is he or she coping in this particular way? These questions apply to coping with dying as well as to coping with all other challenges in living. For that reason, although there are significant differences between death and other sorts of stressors or losses, how one copes with the "little deaths" (Purtillo, 1976) and other stressful challenges throughout life may be indicative of how one is likely to cope with the large crises involved in death itself.

Coping with Dying: Who Is Coping?

Coping with dying typically involves more than a single individual. When we reflect on such coping, most often we think immediately of the ill person, the principal actor who is at the center of the coping challenge. This is where we should always begin, but we should not end there because coping with dying is not solely confined to ill and dying persons. Coping with dying is also a challenge for others who are drawn into such situations. These include the family members and friends of the dying person, as well as the volunteer and professional caregivers who attend to the dying person (Grollman, 1995b).

Confronting imminent death and coping with dying are experiences that resonate deeply within the personal sense of mortality and limitation of all who are drawn into these processes. A family member who says to a dying person, "Don't die on me," may be conveying anguish at the pending loss of a loved one. A caregiver who says, "I hope we won't lose Mr. Smith tonight," may be expressing frustration at his or her inability to prevent the coming of death or concern with the consequences that Mr. Smith's death will bring for the caregiver. In the case of families, it is especially important to note that people who are coping with dying do so not only as particular, unique individuals, but also as members of a family system, and as members of society—all of which influence their coping

A hospice chaplain visits a patient at home.

(Rosen, 1990). For example, a conflicted relationship between a parent and a child or between two siblings who have fought for years may generate special issues that need to be addressed in the context of coping with dying.

Coping with dying is usually multifaceted. It involves more than one person, and thus involves more than one set of perceptions of what is going on, more than one set of motivations, and more than one way of coping. Those who wish to understand coping with dying need to identify *each person* who is involved in that activity and listen carefully to what his or her coping reveals. Only by empathic listening can we hope to understand what the coping means for each individual in each particular situation. Only by striving to understand each individual's coping efforts can we hope to appreciate how he or she is interacting in the shared dynamic of the situation. Sensitivity to outward behaviors, to underlying feelings, and to key variables is essential in such listening. (See Box 6.1 for examples of literature on coping with dying.)

Dying Trajectories and Awareness Contexts

Glaser and Strauss (1965, 1968) described two key variables in coping with dying. They are the nature of the dying trajectory and the degree to which those who are involved are aware of and share information about dying. These vari-

Box 6.1 Selected Descriptions of Coping with Life-Threatening Illness

Albom, M. (1997). *Tuesdays with Morrie: An Old Man, A Young Man, and Life's Greatest Lesson.*

Barnard, D., Towers, A., Boston, P., & Lambrinidou, Y. (2000). *Crossing Over: Narratives of Palliative Care.*

Broyard, A. (1992). *Intoxicated by My Illness and Other Writings on Life and Death.*

Cousins, N. (1979). *Anatomy of an Illness as Perceived by the Patient: Reflections on Healing and Regeneration.*

Craven, M. (1973). *I Heard the Owl Call My Name.**

De Beauvoir, S. (1964/1973). *A Very Easy Death.*

Evans, J. (1971). *Living with a Man Who Is Dying: A Personal Memoir.*

Faulkner, W. (1930). *As I Lay Dying.**

Frank, A. W. (1991). *At the Will of the Body: Reflections on Illness.*

Gunther, J. (1949). *Death Be Not Proud.*

Hanlan, A. (1979). *Autobiography of Dying.*

Jury, M., & Jury, D. (1978). *Gramps: A Man Ages and Dies.*

Kelly, O. (1975). *Make Today Count.*

Lerner, G. (1978). *A Death of One's Own.*

Lerner, M. (1990). *Wrestling with the Angel: A Memoir of My Triumph over Illness.*

MacPherson, M. (1999). *She Came to Live Out Loud: An Inspiring Family Journey Through Illness, Loss, and Grief.*

Mandell, H., & Spiro, H. (Eds.). (1987). *When Doctors Get Sick.*

Quindlen, A. (1994). *One True Thing.**

Rosenthal, T. (1973). *How Could I Not Be Among You?*

Ryan, C., & Ryan, K. M. (1979). *A Private Battle.*

Schwartz, M. (1999). *Morrie: In His Own Words.*

Tolstoy, L. (1884/1960). *The Death of Ivan Ilych and Other Stories.**

Webster, B. D. (1989). *All of a Piece: A Life with Multiple Sclerosis.*

Weisman, M-L. (1982). *Intensive Care: A Family Love Story.*

Wertenbaker, L. T. (1957). *Death of a Man.*

Zorza, V., & Zorza, R. (1980). *A Way to Die.* ■

*Titles marked with an asterisk are fiction.

ables describe both the individual situation and the social context within which coping with dying takes place.

All dying persons do not move toward death at the same rates of speed or in the same ways. Processes of dying or coming to be dead have their own distinctive characteristics in each individual case. As we saw in Chapter 2, Glaser and Strauss (1968) suggested that we should understand *dying trajectories* in terms of two principal characteristics: duration and shape (see Figure 2.4). Some trajectories involve an up-and-down history of remission, relapse, remission, and so on—often in a rather unpredictable way. Other dying trajectories make relatively steady progress toward death. In some cases, the dying trajectory may be completed in a very brief, even instantaneous, span of time; in other cases, it may be slow, extending over a period of weeks, months, or even years.

Obviously, there are variations on these simple patterns. For example, the time when death will occur or the moment when the process will resolve itself so that its ultimate outcome is clear may or may not be predictable. We may know that the person will die, when the death will occur, and how it will take place, or we may be unclear about one or more of these points.

Awareness contexts have to do with social interactions among those who are coping with dying. Glaser and Strauss (1965) argued that once a person in our society is discovered to be dying, the relationships between that person and his or her close associates and health care providers can take at least four basic forms.

1. *Closed awareness* is a context in which the person who is dying does not realize that fact. The staff, and perhaps also the family, may know that the person is dying, but that information has not been conveyed to the dying person, nor does he or she even suspect it. Many have thought (and some still do) that it is desirable not to convey diagnostic and prognostic information to dying persons. In fact, this sort of knowledge usually cannot be hidden for long. Communication is achieved in complex, subtle, and sometimes unconscious ways, and awareness is likely to develop at several levels. For example, changes in one's own body associated with progression of the disease, along with alterations in the behaviors of others or changes in their physical appearances, often lead to gradual or partial recognition that all is not well.
2. *Suspected awareness* identifies a context in which the ill person may begin to suspect that he or she has not been given all of the information that is relevant to his or her situation. For a variety of reasons—for example, tests, treatments, or other behaviors that do not seem to correspond with the supposed problem—the person who is ill may begin to suspect that more is going on than is being said. This may undermine trust and complicate future communications.
3. *Mutual pretense* describes a context that was once (and may still be) quite common, in which the relevant information is held by all the individual parties in the situation but is not shared between them. In other words, mutual pretense involves a kind of shared drama in which everyone involved acts out a role intended to say that things are not as they know them to be. "It is the horse on the dining-room table," as Kalish told us in the Prologue to this book. As mutual pretense is lived out, it may even be conducted so as to cover over embarrassing moments when the strategy of dissembling or evading the truth fails temporarily. This is a fragile situation; one slip can cause the entire structure to collapse. Mutual pretense requires constant vigilance and a great deal of effort. Consequently, it is extremely demanding for everyone involved.
4. *Open awareness* describes a context in which the dying person and everyone else realizes and is willing to discuss the fact that death is near. Those who share an open awareness context may or may not actually spend much time discussing the fact that the person is dying. On some occasions, one or the other person may not want to talk about it right then. After all, as has aptly been said, "No one is dying 24 hours a day." But there is no pretense; when persons are ready and willing to discuss the realities of the situation, they are able to do so.

These are four different types of awareness contexts; they are not steps in a linear progression from inhibitedness to openness. The point is that social interactions and coping with dying are likely to be affected by awareness contexts.

Each awareness context brings with it some potential costs and some potential benefits. At some moments, for example, the anxiety and grief of the family member (or staff person) raised by the oncoming death of a loved one may make discussion of that event too difficult to endure. Avoidance of reality can get some people through a difficult moment and thus may, in certain circumstances, be a productive way of coping for that moment.

In general, however, open awareness allows for honest communication if participants are ready for such interaction. It permits each involved person to participate in the shared grief of an approaching loss. Important words of concern and affection can be spoken. Ancient wounds can be healed. Unfinished business—between the dying person and his or her family members, friends, or God—can be addressed. These benefits come at the cost of having to admit and face powerful feelings (such as anger, sadness, perhaps guilt) and recognized facts (for instance, tasks not completed, choices unmade, paths not taken). This can be quite difficult and painful. Nevertheless, for many persons these costs are preferable to those associated with lack of openness. Always, one balances costs against benefits in both the short and long run.

On the basis of these understandings of coping, dying trajectories, and awareness contexts, we turn next to two principal types of models that have been proposed to explain coping with dying.

Coping with Dying: A Stage-Based Approach

The best-known model of coping with dying is the *stage-based model* put forward by the Swiss-American psychiatrist Dr. Elisabeth Kübler-Ross (Gill, 1980; Kübler-Ross, 1997). In her book *On Death and Dying* (1969), Kübler-Ross reported the results of a series of interviews that focused on psychosocial reactions in persons who were dying. She developed a theoretical model of five stages in such reactions (see Table 6.2). Kübler-Ross understood these stages as "defense mechanisms" that "will last for different periods of time and will replace

Table 6.2 Kübler-Ross's Five Stages in Coping with Dying

Stage	Typical Expression
Denial	"Not me!"
Anger	"Why me?"
Bargaining	"Yes me, but . . . "
Depression	
Reactive	Responding to past and present losses
Preparatory	Anticipating and responding to losses yet to come
Acceptance	Described as a stage "almost void of feelings"

SOURCE: Based on Kübler-Ross, 1969.

each other or exist at times side by side" (p. 138). In addition, she maintained that "the one thing that usually persists through all these stages is *hope*" (p. 138).

In other words, Kübler-Ross argued that people who are dying are people who are in a stressful situation. Because they are living people, like people in other stressful situations, they employ or develop a number of different ways of responding to that situation. Some people when confronted with an object that blocks their forward journey speed up their engines and charge full speed ahead, crashing into and perhaps through the barrier. Other persons who encounter a roadblock back away and try to find some way around it. Others simply remain stationary, not moving forward, not seeking a way around. Still other people go off in some different direction, seeing the roadblock as something that cannot be overcome and that demands some other road be taken. So dying persons may cope by withdrawing, or by becoming angry, or by finding what has occurred in their lives up to now that might make death acceptable. One major point to be underlined again is that *different people cope in different ways.*

Kübler-Ross's stages had an immediate attractiveness for many who read about or heard of this model. Her work helped to bring dying persons and issues involved in coping with dying to public and professional attention. She also made it possible for others to go beyond her initial report. In particular, her model identified common patterns of psychosocial responses to difficult situations, responses with which we are all familiar. In addition, it drew attention to the human aspects of living with dying, to the strong feelings experienced by those who are coping with dying, and to what Kübler-Ross called the "unfinished business" that many want to address. Kübler-Ross said that her book is "simply an account of a new and challenging opportunity to refocus on the patient as a human being, to include him in dialogues, to learn from him the strengths and weaknesses of our hospital management of the patient. We have asked him to be our teacher so that we may learn more about the final stages of life with all its anxieties, fears, and hopes" (xi).

Three important lessons follow from this approach (Corr, 1993a):

1. Those who are coping with dying are *still alive* and often have unfinished needs that they want to address.
2. We cannot be or become effective providers of care unless we *listen actively* to those who are coping with dying and identify with them their own needs.
3. We need to *learn from* those who are dying and coping with dying in order to come to know ourselves better (as limited, vulnerable, finite, and mortal, but also as resilient, adaptable, interdependent, and lovable).

In turn, these are lessons about all who are dying and coping with dying; about becoming and being a provider of care; and about living our own lives (De Hennezel, 1998).

There are, however, significant difficulties in accepting Kübler-Ross's model as it is presented in her book. Research by others (for example, Metzger, 1979; Schulz & Aderman, 1974) does not support this model. In fact, since the publication of Kübler-Ross's book in 1969, there has been no independent confirmation of the validity or reliability of her model, and Kübler-Ross has advanced no further evidence on its behalf. On the contrary, many clinicians who work with the dying have found this model to be inadequate, superficial, and misleading (for example, Pattison, 1977; Shneidman, 1980/1995; Weisman, 1977). Widespread acclaim in the popular arena contrasts with sharp criticism from scholars and those who work with dying persons (Klass, 1982; Klass & Hutch, 1985).

One serious and thorough evaluation of this stage-based model raised the following points: (1) the existence of these stages as such has not been demonstrated; (2) no evidence has been presented that people actually do move from stage 1 through stage 5; (3) the limitations of the method have not been acknowledged; (4) the line is blurred between description and prescription; (5) the totality of the person's life is neglected in favor of the supposed stages of dying; and (6) the resources, pressures, and characteristics of the immediate environment, which can make a tremendous difference, are not taken into account (Kastenbaum, 2001).

If one thinks for a moment about the traits that Kübler-Ross has described as stages, one can see that they are so broadly formulated that they actually designate a variety of reactions. For example, "denial" can describe the following range of responses: (1) I am not ill; (2) I am ill, but it is not serious; (3) I am seriously ill, but not dying; (4) I am dying, but death will not come for a long time; or (5) I am dying and death will come shortly (Weisman, 1972). Similarly, "acceptance" may take the form of an enthusiastic welcoming, a grudging resignation, or a variety of other responses. Also, the trait of "depression" must mean sadness, not clinical depression, which is a psychiatric diagnosis of illness, not a normative coping process. Further, we know that there are not only five ways in which to react to dying.

In addition, there is no reason to think that the particular five ways identified by Kübler-Ross are linked together as *stages* in a larger process. To some extent, Kübler-Ross agreed with this latter point, insofar as she argued for fluidity, give and take, the possibility of experiencing two of these responses simultaneously, or an ability to jump around from one stage to another. This suggests that the language of "stages," with its associated implications of linear progression and regression, is not really appropriate for a cluster of disconnected coping strategies.

Another problem with this model—for which its author is not wholly responsible—is that many people have misused it. There is some irony in this fact. After all, Kübler-Ross set out to argue that dying persons are mistreated when they are objectified—that is, when they are treated as a "liver case" or as a "cardiac case." Unfortunately, since the publication of *On Death and Dying*, some people have come to treat dying persons as a "case of anger" or a "case of depression," others have told ill persons that they have already been angry and should now "move on" to bargaining or depression, and still others have become frustrated by those whom they view as "stuck" in the dying process. (But if I am stuck in the dying process, does that mean I cannot die?) All of this simply forces those who are coping with dying into a preestablished framework that reduces their individuality to little more than an instance of one of five categories (anger, or depression, or . . .) in a schematic process. That is why Rosenthal (1973, p. 39) when he was coping with his own dying, wrote, "Being invisible I invite only generalizations."

All these points suggest that the language of stages and the metaphor of a linear theory (*first* one denies, *then* one is angry, *then* one might turn to renewed denial, and so on) are simply not adequate as a basis for explaining coping with dying. Furthermore, it is not enough to say that a person is "in denial" or has "reached acceptance" if one is to understand that individual in more than a superficial and potentially misleading way.

Perhaps it would be better simply to speak of a broad range of responses to the experience of dying. Essentially, this is what Shneidman (1973a, p. 7) meant by what he called a "hive of affect," a busy, buzzing, active set of feelings, attitudes, and other reactions, to which a person returns from time to time, now expressing one posture (for example, anger), now another (for example, denial). The person may return to the hive and experience the same feelings again and again, sometimes simultaneously, sometimes one day after another, sometimes with long intervals in between.

Coping with Dying: Task-Based Approaches

Why Suggest a Task-Based Model?

Task-based models of coping with dying seek to avoid metaphors that emphasize a passive or reactive way of understanding such coping. As Weisman (1984) noted, coping involves more than an automatic response or a defensive reaction. Also, a posture of defense is largely a *negative* one; it channels energy into avoiding problems, rather than achieving some kind of adaptive accommodation. That may be useful initially and sometimes on later occasions—for example, as a way of obtaining time in which to mobilize personal or social resources. However, *coping is, or at least can be, an active process, a doing with a positive orientation that seeks to resolve problems or adapt to challenges in living.*

Tasks are work that can be undertaken in coping with dying. When one is coping with dying, like all other work, one can always choose not to take on a particular task. One can proceed with a task, leave it for another time, or work on it for a while and then set it aside. In the face of a series of tasks, one can choose to undertake all or none of them, to attempt this one or that one. The main point is that choice implies empowerment.

Tasks are not merely *needs.* They cannot be reduced to and may include more than needs, even if needs often underlie the task work that one undertakes. The term *task* identifies what a person is trying to do in his or her coping, the specific effort that he or she is making to achieve what he or she requires or desires. A problem with focusing on the language of "needs" is that this often allows the focus to shift to what others might do to help. Assistance from others in support of an individual's coping tasks is often important and may even be necessary, but it usually ought to take second place to one's own coping efforts.

We look at task-based models in order to show that individuals who are coping with life-threatening illness and dying are actors, not just re-actors. They can decide how to cope with their experiences in various ways. This puts the central emphasis on the active efforts that are, at least in principle, open to the person coping with dying. Even when such efforts are not possible in practice (for example, when an individual is unconscious), a task-based model encourages others to see things from the individual's point of view and to arrange or modify their efforts accordingly. This is critical in order to appreciate the complexity, richness, and variability of the human experiences of living with life-threatening illness and coping with dying.

Corr (1992a) and Doka (1993a) have made efforts to develop task-based models for understanding coping with life-threatening illness and dying.

A Task-Based Model for Coping with Dying

Corr (1992a) proposed that four primary areas of task work can be identified in coping with dying. Clues to the identity of these areas of task work come from the four dimensions in the life of a human being: the physical, the psychological, the social, and the spiritual. These four areas of task work are listed in Table 6.3, along with some suggestions about the basic types of tasks in coping with dying that might be associated with each area. Recall, however, that coping involves individualized responses to concrete situations. If so, full understanding of coping with dying must reflect the specific tasks undertaken by each individual who is coping.

Physical Tasks Physical tasks are associated with bodily needs and physical distress—that is, coping with such matters as pain, nausea, or constipation, and satisfying such needs as hydration and nutrition. *Bodily needs* are fundamental to maintaining biological life and functioning. As Maslow (1971) argued, satisfaction of fundamental bodily needs is usually the indispensable foundation on which the work of meeting other needs can be built. In addition, *physical distress* cries out for relief both for its own sake and in order that the rest of life can be appreciated and lived well. For example, individuals who are experiencing intense pain, severe nausea, or active vomiting are unlikely to be capable of rich psychosocial or spiritual interactions at the same time.

We must qualify this, however, since humans can and sometimes do choose to subordinate bodily needs and physical distress to other values. For example, martyrs have endured torture for the sake of spiritual values and some individuals have been known to sacrifice their own lives for the sake of protecting those whom they love. More simply, individuals who are dying may choose to accept a slightly higher degree of pain or discomfort in order to be able to stay at home, rather than entering an institution in which constant supervision by skilled professionals could achieve a higher standard in the management of distressing physical symptoms. Others who are offered the support of in-home services may prefer to be in an institution, where they have less fear of being alone, falling, and lying unattended for hours.

Psychological Tasks A second area of task work in coping with dying concerns psychological security, autonomy, and richness. Like the rest of us, individuals who are coping with dying seek a sense of *security* even in a situation that may in many ways not be safe. For example, if they are dependent on others to provide needed services, they may need to be assured that those providers are reliable.

Table 6.3 Four Areas of Task Work in Coping with Dying

Areas of Task Work	Basic Types of Tasks in Coping with Dying
Physical	To satisfy *bodily needs* and to minimize *physical distress,* in ways that are consistent with other values
Psychological	To maximize *psychological security, autonomy,* and *richness*
Social	To sustain and enhance those *interpersonal attachments* that are significant to the person concerned, and to sustain selected *interactions with social groups within society or with society itself*
Spiritual	To address issues of *meaningfulness, connectedness,* and *transcendence* and, in so doing, to foster *hope*

SOURCE: Based on Corr, 1992a.

Also, most individuals who are coping with dying wish to retain their *autonomy*, insofar as that is possible. Autonomy means the ability to govern or be in charge of one's own life (*auto* = self + *nomous* = regulating). In fact, no one has control over the whole of one's life; each person is limited and all are interdependent in a host of ways. Autonomy designates the shifting degrees and kinds of influence that individuals are able to exercise within everyday constraints. Nevertheless, for most persons, it is important to retain some degree of self-government. Some wish to make the big decisions in their lives on their own; others simply wish to designate who should make decisions on their behalf. Some turn over much of the management of their own bodies to professionals, even while they retain authority over some symbolic decisions. An outsider cannot say in advance how autonomy will or should be exercised; that would undercut the very notion of *self*-regulation.

For many people, achieving a sense of security and autonomy contributes to a *psychological richness in living*. Many who are near the end of life still appreciate opportunities for a regular shave and haircut, to have their hair washed and set, to use a special bath powder, or to dress in a comfortable and attractive way. Some dying persons may find it important to their psychological well-being to have a taste of a favorite food or to continue a lifelong habit of sipping a small glass of wine with meals. The issues involved here refer to what many would describe as *personal dignity*.

Social Tasks A third area of task work in coping with dying concerns two interrelated aspects of social living. Each of us is involved in attachments to other individual persons as well as in relationships to society itself and to its subordinate groups.

One set of social tasks has to do with sustaining and enhancing the *interpersonal attachments* valued by the coping person. Dying individuals often narrow the scope of their interests. They may no longer care about international politics, their former duties at work, or a large circle of friends. Instead, they may increasingly focus on issues and attachments that involve a progressively smaller number of individuals now perceived as most important in their lives. In this way, they gain freedom from responsibilities now judged to be less compelling or more burdensome than before. The scope of their social interests and concerns has shifted to fit their new priorities.

There is no obvious set of interpersonal tasks on which each person *must* focus. Because only the individual can decide which attachments he or she values, these decisions may alter as one lives through the process of coping with dying. However, autonomy is restricted in a fundamental way if the significance of each attachment is not a matter of individual decision-making.

A consequence of this interpersonal dimension of coping with dying is that each person involved will have at least two sets of tasks: one conducted on his or her own behalf and another conducted in relation to the interests of others who are involved. For example, a dying person may face some tasks related to his or her own concerns and others related to the concerns of family members or caregivers. The person may choose to decline further efforts at cure because they are too burdensome and offer too little promise of help; in so doing, that person may be obliged to help family members or caregivers accept this decision and become reconciled to its implications for how soon death will arrive. Similarly, family members may have tasks related to their own concerns, as well as tasks related to their responsibilities to assist the dying person. For themselves, they may seek rest or relief from the burdens of caregiving; for the ill person, it may be important for them to be available to provide companionship and a sense of security. Although only the individual can decide the relative importance of these often-conflicting tasks, it is usually helpful if the dying person and his or her support persons can discuss these matters openly.

A second set of social tasks has to do with *interactions with social groups within society or with society itself.* Society correctly wishes to protect its citizens from harm, to prohibit certain types of behavior, to ensure that property is correctly handed over to legitimate heirs, and to offer certain sorts of assistance and benefit. Social groups have their own religious and cultural rituals, expectations, and prohibitions. Like all events in living, dying implicates people in social systems. These systems are constructed and implemented by individuals, but they represent the interests of the group. Social tasks in coping with dying include interacting with social systems as may seem desirable or necessary, responding to demands that society and its organizations continue to make (for example, hospital bills and income taxes may still need to be paid), and drawing on social

A hospice patient and lover of sailboats is helped into a specially designed craft for individuals with disabilities.

Box 6.2 Fantasy on a Summer Afternoon

One day when I was sailing
quietly up the bay
I listened very intently
And thought I heard a seagull say,
"You've never had it so good,"
You've never had it so good."
And I thought, "You don't do so
badly soaring up there in the blue."
Then I passed a wise old pelican
standing sentinel on a pile.
He blinked his beady eyes and said,
"But it only lasts a little while,
But it only lasts a little while."
And what he said is true. ■

SOURCE: Dr. Alfred King

resources as needed (for example, to obtain hospital equipment, transportation, or "Meals on Wheels" services from charitable organizations).

Spiritual Tasks The spiritual area of task work in coping with dying is more difficult to describe than the other three areas, for several reasons. One is that there is little agreement about just what is meant by "spiritual." Most would agree that what is meant by "spiritual" concerns is not merely limited to or identified with "religious" concerns (see Box 6.2). If spiritual and religious concerns were thought to be identical, that would suggest that someone without a religious connection has no spiritual tasks to work on. However, this belief is untrue and therefore unhelpful. It might even lead caregivers to miss or to ignore important clues about certain crucial tasks with which a dying person is struggling.

Second, modern societies, including North American societies, are increasingly made up of many subcultures, and this is true in spiritual matters, too. Roman Catholics and Muslims, Baptist Protestant Christians and Hindus, Buddhists and Unitarians, Dakota and Zuni Native Americans, atheists and agnostics—these and a large number of others (and variations on all of these) may be found among those whose spiritual tasks we are trying to understand as part of their coping with dying. However, we cannot be expected to know and to understand all of these traditions and positions on spiritual issues.

One helpful way to approach the spiritual concerns of dying persons (and those around them) is to identify common themes running through this area of task work (Doka, 1993b). Most people who think about spiritual issues recognize one or more of the following concerns as frequent components of spiritual task work in coping with dying:

Meaningfulness. People who are coping with dying may seek to identify, recognize, or formulate meaning for their lives, for death, for suffering, and for being human. Several types of questions may be pressing in these circumstances: Is my life meaning-full (and often this means worth-full)? If I must die, what does that mean for the value of my having lived? Why is there so much suffering associated with my dying or with my loved one's dying? What does it mean to be human (and when, if ever, does one stop being human, even if life is still present in some form?)? These questions are thrusts toward wholeness and integration, and away from fragmentation (Nabe, 1987).

Connectedness. Illness, and perhaps especially life-threatening illness, threatens to break those connections that lend coherence to one's life. For example, one can feel disconnected from one's body (why won't it do what I want it to do?), from other persons (why can't they understand how much pain I am in?), and from whatever one holds the transcendent to be (where is God in all this?). It is often important for a person in this situation to reestablish broken connections or to maintain and deepen existing connections. There are psychological and social components to this work, but the spiritual aspect goes deeper or underlies these other dimensions because (again) it is tied to the search for meaning and integrity.

Transcendence. In addition, people working on spiritual tasks are often looking toward a transcendent level or source of meaning and connection. "Transcendence" refers here to that which goes beyond (though it may also be found in) the ordinary, and especially to that which is of ultimate, surpassing worth. This concern is often tied to issues of *hope.* Religious people may work

Spending quality time together at an in-patient hospice facility.

to enrich and deepen their connections with a god or some basic reality (the Atman or the Tao) and may seek to realize some religious hope (to be absolved of sin, or to overcome metaphysical ignorance, or to achieve eternal bliss). Nonreligious people may also focus on transcendent hopes—for example, to find their place in a reality that is more than just the individual's moment in the life of the universe, to become one with the elements, to continue to contribute to the life of the society through one's creations, students, and descendants even after one has died.

The focus of hope may change over time, and how one acts on one's hopes depends on the individual and his or her culture, history, environment, and condition (see, for instance, Tong & Spicer, 1994). One person may be focused primarily on personal aspirations (will I achieve nirvana, will I meet God face to face?), while another person may be more concerned about the welfare of the group (will my descendants continue to contribute to the ongoing life of the group?).

Spiritual task work is as variegated and multiform as is task work in the other three areas. And spiritual tasks are irreducibly individual; one Protestant Christian's spiritual tasks are not necessarily (indeed, are seldom) the same as another Protestant Christian's spiritual tasks. That this is the case is important both for gaining a proper understanding of spiritual task work and for helping persons cope with their spiritual tasks.

An Observation on This Task-Based Model This outline of four areas of task work in coping with dying described areas of potential task work. These areas are general categories of tasks for everyone who is coping with dying (not just the dying person). We pointed out that tasks may or may not be undertaken and that some may be more or less necessary or desirable. We also indicated that individuals need not take up any specific task or set of tasks. On the contrary, a task-based model is intended precisely to foster empowerment and participation in coping with dying. Although individual tasks of this sort may be completed, it is never possible to finish all of the task work that confronts an individual. For the dying person, work with tasks ends with death; for those who live on, these and other tasks may arise in coping with bereavement. These areas of task work may also serve as guidelines for helping those who are coping with dying, as we will see in Chapter 7.

A Task-Based Model for Living with Life-Threatening Illness

Corr's model is one task-based framework for developing and enriching our understanding of experiences of dying and coping with dying. There are other similar approaches that also deserve attention, notably a task-based model for living with life-threatening illness proposed by Doka (1993a). We can best understand Doka's model by first looking at Pattison's (1977) concept of the "living-dying interval" from which Doka drew some of his inspiration.

The Living-Dying Interval Pattison (1977) introduced the notion of a *living-dying interval* to organize our perceptions of the experience of coping with life-threatening illness and dying into a temporal framework. Human experience—of living and of dying—is always encountered as sequential. There are befores, nows, and laters in all of our experiences. A good model of coping with dying ought to throw light on challenges that arise from what has already happened in dying, what is in the process of taking place, and what is yet to come (Stedeford, 1984). This existential, temporal component is the basis of Pattison's approach.

Pattison proposed that the living-dying interval be divided into three phases: (1) an *acute crisis phase* mainly associated with the diagnosis of a life-threatening illness; (2) a *chronic-living-dying phase* between the acute crisis phase and the terminal phase; and (3) a *terminal phase* organized around processes directly resulting in death. Further, Pattison suggested that each of these phases is focused on a different variable: rising anxiety generated by the critical awareness of impending death in the acute crisis phase; a variety of potential fears and challenges in the chronic living-dying phase; and issues concerning hope and different types of death in the terminal phase.

Five Phases in Living with a Life-Threatening Illness and Their Distinctive Tasks Subsequently, Doka (1993a) expanded on Pattison's thinking to construct a model combining phases and tasks in living with life-threatening illness. The model demonstrates how coping tasks differ in that period of time between the everyday, ordinary processes of living prior to the crisis knowledge of death (the point at which each of us could become involved in dying, even though that has not yet actually occurred for most of us) and the point at which death occurs. In his work, Doka expanded Pattison's concept of the living-dying interval into a theory of *five phases* in living with a life-threatening illness: the prediagnostic, acute, chronic, recovery, and terminal phases.

The *prediagnostic phase* is associated with initial indicators of illness or disease. For example, I feel an unusual pain, notice a small growth, or become aware of a decline in my functioning. What will I do about this experience? At first, I might simply ignore the indicator by appraising it as insignificant. Or I might try to minimize my affective (emotional) responses to its presence. Or I might decide to investigate its significance. Perhaps I will ask family members or friends to tell me what to do. In some cultures, I might turn to a medicine man or traditional healer. Within the death system of most modern societies, I might turn to medical or other professional sources of advice for investigation or diagnosis of the potential problem. Some persons consult a physician right away for even the most minor or imagined complaints. Other individuals put a doctor visit off for many reasons—for example, they lack ready access to such advice, distrust the system, do not have medical insurance or personal funds to pay for such advice, or simply hope that things will get better and "it" will go away on its own. These are all ways of coping with a potential life-threatening illness in the prediagnostic phase. They involve tasks of recognizing possible danger or risk, trying to manage anxiety or uncertainty, and developing and following through on a health-seeking strategy.

If a serious but treatable condition is diagnosed, an individual will be confronted with a number of tasks in the *acute phase* of a life-threatening illness. One might try to understand the disease, maximize health and lifestyle, foster coping strengths and limit weaknesses, develop strategies to deal with issues created by the disease, arrange for cure-oriented interventions, explore effects of the diagnosis on one's sense of self and others, ventilate feelings and fears, and/or incorporate the reality of the diagnosis into one's sense of past and future.

The *chronic phase* of living with a life-threatening illness involves tasks like managing symptoms and side effects, carrying out health regimens, preventing and managing health crises, managing stress and examining coping, maximizing social support and minimizing isolation, normalizing life in the face of disease, dealing with financial concerns, preserving one's self-concept, redefining relationships with others throughout the course of the disease, continuing to ventilate feelings and fears, and finding meaning in suffering, chronicity, uncertainty, and decline.

Happily, many life-threatening illnesses do not result in death. In such circumstances, a person enters the *recovery phase*, but that does not free the person from a need to cope. Task work is ongoing because "recovery does not mean that one simply returns to the life led before. Any encounter with a crisis changes us. We are no longer the people we once were" (Doka, 1993a, p. 116). Tasks in the recovery phase include dealing with the aftereffects of illness and anxieties about recurrence, reconstructing or reformulating one's lifestyle, and redefining relationships with caregivers. Matt Ryan faced tasks like these in the vignette near the beginning of this chapter after the successful treatment of his prostate cancer.

However, cure-oriented interventions may no longer have much to offer, especially when potential benefits are balanced against their physical, psychosocial, or spiritual costs. Perhaps no relevant cure-oriented intervention is available, either for the disease itself or for the stage at which it has been discovered and diagnosed. If so, the person enters the *terminal phase*, in which he or she is faced with a new set of tasks, such as dealing with ongoing challenges arising from the disease, its side effects, and treatments, dealing with caregivers and (perhaps) deciding to discontinue cure-oriented interventions or turning to interventions designed to minimize discomforting symptoms, preparing for death and saying goodbye, preserving self-concept and appropriate social relationships, and finding meaning in life and death. This was Jo Ryan's situation after the recurrence of her cancer in the vignette near the beginning of this chapter.

Doka's schema of phases and tasks is intended to apply in principle to any life-threatening illness and to go beyond issues linked directly to cure-oriented interventions. It seeks to be sensitive to the many human—physical, psychological, social, and spiritual—aspects of coping with life-threatening illness. This model also brings to the fore three critical factors that influence all coping activities: (1) the wide variety of social and psychological variables (cultural, social, and personal) that enter into processes of coping with life-threatening illness and dying; (2) the developmental context within which the individual confronts this challenge (which we explore in Part Five); and (3) the nature of the disease, its trajectory and effects, and its treatment.

What Do We Now Know about Coping with Dying?

Kastenbaum and Thuell (1995, p. 176) observed that "strictly speaking, there are no scientific theories of dying, if by 'theory' we mean a coherent set of explicit propositions that have predictive power and are subject to empirical verification. There are distinctive theoretical approaches, however, each of which emphasizes a particular range of experience and behavior." The three approaches that Kastenbaum and Thuell examined are Glaser and Strauss's account of dying trajectories and awareness contexts, the stage-based schema advanced by Kübler-Ross, and the task-based model proposed by Corr.

In the end, Kastenbaum and Thuell called for a contextual theory of dying, one that "would help us to understand the changing person within his/her changing socio-environmental field" (p. 186). Such a theory "would not be a reductionistic approach that attempts to explain complex multilevel phenomena in a simple way," nor would it be "an over-rationalized logico-deductive model that ignores the power of spirit, emotion and relationships" (p. 186). What these authors seem to have in mind is a kind of active model or evolving narrative that would integrate all of the relevant dimensions of all of the relevant individuals who find themselves drawn together in a process of coping with dying. Until that goal is achieved, the insights and theoretical frameworks described in this chapter represent the major contributions to this field thus far and define the present state of our knowledge (see Corr, Doka, & Kastenbaum, 1999).

Summary

In this chapter, we explored coping with dying. In so doing, we sought to describe coping processes in ways that do justice to their many elements and to the many individuals involved in such coping. Coping with dying is a part of coping with living, even though dying presents special issues and challenges. We considered dying trajectories and awareness contexts, as well as stage-based and task-based models for explaining coping with dying. Also, we insisted that any adequate account of coping with dying must refer to the whole human being, to each individual human being, and to all who are involved.

Questions for Review and Discussion

1. Think about some moment in your life when you were quite ill. What was most stressful for you at that time? If you felt fear, what were the sources of your greatest fears? What did you want other people to do for or with you at that time? Now try to imagine yourself in a similar situation, only adding that the illness is a life-threatening one. What would be similar or different in these two situations?

2. One central notion in this chapter is the concept of coping. In what ways in the past have you coped with stressful situations? Choose someone you know well and reflect on how she or he copes with stress. What strengths and limitations do you note in your own ways of coping and in this other person's methods of coping?

3. In our analysis of dying trajectories, awareness contexts, a stage-based model, and task-based models, which elements seemed to you to be most (or least) innovative, interesting, and helpful?

4. If you think about the coping processes of dying persons as involving tasks, how might this model of coping affect your understanding of a dying person? How might it affect your interactions with dying persons?

Suggested Readings

Analyses of stress and coping strategies appear in:

Lazarus, R. S., & Folkman, S. (1984). *Stress, Appraisal, and Coping.*

Monat, A., & Lazarus, R. S. (Eds.). (1991). *Stress and Coping: An Anthology* (3rd ed.).

Selye, H. (1978b). *The Stress of Life* (rev. ed.).

Weisman, A. D. (1984). *The Coping Capacity: On the Nature of Being Mortal.*

Researchers, scholars, and clinicians have written about various aspects of coping with dying in:

Ahronheim, J., & Weber, D. (1992). *Final Passages: Positive Choices for the Dying and Their Loved Ones.*

Basta, L., with C. Post. (1996). *A Graceful Exit: Life and Death on Your Own Terms.*

Davidson, G. W. (1975). *Living with Dying.*

Doka, K. J. (1993a). *Living with Life-Threatening Illness: A Guide for Patients, Families, and Caregivers.*

Glaser, B., & Strauss, A. (1965). *Awareness of Dying.*

Glaser, B., & Strauss, A. (1968). *Time for Dying.*

Heinz, D. (1999). *The Last Passage: Recovering a Death of Our Own.*

Hinton, J. (1967). *Dying.*

Kavanaugh, R. E. (1972). *Facing Death.*

Kübler-Ross, E. (1969). *On Death and Dying.*

Kübler-Ross, E., & Kessler, D. (2000). *Life Lessons: Two Experts on Death and Dying Teach Us about the Mysteries of Life and Living.*

Lynn, J., & Harrold, J. (1999). *Handbook for Mortals: Guidance for People Facing Serious Illness.*

Pattison, E. M. (1977). *The Experience of Dying.*

Rosen, E. J. (1990). *Families Facing Death: Family Dynamics of Terminal Illness.*

Staton, J., Shuy, R., & Byock, I. (2001). *A Few Months to Live: Different Paths to Life's End.*

Tobin, D. (1999). *Peaceful Dying: The Step-by-Step Guide to Preserving Your Dignity, Your Choice, and Your Inner Peace at the End of Life*

Weisman, A. D. (1972). *On Dying and Denying: A Psychiatric Study of Terminality.*

Special problems associated with long-term, chronic diseases are examined in:

Mace, N. L., & Rabins, P. V. (1999). *The 36-Hour Day: A Family Guide to Caring for Persons with Alzheimer's Disease, Related Dementing Illnesses, and Memory Loss in Later Life* (3rd ed.).

InfoTrac College Edition
For more information, explore the InfoTrac College Edition at **http://www.infotrac-college.com/Wadsworth**

Enter search terms: COPING, THE LIVING-DYING INTERVAL, STAGES IN DYING.

Chapter Seven

COPING WITH DYING: HOW INDIVIDUALS CAN HELP

IN CHAPTER 6, WE EXAMINED COPING WITH dying on the part of dying persons and others who are drawn into such experiences. Here, we turn to what can be done to help persons who are coping with dying. After describing the individuals who helped Jo and Matt Ryan when they were coping with Jo's life-threatening illness, we note that helping persons who are coping with dying requires both human presence and the specialized expertise of professionals. Next, we explore four primary dimensions of care and the role of tasks as guidelines for helpers. Finally, we devote separate sections to the topics of effective communication, helping helpers (burnout and self-care), and hope, because these topics underlie and flow naturally from the discussions in this chapter while also leading us on to the subjects of Chapter 8. ■

Individuals Who Helped Matt and Josephina Ryan Cope with Life-Threatening Illness and Dying

Just as Josephina Ryan had helped her husband, Matt, when he was threatened by prostate cancer, Matt tried to be there for Jo when she experienced the onslaught of the cancer that would eventually take her life. But Matt admitted right away that he just didn't know how to be very helpful. He struggled to keep up with practical matters like cleaning the house, doing the laundry, and putting food on the table, but he wasn't good at such chores and his spirits had suffered a hard blow. Jo knew that Matt meant well and she tried to pitch in whenever she could, but her energy level was declining. It was hard to watch Matt wander around the house aimlessly, and she worried about what would happen to him after she was gone.

The Ryans' children tried to help as much as they could. Most of the burden fell on Tom and his wife, since they lived in town. They helped with some of the household chores and took Matt to shop and do other errands. It helped Matt to get out of the house and to see Tom's children, but he always worried about Jo back at the house. In fact, Jo wasn't very good at first at accepting help from Tom and his wife or from her other children when they would fly into town for short visits. She had always been the capable, competent mother in the family doing for others. Her cultural background and personality didn't make it easy for her to let others take over that role and the children complained that she was pushing them away just when they knew she must need help.

Even if Jo had been more open to accepting help, many of the friends and neighbors to whom they might have turned didn't know how to offer to help in really useful ways. Some offered unhelpful advice or empty clichés, while others just withdrew in confusion. The Ryans were fortunate, however, in their longstanding friendship with Sharon and Bill Applegate. Both of the Applegates were retired, Sharon from her work as a nurse's aide and Bill from his position as assistant principal and coach in Matt's high school. Sharon pitched in to help Jo with basic, practical care. She knew that activities like helping to wash and bathe people made them feel better, while also preventing sores and other complications associated with confinement to a bed. Before Jo was confined to her bed, Sharon showed Matt and Tom how to help her get around to exercise stiff muscles and how to transfer her to a wheelchair. Later, she gave them advice on moving and positioning Jo in bed. Sharon also devised little jobs for the grandchildren to help out and suggested activities that they could undertake as "junior helpers."

Bill also helped by just spending time with Matt and taking over some practical chores like cutting the lawn that Matt seemed unable to contemplate any longer. When they were together, Matt and Bill didn't actually talk very much, especially about Jo, but Matt seemed to appreciate his presence and Bill made sure to let Matt know that they could discuss whatever he wanted to talk about. This whole illness thing and the prospect of Jo's dying made Matt feel very overwhelmed and isolated. Bill's interest helped to make things seem just a bit less awful, and sometimes Bill could tell Sharon or others in the family what was on Matt's mind and suggest things they could also do to help.

Jo's death was very sad for Matt and the whole Ryan family, just as it was for Sharon and Bill. But the Applegates were gratified at the funeral when Matt told them that Jo's last wish had been to be at home as long as possible before her death. He knew that wouldn't have been possible without their help, and he wanted them to know how grateful he was for their support in helping him to do everything that could be done for his wife and his family. "You made a very bad time just a little bit better," he said, "and for that, I'll always be grateful."

Caring for Persons Who Are Coping with Dying: Human and Professional Tasks

Caring for persons who are coping with dying is not an activity to be carried out only by people who are specially trained to do so. Certainly, dying persons and others who are coping with dying are people with special needs, some of which can best or perhaps only be met by individuals with special expertise. For example, a dying person may have a special need for a physician's prescription for narcotic analgesics or a sacramental act by a member of the ordained clergy. However, much of the care required is not related to special needs; it involves fundamental concerns common to all living human beings, even though they are concerns that may take on a special intensity under the pressures of coping with dying (see Box 7.1).

For example, dying persons need to eat, they need to exercise their bodies, minds, and spirits, and they need above all to be *cared about, not just cared for*. For most of the 24 hours in each day, the care that dying persons need is not specialized care. This care can be provided by any of us. A hand held, a grief or joy shared, and a question listened to and responded to: these are human moments of caring, and they can be offered by any human being who is willing and able to care. In short, "the secret of the care of patients is still caring" (Ingles, 1974, p. 763; see also Peabody, 1927).

Persons who are dying are most likely to be concerned about such matters as being abandoned, losing control over their own bodies and lives, and being in overwhelming pain or distress. Dame Cicely Saunders, founder of St. Christopher's Hospice in London and initiator of the modern hospice movement, has been reported (Shephard, 1977) to have said that dying persons ask three things of those who care for them: (1) *"Help me"* (minimize my distress); (2) *"Listen to me"* (let me direct things or at least be heard); and (3) *"Don't leave me"* (stay with me; give me your presence).

It is important to recognize the many ways in which we can help those who are coping with dying. Sometimes, what helpers can do is simple and obvious, not dramatic and world-shaking (see Box 7.2). But even when we cannot do something specific to help, all of us—professionals and nonprofessionals alike—can offer an "empathetic presence" by listening to and staying with dying persons and their significant others. This is the lesson that Sharon and Bill Applegate learned as they helped Jo and Matt Ryan.

Box 7.1 Some Thoughts about Caring

The common diagnostic categories into which medicine places its patients are relevant to disease, not to illness. They are useful for treatment, but they only get in the way of care. . . . Caring has nothing to do with categories; it shows the person that her life is valued because it recognizes what makes her experience particular. One person has no right to categorize another, but we do have the privilege of coming to understand how each of us is unique. . . . Terms like pain or loss have no reality until they are filled in with an ill person's own experience. Witnessing the particulars of that experience, and recognizing all its differences, is care. ■

SOURCE: Frank, 1991, pp. 45–49.

To provide adequate care for the dying, we must address the many fears, anxieties, desires, and tasks of dying persons. The same applies to family members and friends of the dying person—those significant others who are also coping with dying. We may be more or less successful in meeting these responsibilities because of pressures of limited time, energy, information, or resources. But if we are serious about providing good care, we ought not to fail to address these needs because of lack of understanding or attention to what is needed by those who are coping with dying (see Box 7.3). In this chapter, we provide information about and draw attention to ways in which help can be provided to those who are coping with dying.

Dimensions of Care

There are four primary dimensions of care for those who are coping with dying: physical, psychological, social, and spiritual (Saunders, 1967; Woodson, 1976). Here, we consider each of these in turn, with special attention to their application to dying persons. These dimensions are also relevant to others who are coping with dying: family members and friends of the dying person, as well as professional and volunteer helpers/caregivers.

Physical Dimensions

For many dying persons, one of the most pressing needs is the control of *physical pain or distress.* When pain is present, it must be properly studied and carefully understood (Benoliel & Crowley, 1974; Wall & Melzack, 1994). One can distinguish between at least two sorts of pain: acute pain and chronic pain.

Box 7.2 The Tale of the Stranded Starfish

As a man walked a desolate beach one cold, gray morning he began to see another figure, far in the distance. Slowly the two approached each other, and he could make out a local native who kept leaning down, picking something up and throwing it out into the water. Time and again he hurled things into the ocean. As the distance between them continued to narrow, the man could see that the native was picking up starfish that had been washed upon the beach and, one at a time, was throwing them back into the water. Puzzled, the man approached the native and asked what he was doing.

"I'm throwing these starfish back into the ocean. You see, it's low tide right now and all of these starfish have been washed up onto the shore. If I don't throw them back into the sea, they'll die up here from lack of oxygen."

"But there must be thousands of starfish on this beach," the man replied. "You can't possibly get to all of them. There are just too many. And this same thing is probably happening on hundreds of beaches all up and down this coast. Can't you see that you can't possibly make a difference?"

The local native smiled, bent down and picked up another starfish, and as he threw it back into the sea he replied, "Made a difference to that one!" ■

SOURCE: Author unknown.

Acute pain is a form of pain that is essential to human life. Those who do not feel acute pain—for example, when they touch a hot stove—are in danger of serious harm. When individuals are ill, physicians often obtain the information they need to make an accurate diagnosis by eliciting careful, specific descriptions of pain or distress. For instance, acute pain associated with kidney stones guides both diagnosis and treatment. Thus, acute pain is not always or completely undesirable, given our present human condition. In fact, it may make possible enhancement of both the quality and the quantity of our lives. Of course, dying persons may experience acute pain, too. They may develop symptoms—including physical pain—that may or may not be directly related to the illness that threatens their lives. In this regard, Saunders reminded caregivers that a toothache hurts just as much when you are dying (*Until We Say Goodbye*, 1980).

Chronic pain, however, does not serve any of these constructive functions. Chronic pain does not assist in diagnosis because the diagnosis has already been made. Nor does chronic pain protect the person from dangers in the environment. It is just there, always there. Dull or invasive, sharp or intermittent, chronic pain forms the backdrop of whatever the person is doing at the moment. When it is intense, it can become the whole focus of attention of those who are experiencing such pain (LeShan, 1964).

In life-threatening illness, chronic pain is often associated with a disease that will lead to death. Proper care of the dying person must involve efforts to manage or at least to diminish distress arising from chronic pain—whatever its

Box 7.3 So Little Left

What is it that you want nurse?
What do you expect of me?

You want me to smile all powdered and clean.
Be pleasant, be nice and don't make a scene.
You want me to get up and eat when you say.
To follow *your* rules all through the day.

BUT WHAT ABOUT ME?

I try to tell you, I push you away.
You don't understand what I'm trying to say.
It doesn't much matter what ever I do.
It always ends with me versus you.
You walk away scowling giving up in defeat,
or give me a shot that just puts me to sleep.

How can I tell you what I feel deep inside?
The words just get lost, I mumble, they hide.
My body has failed me, I have little strength.
These strange surroundings make it so hard to think.

I thank you for all the care that you give.
It's so clear to me, you want me to live.
But to live is the future, I know not of that.
All that I know is right now I feel trapped.
Trapped by my body, trapped by the day,
Trapped by my God that won't take me away.

How could you have helped to relieve some of that?
It would have helped if you would have just sat.

Sat not expecting a thing in return,
not making me drink, not making me turn.
Sat just allowing me to be me,
Nasty or frightened or stubborn, but free.
You see as I see it, I've lost all control.
Except for my mood so that's what I show. ■

SOURCE: From M. Metzgar. Reprinted by permission.

origin. It may not always be possible to eradicate chronic pain totally, but even to reduce such pain from agony to ache is an impressive achievement. Care of the dying has shown that chronic pain can be controlled or at least greatly diminished in most cases (Doyle et al., 1998; Saunders et al., 1995; Twycross, 1994, 1995b). Needless pain in end-of-life care is a tragedy when good research has taught so much about the nature of pain and the role of analgesics and other therapeutic modalities in its management (Melzack, 1990). Appropriate medications and supportive therapy can see to it that chronic pain need not so fill the consciousness of dying persons that they can pay attention to nothing else but their pain.

The challenge for therapeutic interventions is to select just the right drug(s) to meet the need(s) of the individual, to achieve just the right balance of responses to requirements (without under- or overmedication), and to employ an appropriate route of administration. The philosophy of pain management in end-of-life care has often emphasized administration of medications via oral routes (in liquid or capsule form) to avoid the pain of injections. However, both injections and suppositories have been recognized as appropriate in certain cases (for instance, when rapid results achievable by injections are required or when individuals are nauseated and cannot swallow). More recently, these have been supplemented by slow-release analgesic tablets, long-term continuous infusion devices (similar to those used for insulin by some diabetics), and patient-controlled analgesia (whereby individuals have some measure of control and autonomy in administering their own medications, often resulting in less overall medication than might otherwise have been employed).

Drug therapy is not the *only* method of controlling chronic pain. As research leads to a better understanding of the nature of disease, it is evident that most pain has a psychological component. Thus, McCaffery and Beebe (1989, p. 7) wrote, "Pain is whatever the experiencing person says it is, existing whenever the experiencing person says it does." That is, *pain is distress as an individual perceives it.* Pain management may seek to alter the threshold or the nature of that perception, just as it may block the pathways or the effects of a noxious stimulant. Biofeedback, guided imagery, meditation, therapeutic touch, and techniques of self-hypnosis may also assist persons to control their pain or to manage its effects. Also, constructive psychological support may encourage individuals to relax and keep muscles and joints active, thereby helping to lessen the degree of physical pain that occurs when a person remains immobile. These therapies are not in opposition to, but can work alongside, medications and other interventions.

When drug therapies are used, long-standing research has demonstrated that many dying persons, including long-term patients with far-advanced cancer, can tolerate large doses of strong narcotics without becoming "doped up" or "knocked out" (Twycross, 1979b, 1982). The goal is not total anesthesia (unconsciousness), but rather analgesia (an insensibility to pain). This goal can be achieved in most cases by choosing the correct medication(s) for the situation and by carefully titrating or balancing dosages against the nature and level of pain (Storey, 1996; Twycross & Lack, 1989).

If the right drug is used and the dose is titrated or calibrated to the precise level needed to control pain—and *no further*—then the pain is well managed. The right drug is crucial. Pain may arise from a variety of sources—for example, direct damage to tissue, pressure, or inflammation. Each source of pain and each route of transmission may require its own appropriate medication. Also, each drug must be selected in terms of the needs of an individual patient, its method of administration, the time intervals at which it will be given, and potential problems with side effects or interactions with other drugs the person may be taking. For example, some drugs like the narcotic Demerol are quick acting and potent, which makes them useful for dealing with episodes of acute pain. However, such a drug may not retain its efficacy long enough to suit someone with chronic pain. If so, a dying person for whom it is prescribed may be in pain again in two or three hours, well before the next dose is administered. This is *not* effective pain control. Morphine and some other strong narcotics have proven their effectiveness in end-of-life care because their effects last long enough to manage chronic pain until the next dose.

Addiction does not occur, even when strong narcotics are prescribed in high doses for dying persons. This has been shown by well-established research (for example, Twycross, 1976) and should now be well known (Porter & Jick, 1980). The psychological "high" and subsequent craving for steadily escalating doses that characterize addiction are not found. This may have to do with ways in which medications are administered and absorbed in the body: they can be given by mouth in single doses or as a timed-release medication. If necessary, intravenous injections or infusions can be used.

Dying persons may become *physically dependent* on strong narcotics, but that also occurs in other situations—for example, in the use of steroids. Here, dependence means only that one cannot withdraw the drug abruptly or while it is still required without harmful side effects. Such physical dependence without underlying emotional disorder is easily terminated and has long been recognized not to constitute an additional problem ("Medical Ethics," 1963). Otherwise, it is as if the body uses the drug to deal with the pain it is experiencing, and it signals when the drug or dose is not correct. Too small or too weak a dose allows pain to return; too large or too powerful a dose induces drowsiness.

Once individuals learn that their pain really can and will be well managed, the dose provided can often be reduced because they no longer are fearful and tense in the face of *expected* pain (Twycross, 1994, 1995b). Effective drug therapeutics provides a sense of security that reduces anxiety. Addressing such psychosocial components of pain can lower the threshold of analgesia and may make it easier to manage discomfort. Thus relaxation may actually allow individuals to tolerate more pain and accept a lower drug dose.

Dying persons may also experience other physical symptoms that can be just as distressing as or even more distressing than physical pain (Saunders & Sykes, 1993). These symptoms include constipation (a common side effect of narcotics), diarrhea, nausea, and vomiting. Sometimes there is weakness or reduction in available energy, loss of appetite, or shortness of breath. Similarly, loss of hair, dark circles around the eyes, and changes in skin color may also be matters of concern to individuals who place high value on self-image and how they present themselves to others. Also, if someone sits or lies in bed for long periods of time, skin ulcers or pressure sores can become a potential source of added discomfort and risk for infection. Reducing this source of distress has always been a concern of effective care for the dying (Kemp, 1995).

Dehydration illustrates an issue that is frequently encountered in dying persons (Zerwekh, 1983; see also Gallagher-Allred & Amenta, 1993). An intravenous infusion might be used, but that method adds another source of pain to

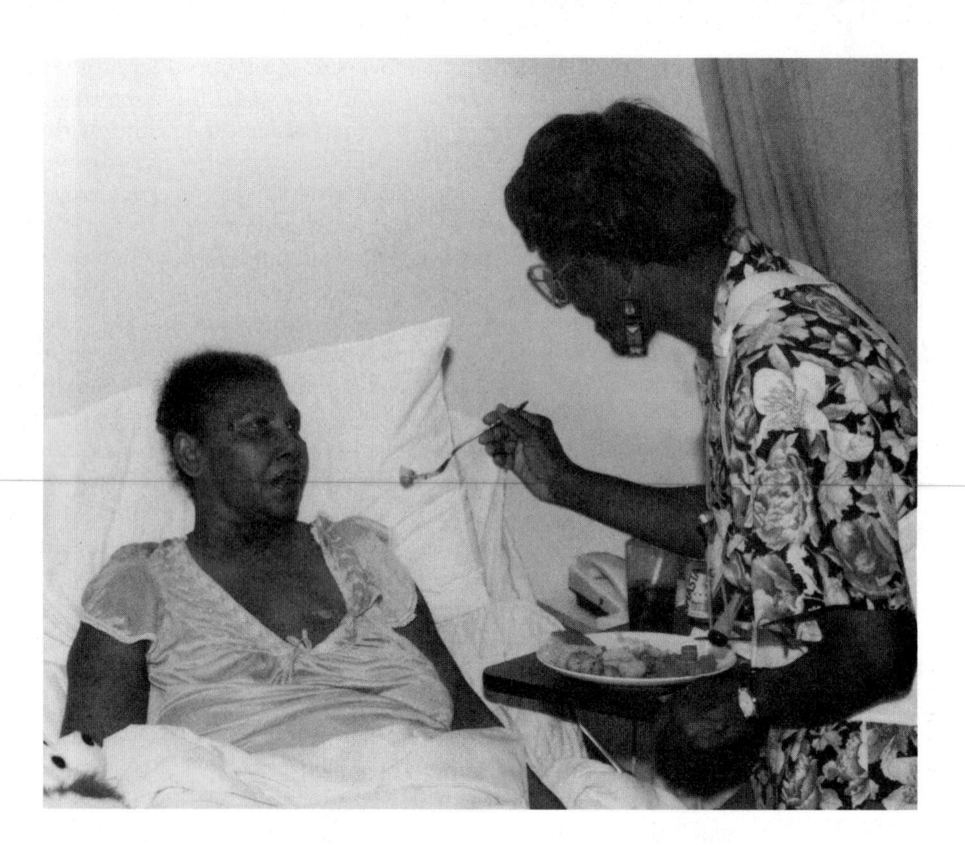

Caring for a basic physical need.

the burdens of ill persons at the end of life. Also, it may overload with fluid a body that is weak and whose organ systems may no longer be functioning effectively. Often, small sips of juice or other fluids, ice chips, or flavored mouth swabs may be enough to maintain quality of life. This shows that effective care for dying persons must address all of their distressing physical symptoms and must do so in ways suited to their current situation. Such care may require intervention on the part of physicians, nurses, and other professional caregivers, but family caregivers and significant others also have important roles to play in these situations, especially when they are shown how to be most helpful to the ill person.

Psychological Dimensions

Another set of concerns revolves around *psychological dimensions* and tasks in coping with dying. Care providers are sometimes even more uncomfortable working with these concerns than with those having to do with physical dimensions in dying persons. It is difficult to be with someone in physical pain, but many would-be helpers are even more uneasy in the face of so-called negative feelings. Nevertheless, someone who is dying is likely to express these sorts of feelings at one time or another. Such a person may experience anger and sadness, anxiety and fear. In the face of such feelings, people often wonder what is the right thing to say or to do.

Frequently, there is no specific or universal right thing to say or to do, but that does not mean there is nothing to say or to do. In fact, one can say and do many things to be helpful. Often, the most helpful thing is simply to be present and listen, making sure that whatever one does say is true, reliable, supportive, and caring (Zerwekh, 1994). To hunt for some way to make all fear, anger, or sadness disappear is to begin a hopeless search. These feelings are real, and they must be lived through.

A student once told us that she believed someone informed of a prognosis of impending death would become sad or depressed, an emotion she thought of as undesirable. She said she would seek any means to prevent it from occurring, or if it did occur, to end it. This is unrealistic. If someone is given unhappy news—of any sort—sadness is a likely and *appropriate* response. Furthermore, some people—including many professional caregivers—too quickly identify sadness with depression. But to realize that one is going to die is to be faced with a loss—and in the face of loss, human beings grieve.

Anger is another feeling that may be particularly discomforting. Our culture often looks on anger as a destructive emotion, rather than an understandable reaction when one's needs are frustrated or one is hurt, a reaction that can be expressed constructively or destructively. Those who are coping with dying often feel lots of anger. They may be angry because of the losses they are experiencing and because others—apparently for no good reason—are enjoying happy, healthy, and satisfying lives. Further, because of physical or other restrictions, a dying person's anger may be limited in the ways in which it can be expressed. Not surprisingly, strong feelings may be projected onto others—that is, directed at whatever or whomever is most readily available, whether or not that is appropriate.

This sort of anger needs to be identified, acknowledged, and expressed. Feelings like this cannot simply be made to go away. Feelings are real; one cannot just stop feeling what one is feeling. Nor is it reasonable to expect that strong feelings should always be suppressed. For example, anger and an outpouring of adrenaline go together; the anger must be worked off, much like the physical rush of adrenaline. When a helper is the object of growls, complaints, or screaming, it may not be very consoling to realize that there is usually nothing personal in such expressions of anger and other strong feelings—but that is often the case.

In such situations, it may be important to learn to be comfortable with one's own discomfort. That is, our task as helpers is not to discover the magical "right" thing to say to make dying persons no longer have such feelings. Letting them talk about why they feel as they do and giving them "permission" to do so through bodily or verbal cues—*really* listening to them—may be the most helpful thing one can do (Nichols, 1995).

In addition, many dying persons have reported that for someone to say to them "I know how you feel" is *not* helpful. For one thing, this is almost certainly not true. Most individuals have not really been in the situation of the other person to whom such a remark is made, and no one can really experience the feelings of another individual. Also, such a remark is often perceived as an attempt to minimize or trivialize the feelings of the person to whom it is addressed.

How can people who are experiencing "negative" feelings be helped? If this question means, How can someone make them stop having those feelings?, the question may say more about our discomfort with their feelings and our need to end that discomfort than it does about the needs of those who are coping with dying. Two things should be noted here. First, *outsiders cannot make anyone feel different or better.* Second, *that may often be an inappropriate goal.* Dying people must live with and through their feelings, just as they must live with and through all of the rest of their life experiences. They can be helped to do that by assistance in identifying their feelings, by acknowledgment of their feelings as appropriate to their particular situations (if that is, in fact, the case), and by permission for them to vent or share their feelings.

There are no magic formulas here. There are no cookbooks for the right behaviors or statements. Nevertheless, what does seem to help people who are coping with dying is for someone to listen to them and to take seriously what they are feeling. This is one thing that can be done to help. Helpers can *be present* to such persons (physically, emotionally, existentially) and can *listen attentively* to what they say (see Box 7.4). If helpers turn off their own internal monologues, if they stop hunting around for the "right" response, and if they just *listen empathetically*, that can help. It helps because it says to the dying person, loudly and clearly, "You matter; you and your feelings are real and important to me." It also helps to hear what the dying person needs, rather than what others think the person needs. Compassion or empathy, which reaches out to understand and feel along with the other person, is quite different from pity, which commiserates with the other individual from a hierarchical and distant standpoint. As Garfield (1976, p. 181) wrote years ago, "The largest single impediment to providing effective psychosocial support to the terminal patient is the powerful professional staff distinction between 'US' and 'THEM.'"

Something else that can be done to help, at least in many instances, is to *touch the person.* Some people are uncomfortable with physical touch. As Hall (1966) noted in his analysis of what he called "proxemics," such people keep a fairly large personal space around themselves, and they may resent and resist intrusion by others into that space. However, sickness may break down some of these barriers. For example, a body massage may be *psychologically* helpful. Often, it is helpful for a friend or concerned person to touch one's wrist or arm, hold one's hand, or give a hug. Not everyone responds favorably to this; each person is an individual with personal expectations and values. Helpers must respect the dying person's values on this point. Seeking permission might be desirable. But for many persons who are coping with dying, gentle touch is psychologically healing.

Many of the psychological tasks of dying persons can be helped by anybody, whether that person is a professional caregiver or not, although some preparation and training may help (Parkes et al., 1996). If there are psychological dimensions of coping with dying that run deeper and that interfere with the individual's quality in living, a professional counselor or therapist may be helpful. Similarly, those who are especially competent to assist with psychological tasks might be called on for help when coping with dying is accompanied by clinical depression, confusional states, or specific forms of mental illness

Box 7.4 On Being a Good Listener

If I am a good listener, I don't interrupt the other nor plan my own next speech while pretending to be listening. I try to hear what is said, but I listen just as hard for what is not said and for what is said between the lines. I am not in a hurry, for there is no preappointed destination for the conversation. There is no need to get there, for we are already here; and in this present I am able to be fully present to the one who speaks. The speaker is not an object to be categorized or manipulated, but a subject whose life situation is enough like my own that I can understand it in spite of the differences between us. If I am a good listener, what we have in common will seem more important than what we have in conflict.

This does not mean that I never say anything, but I am more likely to ask questions than to issue manifestos or make accusations.

SOURCE: Westphal, 1984, p. 12.

One of our most difficult duties as human beings is to listen to the voices of those who suffer. The voices of the ill are easy to ignore, because those voices are often faltering in tone and mixed in message, particularly in their spoken form before some editor has rendered them fit for reading by the healthy. These voices bespeak conditions of embodiment that most of us would rather forget our vulnerability to. Listening is hard, but it is also a fundamental moral act. . . . [Moreover] in listening for the other, we listen for ourselves. The moment of witness in the story crystallizes a mutuality of need, when each is for the other. ■

SOURCE: Frank, 1995, p. 25.

(Stedeford, 1978, 1984). After all, if the goal is to provide whatever care is needed in order to make this time in life as good as possible, the lesson must be that no particular expertise or mode of care should be looked on as irrelevant just because the person happens to be dying.

There is no evidence that coping with dying on its own is associated with psychiatric problems such as suicidal tendencies (Achté & Vauhkonen, 1971; Brown et al., 1986). Thus, Stedeford (1979, pp. 13–14) suggested that as a general rule in the care of those who are coping with dying, "sophisticated psychotherapy is not as necessary as are sensitivity, a willingness to follow the patient rather than lead him, some knowledge of the psychology of dying, and the ability to accept the inevitability of death."

In the end, we are best able to help a dying person or anyone coping with dying when we are able to begin to cope with the reality of our own mortality and our prior experiences with profound losses. Not to do so often complicates our ability to help because it may fail to appreciate whose needs are being addressed. The fundamental criterion for all aspects of caring for dying persons and their family members is that *caring must be made relevant and must be seen to be relevant to the needs and tasks of the person whom one is trying to help.* Caregivers must always ask, "What is the relative value of the various available methods of treatment *in this particular patient?*" (Cade, 1963, p. 3).

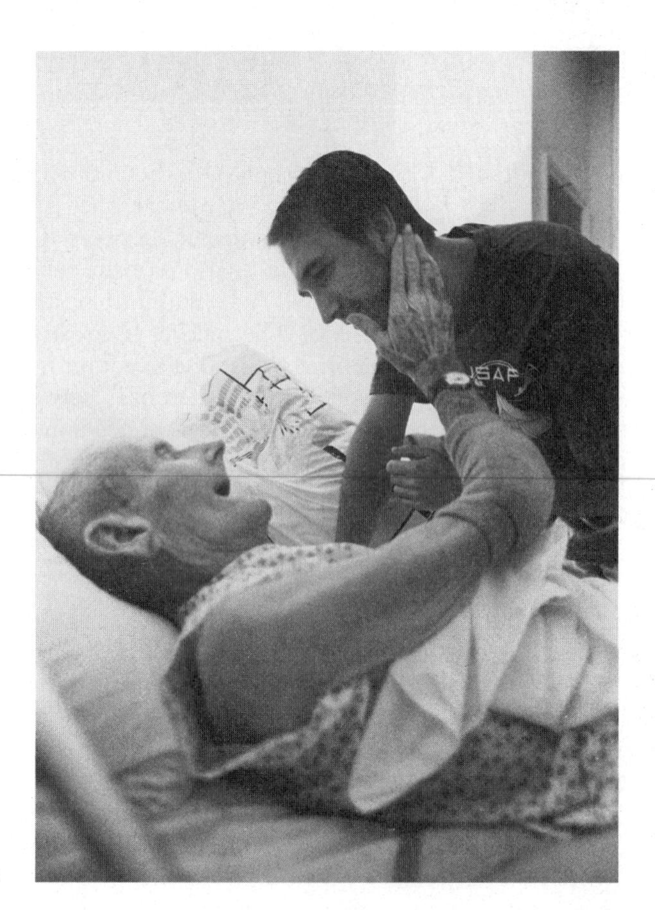

Offering one's presence to a person nearing the end of his life.

Social Dimensions

Social dimensions in coping with dying are often just as pressing as physical and psychological dimensions. These social dimensions are expressed, first of all, in the special relationships that most individuals form with one or more people who occupy cherished roles in their lives. It is to these special people that one brings one's intimate achievements and tribulations. Within these relationships individuals seek safety and security. In their shelter, one makes plans, works through problems, and defines that which is meaningful. Here love is expressed most basically in the sharing of two or more lives. Often, it is sufficient merely to be in the company of such special persons in order to feel a bit better and less beset by the problems of living.

Individuals who are coping with dying can be helped when the relationships that they value are fostered and encouraged. When energy levels are low, they may not be able to sustain all of the relationships that once were important to them. Their circle of personal involvements may change its shape, size, or character, and those who are coping with dying may want to be shown how to uphold the most significant of these relationships. They will want to continue to give care to and to receive care from the special people in their lives. Sensitivity to the identities of these special people, to the nature of their attachments with the person who is coping with dying, and to ways in which such relationships can be maintained and nurtured is an important part of caring and helping.

Social dimensions also include concerns about one's role and place in the family, in the workforce, and in the community at large. For example, economic

A young hospice volunteer reads Field & Stream *with an elderly patient.*

concerns may be or seem to be very important. In our society, many people worry about how their families will survive economically, given the costs of health care and the disappearance of the income that the dying person had formerly provided. There are other concerns, too: Will that project I started at work be completed? What will happen to my business (students, parishioners, clients, customers, stockholders, employees)? How will my spouse be able to cope with being a single parent of young children? Who will take care of my aged parents or aging spouse?

These are the types of questions that arise for many who are dying. One responds in helpful ways to these concerns first by allowing those who are coping with dying to talk about their concerns, and then by being an advocate for such persons. That is, one can listen and try to help these people find resources that may be of assistance with their specific (or not so specific) problems. Sometimes advocacy involves acting on behalf of or in place of others in order to try to serve their needs. Often, advocacy means enabling or empowering individuals to act for themselves in seeking to satisfy their requirements. Note that it can be disempowering to take over the work of coping from the other person; it may be sufficient to help that person recognize his or her options and think about ways to go about accomplishing personal tasks. Social roles offer an excellent opportunity for people to assert and maintain autonomy. Social workers, family therapists, counselors, and lawyers are often able to help in areas of social tasks.

Spiritual Dimensions

Dying persons often face a variety of *spiritual tasks.* Many of these tasks concern a search for meaning, for establishing, reestablishing, and maintaining connectedness with oneself, other persons, and with what the person perceives as the transcendent (Longaker, 1998; see also Chapter 6 in this book). It is important to note that the spiritual dimensions of a person's life are not separate from but rather often underlie and run through physical, psychological, and social dimensions.

Caregivers cannot provide meaning or connectedness for another individual, nor can they give to such individuals an experience or understanding of the transcendent. When asked, one may share one's convictions with others. But when dying persons ask spiritual questions, they may not be interested in our responses. Instead, they are often striving to "tell their own stories" or "sing their own songs" (Brady, 1979).

When we first sat with people and they would raise spiritual issues, we guardedly began to answer them. Sometimes these persons just looked at us and appeared to listen to us; sometimes they went on talking right over our replies. When we stopped talking, they continued with their own thoughts on these matters. Eventually, we learned that individuals often ask questions about what matters to them spiritually as a way of articulating these issues in their own minds. Talking was a way of developing their own thinking, and perhaps they were attempting to determine whether we would allow them to spin out their own answers. Again, what is usually being asked for is for someone to be present, to be empathic, to listen, and to *travel with them on their journey* (Ley & Corless, 1988; Zlatin, 1995).

Helpers can assist in this process. People find meaning, connectedness, and an experience of the transcendent in a variety of ways. Among these are objects (sacred books, a volume of poetry, photographs, icons, sculptures); places (a mosque, a cabin in the woods, one's own home); ritual actions (having a text read, receiving a sacrament, praying, having others lay their hands on you); communities—that is, specific groups of people (a church choir or a support group); particular times (the month of Ramadan, Yom Kippur, Christmas, one's own or a loved one's birthday, an important anniversary in the person's life); teachings and ideas (including perhaps a statement of faith, such as the Apostles' Creed for Christians, the Shahada for Muslims, or the Shema for some Jews); and specific persons (a shaman, rabbi, imam, or family member—perhaps one's child). By attentively asking and listening, caregivers can explore what an individual finds of help and then can arrange either to bring the person to whatever or whomever that might be or to bring it to the person. In this way, a caregiver can help to support the dying person on his or her (*not the caregiver's*) spiritual journey. Spiritual quests are rarely if ever completed, even up to the moment of death. Seeking out meaning, fostering connectedness, and grounding hope can be enriched and deepened throughout the entirety of a person's life. A caregiver's role is to support and sustain this ongoing process.

Spirituality is an essential component in the care of those who are coping with dying.

An important avenue of support for the dying person struggling with spiritual issues may be to enhance that individual's opportunities for creativity (Bertman, 1999). For example, one hospice has developed a rich program that offers creative opportunities in music, literature, drama, visual arts, and metalsmithing (Bailey et al., 1990). Artistic endeavors of this sort reflect specifically human qualities in coping with living and dying. They can be undertaken in diverse settings (in institutions or in homes) where helpers can work together with those who are coping with dying to realize meaning and connectedness.

One last word really has to do with all of the dimensions in which one might seek to help a person who is coping with dying. Because the person has dealt with an issue once does not mean that the issue is now settled. The issue may arise again. Questions like, "Who is going to see to it that my child gets a good education?" or "What does my dying at 26 mean?" are likely to be revisited again and again. Helpers need to be ready to listen to the person, wherever he or she is today, *at this moment.* There is no fixed goal at which the dying person or anyone who is coping with dying—along with those who are listening to that person—has to arrive. Though it may be unwise to put off a question or request—death is always an unexpected visitor—still one can rest assured that as long as there is life there will always be more questions, needs, desires, and concerns. No one ever finishes *all* of the business of life, if for no other reason than that each moment lived brings *new* business.

Tasks as Guidelines for Helping

One reason why we stress a task-based approach to coping with dying in this book is to identify guidelines for helping those who are coping with dying. We can develop such guidelines by focusing on specific tasks that the dying person or other persons affected by his or her dying (a family member, lover, friend, or caregiver) are pursuing. A helper (whether a professional or layperson) can facilitate and assist these persons with their task work. Of course, a person may not wish to have this sort of assistance. Or it may be that the individual is attempting to carry out his or her perceived tasks through some behavior (for example, suicide) that is morally or legally unacceptable to the one who is asked to help. One person's choices of how to live out his or her life do not necessarily impose obligations on others.

Careful observation of the ways in which the individual who is coping with dying perceives and responds to potential tasks can shape specific approaches in helping (see Box 7.5). For example, a dying person may express a need to get in contact with an estranged relative. That might lead a helper to assist in making a telephone call or in writing a letter, or it might become appropriate (if the dying person so wishes) for the helper to make the first contact as an intermediary with the estranged relative.

For a family member caring for a dying person at home, the helper might provide some temporary respite or relief from the physical burdens of care or some time off for psychological or social rejuvenation. The helper might offer to take over some of the physical care in order to provide the family caregiver with some time for uninterrupted sleep or rest. Or the helper might just sit with the dying person so that the family caregiver can leave the confines of the house to shop, see a movie, or seek some other form of rejuvenation. Or perhaps a perceptive helper might offer to take young children out for a day in the park so that a dying person and his or her spouse might have time alone together.

Rosen (1990; and see also Davies et al., 1995) described experiences of families who are facing the death of one of their members. According to Rosen, these experiences form a process consisting of a preparatory phase from the time when symptoms first appear through the initial diagnosis, a middle phase of living with the reality of the fatal illness and its associated caregiving tasks, and a final phase of accepting the imminent death and concluding the process of saying farewell. There are many ways of helping such families at different points in this process. For example, Rosen recommended that helpers make use of a three-generation family tree (a genogram) to identify the family's structure, history, and relationships (see McGoldrick & Gerson, 1985, 1988). This family tree provides a kind of road map for helping by portraying the interpersonal dynamics within the family and the internal resources that helpers might seek to mobilize. Rosen also showed how literary and cinematic materials might be used to help families, as well as practices ("rituals") with which they are familiar and specific suggestions ("coaching") to direct their attention and energies to tasks that they need to address. One caution in these approaches to helping is that the

Box 7.5 Five Themes for Caring and Some Practical Suggestions

Themes:	Practical Suggestions:
1. **Remember** your own limits when you are with a dying person.	Be cautious in supplying answers that you find meaningful—each person has unique experiences and must find his or her own meanings. If asked for your perspectives, do not speak as one who has and intends to give absolute truth, but rather as one who has found some perspectives meaningful in light of your life experiences.
2. **Recognize** that to be facing one's death is a profound experience, which to some degree involves tasks that each individual must carry out for himself or herself.	Be authentically present: this means to be with the person in that particular moment, paying attention to his or her tasks. LISTEN to what the dying person has to say about his or her particular, individual life experiences, including his or her successes, struggles, and failures, as well as his or her search for meaning; allow that person a safe space in which to come to understand those life experiences and that search for meaning. Try to understand the experiences of the other person by carefully listening and then imagining what it is to be that other person at this particular moment. Be attentive to the clues—subtle or obvious—as to what that person wants from you at this particular moment, for example, whether he or she wants to be alone or accompanied (by you or by someone else). Accept silence as a form of presence, too; recognize your discomfort with that silence and resist the impulse to fill it with chatter or teaching.
3. **Respect** the meaning and values of those for whom you are providing care.	Avoid making judgments about the other person's meanings and values. Keep in mind that none of us can fully comprehend what the other's life experiences are and have been, and that none of us is infallible in our own knowledge or understanding.
4. **Reinforce** the person's decision-making capacity and support his or her actual decisions.	Ask questions that help the individual clarify his or her preferences, desires, values, and needs, and help the person make choices based on his or her responses to your questions. Be an advocate for the person with other care providers in seeking to realize his or her decisions.
5. **Reminisce** with the person about his or her life and meaning.	Elicit stories from the person about his or her life experiences. Allow the person to reminisce and support the person as he or she remembers and repeats these stories. Record these stories so that they may be shared. Make available to the person (and significant others) poems, songs, readings, rituals, or prayers that are important to the dying person and that help in the process of remembrance—thus supporting the development of meaning.

SOURCE: Adapted from Colorado Collaboration on End-of-Life Care (no date).

strategies and tactics used by the helper must be carefully adapted to the specific characteristics of the family in question and to its cultural or ethnic background.

These are only a few examples. The principle is that *coping tasks can become guidelines for helpers if these tasks always are appreciated in their concrete, specific, and*

A hospice teen volunteer spends time with a person with a life-threatening illness.

individual circumstances. For example, as they talk together, a dying person and a helper might agree upon a number of coping tasks that could be undertaken. An astute helper will then make it possible for the dying person to determine which (if any) task(s) should be undertaken first and when, and even to change those decisions as time passes. This enhances the autonomy of the dying person and acknowledges the measure of control that he or she still retains at a time when so much may be out of control. Here the helper fosters a sense of security even when much is not safe in the dying person's life.

Individuals who are coping with dying may surprise us with their choices of tasks that are important to them at any given moment. They may be more concerned to have a beloved pet in their company than to permit visits from some human beings who are not very close friends. They may still be preoccupied with how they look or with a diet program. They may find more comfort in talking to a hospital janitor than to a psychiatrist. They may be more grateful to someone who cleans their eyeglasses, gives them a back rub, or trims their ingrowing toenails than to the chaplain who offers spiritual advice. They may be more interested in one last taste of a fast food hamburger and French fries—what the British describe as "a little of what you fancy" (Willans, 1980)—than in the carefully planned nutritional meals from the dietary department.

This range of reactions simply reminds us once again that dying persons are living human beings. They need to sing their own songs, to live out their own lives in ways that they find appropriate and not be "killed softly" by somebody else's song. This is not to imply that helpers should be merely passive. One can suggest things to do, offer options, and provide opportunities. Sometimes it is important to urge people rather strongly to do something they do not want to do but would serve their needs in ways they may not yet have realized or appreciated. Experienced caregivers learn when to be a bit insistent in matters like this and when to back off. However, in the end, decision making must rest primarily with the person being helped, not with the helper.

Helpers of all types need to listen to and be guided by the dying persons; otherwise, they are merely imposing their own agenda on the other person. When one learns that someone is coping with dying, strong feelings well up and one's urge may be to try to make everything right again. Although that is frequently not possible, one should not conclude that nothing is possible. As long as an individual is alive, it is always possible to do something to improve the quality of his or her life. For this, it is desirable to move toward (not away from) the person who is coping with dying.

What one does is not always or even mainly of primary importance. What counts is that one's actions show that one cares. Often, the action can be something simple and concrete. The gesture may not be accepted; it may not even be acknowledged. Dying persons (like everyone else) can be grumpy or exhausted. For those who care, that will not matter too much, because the gesture is made for the sake of the other person, not for one's own sake.

Just as one should begin with the person to be helped wherever he or she is, not where the helper thinks that person should be, so too helpers should begin with themselves wherever they are, with their own talents, strengths, and limitations. Sharing honest emotions or feelings of uncertainty can be a good way to start. Laughing, listening in an interested and nonjudgmental way, and just silently being present are often appreciated. Avoiding insensitive clichés is a good idea (Linn, 1986). Offering help in specific and practical ways is desirable. Conveying one's own sense of hope and sharing (often in nonverbal ways) one's conviction that the life of the other person is and has been meaningful in one's own life can be an eloquent form of caring. Holding a dying person's hand and crying with that person speaks volumes when words are not really possible.

Effective Communication

In the past, our death system often advised us not to speak candidly to dying persons about their diagnoses and prognoses (for example, Oken, 1961; recall our discussion of closed awareness contexts in Chapter 6). It was thought that candor would undercut hope and the will to live or even encourage people to end their own lives. There is, in fact, no evidence that this did or does take place. Even so, the key issue in effective communication is whether specific acts of communication are responsive to the needs of dying persons and are carried out in a thoughtful and caring way (Zittoun, 1990). The content of the communication may not be as important as the ways in which it is expressed and understood. One can brutalize a vulnerable person with the truth, just as one can harm with falsehood.

For the most part, our death system now encourages speaking with greater candor to dying persons about their diagnoses and prognoses (Novack et al., 1979). Many things caused this change, including our contemporary emphasis on informed consent and the patients' rights (President's Commission, 1982; Rozovsky, 1990). Consent to professional intervention or any sort of supportive treatment cannot be freely given unless it is based on information needed to understand the current situation, the nature of the proposed intervention, and its likely outcome(s). Even in the direst of situations, the necessary information can be provided in a caring manner and consent obtained in ways that foster the dignity of all who are involved.

There are two good examples of how to enhance effective communication in coping with dying. First, Buckman (1992) offered a set of suggestions about how to break bad news (see Table 7.1). Never an easy task, it is essential both for the person who needs to know about his or her own situation and for the helper who needs to convey information and confirm that he or she can be relied on in this way. The steps suggested in Table 7.1 are not necessarily a universal scenario, but they do point to a larger literature on preparing helpers to communicate effectively (for example, Buckman, 1988; Cassell, 1985; Faulkner, 1993).

In addition, Callanan and Kelley (1992) explored what they call "nearing death awareness." This concept recognizes that communications from dying persons are too often dismissed as empty or enigmatic expressions of confusion. Instead, Callanan and Kelley argue that such communications may actually reflect either (1) special awareness of the imminence of death and efforts to describe what dying is like as it is being experienced by the individual, or (2) expressions of final requests about what is needed before the individual can

Table 7.1 How to Break Bad News: A Six-Step Protocol

Step 1	Start carefully: get the physical context right; if humanly possible, speak face to face, in an appropriate setting, and with attention to who should be present.
Step 2	Find out how much the person already knows: listen for intellectual understanding, communicative style, and emotional content.
Step 3	Find out how much the person wants to know: determine at what level the person wants to know what is going on; offer willingness to explore matters further in the future.
Step 4	Share the information: start from the person's point of view; have an agenda with desired objectives; share information in small chunks, in plain, nontechnical language; check reception frequently; reinforce and clarify information frequently; check communication levels; listen for the person's concerns; blend your agenda with that of the person.
Step 5	Respond to the person's feelings: identify and acknowledge the person's reactions.
Step 6	Plan for the future and follow through.

SOURCE: Based on Buckman, 1992.

experience a peaceful death. This list draws attention to a special set of communicative tasks undertaken by dying persons and, once more, stresses the indispensable role of active listening.

Effective communication is an important part of fostering hope and quality in living when individuals are coping with dying. It is also important in self-care and in obtaining assistance in meeting the needs of helpers themselves. How one communicates with those one is trying to help can become a model for all helping interactions. The challenge in helping others appears on two basic levels: (1) to keep company with the dying and with others who are coping with dying—even when that requires one to be comfortable with one's own discomfort and to do nothing more than to sit quietly together in silence; and (2) to learn how to identify and respond effectively to the particular physical, psychological, social, and spiritual tasks that are part of a specific individual's coping with dying. The challenge in helping oneself lies in learning to use effective communication to find greater satisfaction in the helping role and to seek from others the professional and personal support that all helpers need.

Helping Helpers: Burnout and Self-Care

A task-based approach to coping with dying reminds helpers that they also have their own coping to consider and that self-care is essential in preventing caregiver burnout (Corr, 1992c; Grollman, 1995b). Helpers, whether they are family members, volunteers, or professionals, are also human beings with needs and limitations. One does not have to be dying to be important. Helpers must not overburden their own resources. Otherwise, they may become unable to give any further assistance. The best helpers are those who operate from a foundation in a rich and satisfying life of their own, not from a sense that they are overwhelmed by stressors and problems of their own (Larson, 1993).

In the videotape *The Heart of the New Age Hospice* (1987), one woman with a life-threatening illness described the foundation for helping others in the following way: "Duty without love is preposterous. Duty with love is acceptable. Love without duty is divine." Helpers cannot operate solely from their own need to be needed. They must care about those whom they are helping, but their love must also include themselves. The best helpers are those who can also take care of themselves and who take time to meet their own needs. In other words, helpers must strive for a balance between too much involvement and too much distance in their interactions with the needs of others (Papadatou, 2000). The desired balance, often called "detached concern" (Larson, 1993) or "detached compassion" (Pattison, 1977), involves entering into the situation of the person being helped in a way that enables the helper to continue to function effectively in the helping role. Such a posture must be achieved in individual ways by each helper and certainly requires considerable self-awareness. Nouwen (1972) made this point by suggesting that caregivers must recognize that they are "wounded healers."

In recent years, *stress and burnout in helpers* have been the subject of much study (for example, Selye, 1978b). One interesting finding is that stress more often arises from the situation within which one is working and the colleagues with whom one works than from the fact that one is working with dying persons and others who are coping with dying (Vachon, 1979, 1987). In each case, then, one must carefully examine the specific sources of stress and the mediators that may modify that stress in various ways (Friel & Tehan, 1980). Thoughtful programs to address stress include such elements as careful staff selection, training, supervision, and support. When such a program is coupled with the development of an individual philosophy of care and attention to one's own needs for care (whether self-care or care from others), helping those who are coping with dying need not be more stressful than many other activities in our society (Harper, 1994; LaGrand, 1980; Lattanzi, 1983, 1985).

Many of the basic elements in an effective program of managing stress and taking care of oneself are found in a series of suggestions set forth in Table 7.2 and in what Hans Selye (1978a, p. 70) called "a kind of recipe for the best antidote to the stresses of life":

Table 7.2 Suggestions for Stress Management and Self-Care

Be proactive: Effective intervention begins with good prevention.

Take charge: Adopt an active strategy of coping focused on one or more of the following—your appraisal of the stressful situation and its sources, what you can do about the situation, or what you can do about your own reactions to the situation.

Set limits: Seek a dynamic balance between demands and resources; limit time and involvements with those you are helping.

Compartmentalize: Put some physical and psychological distance between your home life and your work life.

Develop a stress-hardy outlook:

- Strive to view potentially stressful situations as challenges—that is, as opportunities for growth rather than as threats.
- Strive to balance your commitments to work, family, and friendships.
- Strive to develop the conviction that life's experiences are—within limits—within your control (and a sense of humor that helps to keep stress and striving in perspective).

Practice the art of the possible: Do what you can even though there is always much that you cannot do; be patient and creative.

Improve your communication and conflict resolution skills: Stress often arises when you are caring and compassionate, but do not know what to say or what to do.

Rejuvenate yourself: Employ techniques of exercise, relaxation, and meditation in self-care because stress is unavoidable.

Know yourself: Befriend yourself; be gentle with your inner discomforts.

Maintain and enhance your self-esteem: Develop a positive view of your skills and yourself; doing good can help you to feel good; recognizing your commitment to meaningful work can help you feel better about yourself.

Strengthen your social support: Encouragement, support, and feedback can enhance self-esteem and your sense of self-efficacy.

SOURCE: Based on Larson, 1993.

> The first ingredient . . . is to seek your own stress level, to decide whether you're a racehorse or a turtle and to live your life accordingly. The second is to choose your goals and make sure they're really your own, and not imposed on you . . . And the third ingredient to this recipe is altruistic egoism—looking out for oneself by being necessary to others, and thus earning their goodwill.

Good helpers need to be open to suggestions and support from other persons—even from the dying person or the family they are helping. Indeed, when dying persons are freed from the burden of distressing symptoms and made to feel secure, they can often be very thoughtful and sensitive in caring for those around them. In short, none of us is without needs in coping with someone else's mortality or with our own mortality. We all can benefit from help as we look to our own tasks in coping.

Hope

This brings us to the subject of *hope.* Sometimes it is said that there is no more hope for dying persons, that they are hopeless cases, and that working with the dying must be a hopeless endeavor. Such assertions reveal a narrow understanding of the role that hope plays in human lives (Corr, 1981; Cousins, 1989). We hope for all sorts of things. I hope that someone will (continue to) love me. He hopes that he can have his favorite food for dinner tonight. She hopes to be able to see her sister again. Many of us hope to live as long as we possibly can. Some dying persons hope to live until a special birthday, a holiday, or the birth of a new grandchild. Many hope for an outcome grounded in their spiritual convictions. Perhaps we all hope that our own situation and the situations of those we love will be at least a little bit better while we are dying and after our deaths. Here, hope for a cure may give way to hope for a good dying and death (Webb, 1997). Helpers hope that their interventions will make a difference even in a life that may soon be over. Until death comes, most of us hope that whatever it is that is making us uncomfortable will be reduced or removed from our lives. This last hope—like many other hopes that we may entertain—cannot always be realized. Still, it is only one hope among many.

Few situations in life are ever completely hopeless. So when someone says, "This situation is hopeless," it may just signify a failure of imagination. Often, it represents the point of view of an outsider (for example, a care provider) and his or her judgment that there is no likelihood of cure for the person in the situation. Usually, this type of statement indicates that the speaker has focused exclusively on a single hope or a narrow range of hopes that cannot be realized in a specific set of circumstances. It would be far better to appreciate the therapeutic potential of hope—even in a tongue-in-cheek way (see Box 7.6).

In fact, "hope, which centers on fulfilling expectations, may focus on getting well, but more often focuses on what yet can be done" (Davidson, 1975, p. 49). Hope is a characteristically human phenomenon (Veninga, 1985). But it is fluid, often altering its focus to adapt to changes in the actual circumstances within

Box 7.6 A Tongue-in-Cheek Comment on Hope

After all, hope contains no mono or polyunsaturated fats, cholesterol, sugars, artificial sweeteners, flavors or colors; it's classified as "generally recognized as safe" by the FDA and is a known anticarcinogen. ■

SOURCE: Munson, 1993, p. 24.

which we find ourselves. Again, we must listen carefully to each individual—including hope in those who are trying to help people cope with dying—in order to determine the object of his or her hope. We must also distinguish between hope, which is founded in reality, and unrealistic wishes, which merely express fanciful desires.

Summary

In this chapter, we explored ways in which professionals and laypersons can each contribute to helping those who are coping with dying. We considered four primary dimensions in such care (physical, psychological, social, and spiritual) and we drew on a task-based model as a source of guidelines for helping both others and oneself. Our discussion concluded with some comments on effective communication, helping those who are helping others in their coping with dying, and hope.

Questions for Review and Discussion

1. Think about some moment in your life when someone you loved was quite ill or dying. What was most stressful for you at that time? What did you do or what might you have done that you now think was helpful or unhelpful to the person who was ill or dying?

2. In this chapter, we described four dimensions or aspects of care for the dying: physical, psychological, social, and spiritual. Think about someone you know who was or is dying (or use the example of the Amish man described near the beginning of Chapter 3 or Jo and Matt Ryan whom we described near the beginning of Chapter 6 and again at the outset of this chapter). In the case that you select, how did these four dimensions or aspects of care show up?

3. In this chapter, we pointed out that effective communication is or can be important both for dying persons and for those who are helping such persons. Why is communication important for the dying and their helpers? What makes for effective communication among such people? What is an example from your own experience of poor communication? Of good communication?

4. In this chapter, we suggested that hope is or can be important both for dying persons and for those who are helping such persons. How can hope be important for those who know they will soon be dead or for those who know that the person for whom they are caring will soon be dead? What does hope mean to you?

Suggested Readings

The lives and motivations of two women who have been pioneers in care of the dying are described in:

DuBoulay, S. (1984). *Cicely Saunders: The Founder of the Modern Hospice Movement.*

Gill, D. L. (1980). *Quest: The Life of Elisabeth Kübler-Ross.*

Kübler-Ross, E. (1997). *The Wheel of Life: A Memoir of Living and Dying.*

For guidance on ways in which to help persons who are coping with dying, see:

Bertman, S. L. (Ed.). (1999). *Grief and the Healing Arts: Creativity as Therapy.*

Buckman, R. (1988). *I Don't Know What to Say: How to Help and Support Someone Who Is Dying.*

Buckman, R. (1992). *How to Break Bad News: A Guide for Health Care Professionals.*

Byock, I. (1997). *Dying Well: The Prospect for Growth at the End of Life.*

Callanan, M., & Kelley, P. (1992). *Final Gifts: Understanding the Special Awareness, Needs, and Communications of the Dying.*

Cassell, E. J. (1985). *Talking with Patients: Vol. 1, The Theory of Doctor-Patient Communication; Vol. 2, Clinical Technique.*

Cassell, E. J. (1991). *The Nature of Suffering and the Goals of Medicine.*

Davies, B., Reimer, J. C., Brown, P., & Martens, N. (1995). *Fading Away: The Experience of Transition in Families with Terminal Illness.*

Doyle, D., Hanks, G. W. C., & MacDonald, N. (Eds.). (1998). *Oxford Textbook of Palliative Medicine* (2nd ed.).

Kemp, C. (1995). *Terminal Illness: A Guide to Nursing Care.*

Landay, D. S. (1998). *Be Prepared: The Complete Financial, Legal, and Practical Guide for Living with a Life-Threatening Condition.*

Lynn, J., Schuster, J. L., & Kabcenell, A. (2000). *Improving Care for the End of Life: A Sourcebook for Health Care Managers and Clinicians.*

Melzack, R., & Wall, P. D. (1991). *The Challenge of Pain* (3rd ed.).

Parkes, C. M., Relf, M., & Couldrick, A. (1996). *Counseling in Terminal Care and Bereavement.*

Randall, F., & Downie, R. S. (1999). *Palliative Care Ethics: A Companion for All Specialties* (2nd ed.).

Rosen, E. J. (1990). *Families Facing Death: Family Dynamics of Terminal Illness.*

Saunders, C. M., & Sykes, N. (Eds.). (1993). *The Management of Terminal Malignant Disease* (3rd ed.).

Saunders, C. M., Baines, M., & Dunlop, R. (1995). *Living with Dying: A Guide to Palliative Care* (3rd ed.).

Storey, P. (1996). *Primer of Palliative Care* (2nd ed.).

Twycross, R. G. (1994). *Pain Relief in Advanced Cancer.*

Twycross, R. G. (1995a). *Introducing Palliative Care.*
Twycross, R. G. (1995b). *Symptom Management in Advanced Cancer.*
Wall, P. D., & Melzack, R. (Eds.). (1994). *Textbook of Pain* (3rd ed.).

Support for family and other helpers is discussed in:

Corr, C. A. (1992c). *Someone You Love Is Dying: How Do You Cope?*
Grollman, E. A. (1980). *When Your Loved One Is Dying.*
Harper, B. C. (1994). *Death: The Coping Mechanism of the Health Professional* (rev. ed.).
Larson, D. G. (1993). *The Helper's Journey: Working with People Facing Grief, Loss, and Life-Threatening Illness.*
Vachon, M. L. S. (1987). *Occupational Stress in the Care of the Critically Ill, the Dying, and the Bereaved.*

InfoTrac College Edition
For more information, explore the InfoTrac College Edition at **http://www.infotrac-college.com/Wadsworth**

Enter search terms: BURNOUT, DIMENSIONS OF CARE, EFFECTIVE COMMUNICATION, HOPE.

Chapter Eight

COPING WITH DYING: HOW COMMUNITIES CAN HELP

IN THIS CHAPTER, WE AGAIN CONSIDER HOW to help persons who are coping with dying, but this time we focus on ways that American society has implemented helping principles within formal programs of care. Programs of this sort are typically associated with an *institution*, defined as "a complex interaction of professionals, paraprofessionals, and the public, on informational, economic, and occupational levels, in identifiable physical environments, whose coordinated decisions and actions have magnified public impact" (Jonsen & Helleghers, 1974, p. x). Institutions like this are always based in some physical facility, but it is the services they offer to persons who are coping with dying that are really critical. The primary institutions that are relevant here are hospitals or medical centers, long-term care facilities (often called nursing homes), home health care programs, and hospice programs. Each of these institutions specializes in a particular type of care: hospitals focus on *acute care*, long-term care facilities on *chronic care*, home health programs on *home care*, and hospice programs on *end-of-life care*. But all of these institutions at one time or another become involved in care for persons who are coping with dying.

In this chapter, we ask: (1) What, in principle, are the desirable elements of an institutional program of care for those who are coping with dying? and (2) What, in practice, does each of the four institutions that we have identified contribute to this work in our society? We also outline the historical development and contemporary role of these four institutions, and we try to show how each responds in its own ways to the needs of persons who are coping with dying.

We give particular attention in this chapter to hospice programs because they are the newest social institution offering care for those who are coping with dying, the only one that has been designed specifically for this purpose, and the one that may be least familiar to readers. In its traditional use, the term hospice designated a kind of way station for travelers on a journey, as in St. Bernard's Hospice in the Alps. In its modern use, the term identifies both *a philosophy of care* and *an organized program* that seeks to implement that philosophy.

As *a philosophy or approach to care*, we view hospice as a form of palliative care for those who are coping with dying. Here, we describe the hospice philosophy in terms of ten principles of care. As *an organized, practical program for delivering care* to those who are coping with dying, hospice has developed ways to implement its philosophy both through its own services and in cooperative arrangements with hospitals, long-term care facilities, and various forms of home health care that address (at least in part) similar needs. Both as a philosophy of care and as an organized program of care, hospice has also helped to influence and bring about changes in the American health care system, as we will show in comments on the phrase "palliative care" later in this chapter.

In brief, in this chapter we turn from describing the work of individual helpers (see Chapter 7) to outlining social programs for and principles behind institutional care of those who are coping with dying and to discussing the realities of that care in our death system. We introduce these topics by returning to the example of Matt and Jo Ryan whom we first met in the vignettes near the beginning of Chapters 6 and 7, and by describing growing awareness of the need for better end-of-life care. ■

Social Institutions That Helped Matt and Josephina Ryan Cope with Life-Threatening Illness and Dying

Some of the care that Matt and Josephina Ryan needed was provided by a local hospital. Each of them was diagnosed and received their initial treatments there, and both of them were seen for a time in the hospital's outpatient clinics after their initial surgeries. Matt was fortunate that he needed no further care other than regular follow-up observations. Unfortunately, Jo's situation was more complicated, especially when she faced the demands of her advanced illness. A community home health care program was helpful for a time, with its regular visits from nursing personnel during daytime and weekday hours.

Nevertheless, as her health declined, Jo's needs grew and she was unwilling at that time to remain at home because she was afraid of what might happen and did not want to have her family members take on what she perceived as the burdens of her care.

At that point, the security and gentle pace of a local nursing home that had cared for her mother before her death seemed to offer Jo a good, temporary alternative. She liked the slower pace of the nursing home and even made some friends there at first. But as time went on, Jo found that many of the residents were older than her; some seemed confused and were unable to sustain a relationship. Matt had always been unsure about whether it was a good idea to have Jo stay in any type of facility and he very much missed her at home. The last straw came when one of the residents unwittingly frightened Tom's children, and his family visited less often after that.

Jo felt very much alone and overwhelmed by her problems until someone suggested that she talk with a representative of their local hospice program. That led to a transfer to the hospice inpatient unit. Expert care and the support of the whole hospice team for Jo and her family helped minimize sources of distress and improve their quality of life. Jo's pain and other symptoms were now managed effectively, and both her physical condition and her spirits improved greatly. Jo felt that she had almost miraculously regained control of her life.

Ultimately, with support from the hospice home care team, Jo was even able to go home to be with Matt and her family for several months. In the end, with help from the hospice team, she died in her own bed at home. Before her death Jo marveled that the hospice staff and volunteers took time to just sit and be with her. This form of care seemed so different because the helpers did not spend all of their time talking about disease, treatments, and death.

Recognizing and Responding to the Needs of Persons Who Are Coping with Dying

"What people need most when they are dying is relief from distressing symptoms of disease, the security of a caring environment, sustained expert care, and assurance that they and their families will not be abandoned" (Craven & Wald, 1975, p. 1816). This single sentence itemizes many of the concerns of those who are dying and what they need from institutional programs of care.

During the 1960s and 1970s, some caregivers began to wonder whether care provided to those who were dying was properly recognizing and responding to their needs. Studies conducted in Great Britain (for example, Hinton, 1963; Rees, 1972), Canada (for instance, Mount et al., 1974), and the United States (such as Marks & Sachar, 1973) confirmed that the answer was no. Two points seemed to be central: (1) caregivers did not always realize or acknowledge the level of pain and other forms of distress being experienced by individuals who were dying; (2) caregivers did not always have or believe that they had at their disposal effective resources to respond to the needs of those who were dying. What this meant in practice was that those who were dying were often told:

"Your pain cannot be as bad as you say it is"; "You can't really be feeling like that"; "You will just have to get hold of yourself"; "We cannot offer stronger dosages of narcotic analgesics or you will risk becoming addicted"; "We have to save the really strong medications until they are truly needed"; "There is nothing more that we can do."

It is unfortunate when caregivers who want to help do not have the resources to do so. Thus, many were grateful when new forms of narcotic analgesics became available for use to help dying persons. But it is tragic when the needs of those who are dying are not recognized and when that is compounded by inadequate understanding or misguided fears about whether or how to mobilize available resources to meet those needs.

New perspectives were required on several key points, including:

- The situation of those who are coping with dying (Noyes & Clancy, 1977; Pattison, 1977)
- The nature of pain when one is dying (LeShan, 1964; Melzack & Wall, 1991; Wall & Melzack, 1994)
- Appropriate therapeutic regimes for those who are dying (these were first thought to depend upon certain analgesic mixtures like the "Brompton cocktail" or the unique properties of heroin but were later shown to involve carefully selected narcotics, other medications, and complementary therapeutic interventions [Melzack et al., 1979; Melzack et al., 1976; Twycross, 1976, 1979a])
- The value of holistic, person-centered care and interdisciplinary teamwork (Corr & Corr, 1983; Saunders & Sykes, 1993)
- Ways in which the social organization of programs serving those coping with dying affect the care provided (Saunders, 1990; Sudnow, 1967)

These new elements are all embodied in the hospice philosophy and have been implemented in hospice programs. Some of these elements have also been incorporated in other programs of care for those who are coping with dying.

During the 1990s, increasing interest in end-of-life care was evident in a growing body of literature (for example, Byock, 1997; Webb, 1997) and a study commissioned by the Institute of Medicine (Field & Cassel, 1997). Evidence from large-scale research studies identified ongoing deficiencies in end-of-life care. A key study provided quantitative data from controlled, clinical research conducted in five teaching hospitals in the United States (SUPPORT Principal Investigators, 1995). The SUPPORT (Study to Understand Prognoses and Preferences for Outcomes and Risks of Treatments) project examined end-of-life preferences, decision making, and interventions in a total of 9,105 adults hospitalized with one or more of nine life-threatening diagnoses. The two-year first phase of the study observed 4,301 patients and documented substantial shortcomings in communication, overuse of aggressive cure-oriented treatment at the very end of life, and undue pain preceding death. The two-year second phase of the study compared the situations of 4,804 patients randomly assigned to intervention and control groups with each other and with baseline data from Phase 1. Physicians with the intervention group received improved computer-based prognostic information on their patients' status. Moreover, a specially trained nurse was assigned to the intervention group in each hospital to carry out multiple contacts with patients, families, physicians, and hospital staff in order to elicit preferences, improve understanding of outcomes, encourage better attention to pain control, facilitate advance care planning, and enhance patient-physician communication.

The SUPPORT study used the following criteria to evaluate outcomes: the timing of written "Do not resuscitate" orders; patient and physician agreement (based on the first interview between them) on whether to withhold resuscitation; the number of days before death spent in an intensive care unit either receiving mechanical ventilation or comatose; the frequency and severity of pain; and the use of hospital resources. Results were discouraging. Phase 2 intervention "failed to improve care or patient outcomes" (p. 1591) and led the investigators to conclude that "we are left with a troubling situation. The picture we describe of the care of seriously ill or dying persons is not attractive" (p. 1597). This is disheartening in light of the scope of the study, its capacity to measure targeted outcomes,

the careful design of its interventions, the existence of a well-established professional knowledge base and models within our health system for this type of care, and the degree of ethical, legal, public, and policy-making attention recently directed to issues related to end-of-life decision making and quality of care. Unfortunately, some similar results have been confirmed by other studies drawing on the SUPPORT project (for example, Krumholz et al., 1998).

Another recent study, "Living and Healing During Life-Threatening Illness" (Supportive Care of the Dying: A Coalition for Compassionate Care, 1997), used a qualitative methodology involving focus groups at 11 selected sites in Catholic health care systems across the United States. A total of 407 participants ranging in age from 18 to 93 were brought together between March and June, 1996, in small groups of 3 to 10 persons organized in one of five categories: persons with life-threatening illnesses; personal/family caregivers; bereaved persons; professional caregivers; and community members. The overall results of the study suggested that health care systems in our society needed to change in important ways if they were to serve the needs of persons who are coping with dying. Clearly, there is much to be done at all levels—by individuals to the community and its professionals, and by health care organizations and systems—to improve end-of-life care in our society.

Hospice Philosophy and Principles

Both the Canadian Palliative Care Association (1995) and the National Hospice and Palliative Care Organization (2000) in the United States have established standards for hospice care. Drawing on work by NHPCO, Connor (1998, pp. 3–4) has defined "hospice care" as:

> . . . a coordinated program providing palliative care to terminally ill patients and supportive services to patients, their families, and significant others 24 hours a day, seven days a week. Comprehensive/case managed services based on physical, social, spiritual, and emotional needs are provided during the last stages of illness, during the dying process, and during bereavement by a medically directed interdisciplinary team consisting of patients/families, health care professionals and volunteers. Professional management and continuity of care is maintained across multiple settings including homes, hospitals, long term care and residential settings.

We can summarize the hospice philosophy and its central principles in the following ten points.

1. *Hospice is a philosophy, not a facility—one whose primary focus is on end-of-life care.* In England, the hospice movement began by building its own facilities. This reflected the social situation and health care system in a particular country at a specific time. Going outside existing structures in this way is one classic route for innovation. However, it is not the facility in which hospice care is delivered that is essential; the main thing is the principles that animate services

and the quality of the care itself. The philosophy of care—outlook, attitude, approach—is central in hospice care, along with its focus on persons who are coping with dying (Egan & Labyak, 2001).

2. *The hospice philosophy affirms life, not death.* Dying is a self-limiting condition. Individuals can and will die by themselves, without assistance from others. The hard work is supporting life, not bringing about death. Helping a person to live may be especially difficult when that person is close to death and is experiencing distress in dying. Processes of dying often impose special pressures on quality in living. Hospice cares for and about persons who are coping with dying because they are living and struggling with these special pressures.

3. *The hospice philosophy strives to maximize present quality in living.* We think of hospice as a form of palliative or symptom-oriented care that tries to minimize discomfort. Without abandoning interest in cure, hospice care is focused on other forms of caring when cure is no longer a reasonable expectation. This is not merely the opposite of "active treatment" (an inaccurate phrase that usually is used to mean cure-oriented treatment), for that would make it merely some passive mode of care. In fact, "the care of the dying patient is an active treatment peculiar to the dying patient" (Liegner, 1975, p. 1048). Thus, hospice is an active and aggressive mode of care whose focus is on the alleviation of distressing symptoms, as well as on prospects for personal growth at the end of life, even when the underlying condition from which distress arises cannot be halted or reversed. As Saunders (1976, p. 674) observed, this represents "the unique period in the patient's illness when the long defeat of living can be gradually converted into *a positive achievement in dying*" (our italics).

Art therapy can stimulate creativity even in dying persons.

4. *The hospice approach offers care to the patient-and-family unit.* This means that both the dying person and those whom he or she regards as "family" form the unit receiving care and helping to give care. Hospice care seeks to provide a sense of security and the support of a caring environment for all who are involved in coping with dying—ill persons together with their families, friends, and other involved persons (Egan, 1998).

5. *Hospice is holistic care.* Recognizing that people being served are persons, whole human beings, hospice care assists them in working with their physical, psychological, social, and spiritual tasks. It seeks to enhance quality in living in each of these dimensions.

6. *Hospice offers continuing care and ongoing support to bereaved survivors after the death of someone they love.* Care for family members and friends does not cease with the death of the person they love, as we will see in Chapters 10 and 11 when we discuss how to help the bereaved.

7. *The hospice approach combines professional skills and human presence through interdisciplinary teamwork.* Special expertise in end-of-life care and in the management of distressing symptoms is essential. Expert medical and nursing care are critical. However, the availability of human companionship is equally important. Professional caregivers can offer human presence, but it is often a special gift of hospice volunteers. Appropriate use of one's expertise and one's presence is dependent upon being available and actively listening to understand correctly the needs of dying persons and their family members. Interdisciplinary teamwork demands respect for the special skills and abilities of others, time to exchange information and insights, and a certain amount of "role blurring" in assisting all whom the hospice program is serving.

8. *Hospice programs make services available on a 24-hour-a-day, 7-day-a-week basis.* Hospice seeks to recreate caring communities to help dying persons and their families. Wherever such communities already exist naturally and whenever dying persons and their families are not experiencing significant distress, there may be no need for formal hospice programs. When and where a need does exist, these programs must be available around the clock, just as a caring community is—perhaps through phone contacts or the ability to have a caregiver come to the dying person's bedside wherever that person may be.

9. *Participants in hospice programs give special attention to supporting each other.* Caring for those who are coping with dying and/or bereavement and working within the structure of an interdisciplinary team can be stressful. Thus, hospice programs offer both formal and informal programs of support for their own staff members and volunteers.

10. *The hospice philosophy can be applied to a variety of individuals and their family members who are coping with a life-threatening illness, dying, death, and/or bereavement.* In its modern usage, hospice has primarily been concerned with illnesses like cancer and their implications mainly for older adults. But the hospice philosophy need not be restricted to these conditions. To benefit from the hospice philosophy, there must be time and opportunity to bring services to bear upon the tasks of the patient-and-family unit. Thus, hospice care requires some

advance notice that dying has begun and death is imminent (in a matter of days, weeks, or months), some willingness to accept the benefits and restrictions of hospice care, and an opportunity to mobilize services in particular circumstances. Given these conditions, the hospice philosophy can apply, in principle, to a broad range of diseases at the end of life (such as HIV/AIDS and end-stage renal, cardiac, and Alzheimer's disease) and to situations involving children and adolescents.

Four Programs of Care for Persons Who Are Coping with Dying

Near the beginning of this chapter, we described the experiences of Jo Ryan and her family. We can understand those experiences more fully and come to better appreciate ways in which hospice principles are put into practice by examining the development, role, and functions of the caring institutions and programs that Jo encountered, especially during the last, difficult parts of her life.

Acute Care: Hospitals

In American society, most people receive most of their acute medical care in hospitals, and many people (approximately 50 percent) die there. Hospitals have an ancient origin. The word *hospital* is derived from the medieval Latin *hospitale*, meaning a place of "reception and entertainment of pilgrims, travellers, and strangers" (*Oxford English Dictionary*, 1989, vol. 7, p. 414). *Hospitale* is the basic root of several English terms, including *hostel*, *hotel*, *hospital*, *hospitality*, and *hospice*. In the ancient world, the original places of reception took in pilgrims, travelers, the needy, the destitute, the infirm, the aged, and the sick or wounded. Thus, a broad range of people was served by the ancient *hospitale*. Such institutions were usually associated with some type of religious fraternity or community.

As Western culture became more urbanized and as religious institutions were taken over by secular ones (such as the nation-state or city), hospitals began to change. A division of labor also characterized Western society. Specialization in carrying out tasks became the normal method of operation. No longer did one institution perform many basically different functions; instead, separate institutions now undertook separate functions. These changes took a long time, but they were more or less complete by the end of the 19th century.

In the United States up to the 19th century, care of the sick and dying occurred mainly at home and was provided mainly by family members. Hospitals played virtually no role in such care. In fact, in 1800 there were only two private hospitals in the United States, one in New York and one in Philadelphia (Rosenberg, 1987).

Of course, even in that society, there were persons who were too sick to be cared for at home or who had no one at home to take care of them. If such persons were also poor and could not afford to hire someone to take care of them, they ended up in an *almshouse.* Almshouses were charitable public institutions that housed the insane, the blind, the crippled, the aged, the alcoholic, travelers, and the ordinary workingman with rheumatism or bronchitis or pleurisy. These diverse types of people were freely mixed together. Almshouses most often had large wards, which were usually crowded. Sometimes more than one person had to sleep in a single bed. Because they were usually not well funded, almshouses were typically dark, stuffy, and unpleasant places. Few people entered them voluntarily.

Modern hospitals began to be organized around the beginning of the 19th century. From the outset, they were advocated mainly as having an *educational* function and were not perceived as being primary agents of medical care. These early hospitals had little to offer and were avoided by anyone who could do so. They were expensive for those who could pay their way, "unnatural," and demoralizing. Thus, the physician V. M. Francis (1859, pp. 145–146) wrote just before the outbreak of the Civil War that "the people who repair to hospitals are mostly very poor, and seldom go into them until driven to do so from a severe stress of circumstances. When they cross the threshold, they are found not only suffering from disease, but in a half-starved condition, poor, broken-down wrecks of humanity, stranded on the cold bleak shores of that most forbidding of all coasts, charity."

Until the middle of the 19th century, care provided inside a hospital was usually no better than care that could be obtained elsewhere. The care that was offered mainly involved reporting of symptoms by the patient and "treatment" of such symptoms (usually without much ability to affect their underlying causes) as well as that could be done. This mostly meant allowing the body to heal itself, and in particular not interfering in that process. Basically, what a good hospital provided was a place to rest, shelter from the elements, and decent food. By the time of the Civil War, several dozen hospitals had been founded in the United States. Cities and counties largely built these; only the very poor entered them.

The Civil War during the 1860s brought major changes. For one thing, the understanding of disease changed. Up to this time, as Rosenberg (1987, pp. 71–72) has written, the body was seen as "a system of ever-changing interactions with its environment. . . . Every part of the body was related inevitably and inextricably to every other." Health and disease were seen "as general states of the total organism. . . . The idea of specific disease entities played a relatively small role in this system of ideas and behavior." However, disease now began to be seen as involving specific entities and predictable causes. In the 1860s, Pasteur and Lister contributed to the germ theory of disease. This dramatically changed Western culture's understanding of what caused disease and what could be done to treat disease. Henceforth, science with its theories and technology would change the face of modern medicine. Human bodies were seen as complex machines, disease was thought of as a breakdown in the body's machinery, and therapy involved "fixing" the "malfunctioning part"—or, as we have seen in many cases in the last 25 years, replacing that part. As Rosenberg (1987, p. 85) has written, "This new way of understanding illness necessarily underlined the hospital's importance."

The Civil War itself also taught new ideas. Cleanliness, order, and ventilation were discovered to be of great help in bringing about a return to health. For the first time in American history, people (mostly soldiers) of all social classes experienced care in (military) hospitals. Attitudes toward the hospital were changing.

Immediately after the Civil War, many new hospitals were built. In 1873, there were 178 hospitals in the United States; this number had increased to 4,359 by 1909 (Rosenberg, 1987). Health care—and as a result, dying—was moving into hospitals. (It is interesting to note as an aside that according to Rosenberg [1987, p. 31], one Philadelphia almshouse surgeon complained in 1859 that "dead bodies were often left in the wards and placed directly in coffins while the surviving patients looked on." Some persons believed that this was very hard on the surviving patients, and more or less recommended that such happenings should be hidden from public view. Here is a germ of the idea that Ariès [see Chapter 3] found arising in our time: the denial of death.) From the post–Civil War period on, more and more people would begin to die in hospitals.

This fact produced tension for health care providers and health care recipients alike. As Rosenberg (1987, p. 150) wrote, "Ordinary Americans had . . . begun to accept the hospital. . . . Prospective patients were influenced not only by the hope of healing, but by the image of a new kind of medicine—precise, scientific, and effective." Consequently, hospitals were now expected to be places for the curing of specific diseases. The body's malfunctioning part was to be worked on, made functional, and then the person would get on with his or her life. In this context, death is an unhappy reminder that "scientific" medicine is not always effective—if *effective* is taken to mean capable of producing a cure.

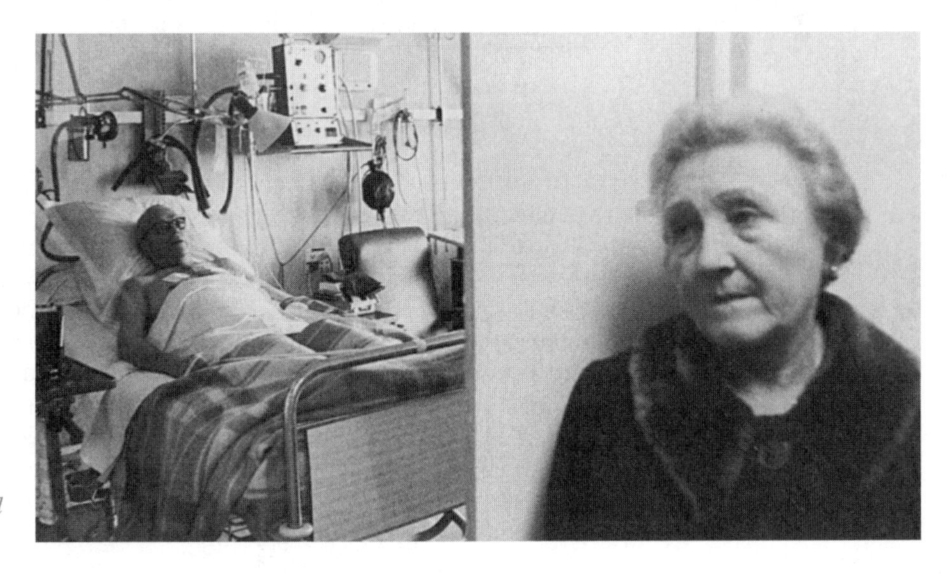

Coping with dying in an institution can intensify feelings of separation and powerlessness.

In this sort of hospital and according to this medical outlook, death is an anomaly, something abnormal. To the health care provider, death may seem to result from personal ineffectiveness. He or she was not able to "fix" the part in the body that was the problem. Thus, death is perceived to involve a kind of failure.

By the end of the 19th century, "moribund patients were systematically transferred to special rooms" (Rosenberg, 1987, p. 292). In some places, whole wards or units were set aside for those who were not expected to recover—out of sight and, to the degree possible, out of mind.

In the 1960s, specific criticisms began to be directed toward the hospital's care (or lack of care) for dying persons. The hospital in our culture is largely an *acute care*, short-term facility. Its purpose is mainly to treat specific diseases and to return people to society with more or less the same functional capacity they had before they became ill. Put simply, hospitals are dominated by medical professionals who see themselves as involved in curing people (Starr, 1982). This is why so many of our hospitals are now called "medical centers" or "health centers."

In our culture, acute care is an expensive business. Diagnostic tools become ever more precise—and costly. The stethoscope is an inexpensive diagnostic tool; the CAT scanner is not. An appendectomy is a relatively inexpensive procedure; a kidney or heart/lung transplant is not. To permit someone to spend time in a hospital when no therapy leading to a cure is available may seem to waste bed space and the time and energy of busy caregivers who have been specially trained in the techniques of cure-oriented intervention. In its historical context, this claim seems to make sense. No wonder economists and health planners became involved in the 1980s in an attempt to make the use of the hospital's expensive services more economically efficient (Stevens, 1989). Consequently, some hospitals were forced to go out of business, reducing their total numbers from nearly 7,000 in 1980 to just over 6,000 in 1998 (U.S. Bureau of the Census, 2000; compare Stolberg, 2001). However, economic efficiency ought not and must not be the sole criterion for acute care institutions. In particular, humane care of dying persons may require bringing additional values into consideration, as Jo Ryan learned when she was in the hospital.

Chronic Care: Long-Term Care Facilities

Another type of institution that Jo Ryan and her family experienced and in which many people die in the United States is the long-term care facility or nursing home. Before the 1930s, there were no nursing homes in this country (Moroney & Kurtz, 1975). They arose as the hospital became more and more an acute care facility and as urbanization helped change the nature of the family from an extended model or group of various relatives living in the same community to a nuclear model usually restricted to husband, wife, and minor children who often lived at a distance from other kin. Also, as average life expectancy increased, many Americans no longer expected to work until just days or hours before their death. They were either unable to work or for various reasons they decided to retire from work well before their death. Many of these people required assistance in caring for themselves and in activities of daily living as they lived out the remainder of their lives. In this, they joined a group of younger *people with chronic diseases or other handicapping conditions* who also experienced problems in taking care of themselves.

These factors led to a situation in which long-term, chronic disability and illness increased while care for people with these conditions became less available. Nursing homes fill this gap in care. In general, they provide a place to live, help with the routine activities of ordinary daily living, and some level of assistance or skilled nursing care. Nursing homes usually do not provide intensive physician care.

Developing mechanisms to offer financial assistance to those who become ill toward the end of their lives played an important part in the development of nursing homes, especially after the passage of the Social Security Act of 1935. With funding available from the personal savings of individuals, from their relatives, from government, and from health insurance and a retirement package (most often provided as a nonsalary benefit by employers), potential providers of care begin to think about offering services to this newly defined population. Primary sources of payment for nursing home residents who are 65 years of age and older now include Medicaid, Medicare, and private sources (such as, private insurance, the resident's own income, family support, social security benefits, and retirement funds).

Until the 1980s, most hospitals did not think of themselves as profit-seeking enterprises. By contrast, many nursing homes have sought both to provide a service and to be a profitable business. Thus, out of a total of 17,000 nursing homes in the United States in 1997 (with 1.8 million beds), 11,400 were owned by their proprietors, while the remaining 5,600 were under voluntary nonprofit, government, or other ownership (U.S. Bureau of the Census, 2000). This puts some pressure on nursing homes, for the sort of care they provide—labor-intensive, round-the-clock care—is expensive. In practice, this has meant that most of those who work in long-term care facilities are nurse aides, thus controlling costs and increasing profits by reducing costs of labor. Since nursing homes often experience high staff turnover, training of new persons, even when such training is minimal, must be constantly repeated. Both for the care provider and the person who is being cared for, this often means that new faces and personalities must be met and learned. This can make the care provided feel discontinuous and uncertain.

In general, long-term care facilities can be divided into several types. (Contact the American Health Care Association at 800-628-8140 or www.ahca.org for a free copy of their pamphlet, "A Consumer's Guide to Nursing Facilities.") First, there are *residential care facilities*, sometimes called shelter care facilities or board-and-care homes. These facilities offer a place to live and to obtain one's basic meals, economies of scale in purchasing, and some companionship for those who are poor, alone, and in need of some attention on more than a short-term basis. Typically, they offer no formal nursing services. As a group, they represent only about 4–5 percent of all long-term care facilities (U.S. Bureau of the Census, 2000).

A second sort of nursing home is the *intermediate care facility*, representing about half of all long-term care facilities. In intermediate care facilities, nursing assistants or aides provide the care with supervision by a professional nurse and with medical guidance or consultation. These facilities serve a segment of the elderly population who require nursing care, together with younger persons who have chronic illnesses or handicapping conditions. Such individuals need assistance with activities of daily living, such as feeding, bathing, and moving around. Some individuals who are confined to a bed or wheelchair need additional help to deal with infirmities and to avoid the development of pressure sores and other debilitating complications.

Finally, there are *skilled nursing care facilities* in which professional nurses under the supervision of a physician provide 24-hour care. These represent nearly half of all long-term care facilities. Failing health in their abilities to care for themselves and to perform activities of daily living typically compromises people in need of skilled nursing care. For example, those in advanced stages of Alzheimer's disease may display disorientation, memory loss, combativeness, and wandering—all of which require constant supervision. Some skilled nursing care facilities serve special populations such as ventilator-dependent patients.

Individuals in nursing homes can generally be divided into two groups: "short stayers," who mostly come from hospitals and who either are rehabilitated and return home or who die in a relatively short period of time; and "long stayers," who are in the home for months or years until they die. The fact that long-term care facilities discharge approximately 30 percent of their residents each year indicates the importance of their rehabilitative role. The occupancy rate in most nursing homes is quite high. Residents in many of these facilities may be very dependent; many are quite elderly, chronically ill, confused, even emotionally disturbed. Such individuals most often lack an available caregiver in the community; they may be single, widowed, childless, and in general, less well off economically than the rest of the population. Although nursing homes provide services to persons needing quite different sorts of care—from those needing brief, intensive rehabilitation to those who are incontinent, mentally impaired, seriously disabled, or very old and very frail—it is the long-term, chronically disabled persons who more and more often occupy nursing home beds.

In 1998, it is estimated that approximately 1.5 million persons 65 years of age or older were residents in long-term care facilities in the United States (U.S. Bureau of the Census, 2000). These residents were overwhelming Caucasian Americans (88.4 percent) and female (75 percent). They included 198,000 people 65–74 years of age (only about 1 percent of individuals in that age group), 528,000 people 75–84 years of age (about 4.4 percent of individuals in that age group), and 738,000 people 85 years of age or older (about 18.2 percent of individuals in that age group). Thus, the notion that to be old in the United States means to be in a nursing home is a misperception; most elderly persons in our society (over 95 percent) do not live in nursing homes. Still, the pressure on long-term care facilities may grow as our population ages and most residents come to need long-term institutional care.

Our society seems content with relatively low overall staff levels of education and compensation in many long-term care facilities. This state of affairs appears to indicate that we do not value properly the increasing importance of such facilities. Nevertheless, many people who work in long-term care

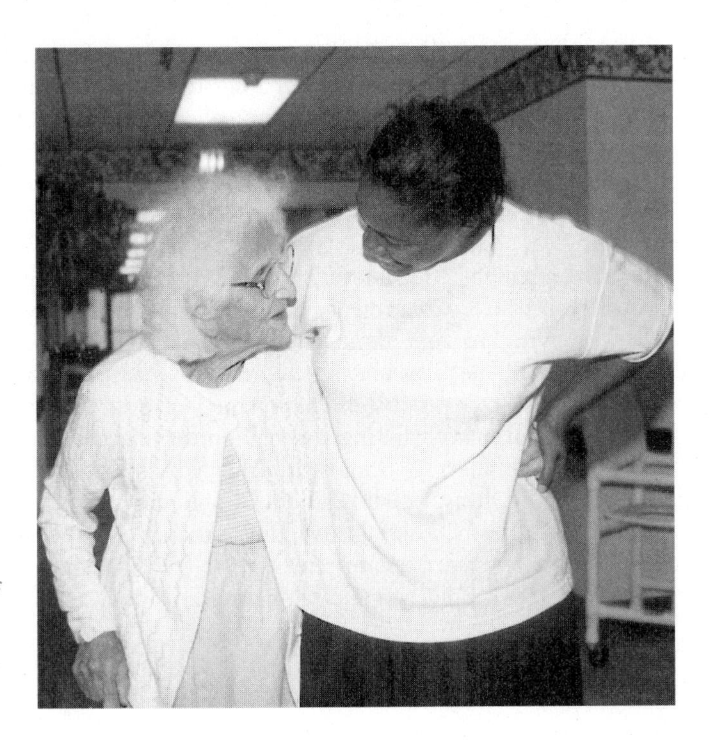

Simply walking together provides physical exercise and strengthens interpersonal bonds.

prefer the slower and more orderly routines of these facilities, along with opportunities to develop long-term personal relationships within them, by contrast with the more hectic pace and rapid patient turnover in acute care (although much of this may not be accurate when these institutions are understaffed).

Many long-term care facilities operate with high standards and quality services for their residents. Still, there are periodic outcries in the media, in the public, and from legislative bodies about the quality of care provided in nursing homes and other long-term care facilities. Many people are dissatisfied with the quality of care in nursing homes, and we are all familiar with aged relatives who plead, "Don't send me to a nursing home."

Quality of living and dying in long-term care facilities can be measured in various ways. One indicator is found in limited contacts between residents and those outside the institution, a situation in which some residents may have no visitors or only a few perhaps on an irregular basis. For many, this suggests disengagement from or diminishment of external social networks. It has also been argued that there is too much isolation when one is dying in a long-term care facility and insufficient attention to bereavement needs of the institutional community, although that may be changing (Shield, 1988). Because of an acute illness or for other reasons, some individuals are transferred from long-term care facilities to acute care hospitals shortly before they die. Nevertheless, approximately 25 percent of all deaths in the United States in 1999 took place in a long-term care facility.

Long-term care facilities provide services that Americans apparently want or need: someone (else) to take care of long-term, chronically disabled, and sometimes dying, people. This may be a choice we are comfortable making. For example, this sort of institutional program was well suited at least for a time to the needs of Jo Ryan and her family. However, an institution designed for long-term care and chronic illness may not be well suited to the requirements of dying persons.

Jo Ryan eventually needed a level and type of services that her nursing home was not able to provide. Situations of this sort contribute to a stereotype often associated with dying persons: alone, afraid, seriously disabled, in unrelieved distress, uncared for, and perhaps uncared about. This stereotype is probably unfair in terms of the actual care provided in many long-term care facilities, but it looms large in the minds of many who may or may not have experienced these institutions with family members or friends. In other words, like hospitals, long-term care facilities do not always provide a comfortable institutional model for dying in our society. Still, both hospitals and long-term care facilities have improved their responses to dying persons in recent years and in many cases have associated themselves with hospice principles or programs of care (NHPCO, 2001b).

Home Care: Home Health Care Programs

Home health care programs have a long history as part of the health care systems in many societies. Such programs can be found in countries like England through its district nurse structure or Canada through its Victorian Order of Nurses (VON). In the United States, many city and county public health departments, the Visiting Nurse Association (VNA), and private home care agencies have traditionally provided home care services.

The rapid growth of home health care in the United States during the last two decades has responded to new needs, together with changes in society and in its health care system. For example, the arrival of HIV infection and AIDS, along with a growing number of frail or confused elders, created new demands for home care. Also, in the 1980s a large number of mental health patients were relocated from psychiatric and other institutions to the community. More recently, federal and other third-party payers placed limitations on inpatient funding (in the form, for example, of "diagnostic-related groups" that capped payment for specific health conditions at a fixed amount), which pressured acute care institutions to discharge patients earlier (often much earlier) than had been previous practice. Some of the factors behind the growth in home health care, such as the desire to limit rising costs in health care by keeping individuals out of expensive institutions as much as possible, are similar to those that gave impetus to the modern hospice movement. In any event, home health care has expanded in many forms, whether it is provided by traditional home health agencies, new home care agencies in the private sector, or newly developed home care departments of hospitals.

Unlike the other three institutions considered in this chapter, home health care programs are not distinguished by a specific kind of illness. All home health care is essentially a form of skilled nursing care (with supplementation in many cases from social services, counseling, pharmacy, physical therapy, home makers, personal care attendants, nutrition, medicine, occupational therapy, and/or speech therapy/audiology). Also, all home health care can be addressed to problems arising from a wide variety of illnesses. The distinctive feature of this form of care is *the location in which it is provided;* home health care programs deliver their services *in the patient's own home.* Medicare, Medicaid, and personal financial resources largely pay for home health care in our society.

Most home health care programs do offer care for dying persons, although they are not primarily or exclusively committed to providing that type of care. Indeed, some staff members in home health care programs have developed broad experience and expertise in caring for dying persons. As caregiving institutions, however, home health care programs usually do not claim specialized expertise in end-of-life care. Most home health care programs that offer skilled nursing care now make services available on a 24-hour-a-day, 7-day-a-week basis. Some home health care programs also offer a multidisciplinary team approach to care, but that may become problematic when third-party payers will not reimburse for some types of services, such as spiritual and/or emotional care. In those circumstances, the home health care program must either depend upon the expertise of its skilled nurses to assess and respond to general family and environmental concerns, or leave additional needs to other community agencies. In short, much home health care is based on diagnostic categories and funding that relate to a desire to control costs, not necessarily to patient or family needs. Of course, these are broad generalizations.

In 1998, there were 13,300 home health care programs in the United States serving nearly 1.9 million patients (U.S. Bureau of the Census, 2000). Some 6,200 of these programs (approximately 47 percent) were owned by their proprietors, about 5,900 (approximately 44.2 percent) were voluntary nonprofit agencies, and less than 1,200 (approximately 8.7 percent) were under government or other ownership.

In recent years, a variety of economic, organizational, and other factors have impacted home health care programs in our society. Although many new home health care programs have been started, some have gone out of business. Others have added a hospice component to their services or may have incorporated some aspects of the hospice philosophy of care in their work. And in some settings, a hospice patient who shows improvement may be discharged to a home health care program until his or her condition worsens and he or she is readmitted to hospice care.

End-of-life Care: Hospice Programs

Hospice programs are the newest addition to the health care system in our society, one that Jo Ryan experienced near the end of her life. As Jo's situation indicates, hospice programs have already become a major way of caring for those who are coping with dying. At the beginning of the 21st century, hospice programs provide an essential service in a cost-effective manner for individuals in our death system. In the United States, however, hospice programs are seldom directly linked to a distinct, identifiable physical environment of the sort that characterizes some other health care institutions. Most hospitals and nursing homes are recognizable facilities in our communities, but hospice programs usually are not so readily identifiable unless they have their own inpatient facility or are associated with a parent institution. That is because hospice is essentially a philosophy of care rather than a facility (as noted earlier in this chapter), and because most hospice care in our society is delivered at home. For this reason, the term "hospice" may be more appropriately used as an adjective to describe a type of care rather than as a noun to identify a place. To appreciate this distinction, we must see how hospice programs developed.

In addition to drawing on age-old human traditions of caring for the dying, hospice programs trace their roots back to medieval institutions that offered rest and support for weary travelers (Stoddard, 1992). In their modern sense, hospice programs offer care for those who are in the final stages of the journey of life. Services are designed primarily to provide care for those who are dying or who have no reasonable hope of benefit from cure-oriented intervention, along with their family members.

One can trace modern hospice care to institutions run by religious orders of nuns in Ireland and England. However, the great impetus came from Dr. (now also Dame) Cicely Saunders who founded St. Christopher's Hospice in southeast London in 1967 (DuBoulay, 1984). Originally a nurse, Dame Cicely retrained as a social worker after injuring her back, and then as a physician in order to pursue her goal of developing and offering better care to the incurably ill and dying. She worked out her views at St. Joseph's Hospice in the East End of London during the 1950s and did research there on medications for the management of chronic pain in those who are dying. Later, she went outside the National Health Service (NHS) in England to found St. Christopher's as a privately owned inpatient facility to implement her theories of clinical practice, research, and education in care of the dying.

At first, it was thought that innovations of this sort could only be undertaken in independent, purpose-built, inpatient facilities. However, in England this original hospice model was later followed by inpatient facilities built with private money and then turned over to the NHS for operation, and eventually by inpatient units within some NHS hospitals (Ford, 1979; Wilkes et al., 1980). England has also seen the development of hospice home care teams designed to support the work of general practitioners and district nurses, as well as hospital support teams that advise on the care of the dying in acute care hospitals (Dunlop & Hockley, 1998) and programs of hospice day care (Wilkes et al., 1978). This development both forms a contrast and is similar to the growth of hospice care as it has developed in North America.

In Canada, Dr. Balfour Mount and his colleagues developed the Palliative Care Service at the Royal Victoria Hospital in Montreal, which came into being in January 1975. This service included an inpatient unit based in a large acute care teaching hospital, a consultation service, a home care service, and a bereavement follow-up program (Ajemian & Mount, 1980). That structure, centered on a hospital-based inpatient unit, seems to be a prominent model for "palliative care" (as the Canadians prefer to call it, since the word "hospice" in French refers to a home for the destitute) in Canada.

In the United States, hospice care began in September 1974 with a community-based home care program in New Haven, Connecticut (Foster et al., 1978; Lack & Buckingham, 1978). Since that time, hospice care has spread across the country. By December 2001, the National Hospice and Palliative Care Organization (NHPCO, 2001c) estimated there were 3,100 operational or planned hospice programs in all 50 states, the District of Columbia, Puerto Rico, and Guam. (For additional information about hospice services, or to find out how to contact a local hospice program, call the Hospice Helpline at 800-658-8898, or contact the National Hospice and Palliative Care Organization, 1700 Diagonal Road, Suite 300, Alexandria, VA 22314; 703-837-1500; fax 703-525-5762; www.nhpco.org).

Hospice programs in the United States in 2000 represented a wide variety of organizational models (NHPCO, 2001c). Approximately 42 percent were independent free-standing agencies, 33 percent were hospital-based, 17 percent were divisions of home health agencies, and 8 percent were based in nursing homes or other auspices. Some 73 percent of hospice programs in the United States were nonprofit in character, 20 percent were for-profit, and 7 percent were government organizations.

In 1982, funding for hospice care was approved as a Medicare benefit (Miller & Mike, 1995). This benefit emphasized home care for elders who qualified for Medicare. Admission criteria typically required a diagnosis of terminal illness, with a prognosis of fewer than six months to live, and the presence of a primary caregiver in the home (although this last requirement no longer applies in most hospice programs). Reimbursement rates are organized in four basic categories: a regular, daily, home care rate (of $110.56 per day as of October 1, 2000); a general inpatient rate (roughly $491.19 per day); $120.23 for short-term respite care; and $644.70 for continuous in-home care (providing for the presence of a trained hospice staff member in specified blocks of time). Each of these rates usually increases over time and is adjusted to take into account different costs in different geographical areas.

Two things are notable about the Medicare hospice benefit, which pays for approximately 65 percent of hospice services (other hospice funding sources include private health insurance, Medicaid, and charitable donations). First, as a federal funding program it emphasizes home care and shifts reimbursement from a retrospective, fee-for-service basis to a prospective, flat-rate basis. Thus, the hospice program receives the amount specified in the regular home care rate for each day in which a dying person is enrolled in its care, regardless of the services it actually provides to that person on any given day.

Second, all monies provided under the Medicare hospice benefit (except for those paid to an attending primary physician) go directly to the hospice program. Thus the program is responsible for designing and implementing each individual plan of care. No service is reimbursed unless it is included in that plan of care and approved by the hospice team, which gives the hospice program an incentive to hold down costs and only to provide care that is relevant to the needs of an individual patient and family unit.

A canine volunteer in hospice care.

The Medicare hospice benefit, which has essentially become a model for other forms of reimbursement for hospice services in the United States, is a desirable option for the individuals who qualify. It is available in all U.S. hospice programs (over 90 percent) that have qualified for Medicare certification. This benefit is subject to change by federal legislation, but it is presently broader than other Medicare benefits and is intended to cover all of the costs of the care provided. Although it does incorporate upper limits on reimbursement to a hospice program, these are expressed in terms of program averages and total benefit days for which the program will be reimbursed, not figures that apply to any particular individual. In fact, as long as a person has been accepted into a Medicare-certified hospice program and continues to qualify for its services, the law prohibits involuntary discharge—whether or not funds are still flowing for reimbursement. In 1997, approximately $2 billion of the Medicare budget of roughly $200 billion was spent on hospice services (NHPCO, 2001). Hospice care is also covered by Medicaid in 43 states and the District of Columbia, as well as by 82 percent of managed care plans and most private insurance plans.

Some have thought that hospice care in the United States has been too closely identified with death. For example, under the Medicare guidelines a patient who enters hospice care must accept the fact that he or she is dying and must agree to forego cure-oriented interventions (although that individual retails the right to withdraw from hospice care at any point). This may be one reason why some minority groups in the United States with strong sanctity of life values, such as African Americans, appear to underutilize opportunities for hospice care.

NHPCO (2001c) estimates that in 2000, hospice programs admitted 700,000 patients and that over 600,000 Americans died while receiving hospice care—approximately 25 percent of all Americans who died that year. In 2000, 56 percent of hospice patients were able to die at home, 16 percent died in a free-standing hospice facility or in a hospice unit, and 19 percent died under hospice care in a nursing home. Average length of enrollment in hospice care in 2000 was 48 days; median length of service was 29 days. According to the

NHPCO (2001c, p. 4), "hospice now cares for over half of all Americans who die from cancer, and a growing number of patients with other chronic, life-threatening illnesses, such as end-stage heart or lung disease" and HIV/AIDS.

Hospice patients in 2000 were described by NHPCO (2001c) as follows:

- Fifty-five percent were female and 45 percent male.
- Eighty-two percent of patients were 65 or older.
- Eighty-two percent were Caucasian Americans, 8 percent were African Americans, and 2 percent were Hispanic Americans.

More than 90 percent of all hospice care hours are provided in patients' homes. In light of the fact that 28 percent of all Medicare costs go toward care of people in their last year of life and almost 50 percent of those costs are expended in the last two months of life (NHPCO, 2001c), hospice care at home often substitutes for more expensive hospitalizations.

Hospice principles have been implemented in different ways in different situations (Saunders & Kastenbaum, 1997). These differences have to do with the needs of particular societies, and especially the structure of their health care and social services systems. In the United States, the hospice emphasis on home care fits with efforts to minimize in-patient care and to encourage home care as more appropriate and more economical. The hospice movement has also made efforts to reach out to underserved groups, through a National Task Force on Access to Hospice Care by Minority Groups. Special issues of the *Hospice Journal* have reflected on hospice care and cultural diversity (Infeld et al., 1995) and on the heritage and future of the hospice movement (Corless & Foster, 1999).

Hospice Care and Palliative Care

Just as the word "hospice" (in its various forms) has its own history and meaning, so, too, do the words "palliative" and "palliation" (and related terms). Originally, "to palliate" meant "to cover with . . . a cloak" (*Oxford English Dictionary*, 1989, vol. 11, p. 101). This meaning can be seen in the practice of covering the casket at a funeral with a cloth called a "pall." In health care, "to palliate" means "to alleviate the symptoms of a disease without curing it."

In this sense, treatment of the common cold is a kind of palliation or palliative care. As we know, there is no cure for the common cold (or for many other everyday maladies), but aspirin, decongestants, antiexpectorants, antihistamines, medications to dry up unwanted secretions, and other interventions (including rest and nutritious food) are usually employed to improve quality of life when individuals have a cold and cough. As a result, symptoms are palliated until the virus that causes the cold works through its own biological trajectory and reaches its natural limits, while the body's own resources rally to repel the invader and restore the person to a healthier condition. In the meantime,

Dear Hospice of Florida Suncoast

Thank you for being there with my mother. You guys are so kind. thank you For being there for my Dad and me. I want to be your Friend. You guys are Awesome. And mom is in heaven. And thank You for All You have Done to make me and my Dad Feel better. You guys Are very specail to us.

Keep Smiling.

With Love From Nina and Frank Sposato.

Even in difficult circumstances there can be feelings of gratitude for help provided.

even though cure is not offered, most people are grateful that their distress is at least partially relieved. Thus, palliative care in all its forms means addressing symptoms rather than their underlying causes (Twycross, 1995a).

As we have already seen, hospice care is a form of palliative care—one that is addressed primarily to distressing symptoms in dying persons who are nearing the end of their lives. In terms of linguistic usage, it might have been more accurate to keep the phrases "palliative care" and "hospice care" separate and to treat the later as a type or subspecies of the former. In fact, at one point in the history of the hospice movement (and perhaps in some contexts today), they were regarded as if they meant essentially the same thing. Thus the World Health Organization (1990, p. 11) regards palliative care as:

> The active total care of patients whose disease is not responsive to curative treatment. Control of pain, of other symptoms, and of psychological, social and spiritual problems, is paramount. The goal of palliative care is achievement of the best quality of life for patients and their families.

More recently, however, many in the medical community have adopted the phrase "palliative care" and used it in ways that are both broader and narrower than the phrase "hospice care." "Palliative care" or "palliative medicine" is now used by these physicians mainly to designate a type of medical care that is addressed to the relief of distressing symptoms (Doyle et al., 1998). However, that need not necessarily imply the full scope and interdisciplinary team approach that typify hospice care (O'Connor, 1999). For example, in this sense of palliative care, there may be no spiritual care, home care visits, bereavement services, or volunteers. In this narrowed meaning of the adjective "palliative," primary emphasis is on the role of the physician and, most often, on hospital-based care. The development of palliative care in this sense in our society in the next few years will depend very much on physician education, the institutional structures within which it is practiced, and reimbursement for this type of care that is offered through managed care programs (NHPCO & the Center to Advance Palliative Care in Hospitals and Health Systems, 2001).

At the same time, this meaning of the phrase "palliative care" may be broader than that of "hospice care," since the former phrase is not necessarily limited to end-of-life care. In this sense, palliative care may apply to many physician-centered efforts to manage pain and other distressing symptoms with or without reference to their origin or their relationship to dying and death. In its richest sense, this meaning of palliative care can bring important resources of pain and symptom management (some of which originated in and have been adapted from the work of the hospice movement) to a broad range of patients; in its most superficial sense, this usage of palliative care may mean little more than traditional forms of physical and psychosocial care.

These are not merely arbitrary shifts in linguistic usage. There are many competing forces behind them. On the one hand, for example, some have chafed at the limits imposed by regulations governing hospice care and by what they perceive to be a "death sentence" that some associate with the word "hospice." On the other hand, there has been a desire to introduce care of distressing symptoms early in the disease process ("to move hospice care upstream," as the saying goes), to fill empty beds in acute care hospitals, and to have an option available for patients and families who want to stop aggressive cure-oriented interventions.

An Institutional Recapitulation

Within the American death system, four institutions currently care for most persons who are coping with dying.

1. *Hospitals* of all sorts (general hospitals, specialized medical or psychiatric institutions, and tertiary-care trauma centers or teaching hospitals) provide *acute care*, emphasizing assessment and diagnosis of illness and disease together with cure-oriented interventions for reversible or correctable conditions. Most hospitals offer a wide variety of medical services through their own internal facilities, such as emergency departments, medical or surgical wards, and intensive care units, or through outpatient departments and clinics. Physicians also offer some types of care in their offices, in community clinics, and in various sorts of specialized centers. Most of these services are not primarily designed for dying persons. Still, a significant portion of hospital-based care is directed toward the last six months of life. Also, approximately 50 percent of all deaths in our society occur in hospitals or are brought to these institutions for confirmation and certification of death. In 1998, 2.6 of every 100 discharges from acute care hospitals resulted from death (Popovic & Kozak, 2000).

2. *Long-term care facilities or nursing homes* offer *long-term care*—that is, custodial, nursing, and rehabilitative care for individuals with chronic illnesses and other disabling conditions. Such institutions do not merely serve the elderly, nor are more than a very small percentage of the elderly in our society residents of such institutions at any one time. Nevertheless, approximately 25 percent of all deaths in our society occur in long-term care facilities.

3. *Home health care programs* of many types (services of county and municipal health departments, the Visiting Nurse Association, private home health care agencies, and home care departments of hospitals) deliver *home care* chiefly in the form of skilled nursing and ancillary care. This care is provided to many different kinds of clients, some of whom may be dying.

4. *Hospice programs* offer *end-of-life care* for dying persons and their families. In our society, that care is most likely to take place in the home, but it may also be delivered in a hospital, a long-term care facility, or a hospice inpatient unit under the supervision of a hospice team, or via a hospice day care program (Corr & Corr, 1992a). Since their inception in the United States, hospice programs have primarily cared for elderly cancer patients, but hospice principles have also been applied to care of children (Armstrong-Dailey & Zarbock, 2001; Corr & Corr, 1985a; Levetown, 2000; Martin, 1989), persons with AIDS (Buckingham, 1992), individuals with motor neuron diseases like amyotrophic lateral sclerosis (ALS or Lou Gehrig's disease) (O'Gorman & O'Brien, 1990; Thompson, 1990), and others who are coping with various life-threatening conditions such as end-stage heart or lung disease. Hospice programs currently care for approximately 25 percent of all people who die in our society.

Summary

In this chapter, we examined ways in which our society provides care for individuals who are coping with dying through formal programs and institutions. We did this by identifying ten principles in the hospice philosophy to serve as a model for such care. Also, we described the historical development of care and its current practice in hospitals, long-term care facilities, home care programs, and hospice programs. We also added some comments on the relationship between hospice care and palliative care.

Questions for Review and Discussion

1. Think about the situation of Jo Ryan as described in the vignette near the beginning of this chapter. Try to focus in particular on her experiences at different points in time: when she first discovered the small lump in her right breast, when she was told that she needed a mastectomy, when she developed cancer again some time later, when she received services from a community home health care program, when she was admitted to a nursing home, when she was transferred to a local hospice inpatient unit, when she went home to be with

her family, and when she neared the end of her life. What types of care did Jo need at these different points in her life? What programs of care were best suited to her needs at these different points?

2. This chapter discussed several different types of care, including that provided by hospitals, long-term care facilities, home health care programs, and hospice programs. Think about being a person with a life-threatening illness (perhaps you can think about someone you know, such as a relative or a friend). What might be the advantages and limitations of being cared for by each of these programs?

3. How would you describe the essential elements in a hospice-type program of care? Why do you think those elements were implemented (at least at first) in different ways in England, Canada, and the United States? Could hospice-type principles be implemented in other institutions (for example, hospitals, long-term care facilities, or home health care programs) in the United States?

4. What sorts of experiences (if any) have you had with hospice programs or with other forms of palliative care?

Suggested Readings

Hospice principles are set forth in many books, such as:

Beresford, L. (1993). *The Hospice Handbook: A Complete Guide.*

Canadian Palliative Care Association. (1995). *Palliative Care: Towards a Consensus in Standardized Principles of Practice.*

Connor, S. R. (1998). *Hospice: Practice, Pitfalls, and Promise.*

Corr, C. A., & Corr, D. M. (Eds.). (1983). *Hospice Care: Principles and Practice.*

Corr, C. A., Morgan, J. D., & Wass, H. (Eds.). (1994). *Statements about Death, Dying, and Bereavement by the International Work Group on Death, Dying, and Bereavement.*

Doyle, D., Hanks, G. W. C., & MacDonald, N. (Eds.). (1998). *Oxford Textbook of Palliative Medicine* (2nd ed.).

Ferrell, B. R., & Coyle, N. (Eds.). (2001). *Textbook of Palliative Nursing.*

Field, M. J., & Cassel, C. K. (Eds.). (1997). *Approaching Death: Improving Care at the End of Life.*

Lattanzi-Licht, M., Mahoney, J. J., & Miller, G. W. (1998). *The Hospice Choice: In Pursuit of a Peaceful Death.*

National Hospice and Palliative Care Organization. (1994). *Standards of Practice for Hospice Programs.*

Saunders, C. M., & Kastenbaum, R. (1997). *Hospice Care on the International Scene.*

Saunders, C. M., & Sykes, N. (Eds.). (1993). *The Management of Terminal Malignant Disease* (3rd ed.).

Saunders, C. M., Baines, M., & Dunlop, R. (1995). *Living with Dying: A Guide to Palliative Care* (3rd ed.).

Stoddard, S. (1992). *The Hospice Movement: A Better Way of Caring for the Dying* (rev. ed.).

Webb, M. (1997). *The Good Death: The New American Search to Reshape the End of Life.*

Hospice principles are applied to situations involving children in:

Armstrong-Dailey, A., & Zarbock, S. (Eds.). (2001). *Hospice Care for Children.*

Corr, C. A., & Corr, D. M. (Eds.). (1985a). *Hospice Approaches to Pediatric Care.*

Martin, B. B. (Ed.). (1989). *Pediatric Hospice Care: What Helps.*

For developments in medicine, hospitals, and long-term care facilities, consult:

Bennett, C. (1980). *Nursing Home Life: What It Is and What It Could Be.*

Gubrium, J. F. (1975). *Living and Dying at Murray Manor.*

Moss, F., & Halamanderis, V. (1977). *Too Old, Too Sick, Too Bad: Nursing Homes in America.*

Rosenberg, C. E. (1987). *The Care of Strangers: The Rise of America's Hospital System.*

Shield, R. R. (1988). *Uneasy Endings: Daily Life in an American Nursing Home.*

Starr, P. (1982). *The Social Transformation of American Medicine.*

Stevens, R. (1989). *In Sickness and in Wealth: American Hospitals in the Twentieth Century.*

InfoTrac College Edition

For more information, explore the InfoTrac College Edition at **http://www.infotrac-college.com/Wadsworth**

Enter search terms: ACUTE CARE, CHRONIC CARE, END-OF-LIFE CARE, HOSPICE CARE, HOME HEALTH CARE, HOSPITALS, INTERDISCIPLINARY TEAMWORK, LONG-TERM CARE FACILITIES OR NURSING HOMES, PALLIATIVE CARE.

Part Four

Bereavement

"TWO-SIDEDNESS IS A FUNDAMENTAL FEATURE of death . . . There are always two parties to a death; the person who dies and the survivors who are bereaved" (Toynbee, 1968a, p. 267). In fact, as we saw in Part Three, the situation is even more complicated than this would suggest. Prior to death, issues in coping with dying concern not only the person who is dying but also his or her family members, friends, and care providers (whether professionals or volunteers). All of these individuals, except the person who dies, are survivors-to-be. For each survivor, "a person's death is not only an ending; it is also a beginning" (Shneidman, 1973a, p. 33).

In this part we examine the experiences of these survivors. Nearly everyone has survived some sort of loss in his or her own life, so we all know something about experiences of loss. In that sense, loss is one of the fundamental experiences in human life. But there are many kinds of loss. Our special concern in Chapters 9–11 is with death-related losses and their consequences.

In Chapter 9, we explain key elements and variables in the experiences of persons who are coping with loss and grief. In Chapter 10, we offer practical advice for individuals who are trying to help bereaved persons. To do this, we draw attention to things that can be said or done (and things that should not be said or done) to help such persons, and we explain the concept of disenfranchised grief. We also describe two examples of organizations that prepare individuals to work in one-to-one helping relationships with bereaved persons and ten principles for facilitating mourning in counseling relationships. In Chapter 11, we turn to ways in which communities within our society have organized themselves to help the bereaved. We also analyze three tasks associated with funeral ritual, and discuss some typical memorial rituals within the contemporary American death system. Finally, we explore aftercare services in the funeral industry, hospice bereavement follow-up programs, and support groups for the bereaved. ■

Chapter Nine

COPING WITH LOSS AND GRIEF

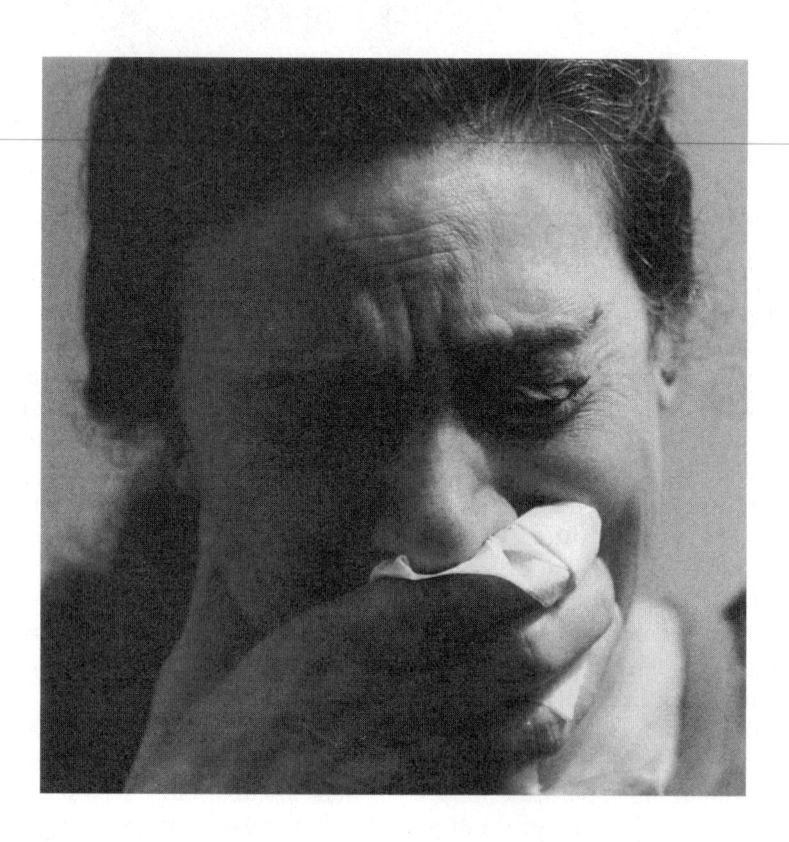

In this chapter, we explore loss and grief as bereaved persons experience them in connection with a death. Our goal is to clarify the nature of these experiences, the language and concepts employed to understand them, and the efforts involved in coping with them. We begin with an example of a grieving person and some comments on the key concepts of loss and bereavement. Next, we analyze grief itself and five variables that influence an individual's grief. Then we consider the related experience of mourning in terms of its normal or uncomplicated dynamics (understood in the theoretical literature as phases, tasks, or processes) and its outcomes. We conclude with brief observations on several related topics: grief and mourning in relationship to gender and families, anticipatory grief and mourning, traumatic loss and death, and complicated grief reactions. ■

Stella Bridgman: Experiencing Her Losses

Stella Bridgman was in her early forties when her 18-year-old son took his own life. His death was the tragic and unfortunate ending to a troubled history involving chemical dependency (starting with marijuana and beer, but escalating to hard liquor, cocaine, and crack) and difficulties at home, in school, and with his part-time job.

Even though her son had a history of erratic and self-destructive behavior, it was a tremendous shock to Stella when she found his body. Her pain was sharp-edged and very powerful. "It was like being punched in the stomach," she said later. Stella experienced a great sense of sadness in losing someone who had been a central part of her life for so many years and whose own life had sprung from her very body. She was also very hurt that her son could reject her (as she viewed it) in this brutal way and spurn the very life that she had given him.

At the same time, Stella was furious at her son for doing this to her and to his 15-year-old sister. She also experienced guilt as she asked herself over and over again whether there was anything in addition to what she had already been doing that she might have done to prevent his death.

The death of her son was not the first loss that Stella had experienced. Her father had died in a distant war when she was a little child; she had not really known him. Her mother, a heavy smoker, had developed lung cancer at a relatively early age and died after a difficult illness a little more than 10 years ago. That was the first death that seemed to have real significance in her life.

The death of her husband in a fiery automobile accident five years later was another harsh experience that left Stella with two young children, a small sum of money from insurance and savings, and no job. She had never anticipated that possibility. All the widows she had known were elderly women. Stella turned to her church, became very protective of her children, and rejoined the workforce.

Eventually, Stella did marry again to a widower whom she met at a church social activity, but her son disliked his new stepfather and the three older siblings who came with him into the new "blended" family.

For Stella, each of the major deaths in her life had a different impact on her. When her mother died, Stella felt like she was experiencing the death of her past. She found it hard to go forward without the support of the parent who had always been with her. When her first husband died, Stella felt like it was the death of her present life, a way of living with which she had become comfortable both before and after her mother's death. But the suicide of her son was like the death of her hopes for the future. Could she cope with this new blow on top of all the others? And could she pull all of her energies together one more time and once again find the strength to live on for herself and for her daughter?

Stella asked over and over: "What did I do?" "Why did this happen?" and "How can I go on?"

Loss and Bereavement

To love is to give "hostages to fortune" (Bacon, 1625/1962, p. 22). Everyone who experiences love or who forms an attachment to another runs the risk of losing the loved person or object and suffering the consequences of loss. If so, then "to grieve is to pay ransom to love" (Shneidman, 1983, p. 29).

Of course, it is in loving that a person shares with others and enriches his or her life. Attachments are those very special, enduring relationships through which individuals satisfy fundamental needs (Bowlby, 1973–1982; Parkes et al., 1993). Stella Bridgman loved the father she had never known, her mother, her two husbands, her own children, and her second husband's children. Not to love in these ways would be to cut oneself off from the rewards of human attachment—to restrict and impoverish one's life. As Brantner (in Worden, 1982, xi) said so aptly: "Only people who avoid love can avoid grief. The point is to learn from it and remain vulnerable to love." To learn about grief and mourning, we begin with some thoughts about loss and bereavement.

Loss

There are *many types of losses* that occur throughout human lives (Viorst, 1986). For example, I may break up with someone I love, be fired or laid off from my job, have to leave my home and relocate, misplace a prized possession, fail in some competition, have a body part amputated, or experience the death of someone close to me. What these losses all have in common is that the individual who loses something is separated from and deprived of the lost person, object, status, or relationship. This is the primary loss—the termination of the attachment or relationship; secondary losses are those that follow from a primary loss.

Death-related losses inevitably involve endings, separations, and other losses, as is evident in the example of Stella Bridgman. What death will mean to a survivor depends on the loss that individual experiences and the ways in which he or she interprets that loss. For example, death may mean the end of the time that I share with my spouse or partner, a separation from one of my parents, or the loss of my child. However I interpret a death-related loss, it is likely to be painful for me because that loss will impact and alter my life in important ways. Even if I am able to view death in the framework of a possible afterlife and eventual reunion with the loved one, or as a transition of the person who died into a realm of ancestors who continue to interact with us, I will still be a person who has been left behind and I am now no longer able to enjoy the physical presence of the person who died. Moreover, losses through death may sometimes be complicated—for example, when dying is long and difficult, or when death is sudden, unexpected, or traumatic.

Losses that are not related to death can also be complicated in their own ways. Such losses may be as hurtful as those arising from death, or perhaps even more hurtful. For example, about half of all marriages in the United States now end in divorce. When that happens, there is often one spouse who wishes to terminate the relationship, another who does not wish to do so or who is less determined on that outcome, and perhaps a third person (such as a child) who is involved in what is happening and directly affected by its implications but not immediately able to influence what is taking place. Each of these individuals will experience different types of losses in the divorce. As in death, there is always loss in divorce, but there may also be elements of deliberate choice, guilt, and blame that are not always associated with a death. Divorce may also be complicated by theoretical (if not practical) opportunities for reconciliation and the inevitable implications of subsequent life decisions by all who are involved in the aftermath of the event. Note that we mention divorce here as only one example of the many types of loss humans may experience that do not involve death itself and yet are quite powerful.

Even a child can face multiple health challenges and losses.

Often, as we reflect on our lives, we can identify the individuals or objects whose loss would mean a great deal to us. However, sometimes the meaning and value of the lost person or object is only fully appreciated after the loss has taken place. In any event, to understand the implications of any experience of loss, we must look back to the *underlying relationships and attachments* on which it is founded.

Bereavement

The term *bereavement* refers to the state of being bereaved or deprived of something. In other words, bereavement identifies the objective situation of individuals who have experienced a loss of some person or thing that they valued (Corless, 2001). Three elements are essential in all bereavement: (1) a relationship with some person or thing that is valued; (2) the loss—ending, termination, separation—of that relationship; and (3) a survivor deprived of the valued person or thing by the loss.

Both the noun *bereavement* and the adjective *bereaved* derive from a less familiar root verb, *reave*, which means "to despoil, rob, or forcibly deprive" (*Oxford English Dictionary*, 1989, vol. 13, p. 295). Thus, a bereaved person is one who has been deprived, robbed, plundered, or stripped of someone or something that he or she valued. In principle, the losses experienced by bereaved people could be of many kinds; in fact, this language is most often used to refer to the situation of those who have experienced a loss through death. In other words, our language tends to assume that bereavement is about death and that death always entails a more or less brutal loss of someone or something that is important to the bereaved person.

Grief

We address here three questions about grief: (1) What is grief? (2) How does grief relate to disease, depression, and guilt? and (3) Is grief a normal or abnormal part of life?

What Is Grief?

Grief is the reaction to loss. When one suffers a significant loss, one experiences grief. The word grief signifies one's reaction, both internally and externally, to the impact of the loss. The term arises from the grave or heavy weight that presses on bereaved survivors (*Oxford English Dictionary*, 1989, vol. 6, pp. 834–835). Not to experience grief for a significant loss is an aberration. It would suggest that there was no real attachment prior to the loss, that the relationship was complicated in ways that set it apart from the ordinary, or that one is suppressing or hiding one's reactions to the loss.

The term *grief* is often defined as *"the emotional reaction to loss."* One needs to be careful in understanding such a definition. As Elias (1991, p. 117) noted, "broadly speaking, emotions have three components, a somatic, a behavioral and a feeling component." As a result, "the term *emotion*, even in professional discussions, is used with two different meanings. It is used in a wider and in a narrower sense at the same time. In the wider sense the term *emotion* is applied to a reaction pattern which involves the whole organism in its somatic, its feeling and its behavioral aspects. . . . In its narrower sense the term *emotion* refers to the feeling component of the syndrome only" (Elias, 1991, p. 119).

Grief clearly does involve feelings and it is certainly appropriate to think of the feeling dimensions of grief. Anyone who has personally experienced grief or who has encountered a grieving person will be familiar with the outpouring of feelings that is a prominent element of most grief. However, it is also important to recognize that *one's reactions to loss are not merely a matter of feelings.* Grief is broader, more complex, and more deep-seated than this narrower understanding of emotions and emotional reactions to loss might imply (Rando, 1993).

Grief can be experienced and expressed in numerous ways (Worden, 2002). These include physical, psychological (affective/cognitive), and behavioral dimensions, represented by:

- *Physical sensations*, such as hollowness in the stomach, a lump in the throat, tightness in the chest, aching arms, oversensitivity to noise, shortness of breath, lack of energy, a sense of depersonalization, muscle weakness, dry mouth, or loss of coordination
- *Feelings*, such as sadness, anger, guilt and self-reproach, anxiety, loneliness, fatigue, helplessness, shock, yearning, emancipation, relief, or numbness
- *Thoughts or cognitions*, such as disbelief, confusion, preoccupation, a sense of presence of the deceased, or paranormal ("hallucinatory") experiences
- *Behaviors*, such as sleep or appetite disturbances, absentmindedness, social withdrawal, loss of interest in activities that previously were sources of satisfaction, dreams of the deceased, crying, avoiding reminders of the deceased, searching and calling out, sighing, restless overactivity, or visiting places and cherishing objects that remind one of the deceased

Grief can also have social and spiritual dimensions, such as:

- *Social difficulties* in interpersonal relationships or problems in functioning within an organization
- *Spiritual searching* for a sense of meaning, hostility toward God, or a realization that one's value framework is inadequate to cope with this particular loss

An illustration of loneliness after loss from Tear Soup *(see Box 10.2).*

To think of grief solely as a matter of feelings is to risk misunderstanding and missing this full range of reactions to loss.

As we seek to grasp the full meaning of grief, we should also note reports that grief can be associated with increased risk of illness or morbidity in bereaved persons (Glick et al., 1974). Other reports (for example, Martikainen & Valkonen,

1996; Steinbach, 1992) suggest that grief may also be a factor in the death of some bereaved persons.

How Does Grief Relate to Disease, Depression, and Guilt?

We can learn more about grief by comparing and contrasting it with three other phenomena: disease, depression, and guilt.

Some writers (such as Engel, 1961) have noted that there are many similarities between *grief* and *disease.* For example, a significant loss may affect a bereaved person's ability to function, at least temporarily. Also metaphors of healing are commonly employed to describe the processes and time required to overcome this impaired functioning. However, there are important distinctions between grief and disease that need to be kept in mind. Grief is a "dis-ease," a discomforting disturbance of everyday equilibrium, but it is not a "disease" in the sense of a sickness or morbid (unhealthy) condition of mind or body. In fact, we believe that most grief is an appropriate and healthy reaction to loss.

Sadness and other common manifestations of grief do resemble some of the symptoms associated with the diagnosis of *clinical depression.* Again, however, grief is a healthy reaction to loss, whereas clinical depression is a mental disorder or disease. Here we agree with Freud (1917/1959a), who long ago recognized the difference between mourning and what he called "melancholia." By mourning, Freud was pointing to the normal processes associated with grief; melancholia is his language for the illness state of depression.

Both grief and clinical depression may involve an experience of being pressed down upon and a withdrawal from the world. However, clinical depression is a complicated or pathological form of grieving characterized by angry impulses toward the ambivalently "loved" person, impulses that are turned inward toward the self (Clayton et al., 1974). Normal grief reactions do not include the loss of self-esteem commonly found in most clinical depression. As Worden (2002, pp. 21–22) observed, "Even though grief and depression share similar objective and subjective features, they do seem to be different conditions. Depression overlaps with bereavement but is not the same. Freud believed that in grief, the world looks poor and empty while in depression, the person feels poor and empty." Other research on grief and depression (for example, Schneider, 1980; Zisook & DeVaul, 1983, 1984, 1985) confirms that they are, in fact, different types of experiences. Thus, Stella Bridgman was beset by her loss and grief, but she was not clinically depressed.

Guilt may be part of the total grief reaction, but it is important and useful to disentangle issues of guilt from the larger grief experience and address them separately. *Grief* is the broad term for reactions to loss; *guilt* refers to thoughts and feelings that assign blame (often self-blame), fault, or culpability for the loss. Guilt experienced by bereaved persons may be realistic or unrealistic. Suggestions of guilt may arise from one's role (for example, that of parent and protector) or from something that one believes he or she should or could have done or not done. For example, even though Stella Bridgman knew that her son had brought on himself many of his own difficulties and finally his death, she agonized over whether she could not or should not have found some way to help him more. Eventually, she realized that she had done all she could and that her son was ultimately responsible for taking his own life.

Unrealistic guilt may be part of a process of *reality testing* induced by a loss in which a temporary acceptance of blame may in the long run prove to be one way of confirming that there was, in fact, nothing that the survivor could have done to prevent the death. By contrast with clinical depression, when guilt is experienced during bereavement, "it is usually guilt associated with some specific aspect of the loss rather than a general, overall sense of culpability" (Worden, 2002, p. 21).

Most Grief Is a Healthy and a Healthful Reaction to Loss

Our view is that *ordinary, uncomplicated grief is a healthy, normal, and appropriate reaction to loss* (see Box 9.1). Bereaved persons may not be at ease with their situation or with themselves, but they are not, on that ground alone, diseased or depressed in any medical or psychiatric sense. Although encounters with death, grief, and bereavement may not be very frequent, usual, or ordinary experiences for many people, they are not *abnormal* or alien in the way disease is foreign to health. Stella Bridgman had experienced several deaths in her life. Each was difficult and demanding in its own way, but in each case she came to realize that her grief was normal and fully warranted by her encounter with loss.

For these reasons, in this book we speak of *signs or manifestations* of grief, not *symptoms.* In itself, grief is not the kind of reaction to loss that should lead us to speak of symptoms, which are indicators of disease. Bereavement and grief simply are not states of disease from which symptoms would arise. Bereavement and grief may be unusual and daunting, but they are not in themselves abnormal, morbid, or unhealthy.

Some people say that if they were to die their friends should have a party and not be sad. This ignores or misrepresents the nature both of grief and of human attachments. It tells people that they ought not to be experiencing what they actually are experiencing or what they may need to experience. Honest reactions to loss are real; they cannot be turned on and off at will. All human beings react to significant losses; few have much control over what those reactions will be right after an important loss. In addition, loss always has social implications for those who go on living (Osterweis et al., 1984). When I love someone, I experience joyful feelings and other reactions that I usually need and want to express. When I lose someone I have loved, I also have feelings and other grief reactions, and I usually need to express or give vent to those reactions, too.

Moreover, after a death only part of our grief is for the person who died. In large measure, our grief is for ourselves as people who have been left behind (see Box 9.2). That is why we experience grief even after a slow, lingering, or painful death when we believe that the dying person has been released from distress and is at last at rest. It is also why we encounter grief even when our theology assures us that the dead person has gone on to a new and better life. Whatever else has

Box 9.1 On the Nature of Grief

Grief is neither a disorder nor a healing process; it is a sign of health itself, a whole and natural gesture of love. Nor must we see grief as a step towards something better. No matter how much it hurts—and it may be the greatest pain in life—grief can be an end in itself, a pure expression of love. ■

SOURCE: May, 1992, p. 3.

To grieve well is to value what you have lost. When you value even the feeling of loss, you value life itself, and you begin to live again. ■

SOURCE: Frank, 1991, p. 41.

happened, as bereaved survivors we have experienced a real loss. It is not selfish or improper to react to that loss with grief; it is simply a realistic human reaction.

We have already noted that experiences of bereavement and grief may be more and more unusual or infrequent in a society in which average life expectancies have been greatly extended and death seems less often to enter our lives. However, we should not misinterpret this by thinking that bereavement and grief are *abnormal* parts of life. Loss, death, and grief are normal and natural parts of human life. Because they may be unusual in our experience and are typically associated with a sense of being out of control, it often appears to bereaved persons that they are losing their minds. This is rarely true. *Reacting and responding to loss is a healthful process, not a morbid one.* It may take courage to face one's grief and to permit oneself to experience one's reactions to significant losses, but ultimately this is done in the interests of one's own welfare (Fitzgerald, 1994; Tatelbaum, 1980).

Of course, loss and grief can befall individuals who already have a psychiatric or physical illness, as well as those who are in good health. So in all cases the appropriateness of one's grief must be assessed on an individual basis. *Grief is very much an individualized phenomenon*, unique in many ways to each particular loss and griever. The same griever is likely to react in different ways to different losses; different grievers are likely to react in different ways to the same loss. Because there is no universal reaction following after any given loss, one person's grief should not be construed as a standard by which others should evaluate themselves. To keep this in mind is to be sensitive and open to the very broad range of manifestations associated with loss. In this way, various normal reactions to loss will not be confused with pathology and the abnormalities of disease.

It is true that loss can sometimes lead to complicated grief reactions that would constitute a disorder warranting therapeutic intervention. For this reason, we will return to the subject of complicated grief reactions at the end of this chapter.

Box 9.2 Mourning Is Properly about the Self, Too

When someone you love has died, you tend to recall best those few moments and incidents that helped to clarify your sense, not of the person who has died, but of your own self. And if you loved the person a great deal . . . your sense of who you are will have been clarified many times, and so you will have many such moments to remember. ■

SOURCE: Banks, 1991, p. 43.

What Makes a Difference in Bereavement and Grief?

Five variables influence experiences of bereavement and grief:

1. The *nature of the prior attachment* or the *perceived value* that the lost person or thing has for the bereaved individual
2. The *way in which the loss occurred* and the *concurrent circumstances* of the bereaved person
3. The *coping strategies* that the bereaved individual has learned to use in dealing with previous losses
4. The *developmental situation of the bereaved person*—that is, how one's being a child, adolescent, adult, or elderly person influences one's grief and mourning (Corr, 1998a)
5. The *support or assistance that the bereaved person receives after the loss* from family members, friends, other individuals, and social institutions (Parkes, 1975b; Sanders, 1989)

We explore the first three of these factors in this chapter, along with the family context for grief. We will discuss social support in Chapters 10 and 11, and we will consider developmental issues in Part Five.

Prior attachments are not always what they seem to be. The full import of a relationship may not be appreciated until it is over. Some relationships are dependent, abusive, ambivalent, distorted, or complicated in many ways. Almost all relationships are multidimensional. A person whom I love is likely to be significant in my life in many ways—for example, as spouse or partner, helpmate, homemaker, sometime enemy, lover, competitor, parent of my children, guide in difficult times, breadwinner, critic, comforter. Each of these dimensions influences my grief experience and may represent a loss that will need to be mourned. Special difficulties may be associated with the death of a person for whom there were or are ambivalent feelings.

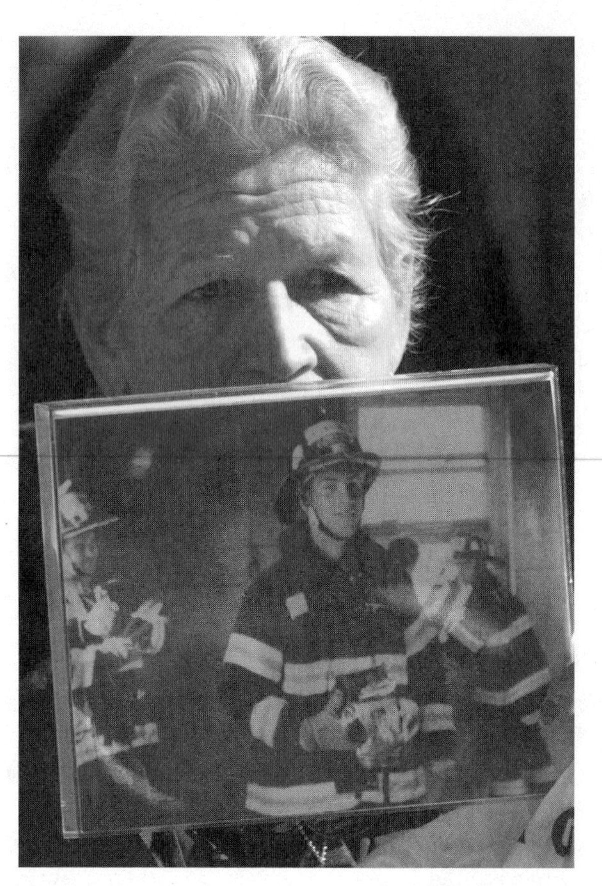

A woman holds a photograph of her firefighter son who was lost on September 11, 2001, at the World Trade Center.

The way in which the loss takes place and the circumstances of the bereaved person are also critical to how we experience grief. As far as *the way in which the loss takes place*, some losses (like the suicide of Stella Bridgman's son and the losses associated with the events of September 11, 2001) occur in sudden, shocking, or traumatic ways. Some losses can be foreseen or predicted; others cannot. Some losses occur gradually and allow time for preparation; others are drawn out and difficult. Some losses are untimely and run contrary to what we expect in the natural order of things; others fit more easily into our sense of the overall patterns of life. In general, deaths that are "off time"—that occur much before or long after our expectations might have prepared us for them—are likely to be among those that we find most difficult (Rando, 1984).

In addition to the characteristics of the loss itself, *the circumstances that surround the bereaved person at the time of the loss* are also influential in shaping the overall bereavement experience. For example, a person who is physically healthy, mentally in top form, and generally at ease with life may be in better condition to cope with loss than someone who is simultaneously beset with a variety of physical, mental, and other challenges in living. By contrast, Shakespeare (*Hamlet*, IV, v: 78) wrote that "when sorrows come, they come not like single spies, but in battalions" and according to a popular saying "it never rains but it pours." What these quotations mean is that losses often do (or at least seem to) compound each other, transforming what might otherwise have been a brief, gentle shower into an extended torrential onslaught. Some losses take place at a time in one's life when other burdens or challenges are heavy. Others are complicated because they are part of a series of losses following rapidly one after another that impact a single survivor. Still other losses involve many deaths at the same time, as in the deaths of several members of an extended family in a single fatal accident. And in the events of September 11, 2001, there were different types of complications arising from multiple deaths in a large-scale disaster. For example, many of the men killed at the World Trade Center in New York City were married and in their 30s and 40s. A significant number of their wives were pregnant at the time. As a result, when their husbands died these women were left on their own to face the problems of pregnancy and giving birth (*St. Petersburg Times*, 2001g).

In Chapter 6, we pointed out that throughout their lives *different individuals are likely to develop different types of coping strategies.* These are our constantly changing efforts to manage perceived stressors. Each of these coping strategies may be more or less effective. Once a significant loss or death occurs, we are likely to cope in ways that make use of the repertoire of coping strategies and skills that we previously acquired. Thus, despite all of the differences between death and other losses in life, it is often a good rule of thumb to ask how someone has coped with other losses earlier in his or her life in order to predict how that person is likely to cope with death and bereavement (Shneidman, 1980/1995). Developing new and more effective coping skills requires more time and energy than are usually available in the immediate aftermath of a death or other significant loss. Thus, Stella Bridgman at first did not believe that her coping skills were adequate to enable her to cope with the loss and grief arising from the suicide of her son.

Mourning: Interpretations and Outcomes

The term *mourning* indicates the processes of coping with loss and grief, and thus the attempt to manage those experiences or learn to live with them by incorporating them into ongoing living (Siggins, 1966). Sometimes this is called "grief work" (Freud, 1959a; Lindemann, 1944; but see Stroebe, 1992) to emphasize the active or effortful nature of the processes of mourning. Settling on a consistent meaning for the word "mourning" is important in light of inconsistencies and disagreements in the use of that term in both everyday discourse and the professional literature (for example, Osterweis et al., 1984; Raphael, 1983), and in the face of larger arguments about how researchers explore and understand the phenomena of bereavement (Stroebe et al., 1994; Wortman & Silver, 1989, 2001).

Stella Bridgman's experiences in the vignette near the beginning of this chapter can help us appreciate the distinction between grief and mourning. As we observed in that vignette, Stella has been deeply impacted by her grief following the death of her son, but she has not yet moved forward very much with her mourning. When we return to her story in Chapters 10 and 11, we will want to see how she is doing and who or what helps her in coping with her losses and grief.

Another way to grasp the meaning of the term "mourning" is to consider the words of Jesus in the Sermon on the Mount: "Blessed are those that mourn, for they shall be comforted." But bereavement, loss, and grief are a burden, not a blessing. If there is any blessing in the experience of bereavement, it can only be in the capacity to mourn and grow through the loss. Only through mourning, through moving toward and working with one's grief, can one find any hope of eventual solace or comfort. Thus Shneidman (1980/1995, p. 179) wrote: "Mourning is one of the most profound human experiences that it is possible to have. . . . The deep capacity to weep for the loss of a loved one and to continue to treasure the memory of that loss is one of our noblest human traits." Here Shneidman and scripture agree on the sense in which mourning can be a blessing for bereaved persons.

As an essential process for those who are experiencing grief, mourning has two complementary forms or aspects. It is both an *internal, private, or intrapersonal process*—our inward struggles to cope with or manage both the loss and our grief reactions to that loss; and an *outward, public, or interpersonal process*—the overt, visible, and shared expression of grief, together with efforts to obtain social support. Some authors (such as Wolfelt, 1996) who prefer to emphasize the distinction between these two aspects use terms like *grieving* for the intrapersonal dimension of coping with loss and reserve the term *mourning* for the interpersonal aspects or social expression of grief. We prefer a single term to designate both aspects of mourning. We use that term to reflect the interacting personal and social dimensions of human beings, both of which are part of most descriptions of mourning.

In the rest of this chapter, we concentrate on the first of these aspects of mourning, its intrapersonal or intrapsychic dimensions. To do so, we give special attention to three types of theoretical models for interpreting mourning (through phases, tasks, and processes; see Table 9.1) and to the question of outcomes in mourning. We will examine public or interpersonal aspects of mourning in Chapters 10 and 11.

Phases in Mourning

Much attention has been paid to mourning in recent years in an effort to understand and explain what it involves. Drawing on work by Bowlby (1961, 1973–82), Parkes (1970, 2001) proposed that mourning involves *four phases:* (1) shock and numbness, (2) yearning and searching, (3) disorganization and despair, and (4) reorganization (see Table 9.1). These phases are said to be elements in an overall process of *realization*—making real in one's inner, psychic world what is already real in the outer, objective world.

Table 9.1 Phase-Based and Task-Based Interpretations of Mourning

Four Phases (Bowlby/Parkes)	Four Tasks (Worden)
Shock and numbness	To accept the reality of the loss
Yearning and searching	To work through the pain of grief
Disorganization and despair	To adjust to an environment in which the deceased is missing
Reorganization	To emotionally relocate the deceased and move on with life

SOURCE: From Parkes, 1970, 2001; Worden, 2002.

Box 9.3 Auden on Grief

Stop all the clocks, cut off the telephone,
Prevent the dog from barking with a juicy bone,
Silence the pianos and with muffled drum
Bring out the coffin, let the mourners come.
Let aeroplanes circle moaning overhead
Scribbling on the sky the message HE IS DEAD,
Put crêpe bows round the white necks of the public doves,
Let the traffic policeman wear black cotton gloves.
He was my North, my South, my East and West,
My working week and my Sunday rest,
My noon, my midnight, my talk, my song;
I thought that love would last for ever: I was wrong.
The stars are not wanted now: put out every one;
Pack up the moon and dismantle the sun;
Pour away the ocean and sweep up the wood;
For nothing now can ever come to any good. ■

Shock and numbness constitute an initial reaction to loss, although they may also recur at other times as one works through one's grief again and again in different circumstances or at a later date. One is shocked or stunned at the impact of the loss (see Box 9.3). It is like being overwhelmed or being knocked off the familiar balance of one's life. One feels dazed or detached, as if one has been overloaded by news of the death and is unable to absorb or take in anything else. The effect is like being encircled by an invisible protective shield. This is similar to the "psychic numbing" or "psychic closing off" experienced by the survivors of the atomic bombing of Hiroshima (Lifton, 1967). Many people also experienced reactions like these in connection with the events of September 11, 2001. The mourner seems to float through life, often unable to take care of basic needs like nutrition, hydration, or making decisions. This is a natural defense against bad news and unwanted pain—but it is almost always a passing or transitory condition.

Yearning and searching represent an effort to return to things as they once were. As the pain of grief penetrates the dissolving barriers of shock and one realizes the magnitude of one's loss, one is unwilling to acknowledge the loss or relinquish what no longer exists. One yearns or pines for a time that is now gone and finds oneself falling into familiar patterns of setting his place at the table or expecting her to come up the driveway at 6:00 P.M. Searching is triggered by a glimpse across a crowded room of someone who resembles him, by a passing whiff of her perfume, by the strains of "our" song (Parkes, 1970). Objectively, yearning and searching are doomed to failure. As Thomas Wolfe (1940) noted

Box 9.4 Andrew and Thomas

A simple question,
Never a problem before.
"**D**o you have any children?"
Really a simple question.
Easy. I say, "Yes," but
What do I say to "How many?"
"**T**wo," my hard-headed
Heart always says.
One is dead.
Must I say only one?
Absolutely not—I have two
Sons. ■

SOURCE: From *The Andrew Poems*, by S. Wagner, p. 36. Copyright © 1994 Shelley Wagner. Reprinted with permission from Texas Tech University Press.

in the title of a posthumously published novel, *You Can't Go Home Again.* The past is simply no longer available as it once was. To grasp that fact is to realize and appreciate the depth, extent, and finality of the survivor's loss.

Disorganization is an understandable reaction to the failure of efforts to reinvigorate the past. If my husband has died, am I still a wife? If my only child has died, am I still a parent? If one child has died, should I subtract that child from the total number of my children (see Box 9.4)? Who am I as a survivor? These are questions of self-identity, but they are joined to practical questions of everyday living. Who will prepare dinner? How will I manage to care for our children without him? What will we do without her weekly paycheck? How can we comfort each other when we are both hurting from the death of our child? Should I sell the house and move back to the town where the rest of my family lives?

Individuals who are disorganized are often unable to concentrate on the challenges that beset them. They are easily distracted or are bewildered when it seems that everywhere they turn new demands are made upon them. They find it difficult to focus their limited energies and to carry out or complete even small projects. It may be a real achievement to get through only a few moments, an hour, or one day at a time. Much that they had previously taken for granted has been called into question. Death has interfered with life. The effect is like walking into someone else's life—shuffling through an unfamiliar landscape, one that is unsettled, chaotic, and confused. The individual feels disoriented and unable to find his or her way.

Reorganization is initiated when one can begin to pick up the pieces of one's life again and start to shape them into some new order. Life is never the same as it once was after a significant loss or death. Once the fabric of one's life has been torn, it may be mended in one way or another, but some differences are always irrevocable. One has to find a new way of living as a person who now is no longer attached in the way in which he or she once was. Attig (2000) has written that bereaved persons are challenged to learn to move from "loving in presence" to "loving in separation." As each aspect of the loss is mourned, "new normals" must be developed for future living. Those who have loved us and who have died would surely want us to find constructive ways in which to reorganize our lives. However, it is we, the bereaved survivors, who have to work that out in real life. Most bereaved persons do achieve some sort of reorganization in their lives. It is a heroic accomplishment because one's former life is put at risk in the highly individual struggle to develop and define a new mode of living.

Some writers have expanded their models of mourning to include five (Weizman & Kamm, 1985), seven (Kavanaugh, 1972), or ten (Westberg, 1971) phases. This phasing seeks to distinguish different aspects of mourning in more precise ways, but it can be confusing when the proposed categories appear to overlap, are difficult to distinguish, or become impractical to apply. The goal in a phase-based model of mourning is not to have the fewest (or the most) elements. Like all theoretical proposals, these models of mourning arise from different concerns, serve different purposes, and should be evaluated in different ways. Many have thought that the four-phase Bowlby/Parkes model satisfies the requirements of clarity, simplicity, and adequacy in helping to understand the complex experiences of mourning.

Some have preferred a simpler account in which the two middle phases of yearning/searching and disorientation are essentially combined so as to result in a three-phase model: (1) shock, (2) a period of intense or active grieving, and (3) reestablishment of physical and mental balance (Gorer, 1965b; Miles, 1984; Tatelbaum, 1980; see Figure 9.1). Similarly, Rando (1993) described three broad phases in mourning: avoidance, confrontation, and accommodation. The number of phases in these models is not as important as whether or not they are useful in helping us to understand the experiences of mourning.

Like stage-based models of coping with dying, phase-based models of mourning have their critics (such as Wortman & Silver, 1989, 2001). Basically, the argument is that these so-called phases are: (1) generalizations drawn from particular populations that may not have been established with sufficient methodological rigor, and (2) may not apply very well beyond the group from which they originated. Some have also thought that a phase-based theory of mourning seems to describe a schema that the mourner is said to "go through" almost in a passive way, as if simple endurance through time and no more were the essence of grief work. This is like thinking of mourning as an experience in which a dirty automobile is hooked up to a car wash line, dragged through the process without exerting any effort, and turned out "clean" at the end. Criticisms of this way of thinking suggest there is much yet to be learned about the basic human experiences of grief and mourning. Should we try to reconfirm a phase-based model or turn instead to another structure, such as those offered by task-based and process-based models of mourning?

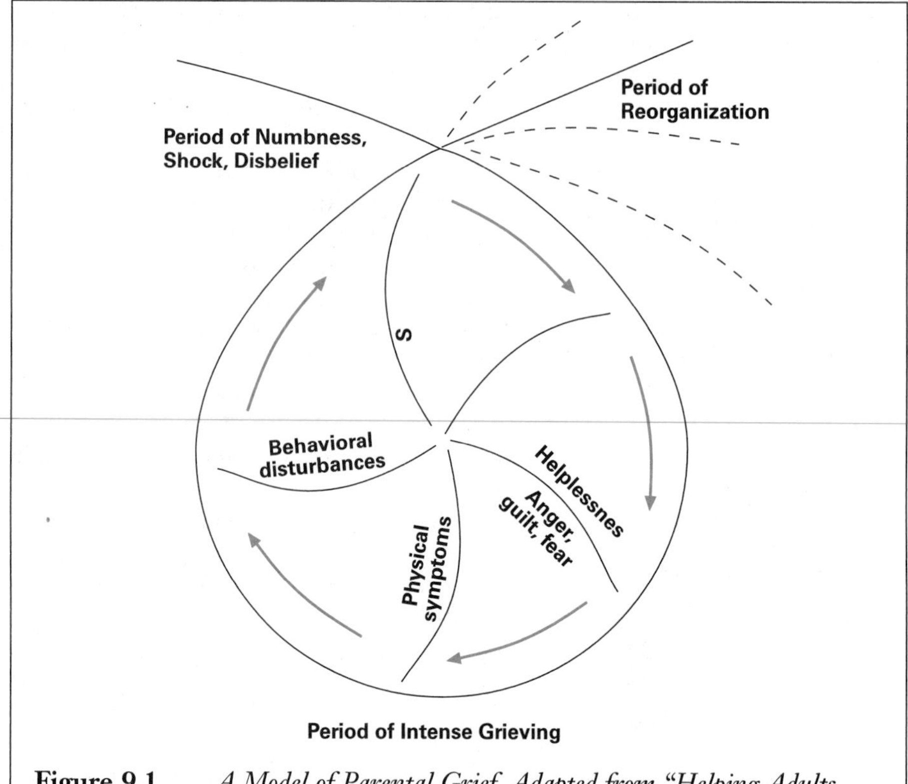

Figure 9.1 *A Model of Parental Grief. Adapted from "Helping Adults Mourn the Death of a Child," by M. S. Miles. In H. Wass and C. A. Corr (Eds.),* Childhood and Death, *p. 220. Copyright © 1984 Hemisphere Publishing Corporation, Washington, D.C. Adapted with permission.*

Tasks in Mourning

Worden (2002) recommended that we think of mourning in terms of tasks, rather than stages or phases. He suggested *four tasks in mourning:* (1) to accept the reality of the loss, (2) to work through the pain of grief, (3) to adjust to an environment in which the deceased is missing, and (4) to emotionally relocate the deceased and move on with life (see Table 9.1). A task-based model of this sort has the important advantage of emphasizing that mourning is an active process (Attig, 1991, 1996), which is similar in some ways to the description of task-based models for coping with dying that we discussed in Chapter 6. Here, examining each of these four tasks in mourning provides another way of understanding the basic dynamics of mourning and their complexities.

Worden's first task involves efforts *to accept the reality of the loss.* These efforts may not be apparent in initial grief reactions, but they underlie all of the long-term work of mourning. When confronted by the death of someone we love, we often feel an immediate sense of unreality. "It can't be true," we say, or "This can't be happening to me." As a temporary or transitional reaction to a significant change in our lives, this is wholly understandable. Nevertheless, making one's loss real and coping with one's grief involve acknowledging and accepting the reality of the death.

To fail to accept the reality of the loss is to move toward delusion and the bizarre. For example, in "A Rose for Emily," a fictional story by William Faulkner (1924/1943), we gradually learn that the female protagonist has kept the body of her dead fiancé in her house and slept in the same bed with it for many years. In a real historical example, Queen Victoria of England had the clothes and shaving gear of her dead husband (Prince Albert) laid out daily long after his death. Efforts like this to mummify or enshrine the possessions or even the body of the deceased—in order to stay connected to that person without changing one's life or so that these possessions will be ready for use when the person returns from what is imagined to be some sort of temporary absence—are really extreme attempts to suspend living at the precise moment of death so as not to face its harsh implications. However, wishing that life could resume at some future moment—unchanged from the way it was in the past—does not make it so.

According to Worden, bereaved persons also face a second task in mourning, *to work through the pain of grief.* As Parkes (2001, p. 191) has written, "anything that continually allows a person to avoid or suppress this pain can be expected to prolong the course of mourning." Productive mourning acknowledges that the pain encountered during bereavement is essential and appropriate. The challenge is to find ways of experiencing this pain that are not overwhelming for the particular individual. Ordinarily, the intensity of a survivor's pain and its tendency to consume the whole of his or her universe decline gradually as healthy mourning proceeds. One mother said: "It had to. You simply couldn't live with that level of pain."

Pain is hurtful, both to individuals and to those around them. Not surprisingly, many try to avoid the pain of grief. Some turn to drugs or alcohol to shroud their distress, but that may only drive it underground in their bodies and psyches. Some people literally try to run away from their grief by fleeing the place where the loss occurred. Others attempt to wipe out all memory and traces of the deceased in order to be relieved of the task of facing the pain of grief after a loss. Ultimately, this strategy of coping through flight is futile. "Sooner or later some at least of those who avoid all conscious grieving break down—usually with some form of depression" (Bowlby, 1980, p. 158).

A society that is uncomfortable with expressions of grief may encourage bereaved persons to flee from its pain by distracting them from their loss or assuring them that the loss was really not all that significant. The wrongheaded message here is that people do not really need to mourn and that they should not "give in" to grief, an experience that is said to be morbid and unhealthy. Sometimes, society reluctantly acknowledges that individuals need to mourn, but then tells them—for example, by commenting that they have "broken down" with grief—that they should only do so alone and in private. Prohibiting people from tasks they need to accomplish—and may need help to learn to accomplish—is, in the end, only hurtful to the individuals in question and to society itself. Mourning is in principle a healthy and healthful process.

The third of Worden's mourning tasks is to *adjust to an environment in which the deceased is missing*. Parkes wrote, "In any bereavement it is seldom clear exactly what is lost" (1987, p. 27). Bereaved survivors must engage in a voyage of discovery to determine the significance of the now-severed relationship, to identify each of the various roles that the deceased played in the relationship, and to adjust to the fact that the deceased is no longer available to fill such roles. This is difficult; a survivor might try to ignore this task or withdraw from its requirements. But life calls us forward. Young children need to be changed, bathed, and fed whether or not a spouse has died. Someone must put food on the table and wash the dishes. Adhering to a posture of helplessness is usually not a constructive coping technique—especially not as a long-term or permanent stance. For many survivors, developing new skills and taking on roles formerly satisfied by the deceased are productive ways of adjusting to loss and growing after a death (Jozefowski, 1999).

Worden describes the fourth task of mourning as one that asks the bereaved person *to emotionally relocate the deceased and move on with life*. Both aspects of this task need careful attention. "Emotional relocation" does not suggest that sur-

Family members need each other and can help each other in their grief.

vivors should "forget" the deceased person and erase his or her memory. That is neither possible nor desirable (Volkan, 1985). Similarly, "moving on with life" does not necessarily involve investing in another relationship—for example, through remarriage or deciding to have another child. Options of this sort are not open to all bereaved persons.

Even when a bereaved person enters into a new relationship, it is important to recognize that no two relationships are ever the same. No new relationship, whatever it may be, will ever be identical to or play the same role in the survivor's life as the one that has now ended. A new relationship never merely takes the place of a previous relationship. A new spouse or child is just that: a new—and different—person who is involved in a new relationship with the bereaved person and who may shape that bereaved person's identity in many new ways.

Clearly, death changes relationships. To think that is not true is to delude oneself. Thus, the fourth task of mourning for the bereaved person is to modify or restructure the relationship with or investment in the deceased in ways that remain satisfying but that also reflect the changed circumstances of life and death. I may continue to love my dead spouse and hold that memory dear in my heart, but it is probably not helpful to act as if he or she is still physically present and available to me in the same ways as before death. Satisfying Worden's fourth task will lead a bereaved person to reconceive his or her own personal identity, restructure his or her relationship with the deceased person in the light of the loss that has taken place, avoid becoming neurotically encumbered by the past in ways that diminish future quality in living, and remain open to new attachments and other relationships. Symbols and symbolic gestures can be important in this fourth task (see Box 9.5).

Like tasks in coping with dying, Worden's tasks in mourning reflect an interpretation of coping (here, mourning) as, in principle, a proactive way of striving to manage one's loss and grief. They depict mourning as involving a set of interrelated tasks, not as a succession of states or phases. Tasks require effort, but that very effort can enable the bereaved person to regain some measure of control over his or her life. Worden (2002, p. 27) wrote that the tasks of mourning "do not necessarily follow a specific order," even though "there is some ordering suggested in the definitions." He believes that mourners must accomplish these tasks before mourning can be completed.

Processes in Mourning

A third way of understanding mourning—*a process-based theory*—can be illustrated by the work of Stroebe and Schut (1999) through what they called *the dual process model.* This model situates mourning firmly in the context of coping and dynamic processes. It emphasizes an oscillation between two complementary sets of coping processes employed by bereaved persons: (1) one set of processes is *loss oriented* or concerned primarily in coping with loss; (2) the other is *restoration oriented* or concerned primarily in coping with "restoration" (see Figure 9.2). *Loss-oriented processes* might involve the intrusion of grief into the life of the bereaved, grief work, the breaking of bonds or ties to the deceased, and overcoming

Box 9.5 Four Widows on Emotionally Relocating Their Deceased Husbands and Moving on with Life

Each one of four widows dealt with her wedding ring in a different way after her husband died. One removed her ring and put it away in her jewelry box. "We were married until death parted us," she said. "Now I am no longer married to him." She did not mean that she no longer loved her former husband, but she wanted to emphasize through her actions that death had separated them and that the separation was a permanent one. A second widow continued to wear her wedding ring on the third finger of her left hand. She knew her husband was dead, but she wanted to emphasize that she still felt connected to him. She felt very content with the legacy of her long, happy, and fulfilling marriage, and she did not intend to look for another husband or a new relationship with another man.

A third widow moved her wedding ring from the third finger of her left hand to her right hand. She did not want to take it off completely or hide it away because it was an important heirloom from her grandmother. Also, she sought an outward sign both to show that she thought of herself as no longer married and to maintain some tangible indicator of a continuing bond with her deceased husband. A fourth widow removed her husband's wedding ring before his body was buried. She had a jeweler refashion it, along with her own wedding ring, into a new piece of jewelry, a pendant that she wore around her neck every day. She said, "I now have a new relationship with my deceased husband, and my lovely pendant symbolizes that new relationship." ■

SOURCE: Based on Corr, 2001a.

resistance to change. *Restoration-oriented processes* might include attending to life changes, doing new things, and avoiding or distracting oneself from grief. Note that "restoration" in this model is not about trying to make real once again the mourner's former world of lived experiences (which no longer exists) or the old assumptive world (which has also been shattered or at least rudely shaken by the loss). Rather, it has to do with efforts to adapt to the new world in which bereaved persons find themselves (Parkes, 1993). What is restored, according to this model, is not a past mode of living, but the ability to live productively in the present and future. Thus, both loss-oriented and restoration-oriented processes address issues of coping; the difference between them is centered on their meaning or focus.

In other words, the dual process model posits an oscillation or interaction between two sets of dynamic and interrelated processes in coping with bereavement. "Working through" one's loss and the grief reactions to the primary loss is thought to represent only one side of this duality; addressing secondary losses and new challenges is the other side of the picture. The dual process model also

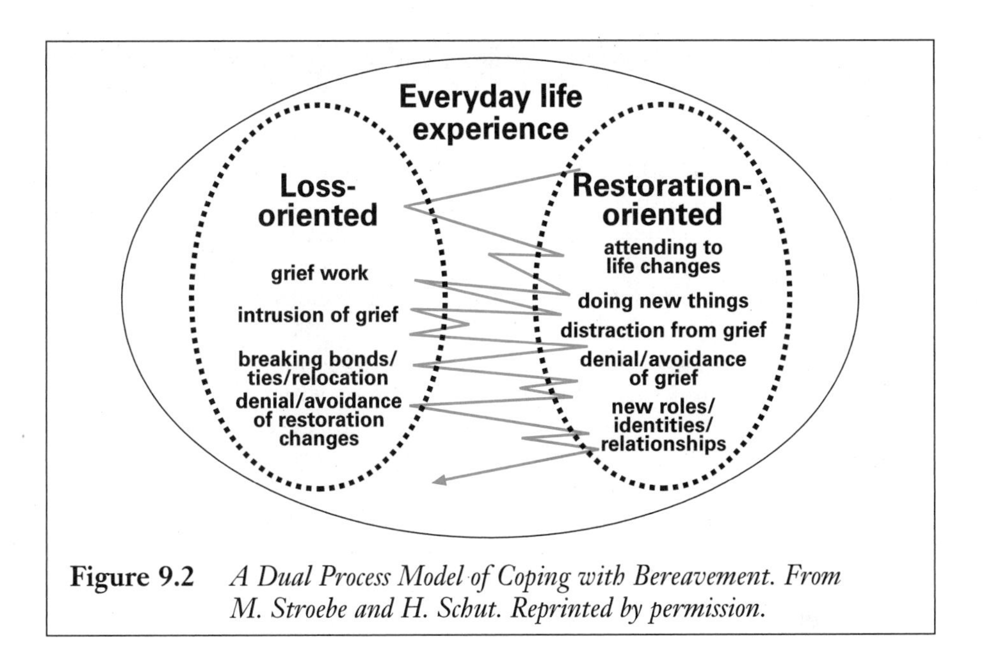

Figure 9.2 *A Dual Process Model of Coping with Bereavement. From M. Stroebe and H. Schut. Reprinted by permission.*

suggests that emphases in coping with bereavement may differ from one cultural group to another, one individual to another, and one moment to another. The main point is that some processes in mourning are more focused on coping with loss itself while other mourning processes are more focused on moving forward with healthy living. Thus, this model emphasizes the effort coping requires of bereaved persons, the potentially active nature of mourning, and the complexity of the processes involved.

Outcomes of Mourning

However mourning is understood or interpreted, the phases, tasks, or processes it encompasses have often been described as leading to recovery, completion, resolution, or adaptation (Osterweis et al., 1984; Rando, 1993). However, it is important to be careful in using these terms to characterize the outcome or goal of an individual's grief work. For example, to *recover* from one's grief seems to suggest that grief is a bad situation like an illness or disease. It also seems to imply that once one is recovered or "healed" one could be essentially unchanged by the experience. Also, *recovery*, *completion*, and *resolution* all seem to suggest a fixed endpoint for mourning, a once-and-for-all closure after which there is or should be no more mourning. If such a fixed endpoint did exist, once it was reached one would then be over and done with mourning. One would have coped successfully and would now be finished responding to loss and bereavement. Also, *adaptation* seems mainly to imply that one has made the best of a bad situation, without necessarily incorporating the changes or the development of

Box 9.6 On Being a Better Person after a Death

Peter and I had discussed how we were going to become better people from this [the death of their father and a brother on the same day]. How, after we received such compassion from our fellow man during this ordeal we had to return it somehow. "We've been touched," we said. We will become gentle human beings who never have a harsh word for anyone and have such patience that people will be astonished by our saintliness or, at the very least, our civility.

Well, that lasted until about the time we got to the airport on the way back from Arlington [National Cemetery, where they had buried their father] and I took a fit that the snack-bar lady only gave me enough cream cheese for half a bagel and wanted to charge me for more.

"Stop, it's just cream cheese," Peter said, delicately shouldering me.

"So, what's your point?" I said.

No, this will not change any of us for the better. ■

SOURCE: Shine, 2000, pp. 216–217.

new ways of functioning that are essential in productive mourning and that may lead to personal growth.

Previously, we criticized views of grief and mourning as disease states. Here, talk about "recovery" seems equally unsuitable unless one uses that term—as the dual process model seems to do with "restoration"—to mean not a return to a former, predeath way of living, but a movement forward to a new way of living in the aftermath of loss. Our point is that mourning can lead to growth as part of coping with loss and grief (although that does not always occur, at least right away; see Box 9.6). If that is so, mourning is more than coming back; it is also learning to go forward (Stearns, 1988).

Fixed endpoints are often assumed without question in attempts to assign a specified time period—for example, several weeks or months, one year—as being necessary or sufficient for mourning. "Time heals," we are frequently told. (This adage fits nicely with comparisons between bereavement and physical wounds.) However, this is really not accurate. There are no fixed endpoints for mourning. Time alone does not heal. What really counts is how that time is used. The central issue is the nature of the activities that constitute productive mourning and the outcomes to which it actually does lead. As one observer commented (S. J. Fleming, personal communication, 9/28/95), "It is not the time we have to use, but the use we make of the time we have."

As a rough guideline or rule of thumb, we might say that mourning is advancing satisfactorily when the survivor is able to think of the deceased person without the same intensity of pain that was previously experienced. Evidence of this ability is usually apparent when the survivor can once again take up tasks of daily living and can invest in life. For most people, this takes much more time than society is usually willing to concede, although for some it may not take as long. Certainly, the first year of bereavement—with all of its anniversaries, special days, and moments that remind the survivor again and again of the absence of the deceased and the loss that has been experienced—is a time of special challenge for the bereaved, a period when "anniversary reactions" may be especially prominent. But there is nothing magic in a single year—a second year of bereavement may be even more difficult as it drives home the finality of the first year's experiences (Clayton, 1973, 1974; Glick et al., 1974; Parkes, 1971).

Perhaps it is better to say with Worden (2002, p. 47): "There is a sense in which mourning can be finished, when people regain an interest in life, feel more hopeful, experience gratification again, and adapt to new roles. There is also a sense in which mourning is never finished." Bereaved persons who are asked, "When did your grief end?" or "When was your mourning over?" often respond: "Never." A bereaved person may rebound from the initial impact of loss and acute grief, or from subsequent eruptions of renewed grief, while never fully completing the work of mourning involved in learning to live with the same loss and grief. This may be more like learning to manage the permanent loss of a limb than allowing a wound to heal.

When bereaved families seven to nine years after the death of a child were asked how they had dealt with the "empty space" in their lives, their responses pointed to three different strategies: (1) "getting over it," (2) "filling the emptiness," and (3) "keeping the connection" (McClowry et al., 1987). In other words, some parents and other family members interpreted their mourning as a way of putting their grief behind them and getting over their reactions to the loss. Others sought to fill up the empty space in their lives, "keeping busy" by redirecting their energies or dedicating themselves to a new focus in their lives. This may be compatible with a periodic sense of the recurrence of the empty space. Still others found it important to maintain their connection to the deceased child or sibling by ensuring that the individual would remain a valued person in their lives as they went on with living. Keeping the connection usually involved integrating the pain and loss into their lives, often by cherishing vivid memories and stories about the deceased child.

This research seems to suggest at a minimum that mourning need not have a single, fixed outcome for all bereaved persons. As a way of coping with loss and grief, mourning is at least partly concerned with work involving "realization" (Parkes, 2001) or making real all of the implications of the loss within one's life. An important part of realization is "unlearning the expected presence of the deceased" (Rakoff, 1974, p. 159). However, another aspect of loss is recognized in Anderson's (1968, p. 5) observation that "death ends a life, but it does not end a relationship." If this is true, as we believe it is, then mourning must also involve "enriched remembrance" (Cantor, 1978; see Box 9.7, which contains many interesting insights even though we might not wish to speak of outcomes of mourning in terms of healing and completion). The concept of "enriched remembrance" seems to involve efforts to restructure the relationship so as to carry its legacy forward with the survivor into his or her new modes of living. In this way, effective mourning frees survivors to live meaningful lives in their new situation—without wholly abandoning what they have lost.

Thus, mourning is a matter of coping with loss and its aftermath, addressing the urgent demands of acute grief, carrying forward the legacy of the relationship

Box 9.7 When Is Mourning Complete?

The emotional pain caused by loss suffered does not move toward forgetfulness. It moves, rather, in the direction of enriched remembrance; the memory becomes an integral part of the mourner's personality. The work of mourning has been completed when the person (or cherished thing) no longer appears as an absence in a barren world but has come to reside securely within one's heart. Each of us must grieve in his or her own manner and at his or her own pace. For many people, one year seems to bring completion. Others require much more or much less time. Periodic waves of grief are often felt for the remainder of one's life. The mourning process must be given the freedom to find its own depth and rhythm; it cannot be artificially accelerated. A loss, like a physical wound, cannot heal overnight. There is no way to hurry the stages of tissue growth and there is no way to speed up the healing process of mourning. But, when mourning has been completed, the mourner comes to feel the inner presence of the loved one, no longer an idealized hero or a maligned villain, but a presence with human dimensions. Lost irreversibly in objective time, the person is present in a new form within one's mind and heart, tenderly present in inner time without the pain and bitterness of death. And once the loved one has been accepted in this way he or she can never again be forcefully removed. ■

SOURCE: From (with minor adaptations) *And a Time to Live: Toward Emotional Well-Being During the Crisis of Cancer,* by R. C. Cantor, pp. 66–67. Copyright © 1978 by Harper & Row, New York. Reprinted by permission of the author.

in an appropriate way into the new postdeath life, and learning to develop and live with "new normals" throughout the rest of the survivor's life. These tasks have been described as centered on "relearning the world" (Attig, 1996) or "meaning reconstruction" (Neimeyer, 2001), even while they are also reported to involve "continuing bonds" or "ongoing connections" with the deceased (Klass et al., 1996). To put this more simply: many bereaved persons have reported that from time to time they have sensed the continued presence of the deceased in their lives or have received after-death communications—and have often taken comfort from those extraordinary or paranormal experiences (LaGrand, 1997, 1999, 2001). One challenge in mourning is to decide what these experiences mean and to find ways to integrate them into healthful, ongoing living.

Grief, Mourning, and Gender

Until recently, much of the research on adult bereavement has been based on women. Reasons for this emphasis include the fact that there are many more widows than widowers, and women are often more willing than men to discuss or share their grief. However, further study of bereaved women and more recent attention to bereaved men has led to contrasting views on grief, mourning, and gender.

For example, there is one view that the way (many? all?) women experience and express their grief and cope with their losses constitutes a "feminine model." An extension of this view is to claim that this feminine model is the "conventional" or right way to grieve. One example of this point of view is provided by Staudacher (1991, p. 3) who argued that "there is only one way to grieve. That way is to go through the core of grief. Only by experiencing the necessary emotional effects of your loved one's death is it possible for you to eventually resolve the loss." In this view, experiencing and expressing emotion—often coupled with a willingness to reach out and accept help—are thought to be essential to healthy bereavement. This is partly about the grief reactions that one has, but the real emphasis is on how those reactions are expressed and on how one copes with loss and grief. However one describes this way of living out one's bereavement, in our society it is often characteristic of bereaved women.

For Staudacher, this description of grief and mourning processes in (many) women has become normative. This so-called "feminine" way of responding to loss and grief is thought to be the "conventional" or only appropriate way; it is what everyone ought to do. As a result, bereaved men are thought to be disadvantaged because they are seen as ignoring their feelings, hiding from their grief, being unwilling to share their emotions, and refusing offers of help. In short, gender favors women in grief. Women mourn correctly and men need to learn to follow that pattern of mourning.

One alternative to this "feminization of grief" is to develop a contrasting theory of "masculine grief" (Golden, 1996; Martin & Doka, 1996, 1998). For example, masculine grief might be said to focus on feelings of anger and guilt, suppressing other emotional responses and hiding vulnerability, an emphasis on thinking about the loss (versus feeling), a desire for solitude, being reluctant to share grief or seek help, valuing self-reliance, assuming the role of protector, seeking to solve practical problems or engage in physical actions, and immersing oneself in work. According to this second view of grief, mourning, and gender, men have their own ways of coping with loss and bereavement, and they ought to be permitted to proceed according to this "masculine" option.

A third view claims that although patterns of grief and mourning may often be related to gender, they are not determined by it. Martin and Doka (2000) now contrast what they had formerly called "feminine" and "masculine" patterns in grief as "intuitive" versus "instrumental," respectively. According to this view, "intuitive" grievers emphasize experiencing and expressing emotion, whereas "instrumental" grievers focus on practical matters and problem solving. The important point for Martin and Doka is this: *the issue is not really one of gender, but of style.* Women and men often express their reactions to loss and cope with their grief in different ways because they have been socialized to perceive themselves and their roles in different ways. But that tendency is not ironclad. All women have not been socialized in a single, rigid way, nor have all men been socialized in a single, contrasting way. Individuals of both genders have different backgrounds, personalities, and ways of living out their lives. As a result, some women are instrumental grievers, and some men are intuitive grievers. The characters of the cold, distant mother and warm, supportive father in the novel and film *Ordinary People* (Guest, 1976) illustrate this point well. Thus a man who grieves by expressing rather than repressing his emotions is not being "effeminate," nor is a woman being "masculine" or not being feminine if she does not share her grief. Such judgments by others merely add another layer of stress to the many difficulties with which bereaved persons are already trying to cope.

Perhaps the most important point in this discussion of grief, mourning, and gender is to legitimize individuality in coping with loss and grief, even as we seek to identify shared patterns among various groups of bereaved persons whose members may or may not be of a specific gender.

Grief, Mourning, and Families

Grief has most often been understood in everyday life and studied in the professional literature as an individual reaction to loss. Until recently, not much attention had been given to the role(s) of families or other similar social groups in bereavement (Brabant, 1996; Shapiro, 1994). In this section, we ask four questions: (1) How are families significant in their members' bereavement? (2) How do families differ in the ways in which they affect their members' bereavement? (3) Do families grieve as a unit? and (4) Do families as a unit cope with loss and grief?

The answer to our first question is that, at a minimum, grief within a family "consists of the interplay of individual family members grieving in the social and relational context of the family, with each member affecting and being affected by the others" (Gilbert, 1996, p. 271). This means that a family system (whatever one may identify as one's "family" and however it may be constituted) almost always provides a context for and will influence its members' experiences of loss, grief, and mourning.

Second, families are different in the ways in which they affect their members' bereavement. To the degree that they are able, families socialize or prepare their members to value relationships, acknowledge losses, express grief, and mourn. However, each family views death-related encounters, attitudes, and practices in its own specific way. Each family also forms relationships within its unit in its own way. For example, extremely enmeshed families will entangle their members very closely with each other, while disengaged families do not offer much support to their members. Some families allow their members considerable freedom in how they express grief and mourning, while other families expect all members to express grief and mourning in the same way. Other family characteristics that may be relevant to the grief of members include: whether the family system engages in open communication or secrecy, the availability of extended family, the family's social and economic resources, the prior role and functioning of the

Grief is expressed in different ways within a multi-generational family.

deceased member in the family system, and the existence of conflicted or estranged relationships at the time of death (Walsh & McGoldrick, 1991a).

Families also differ in their place in a family developmental life cycle (McGoldrick & Walsh, 1991). Losses may occur at different points in what systems theorists portray as a three-generational family life cycle (Carter & McGoldrick, 1988):

- To unattached young adults who are between families
- To young couples who are joining together and creating new family units through marriage
- To families with young children
- To families with adolescents
- To families who are launching children and moving on
- To families in later life

Each of these family types is likely to be coping with different developmental challenges. For example, a new couple may be struggling with issues of commitment to their new family system, while an established couple who are launching children and moving on may be coping with unaccustomed issues of personal and family identity. For a new couple, questions that arise might include: "Can each of us accommodate our previous independence to make a go of our new family unit?" or "Can we work together to become parents and bring children into the world?" By contrast, a couple that is moving on after launching children might ask: "Can we readjust ourselves to take advantage of the opportunities of our new empty nest?" or "Do we still have parental roles to fulfill now that our children have moved away?" In short, families at different points in their life cycle may have different strengths and limitations to make available to their bereaved members. Such families may be affected in different ways and by different sorts of losses.

A third question is whether or not families grieve as a unit. This goes beyond thinking of families only as the context for each of their members' individual grief and mourning. Shapiro (1994) has argued that grief is a family process, but Montgomery and Fewer (1988) contend that this confuses individual and family-level properties. According to Montgomery and Fewer, responses to loss are found in families and families engage in the public or interpersonal processes of mourning, but families do not do the intrapersonal processes of experiencing loss and grief—perhaps for the simple reason that families are not persons. That is why one can often observe significant differences in the grief and mourning of individual family members. Gilbert (1996, p. 273) agrees with this view when she writes: "Families do not grieve. Only individuals grieve. This is done in a variety of contexts, one of which is the family."

Still, it is clear that major losses such as death do bring disorder into family systems and families must cope with that disruption. Death affects the often-unspoken set of assumptions about how life ought to be, well-established roles and relationships, and everyday responsibilities and routines. These and other aspects of family life must be reconsidered and reconstructed (Lamberti & Detmer, 1993; Moos, 1995). In addition, since loss and grief can "have an effect across the boundaries separating one generation from the next," there may be a "multigenerational ripple effect" from a significant death (Detmer & Lamberti, 1991, p. 366).

Following a death, Walsh and McGoldrick (1991a) have argued that two major tasks confront family members and family units: (1) to share acknowledgment of the reality of death and to share the experience of loss; and (2) to reorganize the family system and to reinvest in other relationships and life pursuits. (Note that each of these combines two of the mourning tasks for individuals described by Worden and restates them in family systems terminology; compare Walsh & McGoldrick, 1988.) Acknowledging the reality of death and sharing the experience of loss involve recognition of the loss and its implications, sharing grief reactions, and tolerating individual differences within the family system. Reorganizing the family system requires family members to reconstruct what the family means to them and their sense of identity as a family. In addition, family members must reapportion or abandon activities and roles formerly assigned to the deceased. Reinvestment, as we noted earlier in this chapter, involves restructuring or transforming the relationship with the deceased so as to allow family members to maintain a sense of connection with that person and with their past even as they move toward the future. Open, honest, and supportive communication within the family system is essential to all of these tasks. Family rituals or shared ways of dealing with issues that bring members together, such as memorialization practices, commemorative activities, or prayer, are often useful (Bowen, 1991; Imber-Black, 1991).

Anticipatory Grief and Mourning

The concept of *anticipatory grief* was first introduced by Lindemann (1944) and has since been the subject of various inquiries (for example, Aldrich, 1963; Fulton & Fulton, 1971; Fulton & Gottesman, 1980; Rando, 1986b, 2000; Siegel & Weinstein, 1983). Broadly speaking, anticipatory grief refers to grief experiences that take place prior to but in connection with a significant loss that is expected to take place—for example, grief that occurs in advance of, but somehow still in relation to, impending death. A forewarning of death is a necessary condition for anticipatory grief, but the heart of the matter is the grief reaction to the anticipated, but not yet actually realized, loss.

Some have argued that there can be no such phenomenon as anticipatory grief since the task for a significant other—for example, a wife—is to support and continue to love her husband during the time when he is dying (Parkes & Weiss, 1983; Silverman, 1974). This appears to be an extreme view; on its face, it would deny that the dying husband and/or his spouse could experience grief in reaction to their awareness of his impending death. Edgar Allan Poe provided a clear example of this phenomenon in describing his reactions to his wife's anticipated death (see Box 9.8).

Rando (1986b, p. 24) originally defined anticipatory grief as "the phenomenon encompassing the processes of mourning, coping, interaction, planning, and psychosocial reorganization that are stimulated and begun in part in response to the awareness of the impending loss of a loved one and the recognition of associated losses in the past, present, and future." This is a very broad definition of anticipatory grief that includes both grief reactions and mourning processes. It refers equally to past, present, and future losses. It incorporates a shifting time frame as the dying person moves toward death, and it encompasses the perspectives of both the dying person and his or her survivors-to-be.

One problem with this definition is that the adjective *anticipatory* would seem to be incorrect since the grief in question is not limited solely to future or expected losses. A second problem is that the noun *grief* is inexact since the definition includes both grief and mourning. For those reasons, Rando (1988a) first argued that although the phenomenon of anticipatory grief is real, the term itself is a misnomer. Subsequently, she decided to shift to the phrase *anticipatory mourning* in the title of a later book, *Clinical Dimensions of Anticipatory Mourning* (Rando, 2000).

It seems clear that when a husband is dying, a wife may realize that she has already lost the help that he used to give her around the house (a past loss), that she is currently losing the vigorous ways in which he used to express his love

Box 9.8 An Extract from a Letter by Edgar Allan Poe of January 4, 1848

"You say—'Can you *hint* to me what was the terrible evil' which caused the irregularities so profoundly lamented?' Yes; I can do more than hint. This 'evil' was the greatest which can befall a man. Six years ago, a wife, whom I loved as no man ever loved before, ruptured a blood-vessel in singing. Her life was despaired of. I took leave of her forever & underwent all the agonies of her death. She recovered partially and I again hoped. At the end of a year the vessel broke again—I went through precisely the same scene. Again in about a year afterward. Then again—again—again & even once again at varying intervals. Each time I felt all the agonies of her death—and at each accession of the disorder I loved her more dearly & clung to her life with more desperate pertinacity. But I am constitutionally sensitive—nervous in a very unusual degree. I became insane, with long intervals of horrible sanity. During these fits of absolute unconsciousness I drank, God only knows how often or how much. As a matter of course, my enemies referred the insanity to the drink rather than the drink to the insanity. I had indeed, nearly abandoned all hope of a permanent cure when I found one in the death of my wife. This I can & do endure as becomes a man—it was the horrible never-ending oscillation between hope & despair which I could not longer have endured without the total loss of reason. In the death of what was my life, then, I receive a new but—oh God! how melancholy an existence." ■

SOURCE: From Poe, 1948, vol. 2, p. 356.

for her (a present or ongoing loss), and that she will soon lose the comfort of his presence and the shared retirement that they had planned together (an expected or anticipated loss). Each of these losses may generate its own grief reaction and each may stimulate a mourning process in which one tries to cope with that loss and/or its associated grief reaction. However, these experiences need not be inconsistent with maintaining the loving ties that characterize an attachment between two living people. After all, partners often experience other losses—a job, a beloved home, a loved parent or friend—but continue to love each other through the loss.

We might clarify the meaning of anticipatory grief by adopting a narrower definition, one that limits "anticipatory" grief (and mourning) to reactions to losses that have not yet occurred and are not yet in process—that is, to losses that have not yet moved from expectation to reality. If so, reacting to and coping with dying would become the master concepts in predeath experiences of grief and mourning (Corr & Corr, 2000). Prior to death, one might experience anticipatory grief and mourning related to losses that are expected to take place in the future, other (nonanticipatory) grief reactions and mourning processes that are associated with existing losses (past and present), and reactions to and coping with the new challenges that inevitably arise during dying. This would counterbalance the overemphasis on the effects on postdeath grieving that has unduly dominated discussions of anticipatory grief. Anticipatory grief may affect the quality of postdeath bereavement, but it need not be any more (or less) significant on this matter than all of the other aspects of coping with dying.

Traumatic Loss and Death

A death or loss is properly termed "traumatic" when its circumstances include certain objective elements, such as: "(a) suddenness and lack of anticipation; (b) violence, mutilation, and destruction; (c) preventability and/or randomness; (d) multiple death; and (e) the mourner's personal encounter with death, where there is either a significant threat to personal survival or a massive and/or shocking confrontation with the death and mutilation of others" (Rando, 1993, pp. 568–569). All of these, as we have seen, apply to the losses experienced by the attack on America on September 11, 2001.

First, when the loss or death is *sudden and unanticipated* its shock effects tend to overwhelm a mourner's capacity to cope (Rando, 1996). There is no opportunity to say good-bye and finish unfinished business. Because the event does not seem to make sense, there is often an obsessive effort to reconstruct events so as to comprehend and prepare for them in a retrospective way. Also, traumatic events are often accompanied by intense emotional reactions (fear, anxiety, and a sense of vulnerability and loss of control) and increased physiological arousal. Further, trauma is often followed by major secondary losses, such as having no body to view to confirm the death, a need to rescue others or attend to the wounded, and the demands of legal inquiries.

Second, *violence, mutilation, and destruction* in traumatic events may produce feelings of terror, fear, and anxiety. These feelings may be accompanied by a sense of vulnerability, victimization, and powerlessness. There may also be fantasies of grotesque dying and aggressive thoughts of revenge.

Third, when a traumatic event is perceived as *preventable,* mourners view it as one that could have been avoided. It appears to be both a willful or irresponsibly negligent event as well as an unprovoked violation. As a result, survivors may become angry, outraged, and frustrated. Hence, they strive intensely to find the cause of the event, fix responsibility, and impose punishment. When a traumatic event is perceived as *random,* its unpredictability and uncontrollability can be terrifying. To ward off such terror, mourners and victims often blame themselves for such events, choosing that alternative as a way to defend themselves against the perception that events in the world are truly random and unpredictable, that they cannot be protected against.

Fourth, experiencing *multiple deaths or losses* in a traumatic encounter—especially when they occur simultaneously or in rapid succession as happened on September 11—can produce a form of *bereavement overload* (Kastenbaum, 1969) in which mourners find it difficult to sort out and work through their losses, grief reactions, and mourning processes for each individual tragedy.

Firefighters salute as their colleagues recover the body of a co-worker at the World Trade Center.

Fifth, a mourner's *personal encounter with death* in a traumatic event can involve a significant threat to personal survival or can follow a massive or shocking confrontation with the death and mutilation of others. In the former instance, one is likely to experience fear, terror, heightened arousal, a sense of abandonment and helplessness, and increased vulnerability; in the latter instance, horrifying sensory stimuli (sights, sounds, smells) often produce reactive phenomena, such as nightmares, flashbacks, and intrusive images or memories.

One or more of these five objective elements can usually be found in any traumatic event, whether the event is a *human-induced victimization* (as in the events of September 11, 2001, as well as cases of rape, battering, incest, other criminal assaults, robbery, torture, and terrorism or war-related atrocities) or *a natural disaster* (as in instances of life-threatening disease, serious accidents, earthquakes, hurricanes, tornadoes, and floods). These events result in loss or death that is outside the ordinary range of human experience and that is usually associated with intense fear, terror, and a sense of helplessness (Zinner & Williams, 1999). Many have linked the stress response syndromes that result from traumatic events to *post-traumatic stress disorder* (PTSD)—whose basic symptom categories include reexperiencing the traumatic event, avoiding stimuli associated with the traumatic event or numbing of general responsiveness, and increased physiological arousal—but Prigerson and her colleagues (Jacobs et al., 2000; Prigerson et al., 1999; Prigerson & Jacobs, 2001) have argued that they constitute a distinct form of complicated grief.

Traumatic events have been reported to shatter our *assumptive world*, the "strongly held set of assumptions about the world and the self which is confidently maintained and used as a means of recognizing, planning, and acting"

(Parkes, 1975a, p. 132). In her book, *Shattered Assumptions*, Janoff-Bulman (1992) described an assumptive world as "a conceptual system, developed over time, that provides us with expectations about the world and ourselves" (p. 5). She argued that the fundamental assumptions held by most people in their assumptive worlds are: "The world is benevolent"; "the world is meaningful"; and "the self is worthy." She contended that such beliefs are broad, but not foolhardy, assumptions because they "afford us the trust and confidence that are necessary to engage in new behaviors, to test our limits" (p. 23).

If we consider traumatic events in terms of their effect on our fundamental assumptions, "in the end, it is a rebuilding of this trust—the reconstruction of a viable, nonthreatening assumptive world—that constitutes the core coping task of victims" (Janoff-Bulman, 1992, p. 69). This is the path from being merely a *victim* of a traumatic event to becoming a *survivor* in the full sense of that word. Such a path has elements that are similar to other forms of complicated mourning (Prigerson & Jacobs, 2001). In this case, the mourner will need to cope with both the traumatic aspects of the encounter and the loss and grief found in all bereavement. Thus, Janoff-Bulman (1992) described survivors who have coped effectively with traumatic events and challenges to their fundamental convictions and assumptive worlds in the following ways:

> . . . these survivors recognize the possibility of tragedy, but do not allow it to pervade their self- and worldviews. . . .
>
> [For such survivors] the world is benevolent, but not absolutely; events that happen make sense, but not always; the self can be counted on to be decent and competent, but helplessness is at times a reality. . . .
>
> There is disillusionment, yet it is generally not the disillusionment of despair. Rather, it is disillusionment tempered by hope. . . .
>
> [In the end, this view] involves an acknowledgment of real possibilities, both bad and good—of disaster in spite of human efforts, of triumph in spite of human limitations. (pp. 174–175)

These are the tasks facing many Americans after the terrorist attacks of September 11, 2001.

Complicated Grief Reactions

Thus far in this chapter, we have taken the view that the human experiences of grief and mourning are—at least for the most part—normal and healthy. Still, all human processes can become distorted and unhealthy—usually when they are carried to excess. The phrase *complicated grief reactions* (or complicated mourning) refers to grief reactions or mourning processes that are not only unusual but also abnormal in the sense of being deviant and unhealthy. They may include, but are not limited to, traumatic grief reactions. Describing such experiences as "complicated" respects the difficulties they present without adopting the language of pathology, which seems to many to be unduly judgmental in tone (Volkan, 1970, 1985).

Complicated grief reactions are, in fact, a kind of psychological disorder. They are excessive, distorted, or unproductive (Demi & Miles, 1987). As a result, they overwhelm bereaved persons in a persistent way, lead to maladaptive behavior, or do not move productively toward satisfactory outcomes in mourning. We address these complications here both as a contrast to healthful forms of mourning and as a guide for helpers—whose work is discussed more fully in Chapter 10.

Worden (2002) identified four types of complicated grief reactions:

- *Chronic grief reactions*, which are prolonged in duration and do not lead to an appropriate outcome, as when individuals become aware that they are not making progress in getting back into living again
- *Delayed grief reactions*, in which grief at the time of the loss is then inhibited, suppressed, or postponed, not surfacing again until later, when it will most often appear as an excessive reaction to a subsequent loss or other triggering event
- *Exaggerated grief reactions*, which are excessive and disabling in ways that may lead to the development of a phobia or irrational fear, to physical or psychiatric symptoms, or to aberrant or maladaptive behavior
- *Masked grief reactions*, in which individuals experience symptoms or behaviors—including the complete absence of grief (Deutsch, 1937)—that cause them difficulty but that they do not recognize as related to the loss

In general, complicated grief reactions seem to develop as a result of difficulties in: the relationship with the deceased (for example, ambivalent, dependent, or narcissistic relationships); the circumstances of the death (for instance, uncertainty about or unwillingness to accept the fact of death, or a situation of multiple or traumatic losses); the survivor's own history or personality (such as a history of depressive illness, a personality that employs withdrawal to defend against extremes of emotional distress or that does not tolerate dependency feelings well, or a self-concept that includes being the "strong" one in the family); or the social factors that surround the experience (for example, when a loss is disenfranchised as socially unspeakable or socially negated, or when a social support network is absent).

It is important for helpers to be alert to potential complications in grief and mourning, and to obtain appropriate assistance that would help to untangle complications in grief reactions. However, because of the inevitable individuality of grief reactions, professional assessment is often required both to distinguish idiosyncratic but healthy grief reactions from complicated and unhealthy grief reactions and to intervene in useful therapeutic ways (Rando, 1993).

Summary

In this chapter, we began an examination of central elements involved in the human experiences of loss, bereavement, grief, and mourning. We focused on variables that affect those experiences, paying special attention to how one understands grief and its many manifestations, interpretations of mourning (including models based on phases, tasks, and processes), outcomes of uncomplicated mourning, issues related to gender and families, anticipatory grief and mourning, traumatic loss and death, and complicated grief reactions.

Questions for Review and Discussion

1. Think of a time when you experienced the loss of some person or thing that was important in your life. What made this an important loss for you? Would it have been different if you had lost a different person or thing, or if the loss had occurred in a different way?

2. How did you react to that loss? Try to be as complete as possible in developing this description of your reactions to the loss.

3. How did you cope with that loss? What helped you to cope with that loss or to integrate it into your ongoing living? What was not helpful? Why was it not helpful?

Suggested Readings

Introductory descriptions of loss, grief, and mourning appear in:

Davidson, G. W. (1984). *Understanding Mourning: A Guide for Those Who Grieve.*

Viorst, J. (1986). *Necessary Losses.*

Westberg, G. (1971). *Good Grief.*

Additional analyses of bereavement appear in the following:

Attig, T. (1996). *How We Grieve: Relearning the World.*

Bowlby, J. (1973–82). *Attachment and Loss* (3 vols.): vol. 1, *Attachment;* vol. 2, *Separation: Anxiety and Anger;* vol. 3, Loss: *Sadness and Depression.*

Freud, S. (1959a). *Mourning and Melancholia.* In J. Strachey (Ed. and Trans.), *The Standard Edition of the Complete Psychological Works of Sigmund Freud* (vol. 14, pp. 237–258).

Klass, D., Silverman, P. R., & Nickman, S. L. (Eds.). (1996). *Continuing Bonds: New Understandings of Grief.*

Neimeyer, R. A. (Ed.). (2001). *Meaning Reconstruction and the Experience of Loss.*

Osterweis, M., Solomon, F., & Green, M. (Eds.). (1984). *Bereavement: Reactions, Consequences, and Care.*

Parkes, C. M. (2001). *Bereavement: Studies of Grief in Adult Life* (3rd ed.).

Raphael, B. (1983). *The Anatomy of Bereavement.*

Sanders, C. M. (1989). *Grief: The Mourning After.*

Stroebe, M. S., Hansson, R. O., Stroebe, W., & Schut, H. (Eds.). (2001). *Handbook of Bereavement Research: Consequences, Coping, and Care.*

Special topics in grief and bereavement are examined in the following:

Doka, K. J. (Ed.). (1996b). *Living with Grief after Sudden Loss: Suicide, Homicide, Accident, Heart Attack, Stroke.*

Glick, I., Weiss, R., & Parkes, C. (1974). *The First Year of Bereavement.*

Lagoni, L., Butler, C., & Hetts, S. (1994). *The Human-Animal Bond and Grief.*

Martin, T., & Doka, K. J. (2000). *Men Don't Cry, Women Do: Transcending Gender Stereotypes of Grief.*

Nadeau, J. (1998). *Families Make Sense of Death.*

Parkes, C. M., & Weiss, R. (1983). *Recovery from Bereavement.*

Rando, T. A. (Ed.). (2000). *Clinical Dimensions of Anticipatory Mourning: Theory and Practice in Working with the Dying, Their Loved Ones, and Their Caregivers.*

Rosenblatt, P. C. (1983). *Bitter, Bitter Tears: Nineteenth-Century Diarists and Twentieth-Century Grief Theories.*

Zinner, E. S., & Williams, M. B. (1999). *When a Community Weeps: Case Studies in Group Survivorship.*

InfoTrac College Edition
For more information, explore the InfoTrac College Edition at **http://www.infotrac-college.com/Wadsworth**

Enter search terms: ANTICIPATORY GRIEF AND MOURNING, BEREAVEMENT, COMPLICATED GRIEF REACTIONS (CHRONIC, DELAYED, EXAGGERATED, MASKED), DEATH AND GRIEF, DEATH AND GUILT, DEATH AND LOSS, DEPRESSION, MOURNING, TRAUMATIC LOSS, UNCOMPLICATED GRIEF REACTIONS.

Chapter Ten

COPING WITH LOSS AND GRIEF: HOW INDIVIDUALS CAN HELP

We begin here with the example of Stella Bridgman, the bereaved person whose losses we described at the beginning of Chapter 9. In this vignette, we focus on some of the people around her, and their actions that were or were not helpful to Stella, as a way of enabling us to focus on the basic needs of bereaved people. We then describe some unhelpful messages that are all too often directed to bereaved persons and introduce the concept of disenfranchised grief. Against this, we describe some simple, constructive suggestions for helping the bereaved, and we offer the example of pet loss to show how some losses may be ignored or disvalued and to draw out further guidelines for helpers. We then reformulate Worden's (2002) tasks in mourning to demonstrate how each of us *as individuals* can help bereaved persons with cognitive, affective, behavioral, and valuational tasks. Following that, we describe two programs that prepare individuals to help persons who are coping with loss and grief: Widow-to-Widow programs and the Stephen Ministry. Finally, we describe ten principles that were originally formulated to facilitate uncomplicated grief. These principles were designed to be guidelines for counseling relationships, but they really apply in a more general way to all one-to-one relationships in which one is trying to help a bereaved person. ■

Stella Bridgman: Who Helps a Grieving Person?

When her mother died after a long, lingering illness, Stella Bridgman turned for consolation to her husband, to some relatives and friends who lived nearby, and to her church. They provided enough help to her that she was able to resume a normal life.

But then her first husband died, and it got much worse after her teenage son took his own life. Many of her friends and associates withdrew from her and were not helpful. They felt uncomfortable in the presence of her intense distress, and she felt that she was being badly treated and even stigmatized by some of the ways in which they regarded her as the survivor of a death by suicide.

Some people tried to tell Stella that they knew what she was feeling, but mostly she did not find that helpful. Many people tried hard not to mention her son's name because they thought that would only make Stella feel bad. They found it especially difficult to talk about the way that he had ended his life. Mostly, people tried to avoid Stella and steer clear of any reminders of her loss.

When others withdrew from her, Stella felt isolated and lonely. When others tried not to mention her son's name, Stella perceived this as compounding her initial loss. By not even talking about her son, she feared that people were trying to erase all mention and memory of his life. Above all, Stella felt hurt by these actions of people from whom she had expected assistance and support.

Stella did find one or two people who really helped her. Each of these people simply gave her a hug, lent her an ear in person or by telephone, and just made himself or herself available to Stella. In their presence, Stella knew she didn't have to be careful about what she said or the feelings she expressed. None of them behaved as if they needed to have Stella "get over" her grief. One good friend brought food occasionally or came over once in a while to cook nutritious meals with Stella. Another encouraged Stella to talk about her losses and to go out for walks with her.

Stella knew the story of Job from the Bible. So she was sensitive to the differences between the very proper church elder who told her that "God never gives us burdens heavier than we can bear" and the young clergy person who was wise enough to be silent when Stella needed to express her anger at God for letting these tragedies befall her.

Fundamental Needs of Bereaved Persons

Davidson (1984) has written that bereaved persons need five things: social support, nutrition, hydration, exercise, and rest. Among these, social support is most frequently mentioned and it is often a major postdeath variable in determining complicated versus uncomplicated grief. In Chapter 9, we saw that the variables that make a difference in bereavement and grief include the nature of the prior attachment, the way in which the loss occurred and the concurrent circumstances of the bereavement, the coping strategies that the individual has learned to use in dealing with previous losses, the developmental situation of the bereaved person, and the nature and availability of support for the bereaved person after the loss. In practice, only the last of these is open to alteration after a death has occurred. It is, therefore, the main subject of this and the following chapter.

In the videotape *Pitch of Grief* (1985), an experienced hospice bereavement volunteer observes that the single thing that can most help a bereaved person is the "presence of a caring person." It is not as important what such a person says or does—although there are better and worse things that one might do or say—as that the person does care and is available (Donnelley, 1987). As we have seen throughout this book, listening is a way of giving oneself to the other, of putting aside one's own concerns in order to let the other talk about his or her concerns (see Box 10.1).

The other factors mentioned by Davidson are often ignored in the literature on bereavement. Individuals who are bereaved may experience a disinterest in food and a general loss of appetite. They may also lack energy or the ability to concentrate on the tasks required to prepare nourishing meals. That is one reason that many communities have traditions in which friends and neighbors bring food and drink to the bereaved. In addition to nourishing themselves improperly, sometimes bereaved persons willingly or unwillingly contribute to deficits in their own hydration and nutrition by consuming empty calories or dehydrating liquids like alcohol.

Similarly, bereaved persons need exercise and rest. Some bereaved persons experience insomnia or other disruptions in sleep patterns, whereas other bereaved persons sleep continually without ever feeling really rested. Healthy exercise and a good night's sleep can contribute to a productive mourning process.

Those who seek to help bereaved persons can do much to see that they obtain adequate nutrition, hydration, exercise, and rest.

Unhelpful Messages

All too often, our society conveys unhelpful messages to bereaved persons. Typically, these are clustered around: (1) minimization of the loss that has been experienced, (2) admonitions not to feel (or, at least, not to express in public)

Box 10.1 Listen

When I ask you to listen to me,
And you start giving me advice,
You have not done what I asked.
When I ask that you listen to me,
And you begin to tell me why I shouldn't feel that way,
You are trampling on my feelings.
When I ask you to listen to me,
And you feel you have to do something to solve my problems,
You have failed me, strange as that may seem.
Listen: All that I ask is that you listen,
Not talk or do—just hear me.
When you do something for me
That I need to do for myself,
You contribute to my fear and feelings of inadequacy.
But when you accept as a simple fact
That I do feel what I feel, no matter how irrational,
Then I can quit trying to convince you
And go about the business
Of understanding what's behind my feelings.
So, please listen and just hear me
And, if you want to talk,
Wait a minute for your turn—and I'll listen to you. ■

SOURCE: An anonymous author, reprinted in Landers Daily, *St. Louis-Post Dispatch*, September 19, 1998, p. D3, Creators Syndicate.

the strong grief reactions that one is experiencing, and/or (3) suggestions that one should promptly get back to living and not disturb others with one's grief and mourning.

The first of these clusters of messages may involve the following sorts of statements:

- "Now that your baby has died, you have a little angel in heaven." (But my pregnancy was not intended as a way of making heavenly angels.)
- "You can always have another baby," or "You already have other children." (But how would either of these replace the baby who died?)
- "You're still young, you can get married again." (Yes, but that will not bring back my first spouse or lessen the hurt of his or her loss.)
- "You had a good, long marriage." (Yes, but that only makes me feel all the more keenly the pain of what I have lost.)
- "After all, your grandfather was a very old man." (But that made him all the more dear to me.)

From the standpoint of the bereaved, these messages seem to suggest that the loss was really not all that important or that the deceased person was not truly irreplaceable. One related implication is that bereavement and grief

An illustration of a friend helping a bereaved person from Tear Soup *(see Box 10.2).*

should not be perceived by the individual as such difficult experiences. Another implication is that friends and relatives of the bereaved person, or society as a whole, need not permit the grief-related needs of the bereaved persons to change their daily routines very much.

The second cluster of messages to bereaved persons seeks to suppress the depth or intensity of the grief they are experiencing. For example, such individuals will be told:

- "Be strong," or "Keep a stiff upper lip."
- "You'll be fine," "Don't be always upset," "Put a smile on your face."
- "You're the big man or woman of the family now."
- "Why are you still upset? It's been . . . [four weeks, six months, a year]."
- "What you need to do is to keep busy, get back to work, forget her."

In fact, no one can simply stop experiencing what he or she is experiencing. Feelings and all of the other reactions to a significant loss are real. These grief reactions need to be lived with and lived through. They only change in their own ways and at their own pace. The underlying theme of this second cluster of messages is that it is not good for bereaved individuals to experience some feelings or other grief reactions. Even when grief reactions are acknowledged in principle, it will often be suggested to bereaved persons that they should not experience their reactions in certain (especially public or powerful) ways. The principal theme in such messages is that these ways of experiencing one's grief are unacceptable to those around the bereaved person. In other words, the real message is that your grief is making me or us uncomfortable, and that is inappropriate.

The third set of messages is really a variant of the first two. This set of messages arises from the common practice in American society of what has been called "oppressive toleration." That is the view that people can do or say whatever they wish (or, in this case, experience and express grief in any ways they might want to), as long as they do not disturb others. Accordingly, it is often made clear to bereaved persons in more or less subtle ways—all too frequently, in ways that are very unsubtle indeed—that if they insist, they can grieve as they wish, but in so doing they must take care not to bother those around them or disrupt the tranquility or happiness of society in general. This viewpoint is reflected in business practices that permit a bereaved person to take one or two days off work but then expect that individual to come back to work ready to function as if nothing had happened (Fitzgerald, 1999).

Thus, when people in our society speak of the "acceptability" of grief, they usually mean its acceptability to the group, not to the bereaved person. When President Kennedy was assassinated, American society applauded his widow for the way she dealt with her bereavement in public—not least because she presented a stoic facade to society and to the media, which we could admire but not be disturbed by. It was widely ignored that Mrs. Kennedy's example was not relevant to or workable for most bereaved people and was particularly unhelpful for those having trouble expressing their feelings.

Disenfranchised Grief

Often, the unhelpful messages that we have just described are not merely examples in which individuals have failed in the ways in which they tried (or did not try) to help bereaved persons. Usually, these deficiencies reflect specific social or cultural contexts in which a societal death system conveys to its members—whether in formal and explicit ways or through more informal and subtle messages—its views about what is thought to be socially acceptable or appropriate in bereavement. Social norms of this sort are often hurtful to bereaved individuals when the society and its members disenfranchise their grief and bereavement experiences.

Disenfranchised grief is "the grief that persons experience when they incur a loss that is not or cannot be openly acknowledged, publicly mourned, or socially supported" (Doka, 1989b, p. 4). To disenfranchise grief is to indicate that a particular individual does not have a right to be perceived and/or to function as a bereaved person. The important point here is that disenfranchised grief is not merely unnoticed, forgotten, or hidden; it is socially disallowed and unsupported.

According to Doka (1989b; 2001), grief can be disenfranchised in three primary ways: either the relationship or the loss or the griever is not recognized. Doka also added that some types of deaths, such as those involving suicide or AIDS, may be "disenfranchising deaths" in the sense that they either are not well recognized or are associated with a high degree of social stigma. We witnessed that possibility in the vignette about Stella Bridgman near the beginning of this chapter.

Relationships are disenfranchised when they are not granted social approval. For example, some unsuspected, past, or secret relationships might not be publicly recognized or socially sanctioned. These could include relationships between friends, co-workers, in-laws, or ex-spouses (Scott, 2000)—all of which might be recognized in principle but not in connection with bereavement—as well as relationships that are not always recognized by others as significant, such as extramarital affairs or same-sex relationships. Folta and Deck (1976, p. 235) argued that devaluing of these relationships results from an emphasis in American society on kin-based relationships and roles: "The underlying assumption is that the 'closeness of relationship' exists only among spouses and/or immediate kin." This assumption is not correct. Thus, Folta and Deck concluded "rates of morbidity and mortality as a result of unresolved grief may be in fact higher for friends than for kin" (p. 239).

Losses are disenfranchised when their significance is not recognized by society. These might include perinatal deaths, losses associated with elective abortion, or the loss of body parts. Such losses are often dismissed or minimized, as when one is simply told, "be glad that you are still alive." Similarly, those outside the relationship may not appreciate the death of a pet even though it may be an important source of grief for anyone, regardless of age—child, adolescent, adult, or elder. Also, society often fails to recognize losses that occur when dementia blots out an individual's personality in such a way that significant others perceive the person they loved to be psychosocially dead, even though biological life continues.

Grievers are disenfranchised when they are not recognized by society as persons who are entitled to experience grief or who have a need to mourn. Young children and the very old are often disenfranchised in this way, as are mentally disabled persons.

In addition to these *structural elements of bereavement* (relationships, losses, and grievers), Corr (1998b) has argued that the dynamic or *functional elements of bereavement* (grief and mourning) may also be disenfranchised. For example, a bereaved person might be told by society that the way he or she is experiencing or expressing grief is inappropriate, or that his or her ways of coping with the loss and the grief reaction are unacceptable. Some grief reactions and some ways of mourning are rejected because they are unfamiliar or make others in society uncomfortable.

However it occurs, "the problem of disenfranchised grief can be expressed in a paradox. The very nature of disenfranchised grief creates additional problems for grief, while removing or minimizing sources of support" (Doka, 1989b, p. 7). Many situations of disenfranchised grief involve intensified emotional reactions (for example, anger, guilt, or powerlessness), ambivalent relationships

Losses of many types can evoke grief reactions.

(as in cases of abortion or between persons who were once but who no longer are lovers), and concurrent crises (such as those involving legal and financial problems). Disenfranchisement may remove the very factors that would otherwise facilitate mourning (such as a role in planning and participating in funeral rituals) or make it possible to obtain social support (for example, through time off from work, speaking about the loss, receiving expressions of sympathy, or finding solace within some religious tradition).

Some Constructive Suggestions for Helping

Despite the foregoing, we are not as individuals condemned to hurt bereaved persons or to fail to help them. We can avoid disenfranchising their grief and bereavement, and we can be helpful to them in many ways. For example, after the sudden and unexpected death of his 10-year-old daughter, Rachel, one father drew the following lessons for bereaved persons from his experiences (Smith, 1974, pp. 35–40):

1. Don't blame yourself for what has happened.

2. Don't be brave and strong.
3. Don't try to run away.
4. Don't feel that you owe it to the dead child to spend the rest of your life tied to the place in which he or she lived.
5. Don't feel sorry for yourself.

For helpers, Smith (1974, pp. 47–52) had the following advice:

1. Immediately after a death, *do something specific to help* (for example, notify those who need to be told on the family's behalf, answer the telephone or free family members from other chores that may appear meaningless to them) or make known in other practical ways your willingness to help.
2. Respect preferences that the family may have to be alone.
3. Assist in practical ways through the time of the funeral (for example, help with meals, cleaning, transportation).
4. In the difficult time after the funeral, do not avoid contact with the bereaved.
5. Act normally and mention the name of the deceased person in ways that would have been natural before the death.
6. Permit the bereaved to determine how or when they do or do not wish to talk about the deceased person.
7. Don't try to answer unanswerable questions or to force your religious or philosophical beliefs upon vulnerable bereaved persons.
8. Don't say, "I know how you feel"—no matter how much it may seem to be so, that is never true unless you have walked in the same path.
9. Be available, but allow the bereaved to find their own individual ways through the work of mourning.

Friends are often hesitant and may feel inadequate in approaching someone who is grieving a significant loss. Still, it is better to try to help than to do nothing. In making an effort to help, it is usually a good idea to try to avoid clichés or empty platitudes (Linn, 1986). Sometimes it may be enough to tell the bereaved person: "I don't know what to say to you," or "I don't know what to do to help," but also "What can I do for you right now?" And it can often be most helpful just to sit with or even cry with the bereaved person (see Box 10.2).

Pet Loss

One good example of losses that are often not well appreciated involves pets or companion animals. Exploring these losses briefly can reinforce much of what we have previously indicated about bereavement while also leading to useful lessons for helpers and preparing us to help bereaved persons with their tasks in mourning.

Box 10.2 *Tear Soup*

A book called *Tear Soup: A Recipe for Healing after Loss* (Schwiebert & DeKlyen, 1999) tells the story of "an old and somewhat wise woman whom everyone called Grandy" (p. 1) who has just suffered a big loss in her life. Grandy faces her loss by making "tear soup," filling a soup pot over and over again with her tears, feelings, memories, and misgivings. She knows that the work of making tear soup must be done alone, is typically messy, and "always takes longer . . . than anyone wants it to" (p. 6). The resulting broth is bitter and making it is difficult work, but it has to be done.

Tear Soup affirms all of the feelings and experiences that bereaved people encounter, including their anger at God because they do not understand why this terrible loss has occurred and do not know where God is when they are feeling so all alone. The book rejects foolish advice like telling bereaved persons that if only they had true faith they would be spared their deep sadness, anger, and loneliness. Instead, Grandy continued to trust God and she "kept reminding herself to be grateful for ALL the emotions that God had given her" (p. 29).

Tear Soup notes that people in our society are often not very helpful to the bereaved. They are eager to fix things and feel helpless when they cannot do that—so they want to know when this will all be over. Sometimes those whom one might have thought were one's friends just drop out of sight and stay away. Even worse are individuals who take it on themselves to show the bereaved person how to make tear soup the "correct" way! Grandy teaches us that real help only comes from those special people who can be present and just listen. Their caring presence does not require the bereaved person to be careful about what is said and does not try to talk that person out of whatever he or she is feeling.

Tear Soup also speaks favorably of "special soup gatherings" in which bereaved persons can share stories that lead to both laughter and additional tears, and "where it's not bad manners to cry in your soup or have second helpings" (p. 37). In the end, this little book holds out the hope of a day when one can eventually find it OK to eat something other than tear soup all the time. This does not mean that Grandy is completely finished with her tear soup, but that the hard work of making it is done and she knows that she will survive—even as she keeps a portion of the soup in the freezer to taste a little from time to time. ■

SOURCE: Based on Schwiebert and DeKlyen, 1999.

To begin, we know that relationships between animals and humans take many forms. For example, animals in the wild or in zoological parks are objects of interest to many humans, and humans use other animals as beasts of burden or sources of food. Youngsters in farm communities often learn the skills of caring for animals by raising them to compete in local and state fairs. The story of *Charlotte's Web* (White, 1952) is an example of this latter type of relationship.

In it, a young girl named Fern (and later a spider named Charlotte) saves a pig named Wilbur who is the runt of his litter from various threats to his life.

Some pets become close companions to humans in a variety of specialized ways. As companion animals, they may give unconditional love to a child who finds the world to be sometimes harsh and scary. Since most pets have much shorter life expectancies than do humans, animals often provide opportunities for children and others to learn about loss, sadness, and death. Companion animals may also help children, adolescents, and other humans learn about the responsibilities of caring for another living creature and thereby enhance their self-esteem (Rynearson, 1978). Some animals provide guide services for the disabled, help to guard individuals in dangerous circumstances, comfort those who are lonely and isolated, and bring a spark of joy to residents in long-term care facilities who may otherwise have only limited social contacts outside the institution. When relationships like these are important in one's life, the death or loss of an animal can have a powerful impact on the humans involved.

Some people fail to appreciate or even dismiss close attachments with animals. This attitude can lead to actions—even well-intentioned ones—that make the bereavement experience more difficult. For example, in a story for young readers called *The Accident* (Carrick, 1976), a dog is buried too quickly after a truck kills it. His parents had thought to spare their young son from the burdens of the sad event by burying the dog in the child's absence. They failed to recognize the child's need to share in this important ritual, to act out his love and grief, and to assuage his guilt for not being sufficiently attentive to the dog's whereabouts as they walked together along the highway. Similarly, in books like *Mustard* (Graeber, 1982) and *I'll Always Love You* (Wilhelm, 1985) bereaved children teach adults useful lessons when they turn down opportunities to get a new animal too soon after the death of a beloved pet.

The importance of death-related losses involving pets to the humans who are their companions is strikingly evident in the growing number of pet cemeteries in the United States, which are represented professionally by the International Association of Pet Cemeteries (www.iaopc.com), and in other efforts to memorialize deceased animals (Spiegelman & Kastenbaum, 1990). Loss and grief may also be felt deeply in situations such as when a human being is no longer able to care for an animal and must turn it over to someone else, cannot pay for expensive veterinary services that it would need, must give it up entirely when relocating to new living quarters or to an institution, or faces difficult choices when a sick or feeble animal must be euthanized (Stewart, 1999).

We can learn from this several lessons that really apply not only to pet loss, but to all losses: (1) it is the relationship that is really central to appreciating the loss, not the object of the relationship (in this case, the animal in question); (2) the nature of the death or loss and the way it occurred will affect the bereavement; and (3) the circumstances of the survivor—both developmental (child, adolescent, adult, or elder) and situational (for example, living alone, in a supportive family, or in an institution; having prior bereavement experiences or not)—are also critical. As for helpers, individuals confronted by the death or loss of a pet can be helped and supported, if others will take time to recognize the value of the relationships they have enjoyed with their companion animals, appreciate the challenges they face and the losses they have experienced, and

Memorializing companion animals can provide a measure of solace.

explore with them their resulting needs (Butler & Lagoni, 1996; Kay, 1984; Lagoni et al., 1994; Nieburg & Fischer, 1982).

Helping Bereaved Persons with Tasks in Mourning

"For all bereaved, the central issue in any helping encounter is to learn to build a life without the deceased" (Silverman, 1978, p. 40). One value of Worden's (2002) account of tasks of mourning that we discussed in Chapter 9 is that those tasks can be adopted by individuals who are helping the bereaved as ways of determining how their assistance might most usefully be offered. However,

Worden's tasks are specifically formulated as projects for the bereaved. They need to be adapted in order to serve as guidelines for helpers. We do that here by exploring ways to help bereaved persons with tasks that involve what they know or believe (cognitive tasks), how they feel or react to their loss (affective tasks), how they act (behavioral tasks), and what they value (valuational tasks).

Throughout this process, helpers need to keep one important caution in mind. At a time when so much in a bereaved person's life is out of control and when he or she is so vulnerable to strong feelings, reactions, and pain, outsiders need to be careful not to take over the bereaved person's tasks of mourning and subtly (or not so subtly) shape them in their own ways. Barring outright pathology—which might be identified as involving direct harm that a person is doing to himself or to others—bereaved persons must be permitted to lead the way in their mourning (read Box 10.1 again). This is what Manning (1979) meant by the title of his book *Don't Take My Grief away from Me* and why one often hears cautions against overmedicating bereaved persons.

Cognitive Tasks

Everyone who is bereaved asks questions about what happened. All bereaved persons have a *need for information*. Knowing the facts about what happened is an essential step in making the event real in one's inner world. That is why many bereaved persons go over and over the details of the circumstances in which a death occurred. Outsiders often become impatient with this process. They ask: "What difference does it make if the car that hit her was blue or red? Isn't she still dead?" But that misses the point. Only when a bereaved person can fill in details like this in a personal intellectual mosaic can he or she grasp the reality of its pattern. Until then, the loss seems blank, devoid of color, unlike life, unreal, and untrue. Cognitive and other tasks may be especially important (and sometimes difficult) for bereaved persons who are used to exercising a high degree of control over their environment. Cognitive tasks may also be difficult for bereaved individuals whose social roles (for example, as a clergy person, counselor, or other identified helper) make it hard for them to seek information and assistance from others.

Providing prompt, accurate, and reliable information is a key role for helpers. One day, when Arthur Smith (1974) was 600 miles away from home at a chaplain's conference, he was called to the telephone. His wife's voice simply said, "Rachel died this morning." Smith later wrote, "There is no other way to tell someone that a loved person has died" (p. 8). But in the circumstances, Smith's first reaction was to scan in his mind the list of sick and elderly persons in his parish who might have died. Failing to identify anyone with that name, he asked, "Rachel who?" The deep silence that followed signaled the moment in which Smith began to face the almost inconceivable fact of his daughter Rachel's death and his great loss.

Information is particularly important when the death is unexpected, untimely, traumatic, or self-inflicted. Anything that adds to the shocking qualities of a loss contributes to a sense of unreality, as we saw in the events of September 11, 2001. Protests quickly arise: "Surely, this cannot be happening";

"This sort of thing doesn't happen here"; "This must be some kind of bad dream." Information is often urgently requested: about possible survivors, the cause of the losses, recovery of bodies, and so forth. Sometimes requests for additional information really cannot be answered and are not meant to be answered. Often, they are actually efforts to test reality, to obtain confirmation over and over again that the death has in fact occurred, and perhaps also to confront the hard truth that it will not or may not ever be adequately explained. Testing reality is one way in which bereaved persons move from shock and confusion to other processes of coping constructively with their loss(es) and grief.

For example, even though the ultimate cause of death remains unknown in cases of sudden infant death syndrome, it is important that a "syndrome" or pattern of events can be identified. The postmortem examination and associated investigation on which an appropriate diagnosis of the syndrome rests are critical as a basis for assuring bereaved parents that they did not bring about or in any way cause the death of their child and that nothing could have been done by anyone to prevent the death (see Box 12.1).

Affective Tasks

Helpers can also assist bereaved persons with affective or emotional reactions to the loss. These reactions typically include both feeling and somatic (bodily) components. Most bereaved persons have a *need to express their reactions to a loss or death.* To do this, they may require assistance in identifying and articulating feelings and other reactions that are strange and unfamiliar to them. Some bereaved persons find it difficult to acknowledge or explain their grief reactions. They ask questions of themselves and of others like: "What is happening to me?" "Why is my body reacting in these strange ways?" "Why am I experiencing such odd emotions or such a roller coaster of feelings?" Informed and sensitive helpers can give names to the affective reactions that the bereaved are experiencing. Helpers can also assist in finding appropriate ways to express strong feelings and other reactions. Appropriate ways are ones that are safe for both the bereaved person and for others who may become involved.

Often, what is most needed is the company of a caring person who can acknowledge the expression and validate the appropriateness of the emotional reactions. For example, many bereaved persons have found comfort in reading *A Grief Observed*, the published version of the notebooks in which C. S. Lewis (1976) wrote out his feelings and the kaleidoscope of reactions that he experienced after the death of his wife. He originally wrote only for himself as a way of giving release to his grief, but his description has rung so true with other bereaved persons that his little book provides the normalization and reassurance many desperately need. This model of writing out one's thoughts, feelings, and other reactions to loss has been followed with good results by many bereaved persons who keep a journal or other record of their bereavement experiences (Hodge, 1998; Lattanzi & Hale, 1984). There is an extensive body of writings by bereaved persons (see Box 14.2 in Chapter 14), together with books intended to help the bereaved in these matters (for instance, Grollman, 1977; Rando, 1988b; Sanders, 1992).

Behavioral Tasks

Bereaved persons very often need to act out their reactions to a loss. This behavioral aspect of grief frequently takes the form of activities that reflect a need to *mark or take notice of the death through some external event or action.* For example, nowadays we often see impromptu roadside markers at the sites of motor vehicle accidents (Haney et al., 1997; Reid & Reid, 2001). Another type of behavioral task in bereavement can be observed in *commemorative activities that are designed to remember the life of the deceased or the legacy that he or she has left behind.* One widow described the value of commemorative activities in her comments about letters of condolence that she received from others who had known her deceased husband, even from individuals who were strangers to her (see Box 10.3). The goal of these commemorative activities is to preserve at least in some small measure the memory of the person or thing that has been lost. This may be realized in more or less formal or public ways, but it always involves some act or outward behavior. For example, one might plant a tree in memory of one who has died. This seems to be particularly appropriate because it involves the nurturing of new life in a way that can be revisited from time to time.

Simpler forms of commemoration include attending a wake or funeral, since a prominent part of funeral ritual (see Chapter 11) has to do with commemoration and memorialization of the deceased. Other commemorative gestures might involve putting together a scrapbook of pictures and memories, designing and executing a collage that symbolizes the life of the deceased, writing a poem about the person who has died, or tracing his or her place in a family tree. The point is not so much how the commemoration is accomplished as that something is done to take note of the life that has now ended and its meaning or impact beyond itself.

Valuational Tasks

A fourth area for helping the bereaved has to do with *a need to make sense out of the loss.* The process of finding or making meaning is essential for all human beings. In death and loss, that which had been accepted as a basis for meaning in one's life may have been severely challenged. Mourning initiates the processes of reinvigorating old value frameworks or seeking to construct new ones to take account of the changed realities in our lives.

A prominent example of a member of the clergy struggling to find meaning in a very difficult loss is found in the book, *When Bad Things Happen to Good People* (Kushner, 1981). In this book, Rabbi Harold Kushner described some of the challenges involved in coping with his son's unusual, progressive illness (progeria) and death at a young age. Many who are impacted by this fearsome disease might seek out information about its characteristics and about how other individuals have coped with its implications (for example, from a source like Livneh et al., 1995). What Rabbi Kushner tried to focus on in his book was the task of finding or making meaning out of the events in his family's life. The somewhat unorthodox conclusions he adopted—mainly that God is not

Box 10.3 Condolence Letters

People dread writing letters of condolence, fearing the inadequacy of their words, the pain they must address, death itself. And few people realize, until the death of someone close, what a benediction those letters are.

The arrival of letters about George was a luminous moment of each day. They made me cry. They made me feel close to him. They gave me the sense that the love he inspired in others embraced me. The best were the longer, more specific ones, the ones that mentioned something the writer cherished in George, or recounted some tale from his past that I was unaware of. Others were inexpressibly poignant. At one time I would have avoided writing any such letter, thinking it unkind to dwell on a subject that was the source of such pain, that I would be rubbing salt into a wound. But now I know that it is not unkind. There is so much joy mixed in with the pain of remembering. ■

SOURCE: From *Rebuilding the House* by Laurie Graham, pp. 55–56.

responsible for all the bad things that happen to us—have been a source of consolation to many bereaved people.

Some people have such faith or trust in their basic values that they can incorporate a loss directly or at least be patient until meanings begin to clarify themselves. Others must ask repeatedly the ultimate question: Why? Some ways of making meaning are idiosyncratic; many are widely shared among human beings. Some bereaved persons find consolation in the convictions that they share with a religious community; others turn to a personal philosophy or set of spiritual beliefs. Sometimes answers from any or all of these sources are not readily available. Almost all human beings need some conviction that life truly is worth living even when death has taken someone who is loved.

Programs Designed to Facilitate One-to-One Intervention to Help the Bereaved

Beyond these guidelines for helping bereaved persons with their tasks of mourning, there are several programs in our society that seek to prepare individuals to help the bereaved in one-to-one relationships. A good example of community-based programs that seek to foster one-to-one helping relationships is the "Widow-to-Widow" program, which began in the Boston area (Silverman, 1986). Focusing on a public health perspective and the pivotal idea of bereavement as *transition* (in this case, from wife to widow), this program turned to widows themselves to ask how they viewed and dealt with their needs. As a result, the Widow-to-Widow program was established on the premise—later called "mutual help"—that those who had themselves been bereaved might be in the best position to help others in similar situations. The program was distinguished by the fact that help was offered to every newly widowed person in a community, not only to those who sought it out. Potential helpers (individuals who had been widowed at least two years) gathered to develop their own strategies and procedures with the help of a consultant. The program itself helped to define many of the basic ways of helping bereaved persons. As Silverman (1986, p. 210) noted, "mutual help generally has an advantage over professional help since it does not treat a person as ill and has an image-enhancing emphasis on learning from peers." The Widow-to-Widow program has been replicated in many communities, perhaps most notably in the form of the Widowed Persons Service established in 1974 by the American Association of Retired Persons (AARP; 601 E Street, NW, Washington, DC 20049; tel. 800-424-3410 or 202-434-2260; www.aarp.org).

Other examples of supportive one-to-one helping relationships for the bereaved are those provided by the clergy, church visitors, faith-based social committees, and parish nurses. A prominent example of a faith-based program that seeks to foster such one-to-one relationships is found in The Stephen Ministry (named after a person in the Christian scriptures, Acts 6–8, who provided care to suffering persons). The Stephen Ministries organization (2045 Innerbelt Business Center Drive, St. Louis, MO 63114-5765; tel. 314-428-2600; www.christcare.com) identifies itself as a Christian, transdenominational ministry that provides leadership training through seven-day courses, print and other resources, and ongoing support for Stephen Leaders in enrolled congregations and other organizations. In turn, the leaders prepare members of their organization to be Stephen Ministers who provide direct, one-to-one care to troubled individuals. Since its inception in 1975, this program estimates that it has served thousands of congregations in more than 90 Christian denominations, resulting in more than 250,000 Stephen Ministers who have been trained to serve the needs of persons who are coping with dying, death, or bereavement. Stephen Ministers and members of Widow-to-Widow programs seek to make themselves available to bereaved persons on an individual basis in ways that are consistent with the helping guidelines outlined in this chapter.

Facilitating Uncomplicated Grief: Grief Counseling

Thus far, we have been describing suggestions for "walking alongside" the bereaved person as a fellow human being or fellow griever (see Box 10.4). This reflects our view that grief and mourning are most often normal and uncomplicated. They are adequately served by caring and thoughtful individuals and by the social programs that we have described. Professional intervention is not normally required although it may be helpful.

Box 10.4 For a Time of Sorrow

I share with you the agony of your grief,
The anguish of your heart finds echo in my own.
I know I cannot enter all you feel
Nor bear with you the burden of your pain;
I can but offer what my love does give:
The strength of caring,
The warmth of one who seeks to understand
The silent storm-swept barrenness of so great a loss.
This I do in quiet ways,
That on your lonely path
You may not walk alone. ■

SOURCE: From *Meditations of the Heart,* by Howard Thurman. Reprinted by Beacon Press, Boston.

When professional intervention is indicated, Worden (2002) has proposed an important distinction between *grief counseling* and *grief therapy*. The former has to do with helping or facilitating the work of bereaved persons who are coping with normal or uncomplicated grief and mourning; the latter designates more specialized techniques employed to help people with abnormal or complicated grief reactions. In helping bereaved persons, one must remain alert for manifestations of complicated grief reactions. When those appear, individuals should be referred to appropriate resources for grief therapy (Rando, 1993; Sprang & McNeil, 1995). However, one must not misinterpret normal grief reactions as abnormal or pathological reactions, which would be to misunderstand bereaved persons and to overprofessionalize the help they need.

Most often, grief counseling takes the form of a one-to-one intervention with bereaved persons. As such, it can be offered by anyone who is properly prepared and qualified for this work. As a professional intervention to help persons who are coping with uncomplicated grief and mourning, grief counseling might be offered by psychologists, social workers, clergy, nurses, physicians, counselors, and funeral directors. It is important to note, however, that not all professionals are effective as grief counselors. Grief counseling grows out of caring communities, to which it adds formal understanding of experiences in bereavement and mourning as well as skill in helping individuals with their own coping or problem-solving processes. For such counseling, Worden (2002) identified the following ten principles as guidelines. Many of these principles are also relevant to nonprofessional ways of helping the bereaved.

1. *Help the Survivor Actualize the Loss.* In contrast to the sense of unreality that often accompanies bereavement, this principle recommends an effort "to come to a more complete awareness that the loss actually has occurred and that the person is dead and will not return" (Worden, 2002, pp. 56–57). This is one rea-

While comforting a four-legged friend, a counselor begins a conversation with a teenager and his younger brother after the loss of a loved one.

son why it is so important to identify the bodies of those killed in the collapse of the World Trade Center towers on September 11, 2001. Also, one can simply assist survivors to talk about their losses. Empathic listening and open-ended questions encourage repeated review of the circumstances of the loss, as do visits to the grave site. Immediate family members may be familiar with these details and can often become impatient with their repetition. However, as Shakespeare wrote in *Macbeth* (IV, iii: 209), bereaved persons need to "give sorrow words." A caring helper can aid this important process of growing in awareness of loss and in appreciation of its impact. Still, one must not push survivors too forcefully or too quickly to grasp the reality of a death if it appears that they are not yet ready to deal with it. One must follow the survivor's own cues (see Box 10.5).

2. *Help the Survivor to Identify and Express Feelings.* Many survivors may not recognize unpleasant feelings like guilt, anxiety, fear, helplessness, or sadness, or they may be unable to express their feelings and other reactions to loss in ways that facilitate constructive mourning. A helper can aid bereaved persons to be aware of their reactions to loss and then enable those reactions to find an appropriate focus. For example, some persons may find themselves angry at caregivers who were unable to prevent the death. Others may be angry at other survivors who appear to be insufficiently affected by the death. Still others are

Box 10.5 A Letter to My Family and Friends

Thank you for not expecting too much from me this holiday season.

It will be our first Christmas without our child and I have all I can do coping with the "spirit" of the holiday on the radio, TV, in the newspapers and stores. We do not feel joyous, and trying to pretend this Christmas is going to be like the last one will be impossible because we are missing one.

Please allow me to talk about my child if I feel the need. Don't be uncomfortable with my tears. My heart is breaking and the tears are a way of letting out my sadness.

I plan to do something special in memory of my child. Please recognize my need to do this in order to keep our memories alive. My fear is not that I'll forget, but that you will.

Please don't criticize me if I do something that you don't think is normal. I'm a different person now and it may take a long time before this different person reaches an acceptance of my child's death.

As I survive the stages of grief, I will need your patience and support, especially during these holiday times and the "special" days throughout the year.

Thank you for not expecting too much from me this holiday season.

Love,

A bereaved parent ■

SOURCE: From "A Letter to My Family and Friends" in M. Cleckley, E. Estes, and P. Norton (Eds.), *We Need Not Walk Alone: After the Death of a Child*, Second Edition, p. 180.

angry at themselves for what they have or have not done. Finally, some people are angry (and this is often difficult to admit) at the deceased for dying and leaving the bereaved person behind to face many problems. Thus, Caine (1975) berated her deceased husband for leaving her unprepared, as she felt, to cope with many challenges in life and to raise their children alone.

Questions like "What do you miss about him?" and "What don't you miss about him?" may help the survivor to find some balance between positive and negative feelings. Unrealistic guilt that may be experienced as part of the overall grief reaction may respond to reality testing and lead to the realization that "We did everything we could have done." Many (but perhaps not all) bereaved persons may need to be gently encouraged to express, rather than repress, their sadness and crying. Recognizing strong feelings like anger and blame may help grievers begin to put them into perspective and move on. Similarly, it can be comforting to acknowledge that one did do some positive things prior to the death and may still be able to act in some effective ways even at a time when other things are unsettled or out of control. However, grievers must find their own forgiveness and comfort; helpers only facilitate the process and must seek to do so with sensitivity and care.

3. *Assist Living without the Deceased.* The helper can assist bereaved persons to address problems or make their own decisions. Because it may be difficult to exercise good judgment during acute grief, bereaved persons are often advised not to make major life-changing decisions at such times, such as those involved in selling property, changing jobs, or relocating. Thus, a central lesson in Judy Blume's novel for young readers, *Tiger Eyes* (1981), is the realization that moving from Atlantic City (where her father was killed in the holdup of his 7-Eleven store) to live with her aunt in Los Alamos was ultimately not a productive way for a teenage girl, her mother, and her younger brother to cope with their grief and with each other.

Nevertheless, the role of the helper is not to take over problems and decision making for the survivor. Therefore, when issues arise concerning the making of independent decisions (such as how to deal with sexual needs in bereavement, which may range from needs to be touched or held to problems in attaining intimacy with a new person), the helper's main role is only to assist the survivor in the process of making decisions. This is often best accomplished in a validating and nonjudgmental way. Enabling survivors to acquire new and effective coping skills empowers those who may perceive themselves to be powerless in their bereavement.

4. *Help Find Meaning in the Loss.* Finding meaning in the death of a loved one or in any other important loss in one's life is very much an individual project for a bereaved person. Helpers cannot simply assign meanings to a significant loss or determine what that loss will mean for the survivor. Nevertheless, helpers can assist individuals as they search for a meaning that they can live with or reassign meanings to the changed world in which they now live. Some people find comfort in religious or spiritual convictions that assure them in particular terms or in a general way that some meaning does exist. Others explain why a loss occurred in terms of the way the deceased person had behaved. Still others view losses as events from which they themselves can learn something. Even when a satisfactory reason cannot be assigned to a loss, many find meaning in activities related to the manner of the death that took the loved one away from them. For example, many establish a memorial or a scholarship in the name of the deceased person, while others lobby to minimize handgun violence or drunk driving so that their loved one's death will not have been in vain and in the hope of preventing similar deaths in the future that seem so senseless and unnecessary.

5. *Facilitate Emotional Relocation of the Deceased.* This principle is not only or not always about encouraging the survivor to form new relationships (see Box 9.5). As time passes, that may be appropriate. However, it is important not to do so too quickly in ways that inhibit adequate mourning. The central point of this principle is to "help survivors find a new place in their life for the lost loved one, a place that will allow the survivor to move forward with life and form new relationships" (Worden, 2002, p. 64). This principle (along with others in this list) is well illustrated by "linking objects" that facilitate recognition of loss, expression of grief, restructuring of relationships, and ongoing connectedness. Thus for one son, attending the last game at a baseball stadium (Comiskey Park) in Chicago that was about to be closed revived important recollections of

good times with his father, helped him grieve in ways he had previously avoided, and gave him precious memories to take with him into the future (Krizek, 1992). Restructuring relationships with the deceased does not overthrow, supplant, or dishonor the dead; it encourages survivors to live as well as possible in the future and to live as well as any deceased person who loved and cared for them would have wanted them to live.

6. *Provide Time to Grieve.* It takes time in a rich, many-faceted relationship to restructure attachments and to close doors on aspects of the past that are now over. Intimate relationships develop on many levels and have many ramifications. Mourning, if it is to be adequate to the loss, can be no less complex. Some people regain equilibrium in their lives and quickly return to familiar routines. Thus they may be impatient with a survivor who is moving more slowly or finding it more difficult to deal with his or her loss and grief. They may not appreciate how arduous it is to deal with critical anniversaries or the time around three to six months after the death when so much support offered during the funeral and the early days of bereavement is no longer readily available. Effective helpers may need to be available over a longer period of time than many people expect, although actual contacts may not be frequent.

7. *Interpret "Normal" Behavior.* Many bereaved persons feel that they are "going crazy" or "losing their minds." This is because they may be experiencing things that they usually do not experience in their lives and they may, at least temporarily, be unable to function as well as they have in the past. Help in normalizing grief reactions can be provided by others who are knowledgeable about or experienced with bereavement. Reassurance will be welcomed that unusual experiences, such as hallucinations or a preoccupation with the deceased, are common in bereavement and as a rule do not indicate that one is actually going crazy. Encouragement of this sort guides and heartens the bereaved in their time of travail.

8. *Allow for Individual Differences.* This is a critical principle for helpers. The death of any one person affects each of his or her survivors in different ways. Each survivor is a unique individual with his or her own relationships to the deceased and his or her own personality and coping skills. Each person mourns in his or her own ways. Help in appreciating the individuality of grief reactions and mourning processes is especially important for families or other groups who lose a member. It is even more critical when two parents try to understand the ways in which each of them may be reacting differently to the death of their child. Just as helpers need to respect the uniqueness of each bereaved person whom they seek to assist, so too bereaved persons should respect the individuality of grief and mourning in other persons who have been impacted by the same loss.

9. *Examine Defenses and Coping Styles.* By drawing the attention of bereaved persons in a gentle and trusting way to their own patterns of coping, helpers may enable the bereaved to recognize, evaluate, and (where necessary) modify their behaviors. This is the gentle work of suggesting different ways of coping,

At a candlelight vigil sponsored by MADD (Mothers Against Drunk Driving), a woman holds a photograph of her family as it was before her husband was killed.

not so much directly as by enabling the bereaved person (sometimes through a joint effort) to assess his or her own thoughts and behaviors. Questions such as "What seems to help get you through the day?" or "What is the most difficult thing for you to deal with?" may assist the bereaved person to understand how he or she is coping.

10. *Identify Pathology and Refer*: Most people who engage in helping the bereaved are not prepared to deal with complicated grief reactions on their own because most of us do not possess the specialized skills and expertise of a qualified grief therapist (Rando, 1993; Sanders, 1989; Sprang & McNeil, 1995). However, helpers and counselors can remain alert for manifestations of complicated grief and can play an important role in referring those who need them to appropriate resources. This referral is not a failure; it is a responsible recognition of one's own limitations.

Summary

In this chapter, we reviewed some of the many ways in which individuals can help those who are coping with loss and grief. We noted and explained examples of unhelpful messages to the bereaved, clarified the concept of disenfranchised grief, and introduced examples of pet loss to reinforce positive lessons. We also identified helpful ways in which to assist bereaved persons with tasks in mourning. This sort of assistance essentially constitutes a program for "befriending" the bereaved. We then described the Widow-to-Widow program and The Stephen Ministry as examples of community-based and faith-based programs that prepare individuals to help the bereaved on a one-to-one basis. Further, because the principles underlying professional grief counseling are similar to those that guide everyone who tries to help bereaved persons cope with uncomplicated grief and mourning, we explained ten principles for facilitating uncomplicated grieving.

Questions for Review and Discussion

1. Think of a time when you experienced the death of someone you loved or the loss of something that was important in your life. What did you want others to do with or for you at that time? What was most important: who tried to help, when they tried to help, or how they tried to help?

2. Bereaved persons often report that some individuals were not helpful to them in their bereavement. Think of a time when you needed or sought help from other persons and did not receive it. Why do you think you did not receive the help that you needed or sought? Why do you think people do not always understand how to help bereaved persons? Have you ever found yourself in that situation?

3. Think of the losses that you experienced or that you observed (either directly or through the media) others to experience in connection with the events of September 11, 2001. What types of losses did you notice and what were the main characteristics of those losses?

Suggested Readings

For advice about helping oneself or others in grief, see:

Attig, T. (2000). *The Heart of Grief: Death and the Search for Lasting Love.*

Fitzgerald, H. (1994). *The Mourning Handbook: A Complete Guide for the Bereaved.*

Grollman, E. A. (1977). *Living When a Loved One Has Died.*

Grollman, E. A. (Ed.). (1981). *What Helped Me When My Loved One Died.*

Kushner, H. S. (1981). *When Bad Things Happen to Good People.*

Lewis, C. S. (1976). *A Grief Observed.*

Linn, E. (1986). *I Know Just How You Feel . . . Avoiding the Clichés of Grief.*

Manning, D. (1979). *Don't Take My Grief away from Me: How to Walk through Grief and Learn to Live Again.*

Moffat, M. J. (1982). *In the Midst of Winter: Selections from the Literature of Mourning.*

Neimeyer, R. A. (1998). *Lessons of Loss: A Guide to Coping.*

Rando, T. A. (1984). *Grief, Dying, and Death: Clinical Interventions for Caregivers.*

Rando, T. A. (1988b). *How to Go on Living When Someone You Love Dies.*

Sanders, C. M. (1992). *Surviving Grief . . . and Learning to Live Again.*

Schiff, H. S. (1986). *Living through Mourning: Finding Comfort and Hope When a Loved One Has Died.*

Schwiebert, P., & DeKlyen, C. (1999). *Tear Soup: A Recipe for Healing after Loss.*

Smith, A. A. (1974). *Rachel.*

Smith, H. I. (1999). *A Decembered Grief: Living with Loss When Others are Celebrating.*

Smith, H. I., & Jeffers, S. L. (2001). *ABC's of Healthy Grieving: Light for a Dark Journey.*

Tagliaferre, L., & Harbaugh, G. L. (1990). *Recovery from Loss: A Personalized Guide to the Grieving Process.*

Tatelbaum, J. (1980). *The Courage to Grieve.*

Guidance for professional helpers is provided in the following:

Johnson, J., Johnson, S. M., Cunningham, J. H., & Weinfeld, I. J. (1985). *A Most Important Picture: A Very Tender Manual for Taking Pictures of Stillborn Babies and Infants Who Die.*

Johnson, S. (1987). *After a Child Dies: Counseling Bereaved Families.*

Rando, T. A. (1993). *Treatment of Complicated Mourning.*

Sprang, G., & McNeil, J. (1995). *The Many Faces of Bereavement: The Nature and Treatment of Natural, Traumatic, and Stigmatized Grief.*

Stewart, M. F. (1999). *Companion Animal Death: A Practical and Comprehensive Guide for Veterinary Practice.*

Weizman, S. G., & Kamm, P. (1985). *About Mourning: Support and Guidance for the Bereaved.*

Worden, J. W. (2002). *Grief Counseling and Grief Therapy: A Handbook for the Mental Health Practitioner* (3rd ed.).

Disenfranchised grief and other social implications of grief and bereavement are explored in:

Carter, B., & McGoldrick, M. (Eds.). (1988). *The Changing Family Life Cycle: A Framework for Family Therapy* (2nd ed.).

Doka, K. J. (Ed.). (1989a). *Disenfranchised Grief: Recognizing Hidden Sorrow.*

Doka, K. J. (Ed.). (2001). *Disenfranchised Grief: New Directions, Strategies, and Challenges for Practice.*

Hanson, J. C., & Frantz, T. T. (Eds.). (1984). *Death and Grief in the Family.*

Magee, D. (1983). *What Murder Leaves Behind: The Victim's Family.*

Redmond, L. M. (1989). *Surviving: When Someone You Love Was Murdered.*

Walsh, F., & McGoldrick, M. (Eds.). (1991b). *Living beyond Loss: Death in the Family.*

Walter, T. (1999). *On Bereavement: The Culture of Grief.*

InfoTrac College Edition
For more information, explore the InfoTrac College Edition at **http://www.infotrac-college.com/Wadsworth**

Enter search terms: DISENFRANCHISED GRIEF, GRIEF COUNSELING, GRIEF THERAPY, PET LOSS, TASKS IN MOURNING.

Chapter Eleven

COPING WITH LOSS AND GRIEF: HOW COMMUNITIES CAN HELP

IN THIS CHAPTER, WE AGAIN RETURN TO Stella Bridgman, whose bereavement we learned about in Chapters 9 and 10, this time to consider some of the ways in which she received support and help from her community. In Chapter 10 we focused on what anyone—family members, other relatives, friends, neighbors, or other individuals—might do on their own if and when they were called on to act as a helper to the bereaved. Throughout history, these are the people to whom bereaved persons have most often turned for support and assistance. That way of helping the bereaved often led to and was complemented by support and assistance from social groups within society or from the society itself and its organized programs. We will in this chapter study some of the principal ways in which *communities* in our society have organized *specific social programs to help persons who are coping with loss and grief.*

These community programs include the funeral and memorial rituals that have developed in the American death system. As we will show in this chapter, these rituals have historically taken many different forms, but all are intended to help bereaved persons cope with the disruption and disorientation that arises when someone they love dies. In recent years, other social programs have been developed to help the bereaved, programs that go beyond traditional funeral practices and are also designed to supplement befriending and neighboring. These programs are not meant to take the place of individual help for the bereaved, but they can serve useful roles when such assistance is either not available or not sufficient to the need. In this chapter, we examine three of these societal programs: aftercare programs in the funeral industry, hospice bereavement follow-up programs, and support groups for the bereaved.

Stella Bridgman: Social Support for a Bereaved Person

Stella found consolation at her son's funeral. Although his life in recent years had seemed so troubled, she was surprised that so many of his friends, schoolmates, and co-workers came to the visitation. They told her about what he had meant to them and about their memories of helpful things he had done. When her son was buried next to his father, Stella believed he was finally at peace.

At the funeral and for many months afterwards, the aftercare specialist at the funeral home checked in with Stella from time to time, gave her little pamphlets on loss and grief, suggested some books that she could read, and was available whenever she had questions. Although her son had not been in hospice care, the aftercare specialist referred her to a local hospice bereavement program so that she might also draw on the resources it had to offer.

Four months after her son's death, Stella felt that she was only now experiencing the full impact of his loss. With the encouragement of the aftercare specialist, a friend took her to a meeting of a local chapter of The Compassionate Friends. Stella had heard about this group, but she had thought that it would be too intimidating to go to a meeting on her own. She wondered: Will the group be alien or welcoming? Will it be helpful or not? What if my reactions overwhelm me or I just cannot tolerate the group experience? What if I am physically or emotionally unable to drive home? The presence and support of her friend helped to reduce many of these anxieties.

The group did not draw back when Stella expressed her pain, anger, guilt, and other strong feelings. Members of the group permitted her to give vent to such feelings, and they acknowledged the normalcy of her reactions. Group members also recognized the appropriateness of her questions and validated her experiences as a bereaved parent.

At one meeting, Stella said she felt like she was going crazy. Members of the group agreed that they had often felt that way, too. Stella expressed amazement that other bereaved parents could speak of their dead children without collapsing in tears. How could they go forward with their lives, get through the holidays, and even find it possible to laugh once in a while? Stella tried to tell herself that if these people had also walked "in the valley of the shadow of death" and were now able to find some way to live on, perhaps she could, too. But she could not see how to do that yet.

Over time, just by being themselves these other bereaved parents showed Stella that one can survive horrendous loss and cope effectively with grief reactions, that life can once again become livable. Also, without needing to offer her any advice, the members of the group served as role models and provided Stella with options from which she might choose in determining how to live her own life.

Life Crises and Ritual

Rituals play important roles in the lives of most human beings. Anthropologists and others have studied ritual for nearly a century using various definitions of the key term. For example, Mitchell (1977, p. xi) described *ritual* as "a general word for corporate symbolic activity." The corporate or communal symbolic activity involved in ritual generally has two components: it involves *external (bodily) actions*, such as gestures, postures, and movements, which symbolize interior realities; and it is *social*—that is, the community is usually involved in ritual activity (Douglas, 1970).

One can identify ritual practices of this sort in all human societies. Van Gennep (1961) emphasized the links between ritual and crises or important turning points in human life, such as childbirth, initiation into adulthood, marriage, and death. Because crises involve a significant change or disruption in human life, they threaten the invasion of chaos. Ritual can contribute some degree of ordering or orientation to such events. To the extent that ritual achieves that goal, it helps make the unfamiliar more familiar by providing guidance as to how one should act in these unusual (but not always unanticipated) circumstances. In other words, ritual seeks to "tame" the strange or the unusual experiences in human life to some degree.

Since death is one of the most impressive invasions of disorder and chaos in human life, it is not surprising that throughout history humans have made efforts to bring order into lives that have been affected by death (Bendann, 1930; Puckle, 1926). Archaeologists and anthropologists believe that some of the most ancient artifacts they have discovered had something to do with rituals associated with death and burial. Also, as one moves forward from prehistoric to more recent times, rituals associated with death are found in every societal death system. As Margaret Mead (1973, pp. 89–90) wrote: "I know of no people for whom the fact of death is not critical, and who have no ritual by which to deal with it."

Nevertheless, many individuals in our society make efforts to avoid ritualized practices and appear to act as if they have no need for ritual. They do not come to graduation ceremonies, for example, or they try to avoid attending funerals. As a result, some have suggested that American society is making an effort to do away with all ritualized behavior. That is hardly accurate. In fact, evidence of the felt need for ritual at key moments in our lives can be found in the actions of numerous individuals and communities in our society. For example, the death of a member of the military, a police officer, or a fire fighter is often followed by formal and elaborate funeral, burial, and memorial activities. Officers attend the funeral in full dress uniforms, flags are folded in precise ways and presented to surviving family members, buglers may play "Taps," and a firing squad may shoot into the air in a deliberate way. Similarly, sports teams often wear black armbands after the death of a teammate and a jersey may be "retired" in honor of that individual. In some communities, the death of a prominent or specially admired member may lead to flags being flown at half-staff and a moment of silence being observed at a social activity. Even small social groups, such as a few friends or family members, may be driven to erect an informal roadside memorial to mark the spot at which a loved one or close friend was killed in a motor vehicle accident (Haney et al., 1997). In these and

At the funeral of John Ogonowski, a pilot whose plane was hijacked and crashed into the World Trade Center on September 11, his brother presents a folded American flag to their parents.

numerous other examples, we find that many bereaved people do not suffer alone and in silence. Instead, they take action to draw attention to what has happened, to let their loss and their grief be known, to speak to the public, and to engage the community in their mourning—as we saw in the aftermath of the September 11 attacks on America.

However, not every instance of ritual is equally valuable or effective for all bereaved persons or for all communities. Many cultural groups have their own rituals. Persons who are not members of those groups may not find comfort in such rituals, partly because they do not understand the meaning of the various components of the ritual. Even members of such a group may find little comfort in the ritual because it represents views they do not hold or fails to address what they are experiencing.

In Chapter 4, we offered a description of the main elements that are typical of contemporary American funeral practices. In the next three sections of this chapter, we turn to an analysis of the goals of funeral ritual in contemporary American society, a description of three central tasks associated with such ritual, and some comments on the roles of cemeteries and other forms of memorialization in helping bereaved persons. We want to show how organized social programs of ritual and practice can or might be able to help bereaved persons. In so doing, we take note of criticisms of American funeral rituals.

Funeral Ritual in Contemporary American Society

In our society, some authors (for example, Harmer, 1963; Mitford, 1963, 1998) have severely criticized American funeral and memorial practices. These criticisms have taken different forms. Some contend that funerals are useless and therefore repugnant—a form of fantasized flight from reality (Harmer, 1971). Such critics urge members of society to no longer to take part in funerals at all and to move away from any sort of ritual activity after a death. They would prefer that the time, energy, and money traditionally invested in a funeral be used in some other way. Other critics agree that American funeral practices are overly lavish and expensive (Arvio, 1974; Bowman, 1959) but do not wish to abolish all societal ritual after death. Typically, critics of this second type favor less ostentatious *memorial services* conducted without the presence of the body and often held two or three weeks after the death. These critics substitute one form of ritual for another but are not opposed to all death-related ritual (Irion, 1966, 1971, 1991; Lamont, 1954; Morgan & Morgan, 2001).

Of course, many in our society continue to believe that funerals can and often do serve an important role in human life. Those who hold this view believe that some sort of funeral and burial ritual may help people to make sense of, and to bring order out of, what is potentially a disruptive, stressful, chaotic encounter with death (for example, Jackson, 1966; Raether, 1989). They also argue that funeral and memorial rituals serve a constructive role in grief work (Howarth, 1996; Pine, 1975; Rando, 1985; Romanoff & Terenzio, 1998).

Existing research on these topics reports both criticisms of the funeral industry from clergy (for instance, Fulton, 1961; Kalish & Goldberg, 1978), together with much satisfaction among the general public (Bolton & Camp, 1987; Fulton, 1978; Kalish & Goldberg, 1980; Marks & Calder, 1982). Hyland and Morse (1995) noted that widespread public regard for the comfort offered by funeral service personnel is a striking achievement when one takes into account that most of these services are provided by strangers in circumstances of great stress for the bereaved and during what is usually a relatively short period of contact. Also, research by Canine (1999) concluded that the vast majority of respondents who work in the funeral industry put "service to families" as their first priority. On the basis of this evidence, it cannot be maintained that there is widespread social dissatisfaction with funeral rituals within the American death system or that funeral service practitioners do not act without having the interests of society in mind. Of course, specific individuals and groups must decide about their own participation in funeral rituals and their assessments of these rituals' value. Clearly, opinions may differ in this sensitive area, both on the role of funeral ritual in general and on whether or not a particular funeral ritual provided a useful service in a specific instance.

In the following section, we offer an analysis of three basic tasks that ought to inform productive funeral ritual. Through this analysis, we hope to come to a better understanding of the nature and purposes of funeral and other commemorative rituals. We also want to help you determine for yourself whether or not these rituals are effective in serving significant needs in your life. To that end, note that in planning or taking part in a funeral or other memorial ritual of any kind, it is always appropriate to ask: What do these gestures, these actions, or these words mean or suggest? This question may be difficult to pose when a person is stricken with grief. A better time to think through the rationale for what you might desire in any postdeath ritual is before the ritual is needed. Preplanning that takes account of the individual and social tasks to which funeral and memorial rituals can contribute can be helpful in providing a funeral that successfully meets individual, familial, and societal needs.

Tasks Associated with Funeral Ritual

Scholarly work by anthropologists and sociologists (Durkheim, 1954; Fulton, 1995; Goody, 1962; Malinowski, 1954; Mandelbaum, 1959) uses the language of *functions* to explain funeral rituals. In this book we encourage proactive approaches in which bereaved and other vulnerable individuals can work to regain control over lives that have been impacted by death. Thus, we prefer to interpret funeral and other memorial rituals through a *task-based approach*. Therefore, we propose that these rituals should help bereaved persons themselves and society in general carry out the following three tasks: (1) to dispose

Box 11.1 On the Dangers of Ignoring Death-Related Rituals

The rituals of grief and burial bear the dead away. Cheat those rituals and you risk keeping the dead with you always in forms that you mightn't like. Choose carefully the funerals you miss. ■

SOURCE: Staples, 1994, p. 255.

of the body of the deceased in appropriate ways; (2) to contribute to making real the implications of the death; and (3) to assist in reintegration and meaningful ongoing living (Corr, Nabe, & Corr, 1994). We use these tasks here to explain and evaluate elements of funeral and memorial ritual.

Disposition of the Body

The first task to which funeral ritual should contribute is *to dispose of the body of the deceased in appropriate ways.* To fail in this task is to risk violating both social attitudes and community health—not to mention doing harm to oneself (see Box 11.1). In all societies, the manner in which this task is accomplished requires respect for the body as the remains of someone valued as a human being. Thus, most humans are uncomfortable with allowing the corpse simply to be discarded or left lying around (Iserson, 1994). In addition, dealing with a dead body necessitates behavior in accordance with the religious or philosophical beliefs that an individual and his or her society hold about life and death (Ball, 1995; Kephart, 1950). Disrespect for either of these can result in serious conflict, as dramatized in Sophocles' *Antigone.* In that play, Antigone is concerned that the body of her dead brother must be buried; by contrast, King Creon is concerned that burial of the body will improperly show respect for a rebellious subject.

The question of how to dispose of a human body appropriately in contemporary American society is remarkably complex, as we observed in Chapter 4. Since the United States is a large and diverse society, one finds within it a wide range of religious or philosophical beliefs about the nature of the person, the universe, or any afterlife. Together with or apart from such beliefs, custom is often the guiding force in what many Americans do about disposition of dead bodies.

For example, decisions about embalming, a "visitation" (with or without a "viewing" of the body), whether or not to have a religious or nonreligious funeral or memorial service, cremation, and committal of the body or its cremains to earth burial are often made largely on the basis of the beliefs to which one adheres or the customary practices with which one is familiar. The key point in all of these decisions is the felt need to dispose of human bodies in what is viewed as a respectful and appropriate manner.

Box 11.2 Gordon Parks: The Funeral

After many snows I was home again.
Time had whittled down to mere hills
The great mountains of my childhood.
Raging rivers I once swam trickled now
like gentle streams.
And the wide road curving on to China or
Kansas City or perhaps Calcutta,
Had withered to a crooked path of dust
Ending abruptly at the country burying ground.
Only the giant who was my father
remained the same.
A hundred strong men strained beneath his coffin
When they bore him to his grave. ■

Making Real the Implications of Death

A second task addressed by funeral and memorial ritual is *to contribute to making real the implications of death.* Others sometimes refer to this as "realization" or achieving separation from the deceased. This task may not be as easy as it might seem to an observer who is not personally involved in the process. In fact, disentangling realistic and unrealistic or symbolic and literal elements in bereavement shortly after a death is difficult for many persons (see Box 11.2). That is why it is so important to identify any part of the remains of a deceased person, as in efforts to recover body parts from the rubble of the World Trade Center towers after September 11, 2001. That also explains comments from some bereaved persons in New York City who described others as lucky because at least they had a body to bury. If a bereaved individual is unable to accomplish this task of making real the implications of death, that person's life may be disrupted in some serious ways. Thus, it may be useful to engage in actions that help in the process of recognizing the permanent separation of the dead from the living (in this life, at least).

The funeral can be of assistance in this process of psychological separation of survivors from the deceased (Mandelbaum, 1959; Turner & Edgley, 1976). Some have argued that seeing the dead body may help to make the death real. They bolster this argument with comments to the effect that bereaved survivors often face special challenges in realization when there is no body—for example, when it has been lost at sea, never returned from combat, or consumed in a horrific explosion or fire. Even the presence of some token remains in a closed casket, so it seems, can be helpful to survivors.

Sheri Burlingame prepares to kiss the coffin of her husband, Charles, whose plane was hijacked and crashed into the Pentagon on September 11, 2001.

If in fact funeral ritual is to help with making real the implications of death, then presumably some of the actions and events associated with it should point to the permanence of the separation of the dead from the living. Some have criticized contemporary American funeral practices as failing to support this separation from the deceased. For example, it has been argued that the use of cosmetics and the expensive linings of caskets both seem to promote an image of life rather than of death (Harmer, 1963, 1971; Mitford, 1963, 1998). If it is important to help survivors make the death real for themselves, then contributing to the appearance that the dead person is "asleep," head on a pillow, lying on a mattress, surrounded by beautiful bed linens, may be counterproductive—or so we are told. The tension that seems to be operating here may be between the task of making real the implications of a death and the desire to offer survivors a final, comforting "memory image" of the body of their loved one. Perhaps the challenge is to achieve both of these goals in satisfactory ways.

Some critics (such as Morgan & Morgan, 2001) have argued that many aspects of contemporary American funeral practices draw too much attention to the *body* itself. On this view, making real the implications of death is concerned primarily with taking leave of the *person* as part of an overall process of restructuring relationships with that person. Because a person is not only a body, it is the loss of the person, not his or her body, that is the primary concern.

Issues involved in realization and separation also arise at the place of burial. Sometimes mourners are encouraged to leave the grave site before the body is lowered into the grave. In other cases, cemeteries have encouraged mourners to perform any last rites and take leave of the body at a chapel on their grounds, rather than at the grave site. One can understand some of the motivations behind these practices, such as to allow the cemetery employees to complete their work at their own pace and out of sight of tense mourners, but sending mourners away also distances them from the realities of the death and may thus run counter to the desired work of making real the implications of the death.

A second set of criticisms has been directed toward costs involved in much contemporary funeral practice (Arvio, 1974; Bowman, 1959). Airtight or water-tight metal caskets are expensive objects. Critics have asked: What real purposes are served by such elaborate merchandise? Even if they prevent the body from decaying—and they surely do not when one considers that they could only inhibit the work of aerobic, not anaerobic, bacteria—why is that important?

Answers to these questions seem to reside at the psychological rather than the economic level of mourning. Some persons have argued that spending money for a funeral and burial allows mourners to feel satisfaction in having shown respect and love for the person who has died. After all, expenditures involved in buying a casket and paying the associated costs of a funeral and burial are said to be the third highest financial outlay that most people will make during their lives, exceeded only by the purchase of a house and an automobile. In this sense, expenses associated with a funeral can be seen as a kind of "going-away" present or final gesture of love toward the deceased. At least indirectly, this expenditure may support the realization that the dead person has in fact left the community of the living.

Purchases associated with funerals also represent to some people the last gift or service that they can make to the person who has died. Also, the conviction that the body will be "protected from the elements" may provide some psychological satisfaction to the survivor. This may be true whether or not the merchandise or services actually do accomplish what the buyer thinks they will accomplish. After all, much of what is going on here—especially in its psychological components—is really designed to serve the needs of the living (Jackson, 1963). As one funeral director has written, "Unlike the fast food restaurant, where value is determined solely by cost, the value of death rituals should be determined by the comfort and consolation they provide to the bereaved" (Weeks, 2001, p. 188).

Reintegration and Ongoing Living

Death and Disintegration The death of someone we love leads to disintegration, a breaking apart of the world as it has been known and understood. This leads to a third task facing survivors: *to achieve a new integration and thereby to promote meaningful ongoing living.* For many persons, funeral practices and other activities after a death can play important roles in beginning this process (Malinowski, 1954).

The disintegration that is experienced by bereaved persons may occur at one or more of four levels. First, people who experience the death of an important person in their lives often experience various kinds of *disintegration at the individual level.* They may feel a loss of integrity or wholeness within themselves. They may ask, "Am I going crazy?" Sleep patterns, eating patterns, and health concerns all may be disrupted by the death of a loved person. In short, customary ways in which individuals live in the world and their familiar sense of their own identity can be shredded by a death. The individual then faces the task of pulling himself or herself back together, usually with a somewhat altered if not wholly new identity.

Second, the impact of death may also be evident in *disintegration at the family level.* The death of a person has many meanings for those closest to that person. It may have economic repercussions for the family as a whole, such as the loss of the deceased's income, the loss of an owner of property, and the loss of the person who typically handled certain financial transactions. Death also has consequences for the ways in which those closest to the deceased person relate to each other and to the rest of the world. Members of the family may experience disruptions in their relationships with one another. They may have to renegotiate how they stand in their relationships to each other (how will siblings relate to each other now that the parent has died?) and to the family unit (who will be responsible for which tasks?). Some survivors may lose part of their social identity as the relative (spouse, child, or parent) of the person who died. Death can exacerbate old tensions within a family, just as it may create new tensions. All of these effects are forms of family disintegration associated with death. They impose on members the task of reintegrating the family unit (Friedman, 1980; Goldberg, 1973).

Third, almost all deaths also have implications for *disintegration at the social level.* This is most obvious when a public figure or someone of great social standing dies, such as a president or a celebrity, but the death of any person is likely to cause some measure of social disintegration. Who will make the decisions that person used to make? Who will take over the work associated with that person's job? Who will have to drive more often in the car pool? The structures of society—the whole civic or national society in some cases, but some level of society (the business or school or church) in most cases—will have to be reworked so that society can once again function as an integrated unit.

Fourth, *disintegration at the spiritual level* can involve tasks that are intellectual and perhaps most pressingly emotional. How does one make sense of a world in which this person is no longer present? As a residue of the dying period, there may be anger, frustration, and even despair. For many, this includes an anxiety about or a sense of being alienated from whatever the person holds to be transcendent (for example, God). If the person has certain religious beliefs, those beliefs may be severely challenged ("How could God allow her to die such a painful death?"). Other beliefs may also produce uncertainty and anxiety: What has happened to the loved person now that she is dead? The tasks here concern reconfiguring one's understanding of how the world operates and also renegotiating one's relationship to whatever the person conceived the transcendent to be.

Achieving a New Integration In bringing people together, funeral and related rituals can help to begin the process of *reintegration at the individual level.* Mourners need not see themselves as simply alone. The tasks they need to perform can be accomplished, in part through the aid of persons drawn to their sides by the funeral. Though mourners may feel overwhelmed by the grief and disorientation they are experiencing, they are not simply powerless or adrift on wholly uncharted seas. They cannot change the fact that a death has occurred. However, they can, with the assistance of relatives, friends, and others, decide how to respond to that fact and how to regain some measure of control over the course of their lives.

After a death in contemporary American society, the most obvious sign of *renewed integration at the family level* is often seen in the physical or geographical drawing together of persons who ordinarily see little of each other in their everyday lives. In our society, families are frequently scattered among several towns or states. A funeral is one moment when they are reintegrated, certainly physically, but also often psychologically and emotionally. Sometimes families are heard to remark half jokingly that they only seem to get together (in all of these senses) on the occasion of a funeral.

In some cultural groups, the funeral and other rituals associated with a death go on for months or even years (at different levels of activity during those periods of time). A good example of this is the Jewish tradition of rending one's clothes (*Keriah*), reciting the prayer for the dead (*Kaddish*), and organizing activities in specified ways for particular periods of time. As Gordon (1974, p. 101) has written: "Judaism recognizes that there are levels and stages of grief and so it organizes the year of mourning into three days of deep grief, seven days of mourning [*shivah*], thirty days of gradual readjustment [*Sh-loshim*], and eleven months of remembrance and healing." In practices such as these, the support system is there, again and again, to assist survivors in finding their way through the period of crisis and into the new world that they are entering—a world without the dead person in it.

By contrast, for many individuals in our society, the funeral takes place only a matter of days after the death. After that, participants scatter again, and for many people there is no agreed-upon or designated path through the wilderness of grief and mourning. Integration may be hard to achieve under such circumstances. (Their awareness of the limitations of typical funeral practices in our society may have been part of the motivation that has led many funeral directors to develop "aftercare" programs of support for the bereaved, which we discuss later in this chapter.) In any event, the most important considerations in this situation are how individuals make use of funeral ritual and how they follow up on the beginnings represented by that ritual.

For *reintegration at the social level*, funeral rituals can help to provide a sense that the society is not going to fall apart because of a death. This has been seen in the funeral of many national leaders, like President Kennedy in 1963, but also in the ways in which the funerals and other postdeath activities associated with the death of Diana, Princess of Wales, in 1997, brought together people both locally and around the world. The public ritual of these funerals gave testimony to the ongoing viability of the community and provided opportunities for individuals to rededicate themselves to working on behalf of a better society in the future (Andersen, 1998; Greenberg & Parker, 1965; Wolfenstein & Kliman, 1965).

People come together at a spontaneous memorial in New Jersey with smoke rising from the World Trade Center in the background.

Reintegration at the spiritual level is accomplished for those who hold certain spiritual or religious beliefs if the funeral can help survivors begin to answer their questions about the meaning of the death. Funeral ritual can also help firmly locate the survivors in a supportive faith community. Most religious traditions have agreed-upon and recognized rituals to help survivors in these ways. These rituals offer many believers reassurance about the continued support of God or some value framework in this life and even after it. Whether or not persons have those types of beliefs, the deceased person can be located and secured in the history and memory of the community of those who were touched by that individual through the sharing of stories about the person at a funeral or memorial service.

A funeral, then, can help survivors begin to overcome the individual, family, social, or spiritual disintegration experienced after a death. Achieving a full measure of this type of integration may take much effort and a long time. A funeral, as we typically know it in the United States today, may not go very far toward accomplishing this task, but it can be a beginning.

Cemeteries and Memorialization

Funeral rituals are not the only formal ways in which communities in the American death system try to support and assist persons who are coping with loss and grief. In addition to a visitation, the funeral, and burial or some other form of disposition of the remains, other memorial activities typical of our society are illustrated in cemeteries, memorial sculpture, and memorial photography.

Activities following a death in America have gradually evolved into what has been called a distinctively American way of death (Coffin, 1976; Fales, 1964; Farrell, 1980). To begin with, *cemeteries* serving many groups in American society have developed over time from frontier graves, domestic homestead graveyards, churchyards, potter's fields, and town or city cemeteries (such as the New Haven Burying Ground in Connecticut) especially typical of the 17th and 18th centuries, through what were originally 19th-century rural cemeteries (like Mount Auburn in the Boston area) and lawn-park cemeteries (like Spring Grove in Cincinnati), to memorial parks in the 20th century (like Forest Lawn in the Los Angeles area) (Kastenbaum, 1989b; Sloane, 1991). A similar history, distinguished in its particulars by the unique character of the African-American community, has been documented for African-American burial sites (Wright & Hughes, 1996).

Many American cemeteries are privately owned, whereas others have national (such as those for veterans), public (that is, municipal or county), or religious owners. In the last 100 to 150 years, many cemeteries have stressed an esthetic layout, even a picturesque or pastoral landscape. Some have become major tourist attractions—for example, Forest Lawn Memorial Park in Glendale, California, which has been the object of both literary satire (Huxley, 1939; Waugh, 1948) and scholarly study (French, 1975; Rubin et al., 1979; Zanger, 1980). Recently, American society has also witnessed rapid growth in the number of cemeteries for beloved pets or companion animals (Spiegelman & Kastenbaum, 1990). The diversity and changing character of American cemeteries reflect many different attitudes toward death and the place of final disposition for the body in our society.

Another dimension of memorial activities can be observed in the history of *memorial sculpture*. That history is linked to the evolution of cemeteries, in which wooden or stone markers have given way to marble, granite, and bronze (Forbes, 1927; Gillon, 1972). Some of these markers have been quite plain (providing, for example, only the name and dates of birth/death for the deceased). Others have included artistic icons and three-dimensional sculpture. In times past, grave markers often displayed elaborate and interesting epitaphs (see Box 11.3 for one example; Coffin, 1976; Mann & Greene, 1962, 1968; Reder, 1969; Wallis, 1954). Recently, for esthetic reasons and to keep down

A Native-American burial canoe overlooking Lewis and Clark River in Astoria, Oregon.

maintenance costs, memorial sculpture in American cemeteries has mainly taken the form of religious or abstract objects of art as centerpieces in the landscape, together with flush-to-the-ground markers at individual grave sites. One could also argue that the development of mausoleums in many American cemeteries is an example of a different type of monument making in our society. As in all matters of death, American attitudes toward cemeteries and memorial sculpture are complex and influenced by many factors.

A third area of memorialization, *memorial photography*, developed with the invention and increasingly widespread use of photographic technology from the 19th century onward. Memorial photographs enable survivors to retain a tangible memento of the person and funeral of the deceased (Burns, 1990; Jury & Jury, 1978). They include snapshots taken by relatives, as well as images created and preserved by professional photographers. Also, some people have used videotaping as a way to memorialize a life at the moment of its ending and to establish commemorative links to the past.

Some are uneasy with the idea of memorial photography (Lesy, 1973). However, the extent of this practice and its many variations—such as those depicted in *The Harlem Book of the Dead* (Van der Zee et al., 1978)—testify to the service that it provides to many individuals. In fact, memorial photography can help many survivors simultaneously to distance themselves from the dead, acknowledge the implications of their loss, and carry with them an image of the deceased as they move on in their own lives (Ruby, 1987, 1991, 1995). This directly parallels the three tasks for funeral ritual that we have described in this chapter. Contrasting attitudes toward memorial photography illustrate ten-

Box 11.3 Benjamin Franklin's Epitaph

The body of Benjamin Franklin, Printer
(like the cover of an old book,
Its contents torn out
And stripped of its lettering and gilding)
Lies here, food for the worms.
Yet the work shall not be lost,
For it shall (as he believed) appear once more
In a new and most beautiful edition
Corrected and Revised
By the Author. ■

sions between practices that individuals perceive as helpful in their mourning and public lack of understanding or discomfort with such practices. Efforts to achieve a new understanding of funeral and memorial ritual may help to ease these tensions in our society.

Other Societal Programs to Help the Bereaved

In addition to funeral rituals and memorial practices, we can illustrate some of the ways in which our society has organized itself to help persons who are coping with loss and grief by describing aftercare programs in the funeral industry, hospice bereavement follow-up programs, and key elements that characterize support groups for the bereaved.

Aftercare Programs

In the words of the title of a recent book, many funeral service personnel have come to think of *aftercare* as what they might do *When All the Friends Have Gone* (Weeks & Johnson, 2001). From this perspective, "aftercare" includes any assistance and support offered to the bereaved after the funeral is over and their family members and friends have returned to the familiar patterns of their own lives. Although the term is not limited to the work of funeral services practitioners, it might also become so broad as to be unhelpful. For that reason, the term "aftercare" has come to have a more specific meaning within the funeral services industry. As Johnson and Weeks (2001, p. 5) have observed:

> Funeral home aftercare may be defined as an organized way to maintain a helpful and caring relationship with clients, offer continuing services to client families beyond the expected body disposition and accompanying rituals, and provide death, loss, and grief education to both clients and the community.

A child plays in a cemetery with some distinctive, upright grave markers.

Aftercare in the funeral industry has its roots in the ongoing concern of some funeral directors for the welfare of the bereaved family members of their clients who prior to their deaths had been friends and neighbors in local communities. In this, funeral directors were attuned to the bereavement needs of members of their communities and were willing to offer their empathic presence to the bereaved. Described by Johnson and Weeks as an informal or *"casual" level of aftercare*, it is the first of what they regard as four possible levels of aftercare (see Table 11.1). It involves simply listening while bereaved persons tell their stories, helping them complete paperwork for various bureaucracies and entitlements, and/or providing basic literature (often in pamphlet form) on grief and bereavement. No extra staff are required and costs are minimal.

Table 11.1 Levels and Characteristics of Funeral Home Aftercare Programs

Program Level	Staff	Activities	Cost
Casual (informal)	No extra staff	Visiting, chance meetings, sharing booklists, brochures	Minimal
Fundamental (formal)	Extra staff but no extensive training	Telephone calls, newsletters, socials, dinners, travel	Moderate
Standard (formal)	Extra staff with specific training in bereavement issues	Support group sponsorship/facilitation, lending library, special holiday programs, community education, cards on special days	Substantial
Premier (formal)	Extra staff: master's degree or higher with concentration on counseling and grief/loss issues	Individual counseling, children's programs, in-service training, community advisory boards, spokesperson for media	Substantial to unlimited

SOURCE: From *When All the Friends Have Gone* by O. D. Weeks and C. Johnson (Eds.), p. 9. Copyright © 2001 Baywood Publishing Co. Reprinted with permission.

Aftercare became more formalized as an aspect of funeral services during the 1980s. However, its design and implementation can and do vary greatly in keeping with the needs of the community being served and the resources that it can command. According to Johnson and Weeks, beyond its informal or casual levels, there are three additional formal levels of aftercare: (2) *fundamental aftercare* involving extra staff but no extensive training who offer telephone calls, a newsletter, social meetings, dinner outings, and travel events for the bereaved; (3) *standard aftercare*, which depends on extra staff with specific training in bereavement issues who, in addition to services at the fundamental level, sponsor and/or facilitate support groups, a lending library of selected literature for the bereaved, awareness and critical evaluation of relevant resources in the community, special holiday programs, community education, acknowledgement (through cards or other personal communications) of emotionally difficult days for the bereaved, and referrals to competent mental health providers when necessary; and (4) *premier aftercare*, whose extra staff will have a master's degree or higher with a concentration on counseling and issues related to loss and grief, and who can offer all of the foregoing services as well as the capacity to provide individual counseling, children's programs, in-service training programs for funeral home staff or other professionals in the community, service on local advisory boards, and acting as spokespersons for the media (e.g., when mass or traumatic deaths occur). (Note that when aftercare programs include community education and other services to the public at large they are no longer confined to activities following a specific death and thus go beyond care *after* death.) Resources required for different levels of aftercare may range from minimal for casual or informal aftercare through moderate to quite substantial for the three formal levels of aftercare.

Because aftercare is a relatively recent development in the funeral industry, one knowledgeable member of that industry has noted that "the territory of aftercare is being charted and created through experience and experimentation" (Miletich, 2001, p. 33). The specific form of any aftercare program will depend on the resources that it is allocated, the personnel involved (including their training, personal qualities, and professional skills), and the materials it uses. At present, some are concerned about liability issues for funeral homes that get involved in aftercare (an uncharted area) and, specifically, whether or not it is appropriate for aftercare personnel to describe themselves as "counselors" or "therapists" unless they are otherwise so qualified or licensed in their state. Nevertheless, however aftercare may be defined or described, it has been estimated that nearly 50 percent of all funeral homes in the United States are currently offering some form of aftercare. As we saw in the vignette near the beginning of this chapter, after the death of her son Stella Bridgman benefited from the services of an aftercare coordinator. Thus aftercare is a growing reality in the contemporary American death system as an aspect of community support and assistance for persons who are coping with loss and grief.

Bereavement Follow-up in Hospice Programs

Hospice programs in the United States are required to provide support and counseling for the family members of those whom they serve. This service arises directly out of the hospice philosophy. Since hospice affirms life and is a holistic program of care, it must address the needs of both the dying person and the family members. After death, hospice care is no longer needed by the dying person, but that is not true for family members. In their new roles as bereaved survivors, members of the family must continue to cope with many old problems and they must also address new challenges. Consequently, for many years it has been recognized that hospice programs must include bereavement follow-up services as an essential component of their work (Lattanzi-Licht, 1989).

Not all families need or accept bereavement follow-up from a hospice program. Some may have resources of their own that are adequate to cope with bereavement, whether or not those same resources were sufficient to cope with dying. Moreover, hospice programs do not wish to disable surviving families by making them dependent on hospice services for the remainder of their lives (and few hospice programs would have the resources to sustain such a commitment). Thus, hospice bereavement follow-up is a transitional service designed to assist those family members who wish help in coping with loss and bereavement, usually offered during the first 12 to 18 months after the death of a loved one. Issues that go beyond the capacities of this sort of support, either in their character or duration, would ordinarily require specific evaluation and would likely be referred to professional counseling or therapy.

Programs of bereavement follow-up in hospice care are commonly organized around a detailed plan of care for those who have been identified through careful assessment as key persons in bereavement (Lattanzi-Licht, 1989). This plan of care may be initiated prior to the patient's death and usually encourages participation by family members and staff in meaningful funeral services and rituals. Subsequently, the remainder of the follow-up program is most often conducted through mail, telephone, and/or personal contacts at regular intervals. Care is addressed to specific needs of the bereaved, such as: information about typical patterns or problems in bereavement, grief, and mourning;

acknowledgment and validation of feelings and other grief reactions; suggestions about ways in which to undertake or to join in commemorative and memorialization activities; and a shared conviction that life remains worth living (Souter & Moore, 1989).

Newsletters, cards or letters, individual counseling, annual memorial services, and other social activities are familiar components of hospice bereavement follow-up. Hospice programs also frequently establish support groups for the bereaved or work cooperatively with community organizations that provide such services. In addition, hospice programs typically offer their bereavement services to all members of the community whether or not they cared for the person who died—as we saw in the case of Stella Bridgman. Most of the actual services in hospice bereavement follow-up are carried out by experienced volunteers who have been selected and trained for such work and who are supported by professionals in this field (Parkes, 1979, 1980, 1981, 1987; Parkes et al., 1996).

Support Groups for the Bereaved

Support groups for the bereaved take many forms (Hopmeyer & Werk, 1994; Milofsky, 1980; Wasserman & Danforth, 1988). One type of support group helps bereaved persons mainly through talks and lectures by experts on a variety of practical problems. Groups of this sort try to show their members how to invest their money, complete their income tax returns, cook nourishing meals when they are alone, do small repairs around the home, and so on. One group of funeral homes has named their groups of this type their LIFT program, where "LIFT" indicates "Living Information For Today." Another type of support group focuses on entertainment and social activities, such as holiday parties, visits to restaurants, or bus tours to nearby attractions. Both of these types of groups, whether they emphasize guidance in solving various types of problems or social activities, can be and are meaningful for many bereaved persons. However, they do not take as their principal concern the work of addressing the central issues of grief and mourning.

Support groups whose main concern is to help individuals cope with loss and grief offer support in the broadest sense, but their primary benefits result from the assistance that members of the group give to each other (mutual aid) and from the opportunities that these groups provide for bereaved individuals to help themselves with grief work and tasks of mourning (self-help). An illustration depicting the mutual aid offered by a group known as Parents of Murdered Children (POMC), a national organization with local chapters throughout the country, appears in Figure 11.1. Many groups that function in similar ways have sprung up throughout the United States in recent years in response to a wide variety of loss experiences (see Box 11.4; Hughes, 1995; Pike & Wheeler, 1992). These endeavors may be local and undertaken for a limited period of time, ongoing or open-ended projects of a community agency, chapters of a national organization, or groups sponsored by an aftercare or hospice program (Zulli, 2001). Stella Bridgman found one of these support groups to be of great help in her bereavement.

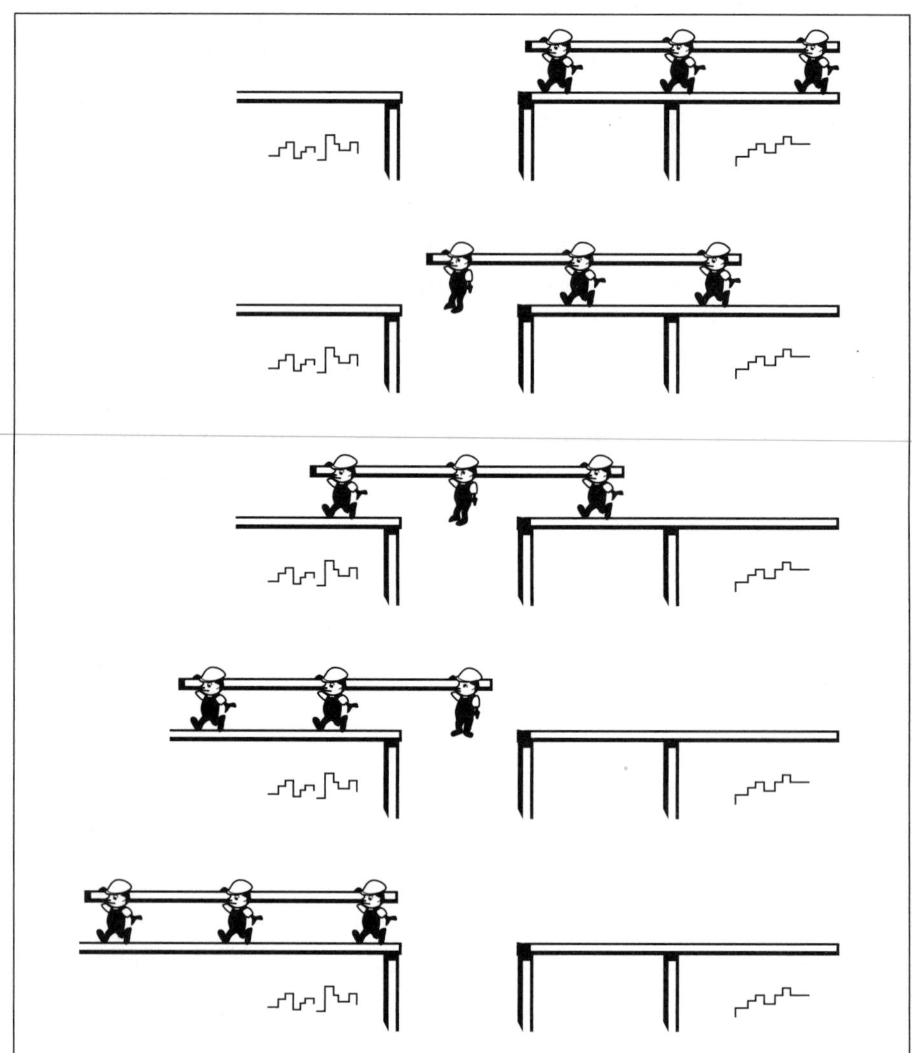

Figure 11.1 *How POMC Helps. Courtesy of the Parents of Murdered Children St. Louis Area-Wide Chapter.*

Principles and Practices in Bereavement Support Groups The very existence and rapid increase of bereavement support groups shows that many bereaved persons need or seek assistance beyond what is readily available to them in their own family or everyday community. By and large, however, what is sought from these groups is not professional counseling or therapy—it is help from others who have shared a similar loss experience. Thus, the essential purpose of these groups is "to provide people in similar circumstances with an opportunity to share their experiences and to help teach one another how to cope with their problems" (Silverman, 1980, p. 40).

Groups of this sort take a variety of forms. They may be time limited or ongoing. They may admit new members at any time or close themselves to additional members once the group has been formed. They may focus their work on all sorts of bereavement or organize themselves around a specific type of loss. They may be led by a bereaved person serving as an experienced volunteer or by a professional facilitator (McNurlen, 1991; Yalom & Vinogradov, 1988).

The question of leadership is important. In dealing with it, it is important to keep in mind the profound differences between grief support groups and therapy groups. These differences arise from the fact that support groups are designed to help otherwise healthy individuals cope with uncomplicated grief reactions, whereas therapy groups are intended to correct psychosocial disorders in individuals who need to restructure their lives in some significant way.

Members of grief support groups come together voluntarily because of the difficulties they encounter in coping with a shared life experience (McNurlen, 1991). Prior to their encounter with loss, such individuals were generally functioning normally. They do not seek to be changed in that, but they do want help in coping with losses that have taxed (often, overtaxed) their capacities.

Some bereavement groups do not permit leadership posts to be held by nonbereaved persons; others assign leadership functions to a professional facilitator (Klass & Shinners, 1983). Always, however, real, substantive expertise in bereavement groups is not perceived as hierarchical; it is found in the members themselves. Thus, members are encouraged to become involved with each other outside the group, and topics for discussion within the group are those that members bring up and choose to share. The focus in the group is not on offering solutions or giving advice but on the process of helping itself—talking about problems, exploring situations, and sharing experiences. This process is often guided by principles such as those in the "Serenity Prayer" (see Box 11.5; also Fox, 1985), which is a frequent component of group ritual. Support groups for the bereaved combine elements of both self-help and mutual aid; one must help oneself, but one does so with the support of others in the group.

Support groups for the bereaved usually have more or less explicit rules or values, such as that confidentiality and a nonjudgmental attitude are to be maintained, advice is not to be given, opportunities are made available for all to speak, side conversations are prohibited, everyone has the right to pass or remain silent, members respect each other's experiences and viewpoints, and meetings start and end on time. Safety issues are a matter of particular concern in groups for vulnerable people. Support groups usually prohibit "putdowns" or evangelization; they are also sensitive to the need to refer for therapy individuals who disrupt the group work or may endanger themselves.

Helping Factors in Bereavement Support Groups Most bereavement support groups are organized around eight helping factors (McNurlen, 1991; Yalom, 1995). Explaining these factors recalls the characteristics of The Compassionate Friends group that helped Stella Bridgman after her son's death.

Bereavement support groups are founded on the shared experience of their members (Borkman, 1976). This shared experience is the basis for a bond through which group members can find *identification* (helping factor 1) with

Box 11.4 Selected Examples of Bereavement Support Organizations

Organization	Description
American Association of Suicidology 4201 Connecticut Avenue NW, Suite 310 Washington, DC 20008 202-237-2280 www.suicidology.org	An information clearinghouse that supplies literature about suicide and local referrals to survivors of suicide
Bereaved Parents of the USA P.O. Box 95 Park Forest, IL 60466 708-748-9184 (fax) www.bereavedparentsusa.org	A national support group with many local chapters serving bereaved parents, grandparents, and siblings
The Candlelighters Foundation 7910 Woodmont Avenue, Suite 460 Bethesda, MD 20814 800-366-2223 www.candlelighters.org	An international network of support groups for parents of children who have or have had cancer
The Compassionate Friends (TCF) P.O. Box 3696 Oak Brook, IL 60522 877-969-0010; 630-990-0010 www.compassionatefriends.org	An international support group with numerous local chapters serving bereaved parents and siblings
Concerns of Police Survivors (COPS) P.O. Box 3199, S. Highway 5 Camdenton, MO 65020 573-346-4911 www.nationalcops.org	A support group for all law enforcement officers and their family members who have been affected by death and bereavement
Make Today Count National Office Mid-America Cancer Center 1235 E. Cherokee Springfield, MO 65804 800-432-2273 (8:00 A.M.–4:30 P.M., Mon–Fri)	A national support group for individuals who are living with life-threatening illness and for their family members
Mothers Against Drunk Driving (MADD) 511 E. John Carpenter Freeway, Suite 700 Irving, TX 75062 800-GET-MADD; 214-744-6233 www.madd.org	Support for those who have been victimized by drunken driving offenses
National Donor Family Council (NDFC) 30 E. 33rd Street New York, NY 10016 800-622-9010; 212-809-2210 www.donorfamily.org	A national resource for information, support, and education about organ and tissue donation and transplantation
National Hospice and Palliative Care Organization 1700 Diagonal Road, Suite 300 Alexandria, VA 22314 800-658-8898; 703-837-1500 www.nhpco.org	A resource for referral to local hospice programs and related services

(continues)

Box 11.4 (cont.) Selected Examples of Bereavement Support Organizations

Organization	Description
National Organization for Victim Assistance (NOVA) 1757 Park Road, NW Washington, DC 20010 800-TRY-NOVA; 202-232-6682 www.try-nova.org	A referral resource for local victim assistance services, plus a 24-hour telephone crisis counseling service
National SIDS Resource Center 2070 Chain Bridge Road, Suite 450 Vienna, VA 22182 703-821-8955 www.circsol.com/sids	A national resource for information about sudden infant death syndrome; referrals to local organizations and support groups for those affected by SIDS
Parents of Murdered Children (POMC) 100 East Eighth Street, Suite B-41 Cincinnati, OH 45202 888-818-POMC; 513-721-5683 www.pomc.com	Support for survivors of homicide
Parents Without Partners, Inc. 401 N. Michigan Ave. Chicago, IL 60611 301-588-9354 www.parentswithoutpartners.org	Services for single parents and their children
SHARE—Pregnancy and Infant Loss Support, Inc. National Office, St. Joseph Health Center 300 First Capitol Drive St. Charles, MO 63301-2893 800-821-6819; 314-947-6164 www.nationalshareoffice.com	A national mutual-help group for parents and siblings who have experienced miscarriage, stillbirth, ectopic pregnancy, or early infant death
Sudden Infant Death Syndrome Alliance 1314 Bedford Avenue, Suite 210 Baltimore, MD 21208 800-221-7437; 410-653-8226 www.sidsalliance.org	An alliance of organizations involved in research and services related to sudden infant death syndrome
THEOS (They Help Each Other Spiritually) International Office, 322 Boulevard of Allies, Suite 105 Pittsburgh, PA 15222-1919 412-471-7779	Support and education for the widowed and their families
Tragedy Assistance Program for Survivors (TAPS) 2001 S Street NW, Suite 300 Washington, DC 20009 800-959-TAPS (8277) www.taps.org	Offers support and assistance to all members of the armed services who have been impacted by death and bereavement
Widowed Persons Service (WPS), American Association of Retired Persons (AARP) 601 E Street, NW Washington, DC 20049 800-424-3410; 202-434-2277 www.aarp.org	Offers programs, literature, and other resources for the widowed

Box 11.5 The Serenity Prayer

God, give us the serenity to accept
what cannot be changed;
Give us the courage to change
what should be changed;
Give us the wisdom to distinguish
one from the other. ■

SOURCE: Fox, 1985, p. 290.

one another. In the group, bereaved individuals find that they no longer are or need be alone. Although they may feel stigmatized or marked out by their loss experience from so many others in the world, within the group they discover that others share similar experiences and that members of the group can learn from each other (Wrobleski, 1984).

Despite all of the uniqueness and individuality of the experience of loss, there is a degree of *universality* (factor 2) found in support groups. In the group, individuals can recognize that they are not alone in their experiences and reactions. Those whom society views as different, shuns, or even stigmatizes because of what has happened to them can be helped by knowing that members of the group do not view them as "bad" or "wrong."

Within the group, long-repressed, pent-up feelings can be let out for as long as necessary. Some people come to bereavement support groups shortly after their loss experience; others join many years later. Whatever the timing, new and old members typically are grateful to the group for permitting them to vent and share such feelings. They need *catharsis* (factor 3) and find opportunity for it in the group.

Individuals also meet other bereaved people within the group from whom they can obtain *guidance* (factor 4) on how they might conduct their own lives after their loss. The group offers such guidance, not primarily through lectures, presentations, or advice, but by providing a forum in which members can describe, exemplify, and live out their experiences with loss and grief. This exchange may or may not validate an individual's personal experiences, but as experiences are shared, important information, guidance, and reassurance are conveyed. For example, most bereaved persons welcome information about grief and mourning processes. Many need to know more about the specific types of losses they have experienced and that may define the nature of the group—for example, about parental bereavement, about homicide and its implications, or about sudden infant death syndrome. Some may need guidance about the social stigma associated with certain kinds of death, such as suicide or AIDS.

A dimension of the group experience that is especially significant for many bereaved persons is the interaction between new members and those who have been participants for some time. Coming to know people who are further along

An illustration of a bereavement support group from Tear Soup *(See Box 10.2).*

in their grief work permits newer members to witness ways in which their more experienced colleagues are managing both their grief and the rest of their lives. Insofar as this demonstrates that things can get better and have gotten better for others, hope is renewed that one's own life might also get better. This *instillation of hope* (factor 5) must be drawn from the group processes by the individual; it cannot simply be injected or imposed from outside.

Existential issues (factor 6), involving large questions such as those concerned with the fairness of life, the benevolence of God, or the basic goodness of the universe, can be raised in bereavement support groups. Answers to such profound questions can seldom be given to one from someone else. More likely, one discovers that one must work out one's own answers or ways of living with such issues and questions, or even with an absence or incompleteness of answers. What a support group can provide in response to these questions is a safe place to recognize that the existential issues raised by loss, grief, and bereavement are legitimate and real, and that different people respond to them in different ways.

The bonding among members in a bereavement support group creates a safe, caring environment in a world that—after a significant personal loss—may appear in so many ways to be unsafe and uncaring. *Cohesiveness* (factor 7) or basic trust develops among members in most support groups, arising from two features of the group experience: the experiences that members share as bereaved persons and the discovery by hurt and vulnerable people that they can help each other simply by sharing their own great losses and pain. "Sharing of experience is the fundamental concept that distinguishes the mutual help experience from other helping exchanges. . . . The essence of the process is mutuality and reciprocity" (Silverman, 1980, p. 10).

Another sort of empowerment is related to *altruism* (factor 8) or giving to others, which is often experienced by those who remain in a bereavement support group for an extended period of time. As they move into leadership roles or find different ways to share with others what they have obtained from their own experiences both in bereavement and within the group, senior members also may find new rewards for themselves. Klass (1985b, 1988) called this the great secret of bereavement support groups: in giving to others, one receives for oneself. Giving and receiving help reciprocally to enhance one's self-esteem. Those who make the transition from intense vulnerability in an early meeting to shared ownership of the group at a later point often interpret their newfound ability to help others as an important element in finding meaning in the life and death of their loved one (Klass, 1985a).

Help Outside the Group Although the main work of support groups for the bereaved occurs within their meetings, that is not the whole of what they have to offer. This point is often neglected. Established, ongoing bereavement support groups like The Compassionate Friends usually set up a network of referral sources for identifying potential new members. Mail or telephone contacts with such individuals may be among the earliest expressions of support that reach a bereaved person.

Sometimes it is enough for the bereaved to know that support groups are available "in case I really need one." That knowledge may be supplemented by regular mailings of a newsletter, which is another mode of support and reassurance that additional help is within reach. Groups may also generate announcements about their activities or reports about loss and grief in the local media. Together with educational conferences and public service endeavors, these are other forms of support that reach beyond the boundaries of the group itself.

Summary

In this chapter, we examined ways in which communities in the American death system have organized specific social programs to offer support and assistance to persons who are coping with loss and grief. This supplements our discussion in Chapter 10 of ways in which individuals can help bereaved persons in one-to-one relationships. In this chapter, we began with an analysis of funeral rituals. Our goal was to show how such organized rituals could help survivors and society with three tasks: to dispose of the body in socially approved ways, to make real the implications of a death, and to begin to move toward reintegration and meaningful ongoing living. We considered criticisms of contemporary American funeral ritual and concluded that the issue is how effectively such rituals help bereaved persons to accomplish these tasks. Individuals and communities who know the options that are available to them in terms of funeral rituals can decide for themselves whether (and, if so, how) or not any specific funeral practice or associated ritual serves their needs or the needs of their social groups. We added to this analysis of funeral ritual a brief exploration of American cemeteries, memorial sculpture, and memorial photography. Then we considered three other prominent social programs in the contemporary American death system that are designed to help the bereaved: aftercare programs in the funeral industry, hospice bereavement follow-up programs, and support groups for the bereaved.

Questions for Review and Discussion

1. In this chapter, we argued that ritual can play an important role in human life. Think about rituals (activities involving symbolic external or bodily actions by a community) that you have experienced either in your own private life or perhaps those that followed the events of September 11, 2001. What purpose(s) do you think these rituals were intended to serve? Why did the persons involved choose to engage in those specific ritual actions?
2. Suppose someone you love has died. What types of activities would you want to have included in a funeral or memorial service? What might or might not be helpful for you at such a moment? Reflect on your answers here and compare them to an actual funeral or memorial service that you have attended (or, if you have not attended such an event, think about what you have heard others say about such events).
3. Many bereaved persons report that they found help in their grief from funeral home aftercare programs, hospice bereavement follow-up programs, or bereavement support groups. Why might that be so? What do you think we could learn from these programs and groups in our own efforts as individuals to help the bereaved? Have you had any personal contact with any of these programs?

Suggested Readings

Information about what happens to human bodies after death is provided by:

Iserson, K. V. (1994). *Death to Dust: What Happens to Dead Bodies?*

Criticisms of American funeral practices can be found in:

Arvio, R. P. (1974). *The Cost of Dying and What You Can Do about It.*

Bowman, L. E. (1959). *The American Funeral: A Study in Guilt, Extravagance and Sublimity.*

Harmer, R. M. (1963). *The High Cost of Dying.*

Mitford, J. (1963). *The American Way of Death.*

Mitford, J. (1998). *The American Way of Death Revisited.*

Waugh, E. (1948). *The Loved One.*

More favorable analyses of funeral practices and information about the work of funeral service personnel are provided by:

Canine, J. D. (1999). *What Am I Going to Do with Myself When I Die?*

Howarth, G. (1996). *Last Rites: The Work of the Modern Funeral Director.*

Irion, R. E. (1966). *The Funeral: Vestige or Value?*

Jackson, E. N. (1963). *For the Living.*

Jackson, E. N. (1966). *The Christian Funeral: Its Meaning, Its Purpose, and Its Modern Practice.*

Lynch, T. (1997). *The Undertaking: Life Studies from the Dismal Trade.*

Margolis, O., & Schwarz, O. (Eds.). (1975). *Grief and the Meaning of the Funeral.*

Pine, V. R. (1975). *Caretaker of the Dead: The American Funeral Director.*

Shaw, E. (1994). *What to Do When a Loved One Dies: A Practical and Compassionate Guide to Dealing with Death on Life's Terms.*

Alternatives to traditional funeral practices are described in:

Irion, P. E. (1968). *Cremation.*

Irion, P. E. (1971). *A Manual and Guide for Those Who Conduct a Humanist Funeral Service.*

Lamont, C. (1954). *A Humanist Funeral Service.*

Morgan, E., & Morgan J. (2001). *Dealing Creatively with Death: A Manual of Death Education and Simple Burial* (14th rev. ed.).

The history and roles of cemeteries, photography, and other memorial practices are described in:

Burns, S. B. (1990). *Sleeping Beauty: Memorial Photography in America.*

Forbes, H. (1927). *Gravestones of Early New England and the Men Who Made Them, 1653–1800.*

Gillon, E. (1972). *Victorian Cemetery Sculpture.*

Ruby, J. (1995). *Secure the Shadow: Death and Photography in America.*

Sloane, D. C. (1991). *The Last Great Necessity: Cemeteries in American History.*

Van der Zee, J., Dodson, O., & Billops, C. (1978). *The Harlem Book of the Dead.*

Wright, R. H., & Hughes, W. B. (1996). *Lay Down Body: Living History in African-American Cemeteries.*

Concerning bereavement support, aftercare, and self-help groups, see:

Hughes, M. (1995). *Bereavement and Support: Healing in a Group Environment.*

Silverman, P. R. (1980). *Mutual Help Groups: Organization and Development.*

Silverman, P. R. (1986). *Widow to Widow.*

Wasserman, H., & Danforth, H. E. (1988). *The Human Bond: Support Groups and Mutual Aid.*

Weeks, O. D., & Johnson, C. (Eds.) (2001). *When All the Friends Have Gone: A Guide for Aftercare Providers.*

InfoTrac College Edition

For more information, explore the InfoTrac College Edition at **http://www.infotrac-college.com/Wadsworth**

Enter search terms: AFTERCARE PROGRAMS, BEREAVEMENT FOLLOW-UP, BEREAVEMENT HELPING FACTORS, BEREAVEMENT SUPPORT GROUPS, DEATH RITUAL, MEMORIALIZATION.

Part Five

Developmental Perspectives

In much of this book, we describe what is common to all or is at least widespread in contemporary American experiences of death. These common factors include death-related encounters, attitudes, and practices that involve and affect nearly everyone in our society, as well as experiences of coping with dying or bereavement in which many or all share, regardless of age or developmental status. However, in addition to sharing in a common human community, each human being is also a member of a distinctive developmental subgroup or cohort. In the four chapters that follow, we consider death-related subjects from this latter perspective: *development across the life course.*

The merits of a developmental perspective first became evident in studies of childhood. Subsequently, it was recognized that developmental processes continue throughout the human life course. Still, more is known about some eras and some aspects of human development than about others.

Many thinkers, such as Freud (1959b), Jung (1970), Havighurst (1953), Bühler (1968), and Neugarten and Datan (1973), have contributed to our understanding of human development. Among such thinkers, Erikson (1963, 1968) is especially well known for describing eight distinguishable eras (sometimes called ages, periods, or stages) in human development (see Table V.1) on p. 298.

According to Erikson, a predominant psychosocial issue or central conflict characterizes each era in the development of an individual ego. These developmental conflicts involve a struggle between a pair of alternative orientations, opposed tendencies, or attitudes toward life, the self, and other people. Successful resolution of each of these developmental struggles results in a leading virtue, a particular strength or quality of ego functioning.

Developmental theorists argue that each normative conflict has a time of special prominence in the life course. Because this timing is controlled by development, not chronology, it only roughly correlates with age. According to developmental theory, failure to resolve the tasks of one era leaves unfinished work for subsequent eras. In other words, a developmental perspective asserts that: (1) developing individuals strive to integrate aspects of their inner lives and their relationships with the social world; (2) the integrative tasks undertaken in this effort depend on the different crises or turning points that unfold as development proceeds; and (3) the way in which the integration is or is not managed determines the individual's present quality of life, potential for future growth, and residual or unresolved work that remains to be achieved.

Erikson's model is not the only developmental framework that might enrich our

Table V.1 Principal Eras in Human Development

Era	Approximate Age	Predominant Issue	Virtue
Infancy	Birth through 12–18 months	Basic trust vs. mistrust	Hope
Toddlerhood	Infancy to 3 years	Autonomy vs. shame and doubt	Will or self-control
Early childhood; sometimes called play age or the preschool period	3–6 years	Initiative vs. guilt	Purpose or direction
Middle childhood; sometimes called school age or the latency period	6 years to puberty	Industry vs. inferiority	Competency
Adolescence	Puberty to about 21 or 22 years	Identity vs. role confusion	Fidelity
Young adulthood	21–22 to 45 years	Intimacy vs. isolation	Love
Middle adulthood or middle age	45–65 years	Generativity vs. stagnation and self-absorption	Production and care
Maturity; sometimes called old age or the era of the elderly	65 years and older	Ego integrity vs. despair	Renunciation and wisdom

Note: All chronological ages are approximate.
SOURCE: Based on Erikson, 1963, 1968.

study of death, dying, and bereavement, and many have noted some of its limitations or added to its details (for example, Kail & Cavanaugh, 2000; Newman & Newman, 1999). The model is limited in its application to different cultural groups; it may apply equally to both sexes only in societies that give equal options to men and women (Gilligan, 1982; Levinson, 1996); and it tends to describe individuals independently of familial or other systemic contexts (McGoldrick, 1988). Still, a developmental perspective does provide an important frame of reference from which to investigate death-related experiences.

In Chapters 12 through 15, we adopt a developmental perspective in order to appreciate the fact that "death is one of the central themes in human development throughout the life span. Death is not just our destination; it is a part of our 'getting there' as well" (Kastenbaum, 1977, p. 43). Our question here is: How or in what ways are death-related experiences distinctive during the principal eras of human development? Chapters 12 through 15 organize answers to that question around four developmental cohorts: children, adolescents, adults, and the elderly. We emphasize the chapters on childhood and adolescence because: (1) many subjects in other parts of this book are already closely associated with adults and the elderly, (2) there is so much that is distinctive in children's interactions with death, and (3) death-related issues in adolescence (which are also distinctive in many ways) are often overlooked or obscured by being merged into discussions of childhood or adulthood. ■

Chapter Twelve

CHILDREN

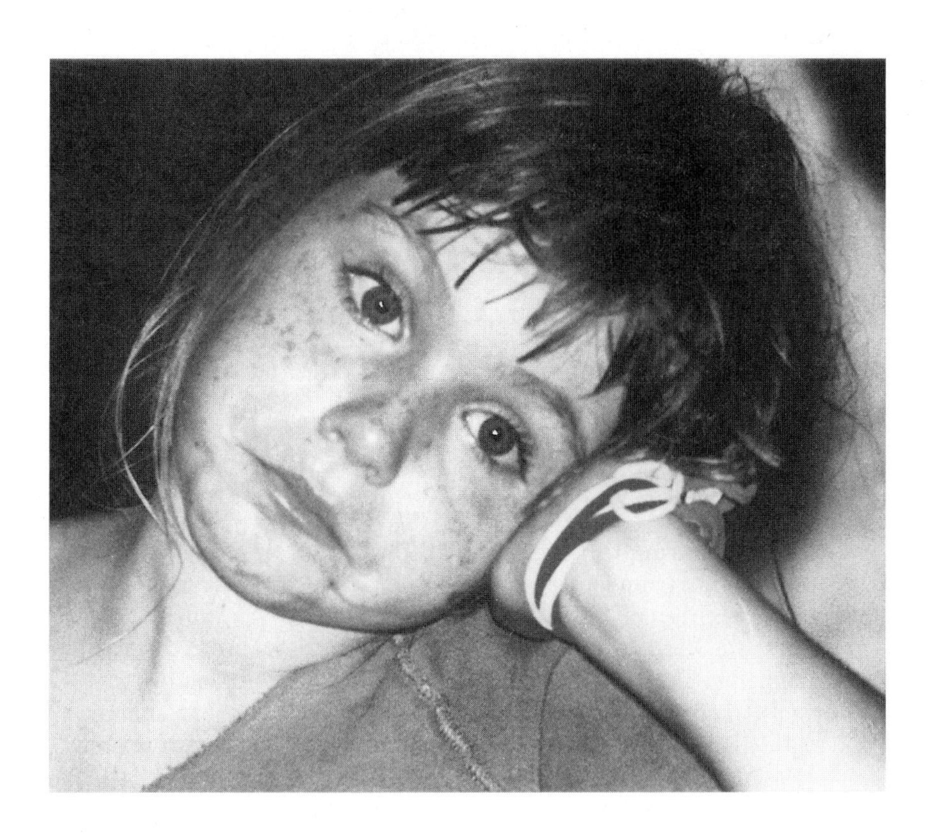

IN THIS CHAPTER, WE EXAMINE INTERACTIONS with death during childhood. In so doing, we focus on young children and adopt a familiar developmental standpoint that views the era of *childhood* as the period from birth to puberty or the beginning of adolescence (*Oxford English Dictionary*, 1989)—roughly, the first 10 to 12 years of life.

Most developmental theorists (like Erikson, 1963, 1968) divide childhood itself into four distinguishable eras: infancy, toddlerhood, early childhood (also called the play age or preschool period), and middle childhood (also called the school age or latency period). (Note that the term *child* can also include the unborn fetus; thus, some writers such as Newman and Newman [1999] and Papalia and her colleagues [1998] identify the prenatal period extending from conception to birth as the first era in the human life course.)

Much still remains to be learned about children and issues related to death, dying, and bereavement. In the current state of our knowledge, we cannot always draw distinctions in death-related matters that parallel divisions between four or more developmental eras in childhood. Moreover, the National Center for Health Statistics (NCHS) provides mortality data in age-related categories and formats that do not always match developmental theorists' distinctions among the various eras within childhood and adolescence. Thus, in this chapter we address childhood as a whole, emphasizing throughout what is unique and distinctive about this whole period and drawing finer developmental distinctions whenever we can. Also, our presentation of mortality data in Chapters 12 and 13 necessarily follows the ways in which NCHS makes that data available.

After a brief vignette illustrating some of the issues that may arise for children within the contemporary American death system, in this chapter we consider additional comments about children and their distinctive developmental tasks, typical encounters with death in American society during childhood, the development of death-related concepts and attitudes toward death during this era, issues related to children who are coping with life-threatening illness and dying, issues related to children who are coping with bereavement and grief, and principles for helping children cope with death. ■

One Child and Death

In the film *And We Were Sad, Remember?* (1979), a young girl named Allison is awakened during the night by a telephone call from her father to her mother. He is calling from a hospital in another town to report that his mother has just died. After the call, Allison's mother explains that Grammie's heart had stopped and she is dead. Allison's mother says that she will drive to Grammie's home tomorrow, and asks whether Allison and her younger brother, Christopher, would like to go with her to Grammie's funeral. She explains what a funeral is and Allison says that she wants to attend. When Christopher wakes, Allison asks him if he would also like to go with her to the "fumeral."

A day or two later, Allison's father tells her that he has arranged for her and Christopher to stay with an adult friend during the funeral and to have a fun adventure. Allison replies that her mother had told her that she could go to the funeral. She insists that she wants to attend and urges him to let her do so. He is quite reluctant, finally agreeing only that he will think about it and decide later. Allison says that whenever he talks like that, it usually means "no."

When the family and friends are all gathered at Grammie's home, Allison and her cousin get into an argument. They are playing with their dolls and acting out a scene involving illness and death. Allison wants to cover the doll that has "died" with a blanket. Her cousin replies that she has been told that dying is like going to sleep. If so, the doll will still need to breathe and cannot do so if the blanket covers its face. The children take their dispute to Allison's father, who only tells them to stop fighting, put the dolls away, and get ready for bed. When Allison insists that he settle their disagreement, he replies in exasperation: "Little girl, you don't have to worry about that for a hundred years!"

Children, Developmental Tasks, and Death

At one time in Western society, children were essentially thought of as miniature adults (Ariès, 1962). After infancy, when they became able to move about more or less independently, their clothing and much of their behavior were expected to be modeled along adult lines. As sensitivity to developmental differences grew, that viewpoint was abandoned in most Western societies, although the Amish (whom we met in the vignette near the beginning of Chapter 3) still follow some of these practices. Now childhood is seen as different from other eras in human development, and additional distinctions are made between different eras within childhood. Thus, developmental theorists identify distinct tasks in four specific eras within childhood: to develop *trust* versus mistrust in infancy, *autonomy* versus shame and doubt in toddlerhood, *initiative* versus guilt in early childhood, and *industry* versus inferiority in middle childhood (see Table V.1; also Papalia et al., 1998).

According to this account, infants who develop a sense of basic trust will become *confident and hopeful* because they will believe that they can rely on people and the world to fulfill their needs and satisfy their desires. Toddlers—often depicted as willful agents in the "terrible twos"—who develop their own legitimate autonomy and independence will learn *self-control* and establish a balance between self-regulation and external dictates. In early childhood, the developmental conflict between initiative and guilt will appear in the form of a challenge to cultivate one's own initiative or desire to take action and pursue goals, but to balance that with the healthy moral reservations that one has about one's plans. Combining spontaneity and responsibility in this way promotes a sense of *purpose or direction* in a child's life. In middle childhood, the developmental conflict between industry and inferiority involves developing one's capacities to do productive work, thereby achieving a sense of *competence* and self-esteem rooted in a view of the self as able to master skills and carry out tasks.

One important aspect of normative development is its variability within specific groups of children. Some youngsters advance in these developmental processes more rapidly than others. Some are delayed in their development by various physical or psychosocial factors. Some are influenced more than others by the social, cultural, economic, or historical contexts in which they find themselves. In short, human development is not an absolutely uniform, lockstep process. In particular, although chronological or age markers (which are relatively easy to determine and appear to be objective) are often used to mark out and evaluate a child's development; in fact, development is not primarily a matter of chronology but one of physical, psychosocial, and spiritual maturation. Thus, some persons who are adult in age and body remain at the developmental level of a young child and must in many (but perhaps not all) ways be appreciated and treated primarily with the latter perspective in mind. Nevertheless, there are broad normative patterns in childhood development whose influences can be seen in typical types of death-related encounters, understandings, and attitudes during childhood.

Encounters with Death during Childhood

"'The kingdom where nobody dies,' as Edna St. Vincent Millay once described childhood, is the fantasy of grown-ups" (Kastenbaum, 1973, p. 37). The realities of life during childhood include both deaths of children and deaths experienced by children (Corr, 1995a).

Deaths of Children

Children between birth and 9 years of age make up 14.1 percent of the total population in the United States. In 1999, this group experienced approximately 36,660 deaths, down by almost 500 deaths from 1998 (Hoyert et al., 2001). In 1999, these deaths represented just over 1.5 percent of the nearly 2.4 million deaths in the country.

Infant Deaths More children die during infancy than throughout the remainder of childhood. In 1999, 27,937 infants died during their first year of life in the United States (see Table 12.1). This is a decline of 434 infant deaths from the 28,371 deaths of infants in 1998. About half of all infant deaths in both years were the result of four principal causes: congenital malformations, disorders related to short gestation and low birth weight, sudden infant death syndrome (SIDS), and newborns affected by maternal complications of pregnancy (Hoyert et al., 2001; Murphy, 2000).

The overall infant mortality rate in the United States in 1999 was 7.1 infant deaths per 1,000 live births (see Table 12.2). Along with the steady decline in

Table 12.1 Number of Deaths during Childhood by Age, Race, and Sex: United States, 1999

	Under 1 Year			1–4 Years			5–9 Years		
	Both Sexes	Males	Females	Both Sexes	Males	Females	Both Sexes	Males	Females
All races	27,937	15,646	12,291	5,249	2,975	2,274	3,474	1,964	1,510
Caucasian Americans, total[a]	18,067	10,197	7,870	3,690	2,084	1,606	2,450	1,376	1,074
Non-Hispanic Caucasian Americans	13,553	7,718	5,835	2,819	1,605	1,214	1,990	1,115	875
Hispanic Americans[b]	4,412	2,411	2,001	882	481	401	464	266	198
African Americans[a]	8,822	4,897	3,925	1,311	746	565	880	519	361
Asian or Pacific Island Americans[a]	705	372	333	166	97	69	96	48	48
Native Americans[a]	343	180	163	82	48	34	48	21	27

[a]Race and Hispanic origin are reported separately on the death certificate.
[b]Includes all persons of Hispanic origin of any race.
SOURCE: Hoyert et al., 2001.

Table 12.2 Death Rates (per 100,000 in the specified population group) during Childhood by Age, Race, and Sex: United States, 1999

	Under 1 Year[a]			1–4 Years			5–9 Years		
	Both Sexes	Males	Females	Both Sexes	Males	Females	Both Sexes	Males	Females
All races	731.4	801.5	658.1	34.7	38.5	30.8	17.4	19.2	15.5
Caucasian Americans, total[b]	596.8	658.1	532.6	30.7	33.9	27.4	15.6	17.1	14.0
Non-Hispanic Caucasian Americans	572.7	636.5	505.6	29.7	32.9	26.2	15.6	17.0	14.1
Hispanic Americans[c]	611.5	655.3	565.9	32.1	34.3	29.8	15.5	14.3	16.1
African Americans[b]	1,551.1	1,694.0	1,403.3	58.9	66.0	51.5	28.0	32.5	23.3
Asian or Pacific Island Americans[b]	388.6	403.4	373.4	23.0	26.6	19.4	11.0	10.6	11.3
Native Americans[b]	808.3	839.5	772.5	51.4	59.4	43.1	21.9	18.9	25.0

[a]Death rates for "Under 1 Year" are based on population estimates; they differ from infant mortality rates, which are based on live births.
[b]Race and Hispanic origin are reported separately on the death certificate.
[c]Includes all persons of Hispanic origin of any race.
SOURCE: Hoyert et al., 2001.

infant deaths in the United States during recent years and a major reduction in deaths from sudden infant death syndrome (see Box 12.1), this is a fine achievement. Nevertheless, infant mortality rates for African Americans remain much higher—about two and one-half times higher—than those for Caucasian Americans or for Hispanic Americans. And, as we noted in Chapter 2, the United States—the richest country on earth—still has an infant mortality rate higher than that of 20 other industrialized countries in the world.

Deaths of Children after Infancy In 1999, 5,249 children between the ages of 1 and 4 years died in the United States, mainly as a result of accidents and congenital malformations (see Table 12.3). In addition, in the same year 7,595 children between 5 and 14 years of age died in our society, mainly as a result of accidents and malignant neoplasms (cancer). Thus, accidents are the leading cause of death in childhood after the first year of life, with motor vehicle accidents becoming proportionately more prominent in later childhood deaths. Throughout childhood, congenital malformations decline in relative significance as leading causes of death, whereas cancer and homicide increase in relative significance. By 1992, human immunodeficiency virus (HIV) infection had become the seventh leading cause of death for children 1 to 4 years of age as well as for those between 5 and 14 years of age (Kochanek & Hudson, 1994), but in 1999 it no longer appeared among the ten leading causes of death in these two age groups.

Among American children who die, there are significant differences between Caucasian Americans and members of other American racial and cultural groups, as well as between males and females (see Tables 12.1 and 12.2). For example, as might be expected, *numbers of deaths* in children between 1 and 4 years of age and between 5 and 9 years of age are much larger among

Box 12.1 Sudden Infant Death Syndrome

Sudden infant death syndrome or SIDS is the leading cause of death in infants from 1 month to 1 year of age. Officially, SIDS is "the sudden death of an infant under one year of age which remains unexplained after a thorough case investigation, including performance of a complete autopsy, examination of the death scene, and review of the clinical history" (Willinger et al., 1991, p. 681). Typically, a healthy baby dies suddenly and tragically with no advance warning. A death of this sort shocks our sensibilities partly because it runs counter to the general pattern of our experiences with death in the United States.

Some cases of SIDS may not be correctly diagnosed—for example, when it is not possible to conduct a thorough case investigation. Nevertheless, identification of this entity as a *syndrome* and its recognition by the World Health Organization as an official cause of death is significant in many ways. A syndrome is a recognizable pattern of events whose underlying cause is unknown. Whenever that pattern is identified, we know that the infant's death did not result from child abuse or neglect and that nothing could have been done ahead of time to prevent the death.

Since there is no way to screen for an unknown cause of death, SIDS deaths have been thought to be unpreventable. Thus, it has been said that the first symptom of SIDS is a dead infant. SIDS strikes across all economic, ethnic, and cultural boundaries, displaying no distinctive or unique associations with risk factors other than those that put all babies in danger, such as teenage pregnancy or parental smoking. The only demographic variable that appears to be critical for SIDS is the fact that it occurs only in infancy—with a noticeable peak in incidence around 2 to 4 months of age and during the winter months. This suggests some associations with infant development and environment, but does not explain SIDS.

In the early 1990s, the American death system mobilized itself in new ways to reduce the risk of SIDS. New research (for example, Dwyer et al., 1995) suggested that infants might be at less risk for SIDS if they were put down for sleep

(continues)

Caucasian Americans than they are among African Americans, Hispanic Americans, Asian Americans, or Native Americans. However, *death rates* are especially high among African-American children in these age groups, as well as among Native-American and Hispanic-American children. In addition, in all racial and cultural groups in our society numbers of deaths and death rates are noticeably higher for male children than they are for female children. Further, after infancy deaths resulting from homicide and HIV infection are disproportionately prevalent among African-American children. All these statistics clearly illustrate the social inequality of death within the contemporary American death system. It is especially hazardous to be an infant, a male child, and an African-American child in our society—and those hazards are compounded when poverty is introduced as an additional variable.

Box 12.1 (cont.) Sudden Infant Death Syndrome

on their backs (supine) or sides, rather than on their stomachs (prone). This recommendation ran contrary to familiar advice that favored sleeping prone in order to reduce the risk that an infant might regurgitate or spit up fluids, aspirate them into an airway, and suffocate. Researchers now believe that any risk of suffocating in this way is far less than that of SIDS.

Accordingly, as early as 1992 the American Academy of Pediatrics (AAP) concluded it was likely that infants who sleep on their backs and sides are at less risk for SIDS when all other circumstances are favorable (for example, firm mattresses and an absence of soft toys nearby). Even though the reasons for that are not yet fully understood, the AAP (1992, p. 1120) recommended that "healthy infants, when being put down for sleep be positioned on their side or back." Subsequently, in June 1994 the federal government initiated the "Back to Sleep" campaign (Willinger, 1995). Dramatic and sustained reductions in SIDS deaths followed: from 1988 to 1999, SIDS rates fell by more than 52 percent leading to a new low in 1999 of 2,648 SIDS deaths (Murphy, 2000; Hoyert et al., 2001). As a result of dramatic changes like this, two separate task forces of the AAP (1996, 2000a) have reaffirmed the recommendation that positioning infants on their back for sleep is the preferred position, although sleeping on the infant's side is an acceptable (though less stable) alternative since it is much better than sleeping on the stomach.

We should not expect that a change in sleep position alone will settle all problems with SIDS, but it will be important if (as expected) this reduction in infant deaths continues and if additional research leads to a better understanding of the causal mechanisms behind SIDS. (Further information about SIDS can be obtained from the SIDS Alliance [1314 Bedford Ave., Suite 210, Baltimore, MD 21208; tel. 800-221-7437 or 800-638-7437, www.SIDSalliance.org] or from the National SIDS Resource Center [2070 Chain Bridge Road, Suite 450, Vienna, VA 22182; tel. 703-821-8955, www.circsol.com]). ■

Deaths of Others Experienced by Children

Deaths of others experienced by children are also a reality of life in our society. No reliable data are available concerning the frequency or patterns of these death-related encounters, and it appears that many Americans often undervalue the prevalence and importance of this type of death for children. The death of a significant other can be an important experience for a child, one with special meaning for his or her subsequent development. In fact, a child may encounter many types of death such as those involving a grandparent, parent, sibling, other relative, classmate, friend, neighbor, teacher, pet, or wild animal.

Loss experiences may differ for individual children. For example, a deceased grandparent or parent might not have lived with or spent much time with a

Table 12.3 Deaths and Death Rates (per 100, 000) during Childhood for the Ten Leading Causes of Death in Specified Age Groups Both Sexes, All Races: United States, 1999

	1–4 Years of Age			5–14 Years of Age		
Rank	Cause of Death	Number	Rate	Cause of Death	Number	Rate
. .	All causes	5,249	34.7	All causes	7,595	19.2
1	Accidents (unintentional injuries)	1,898	12.6	Accidents (unintentional injuries)	3,091	7.8
	Motor vehicle accidents	650	4.3	Motor vehicle accidents	1,771	4.5
	All other accidents	1,248	8.3	All other accidents	1,320	3.4
2	Congenital malformations, deformations, and chromosomal abnormalities	549	3.6	Malignant neoplasms	1,012	206
3	Malignant neoplasms	418	2.8	Assault (homicide)	432	1.1
4	Assault (homicide)	376	2.5	Congenital malformations, deformations, and chromosomal abnormalties	428	1.1
5	Diseases of the heart	183	1.2	Diseases of the heart	277	0.7
6	Influenza and pneumonia	130	0.9	Intentional self-harm (suicide)	244	0.6
7	Certain conditions originating in the perinatal period	92	0.6	Chronic lower respiratory diseases	139	0.4
8	Septicemia	87	0.6	In situ neoplasms, benign neoplasms, and neoplasms of uncertain or unknown behavior	101	0.3
9	In situ neoplasms, benign neoplasms, and neoplasms of uncertain or unknown behavior	63	0.4	Influenza and pneumonia	93	0.2
10	Chronic lower respiratory diseases	54	0.4	Septicimia	77	0.2
. . .	All other causes	1,399	9.2	All other causes	1,701	4.3

SOURCE: Hoyert et al., 2001.

particular child, and a child might not perceive the death of that individual as a very important loss. By contrast, the death of a cherished pet, a childhood friend, or a caring neighbor might be an important event in a child's life.

In addition, children within different cultural, ethnic, and socioeconomic communities in the United States may encounter death in different ways. For example, all too many American children are direct or indirect casualties of familial and community violence (Groves et al., 1993; Kozol, 1995; Nader, 1996), either as immediate victims or as witnesses of violence that may involve multiple losses and traumatic deaths—such as those that occurred on September

Persons with AIDS need understanding, love, and care.

11, 2001. Also, during the early 1990s some American children were members of families in which members died or were dying of AIDS (Levine, 1993; Dane & Levine, 1994), although that number declined near the end of the decade.

Moreover, although few American children experience deaths from starvation, civil disruption, or war, they may witness graphic reports of such deaths on television. In the second week of September, 2001, many American children were exposed to extensive television coverage of the death and destruction caused by terrorist attacks on the World Trade Center in New York City and the Pentagon in the Washington, D.C., area.

Further, Diamant (1994) drew on a study by the American Psychological Association to show that children in the United States who watch two to four hours of television per day will have witnessed fantasized versions of 8,000 murders and 100,000 acts of violence by the time they finish elementary school. Because such fantasies are not real, adults often dismiss them as unimportant. However, they may be very important in the minds of young children, especially those children who have little direct experience with natural human death to put into perspective these surrogate deaths in the media.

The point to emphasize is that children are exposed to these and other death-related events, whether or not adults or society recognize that fact. Curious children are unlikely to ignore such events completely. What is more likely is that the ways in which a child acknowledges and deals with death-related events may not be obvious to adults in their environment. This was evident in the vignette near the beginning of this chapter, when Allison's father failed to understand and respond in helpful ways to her needs. Those who wish to help children in our society need to be sensitive to the many implications of encounters with death during childhood.

In order to appreciate the ways in which children experience death, we will examine two additional topics associated with children's encounters with death: the development of death-related concepts and the development of death-related attitudes in childhood.

The Development of Death-Related Concepts in Childhood

Systematic study of the development of children's understandings of death began in the 1930s (Anthony, 1939, 1940; Schilder & Wechsler, 1934). Since that time, well over 100 research reports on this subject have been published in English alone (Speece & Brent, 1984, 1996; Stambrook & Parker, 1987). We concentrate here on the classic report by Nagy (1948/1959), which exemplifies many of these studies, as well as more recent work by Speece & Brent (1996).

The Work of Maria Nagy

To learn about children's understanding of the concept of death, Maria Nagy (1948/1959) examined 378 children living in Budapest just before World War II. The children were 3 to 10 years of age, 51 percent boys and 49 percent girls, ranging from dull normal to superior in intelligence level (with most falling in the "normal" range). Nagy's methods were as follows: children in the *7-to-10-year-old range* were asked to "write down everything that comes into your mind about death" (p. 4); children in the *6-to-10-year-old range* were asked to make drawings about death (many of the older children also wrote explanations of their creations); and discussions were held with *all of the children*, either about their compositions and drawings, or (in the case of 3- to 5-year-olds) to get them to talk about their ideas and feelings about death. Because of the war, Nagy's results were not published until 1948; they appeared again in 1959 in a somewhat revised form.

Nagy's results (1948, p. 7) suggested three major developmental stages: (1) "The child of less than five years does not recognize death as an irreversible fact. In death it sees life"; (2) "Between the ages of five and nine death is most often personified and thought of as a contingency"; and (3) "In general only after the age of nine is it recognized that death is a process happening in us according to certain laws." Nagy remarked that because "the different sorts of answers can be found only at certain ages, one can speak of stages of development" (1948, p. 7), although she later added that "it should be kept in mind that neither the stages nor the above-mentioned ages at which they occur are watertight compartments as it were. Overlapping does exist" (1959, p. 81). Brief descriptions of each of these stages, using Nagy's own characterizations, will illustrate her results.

Stage 1: There Is No Definitive Death In the first stage of children's conceptual development, Nagy believes that "the child does not know death as such" (1948, p. 7). Either the concept of death has not been fully distinguished from other concepts or its full implications have not yet been grasped. For this reason, *death is not seen as final;* life and consciousness are attributed to the dead. One way in which this occurs is when death is understood either as a departure or a sleep—that is, in terms of continued life elsewhere (departure) or as a diminished form of life (sleep). In Nagy's view, this denies death as a definite and unambiguous concept.

A second way in which the finality of death is not fully grasped is when children "no longer deny death, but . . . are still unable to accept it as a definitive fact" (p. 13). Such children cannot completely separate death from life; they view death as a gradual, transitional process (between dying and being buried or arriving in heaven) or as a temporary situation in which links with life have not yet been completely severed. To Nagy, this meant that life and death are either held in simultaneous relation or they are interpreted as being able to change places with one another repeatedly. In short, although death exists, it is not absolutely final or definitive.

Two points are worth noting about Nagy's description of children who have not grasped the finality or definitiveness of death. First, even when death is interpreted as a kind of ongoing living somewhere else, separation from someone who is loved and consequent changes in the child's life may still be painful. A child does not have to grasp fully the finality of death or the complete cessation of bodily activities in order to react to separation from the dead person. Second, since most children are not satisfied with the simple fact of death as disappearance, they will usually want to know where and how the deceased person continues to live. This curiosity may lead children to speculate about the nature of life in the grave. Because these theories are based on the child's limited life experiences, they may lead to misinterpretations or to feelings of anxiety and fear about what is going on.

Stage 2: Death = A Man According to Nagy, in this second stage *death is imagined as a separate person* (such as a grim reaper, skeleton, ghost, or death angel), or else *death is identified with the dead themselves* so that the children did not distinguish between death and dead persons. Nagy interpreted this concept as a *personification of death*, which means that the existence and definitiveness of death have been accepted although, because of children's strong aversion to the thought of death, death is depicted as a person or reality that is outside or remote from them. In this way, death is conceived of as final, but avoidable or not inevitable and not universal. Those caught by the external force do die; those who escape or get away from the clutches of that force do not die. Later researchers (for example, Gartley & Bernasconi, 1967; Kane, 1979; Koocher, 1973, 1974) emphasized the theme of death's *avoidability* in this stage rather than its personification (which may only be a child's concrete way of representing the avoidability of death through the device of an external figure).

Stage 3: The Cessation of Corporal Life In this third stage, Nagy believed children recognize that death is a process operating within us. Such children view death as both *final and universal*, an aspect of life that is inevitable and not avoidable. Nagy suggested that this reflects a realistic view of both death and the world.

The Work of Mark Speece and Sandor Brent

After reviewing the literature and conducting their own research on children's understandings of death, Mark Speece and Sandor Brent (1994, 1996) concluded that the concept of death is not a simple, uncomplicated notion. It embraces a number of distinguishable subconcepts, each of which is a central aspect in children's concepts of death. Speece and Brent identified five principal subconcepts, some with subordinate components or elements (see Table 12.4).

The theme of *universality* in children's concepts of death is evident in research by Nagy and others, although not always described as a subconcept. It is central to the recognition that *all living things must eventually die*. This is itself a complex point, one that challenges children to bring together three closely

Table 12.4 Subconcepts Embraced by the Concept of Death

Subconcepts
Universality
All-inclusiveness
Inevitability
Unpredictability
Irreversibility
Nonfunctionality
Causality
Noncorporeal continuation

SOURCE: Based on Speece & Brent, 1996.

related notions: all-inclusiveness, inevitability, and unpredictability. *All-inclusiveness* bears on the extent of the group of living things to which the concept of death applies ("Does everyone die?") and points to the fact that no living thing is exempt from death. *Inevitability* has to do with the necessity with which death applies to living things ("Does everyone have to die?") and points to the fact that death is ultimately unavoidable for all living things, regardless of its specific causes. *Unpredictability* relates to the timing of death. If death is all-inclusive and inevitable, one might conclude its timing would be certain and predictable—but that is not the case. In fact, anyone might possibly die at any time. Children and others often shy away from acknowledging the personal implications of this aspect of the universality of death.

Two additional subconcepts, irreversibility and nonfunctionality, are both aspects of the finality of death. *Irreversibility* applies to the processes that distinguish the transition from being alive to being dead and to the state that results from those processes. So, once the physical body of a living thing is dead, it can never be alive again—barring miraculous or magical events and explanations. Medical resuscitation can apply only to a kind of boundary region between being alive and being dead, not to the state of death in which life in a physical body is irreversibly absent. *Nonfunctionality* means that death involves the complete and final cessation of all of the life-defining capabilities or functional capacities (whether external and observable or internal and inferred) typically attributed to a living physical body.

Most researchers agree that universality, irreversibility, and nonfunctionality are all aspects of children's concepts of death. Speece and Brent drew attention to two additional subconcepts—causality and noncorporeal continuation. According to Speece and Brent, the subconcept of *causality* involves comprehending the events or conditions that really do or can bring about the death of a living thing. This subconcept responds to questions like "Why do living things die?" and "What makes living things die?" For Speece and Brent, this requires children to achieve a realistic understanding of the external and internal events or forces that might bring about death—in the face of magical thinking, which suggests that bad behavior or merely wishing could cause someone to die (Fogarty, 2000).

The final component in the concept of death—which Speece and Brent term *noncorporeal continuation*—is reflected in children's efforts to grasp or articulate their understanding of some type of continued life apart from the physical body that has died. This is evident in questions posed by children, such as "What happens after death?" and "Where does your soul or spirit go when you die?"—as well as in the reflections of an 11-year-old girl whose experiences of living with HIV infection prompted her to write, "If only I could talk to someone in Heaven, then they could tell me how it is there, what things there are to do there, and what I should bring" (Wiener et al., 1994, p. 12). Research by Brent and Speece (1993) has shown that children and adults commonly say that some type of continued life form—often, though perhaps not always, a mode of personal continuation—exists after the death of the physical body. This continuation may take many forms, such as the ongoing life of a soul in heaven without the body or the reincarnation of a soul in a new and different body.

Speece and Brent pointed out that many researchers have been disdainful of children's "beliefs in an afterlife" or systematically unwilling to enter into nonnaturalistic aspects of the concept of death.

On the basis of their review of the literature on children's concepts of death, Speece and Brent (1996) concluded, "most studies have found that *by seven years of age* most children understand each of the key bioscientific components—Universality, Irreversibility, Nonfunctionality, and Causality" (p. 43; emphasis added). This conclusion needs to be evaluated in light of Speece and Brent's caution that "age by itself explains nothing. It is rather a convenient general, omnibus index of a wide range of loosely correlated biological and environmental variables." Further, although some researchers (for example, Lonetto, 1980; Schilder & Wechsler, 1934) have maintained that children recognize that death is possible for all other people before they apply it to themselves, Speece and Brent thought it more likely that most children understand their own personal mortality before they understand that all other people die.

Some Comments on Children's Understandings of Death

The work of Nagy and other researchers who have studied the development of death-related concepts in childhood has exposed key elements in the concept of death, such as finality, avoidability versus inevitability, external versus internal forces, and universality. Much of this work has had the great advantage of fitting easily within larger theories or models of developmental psychology, such as those of Jean Piaget (1998; see also Piaget & Inhelder, 1958; Table 12.5). For example, Nagy's characterization of the earliest stages in her account of children's concepts of death agreed with Piaget's observations about an egocentric orientation and several other characteristics of what he calls preoperational thought—such as *magical thinking* (in which all events are explained by the causal influence of various commands, intentions, and forces; see Fogarty, 2000), *animism* (in which life and consciousness are attributed to objects that others think of as inanimate), and *artificialism* (in which it is believed that all objects and events in the world have been manufactured to serve people, a belief that Wass [1984] describes as directly opposed to animism). Similarly, the universality and inevitability that characterize Nagy's final stage conform to Piaget's account of objectivity, generality, and propositional thinking in what he calls the period of formal operations. This finding suggests that children's understandings involve a development or maturation in their capacity to form more and more abstract concepts of subjects like death.

However, research in this field has been plagued by methodological problems, such as lack of precision and agreement in the terms and definitions used for various components of the concept of death, as well as lack of reliable and valid standardized measures for these components. The ensuing literature has not unfairly been characterized as consisting of a "confusing array of results" (Stambrook & Parker, 1987, p. 154). Often, commentators have oversimplified their results, made them more rigid than originally suggested, or applied them uncritically. Many commentators have generalized from studies of particular

Table 12.5 Piaget's System of Cognitive Development

Period and stage[a]	Life period[b]	Some major characteristics
I. Period of sensorimotor intelligence	Infancy (0–2)	"Intelligence" consists of sensory and motor actions. No conscious thinking. Limited language.[c] No concept of reality.
II. Period of preparation and organization of concrete operations		
1. Stage of preoperational	Early childhood (2–7)	Egocentric orientation. Magical, animistic, and artificialistic thinking. Thinking is irreversible. Reality is subjective.
2. Stage of concrete operations	Middle childhood/ preadolescence (7–11/12)	Orientation ego-decentered. Thinking is bound to concrete. Naturalistic thinking. Recognizes laws of conservation and reversibility.
III. Period of formal operations	Adolescence and adulthood (12+)	Propositional and hypodeductive thinking. Generality of thinking. Reality is objective.

[a]Each stage includes an initial period of preparation and a final period of attainment; thus, whatever characterizes a stage is in the process of formation.
[b]There are individual differences in chronological ages.
[c]By the end of age 2, children have attained on the average a vocabulary of approximately 250–300 words.
SOURCE: From "Concepts of Death: A Developmental Perspective" by H. Wass. In H. Wass and C. A. Corr (Eds.), *Childhood and Death*, p. 4. Copyright © 1984 Hemisphere Publishing Corporation. Reprinted with permission.

groups of children (such as Nagy's Hungarian children, who were examined before World War II and before the advent of new cultural forces like television) to other groups of children without taking into account historical or cultural variables in different populations. Speece and Brent (and others, such as Kenyon, 2001; Lazar & Torney-Purta, 1991) have suggested that better research and more nuanced appreciation of results could follow from recommendations to distinguish, standardize, and operationalize key subconcepts within the concept of death.

Adults striving to gain insight into children's understanding of death, to teach children about death, or to provide empathic support to children who are coping with death, must attend to at least four principal variables: developmental level, life experiences, individual personality, and patterns of communication and support (Kastenbaum, 1977). With respect to *development*, cognitive development is not the only relevant variable; maturation is a multidimensional process that applies to all aspects—physical, psychological, social, and spiritual—of a child's life. *Life experiences* are a critical but not yet well-studied factor, even though the quantity and quality of a child's encounters with death are likely to be influential in his or her understanding of death. Each child's *individual personality* will be a powerful variable in the ways he or she can and does think about death. And the death-related thoughts that a child shares with others will depend on his or her ability and willingness to *communicate*, together with the *support* and comfort that he or she receives from those others.

A good example of this effect is seen in quite different challenges that are presented to a child when he or she is asked to explain two simple sentences: "You are dead" and "I will die" (Kastenbaum, 2000; Kastenbaum & Aisenberg, 1972). The first sentence applies to another person at the present time; the second refers back to the speaker, but at some unspecified time in the future. The issues involved in grasping these two sentences are partly conceptual, but they also relate to the potential threat implied in the second sentence and the child's ability to grasp a future possibility. When children strive to understand the concept of death and its various subconcepts, those who have experienced a healthy development, who are able to draw on a fund of constructive personal experiences, whose self-concept is stable and well formed, who communicate openly, and who have adequate support from the adults around them are likely to find themselves in a different and more advantageous position by comparison with children who do not have these resources.

Children do not always think of death as adults do. This does not mean that children have no concept of death. For example, children who think of death as sleep have *an understanding of death*—however undifferentiated it may be from other concepts and however inadequate it may seem in the light of some adult standard—through which they try to make sense of their experiences. As Kastenbaum and Aisenberg (1972, p. 9) noted, "Between the extremes of 'no understanding' and explicit, integrated abstract thought there are many ways by which the young mind can enter into relationship with death." A good way to gain insight into children's understandings of death is to listen carefully to the many questions they ask about this subject (Corr, 1995b, 1996).

The fundamental lesson from research by Nagy and others is that children do make an active effort to grasp or understand death. Nagy (1948, p. 27) added an important corollary: "To conceal death from the child is not possible and is also not permissible. Natural behavior in the child's surroundings can greatly diminish the shock of its acquaintance with death." Allison's father in the vignette at the start of this chapter had not learned this lesson.

The Development of Death-Related Attitudes in Childhood

Children living in the United States today receive many messages about death. The primary sources of these messages are the societal death system that surrounds them and expresses itself, in particular, through the media; their parents, family members, and other persons with whom they come into contact; and their own life experiences.

Many messages from society, parents, and other adults within the contemporary American death system tell children that death is not an acceptable topic for discussion and that children are not permitted to take part in death-related events. Not all societies have transmitted this kind of message to children. For example, as we learned in Chapter 3, among the New England Puritans in colonial America (Stannard, 1977) and in contemporary Amish society (Hostetler, 1994), children were or are expected to take part in both the happy and sad events in a family's life. Any other alternative would have seemed or would still seem undesirable and impracticable.

Death-related situations and experiences may be new to children in American society, as are many other situations in life, but new experiences need not be overwhelming unless children have been taught to view them that way. Just because something is new, it need not be out of bounds from the inquiring mind of a child. The claim that "the child is so recently of the quick that there is little need in his spring-green world for an understanding of the dead" (Ross, 1967, p. 250) does not seem to describe the authentic lives of children in our society. In fact, there is ample evidence in everyday interactions with children and in the scholarly literature (going back as far as the 1920s and 1930s—for example, Childers & Wimmer, 1971; Hall, 1922; Koocher et al., 1976; Schilder & Wechsler, 1934) that *normal, healthy children do have thoughts and feelings about death; they are curious about this subject.*

The specific form of any one child's attitudes toward death, as toward any other significant subject, will relate to the nature of the child's encounters with death and to the developmental, personal, and societal forces that help to shape the child's interpretation and response to a given experience. Even young infants who have little experience or conceptual capacity give clear evidence of separation anxiety. Older children who had no role in a parent's death may nevertheless blame themselves if they believe that something they said or did was somehow magically related to the death. In short, attitudes toward death are complex, even in childhood, and may derive from many sources (Wass & Cason, 1984). To show this, we describe here two arenas in which death-related attitudes are apparent during childhood.

Death-Related Games

Maurer (1966) suggested that the game of peek-a-boo is a classic death-related game in childhood. From the child's egocentric perspective, what happens in this game is that the external world vanishes and then suddenly reappears. As a child focuses on the (apparent) disappearance of the world, he or she may become fearful; its reappearance will often produce delight. From a young child's perspective many experiences like this involve attitudes that are (at least) quite similar to those associated with death.

Further, Rochlin (1967) reported research on children's play activities demonstrating "that at a very early age well-developed mental faculties are functioning to defend oneself against the realization that life may end" (p. 61). Children appear to recognize that their lives might be changed in important ways by death and act on that recognition in the fantasy world of their play. Rochlin's research focused especially on children's games concerned with action, violence, and at least the potential for death. He concluded that "death is a matter of deep consideration to the very young child . . . thoughts of dying are commonplace . . . behavior is influenced by such thoughts" (p. 54). This is not a point to dismiss lightly, since play is the main work of a child's life.

Rhymes, Songs, Humor, and Fairy Tales

Death-related themes appear frequently in children's rhymes and humor. For example, many have sung a little ditty in which "the worms crawl in, the worms crawl out." Others will be familiar with "Ring Around the Rosie," but may not have realized that it is an English song arising from a plague and describing the roseate skin pustules of disease, as a result of which "we all fall down." Even lullabies, like "Rock-a-Bye Baby," are filled with falling cradle themes (Achté et al., 1990), and the child's prayer, "Now I lay me down to sleep," is a petition for safekeeping against death and other hazards of the night.

Children's fairy tales, whether oral or written, are also chock full of references to death (Lamers, 1995). Little Red Riding Hood and her grandmother are eaten by the wicked wolf in the original version of the story, not saved by a passing woodsman or hunter before or after they find themselves in the wolf's stomach (see Box 1.1; Bertman, 1984; Dundes, 1989; Zipes, 1983). The Big Bad Wolf who pursues the three little pigs with threats to huff and puff and blow their houses down dies in a scalding pot of hot water when he falls down the last chimney. Hansel and Gretel (who were left to die in the forest by their parents because there was not enough food) trick the wicked witch and shut her up in the hot oven where she planned to cook them. The wicked stepmother orders the death of Snow White and demands her heart as proof. A gentle kiss may awaken Sleeping Beauty from a state of coma, but the false bride in "The Goose Girl" is put into a barrel lined with sharp nails and rolled until she is dead (Lang, 1904).

Death-related humor and stories of this sort are not necessarily morbid or unhealthful for children. Bettelheim (1977) argued forcefully that they are, in fact, wholesome experiences in which children can work through fears and anxieties related to death in safe and distanced ways. *Death is not absent from the fantasy world of childhood.* Its familiar presence debunks the view that children are simply unfamiliar with death-related thoughts and feelings. Indeed, in the United States today the very powerful force of television entertainment programs repeatedly suggest that the way in which people usually come to be dead is by being killed, only "bad" guys really die, and death itself is not permanent (see Chapter 4).

Children Who Are Coping with Life-Threatening Illness and Dying

Children coping with life-threatening illness and dying frequently experience anxiety. As they acquire information about their condition, their self-concept is likely to change in discernible ways, and they are apt to share an identifiable set of specific concerns associated with dying.

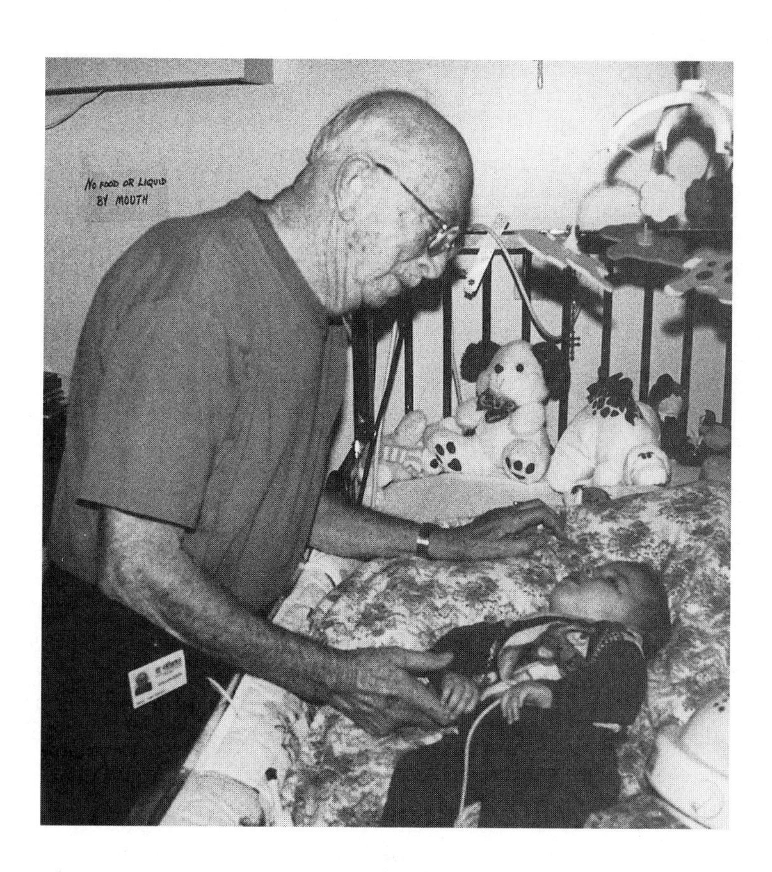

A hospice volunteer visits an ill child.

Anxiety in Ill and Dying Children

When Vernick and Karon (1965) asked, "Who's afraid of death on a leukemia ward?" their answer was everyone—children, family members, and professional caregivers. This finding suggests a basis for coming together and sharing with children.

Still, when Waechter (1971) first began to study ill and dying children, she found a context in which parents and caregivers did not share with the children accurate information about their diagnoses and prognoses. Waechter investigated the attitudes of these children by creating four matched groups of 6- to 10-year-olds: children with chronic disease for which death was predicted; children with chronic disease with a good prognosis; children with brief illness; and nonhospitalized, well children. During an interview, each child was given a projective test (a set of pictures for each of which the child was to develop a story) and a test designed to measure general anxiety.

Waechter demonstrated that anxiety levels in fatally ill children were much higher than those for either of the other two groups of hospitalized children or for the well children and that the fatally ill children expressed significantly more anxiety specifically related to death, mutilation, and loneliness than did other ill children. This was true even though the fatally ill children had not been formally informed of their prognosis. Other studies of ill and dying children have confirmed similar findings (for example, Spinetta & Maloney, 1975; Spinetta et al., 1973; and Waechter, 1984, in the United States; and Lee et al., 1984, in China).

Acquiring Information and Changing Concepts of Self

A different approach was taken by Bluebond-Langner (1977, 1978), who used the methodology of cultural anthropology to identify keen awareness of their situation in hospitalized, terminally ill children with leukemia. Bluebond-Langner identified five stages in the children's process of acquiring information (see the left-hand column in Table 12.6). The sobering—and not surprising—lesson from this portion of Bluebond-Langner's study is that children attend to important experiences in their lives, and acquire information from people and events that impact very closely on them.

Bluebond-Langner's research went one step further. She noted that acquisition of information was coordinated with parallel shifts in self-concept. As the children obtained information, they applied it to a changing understanding of themselves (see the right-hand column in Table 12.6). According to Bluebond-Langner, changes in self-concept were associated with events in the illness process and the information available to the children. Critical points here are the

Table 12.6 The Private Worlds of Dying Children

Stages in the Process of Acquiring Information	Changes in Self-Concept
1. I have a serious illness.	1. From diagnosis (prior to which I had thought of myself as well) to awareness that I am seriously ill.
2. I know the drugs that I am receiving, when and how they are being used, and their side effects.	2. At the first remission, to the view that I am seriously ill—but will get better.
3. I know the purposes of treatments and. procedures	3. At the first relapse, to the view that I am always ill—but will get better.
4. I understand that these treatments, procedures, and symptoms fit together to identify a disease in which there is a cycle of relapses and remissions (i.e., the medicines do not always last as long or work as well as they are supposed to) (does not include death).	4. After several more remissions and relapses, to the view that I am always ill—and will never get better.
5. I understand that the cycle of disease is finite, has an end, and that the end is death—there are only a limited number of drugs and when they stop working, I will die soon.	5. After the death of a leukemic peer, to the realization that I am dying.

SOURCE: Adapted from *The Private Worlds of Dying Children*, by M. Bluebond-Langner, pp. 166 and 169. Copyright © 1978 Princeton University Press.

timing of these changes in relationship to external events and the children's ability to integrate and synthesize information arising from their experiences in order to form new self-concepts.

Children learn from their experiences, from other children, and from the ways in which adults treat them. How could it be otherwise? What they learn is not only abstract information; it has meaning and significance for them. As suggested by Alexander and Adlerstein (1958), the central point may be not so much the content of death conceptions as their significance for the individuals in question. We will pursue this point in Chapter 13. Here we need only observe that children's concepts of death are intimately associated with ways they feel about and interpret both themselves and the world around them.

Issues for Ill and Dying Children

Many advances have taken place in recent years in understanding pain and other distressing symptoms and in their management in different types of life-threatening childhood illnesses (see, for example, Goldman, 1998; McGrath, 1998). The increased understanding has led to official policy statements on care for children with life-threatening illnesses from the Association for Children with Life-Threatening or Terminal Conditions and Their Families (1995) in Britain, the World Health Organization (1998), and the American Academy of Pediatrics (2000b). Nevertheless, recent studies have confirmed deficiencies in the management of pain and other distressing symptoms in many children who are dying (for example, McCallum et al., 2000; Wolfe et al., 2000a).

Psychosocial needs of ill and dying children are likely to focus on the importance of love and security with freedom from pain, freedom from deep-seated feelings of anxiety or guilt, a sense of belonging, a feeling of self-respect, and understanding of self (Masera et al., 1999). From a developmental standpoint, Waechter (1984) noted that preschool children with a life-threatening illness are likely to have principal concerns about the causality of their illness, threats to body image, treatment procedures, and fears of dying, whereas school-age children most often have concerns about the future, education and social relationships, body image, and issues related to hospitalization and procedures. Not surprisingly, much of their anxiety focuses on safety (from pain or other forms of distress, intervention procedures, bodily assault) and security (both within themselves and in relationship to family members, peers, and other important persons) (Sourkes, 1995). Stevens (1998) put much of this more simply by proposing that the emotional needs of dying children will be: (1) those of all children regardless of health, (2) those arising from the child's reaction to illness and admission to a hospital, and (3) those arising from the child's concept of death.

Many of the concerns of dying children emphasize quality in living and the immediate or present-tense implications of various sorts of threats to quality in living. This range of issues fits with the tendency of many children to live in the moment. Moreover, it is important to recognize that cure rates for many illnesses that were once highly lethal for children have changed so dramatically in recent years that for many children the challenge has changed from coping with dying to living with a serious or life-threatening illness (Adams & Deveau, 1993; Doka, 1996a; Koocher & O'Malley, 1981; Spinetta & Deasy-Spinetta, 1981). Thus it has been argued that the work of contemporary pediatric oncologists is guided by the motto "Cure is not enough" and by an emphasis on quality in living among survivors of childhood cancer (Schwartz et al., 1994). Issues that are often central for survivors—or, as some prefer to say, "graduates"—of a life-threatening illness in childhood are: (1) normalization or incorporating the disease experience into one's life history; (2) learning to live with uncertainty—which may lead to a heightened sense of vulnerability, overprotectiveness by adults, and/or a transformation of personal priorities, values, and goals; (3) learning to live with compromise and the ongoing repercussions of disease; and (4) overcoming stigma in social contexts (Ruccione, 1994).

Similar concerns are found in children whose experiences with HIV infection and AIDS have turned into coping with a chronic life-threatening condition (Dane, 1996). In many ways, this is as difficult as coping with acute dying. Thus, one 12-year-old girl had the following to say about contending with the uncertainties posed by HIV infection: "Living with HIV and knowing that you can die from it is scary. . . . I think it is hardest in this order: Not knowing when this will happen. . . . Not knowing where it will happen. . . . Worrying about my family. . . . What will happen to my stuff and my room? . . . Thinking about what my friends will think" (Wiener et al., 1994, p. 24).

Children Who Are Coping with Bereavement and Grief

There once was a scholarly debate about whether or not children are able to grieve after a death (see, for example, Furman, 1973). This debate appears to rest both on a failure to distinguish between grief and mourning, together with an absence of adequate models for childhood mourning. Children certainly experience grief (that is, react to loss). They may cry, get angry, become depressed, have trouble sleeping, regress in their behavior, or react in other ways to loss.

However, children do not always react to loss or express their reactions as adults do (Wolfenstein, 1966). For example, bereaved children may not display their feelings as openly as many adults do, and they may immerse themselves in activities of everyday life such as play and school instead of withdrawing into preoccupation with thoughts of the deceased person (Romond, 1989). As a result, children's grief reactions may be longer in duration and more intermittent in character than those of many adults. The basic issue is how normative developmental tasks influence encounters with loss, and vice versa: Can children feel secure when they are coping with loss and grief? Does healthy development help them in such coping? In ways like these, there may be major differences between bereaved adults and children.

Squib, a little owl, has lost his piece (peace) and is sad.

The real issue for bereaved children is not so much whether they can grieve but the nature of their grief and mourning. That is, what are the central concerns that are likely to preoccupy bereaved children? And what are the tasks of mourning that children face in coping with loss and grief?

Issues for Bereaved Children

Three central issues are likely to be prominent in the grief experiences of bereaved children and may apply to the perceived or real termination of any relationship for children: (1) Did I cause it (death or some other form of loss) to happen? (2) Is it going to happen to me? and (3) Who is going to take care of me? (Worden, 1996). The egocentricity of these issues is obvious. When a child does not rightly understand the causality involved in a loss, perhaps because of ignorance or magical thinking, it is not surprising that issues of origin and endangerment should present themselves.

The death of a parent or other caring adult may especially evoke the first and third of these issues. For example, if Mommy says in exasperation one day, "You'll be the death of me," and is later killed in a car accident, a child may wonder whether the latter event fulfilled the promise of the former. Similarly, when there is widespread discussion of a large-scale trauma, such as happened on September 11, 2001, it is not surprising when children wonder about potential threats to themselves. And when children's welfare depends in so many ways on parents and other adults, we can understand why the death of an important person might lead a child to might wonder who will now provide the care that he or she needs (Donnelly, 1987; Silverman, 2000). As a result, many children who have experienced the death of a parent strive to maintain an emotional connection with the deceased parent by talking to that individual or holding on to symbolic linking objects such as pictures or gifts (Silverman et al., 1992).

If someone dies in the family and a child perceives that Daddy (or the doctor or others) did not or could not prevent that sad event, then the child may be concerned that he or she could experience the same unhappy fate. The death of a sibling or other child may be especially difficult since it seems to strike so close to the child's own self and may rob the bereaved child of emotional support from caregivers (Davies, 1998; Stahlman, 1996; Toray & Oltjenbruns, 1996). A sibling or playmate is equally a companion, competitor, and alter ego. Experiencing such a person's death during childhood may have short-term outcomes in aggressive and attention-seeking behaviors (McCown & Davies, 1995), as well as long-term effects throughout the individual's childhood and later life (Donnelly, 1988; Rosen, 1986).

Children respond to bereavement experiences in ways that suit their particular developmental situation (Fleming, 1985; Furman, 1974; Silverman et al., 1992; Silverman & Worden, 1992a). For example, children who do not appreciate the finality of death may wonder what sort of activities are undertaken by the deceased, who is thought to be somehow alive in a different way or in a different place. By contrast, children who appreciate that death involves irreversibility and nonfunctionality may ask very concrete questions about what happens to a dead body when it stops working.

In their actions, bereaved children may delay beginning their grief work or revealing it to others. In their efforts to cope, children may appear to turn away from death from time to time—for example, to watch television or to go off to school. To adults, this retreat may seem to display lack of awareness, comprehension, or feeling. More likely, it simply involves a short attention span, a failure to realize that the loss is permanent, or a temporary defense against being overwhelmed by the implications of the loss. Usually, strong feelings of anger and fears of abandonment or death are evident in the behaviors of bereaved children. Also, as we noted earlier, children often seem to play death games as a way to work out their feelings and anxieties in a relatively safe setting. Such games are a familiar part of the lives of children; in them, a child can stand safely aside from the harm that comes to the toys or imaginary figures.

In American society, many adults withdraw into themselves and limit communication when they are mourning. By contrast, children may talk to those around them, even to strangers, as a way of watching for reactions and seeking clues to guide their own responses. Similarly, children often ask questions over and over again—"I know that Grandpa died, but when will he come home?"—as a way of testing reality and confirming that what they have been told has not changed. Some questions from children baffle adults: "Where is dead?" "When you die and go to heaven, do you have to do homework, too?" "If Grandpa died and went up to heaven, why is he buried down in the ground?" When viewed from the developmental and experiential perspective of a child, these are quite logical efforts to interpret the meaning of what has happened.

Tasks in Mourning for Bereaved Children

Ill children, dying children, and children who are bereaved may all experience grief. They are all children who are responding to the events and the losses that have occurred or are occurring in their lives. Mourning is the process of attempting to cope or learn to live with loss and grief. This situational or death-related response overlays basic developmental task work. Throughout childhood, the work of mourning may need to be addressed again and again in appropriate ways at different developmental levels. Thus, an individual child may mourn the death of his or her mother, her absence in the months and years that follow, what that subsequently means for being different from schoolmates who have a living mother, and his or her inability to draw on the absent mother's support or to share achievements with her in later school years. Reworking losses and grief responses in this way is quite consistent with maturational processes. Healthy mourning integrates losses in ways that shake off unhealthy obstacles and facilitate ongoing living (Furman, 1973; Furman, 1974).

Fox (1988a, 1988b) identified four tasks that are central to productive mourning in children (see also Trozzi & Massimini, 1999). The first of these tasks is *to understand and try to make sense out of what is happening or has happened.* For this task, children seek information about the death and its circumstances, as well as ways of interpreting or coming to understand its meaning. The second task is *to express emotional and other strong responses to the present or anticipated loss.* This involves the identification and validation of feelings and other strong reactions to loss that the child may be experiencing for the first time, as well as finding appropriate ways that are not hurtful to the child or others to express such reactions. The third task is *to commemorate the life that has been lost through some formal or informal remembrance.* Typically, this involves large muscle activity and some form of memorializing or remembering the life that was lived. The fourth task is *to learn how to go on with living and loving.* This often involves a child's need for permission to find ways to go on with healthy living in the aftermath of a significant loss; it always depends on successfully integrating loss and living. This schema reminds us that bereavement has many dimensions and that children do strive to find effective ways of managing loss and grief.

Baker and his colleagues (Baker & Sedney, 1996; Baker et al., 1992) built on Fox's task-based schema by noting that children's mourning tasks may shift over time in their focus and relative significance. Early tasks are likely to involve an emphasis on trying to understand what has happened and children's needs to protect themselves and their family. Middle-phase tasks usually emphasize emotional acceptance, reevaluation of the relationship (memories and connections), and slowly learning to tolerate painful and ambivalent feelings. Late tasks typically center on forming a new sense of personal identity, constructing a durable internal relationship to the dead person, investing in new relationships, returning to normative developmental tasks and activities, and coping with periodic resurgences of pain.

Helping Children Cope with Death, Dying, and Bereavement

In this section, we organize guidelines for helping children cope with death, dying, and bereavement in four clusters: some general suggestions; a proactive program of education, communication, and validation; helping ill or dying children; and helping bereaved children.

Some General Suggestions

The basic principle in helping children cope with death is more a matter of attitude than one of technique or easily definable skills. As Erikson (1963, p. 269) wrote: "Healthy children will not fear life if their elders have integrity enough not to fear death." Unfortunately, adults often adopt tactics that attempt to insulate children from death-related events, avoid such topics, and deny the finality of death (Becker & Margolin, 1967). In so doing, they block children's efforts to acquire information, express their feelings, obtain support, and learn to cope with sadness and loss.

At the very least, children deserve assistance from their elders in dealing with challenges presented by death. These challenges *will* arise and children *will* attempt to deal with them (see Box 12.2). The only responsible option open to adults is to make available their knowledge, experience, insights, and coping resources to children (McCue & Bonn, 1996; Nussbaum, 1998). As LeShan (1976, p. 3) has written: "A child can live through *anything*, so long as he or she is told the truth and is allowed to share with loved ones the natural feelings people have when they are suffering."

Adults cannot face death for their children or live on their behalf, but adults can prepare children to do this for themselves and can often walk alongside, at least part of the way. "Part of each child's adventure into life is his discovery of loss, separation, non-being, death. No one can have this adventure for him, nor can death be locked in another room until a child comes of age" (Kastenbaum, 1972, p. 37).

Helping children cope with death is an ongoing process, not a unique event that occurs only at one specific point in time. Children often return over and over to issues that concern them. Such issues need to be readdressed as children confront different developmental and situational challenges. It is part of their continuing maturation and socialization, which is carried out in a natural and effective manner when it draws on ordinary events in living and teachable moments, together with children's own questions and initiatives. Adults can

Box 12.2 Being a Child and Being Alone

Do you know the sensation of being a child and being alone? Children can adapt wonderfully to specific fears, like a pain, a sickness, or a death. It is the unknown which is truly terrifying for them. They have no fund of knowledge in how the world operates, and so they feel completely vulnerable. ■

SOURCE: Katzenbach, 1986, p. 322.

also strive to create opportunities for constructive dialogue with and between children. For example, summer camps for children who share an illness (such as cancer) have been shown to help establish relationships that last well beyond the camp sessions and that supplement in constructive ways relationships with healthy peers (Bluebond-Langner et al., 1991).

Adults may need to make special efforts to help children cope with death in a society that has limited experience with natural human death and whose death system all too often inhibits constructive interactions between children and death. This entails accepting certain related responsibilities, such as:

- Undertaking preparation—by initiating a reflective analysis (which no person ever fully completes) of one's own thoughts and feelings about death, and by becoming familiar with basic principles in the body of knowledge that has been developed in this area
- Responding to real needs in children
- Communicating effectively
- Working cooperatively—with children, with other adults, and with relevant institutions in American society (Corr, 1984a)

Cooperative work with and by children is well illustrated by one child who composed a children's version of a widely circulated set of principles formulated for adults by the Center for Attitudinal Healing in California (see Box 12.3) and by another (Gaes, 1987) who wrote *My Book for Kids with Cansur.* Helping can flow from children to adults as well as from adults to children.

A Proactive Program of Prior Preparation

Whenever possible, one helps children best by preparing them ahead of time to cope with issues associated with sadness and loss (Metzgar & Zick, 1996). This help begins with *education* (Stevenson & Stevenson, 1996b). For example, adults can explore with children a relatively safe encounter with death, such as a dead bird found in the woods or a dead fish from the school aquarium. "Teachable moments" that are not highly charged with personal feelings can represent good beginnings for adult-child dialogue (Carson, 1984). Children

Box 12.3 Children's Version of Principles of Attitudinal Healing

1. Love is one of the most important things in life!
2. It is important to get better—so we must not let fear trap us!
3. Giving and receiving are the same thing.
4. Don't live in the past and don't live in the future.
5. Do what you can now. Each minute is for giving love.
6. We can learn to love ourselves and others by forgiving instead of not forgiving. Example: fighting.
7. We can find love instead of fault.
8. If something is the matter outside, don't go crazy because you are safe inside.
9. We are students and teachers to each other.
10. Don't just look at the bad things, look at the good things too!
11. Since love is forever, death need not be scary.
12. We can always see other people as giving love or asking for help. ■

SOURCE: Adapted by Kaycee Poirier, 11 years old, from Shawnigan Lake, BC, Canada, for the Center for Attitudinal Healing, Sausalito, California (415-331-6161). Reprinted with permission.

can also "try out" adult rituals by acting out various sorts of memorializing practices, as in one story about classmates who planted a tree in memory of their teacher's dead son (Simon, 1979). (Note that a child's beloved pet may present quite a different and much less "safe" situation than one arising from a strange, wild animal; see Butler & Lagoni, 1996.)

An extensive body of literature is now available to be read with or by children at all developmental and reading levels (for an annotated list of selected examples, see Box 12.4 and Appendix A; see also Corr, 2000a, 2001c). Also, there is literature for parents, educators, and others who are helping children cope with death (see Box 12.5), and in some areas there may be workshops or college courses on issues related to children and death (Corr, 1980, 1984b, 1992b). Suggestions on how to use these resources are offered in Box 12.6. The underlying principle is that "any subject can be taught effectively in some intellectually honest form to any child at any stage of development" (Bruner, 1962, p. 33). This is well illustrated in an annotated bibliography of children's books about the Holocaust (Rudin, 1998).

Effective education and prior preparation in all forms depend on *effective communication.* Here, the central guideline is "take your cues from the children, answer what they want to know, what they are asking about, in their terms" (Bluebond-Langner, 1977, p. 64). Doka (1996a) suggested organizing one's approach around three questions: "What does a child need to know?" "What does a child want to know?" and "What can a child understand?" Each of these requires careful listening, a process through which adults put themselves in a position to grasp the real concerns of a child and to avoid responding with unnecessary, misleading, or unhelpful information. By employing language that

Box 12.4 Selected Literature for Children about Death, Dying, and Bereavement

Annotated descriptions and complete bibliographical information are provided in Appendix A for the following 60 books and 45 others.

PICTURE AND COLORING BOOKS FOR PRESCHOOLERS AND BEGINNING READERS

About the deaths of pets and other animals:

Brown, L. K., & Brown, M. (1996). *When Dinosaurs Die: A Guide to Understanding Death.*
Brown, M. W. (1958). *The Dead Bird.*
Kantrowitz, M. (1973). *When Violet Died.*
O'Toole, D. (1988). *Aarvy Aardvark Finds Hope.*
Rylant, C. (1995/1997). *Dog Heaven and Cat Heaven.*
Stickney, D. (1985). *Water Bugs and Dragonflies.*
Stull, E. G. (1964). *My Turtle Died Today.*
Varley, S. (1992). *Badger's Parting Gifts.*
Viorst, J. (1971). *The Tenth Good Thing about Barney.*
Warburg, S. S. (1969). *Growing Time.*
Wilhelm, H. (1985). *I'll Always Love You.*

About the deaths of grandparents, parents, and other adults:

Bartoli, J. (1975). *Nonna.*
Carlstrom, N. W. (1990). *Blow Me a Kiss, Miss Lilly.*
Czech, J. (2000). *The Garden Angel.*
Fassler, J. (1971). *My Grandpa Died Today.*
Hazen, B. S. (1985). *Why Did Grandpa Die? A Book about Death.*
Hesse, K. (1993). *Poppy's Chair.*
Zolotow, C. (1974). *My Grandson Lew.*

About the deaths of siblings, peers, and other children:

Bunting, E. (1999). *Rudi's Pond.*
Clardy, A. F. (1984). *Dusty Was My Friend: Coming to Terms with Loss.*
Cohn, J. (1987). *I Had a Friend Named Peter: Talking to Children about the Death of a Friend.*
Dean, A. (1991). *Meggie's Magic.*
Johnson, J., & Johnson, M. (1982). *Where's Jess?*
Schlitt, R. S. (1992). *Robert Nathaniel's Tree.*
Simon, J. (2001). *This Book Is for All Kids, but Especially My Sister Libby. Libby Died.*
Weir, A. B. (1992). *Am I Still a Big Sister?*

About other sorts of death-related events:

Carney, K. L. (1997). *Together We'll Get through This!*
Fassler, D., & McQueen, K. (1990). *What's a Virus Anyway? The Kids' Book about AIDS.*
Fox, M. (1994). *Tough Boris.*
Jordan, M. K. (1989). *Losing Uncle Tim.*
Ladwig, T. (1997). *Psalm Twenty-Three.*
Mellonie, B., & Ingpen, R. *(1983). Lifetimes: A Beautiful Way to Explain Death to Children.*
Shriver, M. (1999). *What's Heaven?*

(continues)

Box 12.4 (cont.) Selected Literature for Children about Death, Dying, and Bereavement

STORYBOOKS AND OTHER TEXTS FOR PRIMARY SCHOOL READERS

About the deaths of pets and other animals:

Carrick, C. (1976). *The Accident.*
Graeber, C. (1982). *Mustard.*
White, E. B. (1952). *Charlotte's Web.*

About the deaths of grandparents, parents, and other adults:

Barron, T. A. (2000). *Where Is Grandpa?*
Bunting, E. (1982). *The Happy Funeral.*
Donnelly, E. (1981). *So Long, Grandpa.*
Douglas, E. (1990). *Rachel and the Upside Down Heart.*
Marshall, B. (1998). *Animal Crackers: A Tender Book about Death and Funerals and Love.*
McNamara, J. W. (1994). *My Mom Is Dying: A Child's Diary.*
Miles, M. (1971). *Annie and the Old One.*
Mills, L. (1991). *The Rag Coat.*
Powell, E. S. (1990). *Geranium Morning.*
Simon, N. (1979). *We Remember Philip.*
Tiffault, B. W. (1992). *A Quilt for Elizabeth.*
Whitehead, R. (1971). *The Mother Tree.*

About the deaths of siblings, peers, and other children:

Alexander, S. (1983). *Nadia the Wilful.*
Chin-Yee, F. (1988). *Sam's Story: A Story for Families Surviving Sudden Infant Death Syndrome.*
Coburn, J. B. (1964). *Annie and the Sand Dobbies. A Story about Death for Children and Their Parents.*
Coerr, E. (1977). *Sadako and the Thousand Paper Cranes.*
Greene, C. C. (1976). *Beat the Turtle Drum.*
Smith, D. B. (1973). *A Taste of Blackberries.*

About postdeath events:

Arnold, C. (1987). *What We Do When Someone Dies.*
Coleman, P. (1996). *Where the Balloons Go.*
Corley, E. A. (1973). *Tell Me about Death, Tell Me about Funerals.*
Goble, P. (1993). *Beyond the Ridge.*
Goldman, L. (1997). *Bart Speaks Out: An Interactive Storybook for Young Children about Suicide.* ■

is meaningful to children, one can minimize confusion of the sort generated by the adults in Agee's *A Death in the Family* (1969), who tried to explain that God had taken the children's father because he had had an "accident." The adults were using this word to mean a fatal automobile mishap, but the children understood it to mean a loss of bladder control, and the adults never realized how

Box 12.5 Selected Literature for Adults About Children and Death

Christ, G. H. (2000). *Healing Children's Grief: Surviving a Parent's Death from Cancer.* New York: Oxford University Press; **Silverman, P. R.** (2000). *Never Too Young to Know: Death in Children's Lives.* New York: Oxford University Press; **Worden, J. M.** (1996). *Children and Grief: When a Parent Dies.* New York: Guilford. Three knowledgeable authors guide professionals in understanding and helping bereaved children.

Corr, C. A., & Corr, D. M. (Eds.). (1996). *Handbook of Childhood Death and Bereavement.* New York: Springer. A comprehensive resource for understanding and helping children in their encounters with death and bereavement.

Emswiler, M. A., & Emswiler, J. P. (2000). *Guiding Your Child through Grief.* New York: Bantam; **Fitzgerald, H.** (1992). *The Grieving Child: A Parent's Guide.* New York: Simon & Schuster; **Trozzi, M., & Massimini, K.** (1999). *Talking with Children about Loss.* New York: Penguin Putnam. Three practical books offer useful advice for parents and other helpers.

Grollman, E. A. (1990). *Talking about Death: A Dialogue between Parent and Child* (3rd ed.). Boston: Beacon. Principles for helping children, a passage to be read together with a child, and guidelines for responding to questions.

Rudman, M. K., Gagne, K. D., & Bernstein, J. E. (1993). *Books to Help Children Cope with Separation and Loss* (4th ed.; vols. 1 & 2 by Bernstein alone, 1977, 1984; vol. 3 with Rudman, 1989.) New Providence, NJ: R. R. Bowker. Informed and sensitive descriptions of hundreds of books for children. Broad topical range, keen evaluations, and guidance about how to use books to help children.

Additional information about death-related literature for children and sources from which books and other items can be purchased are provided by:

Boulden Publishing, P.O. Box 1186, Weaverville, CA 96093-1186; 800-238-8433; fax 530-623-5525; www.bouldenpub.com (offers Boulden publications exclusively).

Centering Corporation, P.O. Box 4600, Omaha, NE 68104-0600; 402-553-1200; fax 402-553-0507; www.centering.org; e-mail to J1200@aol.com (offers their own and other publishers' works).

Compassion Books, 477 Hannah Branch Road, Burnsville, NC 28714; 828-675-5909; fax 828-675-9687; www.compassionbooks.com; e-mail to Heal2grow@aol.com (offers their own and other publishers' works). ■

foolish and perhaps frightening their message about God's responses to wetting your pants seemed to the children.

Effective communication avoids euphemisms and inconsistent or incomplete answers because they so easily lead children into misunderstandings that may be more disturbing than the real facts. More important, effective communication is dependable: the child must be able to rely on what is said, even if it

Box 12.6 Some Guidelines for Adults in Using Death-Related Resources with Children

1. *Evaluate the book or other resource yourself before attempting to use it with a child.* No resource suits every reader or every purpose.

2. *Select resources, topics, and approaches that suit the needs of the individual child.* To be useful, any resource must meet the needs of a particular child.

3. *Be prepared to cope with limitations.* Every resource is likely to have both strengths and limitations. Adapt existing resources to individual purposes.

4. *Match materials to the capacities of the individual child.* Stories, pictures, music, play, drawing, and other options must suit the child's abilities. For example, in using literature, determine the child's reading or interest level. Direct a precocious child to more advanced materials; direct some older children to less challenging titles or invite them to join in partnership with an adult to assess the suitability of simpler materials for younger readers (Lamers, 1986, 1995) so their abilities are not directly challenged by materials that are too difficult for them.

5. *Read or work along with children.* Seize opportunities for rewarding interactions and valuable "teachable moments" from which all can profit (Carson, 1984). Show interest in the child, provide interpretations as needed, and learn from the child. ■

is not the whole of the available truth. Honesty encourages trust, the basis of all comforting relationships. Thus it is better to admit what one does not know rather than to make up explanations that one really does not believe. After all, even good communication can be limited, fallible, and subject to error, as in the case of the children who were eager to attend a funeral in order to see the "polarbears" who would, so they thought they had heard, carry the casket (Corley, 1973; see also Brent, 1978). Although this piece of miscommunication is delightful in some ways, it reminds us that children may not always correctly grasp what they are told. To minimize misunderstandings about death, adults should try to communicate effectively and they should check to determine what a child has grasped by asking the child to explain what he or she understood from the message.

Adults must also consider that children communicate in many ways and at many levels (Kübler-Ross, 1983). They might use: (1) symbolic nonverbal communication—which might take place through artwork of various types; (2) symbolic verbal communication—in which indirect comments about imaginary friends or anthropomorphized figures may really have to do with the child's own concerns; and (3) nonsymbolic verbal communication—which most resembles

literal interchanges between adults. Symbolic communication through art or other media may be particularly important for deep-seated or emotionally charged concerns in young children who lack many verbal skills (Furth, 1988). This was evident in the case of one 6-year-old child who, while he was dying, drew a series of pictures of ships—smaller and darker ships on a progressively darker background as the illness advanced (Grove, 1978).

Validation is a third important element of prior preparation, as well as of support for ill, dying, and bereaved children. Metzgar and Zick (1996) link this to a Native American belief that says: *If you give something a name and a shape, you can have power over it. However, if it remains nameless and shapeless, it will continue to have power over you.* Children who are striving to cope with death-related encounters need validation for their questions, concepts, language, and feelings. Adults can validate these and other aspects of children's death-related experiences by acknowledging them for what they are in a nonjudgmental way. Acknowledgment gives permission to explore what is confused and not yet well articulated. Sharing in such a process is empowering; correcting or "fixing" it is likely to be mistaken and harmful.

Helping Ill or Dying Children

The following principles for communication with ill or dying children provide a solid foundation for helping (Stevens, 1998):

1. First, determine the child's own perception of the situation, taking into account his or her developmental level and experience.
2. Understand the child's symbolic language.
3. Clarify reality and dispel fantasy.
4. Encourage expression of feelings.
5. Promote self-esteem through mastery of age-appropriate tasks and activities.
6. Make no assumptions about what the situation will entail; be open to what each encounter can teach; do not underestimate the child's ability to master life's challenges creatively and with humor and dignity.

Care for ill and dying children is best accomplished through a holistic program of child- and family-centered care (Davies & Howell, 1998). Good examples of this care at a community level include programs like the Ronald MacDonald Houses, home care for dying children, and other forms of pediatric hospice care. *Ronald MacDonald Houses* provide economical, convenient, and hospitable places where families can stay while a child is receiving treatment in a pediatric medical facility. This service minimizes family disruption, reduces financial and logistical burdens (such as those involving travel, finding lodgings, preparing food, and doing laundry), and permits constructive interactions (if not formal counseling) both within and among families who are facing difficult challenges in childhood illness.

Ida Martinson (1976) and her colleagues in Minnesota pioneered programs of *home care for dying children and their families.* Careful research in this project demonstrated that for some children and families it was both feasible and desirable to take the child home to die. Such families typically needed preparation, guidance, and support to mobilize their own resources as well as supplementary assistance to provide needed services. A key point is the recognition by parents of the need for pediatric palliative care (Wolfe et al., 2000b).

In terms of implementation, programs of *pediatric palliative care* have applied hospice principles to various situations involving children (Armstrong-Dailey & Zarbock, 2001; Corr & Corr, 1985a, 1985b, 1985c, 1988, 1992b; Levetown, 2000; Sumner, 2001; Vickers & Carlise, 2000). This has been achieved in various ways (for example, at home, through respite care, in a medical facility) and with various types of staffing (for instance, hospital, hospice, or home care personnel) (Davies, 1999; Howell, 1993; Martin, 1989). Applying these principles in a neonatal intensive care unit (Siegel, 1982; Whitfield et al., 1982) demonstrates that it is not the setting that is critical but the focus on holistic care for the ill child and on family-centered care for parents, siblings, and involved others (Rosen, 1990; Stevens, 1993).

Helping Bereaved Children

The task-based models described earlier for understanding bereaved children (Corr & Corr, 1998b; Fox, 1988a, 1988b; Trozzi & Massimini, 1999) provide a natural agenda for adults who are helping individual children. All bereaved children need information as a foundation for effective grief work. They may need to know about death itself or about the facts surrounding a specific death, or they may need information about common reactions to loss or about coping with death and grief. Adults can provide such information and, in so doing, share their own grief and model good coping strategies. To do this, they must try to view the loss from the child's perspective.

For example, adults often fail to appreciate the importance to a child of the death of a friend or pet (Butler & Lagoni, 1996; Lagoni et al., 1994; Toray & Oltjenbruns, 1996). Also, bereaved adults may all too easily overlook a child's grief on the death of a sibling (Davies, 1998). In each case, it is the relationship in all of its many dimensions—companion, buffer, protector, comforter—that is most important to the child. Adults do well to honor these losses rather than brush them aside as trivial. Respect for the child's experiences can be expressed in attention, honesty, avoidance of euphemisms, support, and (wherever possible) encouragement of the child's involvement in the death or memorialization of a pet.

In all deaths, good memories are as important to bereaved children as they are to adults (Christ, 2000; Jewett, 1982). When possible, one should strive to lay down a fund of such memories before loss or death occurs and help a child while someone else is dying (Smith, 2000). Even when that is not possible, as in cases of unanticipated death, an adult might work with a child after a death to develop and articulate the elements of a legacy that the child can carry forward into the future—for example, by examining a scrapbook or photo album depicting the life of the deceased, or by sharing events from that life in which the child might not have participated. Helping bereaved children might also include assembling a memorial collage, donating to a worthy cause, or planting a living memorial.

In recent years, some have questioned whether children should take part in funeral and burial practices (Corr, 1991; Weller et al., 1988). Suggestions like Grollman's (1967, p. 24) that "from approximately the age of seven, a child should be encouraged to attend" have been misinterpreted to support the viewpoint of Allison's father at the outset of this chapter that children under the age of 7 should be prohibited from attending funerals. In fact, research (Fristad et al., 2001; Silverman & Worden, 1992b) has shown that taking part in bereavement rituals can help children with their grief work.

A basic rule is that no child should be forced to take part in any experience that will be harmful (Emswiler & Emswiler, 2000). However, harm need not

A "teachable moment": a young child at his grandmother's visitation.

occur when adults act on themes underlying all of the suggestions we are describing: prior preparation, support during the event, and follow-up afterward. The child should be told ahead of time what will occur at the wake, funeral, or burial; why we engage in these activities; and what his or her options are for participation. If the child chooses to take part in some or all of these activities, a caring adult should attend to his or her needs during the event. This adult must not be wholly absorbed in personal grief and must be free to accompany a child who might need to arrive late or leave early. After the event, adults should be available to discuss with the child his or her reactions or feelings, answer any questions that might arise, and share their own responses to what has taken place.

Concerns about disruptive behavior by children are no more unique to funerals and burials than they are to graduations and weddings. They can be addressed by providing a special time for children to come to the funeral home when adults are not present or by limiting the role of the children at the funeral service or burial to one appropriate to their interest in and tolerance for public ritual. As Crase and Crase (1976, p. 25) noted: "The wise management of grief in children revolves around the encouragement and facilitation of the normal mourning process while preventing delayed and/or distorted grief responses."

Support groups for bereaved children can assist normal mourning processes after a death (Bacon, 1996; Heiney et al., 1995; Hughes, 1995; Zambelli & DeRosa, 1992). The Dougy Center: The National Center for Grieving Children and

Families (3909 S.E. 52nd Avenue, Portland, OR 97286; tel. 503-775-5683; www.dougy.org), founded in December 1982 by Beverly Chappell, is one of many good models in this field (Chappell, 2001; Corr et al., 1991). The Dougy Center operates groups for children as young as ages 3 to 5 (Smith, 1991) and as old as 19. It has groups for those who have experienced a death of a parent or caregiver; a brother, sister, or close friend; through suicide; or through homicide. It also offers concurrent groups for parents or other adult caregivers of the children being served.

On the principle that grief is a natural reaction to loss—for children as well as for adults—and that each individual has a natural capacity to mourn, those who facilitate groups at The Dougy Center are regarded not as counselors or therapists but as fellow grievers. Their roles are to honor and be available for each child, trust his or her mourning processes, remain alert for signs of complicated mourning processes, walk alongside, and uphold the vision that each bereaved person will once again be able to find a way in life. Other support groups for bereaved children regard facilitators in a more traditional counseling role and adopt a more structured, time-limited agenda for group meetings (for example, Harper et al., 1988; Hassl & Marnocha, 2000; Reynolds, 1992). An approach of this sort may also apply to short-term camps for bereaved children (for example, Stokes & Crossley, 1995). A body of literature describing all of these programs is available for adult helpers (for example, Braza & Bright, 1991; Gaines-Lane, 1995; Whitney, 1991).

Preparing to release eco-friendly helium balloons during a memorial service at a hospice weekend bereavement camp.

Children may also be affected by traumatic death in the form of a homicide, suicide, or mass death caused by a natural disaster or some other form of violent or catastrophic event (Nader, 1996), such as the terrorist attacks on the World Trade Center and the Pentagon on September 11, 2001. Especially when groups of children are involved, it is often important to consider programs of *postvention.* This term, coined by Shneidman (1973b, 1981), was originally applied to interventions designed "to mollify the aftereffects of the event in a person who has attempted suicide, or to deal with the adverse effects on the survivor-victims of a person who has committed suicide" (1973b, p. 385). However, the concept of postvention has since been expanded to apply to after-the-fact interventions focusing on those immediately or indirectly affected by a broad range of traumatic losses.

Principles for postvention with children include: (1) beginning the intervention as soon as possible, (2) implementing a comprehensive and coordinated plan involving affected persons and using relevant resources in the community, (3) providing supportive and caring assistance, (4) anticipating resistance or an unwillingness to cooperate from some persons, (5) expecting individual variations in the nature and timing of traumatic responses, (6) being alert for exaggerated responses that may place an individual's life or health in jeopardy, (7) identifying and changing potentially harmful aspects of the immediate environment, and (8) addressing long-term issues (Leenaars & Wenckstern, 1996). Ideally, postvention should be based on prior planning for coping with crises in schools and communities (Klicker, 2000; Stevenson, 2001) and should be led by a trained professional who—as in all group approaches—should be alert to the need to refer a particular child for individual psychotherapy (Cook & Dworkin, 1992; Crenshaw, 1995; Webb, 1993).

Summary

In this chapter, we studied interactions between children and death in the contemporary American death system. We described distinctive developmental tasks of childhood in order to provide background for our exploration of death-related experiences during childhood. In particular, we noted that among infants and toddlers death rates are high, mainly arising from congenital malformations, sudden infant death syndrome, respiratory distress syndrome, and accidents; in preschool and school-age children, death rates are low, resulting more often from accidents, natural causes, homicide, and communicable diseases. We paid special attention to children's efforts to develop an understanding of the concept of death and its principal subconcepts, as well as to the development of death-related attitudes in childhood.

Next, we explored children's efforts to cope with life-threatening illness, dying, and bereavement. That led us to discuss how to help children cope with death, dying, and bereavement, which included some general suggestions, a proactive program of prior preparation (involving education, effective communication, and validation), and specific remarks about helping ill, dying, and bereaved children. We also identified a number of useful resources for helping children cope with death.

Questions for Review and Discussion

1. The vignette near the beginning of this chapter depicted a father who did not respond in very helpful ways to the death-related concerns of his daughter, Allison. How would you have responded or have wanted him to respond to those concerns?

2. What types of death-related losses did you experience during childhood? What did they mean to you?

3. Try to remember a time when you were a child and you were seriously ill or you experienced an important loss. What were your most significant concerns about that illness or loss? Or perhaps you know a child who has been in such a situation. If so, what were his or her most significant concerns?

4. If you were asked to recommend to adults how they could help children cope with death, what would you suggest? How would your recommendations differ (if at all) for different children or different losses?

Suggested Readings

For developmental perspectives (with or without special reference to death), consult:

Cook, A. S., & Oltjenbruns, K. A. (1998). *Dying and Grieving: Lifespan and Family Perspectives* (2nd ed.).

Erikson, E. H. (1963). *Childhood and Society* (2nd ed.).

Erikson, E. H. (1968). *Identity: Youth and Crisis.*

Kail, R. V., & Cavanaugh, J. C. (2000). *Human Development: A Lifespan View* (2nd ed.).

Newman, B. M., & Newman, P. R. (1999). *Development through Life: A Psychosocial Approach* (7th ed.).

Papalia, D. E., Olds, S. W., & Feldman, R. D. (2000). *Human Development* (8th ed.).

Piaget, J. (1998). *The Equilibration of Cognitive Structures: The Central Problem of Intellectual Development.*

On children and their development, see:

Anthony, S. (1972). *The Discovery of Death in Childhood and After.*

Ariès, P. (1962). *Centuries of Childhood: A Social History of Family Life.*

Lonetto, R. (1980). *Children's Conceptions of Death.*

Papalia, D. E., Olds, S. W. , & Feldman, R. D. (1998). *A Child's World: Infancy through Adolescence* (8th ed.).

General resources on children and death include:

Adams, D. W., & Deveau, E. J. (Eds.). (1995). *Beyond the Innocence of Childhood* (3 vols.).

Corr, C. A., & Corr, D. M. (Eds.). (1996). *Handbook of Childhood Death and Bereavement.*

Grollman, E. A. (Ed.). (1995a). *Bereaved Children and Teens: A Support Guide for Parents and Professionals.*

Papadatou, D., & Papadatos, C. (Eds.). (1991). *Children and Death.*

Wass, H., & Corr, C. A. (Eds.). (1984a). *Childhood and Death.*

Concerning life-threatening illness in childhood, consult:

Armstrong-Dailey, A., & Zarbock, S. (Eds.). (2001). *Hospice Care for Children* (2nd ed.).

Bluebond-Langner, M. (1978). *The Private Worlds of Dying Children.*

Corr, C. A., & Corr, D. M. (Eds.). (1985a). *Hospice Approaches to Pediatric Care.*

Koocher, G. P., & O'Malley, J. E. (1981). *The Damocles Syndrome: Psychosocial Consequences of Surviving Childhood Cancer.*

Levetown, M. (Ed.). (2000). *Compendium of Pediatric Palliative Care.*

Sourkes, B. M. (1995). *Armfuls of Time: The Psychological Experience of the Child with a Life-Threatening Illness.*

Spinetta, J. J., & Deasy-Spinetta, P. (1981). *Living with Childhood Cancer.*

Bereavement and grief in childhood are explored in:

Christ, G. H. (2000). *Healing Children's Grief: Surviving a Parent's Death from Cancer.*

Davies, B. (1998). *Shadows in the Sun: The Experiences of Sibling Bereavement in Childhood.*

Doka, K. J. (Ed.). (1995). *Children Mourning, Mourning Children.*

Doka, K. J. (Ed.). (2000). *Living with Grief: Children, Adolescents, and Loss.*

Fry, V. L. (1995). *Part of Me Died, Too: Stories of Creative Survival among Bereaved Children and Teenagers.*

Rosen, H. (1986). *Unspoken Grief: Coping with Childhood Sibling Loss.*

Worden, J. W. (1996). *Children and Grief: When a Parent Dies.*

For teaching children about death or helping them to cope with death, see:

Cook, A. S., & Dworkin, D. S. (1992). *Helping the Bereaved: Therapeutic Interventions for Children, Adolescents, and Adults.*

Crenshaw, D. A. (1995). *Bereavement: Counseling the Grieving throughout the Life Cycle.*

Deaton, R. L., & Berkan, W. A. (1995). *Planning and Managing Death Issues in the Schools: A Handbook.*

Emswiler, M. A., & Emswiler, J. P. (2000). *Guiding Your Child through Grief.*

Fitzgerald, H. (1992). *The Grieving Child: A Parent's Guide.*

Fitzgerald, H. (1998). *Grief at School: A Guide for Teachers and Counselors.*

Gordon, A. K., & Klass, D. (1979). *They Need to Know: How to Teach Children about Death.*

Grollman, E. A. (1990). *Talking about Death: A Dialogue between Parent and Child* (3rd ed.).

Klicker, R. L. (2000). *A Student Dies, A School Mourns: Dealing with Death and Loss in the School Community.*

McCue, K., & Bonn, R. (1996). *How to Help Children through a Parent's Serious Illness.*

Nussbaum, K. (1998). *Preparing the Children: Information and Ideas for Families Facing Terminal Illness and Death.*

Schaefer, D., & Lyons, C. (1993). *How Do We Tell the Children? A Step-by-Step Guide for Helping Children Two to Teen Cope When Someone Dies* (2nd ed.).

Silverman, P. R. (2000). *Never Too Young to Know: Death in Children's Lives.*

Smilansky, S. (1987). *On Death: Helping Children Understand and Cope.*

Stevenson, R. G. (Ed.). (2001). *What Will We Do? Preparing a School Community to Cope with Crises* (2nd ed.).

Stevenson, R. G., & Stevenson, E. P. (Eds.). (1996b). *Teaching Students about Death: A Comprehensive Resource for Educators and Parents.*

Trozzi, M., & Massimini, K. (1999). *Talking with Children about Loss: Words, Strategies, and Wisdom.*

Wass, H., & Corr, C. A. (Eds.). (1984b). *Helping Children Cope with Death: Guidelines and Resources* (2nd ed.).

Webb, N. B. (Ed.). (1999). *Play Therapy with Children in Crisis: Individual, Group, and Family Treatment* (2nd ed.).

Webb, N. B. (Ed.). (1993). *Helping Bereaved Children: A Handbook for Practitioners.*

Some special situations or subjects are explored in:

Bettelheim, B. (1977). *The Uses of Enchantment—The Meaning and Importance of Fairy Tales.*

Dane, B. O., & Levine, C. (Eds.). (1994). *AIDS and the New Orphans: Coping with Death.*

Lagoni, L., Butler, C., & Hetts, S. (1994). *The Human-Animal Bond and Grief.*

Levine, C. (Ed.). (1993). *A Death in the Family: Orphans of the HIV Epidemic.*

Wiener, L. S., Best, A., & Pizzo, P. A. (1994). *Be a Friend: Children Who Live with HIV Speak.*

InfoTrac College Edition

For more information, explore the InfoTrac College Edition at **http://www.infotrac-college.com/Wadsworth**

Enter search terms: CAUSES OF DEATH IN CHILDHOOD, CHILDREN AND DEATH, COGNITIVE DEVELOPMENT, CONCEPTS OF DEATH OR UNDERSTANDINGS OF DEATH, DEVELOPMENTAL TASKS IN CHILDHOOD, TASKS IN MOURNING.

Chapter Thirteen

ADOLESCENTS

IN THIS CHAPTER, WE EXAMINE INTERACTIONS with death during adolescence. In our society, *adolescence* is an "in between" or transitional period in human development between childhood and adulthood. At one time in American and other societies—and in some societies or cultural groups today—there was no such "in between" period. Coming of age rituals marked a direct and relatively abrupt division between the era of childhood and the reality of adult responsibilities (Ariès, 1962). By contrast, our society has interposed a complex, evolving, and rather special developmental stage between the primary school years and the complete recognition of adult status.

We study death-related experiences in adolescence for their own sake, as well as for what they add to our accounts of childhood and adulthood. In this chapter, we begin with a brief vignette designed to illustrate some of the issues that may arise for adolescents within the contemporary American death system. Then we turn to: the definition and interpretation of adolescence; developmental tasks in early, middle, and late adolescence; typical encounters with death in American society during the adolescent years; death-related thoughts and attitudes during this era of the human life course; issues related to adolescents who are coping with life-threatening illness and dying; issues related to adolescents who are coping with bereavement and grief; special issues concerning suicide and homicide during the adolescent years; and a section on helping adolescents cope with death and bereavement. ■

One Month at Central High School

That April was a tragic time at Central High School. On the third of the month, Tom Adkins and three other boys from Central were killed when a train at a railroad crossing hit the car in which they were riding. The engineer of the train reported that the car had ignored the warning lights and driven around the crossing gates. Neither the train's whistle nor its emergency brakes had been able to prevent the high-speed crash. People said, "Isn't this awful! I can't believe this happened."

Two weeks later, Anthony Ramirez, the star kicker and senior cornerback on the football team, shot himself. Anthony was a good student and was well liked by his teachers and other students. He came from a middle-class family in which the parents and three children seemed closely knit and concerned about each other. That evening the rest of the family had gone to a basketball game in which Anthony's younger brother was playing. It was a bit unusual but not worrisome when Anthony chose to stay at home, saying that he had to study for a test. When the family came home they found Anthony in the garage lying in a pool of blood alongside his father's old hunting rifle, which he had used to end his life. There was no note.

During the postmortem investigation, it turned out that many people were aware of some of what was going on in Anthony's life, but no one knew enough to grasp how badly he really felt. Some of Anthony's friends realized that he always used humor to laugh off inquiries about his feelings and to keep people from getting to know the real person inside his popular image. Anthony's girlfriend acknowledged that their relationship had recently ended but said that she had not recognized how hard he had taken her rejection. Anthony's teachers and coaches talked about the pressures to excel that he always seemed to impose on himself; one remembered an angry outburst followed by a long sullen period occasioned by what Anthony regarded as a bad grade. Anthony's parents and siblings spoke of their own recent preoccupations and their wish that they had realized how depressed he must have been. People said, "If only I had known."

Four days before the end of the month, two freshman girls at Central, Whitney Portman and Shawan Miller, were walking home from the store and found themselves in the middle of a gang fight. The territories of two young gangs overlapped near the intersection where the two girls were walking and a dispute developed over which group had "rights" to sell drugs on that corner. An exchange of gang signs and insults led to some scuffling and a flare up of tempers. Some members of one gang ran into a nearby house, got some weapons, and began shooting when they came out. Whitney and Shawan were shot—they were simply two more victims of the neighborhood in which they lived. One of the girls died, the other was critically wounded. People said, "What can we do to stop this violence?"

The Definition and Interpretation of Adolescence

The term *adolescence* derives from a Latin root *(adolescentia)* that refers to the process or condition of growing up and that designates a "youth" or person in the growing age (*Oxford English Dictionary*, 1989). In contemporary usage, an adolescent is someone who is no longer thought to be merely a child but who is not yet fully recognized as an adult. Thus, adolescents are normally expected to take on more advanced responsibilities than children and are usually accorded special privileges: educational programs for adolescents differ from those for children, and, as they mature, adolescents are ordinarily thought fit to take on work and wage-earning responsibilities, to qualify to drive a motor vehicle, to vote, to drink alcoholic beverages, and to get married (Balk, 1995).

It is overly simple and not quite precise to equate adolescence with the teenage years. Chronology is not an accurate indicator of developmental eras. In fact, most agree that the preteen phenomenon of puberty marks the beginning of the adolescent era. In adopting this marker, however, one must recognize three facts: individuals arrive at puberty at different times (with females typically becoming pubescent at an earlier age than males); puberty itself is more a series of related events than a single moment in time; and it is a historical reality that over the past 150 years the onset of puberty has come earlier in each generation (Kail & Cavanaugh, 2000; Newman & Newman, 1999).

The close of adolescence is less easily designated. In general, the principal developmental task of adolescence is the achievement of individuation and *the establishment of a more or less stable sense of personal identity* (see Table V.1). If so, then adolescence may end when an individual leaves home and his or her family of origin, takes up a career, or gets married. However, these events clearly depend on a variety of individual, cultural, and economic factors, not development alone. Thus, Conger and Peterson (1984, p. 82) aptly observed that adolescence is a physical, social, and emotional process that "begins in biology and ends in culture." Still, to speak too readily of the end of adolescence may be to focus solely on the negative or "closing off" side of the story without necessarily reflecting the positive development of *fidelity* or faithfulness—to self, to

Two images of Andrew, a teenage owl: is he nonthreatening, frightening, or both?

ideals, and to others—that Erikson (1963) proposed as the principal virtue to be achieved in adolescent development.

Apart from the definition of adolescence, there are long-standing disagreements among scholars about how to interpret this era and characterize the adolescent experience (Bandura, 1980; Weiner, 1985). For example, psychoanalytic perspectives have typically highlighted "storm and stress"—focusing on change, turbulence, and difficulties in adolescent life. Anna Freud (1958, p. 275) even wrote, "To be normal during the adolescent period is by itself abnormal." By contrast, empirical research by Offer and his colleagues (for example, Offer, 1969; Offer & Offer, 1975; Offer et. al., 1981; Offer et al., 1988) has produced reports in which large numbers of adolescents from different cultures describe themselves as relatively untroubled, happy, and self-satisfied. On the basis of their review of available empirical research, Offer and Sabshin (1984, p. 101) observed that almost all researchers who have studied representative samples of adolescents "come to the conclusion that by and large good coping and a smooth transition into adulthood are much more typical than the opposite." The voices of adolescents in the published literature (for example, Kalergis, 1998) confirm this depiction of adolescence.

An evolving, transitional period in the life course such as adolescence clearly presents challenges to its interpreters. Responses to these challenges color much that is said about the adolescent era. The danger is that adolescence is "the world's most perfect projective device for adults" (Offer et al., 1981, p. 121; see also Bandura, 1980).

Developmental Tasks in Early, Middle, and Late Adolescence

However one interprets adolescence as a whole, this era can be thought of in terms of three specific developmental subperiods: early, middle, and late adolescence (Blos, 1941, 1979; see Table 13.1). *Early adolescence* (beginning around age 10 or 11 for most individuals and lasting until around age 14) involves decreased identification with parents, increased identification with peers, fascination with hero figures, and growing interest in sexuality. Early adolescence generally centers on efforts to separate from dependency on parents in order to establish new personal ideals and interpersonal relationships (Balk, 1995).

Middle adolescence or "adolescence proper" (roughly ages 14–17) involves developing autonomy from parents, experimenting with "possible selves" or alternative self-concepts, and forging a distinctive, mature identity. Blos (1979) maintained that in striving to gain greater skill at being independent and self-governing, middle adolescents experience a "second chance" or second individuation process. That is, middle adolescents can develop personal or individual resourcefulness by considerably reorganizing the values internalized from their parents, overcoming the egocentrism of childhood and early adolescence, and making choices about the roles and responsibilities they will assume in life.

Late adolescence (roughly ages 17–21 or 22) is ideally the era of stable character formation. For Blos (1979), this involves meeting four distinct challenges: achieving closure in the second individuation process, attaining personal strength by coping successfully with traumatic life events, establishing historical continuity by accepting one's past and freeing oneself for growth and maturity, and resolving one's sexual identity.

This three-part developmental understanding is helpful in appreciating many death-related experiences during the adolescent era.

Table 13.1 Tasks and Conflicts for Adolescents by Maturational Phase

Phase		
Phase I, Early Adolescence	Age:	11–14
	Task:	Emotional separation from parents
	Conflict:	Separation (abandonment) vs. reunion (safety)
Phase II, Middle Adolescence	Age:	14–17
	Task:	Competency/mastery/control
	Conflict:	Independence vs. dependence
Phase III, Late Adolescence	Age:	17–21
	Task:	Intimacy and commitment
	Conflict:	Closeness vs. distance

SOURCE: Fleming & Adolph, 1986, p. 103.

Encounters with Death during Adolescence

The National Center for Health Statistics (NCHS) publishes demographic data on numbers of deaths and death rates in five-year age groupings (10–14 and 15–19 years of age) after early childhood. This format is not consistent with our overall definition of adolescence or with the developmental subperiods that we have outlined. Nevertheless, these data are all that we have available and they do reveal many aspects of typical encounters with death during the adolescent era.

Deaths and Death Rates among Adolescents

Early, middle, and late adolescents make up just over 21 percent of the total population of the United States. In 1999 in the United States, *deaths of adolescents* numbered 4,121 for individuals between the ages of 10 to 14 and an additional 13,778 for those between the ages of 15 to 19 (see Table 13.2). Together, these deaths represented about .07 percent of the nearly 2.4 million deaths in the country for that year. Death rates for these age groups in 1999 were 21.1 per 100,000 for those 10 to 14 years of age and 69.8 for those 15 to 19 years of age (see Table 13.3). These rates are down just a bit from death rates for the same age groups in 1998 and much lower than death rates for every other age

Table 13.2 Number of Deaths during Adolescence, by Age, Race, and Sex: United States, 1999

	10–14 Years			15–19 Years		
	Both Sexes	Males	Females	Both Sexes	Males	Females
All races	4,121	2,528	1,593	13,778	9,780	3,998
Caucasian Americans, total[a]	3,403	1,852	6,154	10,355	7,222	3,133
Non-Hispanic Caucasian Americans	2,498	1,528	970	8,490	5,799	2,691
Hispanic Americans[b]	550	326	224	1,871	1,432	439
African Americans[a]	909	577	332	2,849	2,157	692
Asian or Pacific Island Americans[a]	112	65	47	329	222	107
Native Americans[a]	57	34	23	245	179	66

[a]Race and Hispanic origin are reported separately on the death certificate.
[b]Includes all persons of Hispanic origin of any race.

SOURCE: Hoyert et al., 2001

Table 13.3 Death Rates (per 100,000 in the specified population group) during Adolescence, by Age, Race, and Sex: United States, 1999

	10–14 Years			15–19 Years		
	Both Sexes	Males	Females	Both Sexes	Males	Females
All races	21.1	25.3	16.7	69.8	96.3	41.7
Caucasian Americans, total[a]	19.8	23.5	16.7	66.2	89.5	41.3
Non-Hispanic Caucasian Americans	19.3	23.1	15.4	64.7	85.9	42.3
Hispanic Americans[b]	20.1	23.3	16.7	67.3	99.1	32.9
African Americans[a]	29.4	36.8	21.9	93.6	139.3	46.3
Asian or Pacific Island Americans[a]	13.6	15.4	11.7	40.0	53.4	26.3
Native Americans[a]	22.9	26.9	18.8	104.4	151.8	56.5

[a]Race and Hispanic origin are reported separately on the death certificate.
[b]Includes all persons of Hispanic origin of any race.

SOURCE: Hoyert et al., 2001

group in the population except younger children. In other words, as a group adolescents die in fewer numbers and at lower rates than do infants and adults in our society. Overall numbers of deaths and death rates in our society rise rapidly with increasing age for all adolescents, regardless of gender, race, or ethnicity.

Leading Causes of Death among Adolescents

Following NCHS formats, Table 13.4 provides data on numbers of deaths and death rates for all individuals 15 to 24 years of age who died in the United States in 1999 in terms of the *ten leading causes* of their deaths. Several significant observations arise from these data. First, the three leading causes of death for these young people (accidents, homicide, and suicide) are all human induced; none involves diseases or natural causes. That circumstance is unique to adolescence; for all other eras in human development, there is at least one (usually two or more) disease-related cause among the three leading causes of death. Nearly 74 percent of all deaths among American adolescents occur from these three causes alone and each played a role in the vignette near the beginning of this chapter.

The importance of these three leading causes of adolescent death can be illustrated in another way. If one adds up the number of deaths and the death

Table 13.4 Deaths and Death Rates (per 100,000) for the Ten Leading Causes of Death, 15–24 Years of Age, Both Sexes, All Races: United States, 1999

Rank	Cause of Death	Number	Rate
...	All causes	30,656	81.2
1	Accidents (unintentional injuries)	13,656	36.2
	Motor vehicle accidents	10,128	26.8
	All other accidents	3,528	9.4
2	Assault (homicide)	4,998	13.2
3	Intentional self-harm (suicide)	3,901	10.3
4	Malignant neoplasms	1,724	4.6
5	Diseases of the heart	1,069	2.8
6	Congenital malformations, deformations, and chromosomal abnormalities	434	1.1
7	Chronic lower respiratory diseases	209	0.6
8	Human immunodeficiency virus (HIV) disease	198	0.5
9	Cerebrovascular diseases	182	0.5
10	Influenza and pneumonia	179	0.5
...	All other causes	4,106	10.9

SOURCE: Hoyert et al., 2001.

rates for the fourth through the tenth causes of death in this age group in 1999, the total (3,995 deaths) only slightly exceeds those for suicide alone, the third leading cause of death for this group. (And if we only considered *teenagers*—including individuals younger than 15, but excluding those over 19—accidents, homicide, and suicide would still remain the three leading causes of death, although their relative order of importance would change to accidents, suicide, and homicide.)

Second, human-induced deaths such as those involving accidents, homicide, and suicide most often occur quickly and unexpectedly, and they are frequently associated with trauma or violence. More than three-quarters of all deaths among adolescents are likely to possess these characteristics. For survivors, these deaths are likely to be perceived not only as untimely but also shocking in a way that is especially associated with sudden and unanticipated disaster (Podell, 1989). For adolescent survivors, traumatic deaths that human beings cause or help to bring on themselves and others may have long-term implications for individuation and developmental tasks (Bradach & Jordan, 1995). For example, an adolescent's sense of competence and intimacy might be threatened by remorse arising from carelessness leading to an accidental death, guilt from perceived failure to save a friend from suicide, or anxiety from the homicidal death of a peer.

Third, the largest portion of the total of 13,602 deaths from accidents or unintentional injuries noted in Table 13.4 is made up of motor vehicle accidents (10,128 deaths versus a total of 3,528 for all other accidental deaths). In other words, deaths associated with motor vehicles accounted for nearly 75 percent of all accidental deaths in this age group. Like deaths arising from homicide and suicide, accidental deaths (especially those associated with motor vehicles) are perceived by many adults as preventable. For that reason, survivors often find themselves angry at the behaviors that led to such deaths and anguished over what might have been done to forestall such outcomes.

Fourth, as early as 1988 human immunodeficiency virus (HIV) infection had become the sixth leading cause of death among persons 15 to 24 years of age in the United States and it remained eighth in this ranking in 1999. In view of the long period of asymptomatic infection that typically characterizes the trajectory of HIV infection (see Chapter 20), this statistic is noteworthy. It contrasts with the fact that many who become infected with HIV during their adolescent years are not likely to die until they become young adults. Further, HIV infection is three to five times more prevalent among African-American and Hispanic-American adolescents than among their Caucasian-American counterparts.

In short, today adolescents in America and in many other developed societies are mostly healthy persons. Relative to other developmental groups, they enjoy a very low death rate. The reason is that as a group adolescents have survived the hazards of birth, infancy, and early childhood, and they have not lived long enough to experience the degenerative diseases that are more characteristic of later adulthood.

Two Variables in Deaths of Adolescents: Gender and Race

Useful contrasts can be drawn among adolescents by gender and by race. Tables 13.2 and 13.3 contrast deaths and death rates among adolescent males with those of adolescent females in the United States for 1999. Differences are obvious. Significantly more young males than females die each year. Roughly the same differences apply to accidental deaths in this cohort and to deaths associated with HIV infection, but the difference is more than 6:1 for deaths associated with either homicide or suicide.

When we compare adolescent deaths and death rates among various racial and cultural groups in our society, other important differences emerge (see Tables 13.2 and 13.3). For example, although there are many more deaths of Caucasian Americans in these age groups by contrast with the next largest number (deaths among African Americans), African Americans die at far higher rates. Numbers of deaths in 1999 among younger adolescents are much lower for Hispanic Americans, Asian and Pacific Island Americans, and Native Americans. Death rates among older adolescents are lowest for Asian and Pacific Island Americans, higher among Caucasian Americans and Hispanic Americans, and significantly higher among African Americans, but not yet as high as those for Native Americans. Caucasian Americans are somewhat more likely to die in accidents or from suicide, whereas African Americans are far more likely to die from homicide, diseases of the heart, and HIV infection.

Among all older adolescents (those 15–19 years of age), males are more than 2.4 times more likely to die than females (Table 13.2). Among non-Hispanic Caucasian Americans, this gender differential is only 2.2, but it rises to 3.1 among African Americans in this age group. Differences in death rates between Caucasian-American males and females are at ratios of nearly 3:1 for accidents and HIV infection, more than 4:1 for homicide, and almost 6:1 for suicide. By contrast, differences in death rates between African-American males and African-American females are at ratios of less than 2:1 for diseases of the heart, just over 2:1 for HIV infection, almost 4:1 for accidents, almost 8:1 for homicide, and more than 8:1 for suicide.

Deaths of Others Experienced by Adolescents

There are few reliable sources of data concerning the *deaths of others that are experienced by adolescents.* One early study of more than 1,000 high school juniors and seniors (middle adolescents) reported that 90 percent of those students had experienced the death of someone they loved (Ewalt & Perkins, 1979). In nearly 40 percent of this sample, the loss involved the death of a friend or peer who was roughly their own age. Ewalt and Perkins concluded that "adolescents have more experience with death and mourning than has been assumed" (p. 547). In 20 percent of the sample, the students had actually witnessed a death. A similar study found that when asked to identify their "most recent major loss," 1,139 late adolescent (average age = 19.5) college and university students in New York State reported that the death of a loved one or a sudden death (number = 328) was the most common loss among a total of 46 different types of losses (LaGrand, 1981, 1986, 1988). Clearly, it is not correct to think that contemporary adolescents have no experience with death and bereavement.

In addition, adolescents encounter deaths involving grandparents and parents; neighbors, teachers, and other adults; siblings and friends; pets and other animals; and celebrities and cultural heroes with whom they identify. Adolescence is also the first era in the human life course in which an individual can experience the death of his or her own offspring (Ewalt & Perkins, 1979). Adolescents also report that they encounter a wide variety of loss-related experiences that do not involve death but may nevertheless be very painful, such as the ending of friendships or loving relationships (LaGrand, 1981, 1986, 1988).

Many experiences with death and other losses may have particular significance for an adolescent's developmental tasks. For example, early adolescents who are striving to achieve emotional emancipation from parents may experience complications in those efforts if a parent (or a grandparent to whom they are especially close or who is their surrogate parent) should suddenly die. Such an adolescent may feel abandoned by these adult deaths and may find it hard to attain a feeling of safety in these circumstances.

Similarly, middle adolescents who are seeking to achieve competency, mastery, and control at a time when they enjoy some sense of autonomy may experience a threat to their newfound independence if a friend or other member of their own generation should die (see Box 13.1). The likelihood that the death of another adolescent will be sudden, unexpected, traumatic, and often violent may enhance the threat to the surviving adolescent's own prospects and security. Adolescents who have carried over from childhood the "tattered cloak of immortality" (Gordon, 1986) or who maintain a "personal fable" (Elkind, 1967) of invulnerability may be shaken when confronted by the death of a person of their own age and similar circumstances.

Box 13.1 Who's Andrea?

The spring day dawned crisp and clear on the desert. A beautiful morning . . . sun shining brightly, cheery children shouting and laughing as they bound toward school whilst slowly wakening commuters tap their fingers in rhythm to the FM beat, contemplating the successes of the impending day. It is February the third, a Wednesday, and a wonderful time to be alive.

It is also the anniversary of a devastating event in the life of Marsha, my wife, and I. An endless 2,192 days ago we last hugged our daughter Virginia, an interminable 52,608 hours since we consoled her and swore that everything would be all right. A millennium since we felt her warm touch. When she died, a piece of us died with her. We will never forget her, even when it seems everyone else has.

On most occasions, when we seek to speak to her spirit, we visit the site of the accident that took her life. Today, however, our memories guide us to her resting-place, so that we may place a flower and reaffirm how much we still love and miss her. To speak through our hearts to a daughter who will forever remain 15 years old.

Her remains reside in a quiet, peaceful columbarium on church grounds that few others know about. It is the perfect foyer to heaven. But what is this? Another visitor has already been here, placed a flower, and left a note! Does someone else remember her? As we peer at the words on the tattered paper, authored by "Andrea," it seems as if God Himself has sensed our feelings of abandonment and sent the message.

As we journey home, one question continues to confound us; just who is Andrea? Neither of us can recall a friend of Virginia's named Andrea. Is Andrea really God incognito, or simply a distraught young woman mourning the loss of her friend? One thing is for certain, Andrea, whomever she is, represents validation that Virginia made a difference while she lived on earth. She touched someone so deeply that even 6 years after her death she is remembered, mourned, missed and loved by someone other than her parents and family. It seems a fitting legacy to the days when she walked on the very ground that Andrea, the two of us, and the rest of humanity walk upon today.

Andrea's handwritten note:

> Ginny,
> I love-n-miss you very much and know someday we will see each other again. Your always close in my mind-n-heart. With Love, Andrea. ■

SOURCE: David Stanton, 1999.

Further, late adolescents who are working to reestablish intimacy and commitment with those who are significant in their lives may feel thwarted and frustrated when they encounter the death of a person of a younger generation—for example, a younger brother, sister, friend, or their own child. Dedicating themselves to a relationship with a person of this sort and achieving the closeness that it can involve are stymied when the other person in the relationship dies. Such deaths may rebuff in a disturbing and disempowering way the older adolescent's efforts to reach out to others.

Adolescents are also more likely than children to recognize and understand large-scale perils, such as global tensions, the threat or reality of war, and terrorism. Thus many adolescents were keenly aware of the reality and the implications of the terrorist attacks on the World Trade Center and the Pentagon on September 11, 2001. Many adolescents are also sensitive to violence at home, in their schools, and in the community; ongoing jeopardy associated with nuclear weapons and power plants; and problems involving the environment, such as acid rain, destruction of the world's rain forests, depletion of the ozone layer in the atmosphere, the so-called greenhouse effect involving climatic warming, population growth, and waste disposal.

Death-Related Attitudes during Adolescence

Given the great diversity among adolescents in our society and the breadth of issues associated with death, we should not be surprised to find a wide variety of death-related attitudes held by adolescents. We can begin to examine such attitudes among adolescents in the contemporary American death system by suggesting some of the many factors that influence them.

For *adolescent understandings of death*, researchers generally agree that before or by the beginning of the adolescent era individuals with normal cognitive development are capable of grasping the concept of death and its principal subconcepts (see Chapter 12). Adolescents in Western society are well into what Piaget and Inhelder (1958) called the period of formal operations, which is characterized by propositional and hypothetical-deductive thinking, generality of concepts, and an objective view of reality (Keating, 1990).

However, it is not enough merely to note that adolescents are *capable* of thinking in ways characteristic of adults. Noppe and Noppe (1991, 1996, 1997) have suggested that *adolescent understandings of death may be influenced by ambiguities or tensions arising from biological, cognitive, social, and emotional factors.* First, rapid *biological* maturation and sexual development is associated in many adolescents with an awareness of inevitable physical decline and ultimate death. This tension is represented in high-risk behaviors among many adolescents who seek to defy or "cheat" death (Bachman et al., 1986). Although "the majority of adolescents engage in some risk-taking behavior but do not experience tragic consequences" (Gans, 1990, p. 17), this behavior is particularly hazardous in a world of high-powered automobiles, readily available drugs and firearms, eating disorders, binge drinking, and HIV (Bachman et al., 1986; Bensinger & Natenshon, 1991; Wechsler et al., 1994). Adolescents conflicted by such challenges and possibilities may have reason to look fondly at what they seem to have lost in moving on from the more restricted, apparently simpler, world of childhood.

Second, in the search for one's own identity and reevaluating parental values, an adolescent's newly developed *cognitive* capacities are challenged to take into account the inevitability of death. Thoughts about death in the abstract may or may not coexist with awareness of its personal significance for an individual adolescent (Corr, 1995d). Looking bravely into what the future holds, adolescents may glimpse both positive and negative possibilities. In the end, they must come to appreciate that although there is much they can do to influence the shape of their futures, it is also true that many things are beyond their control.

Third, changing *social* relationships with family members and peers carry potential for both enrichment and isolation. As their relationships enlarge in scope, especially by moving outside of their family of origin, adolescents are challenged to create a viable social life and to avoid a "social death" (Noppe & Noppe, 1991, 1996). A new peer group offers a context in which an adolescent can be comfortable in his or her new identity, but it also imposes scrutiny and its own demands for conformity. This is further complicated when the chosen peer group is a gang that devotes some of its energies to violent behavior and strife with others. Also, in many adolescent peer groups, transient interpersonal difficulties can become sources of anguish and despair. For many adolescents, this may be compounded by moving into new academic and cultural settings, and by specific ethnic influences that may encourage or inhibit certain kinds of public behaviors, such as the expression of grief and other reactions to loss.

Fourth, adolescent *feelings* about development and death are likely to be closely intertwined. Achieving autonomy and individuation during the adolescent years is not only a matter of abandoning parent-child attachments begun in infancy. The real challenge for developing adolescents is to reformulate and make qualitative changes in such attachments, even as they develop new peer group attachments. All of this can involve threats to an adolescent's sense of self-esteem and purpose in life. Developmental feelings of loss and grief—the fear of losing one's self—coexist in many adolescents with feelings of being intensely alive.

The very broad range of adolescent attitudes toward death is reflected in the entertainment media that are so much a part of the lives of many adolescents and preadolescents. For example, video games often involve animated simulations of violence and death, as do movies that are popular with teenagers and young adults. Death-related themes are also prominent in the fast-changing music scene familiar to most adolescents (see Attig, 1986; Plopper & Ness, 1993). When several adolescents were asked to list some of the songs they knew that contain death-related themes, they suggested (among many): "Jumper" by Third Eye Blind, "Adam's Song" by Blink 182, and "Last Resort" by Papa Roach (all about suicide); "Youth of the Nation" by P.O.D. and "Jeremy" by Pearl Jam (both about violence in schools); "Tears in Heaven" by Eric Clapton (about the death of his son); and "I'll Be Missing You" by Puff Daddy and Faith Evans (about death). Since the September 11 attacks, country music stations have also repeatedly aired Alan Jackson's "Where Were You (When the World Stopped Turning)." It is perhaps worth noting, however, a comment by one adolescent who said she does not always listen to the lyrics so much as the music itself. Still, death in many of its forms (not only violence or suicide) is widely present in these lyrics and other media directed to adolescents. You might test that point by taking a moment to think about the death-related attitudes expressed in popular music and other aspects of contemporary culture with which you are most familiar.

A central element in an adolescent's sense of vulnerability or invulnerability has to do not merely with surrogate experiences arising from music written by others but with *lessons learned—or not learned—by adolescents from their own life experiences.* The inability or unwillingness of many adolescents to recognize the personal implications of mortality may have much to do with the limits of adolescent experience and the perspectives that dominate much of adolescent life. This theory is confirmed by an analysis of factors that enter into well-known driving patterns in middle and late adolescence (Jonah, 1986). Two elements are of greatest significance: (1) adolescent drivers may simply not perceive risks that are inherent in their behaviors (such as the likelihood that an accident might occur or that it might result in serious consequences) and thus may inadvertently put themselves into situations fraught with danger; and (2) adolescent drivers may perceive positive utility or value in taking certain risks, such as seizing control over one's life by acting independently, expressing opposition to adult authority and conventional society, coping with anxiety or frustration, or gaining acceptance from a peer group. We saw both of these elements in the vignette near the beginning of this chapter when Tom Adkins and his friends tried (unsuccessfully) to outrun a train in their automobile.

Tolstoy captured the sense of invulnerability found in some adolescents in his classic novella *The Death of Ivan Ilych* (1884/1960, p. 131). As Ivan is dying in midlife, he thinks of his youth: "The syllogism he had learnt from Kiezewetter's Logic: 'Caius is a man, men are mortal, therefore Caius is mortal,' had always seemed to him correct as applied to Caius, but certainly not as applied to himself." In other words, mortality for the young Ivan Ilych was an abstraction, whose personal force and relevance to his own life becomes apparent to him only many years later as he is dying.

However, not all adolescents can put aside threats related to death. In one study (Alexander & Adlerstein, 1958), participants were asked to say the first word that came into their minds in response to a series of stimulus words that included death-related words. Responses were measured in terms of the speed with which they were offered and by association with decreased galvanic skin resistance (increased perspiration or sweating). Participants aged 5 to 8 and 13 to 16 had high death anxiety scores when compared with the scores of 9- to 12-year-olds. The researchers concluded that death has "a greater emotional significance for people with less stable ego self-pictures" (p. 175).

This seems to suggest that death-related threats have greatest personal significance at times of transition in human development and, within adolescence, at times of decreased stability and self-confidence. This is consistent with a report that death anxiety is highest in teenagers and most closely associated with fears of loss of bodily integrity and decomposition (Thorson et al., 1988). For many individuals, early adolescence is a time of little sense of futurity and a high degree of egocentrism (Elkind, 1967). Thus, a key variable in adolescent attitudes toward death may be the level of maturity that the adolescent has achieved (Maurer, 1964), with greater maturity being associated both with "greater sophistication and acknowledgement of the inevitability of death as well as with enjoyment of life and altruistic concerns" (Raphael, 1983, p. 147).

Box 13.2 Two Experiences as a Teen Hospice Volunteer

In my first volunteer experience with hospice, I served as a teen mentor to a 12-year-old boy with a life-threatening illness known as tricuspid atresia. This disease made him prone to congestive heart failure and irregular heartbeats, and therefore limited his physical activity. As a teen mentor, I provided emotional support for this boy by helping him identify his other interests and by taking his mind off his illness. I visited him weekly and often assisted with homework, took him fishing, or simply talked with him about life. It was a truly incredible feeling to see him smile and to know that I made a difference in his life. Realizing that I contributed to the life of another, I gained a greater satisfaction with my own life, as well as a greater appreciation for its many gifts. . . .

One of the greatest challenges I encountered in my work with the terminally ill was through my unique friendship with a 107-year-old hospice patient named Joe, and having that friendship come to an end in November 1998. It was indeed a challenge to grow close with Joe, knowing that our time together would be short. I overcame this challenge by focusing on Joe's life—a century of memories, history, and accomplishments. Each time I visited with Joe I was guaranteed to learn something new, whether it was a history lesson or a lesson on life. I felt that Joe, like all terminally ill patients, should live until he died, so I brought him lunch on occasion and shared pictures with him. When the time came for Joe to pass on, it was extremely difficult to focus on life amidst oxygen machines and tube feedings, yet I continued to hold his hand through it all. On one of Joe's last evenings, he told a friend and I that we were "the best gifts a man could ask for," and that he would never forget us. It was at that moment that the familiar hospice message, "Every day is a gift," truly touched me. From Joe, I learned to cherish this gift of life and to help other hospice patients do the same by offering my compassion during the last stages of their lives. ■

SOURCE: Copyright © 2000 by Education Development Center, Inc. Reprinted with permission. Corace, B., "End-of-Life Care: A Personal Reflection." In *Innovations in End-of-Life Care: Practical Strategies and International Perspectives*, Volume 2, M. Z. Solomon, A. L. Romer, K. S. Heller, and D. E. Weissman (Eds.). Larchmont, NY: Mary Ann Liebert Publishers, 2000, 81–82. This essay was originally published in Volume 2, Number 4 of the online version of *Innovations in End-of-Life Care* at www.edc.org/lastacts.

In short, many adolescents manifest a tendency to live in the moment and not to appreciate personal threats associated with death. The key issue for these adolescents may not arise directly from their capacity to think about death but rather from ways in which the significance of death-related concepts is or is not related to their personal lives. This may not apply to adolescents who have broad and personal experiences with death. For example, some adolescents who have been prepared for and supported in their work as hospice teen volunteers have learned important lessons from those activities (see Box 13.2). In general, however, most adolescents struggle to grasp the personal significance of death by confronting a paradox: they want to keep their feelings in perspective and distance themselves from intense death-related experiences, while, at the same time, they attempt to find meaning in abstract concepts of death by applying them in ways that have personal reference and meaning.

Adolescents Who Are Coping with Life-Threatening Illness and Dying

Because dying and adolescence are both transitional experiences, Papadatou (1989, p. 28) has wisely noted that "it could be argued that seriously ill adolescents experience a double crisis owing to their imminent death and their developmental age." In particular, dying adolescents need to live in the present, to have the freedom to try out different ways of coping with illness-related challenges, and to find meaning and purpose in their lives and in their deaths (Stevens & Dunsmore, 1996a). For most adolescents, effective coping with a life-threatening illness requires information about the disease, involvement in the planning of treatment, and participation in decision making (Cassileth et al., 1980; Dunsmore & Quine, 1995).

Among individuals 15 to 24 years of age, cancer is the fourth leading cause of death (third among females) (Bleyer, 1990), followed at a distance by heart disease, congenital malformations, chronic lower respiratory diseases, HIV infection, cerebrovascular diseases, and influenza and pneumonia (see Table 13.4). All discussions of life-threatening illness and dying during adolescence must take into account the distinctive characteristics of the disease in question and the context surrounding individual adolescents.

The needs and reactions of adolescents associated with life-threatening illness and dying have been described in a variety of ways (Adams & Deveau, 1986; Waechter, 1984). Perhaps one useful rule of thumb is the reminder that adolescents "are not so much afraid of death as of the dying" (Stevens & Dunsmore, 1996a, p. 109). Having a life-threatening illness begins a pattern of loss for adolescents, leading to experiences of loss or alteration in: their sense of themselves as "pre-diagnosis persons"; body image; lifestyle (for example, a perception of being in control and not unreasonably vulnerable may turn into one of vulnerability and overprotectiveness by adolescents and the adults around them); everyday school activities; independence; relationships with parents, siblings, and friends; and sense of certainty about the future.

Stevens and Dunsmore (1996a) drew on their extensive work with ill and dying adolescents to observe that early adolescents with a life-threatening illness are likely to be especially concerned about physical appearance and mobility and to rely on authority figures. Middle adolescents typically focus on what the illness will mean for their ability to attract a girlfriend or boyfriend, on emancipation from parents and authority figures, and on being rejected by peers. Late adolescents may be most concerned with how the illness will affect their lifestyle and their plans for a career and relationships. All adolescents are likely to differ in their reactions to a life-threatening illness and in how they

Box 13.3 Only a Sibling

How do you tell someone you love
You don't want them to die
How can I try to be normal
I know I will cry

How do I cope with my anger
At life, at God and sometimes even at you
How can I put a smile on my face
While my insides are ripping in two

How can I tell you I'm frightened
Of the skeleton my brother's become
Tired and thin from your battle
A war that I'm scared cannot be won

How can I tell you I love you
When all our lives it's going unsaid
How do I stop you from drowning
When the water's already over my head

Every wince stabs me too, with pain
Why cannot I tell anyone how I feel
When I feel like I'm going insane

How can I think of my future
When it's possibly a future without you there
Why do I feel so damn helpless
And my problems too insignificant to share

How do I tell you big brother
That I'm scared of what's happening to you
Why cannot anyone seem to understand
That your dying is killing me too. ■

SOURCE: From "Only a Sibling," by Tammy McKenzie (nee McGowan), CanTeen Newsletter.

express those reactions at different points in the disease trajectory and in different contexts (for example, at home, in the hospital).

Life-threatening diseases impact both the ill adolescent and those who are involved with that adolescent. We see this in two examples of sibling reactions to such situations: a poem by an Australian adolescent (Box 13.3) and a chronicle of the challenges facing healthy adolescents whose ill sibling is coping with cystic fibrosis (see Table 13.5). The challenge for both ill adolescents and those around them is to learn how to live with progressive, life-threatening diseases

Table 13.5 Well Siblings' Views of Cystic Fibrosis and Their Own Sibling's Condition

Disease Trajectory	Well Siblings' Views
Diagnosis	A serious illness
First year following diagnosis	
First annual examination	A condition one does things for
Months/years following first annual examination (without a major exacerbation)	
First major exacerbation	A disease, not merely a condition
Succeeding exacerbations and other illnesses, with periodic hospitalizations	A series of episodes of acute illness and recovery
Frequent exacerbations, episodes of other diseases, and hospitalizations	Questions emerge about cure, course of the disease, control of it, and efficacy of treatment
Development and increase in complications	Chronic, progressive, incurable disease that shortens the life span. (This view does not apply to one's own sibling—at least not in the near future.)
Increased deterioration	Chronic, progressive, incurable disease that shortens the life span. (In some cases this view now applies to one's own sibling.)
Terminal phases	Chronic, progressive, incurable disease that shortens the life span. (In all cases this view now applies to one's own sibling.)

SOURCE: From "Living with Cystic Fibrosis: The Well Sibling's Perspective," by M. Bluebond-Langner, *Medical Anthropological Quarterly*, *5*(2), June 1991, American Anthropological Association. Reprinted with permission. Not for sale or further reproduction.

(Koocher & O'Malley, 1981; Spinetta & Deasy-Spinetta, 1981). This requirement places great demands on individual and familial resources and on processes of communication within the family, especially when the dying trajectory is drawn out, as in HIV infection and AIDS (DiClemente et al., 1996). Not surprisingly, adolescents need defenses in such situations and often seek to play an active role in coping with the challenges they face (Dunsmore & Quine, 1995; Spiegel, 1993).

Society may not be very knowledgeable about or helpful to those who are coping with such experiences because of its limited encounters with life-threatening illnesses and deaths from natural causes during adolescence. However, the basic principles are clear: honest and effective communication, good symptom control, and vigorous responses to specific concerns (Stevens & Dunsmore, 1996b). These guidelines enable ill adolescents to live out their lives in their own ways and to maintain valued involvements with peers, school, and families—the ordinary milieu of adolescent life. Papadatou (1989, p. 31) offered this thought to helpers who wish to approach adolescents and their families when they are coping with life-threatening illness: "We must also believe that we are not helpless or hopeless, but have something valuable to offer: an honest and meaningful relationship that provides the adolescent with a feeling that we are willing to share his journey through the remainder of his life."

Adolescents Who Are Coping with Bereavement and Grief

Adolescents may experience bereavement through the death of a significant person in their lives: for example, a celebrity whom they admired such as Kurt Cobain, the grunge rocker who took his own life; Eazy-E (Eric Wright), the gangsta rapper and cofounder of the group N.W.A. who died of AIDS; Selena, the Tejano singer, who was shot to death; or Aaliyah, who was killed in a plane accident. In the research literature on adolescent bereavement, the deaths of a sibling or parent have been the principal objects of study (Balk, 1991a, 1991b; Fleming & Balmer, 1996); surprisingly little attention has been given to the death of an adolescent's friend (Oltjenbruns, 1996) or pet, or to experiences of bereaved adolescent parents (Barnickol et al., 1986; Welch & Bergen, 2000). Still, useful lessons can be drawn from existing research on adolescent bereavement (Balk, 1991a; Balk & Corr, 2001).

Three key variables in adolescent bereavement are self-concept, depression, and age. In his research on bereaved siblings, Balk (1990) reported that high *self-concept* scores were correlated with less depression, fear, loneliness, and confusion; average self-concept scores were correlated with more depression, loneliness, and anger; and low self-concept scores were correlated with more confusion but less anger. In other work on adolescent sibling bereavement, Hogan and Greenfield (1991) reported an inverse relationship between intensity of bereavement and self-concept scores; that is, high self-concept scores correlated with low intensity of grief, and vice versa. An ongoing attachment to the deceased sibling was also identified in the lives of many bereaved adolescents (Hogan & DeSantis, 1992).

Adolescents need support from their peers when they are coping with loss and grief.

A study of Canadian high school students who experienced the death of a parent revealed that higher *depression* inventory scores were found in bereaved versus nonbereaved adolescents, adolescents without religious beliefs, and those with lower scores of perceived social support (Gray, 1987).

In terms of *age*, another study of sibling bereavement among Canadian adolescents reported that older bereaved adolescents experienced more psychological distress and were more likely to talk with friends, whereas younger bereaved adolescents experienced more physiological distress and were less likely to talk with friends (Balmer, 1992).

In brief, low self-concept and depression may foreshadow difficulties in adolescent bereavement, whereas greater developmental maturity is associated with increased, but relatively transient, psychological distress. The ability to talk with friends about the bereavement and perceived social support are constructive factors. In general, "perhaps the most salient feature of adolescent adjustment following death is the *resiliency* evidenced by the bereaved participants in the face of traumatic loss" (Fleming & Balmer, 1996, p. 153; emphasis added). Bereavement during adolescence does not of itself predispose one to ongoing psychological difficulties; it may actually help many adolescents to become more emotionally and interpersonally mature. However, bereavement may be problematic for vulnerable adolescents by reinforcing conditions they bring to their experience that predispose them to difficulty.

Adolescent grief is manifested in many ways, such as confusion, crying, feelings of emptiness and/or loneliness, disturbances in patterns of sleep and eating, and exhaustion (Balk, 1983). However, as Jackson (1984, p. 42) has written, "Adolescents are apt to think that they are the discoverers of deep and powerful feelings and that no one has ever loved as they love." If so, adolescents may assume that their grief is similarly unique and incomprehensible—to themselves and to others. Consequently, adolescents may only express their grief in brief outbursts or may actively suppress it because they fear loss of emotional control and do not want to be perceived by others as being out of control. However, some bereaved adolescents can reach into themselves in powerful ways to express their grief, as illustrated by the comments of one hospice teen volunteer about the death of her own grandfather (see Box 13.4).

Bereaved adolescents appear to be helped in coping with their grief by activities that reduce stress (playing a musical instrument, keeping busy, or releasing pent-up emotions); their own personal belief systems; support from parents, other relatives, or friends; and professionals or mutual support groups who can normalize grief reactions (Balk, 1991c; Balk & Hogan, 1995; Hogan & DeSantis, 1994). Complications may arise as a result of ambivalent relationships with the deceased or with other survivors; a tendency of some adolescents to idealize the deceased, which may complicate mourning with guilt and self-blame; a possibility that the relationship or the grief may be unacknowledged or disenfranchised by society; the intense, if sometimes relatively transitory, quality of adolescent feelings; the desire to fit in and not be different from peers; or lack of support from peers and adults.

As in coping with life-threatening illness and dying during adolescence, bereavement for adolescents involves a double crisis in which situational tasks overlay and in many respects parallel normal developmental tasks (Sugar, 1968). For bereaved adolescents, in other words, experiences involving protest/searching, disorganization, and reorganization (as we described in

Box 13.4 A Hospice Teen Volunteer and the Death of Her Grandfather

My grandfather was diagnosed on January 13, 2000, with cancer of the colon, spleen, and lymph nodes. He died one month later on February 12. Needless to say, there was an extremely limited time period between his diagnosis and death in which we could prepare for the dreaded reality of the situation. However, since I have been trained as a hospice volunteer, I have learned that death can be approached as a celebration of life. I feel that I was able to celebrate my grandfather's life with him during the final moments that we did have together, and for that I am thankful. When I visited him two weeks before he died, Grandpa and I talked a lot, and I would simply sit by his bedside and hold his hand. Although it grew increasingly difficult for him to speak to us, he reminisced with me about a few of his early childhood memories, and commented on the incredible change that has taken place in the morals and values from his generation to mine. He told me how proud he was of me, and how he so hoped to know where Michael [her brother] and I would be going to college. Shortly after we had to go home . . . he grew so weak that he could no longer talk on the phone with me. To make up for that lack of communication, I e-mailed my grandpa every day until he died. My grandma printed out each of the e-mails and read them to him in his bed. I told him how much I loved him, how proud I was to be his granddaughter, and how much he had taught me, growing up. Grandpa and I had been writing letters back and forth for the past ten years. I have kept each of his letters and put them into an album. I will forever cherish those precious letters, as they allow me to remember the special times and conversations I had with my grandfather. ■

SOURCE: Copyright © 2000 by Education Development Center, Inc. Reprinted with permission. Tibbets, E., "Learning to Value Every Moment." In *Innovations in End-of-Life Care: Practical Strategies and International Perspectives*, Volume 2, M. Z. Solomon, A. L. Romer, K. S. Heller, and D. E. Weissman (Eds.). Larchmont, NY: Mary Ann Liebert Publishers, 2001, 78–79. This essay was originally published in Volume 2, Number 4 of the online version of *Innovations in End-of-Life Care* at www.edc.org/lastacts.

Chapter 9) are often intertwined with normative developmental tasks of establishing emotional separation, achieving competency or mastery, and developing intimacy. If one accepts Coleman's (1978) account of "focal theory"—which holds that most adolescents cope with stressors by concentrating on resolving one crisis at a time—it follows that the double crisis of adolescent bereavement (without further complications, such as a traumatic death, a suicide, or the death of one's own child) is especially challenging both for young copers and for their helpers, who may be trying to determine which aspects of adolescent coping emerge from development and which from bereavement (Corr, 2000b; Garber, 1983).

This perspective suggests that adolescent mourning may not exactly parallel similar processes in adults. Paradoxically, adolescent mourning is likely to be both continuous and intermittent, encompassing as it typically does both grief that comes and goes and an overall process that may involve an extended period of time (Hogan & DeSantis, 1992). In personal relationships and in their social systems, adolescents' bereavement is likely to involve secondary losses and incremental grief. The role of family dynamics and long-term consequences of death for adolescent development both deserve further exploration (Balmer, 1992; Hogan & Balk, 1990; Lattanzi-Licht, 1996; Martinson et al., 1987; Meshot & Leitner, 1993).

Adolescents, Suicide, and Homicide

Suicide and Adolescents

Suicidal behavior among adolescents has attracted much attention in recent years (for example, Lester, 1993; Peck et al., 1985; Stillion & McDowell, 1996) for two primary reasons: (1) to many, adolescence seems to be a healthy and productive era during which the individual evolves from child to adult and finds important openings to the future; and (2) during the period between 1960 and 1990, suicide rates among middle and late adolescents increased significantly (see Figures 13.1 and 13.2)—more rapidly, in fact, than for any other age cohort during the same period of time (Holinger et al., 1994; Maris, 1985).

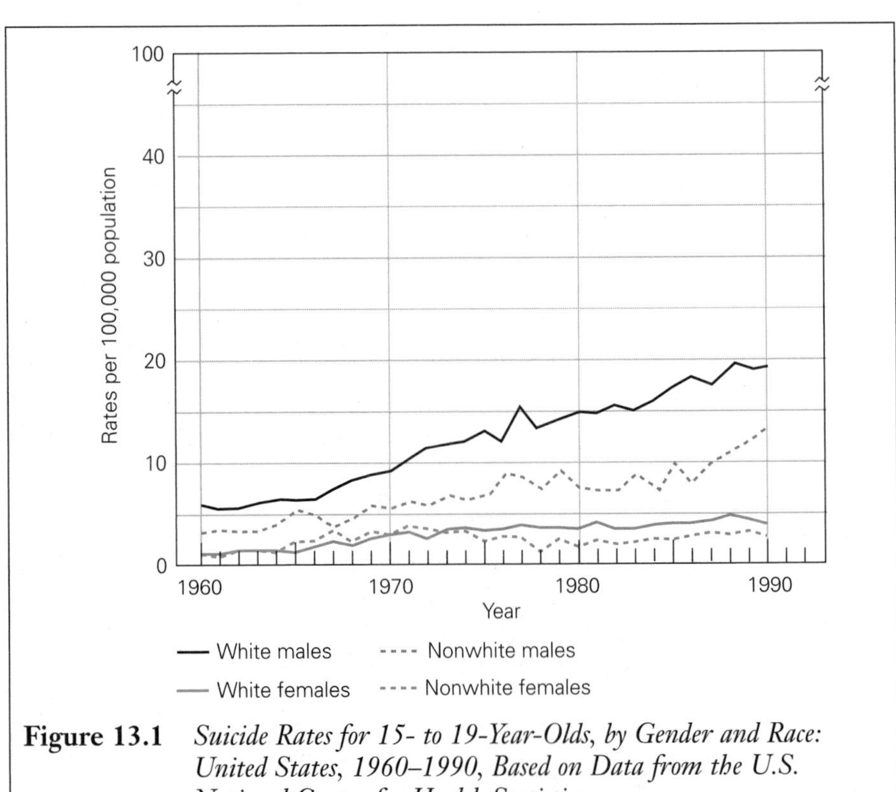

Figure 13.1 *Suicide Rates for 15- to 19-Year-Olds, by Gender and Race: United States, 1960–1990, Based on Data from the U.S. National Center for Health Statistics.*

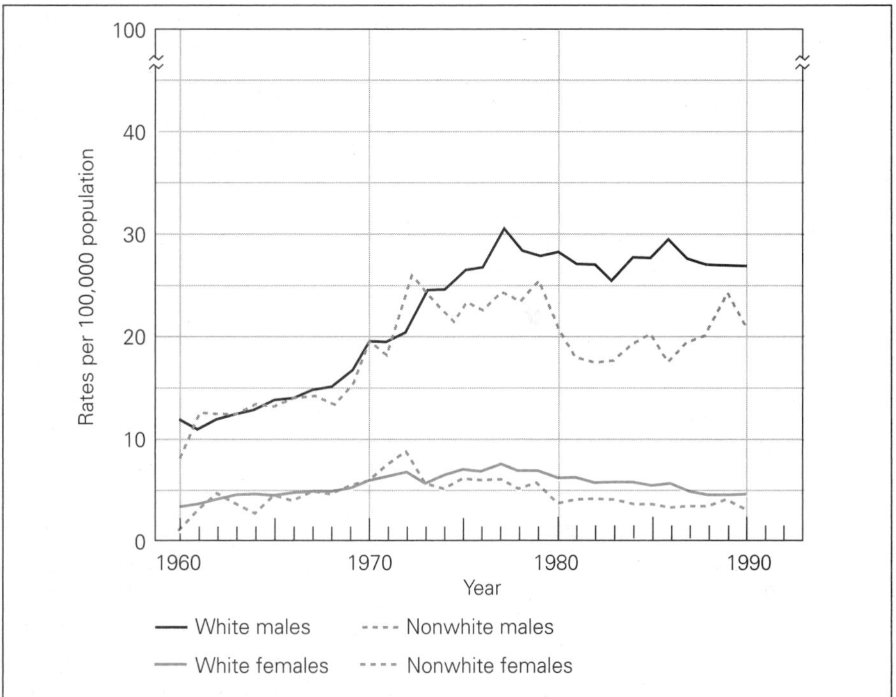

Figure 13.2 *Suicide Rates for 20- to 24-Year-Olds, by Gender and Race: United States, 1960–1990, Based on Data from the U.S. National Center for Health Statistics.*

During the last half of the 1990s, however, suicide rates for middle and late adolescents between 15 and 24 years of age in the United States have displayed a downward trend. According to the best data available (McIntosh, 2001), between 1990 and 1995 suicide rates ranged from a low of 13.0 to a high of 13.8 per 100,000 in this age group. In 1996, these rates declined to 12.0 suicides per 100,000, and continued to decline in 1997 and 1998 with rates of 11.4 and 11.1, respectively. Also, as shown in Table 13.4, the suicide rate for this age group in 1999 was 10.3 per 100,000. This trend is quite promising, even though suicide in 1999 still caused the deaths of 3,901 persons between the ages of 15 and 24. Along with 244 deaths during the same year that were identified as caused by suicide in early adolescents and preadolescent children 5 to 14 years of age, there is ample reason for concern about youth suicide.

In addition to the fact that the suicide rate for adolescents increased more rapidly than that of any other age group during the period 1960–1990, "the second important characteristic of adolescent suicidal behavior is the dramatic sex difference in suicide attempts versus completions" (Stillion & McDowell, 1996, p. 119). According to reliable estimates, the vast majority (about 75 percent) of all adolescent suicide attempters are female, whereas the largest majority (approximately 85 percent) of adolescent suicide completers are male. These and other disparities in suicidal behavior among adolescents—for example, between female and male attempters, between male and female completers, between late and middle adolescents, and between Caucasian-American and African-American adolescents—suggest that we still have much to learn in order to understand more clearly the dynamics behind such phenomena.

It may seem paradoxical that since the middle of the 20th century in the United States self-inflicted death should have become the third leading cause of death among adolescents, in an era of human development that is often perceived by outsiders to be satisfying and promising. In fact, as we saw in the example of Anthony Ramirez in our vignette near the beginning of this chapter, suicide is often chosen by adolescents who do not share the rosy view of their situation that may be held by others, who are overburdened by stresses, who are unable to identify constructive options to resolve their problems, or who are depressed that life is good and promising for others (Jurich & Collins, 1996).

Suicidal behavior in adolescents and others is often complex; it may arise from many factors (Allberg & Chu, 1990; Kirk, 1993; see also Chapter 17 in this book). For that reason, one should not oversimplify the situation of adolescents who attempt or complete actions that may end their lives. Nevertheless, it is often possible to identify adolescents who are at risk for suicide (Garrison et al., 1991). Prominent factors include: inadequacies or alterations in relationships between adolescents and significant others, such as parents and family members, peers, schoolmates, or co-workers; potent pressures among adolescents to conform to peers; inexperience in coping with problems; and dysfunctional behavior. All of these factors are associated with ineffective communication, inadequate coping skills, and the specific problems of developing adolescents. In addition, there is evidence to support the claim that gay and lesbian youth are at high risk for suicidal behavior (Gibson, 1994). This might be due to a variety of factors, including the attitudes of many members of our society toward gay and lesbian persons. More broadly, adolescents "who experience a wide gulf between who they are and who

Depressed adolescents who feel that their lives are going nowhere may turn to life-threatening behavior.

they want to become are at risk for low self-concepts, self-hatred, depression, and suicidal behavior" (Stillion et al., 1989, p. 194). Such adolescents may be unable to express their needs, solve their personal problems, or obtain the assistance that they require.

Adolescents who can neither resolve their problems nor put them into a larger perspective can become isolated and depressed. Since depression is frequently associated with feelings of helplessness and hopelessness, such adolescents may become desperate. Self-destruction may appear to them to be their only available option. *Most often, this does not reflect a wish to be dead.* In fact, like others, many suicidal adolescents are ambivalent in their feelings about life and death and may be unclear about the personal finality of death. What may be most significant in such adolescents is their *overpowering urge to escape from a stressful life situation* (Berman, 1986; Berman & Jobes, 1991).

Adolescents who are ambivalent about ending their lives often attempt to communicate their need for help in some way or other. For example, they may begin to give away cherished possessions or speak vaguely about how things would be better if they were no longer around. However, these may not be very effective ways of getting across the desired message. After all, the ability to achieve effective communication is directly related to an ability to cope with problems. An adolescent who can describe his or her problems to others has usually made an important step toward managing them. Nonetheless, those to whom an adolescent tries to communicate his or her feelings may not recognize such messages as cries for assistance, because many adolescent communications are exaggerated, because this particular message may be obscure, or because those who are living healthful lives may be unable or unwilling to grasp the desperation associated with the message.

Even when outsiders cannot prevent adolescents from attempting or completing suicide, much can be done to minimize the likelihood of such behaviors. Efforts to increase self-esteem, foster the ability to make sound decisions, and enhance constructive coping skills in adolescents are all desirable. School-based education and intervention programs for teachers, counselors, parents, and adolescents are designed to teach about warning signs of suicide and practical strategies for offering help, such as peer counseling and crisis intervention (Berkovitz, 1985; Leenaars & Wenckstern, 1991; Poland, 1989; Ross, 1980, 1985; Stevenson, 2001; Stevenson & Stevenson, 1996a). The important thing about such programs is that the individuals to whom they are addressed are ideally positioned to identify and assist adolescents who might engage in suicidal behavior.

Some have been concerned that education about suicide may produce the very behaviors it is designed to minimize. This is one version of the so-called "contagion theory," whereby it is thought that mentioning suicide is likely to infect the hearer with a tendency to engage in this behavior. In recent years, this concern has been associated with "cluster" or "copycat" suicides—that is, situations in which the example of others and/or reports in the media seem to have established models for troubled youth. In fact, no reliable evidence supports these views (Ross, 1985; see also Chapter 17 in this book).

What is critical for adolescents is not only exposure to knowledge about suicide or even to the suicidal behavior of others, but also anything they might perceive as giving approval to life-threatening behavior (Berman, 1988; Davidson & Gould, 1989). This exposure is precisely what is not found in education that is frank about the negative consequences of suicidal behavior. Such education teaches adolescents that *suicide is a permanent solution to a temporary problem.* It mobilizes resources for resolving problems in other ways and directs attention to the great pain that is a common and widespread legacy of adolescent suicide. Talking about suicide in a constructive educational format is far more likely to clear the air and minimize suicidal behavior than to suggest or encourage such behavior (Stillion & McDowell, 1996).

Crisis intervention programs offer a useful model of intervention to minimize suicidal behaviors in adolescents and others (Fairchild, 1986; Hatton & Valente, 1984). Such programs are directed precisely at those who are ambivalent about ending their lives. They encourage such persons to initiate telephone contact with the helping agency. Many of the volunteers who respond to such contacts are themselves adolescents who have been selected, trained, supervised, and supported in such work (Valente & Saunders, 1987). These volunteers offer a caring presence, an attentive companion during what is most often a limited period of crisis, a helper who can evaluate needs and aid in identifying alternative strategies for resolving problems, and a guide to additional resources for further assistance.

One area of adolescent suicide that is not well understood has to do with those who are left behind when someone completes a suicide (Valente & Sellers, 1986). Grief following the suicide of an adolescent is likely to be intense. This applies to all who are so bereaved but especially to adolescent peers: "Adolescent suicide is a particularly toxic form of death for peers who are left behind" (Mauk & Weber, 1991, p. 115). Adolescent peer bereavement is frequently complicated by feelings of guilt, rejection, frustration, anger, and failure. Quite often, it is also overlaid by societal disapproval, labeling, and stigma—all of which add to the burdens of grief and mourning. Adolescents who endure such experiences deserve sensitivity, care, and sup-

Adolescents, guns, and violence—a lethal mixture.

port in their bereavement. They should also be helped to celebrate and commemorate the life of their deceased friend (Rubel, 1999). Postvention programs, designed to address the specific needs of early and middle adolescents (Hill & Foster, 1996) or later adolescents in college settings (Rickgarn, 1994, 1996), are useful both as interventions after a suicide or other traumatic death and as forward-looking preventive efforts designed to minimize self-destructive behavior in the future.

Homicide and Adolescents

Like suicide, homicide is a major cause of death among adolescents, one that has been increasing in relative significance in recent years and one characterized by significant gender and ethnic differences. In 1999, homicide was only the fourteenth leading cause of death for the population as a whole, but it remained the second leading cause of death for middle and late adolescents. In terms of absolute numbers, there were 4,998 homicide deaths in 1999 in our society among individuals 15 to 24 years of age—almost 30 percent of the total number of such deaths in the entire country that year in a group that represents less than 14 percent of the total population (Hoyert et al., 2001).

During the period from 1960 to 1990, the United States experienced a tripling or quadrupling of homicide rates among middle and late adolescents overall. In addition, homicide rates were significantly higher for males as contrasted with females in this age group, and for African Americans as contrasted with Caucasian Americans. In other words, like suicide, *homicide is far more a male than a female phenomenon*—by almost a 6:1 ratio. However, unlike suicide, *homicide is far more an experience of African Americans than Caucasian Americans.*

Since 1991, there has been a downward trend in homicide deaths in the United States for the population as a whole (see Chapter 4). Nevertheless, in 1999 homicide remained the leading cause of death for African-American males 15 to 24 years of age, and the second leading cause of death for African-American females in the same age group. From an international standpoint, youth homicide rates are far higher in the United States than in any other country in the world (Fingerhut & Kleinman, 1989).

Homicide among adolescents is complex in both its implications and its origins (Busch et al., 1990). Homicide and other forms of trauma have negative effects on a variety of adolescent populations. Foremost among these are the people who are killed, the *primary victims* of the violence (some of whom may be "innocent bystanders," such as the two girls in the vignette near the beginning of this chapter). In addition, adolescent homicide can have negative effects on a broad range of *secondary victims*, such as relatives, friends, those who witness such violence, and even perpetrators of homicides themselves (Shakoor & Chalmers, 1991). This experience may be especially significant for the individuation and developmental tasks of surviving adolescents (Bradach & Jordan, 1995).

Homicide is a phenomenon especially (although not exclusively) prevalent in urban settings (Ropp et al., 1992). As a general rule, most perpetrators and victims of adolescent homicide are likely to come from the same ethnic or racial background, leading to the observation that this type of death is primarily intramural in character (Barrett, 1996). Firearms are involved in the majority of homicide deaths (Fingerhut et al., 1991). In each of these respects, homicide involving adolescents is essentially an extreme form of violence undertaken or experienced by adolescents in their own homes, schools, or communities (APA, 1993; National Research Council, 1993). Dysfunctional home environments along with violent communities beset by gang and drug-induced criminal activities are settings of real and chronic danger for many poor urban youth in American society (Kozol, 1995). The interplay between homicide and social structure is apparent in reports of lethal violence in the Latino community in Chicago (Block, 1993) and in declining rates of both homicide and suicide resulting from restrictive licensing of handguns in the District of Columbia (Loftin et al., 1991).

Adolescent homicide involving middle-class, socially advantaged, suburban, Caucasian Americans (including females) has recently been brought to public attention by media coverage of school shootings in our society. For example, many Americans are aware that schoolchildren killed other schoolchildren and teachers in late 1997 in Pearl, Mississippi, and Paducah, Kentucky; in 1998 in Jonesboro, Arkansas, Springfield, Oregon, and Edinboro, Pennsylvania; in April of 1999 at Columbine High School in Littleton, Colorado; and in March of 2001 at Santee High School in Santee, California. These are, of course, only a few of the most publicized incidents of this type. However, these events are relatively rare and do not take away from the fact that schools are among the safest places for children in our society. What they do point out is that even in such settings death can intrude in ugly ways.

In fact, it is urban, African-American and Hispanic-American males who are most at risk for becoming perpetrators or victims of adolescent homicide. In the words of Holinger and colleagues (1994, p. 182), "Youth homicide most often involves poverty and the apparently related interpersonal, domestic, and gang-related violence; victims and perpetrators share similar characteristics. Character disorders (e.g., impulse control, sociopathic problems) appear common to both victims and perpetrators of youth homicide." One important feature of adolescent homicide is that it typically occurs in contexts of peer and social influence (Barrett, 1996). Violent adults often act alone; violent adolescents usually act in groups. In some adolescent peer groups, violent behavior seems to be accepted, encouraged, and even regarded as a kind of rite of passage into the group.

The far-reaching implications of adolescent homicide in many communities in America have led some (for example, Fingerhut & Kleinman, 1989; Sullivan, 1991) to conclude that such homicide should be regarded not principally as a criminal justice issue but rather as *a public health crisis.* Barrett's (1996) review of attempts to explain adolescent homicide revealed them to be as numerous as the multitude of economic, political, racial, sex role, and other factors that appear to be associated with these behaviors. Such explanations include the disputed claim that there is a subculture within some African-American ghetto communities that models and sanctions violence; "black rage" theories that violence results from inadequate ability on the part of younger, nonwhite males to control impulses and cope with anger arising from economic deprivation, poverty, and discrimination; the ready availability of alcohol, drugs, and cheap handguns in America; and the failures of many social institutions, often coupled with what appears to be lack of interest in or a punitive attitude toward "difficult" adolescents.

These and other explanations for the startling level of homicide among American adolescents go beyond our scope in this book. Clearly, there is much that American society and its death system need to do to reduce levels of violence among adolescents and to bring down both the number and rate of homicide deaths in this group. In light of the complexities of both adolescent homicide and suicide, no simple solution is likely to be found. Holinger and colleagues (1994) synthesized their research on suicide and homicide among adolescents in four central recommendations: (1) gun control to limit the ready availability of firearms; (2) public education concerning the origins of these behaviors, together with what is already known about treatment and prevention strategies; (3) better training of professionals; and (4) more and better research on etiology and treatment. Barrett (1996) proposed similar recommendations, along with a multilevel program of empowerment on the part of religious institutions and local communities; renewed assumption of responsibility on the part of African-American and Hispanic-American adult males; active involvement by parents and educational institutions in the constructive socialization of youth; systematic education about the risk of lethal confrontations and the development of skills in conflict management; reformation of correctional systems; and advocacy of policies of social justice to ameliorate poverty and social distress.

Helping Adolescents Cope with Death and Bereavement

Adolescents can be helped in their efforts to cope with death through education and preparation prior to the fact (both while they are adolescents and in their earlier childhood) and through support and constructive intervention at the time of and after a death.

Education and Prior Preparation

Parents and other adults influence adolescent coping with death through the foundations they lay down in childhood and the environments they help to create in which adolescents function. Open lines of communication, sharing of thoughts and feelings, role modeling, and other constructive socialization processes enable adolescents to feel secure in themselves and to find satisfaction in the rewards of living, even as they also take account of issues related to loss and death.

McNeil (1986) suggested the following guidelines for adult communications with adolescents about death:

1. Take the lead in heightened awareness of an adolescent's concerns about death and in openness to discussing whatever he or she wishes to explore.
2. Listen actively and perceptively, with special attention to the feelings that appear to underlie what the adolescent is saying.
3. Accept the adolescent's feelings as real, important, and normal.
4. Use supportive responses that reflect acceptance and understanding of what the adolescent is trying to say.
5. Project a belief in the worth of the adolescent by resisting the temptation to solve his or her problems and by conveying an effort to help the adolescent find his or her own solutions.
6. Take time to enjoy the company of the adolescent and to provide frequent opportunities for talking together.

Communications of this sort can be supplemented by proactive programs of death education in secondary schools (for example, Crase & Crase, 1984; Rosenthal, 1986; Stevenson & Stevenson, 1996a) and at the college level (for example, Corr, 1978). An extensive body of death-related literature is directed toward and can be helpful to middle school, high school, and other young readers (see Box 13.5 and Appendix B; see also Lamers, 1986). Also, principles set forth in literature for adults about children and death (as suggested in Chapter 12) may be relevant to adolescents, with suitable modifications, and there is literature for adults that deals directly with adolescents and death (for example, Corr & Balk, 1996; Corr & McNeil, 1986). In all programs of education and support for adolescents, careful attention must be paid to the goals that one seeks to achieve and to the needs and experiences of adolescents. In her account of processes in designing a course on death, dying, and bereavement for adolescents, Rosenthal (1986) advised educators to make decisions about possible topics, objectives, materials, methods, and evaluation procedures in terms of three primary aspects of death-related education for adolescents: information, self-awareness, and skills for helping. The important thing is to reach out and make constructive contacts with vulnerable adolescents before they become isolated and alienated.

Support and Assistance after a Death

After the death of Diana Princess of Wales in 1997, one father is reported to have told one of her son's classmates: "It will be your duty never to mention her. . . . You must pretend that nothing has happened and just carry on" (Andersen, 1998, p. 250). This advice is foolish and unhelpful. It can be contrasted with a constructive program that helps bereaved adolescents to obtain accurate information about a loss and begin the process of interpreting and integrating that loss into their ongoing lives; identify affective and other responses to a death, express their feelings in safe and manageable ways, and

Box 13.5 Selected Literature for Adolescents about Death, Dying, and Bereavement

Annotated descriptions and complete bibliographical information are provided in Appendix B for the following 36 books and 22 others arranged under headings for middle school and high school readers.

About life-threatening illness and confronting death as a young person:

Barnouw, D., & Van der Stroom, G. (Eds.). (1989). *The Diary of Anne Frank: The Critical Edition.*

Deaver, J. R. (1988). *Say Goodnight, Gracie.*

Girard, L. W. (1991). *Alex, the Kid with AIDS.*

Gunther, J. (1949). *Death Be Not Proud: A Memoir.*

Hughes, M. (1984). *Hunter in the Dark.*

Maple, M. (1992). *On the Wings of a Butterfly: A Story about Life and Death.*

Paterson, K. (1977). *Bridge to Terabithia.*

Richter, E. (1986). *Losing Someone You Love: When a Brother or Sister Dies.*

Wiener, L. S., Best, A., & Pizzo, P. A. (Comps.). (1994). *Be a Friend: Children Who Live with HIV Speak.*

About suicide in adolescence:

Arrick, F. (1980). *Tunnel Vision.*

Geller, N. (1987). *The Last Teenage Suicide.*

Klagsbrun, F. (1976). *Too Young to Die: Youth and Suicide.*

About experiencing the death of a parent, grandparent, or other adult:

Agee, J. (1969). *A Death in the Family.*

Blume, J. (1981). *Tiger Eyes.*

Brisson, P. (1999). *Sky Memories.*

Cleaver, V., & Cleaver, B. (1970). *Grover.*

Craven, M. (1973). *I Heard the Owl Call My Name.*

Dragonwagon, C. (1990). *Winter Holding Spring.*

Farley, C. (1975). *The Garden Is Doing Fine.*

Fox, P. (1995). *The Eagle Kite.*

Greenberg, J. (1979). *A Season In-Between.*

Lewis, C. S. (1976). *A Grief Observed.*

Little, J. (1984). *Mama's Going to Buy You a Mockingbird.*

Mann, P. (1977). *There Are Two Kinds of Terrible.*

Martin, A. M. (1986). *With You and Without You.*

Tolstoy, L. (1960). *The Death of Ivan Ilych and Other Stories.*

About loss, coping, and death-related education for adolescents:

Bode, J. (1993). *Death Is Hard to Live With: Teenagers and How They Cope with Death.*

Heegaard, M. E. (1990). *Coping with Death and Grief.*

McCaleb, J. (1998). *Our Hero, Freebird: An Organ Donor's Story.*

O'Toole, D. (1995). *Facing Change: Falling Apart and Coming Together Again in the Teen Years.*

Rofes, E. E. (Ed.), and the Unit at Fayerweather Street School. (1985). *The Kids' Book about Death and Dying, by and for Kids.*

Romond, J. L. (1989). *Children Facing Grief: Letters from Bereaved Brothers and Sisters.*

Rudin, C. (1998). *Children's Books about the Holocaust: A Selective Annotated Bibliography.*

Scrivani, M. (1991). *When Death Walks In.*

Shura, M. F. (1988). *The Sunday Doll.*

Traisman, E. S., & Sieff, J. (Comps.). (1995). *Flowers for the Ones You've Known: Unedited Letters from Bereaved Teens.*

(continues)

Box 13.5 (cont.) Selected Literature for Adolescents about Death, Dying, and Bereavement

Additional information about death-related literature for middle school and high school readers, as well as sources from which books and other items can be purchased, are provided by:

Boulden Publishing, P.O. Box 1186, Weaverville, CA 96093-1186; 800-238-8433; fax 530-623-5525; www.bouldenpub.com (offers Boulden publications exclusively).

Centering Corporation, P.O. Box 4600, Omaha, NE 68104-0600; 402-553-1200; fax 402-553-0507; www.centering.org; e-mail to J1200@aol.com (offers their own and other publishers' works).

Compassion Books, 477 Hannah Branch Road, Burnsville, NC 28714; 828-675-5909; fax 828-675-9687; www.compassionbooks.com; e-mail to Heal2grow@aol.com (offers their own and other publishers' works). ■

find their own ways of coping; take active roles in funeral practices and commemorate losses in constructive ways; and find ways to go on with healthy and productive living (Fitzgerald, 2000).

Counseling interventions with adolescents should be guided by two principles: (1) provide a safe environment in which the adolescent can explore difficulties; and (2) assist with the process of addressing the developmental and situational tasks that are often closely interrelated in adolescent bereavement (Calvin & Smith, 1986). This latter principle means that it must be the adolescent, not the counselor, who works out acceptable solutions to challenges in his or her own life. Educators can assist when they themselves understand the nature of bereavement, grief, and mourning. More detailed guidance for counselors is provided by a number of authors (Balk, 1984; Fitzgerald, 1998; Floerchinger, 1991; Gray, 1988; McNeil et al., 1991; Valentine, 1996; Zinner, 1985). Programs of postvention (described in Chapter 12 for children) have been developed for adolescents at both the secondary (Hill & Foster, 1996) and postsecondary (Rickgarn, 1994, 1996) levels.

Adolescents who are unwilling to talk to parents, counselors, or other adults may find it more congenial to address their death-related concerns in the context of a support group populated by peers with similar experiences (Tedeschi, 1996). By establishing a community of bereaved peers, groups of this sort dispel the stigma of being "different" or marked out by a death. This overcoming of isolation from others is important in all bereavement, but especially so in a developmental era like adolescence, in which struggles with identity and the need for peer validation is so characteristic. Support groups can provide important information to bereaved adolescents, offer help with tensions involving containing and expressing emotions, assist in confronting life's hard lessons, and confirm the fundamental message that it is only natural to experience grief in connection with a significant loss.

Many adolescents recognize that there can be positive outcomes even in the wake of intense tragedy, such as a deeper appreciation of life, greater caring

Expressing grief and finding support can help a bereaved adolescent.

for and stronger emotional bonds with others, and greater emotional strength (Oltjenbruns, 1991). Adults can help to encourage such outcomes in adolescents and can learn important lessons from them in their own lives.

Summary

In this chapter, we explored interactions between adolescents and death within the contemporary American death system. We noted how the distinctive developmental tasks of early, middle, and late adolescence have a direct bearing on how adolescents relate to death. These tasks influence encounters with death among adolescents (we noted that adolescence is an era characterized by low death rates especially associated with human-induced deaths resulting from accidents, homicide, and suicide) and attitudes of adolescents toward death (which generally combine a strong emphasis on the present and a tendency to resist recognition of the personal significance of death). We described issues that confront adolescents who are coping with life-threatening illness and dying, as well as those encountered by adolescents who are coping with bereavement and grief. We gave special attention to issues related to suicide, homicide, and violence in adolescent life. Finally, we suggested ways to help adolescents who are coping with death and bereavement.

Questions for Review and Discussion

1. The vignette near the beginning of this chapter describes three shocking encounters with death at Central High School. Did you have any experiences like these during your high school years? If so, what did the administrators, teachers, parents, and other students at your school do to cope with those experiences?
2. What sorts of death-related losses have you experienced in your own adolescence, and what did they mean to you?
3. During your own adolescence, have you been seriously ill or have you experienced an important loss? If so, what were your most significant concerns about that illness or loss? Or perhaps you know an adolescent who has been in such a situation. If so, what were his or her most significant concerns?

4. If you were asked to recommend to adults how they could help adolescents cope with death, what would you suggest? How would your recommendations differ (if at all) for different adolescents or different losses?

Suggested Readings

General resources on adolescents, their development, and death include:

Balk, D. E. (1995). *Adolescent Development: Early through Late Adolescence.*

Corr, C. A., & Balk, D. E. (Eds.). (1996). *Handbook of Adolescent Death and Bereavement.*

Corr, C. A., & McNeil, J. N. (Eds.). (1986). *Adolescence and Death.*

Kalergis, M. M. (1998). *Seen and Heard: Teenagers Talk about Their Lives.*

Offer, D., Ostrov, E., & Howard, K. I. (1981). *The Adolescent: A Psychological Self-Portrait.*

For life-threatening illness in adolescence, consult:

Krementz, J. (1989). *How It Feels to Fight for Your Life.*

Pendleton, E. (Comp.). (1980). *Too Old to Cry, Too Young to Die.*

Bereavement and grief in adolescence are explored in the following:

Balk, D. E. (Ed.). (1991b). Death and adolescent bereavement [Special issue]. *Journal of Adolescent Research.*

Baxter, G., Bennett, L., & Stuart, W. (1989). *Adolescents and Death: Bereavement Support Groups for Secondary School Students* (2nd ed.).

Fairchild, T. N. (Ed.). (1986). *Crisis Intervention Strategies for School-Based Helpers.*

Fitzgerald, H. (1998). *Grief at School: A Guide for Teachers and Counselors.*

Fitzgerald, H. (2000). *The Grieving Teen: A Guide for Teenagers and Their Friends.*

Fry, V. L. (1995). *Part of Me Died, Too: Stories of Creative Survival among Bereaved Children and Teenagers.*

Grollman, E. A. (1993). *Straight Talk about Death for Teenagers: How to Cope with Losing Someone You Love.*

Teaching adolescents about death or helping them to cope with death is examined in:

Stevenson, R. G. (Ed.). (2001). *What Will We Do? Preparing a School Community to Cope with Crises* (2nd ed.).

Stevenson, R. G., & Stevenson, E. P. (Eds.). (1996b). *Teaching Students about Death: A Comprehensive Resource for Educators and Parents.*

Suicide and life-threatening behavior among adolescents and children are explored in the following:

Klagsbrun, F. (1976). *Too Young to Die: Youth and Suicide.*

Lester, D. (1993). *The Cruelest Death: The Enigma of Adolescent Suicide.*

Orbach, I. (1988). *Children Who Don't Want to Live: Understanding and Treating the Suicidal Child.*

Peck, M. L., Farberow, N. L., & Litman, R. E. (Eds.). (1985). *Youth Suicide.*

Pfeffer, C. R. (Ed.). (1986). *The Suicidal Child.*

Pfeffer, C. R. (Ed.). (1989). *Suicide among Youth: Perspectives on Risk and Prevention.*

Rubel, B. (1999). *But I Didn't Say Goodbye: For Parents and Professionals Helping Child Suicide Survivors.*

Stillion, J. M., & McDowell, E. E. (1996). *Suicide across the Life Span: Premature Exits* (2nd ed.).

InfoTrac College Edition
For more information, explore the InfoTrac College Edition at **http://www.infotrac-college.com/Wadsworth**

Enter search terms: ADOLESCENTS AND DEATH, CAUSES OF DEATH IN ADOLESCENCE, DEVELOPMENTAL TASKS IN ADOLESCENCE, HOMICIDE AND ADOLESCENTS, SUICIDE AND ADOLESCENTS.

Chapter Fourteen

ADULTS

FOR MANY ADULTS IN AMERICA, JANUARY 1, 1996, was an important day. On that date, the first members of the so-called Baby Boom generation—individuals born in or after 1946—turned 50 years old. In and of itself, age 50 has no special developmental importance, but it is often perceived as culturally significant in our society. Perhaps what is important developmentally is that this unusually large generational cohort is now moving well into middle adulthood. What will be even more important from death-related perspectives and many other points of view will be when these "Boomers" move into older adulthood.

Our task in this chapter is to examine interactions with death not only for the Baby Boomers but also for all of the adults in our society. *Adulthood*—regarded by many as the "prime of life"—is a lengthy era in human development filling some 40 to 45 years from the close of adolescence to the beginning of "old age" or the era of the "elderly." As a result, it may be most useful to think of human adults both in themselves and as *middle-escents* or *members of the sandwich generation*—individuals situated in terms of developmental eras between their younger counterparts (children and adolescents), on one hand, and their older predecessors (the elderly), on the other.

Despite notable differences among themselves, adults share many issues arising from new elements in family relationships, work roles, and an evolving set of death-related concerns. Nevertheless, because a large number of variables impact the lives of adults during their lengthy adulthood, and because many developmental aspects of adulthood have not been well or broadly studied, it is wise to be cautious in making generalizations about adult humans and their experiences.

In this chapter, one woman writes about the death of her father. Then, we consider the distinctive developmental tasks of young and middle adults; typical encounters with death in American society during the adult years, death-related attitudes during this developmental era, issues related to adults who are coping with life-threatening illness and dying, issues related to adults who are coping with bereavement and grief, and special issues concerning HIV infection and AIDS. We have offered principles for helping adults cope with dying, death, and bereavement throughout this book in appropriate topical chapters. ■

A Christmas Letter, 1998

Dear Friends,

This year, instead of just sending a store-bought Christmas card, writing a Christmas poem, or telling a Christmas story, I decided to write and share a very special LIFE story. This is a real departure for me, but the daughter and the writer in me says this is a story that needs to be told.

To begin this LIFE story fairly, I need to go back to a time a little over three years ago. On May 7, 1995, you might remember my mother died after a long and often difficult struggle with emphysema. In June of that same year my daughter was born, although at that time she wasn't yet my daughter. It wasn't until Halloween that I received permission to go to China and complete her long-awaited adoption. As I left for China, I felt both joy and trepidation for the journey I was about to embark upon, together with concern for my father. I had no idea just how long to plan for my China adventure. How long would it be before I could return home with a beautiful bundle of joy and life in my arms to introduce to her grandfather, who seemed to be such a lonely traveler as he wandered the dark roads of his grief following Mom's death?

Thanksgiving became our target return date. Because my sister and brother-in-law lived in Hong Kong, we could stay with them the extra time to make that date work. My ulterior motives for choosing that date were both to give Dad something to look forward to and to remind him that even in times of pain there are still things for which to be truly thankful.

So much has happened since that Thanksgiving day. Immediately as we (Tian Tian and I) disembarked the plane and Dad looked into her eyes, we became a special, albeit unusual, and complete family unit. We would never again be a 40+-year-old single, professional, self-employed, independent daughter; a lovable (but sometimes gruff), independent, 80+-year-old, grieving widower and father, grandfather, and great-grandfather who sometimes found himself questioning the reason to live; or an abandoned now 5-month-old little girl from a country that didn't seem to know how to love or respect little girls. From that day forward, our lives became entwined in ways I didn't know were possible. Dad reclaimed his spark for living; somehow that little girl reminded him to open his eyes and see life again in all its glory.

It is hard to believe looking back that it could be humanly possible to fit all the flurry of activity and experiences that we have had together into just three years. We have been continually challenged by life's lessons and asked to learn from all of its teachable moments, good and bad. The last year has been the longest because it seems like we have continually been moving from one medical crisis to the next. It was around this time last year that it became clear to all of us that something had to change. It had become too hard on Tian Tian and me to live between houses. Dad had his and we had ours, but neither were really suitable for all of us to live in together. Besides that, Dad suddenly announced that he wanted to live and die in a house with a view of the water. So we bought a new house together. As if my hands weren't full already with a then 2-and-a-half-year-old, an 83-year-old, my private practice, and my dog. Now I added packing up and selling two houses, and unpacking and organizing a new house (with two households' worth of everything). We moved in the end of January and started painting, wallpapering, cleaning, and remodeling (while still living with Dad part time), and then in March, for his birthday, we had our official birthday, St. Patrick's Day, and open house party.

After that, we were officially a one-house family (except Dad's house still hasn't sold; mine sold in two days). It was great and I was looking forward to having another adult around for a long time. We got along so well and I think for the first time since Mom died it really felt like family again. We started making plans for how we were going to decorate for Christmas and what flowers we wanted blooming now and what we needed to plant for spring (Dad always loved his garden and, when he was able, loved gardening).

But I guess that wasn't to be. Shortly after we got him moved in here, all the medical stuff started up again, except this time it wasn't his heart or broken bones like last year. Instead, he developed a stricture in his esophagus and couldn't swallow—so he needed a gastrostomy tube and tube feedings. That, along with the intestinal yeast that he had continually battled for over two years, took all the strength he had left. The Dad I knew who most all of my life had been 6 feet, 4 inches tall and 220+ lbs. was reduced to a death weight of less than 100 lbs.

Even so, he kept battling until late August, when he apologized to me for being tired and just wanting to let go. That was after three hospital stays for either pneumonia or sepsis during summer. Finally, I asked him if he wanted to go home—after all, we chose the house we did because he wanted to live and die in a house with a view. He beamed all over when he said, "Could I?" By the end of the next day, my living room had been turned into a hospice room and Tian Tian and I had our roommate back. I had put my practice on hold a week earlier, so we just became homebodies.

That was about the time that a friend called. All he wanted was some pictures for his new book, but instead he got to hear my sad story. And God love him, he took it upon himself to do something I don't think I would have ever had the energy (or courage) to do. He put out the call to friends and colleagues in the Association for Death Education and Counseling. So many people responded. I was so touched and I want each and every one of you to know what an incredible gift your words, hugs, and warm wishes were. It was just about that time that I was really questioning if I had the strength to go on, but your energy helped me get through what turned out to be a very beautiful, proud, peaceful death.

Dad died on September 2nd, just about sunset, while I was playing Barbra Streisand's "Papa Can You Hear Me." Tian Tian was lying in bed with him while my eldest sister and I were sitting at his side. He simply just sighed and it was over. But then two of the most amazing things happened—Tian Tian suddenly announced (after I told her Granddad was dead) that "Granddad needs a go away tea party." So we had one. We put a pillow and TV tray on his tummy and ate chocolate kisses and drank orange pop out of her tea set (that he had bought for her). Then I told her I was going to give Granddad a bath and wash his hair. I asked if she wanted to help. She did and all went well until I turned him toward her and my sister, so I could wash his back, and his head flopped down right next to hers. Listening to her response was when I lost it: she reached up, lovingly kissed him on the nose, and said, "It's OK Granddad, all your boo boos are all gone now." In that instant, I knew that all my years of teaching, studying, and working with kids' grief had paid off. I had done good and we were going to get through this.

At some later date, the writer in me will have to write about this. The experience was so filled with stories, including Tian Tian trying out the caskets at the funeral home the next day. But right now I'm just glad to have found enough of my brain to write this much of this LIFE story as a THANK YOU note to each of you. I hope none of you mind being a part of a community thank you and Christmas letter. But I am practicing what I preach and being good to myself. Writing individual notes right now is more than I can handle. So this will have to do and soon I will try to touch base with you personally.

Margaret M. Metzgar & Tian Tian

Adults, Developmental Tasks, and Death

Adulthood is the longest single era in human development, extending from the early twenties to age 65. According to developmental theorists, this 40-year period includes two 20-year generational cohorts and two distinguishable eras: *young adulthood* (roughly ages 21 or 22 to 45) and *middle adulthood* or middle age (ages 45 to 65). According to Erikson (1963, 1968), the principal normative developmental task in young adulthood is to achieve *intimacy* (versus the danger of isolation), whereas the major developmental task of middle adulthood is *generativity* (versus the danger of stagnation or self-absorption).

In other words, adulthood is a period of exploring and exploiting the identity established in earlier stages of development through choices about one's lifestyle, relationships, and work (Kail & Cavanaugh, 2000; Newman &

Newman, 1999; Papalia et al., 1995). Decisions made in the vitality of young adulthood chart much of the remaining course of human life in terms of relationships, vocation, and lifestyle. Those decisions enable humans to know themselves in much fuller ways than were possible during adolescence. In middle age, one typically conserves and draws on personal, social, and vocational resources that were established earlier. The transition in midlife from young to middle adulthood can be focused on what is past and gone (youth and its distinctive opportunities), or it can lead to a renewed appreciation of life as one achieves a new understanding of one's self and determines how to live out the remainder of one's life. Once depicted as a tumultuous crisis, *the midlife transition* is now generally thought of as a more or less calm transition in which individual perceptions of responses to events are central (Hunter & Sundel, 1989).

One good example of professional success in early adulthood can be seen in the career of Michael Jordan. From his college years at the University of North Carolina until the announcement on January 13, 1999, of his retirement from being an active player in professional sports, Michael had a spectacular career in basketball. In sports, as a celebrity figure, and in the world of advertising, Michael earned untold riches. His personal life seems to have been equally satisfactory apart from the tragic murder of his father. Following retirement, his challenge was to find ways to avoid stagnation and self-absorption, and to continue to lead a meaningful and productive life. On September 26, 2001, Michael announced that he would pursue that challenge in part by reversing his retirement decision, returning as an active player for the Washington Wizards, and donating his first year's salary of $1 million to the relief efforts resulting from the terrorist attacks on America of September 11, 2001.

Within the broad division between early and middle adulthood, Levinson (1978) distinguished several "seasons" or qualitatively distinct eras in human development, with boundary zones, periods of transition, and characteristic issues. In *young adulthood*, this involves an early adult transition from pre-adulthood, a novice phase in which one enters the adult world and is involved in "forming a dream," an internal transition at about age 30, and a period of "settling down." Similarly, *middle adulthood* can be depicted in terms of another novice or introductory period, an internal transition around age 50, and a concluding period, followed by a further transition into old age or late adulthood. The boundary between young and middle adulthood for Levinson is the celebrated midlife transition, during which the individual reappraises the past and terminates young adulthood, modifies the life structure and initiates middle adulthood, and seeks to resolve four principal polarities: tensions between young/old, destruction/creation, masculine/feminine, and attachment/separateness.

It is only fair to note that much of the original research on adulthood was confined to male subjects. However, in a later, posthumously published study, Levinson (1996) reported results from detailed interviews with 45 women conducted in the period 1980–82. This study examined three groups of young adult women: homemakers, women with careers in the corporate-financial world, and women with careers in academia. As a result of this study, Levinson (1996, p. 36) concluded that the "alternating sequence of structure building-maintaining periods and transitional periods holds for both women and men."

This is the schema of developmental seasons he identified in earlier studies of male adults.

Gilligan (1982) was among the first prominent researchers to argue that the course of human development in females is likely to differ in significant ways from that of their male counterparts. For example, both male and female adults can find themselves caught between pressures from older and younger developmental cohorts (parents and children; see Margaret Metzgar's Christmas letter near the beginning of this chapter). However, responses to issues facing the sandwich generation can be expected to differ in important ways for males and females. For example, in situations involving care of an elderly relative or an ill child, adult males historically would mainly have been expected to provide economic and logistical support, whereas responsibility for practical hands-on care and nurturing would have been assigned to adult females. For many in this generation, this is still the case.

It has been argued that these traditional divisions of roles by gender are no longer accurate for many people in contemporary American society, in part because many women have assumed new responsibilities outside the home in the workforce. Nevertheless, significant differences are still likely to exist between men and women, resulting largely from the ongoing influence of gender splitting or differences in the social roles and responsibilities that are assigned to males and females. Many women who work outside the home are expected to assume a "second shift" or double burden in which men may help out more but do not generally assume responsibility for domestic chores and caregiving. Thus, Levinson (1996) concluded that thorough descriptions of adult life need to take into account both developmental and gender factors. The point is that common aspects in adult development may coexist with differences arising from gender, historical variables, and other factors.

Encounters with Death during Adulthood

Deaths and Death Rates among Adults

Adults between the ages of 25 and 64 make up just over half of the total population of the United States. In 1999, this group experienced 522,275 deaths (Hoyert et al., 2001), which is 21.8 percent of the total of nearly 2.4 million deaths in the U.S. that year. Table 14.1 provides numbers of deaths in 1999 according to ten-year age groupings from ages 25 to 64 by sex, race, and Hispanic origin. It is obvious that overall numbers of deaths rise rapidly throughout this 40-year period. Further, as shown in Table 14.2 an even steeper increase is found in preliminary death rates for young and middle adults, which rise by a factor of more than nine times during adulthood (from 108.3 deaths per 100,000 for those 25–34 years of age in 1999 to 1,021.8 for those 55–64 years of age). These patterns of rapid increase in numbers of deaths and death rates apply across the board to all segments of the adult population in our society: adults as a category, as well as male and female adults,

Table 14.1 Number of Deaths during Young and Middle Adulthood, by Age, Sex, Race, and Hispanic Origin: United States, 1999

	Ages 25–34			Ages 35–44		
	Both Sexes	Males	Females	Both Sexes	Males	Females
All races	41,066	28,276	12,790	89,256	57,118	32,138
Caucasian Americans, total[a]	29,400	20,549	8,851	65,607	42,914	22,693
Non-Hispanic Caucasian Americans	23,986	16,449	7,537	57,630	37,291	20,339
African Americans[a]	10,115	6,723	3,392	21,041	12,567	8,474
Hispanic Americans[b]	5,397	4,084	1,313	7,798	5,476	2,322
Asian or Pacific Island Americans[a]	906	586	320	1,581	992	589
Native Americans[a]	645	418	227	1,027	645	382

	Ages 45–54			Ages 55–64		
	Both Sexes	Males	Females	Both Sexes	Males	Females
All races	152,974	95,659	57,315	238,979	142,724	96,255
Caucasian Americans, total[a]	117,011	73,908	43,103	193,582	116,537	77,045
Non-Hispanic Caucasian Americans	106,808	67,151	39,657	180,793	108,692	72,101
African Americans[a]	31,759	19,298	12,461	39,476	22,769	16,707
Hispanic Americans[b]	9,876	6,497	3,379	12,319	7,490	4,829
Asian or Pacific Island Americans[a]	2,876	1,608	1,268	4,247	2,508	1,749
Native Americans[a]	1,328	845	483	1,674	920	754

[a]Race and Hispanic origin are reported separately on the death certificate.
[b]Includes all persons of Hispanic origin of any race.

SOURCE: Hoyert et al., 2001.

and Caucasian-American, Hispanic-American, African-American, Asian-American, and Native-American adults.

Notable features of changing mortality patterns in the United States during adulthood can be highlighted in three comparisons. First, middle adults die in much larger numbers and at higher rates than do young adults. In 1999, three times as many Americans died in middle age as in young adulthood. This

Table 14.2 Preliminary Death Rates (per 100,000) during Young and Middle Adulthood, by Age, Sex, Race, and Hispanic Origin: United States, 1999

	Ages 25–34			Ages 35–44		
	Both Sexes	Males	Females	Both Sexes	Males	Females
All races	108.3	150.2	66.9	199.2	256.7	142.5
Caucasian Americans, total[a]	96.6	134.6	58.4	177.6	231.5	123.3
Non-Hispanic Caucasian Americans	93.4	128.4	58.6	176.6	228.2	124.8
African Americans[a]	191.4	268.4	122.0	372.4	473.7	282.7
Hispanic Americans[b]	103.2	151.6	51.8	164.3	226.1	99.9
Asian or Pacific Island Americans[a]	49.1	68.5	32.2	85.3	112.8	60.4
Native Americans[a]	172.7	218.5	124.7	286.5	362.7	211.5
	Ages 45–54			**Ages 55–64**		
	Both Sexes	**Males**	**Females**	**Both Sexes**	**Males**	**Females**
All races	427.3	546.8	313.2	1,021.9	1,280.2	786.5
Caucasian Americans, total[a]	386.9	494.3	281.8	961.6	1,200.3	739.2
Non-Hispanic Caucasian Americans	387.0	491.7	284.5	972.2	1,208.1	751.0
African Americans[a]	808.6	1,082.4	580.9	1,683.2	2,244.1	1,255.4
Hispanic Americans[b]	339.0	456.4	226.8	733.9	963.0	536.0
Asian or Pacific Island Americans[a]	210.3	252.4	173.6	558.8	703.8	431.6
Native Americans[a]	518.3	682.3	365.0	1,130.2	1,321.8	960.4

[a]Race and Hispanic origin are reported separately on the death certificate.
[b]Includes all persons of Hispanic origin of any race.

SOURCE: Kochanek et al., 2001.

increase occurred in a middle-aged population that was more than 27 percent smaller than the population of young adults. Second, each successive ten-year cohort of adults experiences a larger number of deaths and a higher death rate. Third, the very high infant death rates for the population as a whole (discussed in Chapter 12) are not exceeded until the final ten-year cohort in middle adulthood (those 55–64 years of age).

Leading Causes of Death among Adults

Table 14.3 shows that the leading causes of death change in interesting ways with age during adulthood. For young adults (ages 25–44), the three leading causes of death in 1999 were accidents, cancer, and diseases of the heart—together representing nearly half of all deaths in this cohort—followed by suicide and HIV disease. Homicide and suicide are relatively more significant during the first half of this era (ages 25–34), whereas cancer and heart disease

Table 14.3 Preliminary Number of Deaths and Death Rates (per 100,000) for the Ten Leading Causes of Death during Young and Middle Adulthood, Both Sexes, All Races: United States, 1999

	Ages 25–44			Ages 45–64		
Rank	Cause of Death	Number	Rate	Cause of Death	Number	Rate
...	All causes	130,340	157.5	All causes	391,994	662.2
1	Accidents (unintentional injuries)	26,836	32.4	Malignant neoplasms	135,748	229.3
	Motor vehicle accidents	13,531	16.4			
	All other accidents	13,304	16.1			
2	Malignant neoplasms	20,734	25.1	Diseases of the heart	99,035	167.3
3	Diseases of the heart	16,542	20.0	Accidents (unintentional injuries)	18,799	31.8
				Motor vehicle accidents	8,347	14.1
				All other accidents	10,451	17.7
4	Intentional self-harm (suicide)	11,496	13.9	Cerebrovascular diseases	15,210	25.7
5	Human immunodeficiency virus disease (HIV)	8,905	10.8	Chronic lower respiratory diseases	14,395	24.3
6	Assault (homicide)	7,417	9.0	Diabetes mellitus	13,826	23.4
7	Chronic liver disease and cirrhosis	3,696	4.5	Chronic liver disease and cirrhosis	11,989	20.3
8	Cerebrovascular diseases	3,417	3.8	Intentional self-harm (suicide)	7,924	13.4
9	Diabetes mellitus	2,512	3.0	Human immunodeficiency virus disease (HIV)	4,992	8.4
10	Influenza and pneumonia	1,389	1.7	Septicemia	4,400	7.4
...	All other causes	27,666	33.4	All other causes	65,676	111.0

SOURCE: Kochanek et al., 2001.

become more important during the second half of the era (ages 35–44). This shift signals a decline during young adulthood in the relative significance of human-induced deaths (those arising from accidents, homicide, and suicide) and a parallel rise in the relative significance of degenerative diseases (such as cancer and heart disease)—trends that continue throughout the remainder of the human life course.

During middle adulthood (ages 45–65), cancer and heart disease accounted for almost 60 percent of all deaths in our society in 1999, followed at a great distance by accidents and a series of degenerative diseases (cerebrovascular diseases, chronic lower respiratory diseases, diabetes mellitus, and chronic liver disease and cirrhosis). Among cancer deaths in adults, leading causes for both sexes are cancer of the respiratory and intrathoracic organs (lung cancer), followed by prostate and colon/rectum cancer for males and by breast and colon/rectum cancer for females.

Rates for accidental death throughout early and middle adulthood are lower than those in adolescence, but other forms of accidents than those involving motor vehicles become steadily more significant as causes of death throughout adulthood. Death rates for homicide decline during adulthood, although death rates from suicide remain roughly steady.

During the 1980s, a new factor appeared in encounters with death—human immunodeficiency virus (HIV) and acquired immune deficiency syndrome (AIDS)—and soon became especially significant during young adulthood and middle age (see Chapter 20). By 1994, HIV infection was the leading cause of death for young adults 25 to 44 years of age, accounting for some 30,260 deaths (Singh et al., 1995). By 1999, however, HIV infection had fallen to become the fifth leading cause of death during young adulthood, with less than 9,000 deaths (Hoyert et al., 2001). That decline of more than 70 percent in deaths in this age group in a five-year period is due to many factors, such as better education about HIV and AIDS, more effective prevention measures, and better care for infected persons. In 1999, HIV infection was also the ninth leading cause of death among middle adults, with about 5,000 deaths.

Two Variables in Deaths of Adults: Gender and Race

Tables 14.1 and 14.2 indicate contrasts by gender and race in number of deaths and death rates among adults in the United States. For gender, the main difference is that adult males die far more frequently and at much higher rates than females do in our society. Both male and female young adults (ages 25–44) experience significant numbers of deaths from accidents, HIV infection, and homicide, but males are more prone to heart disease and suicide than females, whereas the influence of cancer as a cause of death appears much earlier among females than males. As males and females proceed into middle adulthood (ages 45–64), degenerative diseases become more prominent as leading causes of death in both groups.

In both young and middle adults, there are a much larger *number* of deaths among Caucasian Americans than among African Americans, Hispanic Americans, Asian and Pacific Island Americans, and Native Americans. However, African Americans (and, to a lesser extent, Native Americans) experience much higher death *rates* than Caucasian Americans. In all of these racial and cultural groups, males greatly exceed females in both absolute numbers of deaths and death rates. In terms of causes of death, HIV infection and homicide are more typical causes of death among African Americans, whereas suicide is more prevalent among Caucasian Americans.

Attitudes toward Death among Adults

Some features of adult encounters with death are particularly significant in shaping attitudes toward death—especially during middle adulthood. The years of the late twenties and early thirties are likely to be times of more stability in self-understanding compared to adolescence. As a result, anxiety about one's own death and defenses against that realization appear to be a less prominent feature of young adulthood than of adolescence. Of course, this may change if new or different encounters with death generate new threats and anxieties. Also, general patterns of death-related attitudes begin to alter for many persons in our society as they move into middle adulthood.

For example, typical encounters with death during adulthood are likely to increase as the next-older generation begins to experience higher death rates. The deaths of Margaret Metzgar's mother and father described in the vignette near the beginning of this chapter are examples of events that are likely to confront a middle-aged adult in the United States today. This, together with issues arising from their developing children, is what is meant when we speak of the *sandwich generation*, a group that often feels trapped by new and different pressures arising simultaneously from both the older and younger generations that surround it on either developmental front.

In the case of younger adults, death-related worries and concerns are most likely to relate to the deaths of others. However, as one progresses developmentally and/or, more significantly, as one learns from one's own life experiences, one typically encounters a newly personalized sense of mortality (Doka, 1988). This recognition occurs particularly in two ways: through encounters with the deaths of parents, peers, siblings, and spouses, often for the first time in one's life and especially as a result of natural causes; and through one's own newly emerging realization of oneself as a mortal creature who could die at any time and who will die someday.

Peers, siblings, or a spouse can die at any time, but in adulthood it is more likely that they will die of natural causes (such as heart attack, cancer, or stroke). When that happens, their adult survivors cannot easily dismiss death as the result of ill fortune or external forces—both of which might, in principle, be avoided. Similarly, when adults begin to sense the limits of their bodily capacities or to recognize problems associated with aging or lifestyle, their personal sense of invulnerability must diminish. At this time adults begin to make a retrospective assessment of their achievements, to realize that they have already passed through half or two-thirds of average life expectancy, to appreciate that the future does not stretch endlessly ahead without any real possibility of a horizon or end point, and to entertain prospective thoughts of retirement and eventual death. This can lead to a reappraisal of personal values and priorities, which may result in an enriched capacity for love and enjoyment and a richer, more philosophical sense of meaning in one's life—or it may have less positive results (Jacques, 1965). In short, the implications of death play a prominent role in the reevaluation of life and self that characterizes middle age.

As young and middle-aged adults turn to thoughts of their own death, they are likely to think of what that will mean for their children, family members, or significant others, as well as for the vocational and other creative projects that have occupied so much of their time and energy since becoming adults.

To all of this, HIV infection and AIDS have added the lethal specter of an infectious disease, but one whose shadow has changed significantly in form and power during the last half of the 1990s. Someone once said to us: "There was a world before the discovery of AIDS, and there is a world after the discovery of AIDS. But things will never be the same after the discovery of AIDS." If so, then life is irrevocably altered for adults and many others. Moreover, the Desert Storm war in Kuwait and Iraq in 1991, ongoing tensions and hostilities with Iraq, the assignment of members of the American military to peacekeeping duties in various portions of the former Yugoslavia, the act of domestic terrorist involved in the bombing of the federal building in Oklahoma City in 1995, the terrorist attacks on the World Trade Center and the Pentagon in September 2001, and subsequent warfare in Afghanistan, each had a special impact on many mature adults. The older reservists who were called up for various war or peacekeeping situations because of their special skills were in a different situation from many younger volunteers who were already serving on active duty. And the hundreds of firefighters and police officers who lost their lives at the World Trade Center or who worked as rescuers there were all adults in their active middle years.

In recent years, in other words, a number of new death-related perils have been presented to young and middle adults. Some (such as issues related to the nuclear threat or to the environment) are shared with all who inhabit the planet. Others (such as those involving war, alcoholism, or drug abuse) apply mainly to individuals in specific localities or roles. Still others (such as the deaths of significant age-mates from natural causes and the implications of an emerging sense of personal mortality) are particularly relevant to those in the long middle years of life. In general, however, one might say that death-related events often confront young adults with frustration and disappointment, even as they take on a very personal tone for middle adults with interpersonal implications for their loved ones.

Adults Who Are Coping with Life-Threatening Illness and Dying

Coping as a Young Adult

If the basic developmental task in young adulthood is that of achieving intimacy, then, as Cook and Oltjenbruns (1998) suggested, life-threatening illness and dying challenge the needs of young adults to develop intimate relationships, express their sexuality, and obtain realistic support for their goals and future plans.

"*Intimacy* involves the ability to be open, supportive, and close with another person, without fear of losing oneself in the process. The establishment of intimacy with a significant other implies the capacity for mutual empathy, the ability to help meet one another's needs, the acceptance of each other's limitations, and the commitment to care deeply for the other person" (Cook & Oltjenbruns, 1998, p. 329). In short, intimacy depends on a sense of one's own identity and trust in the other.

To achieve quality in living, young adults who are seriously ill or dying still need to pursue and maintain intimacy. In general, an inability to develop intimate relationships results in isolation. As we saw in Chapter 6, abandonment and isolation are the principal concerns of individuals who are coping with dying. Thus, life-threatening illness and dying directly challenge the main developmental task of young adulthood.

Young adults seek to develop intimate relationships with others primarily through reciprocal self-disclosure. This process may, but need not, be compromised when young adults are ill or dying. In fact, intimacy is a critical element in the lives of young adults who are seriously ill or dying—for themselves, for their family members and friends, and for their professional caregivers. When there is difficulty in achieving or maintaining intimacy, all concerned must reexamine barriers (such as death-related fears or lack of information about the person's disease) and consider what may be gained by renewed efforts to risk sharing in a pressured and precious time.

Many couples express their intimacy most naturally through *sexuality*. Not confined to sexual intercourse, sexuality includes a broad range of thoughts, feelings, and behaviors. Such expressions of sexuality in the lives of seriously ill and dying adults should be fostered (Lamb, 2001). To do so may involve decisions about grooming or dressing, a gentle touch or caress, open discussion of physical and psychological needs, and other aspects of feeling positive about oneself. Nonjudgmental attitudes, privacy, and efforts to adapt to changes brought about by disease and treatment (for example, mastectomy or colostomy) can all be helpful in this area.

For young adults, a life-threatening illness may threaten *goals and future plans* in many areas, such as getting married, having children, and pursuing educational or vocational aspirations. If so, young adults must reevaluate their plans and determine what may be appropriate in their new situation. They may

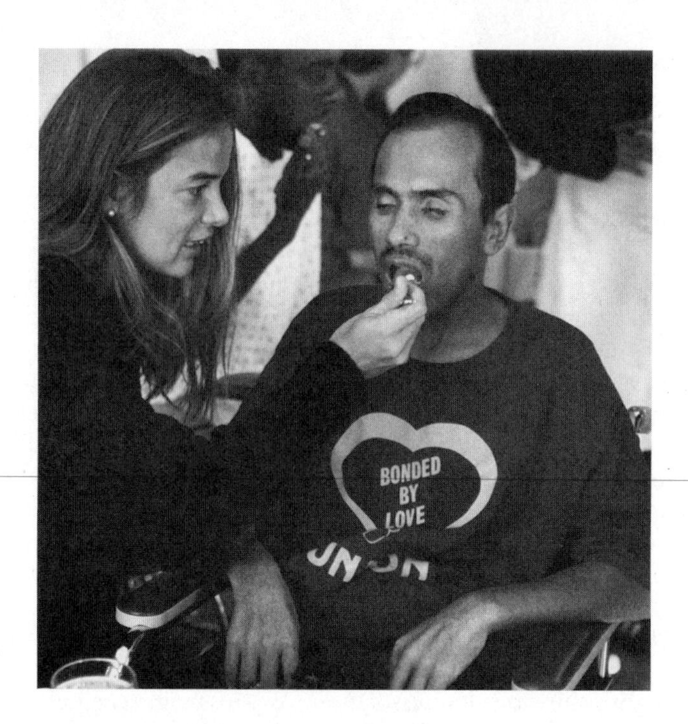

A young adult helps a peer who is close to death.

appreciate assistance from those who can clarify the realities of the situation, while also supporting their autonomy and decision-making processes. In this way, one respects efforts to satisfy important personal and developmental needs, while also recognizing constraints on former hopes and dreams.

Coping as a Middle-Aged Adult

According to Erikson (1963, 1968), the principal developmental task for middle-aged adults is the pursuit of *generativity.* In terms of life-threatening illness and dying, this means that the needs of the dying at midlife involve reevaluating one's life, continuing in one's roles, and putting one's affairs in order (Cook & Oltjenbruns, 1998). Reassessment, conservation, and preparation are characteristic activities of all middle-aged adults. They involve "stock-taking" (Butler & Lewis, 1982), efforts to sustain generativity as an alternative to self-indulgence and stagnation (Erikson, 1963), and a need to prepare for the future and to carry out one's responsibilities to others. Awareness of a life-threatening illness and challenges involved in coping with dying are likely to heighten, rather than to thwart, these developmental processes.

In middle adulthood, questions of *reevaluation* relate to the meaning and direction of one's life. Such questions become more, not less, poignant and urgent under the dual stimuli of illness and maturation. One person might more vigorously pursue a creative, vocational, or personal project established in young adulthood in recognition of new pressures that may now threaten its completion. Another midlife adult might decide to change earlier projects and to strike out in new directions or relationships. In either case, the individual might experience grief over what he or she has not attained, along with some overshadowing awareness of other losses yet to come.

However they choose to look toward a future that may now be perceived as more clouded and less extensive than it was before, middle-aged adults who are coping with life-threatening illness or dying can be expected to consider the prospects for *continuation* or enduring value in the legacies that they have been establishing for the future. Again, they may strive more diligently to achieve such goals, alter their form in ways that appear more satisfying or more achievable, or choose to settle for what has already been achieved. Insofar as possible, it would be desirable to support constructive processes of generativity in ill and dying midlife adults by enabling them to continue to take part in meaningful roles and relationships in suitable ways.

Looking to the future within a context of life-threatening illness or dying, and in light of developmental tasks of middle adulthood, typically leads midlife adults to strive to *put their affairs in order.* Most often, this involves an effort to continue to meet responsibilities to those whom they love and to ensure such obligations are met after the individual dies. Life-threatening illness and dying threaten one's ability to meet such commitments but need not render them completely impossible. With support, one can strive to influence the future to the degree possible or to arrange for others to assume specific responsibilities on one's behalf. This can take the form of making a will, disposing of property, or conveying important wishes and messages. In this regard, activities such as those involved in planning one's own funeral and burial arrangements can represent a healthy vitality in continuing to fulfill prized roles and an ability to minimize postdeath disruptions or burdens on others.

Adults Who Are Coping with Bereavement and Grief

Members of an aging, sandwich generation may find themselves beset with potential death-related losses on all sides. Young and middle-aged adults may suffer a full range of deaths, including those of their parents and grandparents; their spouses, siblings, and friends; their children; and themselves. This is itself distinctive in some respects: children and most adolescents do not experience the deaths of their own children, and the parents of most elderly adults have predeceased them. What is most characteristic of bereavement in young and middle adults is the very real potential for so many kinds of death-related losses. Even the birth of a child who is impaired in some way may present adult parents with losses, challenges, and opportunities that they must meet (see Box 14.1).

Each loss is difficult in its own way. However, research by Sanders (1979) showed that adult bereavement is usually impacted most significantly by the

Box 14.1 Welcome to Holland

I am often asked to describe the experience of raising a child with a disability—to try to help people who have not shared that unique experience to understand it, to imagine how it would feel. It's like this. . . .

When you're going to have a baby, it's like planning a fabulous vacation trip—to Italy. You buy a bunch of guidebooks and make your wonderful plans. The Coliseum. The Michelangelo David. The gondolas in Venice. You may learn some handy phrases in Italian. It's all very exciting.

After months of eager anticipation, the day finally arrives. You pack your bags and off you go. Several hours later, the plane lands. The stewardess comes in and says, "Welcome to Holland."

"Holland?!?" you say. "What do you mean, Holland?? I signed up for Italy! I'm supposed to be in Italy. All my life I've dreamed of going to Italy."

But there's been a change in the flight plan. They've landed in Holland and there you must stay.

The important thing is that they haven't taken you to a horrible, disgusting, filthy place, full of pestilence, famine and disease. It's just a different place.

So you must go out and buy new guidebooks. And you must learn a whole new language. And you will meet a whole new group of people you would never have met.

It's just a different place. It's slower-paced than Italy, less flashy than Italy. But after you've been there for a while and you catch your breath, you look around . . . and you begin to notice that Holland has windmills . . . Holland has tulips. Holland even has Rembrandts.

But everyone you know is busy coming and going from Italy . . . and they're all bragging about what a wonderful time they had there. And for the rest of your life, you will say, "Yes, that's where I was supposed to go. That's what I had planned."

The pain of that will never, ever, ever go away . . . because the loss of that dream is a very, very significant loss.

But . . . if you spend your life mourning the fact that you didn't get to Italy, you may never be free to enjoy the very special, the very lovely things . . . about Holland. ■

death of a child, a spouse, and a parent—in that order. This finding is consistent with a familiar saying among bereaved adults, who report that "the death of my parent is the death of my past; the death of my spouse is the death of my present; the death of my child is the death of my future." What bereavement means to adults can be seen in the following analyses of different types of death encountered during adulthood and in what some bereaved adults have written about their experiences (see Box 14.2).

Box 14.2 Selected Descriptions of Bereavement Experiences during Adulthood

About the death of a child:

Bramblett, J. (1991). *When Good-Bye Is Forever: Learning to Live Again after the Loss of a Child.*

Claypool, J. R. (1974). *Tracks of a Fellow Struggler: How to Handle Grief.*

Donnelly, K. F. (1982). *Recovering from the Loss of a Child.*

Evans, R. P. (1993). *The Christmas Box.*

Guest, J. (1976). *Ordinary People.**

Koppelman, K. L. (1994). *The Fall of a Sparrow: Of Death and Dreams and Healing.*

Kotzwinkle, W. (1975). *Swimmer in the Secret Sea.**

Leach, C. (1981). *Letter to a Younger Son.*

Simonds, W., & Rothman, B. K. (Eds.). (1992). *Centuries of Solace: Expressions of Maternal Grief in Popular Literature.*

Smith, A. A. (1974). *Rachel.*

Stinson, R., & Stinson, P. (1983). *The Long Dying of Baby Andrew.*

Wagner, S. (1994). *The Andrew Poems.*

About the death of a spouse, peer, or friend:

Brothers, J. (1990). *Widowed.*

Caine, L. (1975). *Widow.*

Elmer, L. (1987). *Why Her, Why Now: A Man's Journey through Love and Death and Grief.*

Evans, J. (1971). *Living with a Man Who Is Dying: A Personal Memoir.*

Graham, L. (1990). *Rebuilding the House.*

Guest, J. (1997). *Errands.**

Lewis, C. S. (1976). *A Grief Observed.*

Smith, H. I. (1996). *Grieving the Death of a Friend.*

Wertenbaker, L. T. (1957). *Death of a Man.*

About the death of a parent:

Anderson, R. (1968). *I Never Sang for My Father.**

De Beauvoir, S. (1973). *A Very Easy Death.*

Donnelly, K. F. (1987). *Recovering from the Loss of a Parent.*

Jury, M., & Jury, D. (1978). *Gramps: A Man Ages and Dies.*

Smith, H. I. (1994). *On Grieving the Death of a Father.*

About one's own struggles with life-threatening illness:

Broyard, A. (1992). *Intoxicated by My Illness, and Other Writings on Life and Death.*

Hanlan, A. (1979). *Autobiography of Dying.*

Lerner, G. (1978). *A Death of One's Own.*

Tolstoy, L. (1960). *The Death of Ivan Ilych and Other Stories.**

Underwood, M. (1995). *Diary of a Death Professional.*

*Titles marked with an asterisk are fiction.

Death of a Child

Fetal Death Along with some adolescent parents, many adults experience the death of a child in the uterus or during the birthing process. In general, these may be called *fetal deaths*, a category that includes what are popularly termed miscarriages, stillbirths, or spontaneous abortions. Fetal deaths are usually distinguished from elective abortions. Fetal deaths may take place at various times during gestation or (as perinatal deaths) during the birthing process. Although data are not readily available on all forms of fetal death, one source has reported that "each year in the United States, out of an estimated 4.4 million *confirmed* pregnancies, there are more than half a million miscarriages, [and] twenty-nine thousand stillbirths" (Davis, 1991, xiii; italics in original).

Some have believed fetal death experiences had minimal impact on the parents and did not generate a significant grief reaction. Parents were offered false consolation: "Now you have a little angel in heaven" or "You can always have another child." Such easy dismissal of the losses in a fetal death reflects ignorance and the discomfort of outsiders. It is often bolstered by an erroneous claim that there could not be much grief when there had not been real bonding with the infant. In fact, during pregnancy most parents begin to actively reshape their lives and self-concepts to accommodate the anticipated baby. Such parents observe the movements of the fetus in the womb (now with the aid of new imaging technologies), explore potential names for the baby, plan accommodations, and develop dreams. When the death occurs in the uterus, it is often important to complete a process of bonding that is already under way in order to enhance opportunities for productive grief and mourning (Lamb, 1988). Parental grief associated with fetal or infant death is a reality that is related not to the length of a baby's life but to the nature of the attachment (Borg & Lasker, 1989; DeFrain et al., 1986; Lafser, 1998; Peppers & Knapp, 1980). We must recognize the depth of the parents' grief and how they cope with their losses (Allen & Marks, 1993); otherwise, the grief may be disenfranchised (Doka, 1989b).

Thus, programs have emerged in which parents and other family members are permitted (if they wish to do so) to see and hold their dead infant, name the child, take pictures (Johnson et al., 1985; Reddin, 1987; Siegel et al., 1985), retain other mementos (such as a blanket, name tag, or lock of hair), obtain information from a postmortem examination, and take part in rituals that validate the life

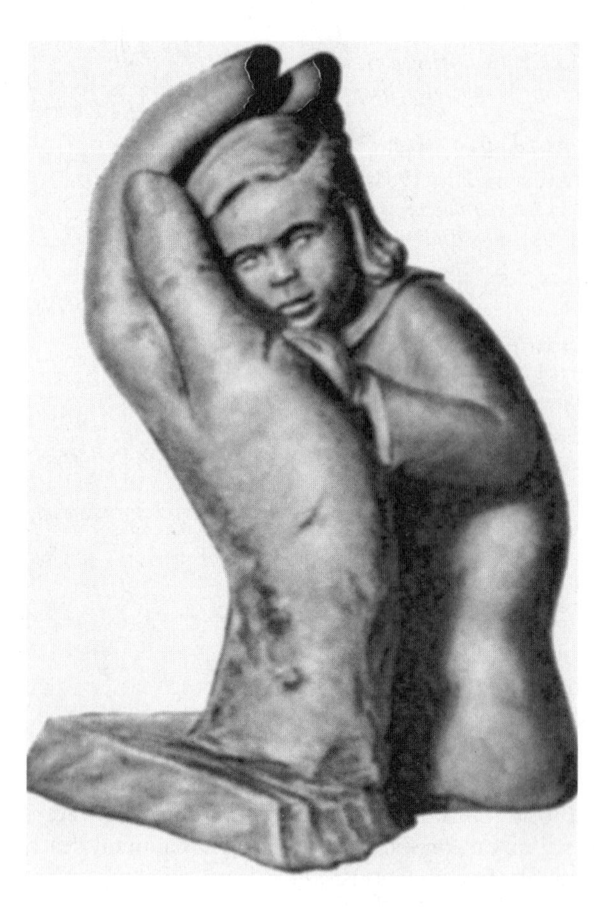

"See! I will not forget you . . . I have carved you on the palm of my hand" (Isaiah 49:15).

and the loss. Such practices provide opportunities to interact with the baby, to share experiences, and to strengthen a realistic foundation for mourning. Implementing such practices requires attention to detail and sensitivity to individual preferences. The key is to understand the meaning of the loss for the survivors and then to provide appropriate support. The aim is to affirm that the child and his or her abbreviated life were real and have value, and to honor the need of survivors.

In cases of elective abortion when the parents feel unable or unwilling to bring the baby to term, or in cases of infant adoption, when the child is given over shortly after birth to be raised by others, one often experiences a lingering sense of loss and grief (Doane & Quigley, 1981; Peppers, 1987). When one chooses (deliberately or ambivalently) to abort, even if one believes that the fetus is not yet a human child, one often feels a sense of loss that must be mourned. To opt for adoption, even in light of the conviction that one is really not able to rear this child, may also leave one with feelings of pain or regret. Neither elective abortion nor adoption need result in grief that incapacitates. It is wrong, however, to assume that these are easy, painless decisions and to dismiss out of hand the implications for parents of events and decisions that close off opportunities involving what is or would become their biological offspring.

Neonatal and Other Infant Deaths After birth, the principal causes of death during infancy present contrasting scenarios for parents and significant others. On one hand, congenital malformations, disorders related to short gestation and low birth weight, and respiratory distress syndrome (RDS) may involve a struggle for life, the intervention of professionals and advanced technology prior to the death, and lingering implications of genetic origins and other forms of responsibility. In such circumstances, the death of the infant is likely to occur in an institutional context, when the parents are perhaps excluded or not present. On the other hand, sudden infant death syndrome (SIDS) will likely involve none of these factors, since it is the prototype of an encounter whose first symptom is death, as well as a death arising from an unknown cause that mostly occurs at home and for which parents often feel guilty in terms of what they did or did not do (see Box 12.1; Corr et al., 1991; DeFrain et al., 1991).

For survivors, neonatal and other infant deaths have in common the untimely and perhaps unheralded death of a vulnerable individual (Delgadillo & Davis, 1990). Even though pregnancy, the birthing process, and infancy are known to be times of risk for the offspring, a common societal belief is that tiny babies should not die. Thus, it is often said in the wake of such a death that "it's just not fair." The hard fact is that "none of us is guaranteed long life, only a lifetime" (Showalter, 1983, x).

The specific impact of various sorts of infant deaths will depend on diverse factors that enter into the mode of death and the situation of survivors. For example, the death of an infant in a neonatal intensive care unit can be an excruciating experience for professionals and parents alike. The experience may be even more difficult if there is conflict between professional care providers and family members (or between family members themselves) about care goals (Stinson & Stinson, 1983). Some bereaved mothers may prefer to remain on a maternity ward because of the staff's expertise in postpartum care, whereas others may wish to be relocated in order not to be confronted with happy parents interacting with newborn babies.

In most cases involving the death of an infant, a variety of issues arise for the parents and others involved. These issues include feelings of responsibility, loss of the idealized baby, loss of a part of oneself and one's future, lack of memories and rituals of mourning, and lack of social or professional support (Davis, 1991). Even when support is offered, it may not match the parents' needs or be available for as long as they require (Brabant et al., 1995).

The death of an infant and the unique ways in which surviving parents may experience and express their grief responses may create or add to existing strains on parental relationships (Bramblett, 1991; Schwab, 1990). Single parents also face special challenges when they must cope with an infant's death on their own (Wyler, 1989). Most of these bereaved parents display amazing resilience in finding ways to go on with productive living (Knapp, 1986; Miles, n.d.). Such parents deserve the best that can be offered in terms of information (for example, about the nature of the infant's death and about parental loss and grief), professional support, and contact with those who have had similar experiences (Brabant et al., 1995; Donnelly, 1982; Johnson, 1987; Klass, 1988; Schiff, 1977). In many cases, one key area of decision making involves whether (and, if so, when) to consider undertaking another pregnancy and how to help subsequent children relate to the older sibling who died before they were born (Schwiebert & Kirk, 1986). In all cases, it is important to help bereaved parents identify their own needs and not to overburden them with criticisms or expectations of others.

Deaths during Childhood and Adolescence A child or adolescent may die in many ways—for example, through some sort of accident (often involving a motor vehicle), as a result of homicide or suicide, through natural causes, even through social conflict, terrorism, or war. Typically, these deaths take place suddenly and without much warning or opportunity for preparation. In all cases, they involve multiple dimensions: loss of the life of the child, loss of what was or is a part of the self, loss of the hopes and dreams that the child represents, and a search for meaning (Klass, 1999; Wheeler, 2001).

Pain associated with the death of a child is often extraordinarily deep, pervasive, and enduring (Davies et al., 1998). Charles Dickens (1848/1963, p. 274) recognized this fact in his novel *Dombey and Son* when he put the following exclamation into the mouth of a bereaved father: "And can it be that in a world so full and busy, the loss of one weak creature makes a void in any heart, so wide and deep that nothing but the width and depth of vast eternity can fill it up!" Only a few years earlier than Dickens, Ralph Waldo Emerson made a similar point after the death of his son when he wrote in his journal on January 28, 1842, "sorrow makes us all children again" (Emerson, 1970, p. 165). Much the same is evident both in a best-selling story centered on a long-past but not-forgotten experience of the death of a child, *The Christmas Box* (Evans, 1993) and in a prizewinning book of poems by a bereaved mother, *The Andrew Poems* (Wagner, 1994; see Box 14.3). All of the resources that an individual and a family can command are required to cope with such a deep and intimate experience (Rosof, 1994).

Box 14.3 Shelly Wagner: The Tie

At night, I imagine
lying on my side next to him,
my arm under his head,
whispering in his ear,
smoothing the child-sized red tie
that lies on his chest
like an upside-down
exclamation mark.
I put off buying him
men's clothing,
but for Easter
he wanted a tie—
a red one
and a navy blue blazer.
Now, just under six years old,
he is buried
wearing it forever—
as old a man
as he will ever be.
At night,
lying next to my husband,
I back into
the curved question mark
of his body
and ask,
"What is Andrew like now?"
He always whispers,
"His coat and tie are the same."

SOURCE: From *The Andrew Poems,* by S. Wagner, p. 36.

A special problem for parents who have experienced the death of a child arises from simple, everyday questions like "How many children do you have?" The difficulty is partly a matter of how the bereaved parent should view his or her own identity ("Am I still a parent?" "What does this death mean for me?") and partly an issue of how much of one's personal life one might or should be willing to disclose to the person who posed the question. Above all, the challenge is how to be faithful to the deceased child and to his or her memory. Bereaved parents meet this challenge often and in different ways, but not so easily as it may seem to those who have not been bereaved (see Box 14.4).

When the child's death has come about by some form of more or less deliberate behavior (for example, suicide or homicide), by inadvertence (for

Box 14.4 How Many Children Do You Have?

It is early fall and I am standing in line at the grocery store. As I turn around to check the items in my cart, the woman behind me notices that I am very pregnant. "Is this your first child?" she asks innocently. Tears form in my eyes as I try to decide what to answer. If I say no, this will lead to the inevitable question: "How many children do you have?" Am I up for the possible reaction to my answer? Am I ready to bring up old feelings and memories? That day, I decide yes.

I turn to the woman and say, "This is my second child. My first child, my son, died in October of 1985 of Sudden Infant Death Syndrome." She puts her hand on my shoulder and tells me how sorry she is. She asks me some questions about our son and about SIDS. I appreciated so much the opportunity to talk about our son, Brendan, and SIDS, even to a complete stranger!

Unfortunately, that is not always the response I receive. Many times people will mumble something unintelligible and walk away. That is okay, too. I understand how difficult it is to hear about a baby dying—no one likes to hear about that.

Responses among bereaved parents will differ when they are asked how many children they have. In most cases, I will tell people I have a son who died, and two daughters.

There have been situations when I haven't mentioned Brendan. This is okay—it doesn't mean I don't love him or that I deny that he ever existed. It doesn't mean that I am a bad mother. What it does mean, is that, for the moment, I choose not to share Brendan. Early in my bereavement, I told everyone about Brendan's life and death. More than twelve years later, I have learned to cope with his absence and do not feel the need to mention him every time I meet someone new.

There are many ways in which my family and I keep his memory alive. As bereaved parents, we decide what is right for each of us. When we choose to mention our deceased children, we may make some people uncomfortable, but we may also have the opportunity to educate others. If we choose not to mention our deceased children, that does not mean that we deny them or that we should feel guilty. The only correct choice is what feels right to the bereaved parent. ■

SOURCE: Maruyama, N. L. (1998). How many children do you have? *Bereavement Magazine 12*(5), p. 16. Reprinted with permission from Bereavement Publishing, Inc., 5125 North Union Boulevard, Suite 4, Colorado Springs, Colorado, 80918; tel. 888-604-4673.

instance, accidents), or by irresponsible behavior (such as drunken driving), elements of responsibility, anger against the person responsible, guilt, or blame (by oneself or by others) may enter into the bereavement experience. Such elements can be expected to add to the burdens of parental grief and mourning (Bolton, 1995; Chance, 1992).

Guilt in Parental Bereavement Guilt is in part the conviction that one has done wrong by violating some principle or responsibility. Guilt may be realistic and well founded or unrealistic and unjustified (Stearns, 1985). Typically associated with guilt are lowered self-esteem, heightened self-blame, and a feeling that one should make retribution for the supposed wrong. Guilt is by no means exclusive to parental bereavement, but it is almost always—at least initially—a prominent part of such bereavement.

Miles and Demi (1984, 1986) suggested that guilt in parental bereavement arises from feelings of helplessness and responsibility. These feelings lead parents to ask how their past and present actions and feelings might have contributed to the child's death. Inevitable discrepancies between ideal standards and actual performance can culminate in guilt feelings. How that works itself out in individual cases depends on parental, situational, personal, and societal variables. For bereaved parents, there are at least six potential sources of guilt:

1. *Death causation guilt*, related to the belief that the parent either contributed to or failed to protect the child from the death
2. *Illness-related guilt*, related to perceived deficiencies in the parental role during the child's illness or at the time of death
3. *Parental role guilt*, related to the belief that the parent failed to live up to self-expectations or societal expectations in the overall parental role
4. *Moral guilt*, related to the belief that the child's death was punishment or retribution for violating a moral or religious standard
5. *Survival guilt*, related to violating the standard that a child should outlive his or her parents
6. *Grief guilt*, related to the behavioral and emotional reactions at the time of or following the child's death—that is, feeling guilt about how one acted at or after the time of the child's death

In the case of a bereaved parent, one must identify and address any of these elements of guilt that might appear in the overall bereavement experience. Each needs to be addressed in the mourning process.

Gender and Role Differences in Parental Bereavement Fathers and mothers are different; married, unmarried, and divorced parents are different. Each bereaved survivor is distinguished by his or her gender, role(s), and individual characteristics. Each of these distinguishing factors may and likely will influence the bereavement experience (Schwab, 1990). For example, according to traditional gender-based roles in American society, expression of strong feelings was sanctioned for females but discouraged for males. Similarly, wives were expected to remain at home, while husbands went out to work. Although such gender-based roles do not apply in all relationships and are changing in many areas of society, factors like these may encourage different types of grief experiences for mothers and fathers. Even simply as two different individuals, at any given time spouses may be coping with loss and grief in different ways and may not be available to support each other as they otherwise do in healthy marital relationships (Schatz, 1986; Simonds & Rothman, 1992). Consequently, bereaved parents need to be tolerant of and patient with each other (Rosenblatt, 2000, 2001). Assistance from empathetic friends, other bereaved parents (for example, through a support group like The Compassionate Friends), and/or an experienced counselor may be helpful.

As gender expectations are altered, as social roles change, and as individual differences are permitted freer expression, responses to bereavement are likely to be affected. A single parent and a surviving couple will be alone in different ways after the death of their child. Divorced or widowed parents whose child dies may face competing demands from grief and surviving children. A young parent and a grandparent may not always be able to help each other in mourning. We must appreciate the many factors that enter into individual experiences of parental bereavement during adulthood.

Death of a Spouse, Life Partner, Sibling, Peer, or Friend

Pair relationships can be very important in human life. Among adults, pair relationships may be established and carried over from childhood or adolescence, or newly formed during the adult years. Such relationships may be of many types; those involving marital ties are not the only model. One may have special bonds with many other adults, such as a brother or sister, other relative, friend, coworker, lover, or life partner (heterosexual, gay, or lesbian). The relationship may be overt or hidden, continuous or intermittent, satisfying or complicated, healthy or abusive. There are perhaps as many variables in adult-to-adult relationships as there are in the individuals involved and in the ways they interact.

The dimensions of an adult's bereavement occasioned by the death of someone who is also an adult will depend, in the first place, on the intimacy and significance of the roles that the deceased played in the survivor's life. For example, the sibling relationship is typically the longest and most enduring familial relationship. Where that relationship is especially close, the death of one sibling may involve both his or her loss and the loss of an important part of the surviving sibling's identity (see Box 14.5). Much the same is true in spousal or other intimate friendships in which two individuals have established a relationship that gradually becomes an important and enduring part of their identity (Sklar & Hartley, 1990; Smith, 1996). The deceased individual is no longer alive to receive love, his or her contributions to the relationship go unfulfilled, the comforting presence to which one formerly turned for love and solace is no longer available, and plans that the couple had made for the future may now go unrealized. Thus, after the death in 1998 of his wife, Linda, Paul McCartney is reported to have said that he had lost his best friend. Some of Al Joyner's experiences after the death of his wife, FloJo, reflect issues encountered by many bereaved adult spouses (see Box 14.6).

Death of a fellow adult—a spouse, sibling, peer, or friend—can change the world, the other, and the self for a bereaved adult. The death of only one person like this can entail many emotional, social, financial, spiritual, and other losses. It can also precipitate renewed struggles with identity (DiGiulio, 1989; Golan, 1975). Much will depend on how the death occurred, on the perspective of the survivor, and on social norms. For example, if it was an ex-spouse

Box 14.5 Cokie Roberts on the Death of Her Sister

At some point during Barbara's illness I began preparing myself for a different vision of my old age. Without really thinking about it, I had always assumed we'd occupy adjacent rockers on some front porch, either literally or figuratively. Now one of those chairs would be empty. Intellectually I understood that. But every time some new thing happens that she's not here for, emotionally it hits me all over again—that sense of charting new territories without the map of my older sister.

And here's what I didn't expect at all—not only was I robbed of some part of my future, I was also deprived of my past. When a childhood memory needed checking, all my life I had simply run it by Barbara. Now there's no one to set me straight. My mother and brother can help some. My brother and I have, in fact, grown a good deal closer since our sister died; after all, without him, I would not only not have a sister, I would not be a sister. But Tommy didn't go to school with me, share a room with me, grow up female with me. Though I love him dearly, he is not my sister.

There it is. For all of the wonderful expressions of sisterhood from so many sources, for all of the support I both receive and provide, for all of the friendships I cherish, it's not the same. I only had one sister.

SOURCE: Roberts, 1998, pp. 16–17.

who died, is the survivor to be thought of as a widow or widower (Campbell & Silverman, 1996; Kohn & Kohn, 1978; Stillion, 1985)?

Death of a Parent or Grandparent

Adults typically emancipate themselves in some measure from parental and family bonds. For example, they may move away from parental influences, either geographically or psychosocially. Usually, but not always, they reestablish new relationships with parents, grandparents, and other family members, revising the relationships that characterized their childhood. In any case, adults have unique relationships—simple, ambivalent, or complicated though they may be—with their own parents and grandparents throughout their adult lives. These members of an older generation often are sources of advice, support, and assistance to their adult children and grandchildren.

In our society, most adults expect their parents and grandparents to precede them in death, and in fact this is the most common form of bereavement during adult life. Nevertheless, when such deaths do occur, they often are difficult experiences for survivors (Horowitz et al., 1984; Moss & Moss, 1983; Myers, 1986; Smith, 1994). They involve the loss of a lifelong relationship, full of shared (playful and sorrowful) experiences. The surviving adult may also perceive the death as the removal of a "buffer" or source of generational "protection" against his or her own personal death (Akner & Whitney, 1993; Angel, 1987). Literature on motherless daughters (Edelman, 1994), fatherless daughters (Simon, 2001), and fatherless sons (Chethik, 2001; Smith, 1994) describes special complications that may apply to each of these bereavement situations. Sometimes, the death may be perceived as the completion of a long, full life or as a release from suffering. Just as easily, however, it may involve lost opportunities or unfinished business and a failure to experience certain developmental or situational milestones by the deceased, the adult survivor, or the survivor's children. For example, following the death of a parent or grandparent the adult child no longer has an opportunity to renew or extend relationships with the deceased person on an adult-to-adult basis. Difficult and important issues may be left unresolved. In these and other ways, the death of a parent almost inevitably gives his or her adult children a "developmental push" (Osterweis et al., 1984) in which they feel with additional force their own finitude and the weight of their own responsibility as members of the now-oldest living generation.

FloJo: Florence Griffith Joyner in a moment of athletic triumph.

Summary

In this chapter, we explored many aspects of interactions between young and middle-aged adults and death within our society. We noted how the distinctive developmental tasks of young adulthood (striving to achieve intimacy versus isolation) and middle age (striving to achieve generativity versus stagnation) have a direct bearing on how adults relate to death. These tasks influence encounters with death among young and middle-aged adults (we noted an accelerating increase in death rates involving diseases of the heart and cancer) and attitudes of adults toward death (concern about the deaths of others in young adults and the appearance of a newly personalized sense of mortality in middle adults). We also explored some of the main concerns that arise when young and middle-aged adults are coping with life-threatening illness and dying. Finally, we reviewed the most typical of the many types of bereavement encounters that adults may experience and some of their implications.

Box 14.6 The Death of Florence Griffith Joyner and Its Aftermath

Florence Griffith Joyner, known to friends and fans as "FloJo," died unexpectedly on September 21, 1998, at the age of 38 (Gregorian, 1998).

FloJo was known for her athletic abilities and flamboyant style. She set new world records in track while winning three gold medals and a silver medal at the Olympic Games in Seoul in 1988.

FloJo's husband, Al Joyner, and his sister, Jackie Joyner-Kersee, experienced the sudden death of their mother at the age of 37 as a result of cerebrospinal meningitis. But Al said that tragic event did not prepare them for FloJo's death (Brennan, 1998).

On September 21, 1998, Al woke at 6:30 A.M. to the sounds of the bedroom alarm clock. When he went to wake his wife, in bed with their 7-year-old daughter, Mary, Al experienced what he later said was "the most hopeless moment of my life" (Brennan, 1998, p. 5E).

A postmortem examination determined that FloJo had died in her sleep of an epileptic seizure.

Several weeks after FloJo's death, Al was reported to have said: "If Mary were not here, I really think I would do something stupid. I feel like I have nothing to live for, until I think of her" (Brennan, 1998, p. 5E).

Al also said that he has not had his wife's mobile telephone service disconnected. In fact, from time to time he calls that number just to hear the voice of Florence on the answering tape saying, "This is Florence. I can't talk to you right now. Please leave a message." ■

Questions for Review and Discussion

1. Think back to Margaret Metzgar's situation as she described it in the vignette near the beginning of this chapter. What types of losses and deaths was Margaret coping with? If you were her friend, how would you try to help her cope?
2. What sorts of death-related losses are most typical in adulthood, and what do such losses usually mean to adults?
3. What sort of losses have you experienced as an adult? How did you respond?
4. Do you know an adult who has experienced significant death-related losses? What were those losses like for that person? What did you do or what could you have done to help?

Suggested Readings

Concerning life-threatening illness in adulthood, consult:

Armstrong, L., & Jenkins, S. (2000). *It's Not about the Bike: My Journey Back to Life.*

Cousins, N. (1979). *Anatomy of an Illness as Perceived by the Patient: Reflections on Healing and Regeneration.*

Frank, A. W. (1991). *At the Will of the Body: Reflections on Illness.*

Bereavement and grief in adulthood are explored in several ways:

In terms of the death of a child:

Allen, M., & Marks, S. (1993). *Miscarriage: Women Sharing from the Heart.*

Bolton, I. (1995). *My Son, My Son: A Guide to Healing after a Suicide in the Family.*

Borg, S., & Lasker, J. (1989). *When Pregnancy Fails: Families Coping with Miscarriage, Stillbirth, and Infant Death* (rev. ed.).

Chance, S. (1992). *Stronger than Death.*

Corr, C. A., Fuller, H., Barnickol, C. A., & Corr, D. M. (Eds.). (1991). *Sudden Infant Death Syndrome: Who Can Help and How.*

Davis, D. L. (1991). *Empty Cradle, Broken Heart: Surviving the Death of Your Baby.*

DeFrain, J., Ernst, L., Jakub, D., & Taylor, J. (1991). *Sudden Infant Death: Enduring the Loss.*

DeFrain, J., Martens, L., Story, J., & Stork, W. (1986). *Stillborn: The Invisible Death.*

Donnelly, K. F. (1982). *Recovering from the Loss of a Child.*

Ilse, S. (1989). *Miscarriage: A Shattered Dream.*

Jimenez, S. L. M. (1982). *The Other Side of Pregnancy: Coping with Miscarriage and Stillbirth.*

Klass, D. (1988). *Parental Grief: Solace and Resolution.*

Klass, D. (1999). *The Spiritual Lives of Bereaved Parents.*

Knapp, R. J. (1986). *Beyond Endurance: When a Child Dies.*

Lafser, C. (1998). *An Empty Cradle, a Full Heart: Reflections for Mothers and Fathers after Miscarriage, Stillbirth, or Infant Death.*

Osmont, K., & McFarlane, M. (1986). *Parting Is Not Goodbye.*

Panuthos, C., & Romeo, C. (1984). *Ended Beginnings: Healing Childbearing Losses.*

Peppers, L. G., & Knapp, R. J. (1980). *Motherhood and Mourning: Perinatal Death.*

Rando, T. A. (Ed.). (1986a). *Parental Loss of a Child.*

Rosenblatt, P. C. (2000). *Parent Grief: Narratives of Loss and Relationship.*

Rosenblatt, P. C. (2001). *Help Your Marriage Survive the Death of a Child.*

Rosof, B. D. (1994). *The Worst Loss: How Families Heal from the Death of a Child.*

Simonds, W., & Rothman, B. K. (Eds.). (1992). *Centuries of Solace: Expressions of Maternal Grief in Popular Literature.*

In terms of the death of a spouse, friend, or peer:

Campbell, S., & Silverman, P. (1996). *Widower: What Happens When Men Are Left Alone.*

Kohn, J. B., & Kohn, W. K. (1978). *The Widower.*

Lewis, C. S. (1976). *A Grief Observed.*

Stroebe, W., & Stroebe, M. S. (1987). *Bereavement and Health: The Psychological and Physical Consequences of Partner Loss.*

In terms of the death of the adult's parent or grandparent:

Akner, L. E., with C.V. Whitney. (1993). *How to Survive the Loss of a Parent: A Guide for Adults.*

Angel, M. D. (1987). *The Orphaned Adult.*

Chethik, N. (2001). *FatherLoss: How Sons of All Ages Come to Terms with the Deaths of Their Dads.*

Edelman, H. (1994). *Motherless Daughters: The Legacy of Loss.*

Myers, E. (1986). *When Parents Die: A Guide for Adults.*

Simon, C. (2001). *Fatherless Women: How We Change after We Lose Our Dads.*

Smith, H. I. (1994). *On Grieving the Death of a Father.*

InfoTrac College Edition
For more information, explore the InfoTrac College Edition at **http://www.infotrac-college.com/Wadsworth**

Enter search terms: ADULTS AND DEATH, CAUSES OF DEATH IN ADULTHOOD, DEVELOPMENTAL TASKS IN ADULTHOOD, "SANDWICH" GENERATION.

Chapter Fifteen

THE ELDERLY

IN THIS CHAPTER, WE STUDY THE ELDERLY—those who are 65 years of age and older—and their experiences with death. These "golden-agers" or "senior citizens" represented approximately 12.4 percent of the total population of the United States in 1999. Because the elderly are a growing portion of America's population whose number is expected to rise from around 35 million in 1999 to 62 million in 2025, some have spoken of the "graying" of America. In many societies, these elders would be thought of as the repository of social wisdom, but America's youth-oriented society does not typically take this view. Thus, the position of the elderly is more ambiguous and less honored by much of our society.

With the emergence of a body of gerontological and geriatric knowledge about older adults, much has been learned about the developmental tasks and other issues that distinguish them from other members of American society. In particular, it has been recognized that aging is not identical with pathology. Becoming an older adult is often marked by a variety of biological, psychological, and social changes—but the majority of elderly persons in the United States are living vigorous, productive, and satisfying lives. NBC news correspondent Tom Brokaw (1998) has called our elders *The Greatest Generation*, and former President Jimmy Carter (1998) has written about *The Virtues of Aging*. One notable example of achievement by an elderly American occurred on October 29, 1998, when John Glenn—the first American to orbit the earth on February 20, 1962—went back into space at the age of 77 after successful careers in the military, as an astronaut, and as a United States senator.

Nevertheless, American society often gives evidence of what Butler (1969) called *ageism*, which he (1975, p. 12) defined as "a process of systematic stereotyping of and discrimination against people because they are old." In fact, it is wrong, unfair, and potentially harmful to the elderly when they are casually lumped together, when their lives are devalued, and when appreciation is lacking for what they have in common with all other human beings. Against this stereotyping, it is desirable to acknowledge the shared humanity, the significant contributions and human values, and the great diversity to be found in this portion of the population. If it is true that "human beings are more alike at birth than they will ever be again" (Stillion, 1985, p. 56), then it should also be true that human beings are most unalike in older adulthood, in view of the many years in which each elder has had to work out his or her long story.

Senator John Glenn after returning from space on November 8, 1998; in the background is a poster of Glenn in his 1962 Mercury 7 spacesuit.

Research on late adulthood has demonstrated that it is not appropriate to speak of "old age" without qualification. In fact, the elderly are neither a static nor a monolithic segment of the population (Erikson et al., 1986; Havighurst, 1972). As one researcher has reported, "old people do not perceive meaning in aging itself, so much as they perceive meaning in being themselves in old age. Thus . . . [the central issue is] how old people maintain a sense of continuity and meaning that helps them cope with change" (Kaufman, 1986, pp. 13–14).

We begin this chapter with a brief vignette describing the companionship that two elderly Americans found in each other's company. Next, we consider in turn the distinctive developmental tasks of the elderly, typical encounters with death in American society during the later adult years, attitudes toward death during this era of human development, issues related to elders who are coping with life-threatening illness and dying, issues related to elders who are coping with bereavement and grief, and special issues concerning suicide among the elderly. Principles for helping older adults cope with dying, death, and bereavement appear throughout this book in appropriate topical chapters. ■

Lives Crowned by Love

He calls her Miss America. Sometimes she calls him John, the name of her deceased husband. . . . Francis Eldridge is 92. Marie Franzen is 97. Both lived full and happy lives before they met nine years ago. Francis was married to his Edyth for 58 years. Marie was married to John for 64.

Neither was looking to begin again when they were introduced during lunch at the Seminole Senior Center. . . . Instead they became soul mates. Francis remembers what happened later, at Marie's home. "She was having trouble lifting a window," he says. "I went by to fix it and never left."

They decided against marriage, but after a month Francis moved into Marie's Seminole bungalow. . . . Francis loved Marie's cooking. Her beef stew, Hungarian goulash and stuffed cabbage pushed his weight up to a robust 175 pounds.

Then Marie was diagnosed with Alzheimer's. But as long as Francis was around, Marie eventually found the words she intended to say.

Everything changed in March of 1999 when Francis developed a severe case of pneumonia that landed him in the Largo Medical Center for three weeks.

He was released from the hospital too weak to take care of himself and Marie. He moved in with his daughter, Sylvia Whitney . . . Marie moved into Crystal Oaks [a nursing home].

"He was happy to be with me, but he missed her so much," says Whitney. "I would take him to visit her once or twice a week, but he kept losing weight. Marie is the only woman—besides my mother—that my dad ever cared about."

As Francis shriveled, Marie languished. "He dropped to 114 pounds; she was lost," says Whitney. Out of desperation, she moved Francis to Crystal Oaks to live with Marie.

Francis is back up to 137 pounds. No one expects Marie's Alzheimer's to go away, but she now has longer stretches of clarity.

"You don't know what your feelings can do to your body," says Francis as he and Marie soak up the sun on a green metal bench in front of Crystal Oaks. They come here each morning after breakfast to hold hands and say hello to all who pass. . . .

The two are teasing each other about their dancing when Francis' black wrist watch begins to talk. "Ten forty-two," it says in a monotone. This is followed by a recording of a crowing rooster. Francis and Marie are both legally blind. They depend on the rooster to tell them when to go inside.

They shuffle along the polished floors until they come to the large water fountain they use as a landmark. "When we find the fountain, we've found our room," says Marie.

Inside, she has a collection of teddy bears. Friends bring them as gifts, and Marie keeps them for a while before passing them on to visitors and friends. But the small white bear dressed in blue never leaves the room. It was a gift from Francis.

When they melt into Marie's single bed for their daily noontime rest, the bear is there too. They will spend the next hour wrapped in each other's arms, Miss America and her darling John. (Source: "Lives Crowned by Love" by

Jamie Francis, p. 1D in the Floridian, *St. Petersburg Times*, March 9, 2001, Reprinted by permission.)

The Elderly, Developmental Tasks, and Death

In Erikson's (1959) original schematization, the last era in the human life course was named *senescence*. This term had been used earlier by Hall (1922) to designate the last half of human life. The word itself identifies the process of growing old, and thus by transference designates the old or the elderly themselves. Unfortunately, senescence is etymologically linked to the terms senile and senility, which now designate not merely the condition of being old but the presence of cognitive impairment often mistakenly associated with old age. This linkage between normative developmental eras and pathology is generally not accurate and thus undesirable. Perhaps to avoid such implications, Erikson later (1963, 1982) spoke about this period as the era of *maturity* or one in which human development is "completed."

Different developmental theorists describe the principal developmental task of late adulthood in similar ways. Erikson (1963, 1982) described this task as involving *the achievement of ego integrity versus despair or disgust*, Maslow (1968) spoke of *self-actualization*, and Birren (1964) wrote about *reconciliation*. In each of these languages, the principal developmental work of old age involves the attainment of an inner sense of wholeness. Successfully resolving earlier developmental tasks and coming to terms with one's past helps older adults achieve the balance and harmony in this wholeness (integrity means being whole or undivided), which emerges from a process of introspection, self-reflection, and reminiscence that Butler (1963) called "life review" (compare Woodward, 1986).

In this process of heightened interiority, past experiences are spontaneously brought to consciousness, reviewed and assessed, and perhaps reinterpreted or reintegrated. The aim is to resolve old conflicts and to achieve a new sense of meaning, both as an accounting to oneself of one's past life and as a preparation for death. If this process is successful, it results in integrity and wisdom (Erikson & Erikson, 1981). If not, it yields a sense of despair because one is not satisfied with what one has done with one's life and does not feel that sufficient time or energy remains to alter directions and compensate for the ways in which one has lived.

Customarily, the elderly in our society have been thought of as those who are 65 years of age or older (perhaps in part because many faced a social marker of mandatory retirement at that age). In the 21st century, however, the situation is more complicated than this. For example, we saw in Chapter 2 (see Table 2.4) that persons reaching age 65 in the United States in 1999 had an estimated average life expectancy of an additional 17.7 years (19.1 years for females; 16.1 years for males) and that such averages had been trending upward in recent years. In fact, the portion of those in the very oldest segment of our society, our centenarians, is projected to grow most rapidly of all during the first half of the 21st century (see Figure 15.1 and Gertner, 2001). Thus, a book entitled *Living to 100: Lessons in Living to Your Maximum Potential at Any Age* (Perls et al., 2000) and its companion Web site (www.livingto100.com) argue that there is much to learn from those over 100 years of age in terms of how all of us might live our lives. (See Box 15.1 for some thoughts about increasing your life expectancy.)

In short, many elders—especially in the 65- to 74-year-old age group—possess relatively good health, education, purchasing power, and free time and are politically active (Neugarten, 1974; Thorson, 2000a). This suggests the need to draw important distinctions within the elderly between the "young old" (those 65–74 years of age), the "old" or "old old" (those 75–84 years of age), and the "oldest old" or "very old" (those 85 years of age and older). Some have spoken of the very old as the "frail elderly," but that is a health category, not a developmental designation—elderly persons of any age (as well as younger persons) may or may not be frail. In any event, there clearly are different social cohorts among the elderly and distinctive developmental tasks in this evolving population.

Encounters with Death among the Elderly

Deaths and Death Rates among the Elderly

Individuals who are 65 years of age or older experienced a total of almost 1.8 million deaths in 1999. That represented about 75 percent of the nearly 2.4 million deaths in the country in the year in a group that makes up only 12.4 percent of the total U.S. population.

Table 15.1 provides an overview of numbers of deaths and death rates in the United States in 1999 for individuals 65 to 74 years of age, 75 to 84 years of age, and 85 years and older. By comparing these data, one can see that

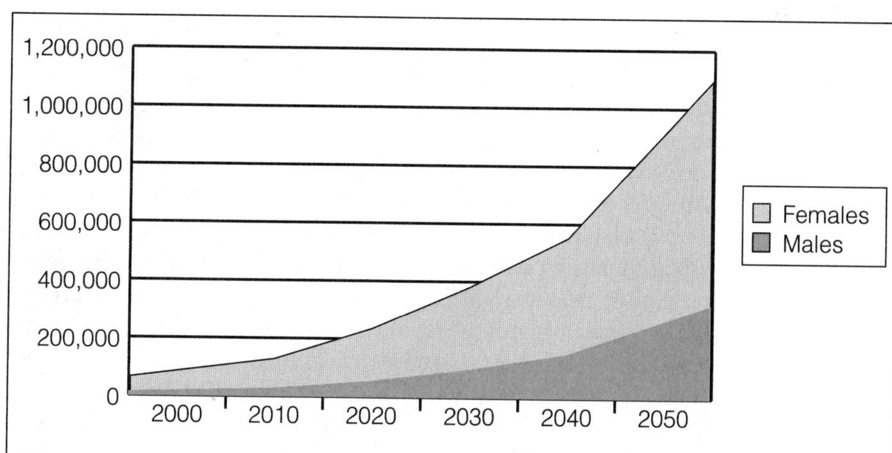

Figure 15.1 *Actual and Projected Centenarian Populations by Gender, United States, 2000–2050. SOURCE: U.S. Bureau of the Census, National Population Projections, 2001.*

Box 15.1 Some Thoughts about Increasing Your Life Expectancy

Some suggestions for increasing your life expectancy:

- Have a pool of "good" genes (choose your parents wisely!)
- Keep your blood pressure low; take an aspirin a day
- Participate in regular exercise and maintain your weight
- Avoid a diet high in protein and high in saturated fats; limit coffee drinking
- Do not smoke cigarettes or use other tobacco products; avoid secondhand smoke
- Limit your use of alcohol products to not more than two drinks per day
- Avoid excessive exposure to the sun
- Practice effective stress management techniques and maintain a good sense of humor
- Engage in rewarding hobbies
- Enjoy many friends (of all age groups) and share gratifying activities with them

If you could reach age 100 or more:

- What would you want to do?
- What would be your goals?
- How would you plan to support yourself financially?
- What health problems would you anticipate?
- With whom would you want to live?
- Where would you choose to live?
- What living facilities would you desire?

numbers of deaths rise rapidly from totals for those 65 to 74 years of age to totals for those 75 to 84 years of age, and then decline for the much smaller population of those 85 years of age and older. This curve continues the general pattern of a steady and rapid increase in numbers of deaths throughout the whole of adulthood in American society, at least up to age 85 and older.

Similar patterns are true of death rates among elders. In 1999, very high overall death rates for elders who were 65 to 74 years of age rose to exceptional heights of nearly 15,500 per 100,000 for elders who were 85 years of age or older. Similar increases in death rates appeared in all segments of the elderly population. All of these figures are greatly in excess of the overall mortality rate in the United States, which was 877.0 per 100,000 in 1999. In short, death is very much a part of the life of the elderly in American society. Since human beings are mortal and cannot live indefinitely, the longer one lives the closer one comes to the limit of the human life course.

Table 15.1 Number of Deaths and Death Rates (per 100,000), Ages 65 and Older, All Races, by Age and Sex: United States, 1999

	Number of Deaths			Death Rates		
	Both Sexes	Males	Females	Both Sexes	Males	Females
65–74 years	452,600	254,920	197,680	2,484.3	3,109.3	1,972.9
75–84 years	698,590	340,970	357,620	5,751.3	6,999.8	4,915.4
85 years and older	646,141	209,989	436,152	15,476.1	16,931.3	14,861.1

SOURCE: Hoyert et al., 2001.

Leading Causes of Death among the Elderly

Preliminary data concerning the ten leading causes of death (along with numbers of deaths and death rates for each of those causes) for all individuals in our society who were 65 years and older in 1999 are given in Table 15.2. With only three exceptions (influenza and pneumonia, accidents, and septicemia) all of these ten leading causes of death for older adults in our society are chronic or degenerative diseases. This pattern extends throughout older adulthood: as in young and middle adulthood, degenerative diseases are increasingly prominent as leading causes of death, whereas human-induced deaths and communicable diseases decline in relative significance. In general, leading causes of death are essentially the same for both male and female elders, with only minor differences in their relative significance.

Nevertheless, other causes of death among the elderly are also of interest. Numbers of accidental deaths increase significantly (from 18,924 to 32,147) from middle to late adulthood, whereas death rates nearly triple (from 31.8 to 93.1 per 100,000). Among the elderly, accidental deaths related to motor vehicles are far less frequent than all other accidental deaths (7,779 versus 24,368). In terms of overall *numbers*, homicide, HIV infection, and suicide are not included among the ten leading causes of death for older adults, although the highest *rates* of suicide in the whole of American society have been found for many years among elderly persons age 85 and older (19.2 per 100,000 in 1999).

Two Variables in Deaths of the Elderly: Gender and Race

Table 15.1 also reveals contrasts by gender in number of deaths and death rates among the elderly. At first, males die in larger numbers than females, but that changes as individuals reach 75 years of age and older. Because more American females live to an advanced age than males, there are more of them to die among the "oldest old" in our society. Thus, in 1999 there were over 78,000

Table 15.2 Preliminary Number of Deaths and Death Rates (per 100,000) for the Ten Leading Causes of Death for Those 65 Years of Age and Older, Both Sexes, All Races: United States, 1999

Rank	Cause of Death	Number	Rate
. . .	All causes	1,797,451	5,204.0
1	Diseases of the heart	607,255	1,758.1
2	Malignant neoplasms	390,070	1,129.3
3	Cerebrovascular diseases	148,580	430.2
4	Chronic lower respiratory diseases	108,106	313.0
5	Influenza and pneumonia	57,270	165.8
6	Diabetes mellitus	51,846	150.1
7	Alzheimer's disease	43,990	127.4
8	Accidents (unintentional injuries)	32,147	93.1
	Motor vehicle accidents	7,779	22.5
	All other accidents	24,368	70.6
9	Nephritis, nephrotic syndrome, and nephrosis	29,937	86.7
10	Septicemia	24,621	71.3
. . .	All other causes	303,629	879.1

SOURCE: Kochanek et al., 2001.

more deaths in the oldest group of American females than among females 75 to 84 years of age. Similarly, death rates for males remain consistently higher throughout older adulthood than those for females.

In terms of race and Hispanic origin, numbers of deaths climb sharply among "young old" and "old" Caucasian-American elders before falling somewhat among those 85 years of age and older (Hoyert et al., 2001). This trend reflects a crossover effect in which the population of the "oldest old" who remain alive in our society is less numerous than any other ten-year age group. Much smaller numbers of deaths among African-American, Hispanic-American, and Asian-American elders rise only modestly at first in these age groups and then decline in relatively steeper fashion. Only among Native-American elders are numbers of deaths slightly higher among those 65 to 74 years of age than among their older counterparts. In all these groups, death rates rise steadily throughout older adulthood and male elders have higher death rates than their female counterparts.

Attitudes toward Death among the Elderly

There is general and long-standing agreement in the research literature that the elderly are significantly less fearful of death than younger persons (for example, Bengtson et al., 1977; Kalish & Johnson, 1972). Of course, "fear of death" is not an uncomplicated notion (as we saw in Chapter 3), and older adults may differ among themselves in this regard. Also, variables that tend to

reduce or threaten quality of life in the elderly, such as poor physical and mental health, being widowed, or being institutionalized, appear likely to be inversely associated with fear of death (Marshall, 1975; Swenson, 1961; Templer, 1971). Nevertheless, many studies (such as Kastenbaum, 1967; Matse, 1975; Saul & Saul, 1973) have shown that elderly persons often talk about aging and death (see Box 15.2), even within fairly restrictive institutional environments that may not encourage such discussions.

Kalish (1985a) proposed three explanations for the relatively low level of fear of death among older adults: (1) they may accept death more easily than others because they have been able to live long, full lives; (2) they may have come to accept their own deaths as a result of a socialization process through which they repeatedly experience the deaths of others; and (3) they may have come to view their lives as having less value than the lives of younger persons and thus may not object so strenuously to giving them up. For any of these reasons, death may seem to an elderly person to represent less of a threat than, for example, debility, isolation, or dependence. As a result, most elders want to die at home, without pain, and without becoming a burden on their families.

Box 15.2 Jenny Joseph: Warning

When I am an old woman
I shall wear purple
With a red hat which doesn't go, and doesn't suit me.
And I shall spend my pension on brandy and summer gloves
And satin sandals, and say we've no money for butter.
I shall sit down on the pavement when I'm tired
And gobble up samples in shops and press alarm bells
And run my stick along the public railings
And make up for the sobriety of my youth.
I shall go out in my slippers in the rain
And pick the flowers in other people's gardens
And learn to spit.

You can wear terrible shirts and grow more fat
And eat three pounds of sausages at a go
Or only bread and a pickle for a week
And hoard pens and pencils and beermats and things in boxes.

But now we must have clothes that keep us dry
And pay our rent and not swear in the street
And set a good example for the children.
We must have friends to dinner and read the papers.

But maybe I ought to practice a little now?
So people who know me are not too shocked and surprised
When suddenly I am old, and start to wear purple. ■

SOURCE: "Warning" from *Selected Poems*, Bloodaxe Books Ltd.

Elders Who Are Coping with Life-Threatening Illness and Dying

Four specific needs of older adults who are coping with life-threatening illness or dying have been identified by Cook and Oltjenbruns (1998, p. 346): "maintaining a sense of self, participating in decisions regarding their lives, being reassured that their lives still have value, and receiving appropriate and adequate health care services."

Maintaining a Sense of Self

Preserving and affirming the value in the identity established in one's developmental work throughout life is an important task for individuals involved in transitions and reassessments like those that characterize developmental work in older adulthood. One's sense of integrity is founded on one's self-concept and self-esteem. As we have already noted, in the elderly this reassessment is typically pursued through the processes of life review—reflection, reminiscence, and reevaluation (Kaufman, 1986).

For elderly persons who are coping with life-threatening illness or dying, these processes need not be eliminated, although they may be curtailed by distress, lack of energy or ability to concentrate, absence of social support, and what often appear to be societal tendencies to devalue aging and the elderly. Against these inhibiting factors, family and professional caregivers can encourage life review activities in a number of ways. For example, they can directly participate by listening and serving as sounding boards or by providing stimuli such as photographs and prized mementos. Enabling ill or dying elders to remain at home or to retain and express their individuality within an institution is another way of affirming the person's uniqueness and value. Hospice programs often encourage ill or dying elders to identify achievable goals in craftwork or other ways of making tangible gifts to give to others. Passing on such gifts or valued personal items can be a cherished activity in itself and a way of leaving behind an enduring legacy. Accepting such gifts with warmth and appreciation is not an expression of a wish for the death of an elder but rather an act of affection.

Participating in Decisions about Their Lives

In Western society, autonomy or the ability to be in charge of one's own life is a prized value for many individuals. This may be particularly true for elderly persons, who may already have experienced a number of losses and who are often concerned with issues related to dependence. Older adults often see continuing to take part in decisions about their own lives, insofar as that is possible, as desirable. They may have a very broad and active role in such decision making, or that role might be highly constrained and largely symbolic. Nevertheless, it will usually be regarded as important and should be sustained as much as possible (see Box 15.3).

Fostering autonomy may require delicate negotiations among the individual elder, his or her family members, and professional care providers (Norlander & McSteen, 2001). For example, many older adults in the United States desire to and in fact do remain in their own homes. For such individuals, the decision to enter a long-term care facility may become a matter of contention between elders and other family members; in some cases, it may lead to a kind of learned helplessness when the elder's wishes are not supported or validated (Solomon, 1982).

As a culture, American society has long valued individualism and autonomy. However, it is only lately that our society has gradually come to realize—in theory, at least—the need for autonomy and the values that it represents for elders specifically. Thus, according to the Patient Self-Determination Act, which went into effect in 1991, individuals who enter a health care facility must be informed of their rights to fill out a living will or health care proxy, grant someone their durable power of attorney in health care matters, or otherwise

Box 15.3 Jimmy Carter, on Aging and Facing Death

We are not alone in our worry about both the physical aspects of aging and the prejudice that exists toward the elderly, which is similar to racism or sexism. What makes it different is that the prejudice also exists among those of us who are either within this group or rapidly approaching it. When I mentioned the title of this book to a few people, most of them responded, "Virtues? What could possibly be good about growing old?" The most obvious answer, of course, is to consider the alternative to aging. But there are plenty of other good answers—many based on our personal experiences and observations. . . .

Perhaps the most troubling aspect of our later years is the need to face the inevitability of our own impending physical death. For some people, this fact becomes a cause of great distress, sometimes with attendant resentment against God or even those around us. . . .

We can either face death with fear, anguish, and unnecessary distress among those around us or, through faith and courage, confront the inevitable with equanimity, good humor, and peace. When other members of my family realized that they had a terminal illness, the finest medical care was available to them. But each chose to forego elaborate artificial life-support systems and, with a few friends and family members at their bedside, they died peacefully. All of them retained their life-long character and their personal dignity. During the final days of their lives they continued to enjoy themselves as well as possible and to reduce the suffering and anguish of those who survived. My older sister Gloria was surrounded by her biker friends and talked about Harley-Davidsons and their shared pleasures on the road. Her funeral cortege, in fact, was a hearse preceded by thirty-seven Harley-Davidson motorcycles. Until the end, my brother Billy and my mother retained their superb sense of humor, and my youngest sister, Ruth, was stalwart in her faith as an evangelist.

Rosalynn and I hope to follow in their footsteps, and we have signed living wills that will preclude the artificial prolongation of our lives. ■

SOURCE: Carter, 1998, pp. 8–9, 82, 85–86.

have their wishes about treatment recorded and respected (Annenberg Washington Program, 1993; Cate & Gill, 1991). This procedure contributes to positive mental health and general satisfaction with life (Rodin & Langer, 1977). In other words, encouraging elders to participate in decision making about their own lives works against premature psychosocial and even physical decline and death—in elders who may have felt beset by loss of control and other external or internal pressures that undermine autonomy and quality of life and that foster hopelessness, helplessness, and "giving up" (Maizler et al., 1983; Schulz, 1976; Verwoerdt, 1976).

Being Reassured That Their Lives Still Have Value

As already noted, in a youth-oriented society ageism can foster discrimination against and devaluation of the lives of older adults. Combined with losses that such elders may have experienced, such as those involved in retirement or in bodily functioning, this attitude may encourage older persons to depreciate their own value and sense of worth. Life-threatening illness or dying may compound this process of devaluation by elders and others. Reduced contacts with significant others may lead to isolation and justified or unjustified concerns about social death even when physical death is not imminent. At least for some elders, a lasting dimension of quality of life involves the possibility or impossibility of expressing one's sexuality and sexual needs (Verwoerdt et al., 1969; Weinberg, 1969). Sexuality may take the form of sexual intercourse, but often it involves no more than simple touching or hugging, as we saw in the vignette near the beginning of this chapter.

The hospice philosophy, with its emphasis on life and maximizing present quality in living, points the way to an antidote to this sort of devaluation of the lives of elderly persons. Conveying to older adults—even those who are coping with life-threatening illness and dying—that their lives are still valued and appreciated, that they are important to and have much to teach others, and that they can still find satisfaction in living can enhance their sense of self-worth. Simple things like not talking down to elders, or assuming deafness or incompetence on their part, can do much to foster self-esteem and dignity. Showing

Hospice teen volunteers help a patient record precious memories as part of a lifetime legacies project.

family members how to be involved in constructive ways in the life and care of an ill or dying elder can improve present quality in living and diminish feelings of guilt or frustration for all concerned (Kaufman, 1986).

Receiving Appropriate and Adequate Health Care

Studies conducted some time ago in both the United States (Sudnow, 1967) and Great Britain (Simpson, 1976) demonstrated that older adults who were brought to hospital emergency rooms in critical condition were likely to receive care that was not as thorough or vigorous as that provided to younger persons. This finding raises questions of equity, particularly for those who are critically ill, dying, and vulnerable. Constructive lessons drawn from the life-affirming orientation of hospice programs, as well as positive developments in geriatric medicine and in gerontological specializations in other fields such as nursing and social work, can do much to change this situation. Older adults who are coping with life-threatening illness or dying have helped to create and support societal health care and welfare systems. In return, such systems should address their health care needs appropriately. Through political action and organizations such as the American Association of Retired Persons, elders are mobilizing to try to ensure that these needs are addressed.

Elders Who Are Coping with Bereavement and Grief

Most older adults encounter many occasions for bereavement. We illustrated some of these in the vignette near the beginning of this chapter. Not all of these losses are directly associated with death. However, death-related losses alone offer a broad array of challenges for many elderly persons in the form of the deaths of spouses, siblings, friends, and peers; the deaths of "very old" parents who may have lived to such advanced old age that their children have now reached "young old" status; the deaths of adult children; and the deaths of grandchildren or great-grandchildren. In addition, there is the special poignance of the death of a pet or companion animal when its owner is an older adult, and the impact of physical disability or psychosocial impoverishment. In fact, as Kastenbaum (1969) noted, older adults are likely to experience losses in greater number, variety, and rapidity than any other age group. Consequently, the elderly are often exposed to "bereavement overload," a situation in which they do not have the time or other resources needed to process their grief and mourn one significant loss effectively before another occurs. For such older persons, grief is a constant companion.

Illness, Disability, and Loss

Older adults may be grieving as a result of the many "little deaths" that they have experienced throughout life or in later adulthood. Among these are losses associated with illness of various sorts. Not every elderly person experiences such losses, but many live with one or more illness-related burdens. For example, high blood pressure and constriction or obstruction in the arteries are common in many elderly persons, as are certain forms of cancer (lung and prostate cancer in males; lung and breast cancer in females). Even when these conditions are not fatal, they may restrict quality of life. Chronic health problems, such as those involved in arthritis, emphysema, and diabetes, have similar effects.

Some long-term degenerative diseases, such as Alzheimer's and Parkinson's diseases or amyotrophic lateral sclerosis (often called "Lou Gehrig's disease" in the United States), have special import for losses in the elderly. These diseases may manifest themselves in ways that are physical (for example, through pain or loss of muscle control), psychological (for instance, through confusion), social (for example, through loss of mobility, institutionalization, and limited capacity for social exchanges), and/or spiritual (as in questions about the meaning of one's life and the goodness of a universe in which these losses occur). They affect both the individual person—for example, the elder with Alzheimer's disease who may be aware of his or her declining mental function—and those who love and must care for a person who may become unable to perform even the most basic activities of daily living (Kapust, 1982; Mace & Rabins, 1999). Often, these diseases generate the very special problems of complicated or "ambiguous" loss (Boss, 1999) and psychosocial death involved in what Toynbee (1968a, p. 266) has termed "the premature death of the spirit in a human body that still remains physically alive." These issues stand alongside very difficult problems of decision making, appropriate modes of care, and costs.

Less dramatic, but still significant in terms of well-being, are the accumulated losses or deficits that elders often experience in effective functioning. These can include sensory and cognitive impairments, oral and dental problems, loss of energy, reduced muscle strength, diminished sense of balance, and problems related to osteoporosis, arthritis, or sexual functioning. Specific losses of this sort and their combined effect on an individual elder can reduce quality in living and generate regret on the part of that person, family members, and care providers for what has been lost.

The Death of a Spouse, Life Partner, Sibling, Friend, or Other Significant Peer

Surviving the death of a spouse, sibling, life partner, friend, or other significant peer is a common experience in older adulthood (Bennett & Bennett, 2001). The individual who has died may be a marriage partner, a brother or sister, an individual of the same or opposite sex with whom one has lived for some time and formed a stable relationship, or a special friend or peer. One problem for some elders (particularly among the "very old" group) may be the loss through death or incapacitation of most or all of the members of one's family of origin. Survivors of losses of this type constitute a special group of "lonely oldies" whose particular form of loneliness and deprivation may not be assuaged even by the joy they find in the presence and attention of members of younger generations.

In general, sustaining roles and relationships is crucial for most bereaved elders. The most important of these roles and relationships may include companionship, someone with whom one can talk, someone with whom to share burdens, pleasures, and sexual gratification, and someone to offer presence and care in the future as one's own needs increase (Lopata, 1996; Lund, 1989). When the relationship with the partner is such that their lives are closely interwoven, "the loss of one partner may cut across the very meaning of the other's existence" (Raphael, 1983, p. 177). Of course, most relationships with a partner are complicated in some ways and are not without conflict. Still, every older adult experiences multiple losses in the death of a significant peer, and those who have experienced the death of a spouse or life partner may be at higher risk during the following year for increased morbidity and mortality (from illness or suicide, for example) (Glick et al., 1974; Stroebe & Stroebe, 1987).

The death of a spouse or close companion in late adulthood often generates bereavement experiences of separation and deprivation, involving grief (including yearning, pain, and anger), isolation, and loneliness (Worden, 2002). In our society, the burdens of survival following the death of a spouse most often fall upon women (Hurd & Macdonald, 2001). In the United States, women outlive men on the average and women most often marry men who are their own age or older. In addition, widowers are more likely than widows to remarry (Carey, 1979), partly because of the relative availability of potential spouses for elderly males (and the opposite for elderly females), and because widowed males often do not do well physically or mentally outside of marriage. However, it is not the case that all widowed elders wish to marry again. Emotional ties to the deceased are likely to persist and memories may be cherished by both sexes (Moss & Moss, 1984). Thus, it may not so much be the experience of bereavement as its expression that is influenced by gender roles.

Both in place of or as a supplement to other forms of social support, self-help groups (Lund et al., 1985; Yalom & Vinogradov, 1988) and widow-to-widow programs (Silverman, 1969, 1986) have been found to be very helpful for bereaved elders, as we saw in Chapters 10 and 11. Social interventions of this type typically serve the full range of bereaved persons who have experienced certain kinds of losses (not only those evaluated as "high risk") and do so on a foundation of shared experience. Through these interventions, individuals who have had similar bereavement experiences can share feelings and problems and can encourage each other to regain control in living by evaluating options and alternatives represented in the lives of the others. Also, bereaved elders can obtain helpful information about loss, grief, and living.

The Death of an Adult Child

To a parent, one's offspring always remains one's child in some important ways despite his or her age. In the United States, as average life expectancy increases, it becomes increasingly likely that middle-aged and elderly parents may experience the deaths of their adult children. For example, many young adults in their twenties and thirties who die in accidents or from communicable diseases and individuals in their forties, fifties, and sixties who die of degenerative diseases may leave behind a surviving parent (Rando, 1986b). In fact, one study (Moss et al., 1986) reported that as many as 10 percent of elderly persons with children had experienced the death of a child when the parent was 60 years of age or older.

For such a parent, the grief felt at this type of loss may be combined with special developmental complications (Blank, 1998; Brubaker, 1985; Moss et al., 1986). For example, surviving parents may feel that the death of an adult child is an untimely violation of the natural order of things, in which members of the older generation are expected to die before the younger (see Box 15.4). Such parents may experience survivor guilt and may wish to have died in place of their child. In addition, there may be special hardships if the adult child had assumed certain responsibilities as helper or care provider for the parent. After the death, these needs will have to be met in some other way, and the parent may face an increased likelihood of institutionalization or of diminished social contacts. How family legacies will be carried forward is less certain. The parent may also join to his or her own sense of loss added regret and grief for the pain that the spouse or children of the adult child are experiencing. In some cases, the older survivor may be obliged to take over the care of surviving grandchildren.

The Death of a Grandchild or Great-Grandchild

If it is more likely that children and adolescents will have living grandparents and great-grandparents because of increased life expectancy among older adults, then it is also more likely that these older adults will experience the death of one of their grandchildren or great-grandchildren. This area of bereavement is not well-studied, even though it is recognized that cross-generational relationships between grandchildren and grandparents can involve special bonds of intimacy (Wilcoxon, 1986).

Grandparents have been described as "forgotten grievers" (Gyulay, 1975), both connected to and distanced from events involving the fatal illness, death, or bereavement of a grandchild. The grief of such grandparents responds to their own losses, to the losses experienced by their son or daughter, and to the losses experienced by the grandchild. Such grief may contain elements of hurt over such an "out of sequence" death, anger at parents who perhaps did not seem to take adequate care of the grandchild, guilt at their own presumed failure to prevent the loss or death, and resentment at God for letting such tragic

Box 15.4 Lament of a Man for His Son

Son, my son!

I will go up to the mountain
And there I will light a fire
To the feet of my son's spirit,
And there will I lament him;
Saying,
O my son,
What is my life to me, now you are departed!

Son, my son,
In the deep earth
We softly laid thee in a Chief's robe,
In a warrior's gear.
Surely there,
In the spirit land
Thy deeds attend thee!
Surely,
The corn comes to the ear again!

But I, here,
I am the stalk that the seed-gatherers
Descrying empty, afar, left standing
Son, my son!
What is my life to me, now you are departed? ■

SOURCE: From *The American Rhythm* by Mary Austin.

events occur (Galinsky, 1999; Reed, 2000). All of these reactions may be complicated in a situation in which there is unwillingness to acknowledge certain causes of death (such as suicide or HIV infection) or to discuss openly the circumstances of the death. Finally, there may be conflicts between grandparents and one or more surviving parent—for example, when members of the older or younger generation blame the others for a perceived failure to prevent the death or when grandparents are drawn into or otherwise affected by disputes between the surviving parents.

Loss of a Pet

We discussed pet loss in Chapter 10, but it is important to note that loss of a pet or companion animal can be of great and special importance in the lives of older adults. Companion animals can be sources of unconditional love, as well as objects of care and affection in the lives of many elderly persons. Some of these animals protect and aid the handicapped. In recent years, others have become welcome visitors in many nursing homes, long-term care facilities, and other institutions. In these roles, companion animals can relieve loneliness, contribute to a sense of purpose, and enhance self-esteem (Rynearson, 1978).

When an elderly person's companion animal dies, it becomes immediately obvious that the key point is the relationship with that animal, rather than its intrinsic value (Kay, 1984; Lagoni et al., 1994; Nieburg & Fischer, 1982). Such a loss can represent a major bereavement for an elderly person who may otherwise have only limited social contacts (Quackenbush, 1985; Shirley & Mercier, 1983) and thus should not be dismissed as insignificant. Similar losses and grief may occur when an older adult is no longer able to care for an animal, cannot pay for veterinary services that it needs, cannot take it along when relocating to new living quarters or to an institution, or must have a sick or feeble animal euthanized (Kay et al., 1988). Older adults may also be concerned about what will happen to a prized pet if they should die.

Suicide among the Elderly

The highest rates of suicide in the United States are found among the elderly. In 1999, these rates were 18.3 per 100,000 in those who were 75 to 84 years of age and 19.2 per 100,000 in those who were 85 years of age and older (Hoyert et al., 2001). Both of these figures, as well as a suicide rate of 15.9 per 100,000 for all elders at or over 65 years of age, are considerably beyond the overall rate of 10.7 suicides per 100,000 for the U.S. population as a whole. Among elderly persons, Caucasian-American males are by far the most likely to take their own lives. In general, older adults are far more deliberate in suicidal behavior than their younger counterparts, they are unlikely to ask for help that might interfere with their decision, and they are unlikely to fail to complete the suicidal act once they have undertaken the attempt (Butler & Lewis, 1982; Farberow & Moriwaki, 1975; McIntosh, 1985). Therefore, any indicators of suicidal tendencies on the part of elderly persons should be taken seriously and evaluated carefully.

The single most significant factor associated with suicidal behavior in the elderly is depression (Leenaars et al., 1992; Osgood, 1992). Another important variable may be institutionalization in a long-term care facility (Osgood et al., 1991). Older adults may begin to contemplate suicide: when the life review process results in a sense of despair about the meaning of their lives; when they experience physical or mental debility; when they experience the death of a spouse or other significant person (especially a person on whom they had been dependent for care and support); or when confinement in an institution seems to undermine control over their lives. In these circumstances, some may come to consider suicide an acceptable alternative to continued living under what appear to those individuals to be unsatisfactory conditions. Other factors—such as the impact of an unwanted layoff or retirement on males whose identity had hitherto been greatly dependent on their vocational roles (a factor that is increasingly likely to impact women as they move into similar vocational roles), previous dependency on a now-deceased female caretaker (Campbell & Silverman, 1996; Kohn & Kohn, 1978), or social isolation—appear to account for much higher rates (rising with age) of male than female suicides among the elderly (Miller, 1979; Osgood, 1992).

In American society, there are a number of obstacles to interventions designed to minimize the likelihood of suicidal behavior among the elderly. Some of these obstacles arise from efforts to apply interventions that have been successful with younger persons in ways that are inappropriate to the developmental situation of older adults. For example, claims that suicide is a permanent solution to a temporary problem apply more aptly to impulsive decisions by adolescents than to decisions arising from an elder's long deliberation. Equally, advice to concentrate on a promising future or to consider interpersonal obligations to others seems better suited to younger persons than to elders with less rosy expectations and diminished social relationships. Again, arguing that suicide terminates life prematurely and cuts short a full life is less obviously relevant to a person in old age. Also, some argue that efforts intended to thwart suicidal behavior in the elderly are inappropriate assaults on the autonomy of older adults, although others make a vigorous case that too-ready tolerance of suicide among the elderly may reflect lack of interest in the lives of such individuals (Moody, 1984; Osgood, 1992).

In the end, suicidal behavior among the elderly needs to be understood within the broad physical, psychosocial, and developmental situation of older adults in American society (Osgood, 2000). Particular attention must be paid to social attitudes associated with ageism, a devaluation of worth and meaning in the lives of the elderly, and an unresponsiveness to the needs of older adults. Significant changes in these and other socio-cultural factors will be required to alter suicidal behavior in the elderly.

Summary

In this chapter, we explored many aspects of interactions between elderly persons and death in our society. We saw that the distinctive developmental tasks of older adulthood (striving to achieve ego integrity versus despair) have a direct bearing on how elders relate to death. These tasks influence encounters with death among the elderly (we noted high death rates mainly brought about by long-term degenerative diseases) and attitudes of older adults toward death (in general, manifesting less anxiety than younger persons). We noted the importance for elders coping with life-threatening illness and dying to maintain a sense of self, participate in decisions regarding their lives, be reassured that their lives still have value, and receive appropriate and adequate health care services. We considered that older adults may find themselves coping with bereavement and grief as a result of illness, disability, and loss; the death of a spouse, sibling, or other significant peer; the death of an adult child; the death of a grandchild or great-grandchild; or the loss of a pet or companion animal.

We also observed that high rates of suicide among the elderly are strongly associated with depression.

Questions for Review and Discussion

1. Think back to the situation of the elderly couple described in the vignette near the beginning of this chapter. What types of losses did they experience? How did those losses affect them? How did they help each other?

2. Do you know an elderly person who has experienced significant death-related losses? What were those losses like for that person? How did you or could you help such a person?

Suggested Readings

On aging and the elderly, consult:

Butler, R. N. (1975). *Why Survive? Being Old in America.*

Erikson, E. H., Erikson, J. M., & Kivnick, H. (1986). *Vital Involvements in Old Age.*

Nouwen, H., & Gaffney, W. J. (1990). *Aging: The Fulfillment of Life.*

Perls, T. T., Silver, M. H., & Lauerman, J. F. (2000). *Living to 100: Lessons in Living to Your Maximum Potential at Any Age.*

Thorson, J. A. (2000a). *Aging in a Changing Society.*

Thorson, J. A. (Ed.). (2000b). *Perspectives on Spiritual Well-Being and Aging.*

On death and the elderly, consult:

Campbell, S., & Silverman, P. (1996). *Widower: When Men Are Left Alone.*

Galinsky, N. (1999). *When a Grandchild Dies: What to Do, What to Say, How to Cope.*

Hurd, M., & Macdonald, M. (2001). *Beyond Coping: Widows Reinventing Their Lives.*

Leenaars, A. A., Maris, R. W., McIntosh, J. L., & Richman, J. (Eds.). (1992). *Suicide and the Older Adult.*

Lopata, H. Z. (1996). *Current Widowhood; Myths and Realities.*

Lund, D. A. (1989). *Older Bereaved Spouses: Research with Practical Applications.*

Norlander, L., & McSteen, K. (2001). *Choices at the End of Life: Finding Out What Your Parents Want Before It's Too Late.*

Osgood, N. J. (1992). *Suicide in Later Life: Recognizing the Warning Signs.*

Osgood, N. J., Brant, B. A., & Lipman, A. (1991). *Suicide among the Elderly in Long-Term Care Facilities.*

Reed, M. L. (2000). *Grandparents Cry Twice: Help for Bereaved Grandparents.*

Stroebe, W., & Stroebe, M. S. (1987). *Bereavement and Health: The Psychological and Physical Consequences of Partner Loss.*

InfoTrac College Edition
For more information, explore the InfoTrac College Edition at **http://www.infotrac-college.com/Wadsworth**

Enter search terms: AGEISM, CAUSES OF DEATH IN THE ELDERLY, DEVELOPMENTAL TASKS IN THE ELDERLY OR IN OLDER ADULTS, EGO INTEGRITY, "GRAYING" OF SOCIETY, OLDER ADULTHOOD, PET LOSS, SENESCENCE, SUICIDE AND THE ELDERLY, SURVIVOR GUILT.

Part Six

Legal, Conceptual, and Moral Issues

In Chapters 16 through 19, we address legal, conceptual, moral, religious, and philosophical issues that are directly related to dying, death, and bereavement. Issues related to the law, suicide, assisted suicide and euthanasia, and questions of ultimate meaning are brought together here because they pose markedly pressing conceptual and moral challenges. Thus, in addressing these issues, one must undertake two parallel struggles: first, to *understand* the facts and implications of the situation at hand, along with the options that are available; second, to *choose* one's values and a particular course of action within the situation.

We begin with *legal issues* because the law is the most explicit framework of rules and procedures that a society establishes within its death system. Thus, in Chapter 16 we describe what the American legal system requires or permits before, at the time of, and after death.

In Chapter 17, we seek to clarify the concept of *suicide*, provide data about some common patterns in suicidal and life-threatening behavior, describe some perspectives that may help to explain this behavior, discuss its impact on bereaved survivors, suggest constructive ways to intervene to minimize the likelihood of a completed suicide, and introduce the concept of rational suicide.

In Chapter 18, we clarify the concepts of *assisted suicide and euthanasia*, describe moral and religious arguments that have been advanced to favor or oppose such activities, and illustrate what they might mean for social policy through examples taken from the Netherlands and the state of Oregon.

In Chapter 19, we address questions of ultimate values by examining *the meaning and place of death in human life.* Many religious and philosophical perspectives seek answers to these questions. Such perspectives are frameworks within which both individuals and particular societies approach death-related experiences. ■

Chapter Sixteen

LEGAL ISSUES

EVERY SOCIETY DEVELOPS A MORE OR LESS formal system of law to serve its interests as a community and to promote the welfare of its members. Such a system may include both written and unwritten rules and procedures. These rules and procedures reflect values upheld by a society as well as ways in which it organizes itself to implement those values. In contemporary America, a formal set of rules and procedures governing social conduct is embodied in our legal system.

Any system of societal rules and procedures is likely to function most effectively when social values are well established and when it is responding to familiar events. It may be less effective when there is a lack of consensus about social values, when the values are in flux, or when progress poses new problems not easily addressed by existing legal frameworks. In recent years in the United States, challenges to the legal system have arisen from all three of these circumstances: there is disagreement in our heterogeneous population about some social values, other social values appear to be in transition, and new challenges have arisen from new circumstances and from new medical procedures and technology.

In this chapter, we discuss ways in which American society has organized itself through its legal system to deal with issues relating to death, dying, and bereavement. Our vignette describes the death in 1992 of the wife of Dr. Kenneth Moritsugu and the subsequent death in 1996 of one of his daughters, as well as what he did to carry out their wishes for organ donation. We then offer brief comments on the American legal system before taking up three important clusters of legal issues: (1) those concerned with issues that arise prior to death, such as advance directives for treatment of the dying; (2) those that arise at death itself, such as definition, determination, and certification of death; and (3) those that may have been initiated prior to death but whose real force is exerted in the aftermath of death, such as organ, tissue, or body donation, and issues concerning disposition of one's body and property. ■

Donor Husband, Donor Father

It was October 28, 1992, and Kenneth Moritsugu, M.D., M.P.H., was returning to his home in Silver Spring, Maryland, from Baltimore. He had taken his aunt and sister, visiting from Hawaii, on a day trip to visit art museums and the Inner Harbor—a mammoth shopping complex along the waterfront. His wife, Donna Lee, had elected to stay home.

As the three approached the end of their commute, traffic slowed. An accident had taken place, they thought. A long, tedious drive lay ahead as every car strained to advance.

As they approached the scene of the accident, Dr. Moritsugu looked out his window. He noticed the similarities in the wrecked vehicle and the car at home, the one Donna Lee drove. Panic set in as he realized the crushed vehicle on the road was in fact his wife's.

At the hospital, he learned Donna Lee was brain dead and would never recover. "Several years before, we had talked about what we should do when the other died," Dr. Moritsugu recalled. "We had both said we wanted to donate. When the concept was brought up in that deepest, darkest moment, the memory of that conversation came back to me, and I had the privilege of carrying out her wishes. Because of her, many other individuals are surviving today."

A year later, Dr. Moritsugu, Assistant Surgeon General of the United States and Medical Director of the Federal Bureau of Prisons of the U.S. Department of Justice, began a personal crusade to encourage organ and tissue donation. . . .

[Dr. Moritsugu] has suffered the bittersweet solace of donation not only once, but twice.

In 1996 Dr. Moritsugu's 22-year-old daughter, Vikki Lianne, was struck by an automobile while crossing the street. She, too, was declared brain dead and her organs donated.

It was only later that Dr. Moritsugu learned that Vikki Lianne and his older daughter, Erika Elizabeth, had made the commitment to donate their organs shortly after their mother's death. They had learned how much the donations had meant to others, and they had seen the comfort it had brought their family.

"It makes me proud," Dr. Moritsugu said. "We talk about donation as affecting one person, but there are ripples. Each donation affects so many more people—family, friends, colleagues."

Dr. Moritsugu is quick to point out that he should not be credited for the donations. "I didn't do anything," he noted. "I was just someone who happened to be there. They [Donna Lee and Vikki Lianne] are the ones who made the miracle."

Through Donna Lee:

- A marine biologist engaged in research on the effects of environmental pollution received a new heart.
- A 35-year-old diabetic hospital custodian received a kidney and pancreas.
- An 11-year-old child on dialysis, failing in school, received the other kidney. He is now making straight As and is on his way to college.
- A retired schoolteacher received a new liver.
- A young retarded woman who had lost her sight due to an accident received a cornea, while the other cornea provided new vision to a 49-year-old government worker.

Through Vikki Lianne:

- A mother of five received a new heart.
- A widow with four children received a lung.
- A 59-year-old man, an active volunteer with a local charitable organization, received a liver.
- A widower with one daughter received a kidney.
- A married, working father of several children received the other kidney.
- A 26-year-old man and a 60-year-old woman received her corneas. (Source: From "Donor Husband, Donor Father: UNOS Board Member Kenneth Moritsugu Looks Beyond Tragedy to Serving Others." UNOS Update. [Special Edition, Spring], p. 26. Reprinted with permission.)

American Society and Its Laws

In the United States, our federal system assigns certain obligations (such as foreign relations and defense) to the national government and reserves most other responsibilities to the authority of the individual states and their subordinate entities. For most issues related to death, dying, and bereavement, state law governs what is to be done and how it is to be done. Given the diversity cherished by our states, different laws and procedures apply in different states. Some states might even have no legislation on a given subject. Thus, this chapter can only address legal issues and structures in a general way. Individuals should seek competent legal advice that is appropriate to their particular circumstances.

The establishment of *legislation* is often a slow and complicated process subject to political pressures, competing interests, and social circumstances. When values in society are changing or when there is no consensus on social values, the process of embodying and codifying those values in legislation may not go forward easily. Difficult cases may frustrate a society in its process of determining how to implement its values. This is particularly true in cases that involve fast-moving advances in medical technology and procedures.

When no specific legislation covers a specific subject, decisions must still be made in individual cases. One way this is done is by drawing on precedents set by prior court decisions. Such prior decisions and precedents constitute *case law.*

When neither the legislature nor the courts in their prior decisions have addressed a topic, the legal system turns to *common law.* Originally, this was a set of shared values and views drawn from English and early American legal and social history. In practice, it is typically represented in a more formal way by the definitions contained in standard legal dictionaries. *Black's Law Dictionary* (Black, 1999) is one well-known example of this type of organized expression of common law.

It is important to be clear about which type(s) of legal rules and procedures apply to any given issue. The principles set forth here constitute the broad legal and social framework within which a large spectrum of moral, social, and human issues are addressed in American society. This legal framework is an important part of the contemporary American death system, but only one such component. Some death-related issues, such as cemetery regulations and cultural or religious rituals, are not directly addressed by the legal system. Other issues, such as assisted suicide and euthanasia (see Chapter 18), have challenged our legal system and remain wholly or partly outside its framework.

Legal Issues before Death

The term *advance directives* applies to a wide range of instructions that one might make orally or set down in writing about actions that one would or would not want to be taken if one were somehow incapacitated and unable to join in making decisions (Cantor, 1993). Of course, any advance directive depends on an individual's willingness to address ahead of time the implications of death for his or her life and the lives of his or her family members and friends. Many people are reluctant to consider issues of this sort, perhaps because they involve contemplating the implications of one's own mortality. Our vignette at the outset of this chapter makes clear that Donna Lee and Vikki Lianne Moritsugu had at least discussed organ donation with some family members before their untimely deaths.

Since the end of 1991, federal legislation in the form of the Patient Self-Determination Act has required that individuals being admitted to a health care institution that receives federal Medicare or Medicaid funds be informed of their right to accept or refuse treatment and to execute an advance directive. Such individuals must also be told about the options available to them to implement those rights (Annenberg Washington Program, 1993; Cate & Gill, 1991; Kapp, 1994). Even so, many do not exercise their right to complete an advance directive—but that, too, is within their rights.

Some advance directives are intended to come into force at the time of one's death—for example, directives on organ and tissue donation, the disposition of one's body, or the distribution of one's estate. We discuss those directives later in this chapter. First, we consider advance directives that bear upon decisions about treatment before death. Advance directives of this sort include living wills, durable powers of attorney in health care matters, and the "Five Wishes" document.

Living Wills

Living wills were originally developed in the early 1970s as a means whereby persons who were competent decision makers could express their wishes to professional care providers, family members, and friends about interventions that they might or might not wish to permit in the event of a terminal illness. In particular, living wills are intended to convey a set of prior instructions for situations in which a terminal illness has left an individual unable to make or to express such decisions.

As originally formulated, living wills had no legal standing and could take any form. At that time, a "living will" was simply any sort of document through which an individual could express various wishes about treatment prior to death. The common threads of these early living wills were: (1) a concern about the possibility or likelihood of finding oneself in a situation in which the mode of dying would leave one unable to take part in making important decisions; and (2) a concern about the context of dying in which one might be in an unfamiliar or alien environment, among strangers or others who might have their own individual or professional views of what should or should not be done, and who might not understand, appreciate, or agree with the wishes of the person who wrote the living will.

In response to concerns of this sort, early living wills usually combined a desire expressed by those who composed and signed them; a request that the desire be given serious consideration by those providing care to the signers; and an effort to share responsibility for certain decisions made in specified situations. For this last point, living wills could be understood as an effort by those who composed them to protect health care providers from accusations of malpractice as well as from civil liability or criminal prosecution. However we interpret their context, living wills represent a desire to promote individual autonomy in death-related matters by thinking ahead about issues of life and death, formulating one's views concerning important decisions, and communicating them to others (Alexander, 1988).

In the absence of legal standing or requirements, individuals and organizations could formulate living wills any way they wished. An organization called

Choice in Dying undertook one early effort to standardize the form and language of living wills. That organization produced various versions of a living will that have been widely distributed. In March 2000, Choice in Dying merged into the Partnership for Caring: America's Voices for the Dying (1620 Eye Street NW, Suite 202, Washington, DC 20006; tel. 800-989-9455 or 202-286-8071; www.partnershipforcaring.org) from which living wills and other end-of-life resources (such as Choice in Dying, 1996) can be obtained. The key passages in these living wills are a directive to withhold or withdraw treatments that merely prolong dying when one is in an incurable or irreversible condition with no reasonable expectation of recovery, and a directive to limit interventions in such circumstances to those designed to provide comfort and relieve pain.

Note that living wills characteristically do not call for direct killing or active euthanasia. Most often, they explicitly state: "I am not asking that my life be directly taken, but that my dying be not unreasonably prolonged." Most living wills are primarily intended to refuse certain kinds of cure-oriented interventions ("artificial means" and "heroic measures") when they are no longer relevant ("futile care"), to request that dying be permitted to take its own natural course, and to ask that suffering associated with life-threatening illness be mitigated with effective palliative care, even if such palliative care should have a collateral or side effect of hastening the actual moment of death.

The broad legal context for living wills is the well-established right to privacy and the right of competent decision makers to give or withhold informed consent, to accept or refuse interventions even when that might affect the timing of the individual's death (Alderman & Kennedy, 1995; Cantor, 1993; President's Commission, 1982, 1983a, 1983b; Rozovsky, 1990).

In 1976, the California legislature enacted the first "natural death" or "living will" legislation. Since then, similar legislation (sometimes with local variations) has been passed in all 50 states and the District of Columbia. Typically, such legislation: (1) specifies the conditions under which a competent adult is authorized to sign a document of this type; (2) stipulates the form that such a document must take in order to have legal force; (3) defines what sorts of interventions can or cannot be refused—for example, interventions undertaken with a view toward cure, which may or may not include hydration or nutrition; (4) authorizes oral or written repudiation of the signed document by the signer at any time; (5) requires that professional care providers either cooperate with the document's directives or withdraw from the case and arrange for alternative care (consenting to do so is thus legally protected, whereas failure to do so is theoretically subject not merely to potential malpractice liability but also to penalties that could extend to loss of professional licensure); and (6) stipulates that death resulting from actions authorized by the legislation is not to be construed for insurance purposes as suicide.

A presidential commission (President's Commission, 1982) and other agencies have proposed models for legislation on this subject. These proposals typically: (1) relate to all competent adults and mature minors—not only those who are dying; (2) apply to all medical interventions and do not limit the types of interventions that may be refused; (3) permit the designation of a surrogate or substitute decision maker in a manner similar to that described in the following section; (4) require health care providers to follow the directives of the individual and incorporate sanctions for those who do not do so; and (5) stipulate that palliative care be continued for those who refuse other interventions. This model goes beyond the scope of early living wills and incorporates features now more typical of durable powers of attorney.

Historically, living wills have not been without their limitations or potential difficulties (Culver & Gert, 1990; Robertson, 1991). Like any documents written down in advance of a complex and life-threatening situation, living wills may not anticipate every relevant feature that may arise. Partly for this reason, their significance and force may be subject to interpretation and/or dispute among the very family members and professional care providers whom they seek to guide (Colen, 1991; Flynn, 1992).

Durable Powers of Attorney in Health Care Matters

Because of limitations and potential difficulties associated with living wills, some have preferred an alternative approach. One alternative is found in state legislation that authorizes a *durable power of attorney for the making of decisions in health care matters.* "Power of attorney" is a well-established legal doctrine whereby one individual authorizes another individual (or group of individuals) to make decisions and take actions on behalf of the first individual in specific circumstances or for a specified period of time. For example, a power of attorney might authorize an individual to sign a contract on my behalf to close the sale of my house at a time when I am not available to do so. Historically, a power of attorney or authorization to act in place of some individual continued only while that person remained competent. A "durable" power of attorney is one that endures until it is revoked; that is, it continues in force even (or especially) when the individual who authorized the designation is no longer able to act as a competent decision maker. A durable power of attorney in health care matters (sometimes called a "health care proxy") is one that is concerned with issues of health care.

Advocates argue that a durable power of attorney has two significant advantages over other written or oral directives, such as a living will. First, it empowers a surrogate or substitute decision maker to make decisions on behalf of some individual in any and all circumstances that the document covers. Second, the surrogate decision maker can be instructed to refuse all interventions, to insist on all interventions, or to approve some interventions and reject others. The first advantage attempts to minimize problems arising from changing circumstances and competing interpretations of written documents; the second allows the person authorizing the surrogate—and the surrogate—some degree of freedom in choosing which interventions to accept and which to refuse.

Durable powers of attorney in health care matters were first authorized in the state of California in 1985. Similar legislation has since been approved in nearly all states and the District of Columbia. Sample documents and booklets explaining durable powers of attorney in health care matters are available from the Partnership for Caring, the American Bar Association, and the American Association of Retired Persons. Note that to be effective any durable power of attorney must satisfy the legislative requirements of the legal jurisdiction within which it is to be enforced. Competent legal advice should be sought to confirm this. Interested parties are usually advised (wherever possible) to complete both a state-authorized living will (providing general guidance to decision makers) and an appropriate durable power of attorney for health care (authorizing discretion within those guidelines on the part of a health care agent or substitute decision maker).

Five Wishes

In 1997, the Florida Commission on Aging with Dignity created a new document called "Five Wishes" that combines many of the best elements of living wills and durable powers of attorney in health care matters. This document is specifically designed to be easy to understand, simple to use, personal in character, and thorough. As the cover page of the document says, it "is a gift to your family members and friends so that they won't have to guess what you want." "Five Wishes" asks the person filling out the document to express his or her wishes about the following issues and provides guidance in relation to each of these issues: (1) the person I want to make health care decisions for me when I can't make them for myself; (2) the kind of medical treatment I want or don't want if I am close to death, in a coma, or have permanent and severe brain damage and am not expected to recover from that situation, or am in another condition under which I do not wish to be kept alive; (3) how comfortable I want to be; (4) how I want people to treat me; and (5) what I want my loved ones to know.

Because of widespread interest in "Five Wishes," a cooperative effort was undertaken with the American Bar Association Commission on Legal Problems of the Elderly to develop a revised version structured to meet the legal requirements of other jurisdictions. At this writing, one million copies of the "Five Wishes" document have been distributed. It is valid in 35 states and the District of Columbia; elsewhere it can be used to help individuals offer guidance to their care providers. The entire "Five Wishes" document, along with a video and accompanying booklet (Aging with Dignity, 2001), can be obtained for a nominal fee from Aging with Dignity (P.O. Box 1661, Tallahassee, FL 32302-1661; tel. 888-5-WISHES or 850-681-2010) or ordered from their Web site www.agingwithdignity.org.

Legal Issues at Death

The central issues that relate to death itself and the time at which it occurs are definition, determination, and certification of death.

Definition of Death

Definition of death reflects the fundamental human and social understanding of the difference between life and death. This distinction underlies all issues related to determination and certification of death. These issues all involve approaches designed to identify whether or not the condition that society has defined as death exists. Above all, determination of death must be based on a definition that discriminates between real and only apparent death. This definition is essential in order to be as clear as possible about who is to be included among those who are alive or dead. It would be just as wrong to treat the dead as if they were living, as it would be to treat the living as if they were already dead. The dead are no longer alive; the living are not yet dead.

The difference between being alive and being dead is of course a profoundly important one. Aristotle called death a kind of destruction or perishing that involves a change from being to nonbeing (see *Physics*, bk. V, ch. 1; *Metaphysics*, bk. XI, ch. 11). He meant that death involves a change in the very substance of the being. When a human being dies an important consequence follows: there is no longer a human being present—instead, there is only a body or a corpse. Because the corpse is still an object deserving honor and respect it is not simply to be discarded in a cavalier or thoughtless manner. However, it is also important not to confuse the remains with a living human person (Nabe, 1981). That is why two distinct things can be said after a death of a loved one: "These are the hands that held and caressed me" and "Everything that was essential to the person whom I knew and loved is no longer here."

How can we define the condition that we call death, the condition that is the opposite of life? Here is one answer:

> An individual who has sustained either (1) irreversible cessation of circulatory and respiratory functions, or (2) irreversible cessation of all functions of the entire brain, including the brain stem, is dead. (President's Commission, 1981, p. 73)

That definition was codified in the Uniform Determination of Death Act (UDDA; reprinted in Iserson, 1994, p. 611) and has since been adopted (as such or in a closely modified form) by many state legislatures.

Several points in the UDDA are critical:

1. It speaks of "an individual," not "a person," because whether or not a person is present is precisely the issue.
2. It requires *irreversible*—not merely temporary or reversible—cessation of the designated functions.
3. It recognizes the possibility of situations in which external interventions mask or hide the precise status of respiratory and circulatory functions—in which it may be unclear whether or not the individual is actually sustaining those functions spontaneously or is at least capable of doing so.
4. In such circumstances, the UDDA requires evaluation of the capacities of the central nervous system—which is the body's command and control center—because the definition recognizes that under normal circumstances,

the life of the central nervous system ends shortly (a matter of a few minutes) after respiratory and circulatory functions are brought to a halt.

5. Finally, and most important, in such circumstances, it concludes that irreversible cessation of all functions of the brain and brain stem (which controls autonomic activities, such as respiration and circulation) is the condition understood as death.

Some have proposed that the irreversible loss of the capacity for bodily integration and social interaction is sufficient to define the death of a human being (Veatch, 1975, 1976). This proposal focuses on neocortical or upper brain activity as definitive of the presence or absence of human life, to the exclusion of lower brain or brain stem activity. It contends that the human person may be dead even when bodily or vegetative functioning remains. In other words, this proposal would regard the presence of a "persistent vegetative state" as the equivalent of death (Gervais, 1986).

Critics have charged that this proposal could lead, in the extreme, to a situation in which society would be asked to bury a body that demonstrated no upper brain function but in which there was spontaneous respiratory and circulatory function (Ramsey, 1970; Walton, 1979, 1982). More realistically, this situation would call not for immediate burial but for the removal of artificial support, including artificial means of providing nutrition and hydration, on the grounds that the individual was no longer alive *as a human being*. All of these decisions depend on a concept or definition of death; if one conceded that the individual was alive and still proposed to remove artificial support, one would be advocating some form of euthanasia (see Chapter 18).

Both the UDDA and the proposal from the President's Commission also include the following sentence: "A determination of death must be made in accordance with accepted medical standards."

Determination of Death

Determination of death has to do with deciding whether or not death has actually occurred, establishing the conditions under which it took place, evaluating the nature of the death, and confirming whether or not further investigation is required. This process is similar to the work of referees in organized sports. Those involved in determination of death are expected to contribute expertise about the subject and good judgment in applying their expertise to individual cases. Like referees, those who determine that death has occurred do not make the rules. Their role is to apply tests or criteria in an expert manner to arrive at the best decisions possible. They may also help to develop new and better ways of determining death.

Traditional tests applied to determine whether or not someone has died are well known. In times past one might hold a feather under an individual's nostrils and observe whether it moved when he or she exhaled or inhaled. Sometimes a mirror was used in a similar way to observe whether moisture contained in exhalations from a warm body condensed on its cool surface. One could also place one's ear on the chest to listen for a heartbeat or touch the body at certain points to feel for arterial pulsation. Over time, more sensitive and discriminating tests have been developed. For example, stethoscopes make possible a more refined way of listening for internal body sounds.

In all cases, the tests used to determine death depend on established procedures and available technology. These tests vary from place to place and from time to time (Shrock, 1835). The complex testing procedures of a highly developed society are not likely to be available in the rudimentary health care system of an impoverished country, just as the advanced technology of a major urban medical center is not likely to be found in a sparsely populated rural area. Determination of death is closely related to the state of the art or prevailing community practices in a particular setting. Although they can vary, procedures to determine death in American society are clearly adequate for the vast majority of deaths. Still, as might be expected, determination of death is inevitably subject to human limitations and fallibility.

Sometimes, advanced life-support systems make it unclear whether or not death has actually occurred. Are the support systems sustaining life itself or some limited bodily functions? Especially, are they sustaining or merely imitating vital bodily functioning? When a respirator forces air into a body and then withdraws it, is that body breathing or merely being ventilated? Is that body alive, or does it merely present the appearance of being alive?

Questions of this sort led an ad hoc committee of the Harvard Medical School (Ad Hoc Committee, 1968) to develop the following criteria for irreversible coma as a basis for certifying that death has occurred:

1. *Unreceptivity and unresponsivity.* Neither externally applied stimuli nor inner need evokes awareness or response.
2. *No movements or breathing.* Observation over a period of at least 1 hour does not disclose spontaneous muscular movement, respiration, or response to stimuli. For individuals on respirators, one must turn off the machine for a specified period of time and observe for any effort to breathe spontaneously.
3. *No reflexes.* A number of reflexes that can normally be elicited are absent. For example, pupils of the eye will be fixed, dilated, and not responsive to a direct source of light. Similarly, ocular movement (which normally occurs when the head is turned or when ice water is poured into the ear) and blinking are absent.
4. *Flat electroencephalogram.* The electroencephalograph (EEG) is a machine that monitors minute electrical activity in the upper brain (cerebrum). A flat EEG reading suggests the absence of such activity. The Harvard Committee indicated that the EEG has its primary value in confirming the determination that follows from the previous three criteria.

The Harvard Committee added "all of the above tests shall be repeated at least 24 hours later with no change" (p. 338).

To apply the Harvard criteria properly, one must exclude two special conditions: hypothermia, in which the temperature of the body has fallen below 90 degrees Fahrenheit; and the presence of central nervous system depressants, such as barbiturates. In both of these special conditions, the ability of the body to function may be masked or suppressed in such a way as to yield a false negative on the Harvard Committee's tests.

The first three of the Harvard Committee's criteria are essentially sophisticated and modernized restatements of tests that have traditionally been employed in determination of death. The fourth criterion adds a new test in a confirmatory role—not as an independent test in its own right. Requiring that all four tests be repeated after a 24-hour interval indicates the committee's desire to proceed with great care in this important matter.

The limits of the committee's work are clear in its own stipulation: "We are concerned here only with those comatose individuals who have no discernible central nervous system activity" (p. 337). In other words, these criteria are not intended to be applied to all determinations of death. Rather, they represent an effort to define "irreversible coma." A negative outcome resulting from a careful application of the Harvard criteria (two sets of four tests each, separated by a 24-hour period) is intended to demonstrate the presence of irreversible coma, and irreversible coma is to be understood as a new indicator that death has occurred.

The President's Commission (1981, p. 25) observed that the phrase "irreversible coma" may be misleading here since any coma is a condition of a living person, while "a body without any brain functions is dead and thus beyond any coma." This observation reminds us of the difficulty of being clear about language and concepts in matters of this sort.

There would have been no need for criteria of the kind proposed by the Harvard Committee if irreversible coma had not become an object of some puzzlement in modern society. In times past, individuals in irreversible coma would simply have begun to deteriorate. There would have been no way to sustain even the limited functioning that they had or seemed to have. More recently, interventions resulting from advances in modern medical technology have made it possible to sustain the reality or the appearance of vital bodily functioning. The Harvard criteria are intended to identify situations in which life only appears to continue and to equate such situations with death.

Since the Harvard criteria first appeared in 1968, their implementation in some circumstances has been modified and additional or alternative tests, such as cerebral angiograms to test for blood flow in the brain, have sometimes been employed. That modification is only to be expected as experts develop new tests and devise new ways to evaluate whether individuals are alive. In fact, various approaches to determination of death might or might not all relate to the same definition of death. That is because determination of death is a separable matter from the more fundamental question of definition of death.

Certification of Death: Death Certificates, Coroners, and Medical Examiners

Most people in North America and in other developed countries die under the care of a physician—for example, while they are in health care institutions (such as hospitals or long-term care facilities) or in organized programs of hospice or home care. In such circumstances, a physician or other authorized person usually determines the time and cause of death, together with other significant conditions. That information is recorded on a form called a *death certificate*, which is then signed or certified by the physician or other authorized person (Iserson, 1994).

Death certificates are the basis for much of the record keeping and statistical data concerning mortality and health in modern societies (Shneidman, 1973a). They serve a broad range of public and private functions, such as claiming life insurance and other death benefits, disposition of property rights, and the investigation of crime.

Most state certificates of death (see Figure 16.1) are modeled after a standard, single-page form containing the following categories of information: personal information about the deceased and the location of his or her death; the names of his or her parents, together with the name and address of the person who provided this and the previous information; causes and conditions of death; certification of death and information about the certifier; and information about disposition of the body (whether by burial, cremation, removal, etc.), together with the signature of a funeral director. When completed, a death certificate is delivered to a local (usually county) registrar, who signs the form, records it, and provides a permit for disposition of the body.

Every death certificate classifies the *manner of death* in four basic categories: natural, accidental, suicide, or homicide. This system of classification is known as the "NASH" system, based on the first initials of these four terms. Some deaths may also be categorized as "undetermined" or "pending investigation." Deaths come under the jurisdiction of a coroner or medical examiner if the person who died was not under the care of a physician, if the death occurred suddenly, if there is reason to suspect foul play, and in all cases of accidents, suicide, or homicide (Iserson, 1994). The function of a coroner or medical examiner is to investigate the circumstances and causes of such deaths. Coroners and medical examiners are empowered to take possession of the body (or to release it to family members for donation or other forms of disposition), to conduct various kinds of investigations, and to hold an inquest or coroner's jury, which is a quasi-judicial proceeding designed to determine the cause of a death.

The term *coroner* goes back to medieval times in England, where it identified the representative of the crown (*corona* in Latin). Originally, the coroner's function was to determine whether the property of the crown—that is, the deceased—had been unlawfully appropriated or killed. In modern societies, coroners are usually individuals who have been elected to office. They are not normally required to have any special qualifications other than being adult citizens of their elective jurisdiction. Many—but not all—coroners or deputy coroners in the United States, particularly in rural areas, are funeral directors. By contrast, *medical examiners* are appointed to their positions and are required to be qualified medical doctors (usually forensic pathologists). Some states have eliminated the office of coroner and have replaced it with the medical examiner. Other states continue to maintain a coroner system, often with medical examiners in large, urban centers.

TYPE OR PRINT IN PERMANENT BLACK INK

CERTIFICATE OF DEATH
FLORIDA

LOCAL FILE NO.

DECEDENT

1. DECEDENT'S NAME — FIRST — MIDDLE — LAST | 2. SEX

3. DATE OF DEATH *(Month, Day, Year)* | 4. SOCIAL SECURITY NUMBER | 5a. AGE-Last Birthday *(years)* | 5b. UNDER 1 YEAR: Months, Days | 5c. UNDER 1 Day: Hours, Minutes

6. DATE OF BIRTH *(Month, Day, Year)* | 7. BIRTHPLACE *(City and State or Foreign Country)* | 8. WAS DECEDENT EVER IN U.S. ARMED FORCES? *(Yes or No)*

9a. PLACE OF DEATH *(Check only one: see instructions on other side)*
HOSPITAL: _ Inpatient _ ER/Outpatient _ DOA OTHER: _ Nursing Home _ Residence _ Other *(Specify)*
9b. INSIDE CITY LIMITS? *(Yes or No)*

9c. FACILITY NAME *(If not institution, give street and number)* | 9d. CITY, TOWN, OR LOCATION OF DEATH | 9e. COUNTY OF DEATH

10. GIVE KIND OF WORK DONE DURING MOST OF WORKING LIFE. DO NOT USE RETIRED

10a. DECEDENT'S USUAL OCCUPATION | 10b. KIND OF BUSINESS/INDUSTRY | 11. MARITAL STATUS — Married, Never Married, Widowed, Divorced *(Specify)* | 12. SURVIVING SPOUSE *(If wife, give maiden name)*

13a. RESIDENCE — STATE | 13b. COUNTY | 13c. CITY, TOWN, OR LOCATION | 13d. STREET AND NUMBER

13e. INSIDE CITY LIMITS? *(Yes or No)* | 13f. ZIP CODE | 14. WAS DECEDENT OF HISPANIC OR HAITIAN ORIGIN? *(Specify No or Yes — If yes, specify Haitian, Cuban, Mexican, Puerto Rican, etc.)* _ No _ Yes Specify | 15. RACE — American Indian, Black, White, etc. Specify | 16. DECEDENT'S EDUCATION *(Specify only highest grade completed)* Elementary/Secondary (0-12) | College (1-4 or 5+)

PARENTS

17. FATHER'S NAME *(First, Middle, Last)* | 18. MOTHER'S NAME *(First, Middle, Maiden Surname)*

19a. INFORMANT'S NAME *(Type/Print)* | 19b. MAILING ADDRESS *(Street and Number or Rural Route Number, City or Town, State, Zip Code)*

DISPOSITION

20a. METHOD OF DISPOSITION
_ Burial _ Cremation _ Removal from State
_ Donation _ Other *(Specify)*
20b. PLACE OF DISPOSITION *(Name of cemetery, crematory, or other place)* | 20c. LOCATION — City or Town, State

21a. SIGNATURE OF FUNERAL SERVICE LICENSEE OR PERSON ACTING AS SUCH ▶ | 21b. LICENSE NUMBER *(of Licensee)* | 21c. NAME AND ADDRESS OF FACILITY

CERTIFIER

To be Completed by CERTIFYING PHYSICIAN Only:
22a. To the best of my knowledge, death occurred at the time, date and place and due to the cause(s) as stated.
(Signature and Title) ▶
22b. DATE SIGNED *(Mo., Day, Yr.)* | 22c. HOUR OF DEATH M
22d. NAME OF ATTENDING PHYSICIAN IF OTHER THAN CERTIFIER *(Type or Print)*

To be Completed by MEDICAL EXAMINER:
23a. On the basis of examination and/or investigation, in my opinion death occurred at the time, date and place and due to the cause(s) and manner as stated.
(Signature and Title) ▶
23b. DATE SIGNED *(Mo., Day, Yr.)* | 23c. HOUR OF DEATH M
23d. MEDICAL EXAMINER'S CASE # _ _ • _ _ • _ _ _ _ _

24. NAME AND ADDRESS OF CERTIFIER (PHYSICIAN, MEDICAL EXAMINER) *(Type or Print)*

25a. SUBREGISTRAR — SIGNATURE AND DATE ▶ | 25b. LOCAL REGISTRAR — SIGNATURE ▶ | 25c. DATE REGISTERED

CAUSE OF DEATH BY CERTIFIER

26. PART I. Enter the diseases, injuries, or complications that caused the death. Do not enter the mode of dying, such as cardiac or respiratory arrest, shock, or heart failure. List only one cause on each line. | Approximate Interval Between Onset and Death

IMMEDIATE CAUSE (Final disease or condition resulting in death) →
a. ____ DUE TO (OR AS A CONSEQUENCE OF):
Sequentially list conditions, if any, leading to immediate cause. Enter UNDERLYING CAUSE (Disease or injury that initiated events resulting in death) LAST.
b. ____ DUE TO (OR AS A CONSEQUENCE OF):
c. ____ DUE TO (OR AS A CONSEQUENCE OF):
d. ____

PART II. Other significant conditions contributing to death but not resulting in the underlying cause given in Part I | 27a. WAS AN AUTOPSY PERFORMED? *(Yes or No)* | 27b. WERE AUTOPSY FINDINGS USED TO COMPLETE CAUSE OF DEATH? *(Yes or No)* | 28. CASE REPORTED TO MEDICAL EXAMINER? *(Yes or No)*

29. IF FEMALE, WAS THERE A PREGNANCY IN THE PAST 3 MONTHS? _YES _ NO | 30a. IF SURGERY IS MENTIONED IN PART I or II ENTER CONDITION FOR WHICH IT WAS PERFORMED | 30b. DATE OF SURGERY *(Mo., Day, Year)*

31. PROBABLE MANNER OF DEATH *(Specify)* Natural, accident, suicide, homicide, or undetermined. | 32a. DATE OF INJURY *(Month, Day, Year)* | 32b. TIME OF INJURY M | 32c. INJURY AT WORK? (Yes or No) | 32d. DESCRIBE HOW INJURY OCCURRED

32e. PLACE OF INJURY — At home, farm, street, factory, etc. *(Specify)* | 32f. LOCATION *(Street and Number or Rural Route Number, City or Town, State)*

Margin: 7; 9a; 9bde; 13; 20a; Part Ia.; Part II; 32e; 32f

State of Florida, Department of Health, Vital Statistics

DH 512, 9/96 (Replaces HRS Form 512)

Figure 16.1 *An Example of a Death Certificate*

Legal Issues after Death

Following a death, there are two broad areas of legal concern: anatomical gifts involving the donation of body organs, tissues, and/or one's entire body; and the disposition of one's body and property or estate.

Organ, Tissue, and Body Donation

Background: Which Organs Can Be Donated? The modern era of *organ and tissue donation* began in the 1950s, when a combination of advances in knowledge, technology, pharmacology, and practice made it possible for biomedical scientists and clinicians to transplant specific organs and tissues from one individual to another (Dowie, 1988; Fox & Swazey, 1974, 1992). One key advance involved learning how to classify or type and compare human tissues so as to achieve the greatest likelihood of success in matching the biological characteristics of donor and recipient. Another major breakthrough—which has been called "the most notable development in this area" by the United Network for Organ Sharing (UNOS; www.unos.org)—occurred when an immunosuppressant medication (cyclosporine) was developed in the mid-1970s and approved for commercial use in November 1983. Effective immunosuppression prevents the recipient's immune system from attacking and rejecting the transplanted organs as a foreign body. These advances made transplantation of human organs and tissues a real option for transplant recipients to save or enhance the quality of their lives.

Major organs that can currently be transplanted are listed in the top line of Table 16.1. They include: individual kidneys, livers, and hearts; entire lungs, pancreas, and intestines, or portions thereof; and joint transplants of a heart/lung or kidney/pancreas.

Why Is There a Need for Organ Donation and Transplantation? The growing need for transplantable human organs arises from nonfunctioning or poorly functioning organs in potential recipients. Also, with better screening practices and diagnostic techniques, individuals who might benefit from transplantation are now being identified earlier and more effectively than they would have been previously. In addition, transplant centers have improved their technical abilities to transplant major organs (Frist, 1989, 1995; Maier, 1991).

Recognizing these developments, in 1984 Congress enacted the National Organ Transplant Act (NOTA). Among other things, NOTA established the national Organ Procurement and Transplantation Network (OPTN) to facilitate the procurement and distribution of scarce organs in a fair and equitable way by matching donated organs with potential recipients. The United Network for Organ Sharing currently administers the OPTN under contract to the Division of Transplantation in the Department of Health and Human Services. NOTA also established the Scientific Registry of Transplant Recipients, a system to measure the success of transplantation by tracing recipients from time of transplant to failure of organ (graft) or patient death.

Table 16.1 Number of Individuals (Patients or Registrations) on the National Transplant Waiting List as of December 31, 2001, by Organ, Gender, Race, and Age[a]

Number Percentage	Kidney	Liver	Pancreas	Kidney-Pancreas	Intestine	Heart	Heart-Lung	Lung	Total
Total:[b]	50,803	18,744	1,220	2,454	180	4,123	212	3,795	79,367
By Gender:									
Females	22,807	8,111	587	1,123	84	912	119	2,204	35,947
	42.6	42.5	47.2	43.9	46.2	22.0	56.1	57.4	42.4
Males	30,753	10,955	656	1,434	98	3,225	93	1,637	48,851
	57.4	57.5	52.8	56.1	53.8	78.0	43.9	42.6	57.6
By Age:									
0–5	85	569	6	1	93	132	13	18	917
	0.2	3.0	0.5	0.1	51.1	3.2	6.1	0.5	1.1
6–10	136	208	1	0	22	38	6	49	460
	0.3	1.1	0.1	0.0	12.1	0.9	2.8	1.3	0.5
11–17	486	365	6	1	21	73	17	152	1,121
	0.9	1.9	0.5	0.0	11.5	1.8	8.0	4.0	1.3
18–49	25,762	6,901	1,036	2,131	32	1,191	145	1,757	38,955
	48.1	36.2	83.3	83.3	17.6	28.8	68.4	45.7	45.9
50–64	20,696	9,128	191	417	14	2,188	30	1,743	34,407
	38.6	47.9	15.4	16.3	7.7	52.9	14.2	45.4	40.6
65+	6,395	1,895	3	7	0	515	1	122	8,938
	11.9	9.9	0.2	0.3	0.0	12.4	0.5	3.2	10.5
By Race or Ethnicity:									
Caucasian Americans	22,664	13,954	1,070	1,879	114	3,201	160	3,189	46,231
	42.3	73.2	86.1	73.5	62.6	77.4	75.5	83.0	54.5
African Americans	18,809	1,409	95	412	38	550	26	384	21,723
	35.1	7.4	7.6	16.1	20.9	13.3	12.3	10.0	25.6
Hispanic Americans	7,778	2,534	60	207	25	289	18	189	11,100
	14.5	13.3	4.8	8.1	13.7	7.0	8.5	4.9	13.1
Asian Americans	3,007	757	9	35	3	58	3	42	3,914
	5.6	4.0	0.7	0.9	1.1	0.9	1.9	0.9	4.6
Others	1,302	412	9	24	2	39	5	37	1,830
	2.4	2.2	0.7	0.9	1.1	0.9	2.3	0.9	2.2

[a]Some patients are multiply listed at different transplant centers for the same organ or at the same transplant center for multiple organs (e.g., kidney and heart). The data in this report are not adjusted for multiple listings at different centers. However, the data are adjusted for multiple listings at the same center; thus, a patient is counted only once per center, per organ. The degree of multiple listing of the same patient at different centers has been difficult to determine accurately, but is estimated to involve less than five percent of all patients and appears to have declined over time.

[b]The numbers in this line represent current estimates of patients listed on the waiting list. Note that the overall total in this line (= 79,367) is less than the sum of the organs (= 81,531) because some patients are listed for multiple organs. Such patients are counted separately under each organ for which they are waiting, but only once in the overall total. All other figures in the remainder of this table reflect numbers of registrations (whose total = 84,798) rather than numbers of patients.

SOURCE: Adapted from data from United Network for Organ Sharing, 2002, www.unos.org.

The need for organ transplantation is evident from Table 16.1, which provides data on the number of patient registrants by gender, age, and race or ethnicity on the National Transplant Waiting List in the United States as of May 31, 2001. Among these registrants, most are waiting for kidneys and livers, there are nearly three males for every two females, the largest numbers by age are 18–49 years old (followed closely by those 50–64 years of age), and the largest numbers by race or ethnicity are Caucasian Americans and African Americans. The number of registrants on lists like these increases each month.

Sadly, more than 15 registrants on the National Transplant Waiting List currently die every day in the United States because no suitable organs become available for transplantation. In 2000, 5,597 registrants (7.3 percent of the total) were removed from the waiting list because of death.

The growing need for organ donation and transplantation can be seen from Table 16.2, which reports end-of-year data for numbers of patient registrations on the National Transplant Waiting List from 1988 through 2000, as well as the number of transplants accomplished and the numbers of donors from whom organs were recovered in each of those years. These data and Figure 16.2 show that from 1988 to 2000 in the United States the number of patient registrations on the list has increased by over 360 percent, whereas numbers of transplants and donors have increased only about 81 percent and 96 percent, respectively. In other words, during this time period the United States has witnessed a gradual or incremental increase in the availability of transplantable organs, while there has been a huge growth in the need for such organs.

As a result, *the single largest obstacle to organ transplantation today is the scarcity of transplantable organs.* Because there would be no organ transplantation if there were no organ donation, it is useful to look more closely at some facts about organ donation and at efforts to increase the numbers of donated organs.

Who Can Donate and How Is Donation Accomplished? Organ donation is only possible when: (1) the organ in question is not uniquely vital to the donor's health; or (2) the donor is already dead when the organ is retrieved from his or her body. *Living donors* can offer replaceable materials (such as blood or blood products), one of a pair of twinned organs (such as kidneys), or a portion of certain organs (such as a liver, lung, or pancreas). *Non-living donors*—individuals who have died prior to donation and the subsequent recovery of their organs—can donate all of these and other transplantable organs and tissues, as we saw in the vignette near the beginning of this chapter. It is crucial, however, that conditions preceding, at the time of, and immediately following the death must not damage the organs or otherwise render them unsuitable for transplantation. For nonliving donors, this means that organs must be recovered shortly after the death of an otherwise healthy donor and before they have begun to deteriorate (the time frame depends on the particular organ in question).

In most instances, a nonliving donor will have died of external trauma to the head (as might be associated with an accident, homicide, or suicide) or a cerebrovascular incident (for example, a cerebral hemorrhage), and will have been pronounced dead ("brain dead"). Often, some bodily functions in a potential organ donor are artificially sustained by external intervention for a limited

Table 16.2 Number of Patient Registrations on the U.S. National Transplant Waiting List, Number of U.S. Transplants, and Number of U.S. Organ Donors, End of Year 1988–2000

Year	1988	1989	1990	1991	1992	1993	1994
Number of Patient Registrations on the National Transplant Waiting List	16,026	19,095	20,481	23,198	27,563	31,355	35,271
Number of Transplants							
Nonliving donors	10,803	11,225	12,879	13,327	13,559	14,735	15,206
Living donors	1,823	1,918	2,213	2,423	2,572	2,899	3,086
TOTAL:	12,626	13,143	15,002	15,750	16,131	17,634	18,292
Number of Donors							
Nonliving donors	4,080	4,012	4,509	4,526	4,520	4,861	5,100
Living donors	1,827	1,918	2,124	2,425	2,572	2,906	3,102
TOTAL:	5,907	5,930	6,633	6,951	7,092	7,767	8,202

Year	1995	1996	1997	1998	1999	2000	Total
Number of Patient Registrations on the National Transplant Waiting List	41,179	46,925	53,123	60,299	67,079	73,951	515,545
Number of Transplants							
Nonliving donors	15,902	15,965	16,253	16,943	16,946	17,255	190,998
Living donors	3,438	3,735	4,009	4,473	4,768	5,653	42,920
TOTAL:	19,340	19,700	20,262	21,416	21,714	22,908	233,918
Number of Donors							
Nonliving donors	5,359	5,416	5,477	5,799	5,822	5,984	65,465
Living donors	3,458	3,756	4,021	4,496	4,748	5,600	42,953
TOTAL:	8,817	9,172	9,498	10,295	10,570	11,584	108,418

SOURCE: Adapted from United Network for Organ Sharing, 2001, www.unos.org

period of time in order to preserve the quality of transplantable organs while decisions are made about donation, a search for appropriate recipients is undertaken, and a potential recipient is prepared to receive a transplant (Albert, 1994). This does not mean that an already-dead donor is "being kept alive"; only some biological functions are being supported externally, not the life of the person.

As shown in Table 16.2, the ratio of living to nonliving donors has gradually increased from 31/69 percent in 1988 to 48/52 percent in 2000. That seems to reflect an increased willingness among living donors, whether or not they are related by blood or marriage to a potential recipient, to offer a part of their bodies for transplantation. At the same time, the ratio of transplants from living donors to those from nonliving donors has only increased from 14/86 percent in 1988 to 25/75 percent in 2000. The simple reason for this is that a

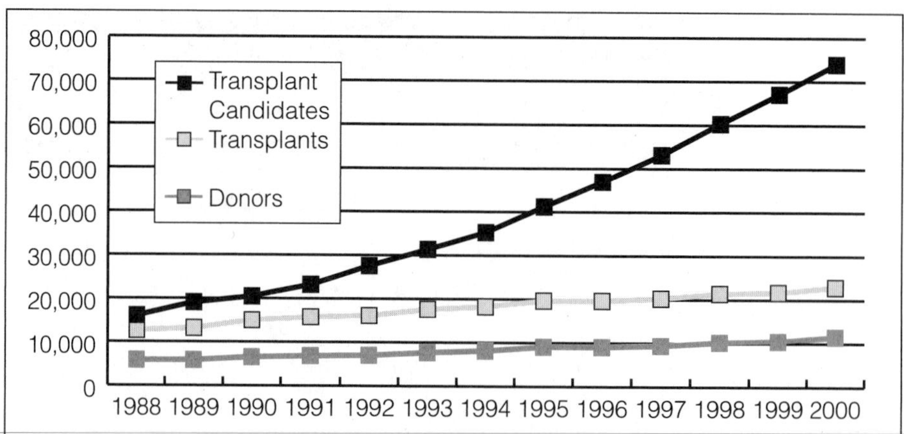

Figure 16.2 *Transplant Candidates, Organ Transplants, and Organ Donors, United States, 1988–2000. Source: Adapted from data from United Network for Organ Sharing, 2002, www.unos.org.*

living donor can only donate one of a pair of organs or a portion of an organ to a single recipient, whereas a nonliving donor can donate 6 to 8 major organs along with ocular components and numerous other tissues that can affect the lives of a large number of recipients (as we saw in the vignette near the beginning of this chapter).

Living donation has many advantages. The donor's medical history is known, an extensive evaluation can be done beforehand, the organ is removed under elective circumstances, and the donated organ is out of the body only a very short period of time. Consent to donate is obtained directly from potential living donors, but only after a suitable screening and evaluation process to determine that they understand the procedure that will be undertaken, are consenting freely, are a good tissue match to the potential recipient, are likely to be able to withstand the donation process, and can be expected to cope effectively with the aftermath of the experience however that might work out (The Authors for the Live Organ Donor Consensus Group, 2000).

In the case of a nonliving donor, consent to donate is a bit more complicated. First, an effort will be made to "decouple" determination of death from issues associated with organ donation. Health care professionals who are not part of the transplant team and are not involved in caring for potential transplant recipients will strive to save the life of the potential donor, determine whether or not (and when) that individual is brain dead, and communicate that determination to the individual's next of kin. Insofar as possible, an effort will be made to inform family members of their loved one's death and give them time to absorb that fact before issues associated with donation are raised. Meticulous determination of death balances the legal, medical, and human interests of the potential donor and his or her family members with the practical interests of the recipient.

Second, because the American death system does not employ a policy of "presumed consent" for donation of major organs (whereby organs can be retrieved unless there is a written directive to the contrary from the decedent or next of kin that specifically refuses donation), explicit permission for donation will be sought from an appropriate source in accordance with the requirements of the Uniform Anatomical Gift Act (UAGA, 1968, with amendments in 1987; Wendler & Dickert, 2001).

In general, once a person has died, he or she no longer owns his or her body—for the very good reason that he or she is no longer a living person who can exercise such ownership. To deal with this, the UAGA (reprinted in Iserson, 1994, pp. 615–618, and passed with only slight variations by all of the state legislatures in the United States) allows persons to make known before their deaths their wishes about the donation of their organs. To do this, the act designates: who may execute an anatomical gift; who may receive such donations and for what purposes; how such an anatomical gift may be authorized, amended, or revoked; and the rights and duties at death of a donee—that is, an individual or organization to whom such a gift is made. Under the provisions of the UAGA an individual who is of sound mind and 18 years of age or older can donate all or any part of his or her body, the gift to take effect on his or her death and to be made for the purposes of health care education, research, therapy, or transplantation. The UAGA seeks to eliminate conflicts of interest, for example, by requiring that different care providers serve a potential donor and a potential recipient.

Unless there is actual notice that a decedent did not wish to donate, under the UAGA organ donation from a nonliving donor may be authorized by a health care surrogate; the donor's spouse; an adult son or daughter; either parent; an adult brother or sister; a legal guardian; or any other person authorized or under obligation to dispose of the body. In principle, the order of priority in this list of persons is important; actual notice of opposition on the part of an individual of the same or a prior class would prevent a donation. In other words, a surviving spouse's decisions about donation would take precedence over those of the decedent's parents or adult children, whereas decisions authorized by a health care surrogate would take precedence over those of any relative.

In practice, it may be unlikely that an anatomical gift of any sort would be accepted if there were objections from any of the individuals listed in the previous paragraph. Even if the deceased had indicated a wish to donate, outsiders would ordinarily be unwilling to enter into conflicts between family members, and only a relatively short period of time is usually available for the resolution of such matters.

Under a government regulation called the Medicare and Medicaid "Conditions of Participation" that went into effect in 1998, hospitals must: (1) report to their local or regional Organ Procurement Organization (OPO) all patients whose deaths are imminent or who have died in the hospital; (2) ensure the right of next of kin to choose donation; and (3) arrange for trained personnel (members of the OPO's staff or hospital personnel whom they have trained for this purpose) to offer the opportunity to donate (U.S. Department of Health and Human Services, 1998, 2000). As might be expected, trained procurement professionals (often working with ICU nurses) have been shown to be most effective in introducing the opportunity for donation (Evanisko et al., 1998; Siminoff et al., 1995). Nevertheless, it is well recognized that individuals cannot and should not be coerced to donate organs, either their own or those of a deceased relative, and that equal respect should be given to both decisions to donate and decisions not to donate (Iserson, 1994).

The "Conditions of Participation" regulation has the goal of seeking to increase the number of donated organs. In addition, its purpose is to ensure that family members will be given an appropriate opportunity to know about and consider donation at a time when they have been victimized by the death of a loved one and when so little else is within their control. Many have reported that helping others by making a "gift of life" was the single positive aspect in this difficult experience, a way of continuing the legacy of the donor's life and finding some measure of solace in their own bereavement (see Box 16.1).

Efforts to Increase Organ Donation In recent years there have been many efforts to educate the public about organ donation and transplantation, to broaden criteria for acceptable donors, to encourage more living donors, and to try to obtain more donors from among the estimated 12,000 to 15,000 deaths occurring in the United States every year that could yield suitable donor organs (Gortmaker et al., 1996). For example, word of mouth and public education projects have sought to dispel myths about organ donation by emphasizing facts such as the following: "brain-dead" individuals cannot return to life; donor families incur no costs to donate; human organs and tissues cannot legally be bought or sold in the United States; organ donation usually has no substantive effect on desired funeral practices, other than the possibility of a brief delay; donation and transplantation are encouraged and supported (or at least not opposed) by nearly all religious communities in the United States; members of some minority groups whom research has shown to have lower rates of donation than the general population (Callender et al., 1991; Wheeler & Cheung, 1996) are most likely to find a close tissue match with other members of similar groups and gene pools; and a large and growing number of individuals on the National Transplant Waiting List are in desperate need of a transplanted organ. Public education efforts like these are summarized in the slogan, "*Don't take your organs to heaven . . . heaven knows we need them here!*"

Other educational efforts have encouraged potential donors to sign, date, and have witnessed an organ donor card. Donor cards can be obtained from the federal government's Division of Transplantation (tel. 888-90-SHARE; www.organdonor.gov) or local, regional, or national organizations, such as the Coalition on Donation (tel. 800-355-SHARE; www.shareyourlife.org), UNOS (800-355-SHARE; www.unos.org), or the National Kidney Foundation (800-622-9010; www.kidney.org). Many states also have a donor card on the reverse side of their automobile driver's licenses and/or computer registration systems through which one may indicate willingness to donate at the time of obtaining or renewing a driver's license. The goal of these cards and systems is to sensitize the public to the need for transplantable organs, to encourage dialogue about donation among family members, and to have a readily accessible way to determine willingness to donate when death occurs.

However, none of these approaches on its own is really sufficient. It is also not enough to include wishes about donation in one's last will and testament,

Box 16.1 The Best Part of the Worst Day of My Life

I want to tell you about a woman who enriched the lives of everyone who knew her, and who, through her foresight, is even now enriching the lives of people she never even met. I want to tell you about my late wife Carolyn.

Carolyn was a cheerful person, and an optimist. She had boundless energy, and she loved life and all it had to offer. I was the cautious one who worried. Carolyn usually assumed that things would turn out all right, and they generally did.

That's why it took me by surprise about 7 years ago when she came home with a new driver's license and told me that she had registered as a donor. "If I die," she told me, "I want to help people."

Until that moment, I never had any problem with the idea of organ donation. In my mind, it had always been something that happened to other people. Carolyn's statement forced me to think about the possibility of her death, and how I would feel about donating her organs.

I was uncomfortable, and I told her this. In fact, I asked her to change her mind. She smiled slyly, "It's my body, and this is what I want!" I was disturbed, and I said, "OK, if it's on your license, then that's fine, because I don't think I could make that decision."

Up to this point, everything on her side had been light and joking. Now she became serious. "Doug," she told me, "no matter what is on my license, if anything happened to me, you would have to give your consent. That's why I'm telling you."

I remember my reply very clearly. "Carolyn, do you realize what you're asking me? On what would be the worst day of my life, you're asking me to undergo that additional ordeal?" But, she was adamant. I was surprised how strongly she felt about it. I had initially thought it was a whim, but it was clearly something that she had given a lot of thought, and in the end, I had to promise.

That was 7 years ago, and in the meantime, I thought about it myself to the point where I realized that I agree with her. Having moved to Maryland, last January I went to get a new driver's license, and after a moment's hesitation, I, too, signed up to be a donor. Like a little boy, when I got home I proudly showed Carolyn my new license with the words DONOR / YES. It's strange to me now to remember how big her smile was, but that's the way Carolyn was with things that she cared deeply about.

Just two short months later, the worst day of my life arrived. On Friday, March 23rd I was in Louisville, Kentucky helping my mother make funeral arrangements for my grandmother who had died the day before. Just before noon, I got a call that Carolyn had collapsed at work and been rushed to the hospital with a massive heart attack. I was able to speak to her briefly, giving me hope, but ninety minutes later, after a brave struggle, she died.

Shortly afterwards, talking to my father by phone, he relayed the question that I hoped I'd never have to answer. Did I want Carolyn to be a donor? At

(continues)

Box 16.1 (cont.) The Best Part of the Worst Day of My Life

that moment I realized the great gift that Carolyn had given me with our conversation of 7 years ago. I didn't have to think. I knew. She wanted to help others, and I wanted that too. I gave my consent.

Then there were two things I had to do. One filled me with sorrow, but the other buoyed my spirit. I knew that I had to get myself back to Maryland to see Carolyn and spend some time with her, and, I knew that I had to hold myself together so that I could make the arrangements for her to be a tissue donor.

I think we've all heard it said that the body of a dead loved one doesn't really matter. The body is not the person; it's just an empty vessel. I can tell you that the time I spent with Carolyn there in the basement of the hospital, I felt very differently. It's true that it wasn't animated with her fabulous spirit, but this was the body of my wife, my soul-mate, my best friend. It's how I had known her all our life together. If this was just an empty vessel, then I wouldn't care what was done with it. But I did care—very much.

I still felt so much love for Carolyn, and I knew that I could express this to her through the loving and respectful disposition of her body. And it was so important to her that her body be used to improve the lives of others. Making the arrangements for her to be a tissue donor was an act done out of love: her love of life, our love for the unknown people who would be helped, and my love for her.

Most people are familiar with organ donation, such as a heart or a kidney. Before the day Carolyn died, I, like most people, had never heard of tissue donation. Carolyn told me, "If I die, I want to help people." Sadly, her death has come to pass, but the sorrow I feel over the loss of Carolyn is lightened by the knowledge that people have been helped. Already, two people have had their sight restored, and two others have received either life-saving or life-prolonging heart valve transplants.

If I could speak to these people, I would tell them two things. First, this gift you have received was given to you with great love by Carolyn and by me. Always know that wherever you are, there are two beings who love you profoundly. Second, please don't ever feel guilty about what you have received. Nothing could save Carolyn. You have given me a great gift by making it possible for something life-affirming to come out of her death.

On March 23rd [2001], my beloved Carolyn died. It has been a great source of comfort to me to know that through her compassion and her wisdom, two people are living richer lives, two people are leading longer lives, and, perhaps, somewhere, a family has been spared the anguish that nothing could spare mine. We must all take responsibility to spread the word about donation among our friends and colleagues so that people in need are helped, and so that families in grief can benefit from the comfort that donation brings. Perhaps for them, it will be like it was for me: the best part of the worst day of my life.

Douglas Harrell ■

Make your wishes about organ and tissue donation known to your family members.

because wills are generally not officially read for some time after a death and thus are not a good vehicle for this time-sensitive purpose. What those who wish to be organ donors should do is discuss this matter with their next of kin. As the slogan says: "*Share your life. Share your decision.*" The reason for this is that, regardless of any written or oral expression of wishes an individual might make, next of kin are likely to be key decisions makers (Iserson, 1994; Williams, 1989). *Lack of discussion among family members about their wishes appears to be the single most significant barrier to donation.* Therefore, for those who wish to donate: (1) do not rely on only one method of communicating your wishes—employ as many methods as possible; and (2) convey your wishes in clear and unambiguous ways to your next of kin.

Xenotransplantation and Non-Heart-Beating Donors Two other efforts to enlarge the pool of potential organ donors involve xenotransplantation and what are called "non-heart-beating donors." *Xenotransplantation* is transplantation across species—that is, from animals to humans. At present, xenotransplantation has been successful in cases like heart valves from pigs, but that success has been limited to certain tissues. *Non-heart-beating donors* are individuals in permanent vegetative states who are not yet dead but for whom competent decision makers (their next of kin or those authorized to act for them as substitute decision makers) might decide: (1) to withdraw life-sustaining interventions; and (2) to authorize donation. In such circumstances, the interventions will be withdrawn and a brief interval will be allowed during which the individual is observed to determine whether or not he or she resumes body functions without support; if not, the individual will be pronounced dead and interventions will be resumed as needed to permit recovery of donated organs. From 1993 to 2000 in the United States, organs were recovered from a total of 581 non-heart-beating donors.

After Donation and Transplantation Offering the opportunity to donate human organs should be accompanied by a suitable program of bereavement follow-up for both living donors and members of donor families. Principles underlying appropriate practices before and after death have been set forth in "A Bill of Rights for Donor Families" (see Figure 16.3), and many procurement organizations now do good work in implementing such principles (Maloney & Wolfelt, 2001). The Executive Committee of the National Donor Family Council has written an article about its work (Corr et al., 2001) and has available both free booklets and a quarterly newsletter for donor families (800-622-9010; www.donorfamily.org). (In addition to the NDFC, the National Kidney Foundation (NKF) sponsors programs for living donors (www.livingdonors.org) and the transAction Council for transplant recipients (www.transplantrecipients.org).) National communication guidelines (NKF, 1997) have also been developed so that donor families can obtain appropriate information about the consequences of their decision to donate and transplant recipients can express thanks for the gift that they have received (Corr, Nile, et al., 1994). Research by Albert (1998) suggests that appropriate contacts can benefit both donor family members and transplant recipients.

At the national level, since 1994 there has been an annual National Donor Recognition Ceremony to recognize the difficult decisions made by organ and tissue donors and their families (note the "Gift of Love, Gift of Life" inscription and medal on the photo of Karen Musto's gravestone on p. 450; see also Musto, 1999). Also, since January 1995 a National Donor Family Quilt, entitled "Patches of Love" and consisting of individually designed 8-inch quilt squares, has become an effective way for donor families to commemorate their loved ones, participate in an international program of memorialization, and contribute to public awareness and education about tissue and organ donation (Corr, 2001b).

Tissue Donation and Transplantation In addition to human organs, it is also possible to transplant human tissues such as skin grafts for burn and accident victims, heart valves and aortic patch grafts to sustain heart functioning, saphenous and femoral veins that are used in cardiac bypass surgery, eye and ocular components to restore or improve sight, and bone and connective tissue grafts that make possible periodontal and trauma reconstructions, as well as orthopedic and neurosurgical procedures such as spinal fusions. Because blood and fat

Bill of Rights for Donor Families

Donor families have the right:

▲ 1. To a full and careful explanation about what has happened to their loved one, his or her current status, and his or her prognosis.

▲ 2. To be full partners with the health care team in the decision-making process about the care and support given to their loved one and to themselves.

▲ 3 To a full and careful explanation about the (impending) death of their loved one, with appropriate reference to the concept of cardiac and/or brain death and the basis upon which it has been or will be determined that that concept applies to their loved one.

▲ 4. To opportunities to be alone with their loved one during his or her care and after his or her death occurs. This should include offering the family an opportunity to see, touch, hold, or participate in the care of their loved one, as appropriate.

▲ 5 To be cared for in a manner that is sensitive to the family's needs and capacities by specially-trained individuals.

▲ 6. To have an opportunity to make organ and/or tissue donation decisions on behalf of themselves and of their loved one who has died. This opportunity is to be included in the normal continuum of care by the health care provider after death has been determined and the family has had sufficient time to acknowledge that death has occurred.

▲ 7. To receive information in a manner that is suited to the family's needs and capacities about the need for organ and tissue donation, the conditions and processes of organ and/or tissue donation, and the implications of organ and/or tissue donation for later events, such as funeral arrangements, viewing of the body, and related practices.

▲ 8. To be provided with time, privacy, freedom from coercion, confidentiality, and (if desired) the services of an appropriate support person (e.g., clergyperson) and other resources (e.g., a second medical opinion, advice from significant others, or the services of an interpreter for those who speak another language) which are essential to optimal care for the family and to enable family members to make an informed and free decision about donation.

▲ 9. To have their decisions about organ and/or tissue donation accepted and respected.

▲ 10. To have opportunities to spend time alone with their loved one before and/or after the process of removing donated organs and/or tissues, and to say their "goodbyes" in a manner that is appropriate to the present and future needs of the family consistent with their cultural and religious identity (e.g., a lock of hair)

▲ 11. To be assured that their loved one will be treated with respect throughout the process of removing donated organs and/or tissues.

▲ 12. To receive timely information that is suited to the family's needs and capacities about which organs and/or tissues were or were not removed, and why.

▲ 13. To receive timely information regarding how any donated organs and/or tissues were used, and, if desired, to be given an opportunity to exchange anonymous communications with individual recipients and/or recipient family members. Upon request, donor families should also be given accurate updates on the condition of the recipients.

▲ 14. To be assured that the donor family will not be burdened with any expenses arising from organ and/or tissue donation, and to be given assistance in resolving any charges that might erroneously be addressed to the family.

▲ 15. To receive ongoing bereavement follow-up support for a reasonable period of time. Such support might take the form of: the name, address, and telephone number of a knowledgeable and sensitive person with whom they can discuss the entire experience; an opportunity to evaluate their experience through a quality assurance survey; free copies of literature about organ and/or tissue donation; free copies of literature about bereavement, grief, and mourning; opportunities for contact with another donor family; opportunities to take part in a donor or bereavement support group; and/or the services of a skilled and sensitive support person.

All explanations mentioned in this document should be provided by a knowledgeable and sensitive person in a private, face-to-face conversation whenever possible in a manner suited to the family's needs. Also, these explanations may need to be repeated or supplemented in more than one interchange.

Figure 16.3 *A Bill of Rights for Donor Families. From C. A. Corr, L. G. Nile, and other members of the National Donor Family Council of the National Kidney Foundation, Inc. Copyright © 1994. Reprinted with permission.*

Karen Musto died tragically at age 27; her gravestone marks her as an organ donor.

cells are removed during the processing of donated tissues, there is usually no problem of rejection after transplantation. Also, many tissues can be sterilized, frozen, and kept in storage often for many years. Although more than 400,000 human tissue transplants are accomplished each year in the United States, this form of transplantation may be the least appreciated by the general public.

Conversations about recovery of transplantable tissues may be part of the overall discussion of organ donation or they may occur independently (often in the form of a telephone conversation rather than a face-to-face interaction). In the former instance, a procurement coordinator from an OPO might be the principal professional in the discussion; in the latter instance, a staff member from a specialized eye or tissue bank might fill that role.

Body Donation The basic principles outlined in this section apply to the donation of entire bodies for medical education and research, with some significant differences. For example, in most areas of the United States, there is no longer a shortage of donated bodies for medical education or research. Thus individuals who wish to make a gift of their bodies for these purposes after death should determine in advance that such a gift will be welcomed by its intended recipients (Iverson, 1990). They should also know that if they give consent for both organ/tissue and body donation, the former will generally take precedence over the latter on the principle that seeking to save lives is the first priority. Arrangements can be made for body donation by contacting an appropriate institution—usually the anatomy department of a medical or dental school—and following the procedures that it requires. Institutions receiving donated bodies typically have special procedures for disposing of their remains once such bodies have been used for educational or research purposes (for example, Reece & Ziegler, 1990).

Disposition of the Body

State and local regulations provide a general framework for the disposition of bodies that is principally concerned with recording vital statistics, giving formal permission for the burial or other disposition of a body, preventing bodies or institutions that handle bodies from becoming a source of contamination or a threat to the health of the living, protecting the uses of cemetery land, and governing processes of disinterment or exhumation. Beyond that, regulation of body disposition is essentially a matter of professional practice, social custom, and good taste.

For example, as we indicated in Chapter 4, there is no general legal requirement that bodies be embalmed following a death, although this is common practice among many groups in the United States. Embalming is legally required when bodies are to be transported via common carrier in interstate commerce. It may also be mandated when disposition of a body does not occur promptly and when refrigeration is not available. In other circumstances, as we learned in Chapter 4, the practice of embalming is mainly undertaken to permit viewing of the body prior to or as part of funeral ceremonies. Similarly, concrete grave liners and other forms of individual vaults that are used as the outer liners for caskets in the graves at many cemeteries are typically required not by law but by the cemeteries themselves to prevent settling of the ground and thus to minimize costs of groundskeeping and other maintenance activities in the cemetery.

Disposition of Property: Probate

After a death, it is necessary to distribute property owned by the deceased to others. In general, disposition of personal property is governed by the laws of the state where a person lived at the time of death, whereas disposition of real estate (land and the structures built on it) is governed by the laws of the state where the real estate is located. The process of administering and executing these functions is called *probate*, a term deriving from a Latin word (*probare*, "to prove") that has to do with proving or verifying the legitimacy of a will.

In the American death system, probate courts supervise the work of a decedent's personal representative who is charged to carry out necessary postdeath duties (Manning, 1995; Prestopino, 1992). That representative is called an *executor* if he or she has been named by the decedent in a will or an *administrator* if appointed by the court. Such a representative is responsible for making an inventory and collecting the assets of the estate; notifying parties who may have claims against the estate of the decedent; paying debts, expenses, and taxes; winding up business affairs; arranging for the preparation of necessary documents; managing the estate during the process; distributing the decedent's remaining property to those entitled to receive it; and closing the estate (Dukeminier & Johanson, 1995). Charges levied against the estate may include a commission for the personal representative; fees charged by attorneys, accountants, or others who assist in administering the estate; and court costs.

Many individuals seek to reduce these costs, along with the time consumed by the probate process, by arranging their affairs in ways that minimize involvements with or complexities for the probate process, as we will discuss later in relationship to trusts and other will substitutes.

Wills and Intestacy

Individuals who die without a valid will are said to have died *intestate* or without a testament stating their wishes. In every state, there are laws governing how the estate of an intestate individual will be distributed. These rules vary from state to state but are generally based on assumptions made by state legislators as to how a typical person would wish to distribute his or her property (Atkinson, 1953). For example, a surviving spouse and children are likely to be regarded as preferred heirs, and the decedent's descendants are likely to be given precedence over parents, other ancestors, or their descendants. In the case of an intestate individual with no one who qualifies as an heir under the intestacy statute, the estate *escheats* or passes to the state.

Individuals can gain some measure of control over the distribution of their property through estate planning and a formal statement of their wishes, commonly called a *will.* Each state has regulations on how a will must be prepared and submitted to the probate process. Such regulations are intended to communicate the importance that the state attaches to the process of drawing up a will and to provide an evidentiary basis for proving during the probate process that the document really is the decedent's will and does actually represent his or her intentions. For example, wills are to be drawn up, signed, and dated by adults *(testators)* who are of "sound mind," who are not subject to undue influence, and whose action is witnessed by the requisite number (as provided by state law) of individuals who do not have a personal interest in the will whereby they would benefit from the disposition of the estate for which it provides. In general, through their wills individuals are free to dispose of their property as they wish, subject to exceptions (such as community property laws relating to marriages) that have been enacted by most states to protect certain close family members from total disinheritance.

Holographic wills—those that are handwritten and unwitnessed—are acceptable in many states. However, state law varies significantly on this matter, and wills of this sort may be unreliable if they do not include specific, required language, or if the meaning of their language is ambiguous.

In general, professional legal assistance is usually recommended to draw up and execute a formal, written will in order to ensure that the document does convey its intended meaning and will have legal effect, notwithstanding changes in the testator's circumstances (Manning, 1995; Prestopino, 1992).

Wills can be changed at any time before the testator's death, assuming that the individual remains of sound mind and gives evidence of intent to make the change. This can be accomplished through a supplementary document called a *codicil,* which leaves the previous document intact while altering one or more of its provisions; through a new will that revokes the previous document either explicitly or implicitly; through a formal revocation process that does not establish a new will; or through some physical act, such as divorce, subsequent marriage, or marriage followed by the birth of a child. The most recent, valid will is the document that governs disposition of the decedent's estate. There are many published resources on these subjects, both for legal professionals and for lay readers (for example, Clifford & Jordan, 1994; Esperti & Peterson, 1991; Hughes & Klein, 2001; Magee & Ventura, 1999).

Trusts and Other Will Substitutes

It is both possible and legal to seek to avoid the expense and delay of the probate process by *transferring assets during one's life*. For example, with the exception of certain limited circumstances in which death is imminent, one can simply make an irrevocable and unconditional *gift* of property in which full control of the gift is conveyed to the recipient at the time the gift is made (Brown, 1975). Such gifts can now be made by individuals in amounts as high as $10,000 per year per donee (the receiver of such a gift) without incurring any federal tax liability. Similarly, ownership of real estate (land and the structures built on it) can be directly and immediately transferred through a written *deed*. Both gifts and deeds surrender ownership and benefit of the object of the gift or deed, although some states permit *revocable deeds* or other conditions under which the transfer is not as absolute. Gifts and deeds may reduce the size of an estate that is presented for probate or considered for tax purposes.

Alternatively, one can make *transfers effective at death* that convey possession and complete ownership rights to another person upon the death of the current owner of the property, even though the current owner retains many benefits from and control over the property until his or her death. For example, *joint tenancy with right of survivorship* amounts to an arrangement for transfer of property at death through a form of co-ownership. Under this arrangement, two or more parties possess equal rights to the property during their mutual lifetimes. When one party dies, his or her rights dissolve and the rights of the survivor(s) automatically expand to include that person's previous ownership rights. This process can continue until the last survivor acquires full and complete ownership of the entire property interest. At each stage in the process nothing is left unowned by a living person and nothing is therefore available to pass through the probate process. Joint tenancy with right of survivorship usually avoids delay in getting assets to survivors, but it does not necessarily reduce tax liability.

Life insurance policies are another familiar social vehicle through which assets are transferred from one person to another at the time of the first person's death. Such insurance policies depend on a contractual agreement in which premium payments made by the policyholder result in a payment of benefits to a specified beneficiary by an insurance company upon the death of the insured. Many life insurance policies provide considerable flexibility to the insured as to how the monetary value of the policy can be employed during his or her lifetime, including the power to change beneficiaries before death. Benefits from life insurance policies are not included as taxable assets in the estate of the insured, although they clearly add to the property or estate of the beneficiary.

A *trust* is one of the most adaptable and efficient ways of preserving one's assets from probate. One makes a trust by transferring property to a trustee (usually a third party, such as an officer of a corporation or a bank), with instructions on its management and distribution (Abts, 1997; Esperti & Peterson, 1992). Trustees are legally bound to use the trust property for the benefit of the beneficiaries according to the terms provided in the trust instrument or imposed by law. Typically, the maker of the trust retains extensive use and control over the property during his or her life.

Usually, upon the death of the person who established the trust (the *settlor*), the property is distributed to designated beneficiaries without becoming part of the estate in probate. However, a trust can be established that stipulates other circumstances for distribution of property. For example, a trust might stipulate that the settlor's surviving spouse receives a life estate in the income from the trust assets, with the principal to be distributed to children upon the death of the spouse. Rights to amend or revoke the trust can be retained by the person who established the trust. In addition to these *testamentary trusts*, one can also establish *living trusts*, which are essentially set up for the benefit of the trustor—for example, in case he or she is incapacitated and unable to act on his or her own behalf. Living trusts of this sort are especially useful for single adults with no dependents and with minimal assets.

Estate and Inheritance Taxes

Two basic types of taxes follow upon a death: estate taxes and inheritance taxes. *Estate taxes* are imposed on and paid from the decedent's estate. They could be described as taxes not on property itself but on the transfer of property from a decedent to his or her beneficiaries. This occurs before all remaining assets in the estate are distributed to heirs or beneficiaries. By contrast, *inheritance taxes* are imposed on individuals who receive property through inheritance.

Federal estate tax law applies uniformly throughout the United States. Among many other changes, the Economic Growth and Tax Relief Reconciliation Act of 2001 exempts from federal taxes an unlimited amount of property that is donated to charity, together with other property in the estate valued at $1 million in the year 2002 (an amount that is scheduled to rise to $1.5 million in 2004, $2 million in 2006, and $3.5 million in 2009 until this tax is repealed entirely in 2010—although this law has a "sunset" provision whereby estate taxes will be reinstated in 2011 unless Congress and the President take further action on this matter). Also, one can transfer to a surviving spouse an unlimited amount of property without estate taxes. However, such a transfer may only have the effect of postponing or deferring rather than avoiding taxes, since property transferred in this way that remains in the spouse's possession at the time of his or her death will become part of that individual's estate. Federal gift taxes exempt a cumulative amount of $1 million from 2002 onward, and rates gradually fall from 50 to 35 percent in 2010.

In addition, most states have estate and/or inheritance taxes. These taxes vary from state to state, and they may impose different rates on those who are more closely or more distantly related to the decedent. Thus, it is simply sound and prudent policy for those faced with potential estate and/or inheritance taxes to seek the advice of experts in order to minimize any tax burden that might arise.

Summary

In this chapter, we surveyed legal issues that arise before, at, and after the death of a human being in the United States. In before-death issues, we considered advance directives for health care (living wills, durable powers of attorney in health care matters, and "Five Wishes"). Among legal issues, at death, we examined definition, determination, and certification of death. In after-death issues, we discussed organ, tissue, and body donation; disposition of one's body and property; and wills, trusts, and taxes.

Questions for Review and Discussion

1. Which of the available advance directives (living wills; durable powers of attorney; "Five Wishes") discussed in this chapter seems to you most desirable for situations in which you might be unable to participate in decision making about your medical treatment? Why?

2. Why is it difficult in some cases in contemporary American society to decide whether or not someone is dead? Why is it important to make such a decision?

3. What are your views about donating your body's organs or tissues for transplantation after your death? What about donating the organs or tissues of someone you love? What feelings, beliefs, and values led you to these views?

4. Have you thought about disposition of your body and property if you should die? What have you done about these matters, what do you think you should or might do, or why have you done nothing?

Suggested Readings

For a unique resource on legal and other issues related to dead bodies, see:

Iserson, K. V. (1994). *Death to Dust: What Happens to Dead Bodies?*

Concerning rights to privacy, informed consent, and advance directives, see:

Alderman, E., & Kennedy, C. (1995). *The Right to Privacy.*

Alexander, G. J. (1988). *Writing a Living Will: Using a Durable Power-of-Attorney.*

Annenberg Washington Program. (1993). *Communications and the Patient Self-Determination Act: Strategies for Meeting the Educational Mandate.*

Cantor, N. L. (1993). *Advance Directives and the Pursuit of Death with Dignity.*

Cate, F. H., & Gill, B. A. (1991). *The Patient Self-Determination Act: Implementation Issues and Opportunities.*

Flynn, E. P. (1992). *Your Living Will: Why, When, and How to Write One.*

Sabatino, C. P. (1990). *Health Care Powers of Attorney: An Introduction and Sample Forms.*

Society for the Right to Die. (1991). *Refusal of Treatment Legislation: A State by State Compilation of Enacted and Model Statutes.*

Urofsky, M. I. (1993). *Letting Go: Death, Dying, and the Law.*

Williams, P. G. (1991). *The Living Will and the Durable Power of Attorney for Health Care Book, with Forms* (rev. ed.).

On the topic of defining death, see:

Cantor, N. L. (1987). *Legal Frontiers of Death and Dying.*

Gervais, K. G. (1986). *Redefining Death.*

Veatch, R. M. (1976). *Death, Dying, and the Biological Revolution: Our Last Quest for Responsibility.*

Walton, D. N. (1979). *On Defining Death: An Analytic Study of the Concept of Death in Philosophy and Medical Ethics.*

On the topic of organ donation, see:

Dowie, M. (1988). *"We Have a Donor": The Bold New World of Organ Transplanting.*

Green, R. (1999). *The Nicholas Effect: A Boy's Gift to the World.*

Maier, E. (1991). *Sweet Reprieve: One Couple's Journey to the Frontiers of Medicine.*

Prottas, J. (1994). *The Most Useful Gift: Altruism and the Public Policy of Organ Transplants.*

Concerning personal estate planning and disposition of property, consult:

Abts, H. W. (1997). *The Living Trust: The Failproof Way to Pass Along Your Estate to Your Heirs without Lawyers, Courts, or the Probate System* (rev. ed.).

Armstrong, A., & Donahue, M. R. (2000). *On Your Own: A Widow's Passage to Emotional and Financial Well-Being* (3rd ed.).

Clifford, D., & Jordan, C. (1994). *Plan Your Estate* (3rd ed.).

Esperti, R. A., & Peterson, R. L. (1991). *The Handbook of Estate Planning* (3rd ed.).

Esperti, R. A., & Peterson, R. L. (1992). *The Living Trust Revolution: Why America Is Abandoning Wills and Probate.*

Hughes, T. E., & Klein, D. (2001). *A Family Guide to Wills, Funerals, and Probate: How to Protect Yourself and Your Survivors* (2nd ed.).

Magee, D. S., & Ventura, J. (1999). *Everything Your Heirs Need to Know: Organizing Your Assets, Family History, Final Wishes* (3rd ed.).

Rolcik, K. A. (1998). *Living Trusts and Simple Ways to Avoid Probate: With Forms.*

On professional estate planning and disposition of property, consult:

Atkinson, T. E. (1953). *Handbook of the Law of Wills and Other Principles of Succession* (2nd ed.).

Brown, R. A. (1975). *The Law of Personal Property* (3rd ed., by W. B. Rauschenbush).

Dukeminier, J., & Johanson, S. M. (1995). *Wills, Trusts, and Estates* (5th ed.).

Haskell, P. G. (1994). *Preface to Wills, Trusts, and Administration* (2nd ed.).

Lynn, R. J. (1992). *Introduction to Estate Planning in a Nutshell* (4th ed.).

Manning, J. A. (1995). *Manning on Estate Planning* (5th ed.).

Prestopino, D. J. (1992). *Introduction to Estate Planning* (3rd ed.).

InfoTrac College Edition
For more information, explore the InfoTrac College Edition at **http://www.infotrac-college.com/Wadsworth**

Enter search terms: ADVANCE DIRECTIVES, CORONER, DEFINITION OF DEATH, DETERMINATION OF DEATH, DURABLE POWER OF ATTORNEY IN HEALTH CARE, "FIVE WISHES," INHERITANCE TAXES, INTESTATE, LIVING WILLS, MEDICAL EXAMINER, NON-HEART BEATING DONORS, ORGAN AND TISSUE DONATION AND TRANSPLANTATION, PROBATE, WILLS, XENOTRANSPLANTATION.

Chapter Seventeen

SUICIDE AND LIFE-THREATENING BEHAVIOR

FOR MANY PEOPLE, BEHAVIOR THAT APPEARS to involve a deliberate intention to end one's life is puzzling. Such behavior seems to challenge values that are widely held, although perhaps not often or effectively articulated. The motivations or intentions behind suicidal behavior frequently seem to be enigmatic or incomprehensible. Perhaps for those reasons, when a death occurs by suicide there is often a desperate search for a note, an explanation, or some elusive meaning that must have been involved in the act. Typically, however, there is no single explanation or meaning in all of the individuality and complexities that typify suicidal and life-threatening behavior (see Box 17.1). As Alvarez (1970, xiv) has written: "Suicide means different things to different people at different times." That may be the most tantalizing aspect of it all.

We have already examined some issues related to suicide: in our general discussion of death rates and leading causes of death in

Box 17.1 On Understanding a Suicidal Act

Each way to suicide is its own: intensely private, unknowable, and terrible. Suicide will have seemed to its perpetrator the last and best of bad possibilities, and any attempt by the living to chart this final terrain of a life can be only a sketch, maddeningly incomplete. ■

SOURCE: Jamison, 1999, p. 73.

Chapter 2, and as related to adolescents and the elderly in Chapters 13 and 15. We will discuss assisted suicide, euthanasia, and intentionally deciding to end a human life in Chapter 18. But there still remains much for us to learn here about suicide and life-threatening behavior.

We begin here with brief descriptions of three acts of suicide in order to introduce the issues that we need to discuss. Then we seek to clarify the meaning of suicide and life-threatening behavior, and sketch some common patterns in this behavior. Next, we describe efforts to identify central factors (psychological, biological, and sociological) that might enter into an effort to understand or explain such behavior. Further, we explore the impact that suicide has on survivors and interventions that individuals and social groups can undertake to prevent or at least to minimize suicidal behavior. Finally, we examine whether or not there could be a rational basis for suicide, one that might view suicide as morally appropriate or justifiable. ■

Three Completed Suicides

At the time of his death on July 1, 1961, Ernest Hemingway was 62 years old and a successful journalist, writer of short stories, and novelist. Best known for his longer works of fiction, such as *The Sun Also Rises* (1926), *A Farewell to Arms* (1929), and *For Whom the Bell Tolls* (1940), Hemingway won the Pulitzer Prize for his novella, *The Old Man and the Sea* (1952), and two years later he was awarded the Nobel Prize for literature. The image that he presented to the public was that of a writer, hunter, and sportsman characterized by courage and stoicism—the classic macho male. In his private life, however, Hemingway was subject to severe depression and paranoia, like his father. In the end (also like his father), he used a shotgun to complete his own suicide (Lynn, 1987). This is a notoriously deliberate and effective means of committing suicide. Perhaps it was foreshadowed in the words of a character in *For Whom the Bell Tolls* (1940, p. 468), who said, "Dying is only bad when it takes a long time and hurts so much that it humiliates you."

Ernest Hemingway (1899–1961).

Sylvia Plath (1932–1963) was an American poet and novelist. She was best known for her novel, *The Bell Jar* (1971), which was first published in England under an assumed name in January 1963, only a month before her death. This book has an autobiographical quality in its description of a woman caught up in a severe crisis who attempts suicide. Like the author's poetry, *The Bell Jar* emphasizes conflicts that result from family tensions and rebellion against the constricting forces of society.

The death of Plath's father when she was 8 years old was a significant event in her life, as was what Alvarez (1970, p. 7) called her "desperately serious suicide attempt" in 1953 (in which she used stolen sleeping pills, left a misleading note to cover her tracks, and hid behind firewood in a dark, unused corner of a cellar). Plath also survived a serious car wreck during the summer of 1962, in

Sylvia Plath 1932–1963).

which she apparently ran off the road deliberately. In one of her own poems, Plath (1964) seems to describe these events in the following way:*

I have done it again.
One year in every ten
I manage it—

A sort of walking miracle . . .
I am only thirty.
And like the cat I have nine times to die.

This is Number Three. . . .

In December 1962, Plath separated from her husband—the British poet Ted Hughes, whom she had married in June 1956—and moved to London with her two children, Freda and Nicholas. Early on the morning of February 11, 1963, Plath died.

In the days before her death, Plath's friends and her doctor had been concerned about her mental state. Her doctor had prescribed sedatives and had tried to arrange an appointment for her with a psychotherapist. But Plath convinced them that she had improved and could return to her apartment to stay alone with her children during the night of February 10–11. A new Australian

---

*Excerpted from "Lady Lazarus" in *Ariel* by Sylvia Plath. Copyright © 1963 by Ted Hughes. Copyright renewed. Reprinted by permission of HarperCollins Publishers, Inc. and Faber & Faber Ltd.

au pair (an in-home child care provider) was due to arrive at 9 A.M. on the morning of Monday, February 11, to help with the children and housework.

When the *au pair* arrived and could raise no response at the door of the building, she went to search for a telephone to call the agency that employed her to confirm that she had the right address. After returning and trying the door again, and then calling her employer a second time, the woman came back to the house at about 11 A.M. and was finally able to get into the building with the aid of some workmen. Smelling gas, they forced open the door of the apartment and found Plath's body, still warm, together with a note asking that her doctor be called and giving his telephone number. The children were asleep in an upstairs room, wrapped snugly in blankets against the cold weather and furnished with a plate of bread and butter and mugs of milk in case they should wake up hungry before the *au pair* arrived—but their bedroom window was wide open, protecting them from the effects of the gas.

Apparently, about 6 A.M. Plath had arranged the children and the note about calling her doctor, sealed herself in the kitchen with towels around the door and window, placed her head in the oven, and turned on the gas (Stevenson, 1989). A neighbor downstairs was also knocked out by seeping gas and thus was not awake to let the *au pair* into the building when she arrived.

After Plath's death, Alvarez (1970, p. 34) wrote: "I am convinced by what I know of the facts that this time she did not intend to die." However that may be, interest in Plath's life, chronic suicidality, and death continues today (for example, Gerisch, 1998; Lester, 1998).

Mohamed Atta

The last night. Remind yourself that in this night you will face many challenges . . . Continue to pray throughout this night . . .

Purify your heart and clean it from all earthly matters. The time of fun and waste has gone. The time of judgment has arrived . . . You have to be convinced that those few hours that are left you in your life are very few . . . Be optimistic.

Always remember the verses [from the Koran] that you would wish for death before you meet it if you only know what the reward after death will be.

Everybody hates death, fears death. But only those, the believers who know the life after death and the reward after death, would be the one who will be seeking death . .

Check all of your items—your bag, your clothes, knives, your will, your IDs, your passport, all your papers. Check your safety before you leave . . . Make sure that nobody is following you . . .

In the morning, try to pray the morning prayer with an open heart . . . When you enter the plane:

Oh God, open all doors for me. Oh God . . . I am asking for your help . . . I am asking you to lift the burden I feel . . .

(Taken from a handwritten document found by the FBI in the luggage of one of the September 11 hijackers; Atta, 2001.)

What Is Suicide?

I can become dead by killing myself. If so, I do something to cause my own death, or I do not do something to prevent my own death. No one else is involved in the actions that bring about my death. Hemingway and Plath's deaths are good examples of this. No one else was present, and no one else acted to bring about these deaths. This is part of the meaning of suicide: an individual acts to cause his or her own death.

However, this is not enough by itself to make a death a suicide. Someone might engage in an action that accidentally causes his or her death. For example, a parachutist whose parachute does not open engages in an action that causes his or her own death, but that death is not a suicide. What is missing in this case is the *intention* to die.

Thus, for death to be a suicide, the person carrying out the act must have the *intention* that the act results in death. But determining the intention of someone—even of ourselves—is seldom easy, and suicidal behavior often turns out to be a particularly ambiguous and ambivalent sort of behavior. The intentions of those who engage in suicidal behavior are varied. They may include attempts at revenge (perhaps this was Atta's motivation?), to gain attention, to end some form of perceived suffering, or to end one's life—or, perhaps, some combination of one or more of these and other intentions.

Partly because of this ambiguity in intentions, it is not always clear whether or not a specific situation should be described as a suicide. We can see that in the case of Sylvia Plath and in Alvarez's comment that "this time she did not intend to die." Suppose someone has been warned about a diabetic condition and cautioned to monitor his or her diet. If that person fails to do so and dies in a diabetic coma, was the death caused intentionally? What if someone drove too rapidly for road conditions and died when his or her car crashed into a bridge abutment at high speed with no brake marks on a clear, dry day? Can one unconsciously act to end one's life (do unconscious intentions exist) (Farberow, 1980)? Suicidologists struggle with questions like these and disagree about how to answer them.

Uncertainty about whether or not a particular act was a suicidal one has important consequences for anyone studying this subject. It may have social significance if one fails to include certain acts among those classified as suicidal acts because one is uncertain about them. If so, then statistical data on the number of deaths resulting from suicidal behavior will at best be inaccurate (Evans & Farberow, 1988).

Data on suicide may be inaccurate for other reasons, too. For example, authorities may be reluctant to call a death a suicide in order to give the decedent and his or her survivors the benefit of the doubt and to protect family members from guilt and the social stigma often attached to suicide. Family members and those concerned with their welfare may resist attempts to label a death as a suicide. For reasons like these, it has been suggested that the number of deaths due to suicide may be at least twice the number actual recorded (O'Carroll, 1989). If this is the case, the impact of suicide on individual lives and on society may be seriously misunderstood.

Further, difficulties in recognizing someone's actual intentions may contribute to our failing to recognize suicidal behavior when confronted by it. If one does not believe that someone's intention is to end up dead, or if that person does not express or even denies such an intention, one may pay less attention to that person. Thus, certain forms of life-threatening behavior are sometimes discounted on the grounds that they are *only* a "cry for help" (Farberow & Shneidman, 1965). At a minimum, though, the case of Sylvia Plath shows that life-threatening acts are a desperate way to seek help, and even a cry for help can have lethal consequences, whether or not they were fully foreseen or intended. It is, therefore, important to try to get a clear understanding of suicidal and life-threatening behavior and to become familiar with common patterns of such behavior in our society.

Some Common Patterns in Suicidal Behavior

In 1999, suicide (designated as "intentional self-harm" in the new international classification system) was the eleventh leading cause of death in the United States, accounting for 29,199 deaths and a death rate of 10.7 per 100,000 (Hoyert et al., 2001). During the decade of the 1990s, suicide had been the eighth or ninth leading cause of death in our society, overall numbers of suicide deaths had fluctuated between 30,000 and 31,000 (even while the total population in the United States grew by about 10 percent), and death rates from suicide had declined from 12.4 to 10.7 per 100,000 (see Table 17.1). Also, for some years now the United States has had one of the lowest suicide rates (in the bottom third) in the world (Seltzer, 1994). Thus the new 1999 data on numbers of deaths (assuming that they are reliable) and death rates from suicide represent a continued decline and an additional modest improvement.

Table 17.1 Suicide Rates per 100,000 Population by Age: United States, 1990–1999

Age	1990	1991	1992	1993	1994	1995	1996	1997	1998	1999
5–14	00.8	00.7	00.9	00.9	00.9	00.9	00.8	00.8	00.8	00.6
15–24	13.2	13.1	13.0	13.5	13.8	13.3	12.0	11.4	11.1	10.3
25–34	15.2	15.2	14.5	15.1	15.4	15.4	14.5	14.3	13.8	13.5
35–44	15.3	14.7	15.1	15.1	15.3	15.2	15.5	15.3	15.4	14.4
45–54	14.8	15.5	14.7	14.5	14.4	14.6	14.9	14.7	14.8	14.2
55–64	16.0	15.4	14.8	14.6	13.4	13.3	13.7	13.5	13.1	12.4
65–74	17.9	16.9	16.5	16.3	15.3	15.8	15.0	14.4	14.1	13.6
75–84	24.9	23.5	22.8	22.3	21.3	20.7	20.0	19.3	19.7	18.3
85+	22.2	24.0	21.9	22.8	23.0	21.6	20.2	20.8	21.0	19.2
65+	20.5	19.7	19.1	19.0	18.1	18.1	17.3	16.8	16.9	15.9
Total	12.4	12.2	12.0	12.1	12.0	11.9	11.6	11.4	11.3	10.7

SOURCE: Hoyert et al., 2001; and American Association of Suicidology, www.suicidology.org.

If we compare suicide to homicide as a cause of death in our society, in 1999 there were 12,310 more deaths from suicide than from homicide. That is, more Americans kill themselves than are killed by others. In 1999 there were also many more deaths from suicide than from the 14,802 deaths associated with human immunodeficiency virus (HIV) infection. In fact, there were nearly as many deaths from suicide in 1999 as there were from homicide and HIV combined. By contrast, there were 13,202 more deaths from motor vehicle accidents than from suicide in the United States in 1999.

Some common patterns in completed suicides in the United States have been dramatized in the following ways for the year 1999: an average of one person killed himself or herself every 18 minutes; an average of one elderly person killed himself or herself about every 96 minutes; an average of one young person (15–24 years of age) killed himself or herself just over every two hours and fifteen minutes (American Association of Suicidology, www.suicidology.org, 2001). It has also been estimated that there are 25 attempts at suicide for every completed suicide in our society or an estimated 730,000 suicide attempts in the United States in 1999. Among young people, there may be as many as 100 to 200 attempts for every completed suicide, whereas there may be only four attempts for every completed suicide among the elderly. Moreover, the American Association of Suicidology has estimated that 5 million living Americans have attempted to kill themselves and that each completed suicide intimately affects at least six other people, or a total of some 175,000 persons, each year.

Men carry out a completed suicide more frequently than women, by a ratio of more than 4:1 in a typical recent year. It is also noteworthy, however, that women attempt suicide more frequently than do men, by an estimated ratio of approximately 3:1.

In terms of methods, firearms are the main instruments used to carry out suicide among both men and women. Approximately 62 percent of all men and about 37 percent of all women who committed suicide in 1999 used firearms (Hoyert et al., 2001). The second most common means among men was hanging (including strangulation and suffocation); poisoning was second among women.

A particularly disturbing aspect of suicidal behavior is its frequency among young persons. Between 1960 and 1990, rates more than doubled among individuals who were 15 to 24 years of age, although suicide death rates in this group have since declined from 13.2 to 10.3 per 100,000 through 1999 (see Chapter 13 for a fuller discussion of youth suicide). Although suicide is sometimes portrayed as an urban phenomenon, it has been reported that youth in rural areas have higher rates of suicide, especially in the western part of the United States (Greenberg et al., 1987). Thus suicide can be found among young people everywhere throughout the country. In fact, in 1999 suicide was the third leading cause of death among 15- to 24-year-olds (following accidents and homicide), accounting for 3,901 deaths. This figure represented approximately 13.4 percent of all deaths from suicide in 1999 and about 12.7 percent of all deaths among individuals 15 to 24 years of age (Hoyert et al., 2001). In the same year, suicide was the sixth leading cause of death among 5- to 14-year-olds, accounting for 244 deaths.

Both absolute numbers and death rates for suicide increase as one moves on in the life course (see Table 17.1). For example, among those 25 to 44 years of age in 1999, suicide was the fourth leading cause of death, accounting for 11,572 deaths (8.8 percent of all deaths in this age group) and a death rate of 13.9 per 100,000. By contrast, in the 45- to 64-year-old age group, suicide was the eighth leading cause of death, accounting for 7,977 deaths (only 2.0 percent of all deaths in this age group) and a death rate of 13.4 per 100,000. Among individuals 65 years old and over, suicide was well out of the ten leading causes of death, but it still accounted for 5,489 deaths in 1998 (only 0.3 percent of all deaths in this age group) and a death rate of 16.9 per 100,000 (see Chapter 15 for a fuller discussion of suicide among the elderly). In fact, it is elderly adults—especially elderly white males and others who are over 85—who have by far the highest suicide rates in our society.

In relation to ethnicity, Caucasian Americans most frequently complete a suicidal action; about 90 percent of all suicidal deaths in 1999 involved Caucasian Americans (Hoyert et al., 2001). Among Caucasian Americans, males (with 21,107 suicide deaths in 1999) are most at risk for suicide, even though numbers of suicidal deaths among females exceed those of females in all other ethnic groups by a ratio of nearly 9.5 to 1. In 1999, 5,193 Caucasian-American females died of suicide by contrast with only 548 deaths among all nonwhite females.

In general, African Americans have much lower mortality rates from suicide than Caucasian Americans (5.6 versus 11.7 per 100,000 in 1999). This is true even among young persons, where Caucasian-American youths complete far more suicides than African-American youths (just the opposite of the situation in homicide deaths). However, suicide among African Americans reaches a peak among young adults, and suicide rates are increasing among young African-American males, even more rapidly than among young white males. Among African Americans in 1999, 1,630 males died of suicide versus only 294 females, resulting in a difference in mortality rates of 10.0 versus 1.6 deaths per 100,000 in these two groups.

Information on suicide among Hispanic Americans is even less reliable because that population group is not always easy to identify and trace. For 1999 the National Center for Health Statistics reported 103,740 deaths among Hispanic Americans (Hoyert et al., 2001), but only 1,695 of these deaths resulted from suicide. Still, all reports on deaths by suicide are dependent on available data, and several authors (such as Hoppe & Martin, 1986) have noted that among Hispanic Americans (and African Americans) many deaths that are suicides may not be reported as such (for example, they may be reported as accidents or homicides). Not surprisingly, numbers of suicide deaths among white non-Hispanics in 1999 were nearly 15 times higher than those attributed to Hispanic Americans.

Suicide rates among Asian Americans have not been thoroughly studied, although it is widely thought that since the early 1980s suicide rates in this group have generally been below those of the general population as a whole (McIntosh, 1989). Lester (1994) reported that in his study Asian Americans overall had lower rates of suicide than Caucasian Americans and Native Americans. Among Asian Americans, Japanese Americans had the highest rates, and Filipino Americans had the lowest. Also, Lester reported that Asian-American women had a relatively higher suicide rate compared to men than women in other ethnic groups, and Chinese and Japanese Americans showed a relatively greater increase in suicidal behavior as they aged. As a rule, Asian-American suicide rates are highest among the elderly (McIntosh & Santos, 1981a; Yu, 1986).

It is commonly claimed that there are high suicide rates among Native Americans. However, that claim has been called a myth (Thompson & Walker, 1990), and some (such as Van Winkle & May, 1986) have asserted that it is based on small numbers of suicides over short time spans and among small population bases. (This dispute reveals in another form our dependence on data and statistics to try to understand suicide mortality rates.) In fact, Webb and Willard (1975) determined that there is no single common Native American pattern for suicides, and Thompson and Walker (1990) argued that suicide rates in the various tribes seem mostly closely related to suicide rates in their surrounding populations. If that is correct, then Native American rates of suicide should be compared to rates among others in the areas in which the Native Americans live. Thus, no overall statistic for Native American suicide rates is really reliable, since such rates vary markedly from area to area and tribe to tribe (McIntosh, 1983).

Still, this myth persists and even influences beliefs among Native Americans themselves. Thus, Levy and Kunitz (1987) reported that the Hopi have become concerned about suicide rates among themselves, even though "Hopi suicide rates are no higher than those of the neighboring counties" (p. 932). Furthermore, they found no evidence that Hopi suicide rates are increasing. This finding does not suggest that there should be no concern about suicide rates in any particular Native American group, but only that such rates need to be understood in context if we are to appreciate them properly.

The only generalization about Native Americans that does appear to be valid is that suicide in this group is largely a phenomenon of young males, since suicide rates among the elderly are low in this cultural group (McIntosh & Santos, 1981b; Thompson & Walker, 1990).

With these data about common patterns in suicidal behavior in hand, we can now examine some of the leading interpretations of this behavior—psychological, biological, and sociological—that have been offered to help understand suicide. In each case, part of the work of these interpretations has been to try to elucidate the causes of (or, perhaps better, contributing factors to) suicide.

Explanations of Suicide

As we have suggested, acts of suicide produce an intense urgency in survivors to find an explanation—a reason—for this unsettling behavior. Although this pressure to find a reason is understandable, it is not an easy one to respond to with clarity.

For instance, when terrorists flew airplanes into the World Trade Center, many wanted to know why anyone would do such a thing. At first glance, it appeared that these and other self-destructive and murderous acts were the product of distorted fanatical religious beliefs. Some of what Atta wrote in his letter, such as references to Islamic beliefs about God and an afterlife, appear to support this supposition.

However, this cannot be an adequate explanation of what these individuals did. As Ariel Merari (who heads the Political Violence Research Center at Tel Aviv University and who has studied terrorist violence extensively) argues, there are many religious believers (from all religions) who hold distorted and fanatical beliefs, but who do not engage in such behaviors (Martin, 2001). Merari then looked for other reasons for these acts. First, he noticed that such behavior is not limited to religious believers. Soldiers in World Wars I and II and Japanese pilots during World War II also performed suicidal acts that bore similarities to those in the events of September 11. Second, Merari found that what these people had in common was they belonged to organizations that encouraged them to do these things. In particular, he claims that groups which get members to engage in suicidal/murderous acts share three characteristics: (1) they build up motivation to overcome ambivalence and perform the act, (2) they provide group pressure to stick to the mission, and (3) they get a direct commitment from the individual to perform the act. This last element includes identifying the individual before the group as a "living martyr" and having the individual identify himself (until recently, these acts have nearly always been performed by males) this way, for instance, by writing letters to family members in which he identifies himself as such. Having publicly proclaimed himself as having accepted this role, it is difficult to back out.

Whether or not this explanation is adequate, it demonstrates the difficulty and complexity of providing a single explanation of suicide. Perhaps that is why the three general types of explanations that follow have been offered to help us understand suicide.

Psychological Explanations of Suicide

Leenaars (1990) identified three major forms that psychological explanations of suicide have taken. The first of these is based on Freud's psychoanalytic theory. Freud argued that suicide is *murder turned around 180 degrees* (Litman, 1967) and suggested that it is related to the loss of a desired person or object. Psychologically, the person at risk comes to identify him or her self with the lost person. He or she feels anger toward this lost object of affection and wishes to punish (even to kill) the lost person. However, since the individual has identified his or her self with this object of affection, the anger and its correlated wish to punish become directed against the self. Thus, self-destructive behavior is the result.

A second psychological approach sees the problem as *essentially cognitive in nature.* In this view, clinical depression (suicide is highly correlated with depression) is believed to be an important contributing factor, especially when it is associated with hopelessness. The central issue here is that negative evaluations are a pervasive feature of the suicidal person's worldview. The future, the self, the present situation, and the limited number of possible options that are envisioned by the individual are all viewed as undesirable. Along with these evaluations, impaired thinking is present: such thinking is "often automatic and involuntary . . . characterized by a number of possible errors, some so gross as to constitute distortion" (Leenaars, 1990, p. 162).

A third psychological theory claims that *suicidal behavior is learned.* This theory contends that as a child the suicidal individual learned not to express aggression outward, but rather to turn it back on the self. Again, depression is noted as an important factor, now the result of negative reinforcement from the environment for a person's actions. Furthermore, this depression (and its associated suicidal or life-threatening behavior) may even be seen as being positively reinforced—that is, rewarded by those around the individual. It might be argued, for example, that Ernest Hemingway's depression, as mentioned earlier, was positively reinforced by the example of his father's own suicide (Slaby, 1992). In any event, this theory views the suicidal individual as poorly socialized and maintains that constructive cultural evaluations of life and death have not been learned.

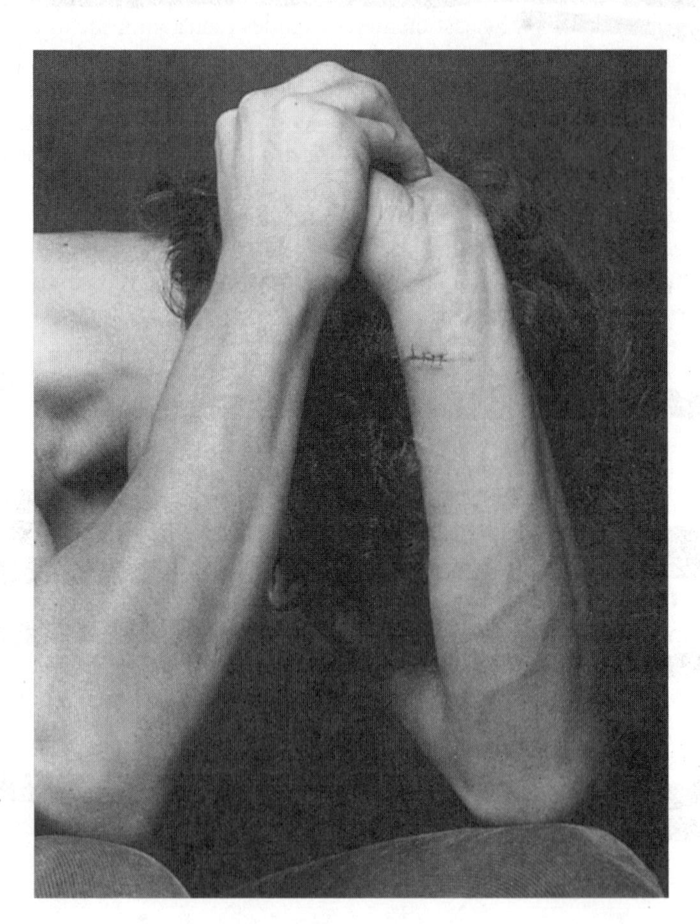

Suicidal behavior is often closely linked to depression.

Jamison (1999) argued that psychopathology is "the most common element in suicide" (p. 100). In particular, she focused on the relationships between "mood disorders, schizophrenia, borderline and antisocial personality disorders, alcoholism, and drug abuse." She believes that these mental illnesses play a (and perhaps *the*) significant role in accounting for suicidal acts. She also described genetic and brain chemistry abnormalities (discussed below), and related these to psychopathological factors. In that discussion, she reiterated her view that even when these other factors are taken into account, they are of most significance when associated with mental illness.

These psychological theories need not be seen as incompatible, of course. Putting them together helps bring our overall understanding of suicide and suicidal behavior more sharply into focus. Since suicide is a complex behavior, it probably makes most sense to see it as arising (at least often) from a complex basis.

Biological Explanations of Suicide

Some studies have sought to discover whether there are biological explanations for suicidal behavior (for example, Roy, 1990). These have typically focused on biological explanations relating to either neurochemical or genetic factors. Some theorists believe that there may be a disturbance in the levels of certain neurochemicals found in the brain, such as a reduction in the level of serotonin (a chemical related to aggressive behavior and the regulation of anxiety) in suicidal individuals. However, such studies have not made clear whether such a decrease is associated with depression, suicidal behavior, or the violent outward or inward expression of aggression.

Other studies (Egeland & Sussex, 1985; Roy, 1990; Wender et al., 1986) have suggested that some predispositions to suicidal behavior may be inherited. For example, a study of adopted children in Denmark looked at the biological families of adopted children diagnosed with "affective disorder" who had completed suicide (Wender et al., 1986). More of these persons who showed signs of "affective disorder" and had completed a suicide had relatives who showed the same signs and actions than was the case for a control group. However, it is uncertain from this study exactly what it is that may be inherited. Perhaps the inherited element is an inability to control impulsive behavior, not suicidal behavior in itself.

Thus, it has not yet been demonstrated that biological factors can be related clearly to suicidal behavior. Nevertheless, continued research into biological explanations of suicide may eventually yield helpful information to add to what is already known about other factors contributing to suicidal behavior.

Sociological Explanations of Suicide

The oldest and best-known attempt to offer an explanation of suicide comes from the work of a French sociologist, Emile Durkheim (1951; Selkin, 1983), originally published in France at the end of the 19th century. Durkheim argued that no psychological condition *by itself* invariably produces suicidal behavior. Instead, he believed that suicide can be understood as an outcome of the relationship of the individual to his or her society, with special emphasis on ways in which individuals are or are not *integrated* and *regulated* in their relationships with society. Durkheim's analysis has been criticized, but his book remains a classic in the literature on suicide (Douglas, 1967; Lester, 2000; Maris, 1969). In it, he identified three primary sorts of relationships between individuals and society as conducive to suicidal behavior, and he made brief reference to the possibility of a fourth basic type of suicide.

Egoistic Suicide The first of these relationships may result in what Durkheim called *egoistic suicide,* or suicide involving more or less isolated individuals. It has been shown that the risk of suicide is diminished in the presence of a social group that provides some integration for the individual (especially in terms of meaning for his or her life). When such integration is absent, loses its force, or is somehow removed (especially abruptly), suicide becomes a more likely possibility.

Durkheim argued for this thesis in the case of three sorts of "societies"—religious society, domestic society, and political society. A *religious society* may provide integration (meaning) for its members in many ways—for example, by means of a unified, strong creed. A *domestic society* (for example, marriage) also seems to be a factor that tends to reduce suicidal behavior by providing individuals with shared "sentiments and memories," thereby locating them in a kind of geography of meaning. In addition, a *political society* can be another vehicle that assists individuals in achieving social integration. When any of these societies—religious, domestic, or political—does not effectively help individuals to find meaning for their lives or when the society disintegrates or loses its influence, individuals may be thrown back on their own resources, may find them inadequate to their needs, and may become more at risk for suicidal and/or life-threatening behavior.

In short, Durkheim's thesis here is that whenever an individual experiences himself or herself in a situation wherein his or her society fails to assist that individual in finding his or her place in the world, suicidal behavior can result. Thus, egoistic suicide depends on an *under*involvement or *under*integration, a kind of disintegration and isolation of an individual from his or her society.

Altruistic Suicide The second form of social relationship that is or may be related to suicide arises from an *over*involvement or *over*integration of the individual into his or her society. In this situation, the ties that produce the integration between the individual and the social group are so strong that they may result in *altruistic suicide* or suicide undertaken on behalf of the group. Personal identity may give way to identification with the welfare of the group, and the individual may find the meaning of his or her life (completely) outside of self. For example, in some strongly integrated societies, there are contexts in which suicide may be seen as a duty. In other words, the surrender of the individual's life may be demanded on behalf of what is perceived to be the welfare of the society.

Durkheim listed several examples found in various historical cultures that involve relationships of strong integration or involvement and that lead to suicidal behavior: persons who are aged or ill (the Eskimo); women whose husbands have died (the practice of *suttee* in India before the English came); servants of social chiefs who have died (many ancient societies). One might think also of persons who have failed in their civic or religious duties so as to bring shame on themselves, their families, and/or their societies—for example, the samurai warrior in Japanese society who commits ritual *seppuku*. Also, involvement in a religious cult led some Americans to altruistic suicide at the People's Temple in Georgetown in British Guyana (1978) and at the Heaven's Gate complex in California (1997).

Anomic Suicide Durkheim described a third form of suicide, *anomic suicide*, not in terms of integration of the individual into society but rather in terms of how the society *regulates* its members. All human beings need to regulate their desires (for material goods, for sexual activity, and so forth). To the extent that a society assists individuals in this regulation, it helps keep such desires under control. When a society is unable or unwilling to help its members in the regulation of their desires—for example, because the society is undergoing rapid change and its rules are in a state of flux—a condition of *anomie* is the result. (The term anomie comes from the Greek *anomia* = *a* [without] + *nomoi* [laws or norms], and means "lawlessness" or "normlessness.")

Anomie can be conducive to suicide, especially when it thrusts an individual suddenly into a situation perceived to be chaotic and intolerable. In contemporary American society, examples of this sort of suicide might involve adolescents who have been unexpectedly rejected by a peer group, some farmers who find that economic and social forces outside their control are forcing them into bankruptcy and taking away both their livelihood and their way of life, or middle-aged employees who have developed specialized work skills and who have devoted themselves for years to their employer only to be suddenly thrown out of their jobs and economically dislocated. For such individuals, *under*regulation or a sudden withdrawal of control may be intolerable because of the absence of (familiar) principles to guide them in living.

Fatalistic Suicide Durkheim only mentions a fourth type of suicide, called fatalistic suicide, in a footnote in his book, where it is described as the opposite of anomic suicide. Fatalistic suicide derives from *excessive regulation* of individuals by society—for example, when one becomes a prisoner or a slave. These are the circumstances of "persons with futures pitilessly blocked and passions violently choked by oppressive discipline" (1951, p. 276). Durkheim did not think that this type of suicide was very common in his own society, but it may be useful as an illustration of social forces that lead an individual to seek to escape from an *overcontrolling* social context.

Suicide: An Act with Many Determinants and Levels of Meaning

In a way similar to Durkheim's claim that suicidal behavior cannot be understood solely by studying the psychology of those who engage in such behavior, Menninger (1938, p. 23) wrote, "Suicide is a very complex act, and not a simple, incidental, isolated act of impulsion, either logical or inexplicable." Both of these theorists saw a completed suicide as an outcome of *many* causes, not only one. Shneidman (1980/1995), Douglas (1967), and others (such as Breed, 1972) also have suggested that a variety of elements may enter into suicidal behavior.

One popular way to reflect the complexity of suicidal behavior is to think of it as involving three elements: *haplessness* (being ill fated or unlucky), *helplessness*, and *hopelessness*. Shneidman (1980/1995) took this understanding forward to a still more complex and precise account by thinking of the factors that lead to suicide in terms of three main components and a triggering process: (1) *inimicality*, or an unsettled life pattern in which one acts against one's own best interests; (2) *perturbation*, or an increased psychological disturbance in the person's life; (3) *constriction*, which appears in "tunnel vision" and "either/or" thinking, and which represents a narrowing of the range of perceptions, opinions, and options that occur to the person's mind; and (4) the idea of *cessation*, of resolving the unbearable pain of disturbance and isolation by simply ending it or being out of it.

These characterizations of suicide can lead to an important conclusion in the search for an understanding of suicidal behavior. As we have noted, there is often a natural impulse among students of suicidal behavior and bereaved family members to look for the cause of a suicide. This need can be illustrated in the efforts of many survivors to find a suicide note that they hope might explain what has happened. In fact, however, there usually is no such single cause. Suicide is most often an act with many determinants and levels of meaning. It may arise from a context of many sorts of causes, among which biological, psychological, and social factors are surely prominent (Lester, 1990a, 1990b, 1992; Maris, 1981, 1988; Maris et al., 1992). In fact, one expert on suicide notes has written that "in order to commit suicide, one cannot write a meaningful suicide note; conversely, if one could write a meaningful note, one would not have to commit suicide" (Shneidman, 1980/1995, p. 58).

The Impact of Suicide

In addition to the individual who dies or who puts his or her life in jeopardy, a suicidal act always affects other people. Reports in the literature from the 1970s and ongoing communications from counselors, therapists, and members of suicide support or bereavement self-help groups have indicated that survivors of the person who has died from suicide almost always have a difficult time dealing with that death (for example, Cain, 1972; Wallace, 1973). The common theme in these reports is that the aftereffects of suicide intensify experiences of anger, sadness, guilt, physical complaints, and other dimensions of grief found in all loss and bereavement. Thus, Lindemann and Greer (1972, p. 67) wrote: "The survivors of a suicide are likely to get 'stuck' in their grieving and to go on for years in a state of cold isolation, unable to feel close to others and carrying always with them the feeling that they are set apart or under the threat of doom."

More recent reports have questioned the adequacy of this account of bereavement following a suicide (for example, Barrett & Scott, 1990; Dunne et al., 1987; Nelson & Frantz, 1996; Silverman et al., 1994). In particular, it has been noted that most of the published studies on this subject have had significant methodological weaknesses (McIntosh, 1987). The size of the study groups has been small. Persons who participate in these studies have often come from clinical sources, from support groups, and from college students (and each of these groups may have people who are atypical in one way or another). For obvious reasons, participants in most studies have been volunteers. Thus, large numbers of survivors who are not members of this kind of group or who have refused to participate (and who may in fact make up the largest group of survivors) have not been studied (Van Dongen, 1990). Also, there have been few comparison studies in which survivors of someone who committed suicide are compared to other bereaved persons (Hauser, 1987). Those studies that have made some comparison between different groups of survivors have yielded inconclusive results (Demi & Miles, 1988; McIntosh, 1987).

Most researchers (such as Barrett & Scott, 1990; Calhoun et al., 1986; Demi & Miles, 1988; Hauser, 1987) themselves warn against making generalizations on the basis of their work. Still, actual empirical study is important to correct impressions that arise from "clinical observation, intellectual conjecture, and theoretical speculation" (Barrett & Scott, 1990, p. 2). Only such study can prevent us from making false generalizations or from stereotyping suicide survivors and thus increasing the difficulty of their mourning by placing expectations on them that they may or may not meet.

Thus, what we can say about the nature of the mourning process for suicide survivors and how it differs from that process for other survivors is still somewhat tentative. Perhaps one of the clearest statements on this subject comes from the work of Barrett and Scott (1990). They pointed out that suicide survivors at least have *more types of issues* to deal with than do other survivors. The survivors of someone's suicide must cope with: (1) the tasks anyone has *after the death of someone to whom one has been close*, (2) tasks related to a death that *arises from some cause other than a natural one* and is often therefore *perceived to have been a death that was avoidable*, (3) tasks associated with *a sudden death*, and finally (4) tasks due to *the suicidal nature of the death*, such as the repudiation of life-affirming values and abandonment issues that it seems to imply.

Some aspects of these tasks are present in the mourning process of suicide survivors more frequently than in the mourning of persons bereaved as a result of other types of death. Blame (of others or of oneself) and guilt (the response to a sense of being at fault), a sense of being rejected by the deceased, and perhaps especially significant, a search for an explanation for why the person acted to end his or her life often play heightened roles in the lives of these mourners (Dunn & Morrish-Vidners, 1988; Reed & Greenwald, 1991; Silverman et al., 1994; Van Dongen, 1990, 1991).

Whereas some have claimed that suicide survivors are themselves subject to self-destructive and suicidal thoughts and actions, other studies have reported that these survivors found a strong deterrent to such actions in realizing how devastating another suicide in the family would be for fellow survivors (Dunn & Morrish-Vidners, 1988; Van Dongen, 1990).

Not all suicide survivors will have to deal with these tasks to the same extent. Some evidence indicates that it is the degree of emotional attachment to the deceased that matters most here (as with all mourning), as much as or even more than the formal nature (parent, sibling, friend) of the relationship (Barrett & Scott, 1990; Reed & Greenwald, 1991), or the type of death.

Although there are few longitudinal studies of survivors of another's suicide, one study of elderly survivors indicated that whereas many mourners of other sorts of death begin to experience a change in their mourning around six months, these survivors take longer to reach that first change. Even after two and a half years, suicide survivors rated their mental health differently than did the survivors of natural deaths or other types of sudden death (Farberow et al., 1992).

One issue affecting the mourning of survivors of another's suicide is the interaction of these survivors with members of their social support group. Some studies indicate that these survivors find less helpful support than do other survivors (Dunn & Morrish-Vidners, 1988; Rudestam, 1987). Rudestam (1987) noted that in one study 84 percent of funeral directors who were interviewed said that people reacted differently to suicide survivors. Such studies imply that suicide survivors may be a good example of persons experiencing disenfranchised grief (see Chapter 10).

Part of the difficulty for such survivors concerns the social rules governing how to behave in this situation. Not only are there fewer social rules to guide people, but the rules that do exist seem to constrain behavior more than those rules governing other mourning situations (Calhoun, Abernathy, & Selby, 1986; Dunn & Morrish-Vidners, 1988; Van Dongen, 1990). Another complicating factor is that the survivors themselves seem often to withdraw from others and do not reach out for or readily accept other people's support (Dunn & Morrish-Vidners, 1988). Thus, survivors may experience the stigmatization association with suicide intrapsychically as much as socially (Allen et al., 1993; Rudestam, 1987).

As we have noted, however, mourning is a process in which people need a support system. If one is to cope adequately with mourning a suicide, then communication, or at least the nonjudgmental presence of others, can be helpful (Bolton, 1995; Chance, 1992; Dunn & Morrish-Vidners, 1988).

Another issue of concern around suicide involves what have been called "cluster" or "copycat" suicides. There is no agreement about how to define such suicides (Davies, 1993; Gould et al., 1990). To the extent that a set of suicides can be seen as being formed by more than chance, such sets occur more frequently among 15- to 19- and 20- to 24-year-olds and perhaps among 45- to 64-year-olds (Gould et al., 1990). However, careful study of such events is still in development.

Although it may be the case that some adolescents are influenced by the experience of an earlier suicide, either directly (by actually knowing someone who has committed suicide) or indirectly (by knowing of a suicide from the media or from other people's accounts), the adolescents who have committed suicide following earlier suicides and who have been carefully studied share other attributes that are at least as likely to account for their behavior as this contact (Davidson et al., 1989). Those attributes include substance abuse, mental illness, losing a girlfriend or boyfriend, witnessing or using violence themselves, damaging themselves physically, being more easily offended, attending more schools, moving more frequently, and having more than two adults who served as parents (Davidson et al., 1989).

Suicide Intervention

In this section we focus on "suicide prevention." However, because one cannot really prevent very determined acts of suicide, it is better to speak here of *intervention aimed at reducing the likelihood of a completed suicide* (Shneidman, 1971; Silverman & Maris, 1995). Many programs have been developed throughout the United States and in other countries to work toward this goal, often using the techniques of *crisis intervention* (consult local crisis intervention programs in your area or contact the American Association of Suicidology's National Hopeline Network, which is staffed 24 hours per day, 7 days per week by trained counselors, at 1-800-SUICIDE). Such programs minister to the needs of persons who feel themselves to be in crisis or who sense an inclination toward suicide. Over decades of work, much has been learned about how persons like this behave. In turn, much has been learned about how others can assist such people—that is, about how to intervene constructively in cases of suicidal or life-threatening behavior (Seiden, 1977).

First of all, mistaken impressions about suicidal behavior must be confronted (see Table 17.2). For instance, many people believe that suicidal persons do not talk about their intentions, that suicide is the result of a sudden impulse, and that mentioning suicide to someone who is emotionally upset may make a suggestion to that person that he or she had not previously entertained. It has long been recognized that these are all erroneous beliefs (Maris, 1981).

People who are thinking about killing themselves most often *do* talk about this. One estimate claims that 80 percent of persons who are inclined toward suicide communicate their plans to family members, friends, authority figures (such as physicians or clergy), or telephone intervention programs (Hewett, 1980, p. 23).

Suicide rarely occurs without warning. It is seldom an action that erupts from nowhere. It is often thought out well in advance and planned for. Frequently, a suicidal person gives many clues about his or her intentions. These clues may or may not be verbal. They might include giving away beloved objects, making changes in eating or sleeping habits, or even displaying a sense of calmness after a period of agitation (calmness because a *decision* has finally been made about what to do).

Table 17.2 Facts and Fables about Suicide

These Statements are *Not* True	These Statements *Are* True
Fable: People who talk about suicide don't commit suicide.	**Fact:** Of any ten persons who kill themselves, eight have given definite warnings of their suicidal intentions. Suicide threats and attempts *must* be taken seriously.
Fable: Suicide happens without warning.	**Fact:** Studies reveal that the suicidal person gives many clues and warnings regarding his suicidal intentions. Alertness to these cries for help may prevent suicidal behavior.
Fable: Suicidal people are fully intent on dying.	**Fact:** Most suicidal people are undecided about living or dying, and they "gamble with death," leaving it to others to save them. Almost no one commits suicide without letting others know how he is feeling. Often this "cry for help" is given in "code." These distress signals can be used to save lives.
Fable: Once a person is suicidal, he is suicidal forever.	**Fact:** Happily, individuals who wish to kill themselves are "suicidal" only for a limited period of time. If they are saved from self-destruction, they can go on to lead useful lives.
Fable: Improvement following a suicidal crisis means that the suicidal risk is over.	**Fact:** Most suicides occur within about three months following the beginning of "improvement," when the individual has the energy to put his morbid thoughts and feelings into effect. Relatives and physicians should be especially vigilant during this period.
Fable: Suicide strikes more often among the rich—or, conversely, it occurs more frequently among the poor.	**Fact:** Suicide is neither the rich man's disease nor the poor man's curse. Suicide is very "democratic" and is represented proportionately among all levels of society.
Fable: Suicide is inherited or "runs in a family."	**Fact:** Suicide does not run in families. It is an individual matter and can be prevented.
Fable: All suicidal individuals are mentally ill, and suicide is always the act of a psychotic person.	**Fact:** Studies of hundreds of genuine suicide notes indicate that although the suicidal person is extremely unhappy, he is not necessarily mentally ill. His overpowering unhappiness may result from a temporary emotional upset, a long and painful illness, or a complete loss of hope. It is circular reasoning to say that "suicide is an insane act," and therefore all suicidal people are psychotic.

SOURCE: From Shneidman & Farberow, 1961, for the U.S. Government Printing Office, PHS Publication No. 852.

Asking someone if he or she is thinking about attempting suicide is not planting an idea that would otherwise not have occurred to the person. Individuals who are depressed or who are severely agitated most likely have already thought about killing themselves. Many suicidologists believe that almost all human beings think about the possibility of suicide at one time or another. Thus, suicide is not an infrequently encountered idea. If the person does not volunteer information about suicidal thoughts or plans, the simplest way to discover this is to ask.

Once suicidal intentions are noticed, intervention can take many forms (Hatton & Valente, 1984). Some practical ways to help suicidal people are summarized in Box 17.2. First, one should note that many suicidal intentions are not long lasting. A primary goal may be to help the person work through a relatively short-term crisis period. That is a basic strategy employed by all crisis intervention programs.

As we have recommended throughout this book, in order to help suicidal persons it is critical to listen to them. Paying attention to and being present for someone who is suffering is an essential step toward helping that person. Others really must hear the feelings being expressed in order to try to understand what this person needs. Part of the listening process is to hear suicidal remarks for what they are and to recognize the several levels or dimensions that each remark may contain. Most crisis intervention workers insist that *every* suicidal remark must be taken seriously.

Once such a remark is heard, the actual intentions and plans should be evaluated. The more the person has thought about suicide, and the more he or she has worked out actual plans for suicide, the more seriously must the remarks be taken. A remark like "Sometimes I just feel like killing myself" with no follow-up is less serious than remarks that indicate someone's having thought out when and how he or she intends to accomplish the act. That becomes even more serious when actual steps have been taken to prepare to implement the plan.

In general, changes in affect are significant. If someone has been depressed but now seems suddenly much lighter in emotional tone, this is not necessarily a time for reduced concern (Farberow, 1983). Suicidal actions actually increase when people are coming out of depression. In such circumstances, they may finally have the requisite energy to act. Similarly, a change toward agitation can signal a crisis.

In listening, attention must be paid to what the person says. This usually means that one should not engage in the process of evaluating in a judgmental way (from one's own point of view) what the person believes or feels. What looks like a problem from the suicidal person's point of view *is* a problem for that person. Telling such individuals that their problems are insignificant is not likely to be of much help. It is more likely to sound as though we are not really hearing them or are unwilling to appreciate the magnitude of the problems that they believe themselves to be facing. Not surprisingly, they may then turn away from us.

Many suicidal persons experience "tunnel vision," a process in which the individual perceives only a very narrow range of possible solutions for resolving the crisis. From this perspective, suicide may seem to be the only available solution. One way to help is to point out other, constructive options for resolving the crisis, such as drawing on inner resources not previously recognized or turning to external resources available in the community that might help with the crisis (whether it is emotional, physical, financial, or whatever).

Finally, specific action is called for. Getting some particular agreement can be helpful, such as: "Will you agree *not* to do anything until I get there?" "Will you go with me to talk to a counselor?" "Will you promise not to harm yourself until after you next see your therapist?" It is also usually important not to let the

Box 17.2 Some Practical Ways to Help Suicidal Persons

■ Take the person seriously; be available to get involved and to listen.

■ Allow the person to express his or her feelings and try to accept them for what they are; be empathetic, calm, and nonjudgmental.

■ Don't be afraid to speak openly about suicide; ask questions like "Have you ever thought about hurting or killing yourself?" You can also offer concrete examples of what leads you to believe the person is close to suicide.

■ Express your concern for the person by listening attentively, maintaining eye contact, moving closer to the person, and touching the person or holding his or her hand, if that seems appropriate.

■ Don't debate with the person whether suicide is right or wrong or whether the person's feelings are good or bad; an argumentative or lecturing posture will distance you from the person.

■ Never challenge a potentially suicidal person to complete the act; don't dare him or her to do it.

■ Find out if the person has a specific plan to carry out a suicidal action or has taken concrete steps to prepare to do so (such as gaining access to the means that might be used to end his or her life).

■ Point out constructive alternatives that are available, but do not offer glib reassurance; stress that suicide is most often a permanent solution for temporary problems.

■ Take action by removing the means (such as firearms or stockpiled pills) that the person might use to end his or her life.

■ Remind the person that although he or she is ultimately responsible for his or her actions, help is available, people do care, and you will try to make connections with helping resources.

■ Get help from people or agencies that are knowledgeable about intervening in crises and preventing suicide.

■ Until you can get such help, try to stay with the person and not leave him or her alone; if you must leave, ask the person to make a contract with you or promise not to take any further steps to end his or her life until you can get help or can return to address the situation further.

■ Do not allow yourself to promise confidentiality or to be sworn to unconditional secrecy; such commitments should be contingent on a contract that the person not act before certain conditions that you set (such as seeking professional help) are met. ■

SOURCE: Based on guidelines from the American Association of Suicidology and the National Depressive and Manic-Depressive Association.

person be alone or to have access to the means intended to be used to commit suicide. In many cases, the involvement of a trained professional will be essential (Leenaars et al., 1994).

One last word: some crisis intervention workers have pointed out that in the end no one can really take responsibility for someone else's life. If a person is seriously determined to end his or her life, ordinarily someone else cannot prevent that event—short of essentially "jailing" the person. Although guilt is a frequently encountered response to suicide, suicide is, finally, an action over which others have little control. It is an option for human beings.

Rational Suicide

We consider next the question of the morality of suicide. Various positions have been taken on this question. Depression, ambivalence, and other strong feelings are central elements in much suicidal behavior. For many persons, these are precisely the elements that justify intervention by others in order to prevent a fatal outcome arising from unstable foundations. The implication is that suicide is an irrational behavior. That might be true in several senses: for example, the behavior might be based on beliefs that cannot be supported ("this humiliation will never end") or on temporary desires that are not compatible with the individual's basic values (Motto, 1980). If a situation involving suicide is correctly described as involving irrational motives, it is difficult to support the view that suicide is a morally appropriate act.

But suppose the person considering suicide is not irrational. That is, could there be a rational basis for suicide (Werth, 1999)? Are there motives for suicide that are lucid, rational, and morally appropriate? These questions have been answered affirmatively in many cultures (see, for example, Box 17.3) and this question was raised in a forceful way by the events of September 11. When we consider the amount of long-range planning and the necessary careful work that had to precede the actual actions on that day (look at Atta's letter again and notice how he spells some of this out), it is difficult to see these acts as not rational—if rational means thought out.

Under a different set of circumstances, Rollin supported a positive response to these questions when she wrote, "The real question is, does a person have a right to depart from life when he or she is nearing the end and has nothing but horror ahead?" (Humphry, 1992, p. 14). Rollin views suicide as a legitimate form of "self-deliverance." This position is based on an assertion that the legitimate scope of an individual's autonomy and self-determination should include the right to end one's life. In fact, it is not illegal to commit suicide in any of the jurisdictions in the United States. This suggests that for many people in our society suicide does legitimately lie within the range of the individual's autonomy.

In general, circumstances involving terminal illness and unendurable suffering are most prominently mentioned in contemporary discussions of the morality of suicide. They are also the circumstances suggested to be ones in which

Box 17.3 A Comment from Seneca on Suicide

But life, as you know, needn't always be held fast. It isn't in living, but in living well, that the good consists. Hence the philosopher-adept [i.e., the wise person] lives as long as he ought, and not as long as he can. . . . The quality of life, not its length, is always his thought. If he encounters a throng of troubles fatal to peace of mind, he sets himself free. . . . It matters not a whit to him whether he procures his end or accepts it, whether it comes slowly or quickly. . . . To die soon or die late matters nothing: to die badly or die well is the important point. But to die well is to escape the risk of living badly. ■

SOURCE: From Seneca, 1932, vol. 1 , p. 239.

"rational suicide" might be thought to be morally appropriate. Proponents of rational suicide may concede that hospice-type care can relieve these sorts of distress in most cases. However, they also argue that options for suicide should remain open to individuals whose distress cannot be relieved by care in the hospice manner as well as to individuals experiencing other forms of suffering that, in their view, render life undesirable (Humphry, 1992).

Some societies also think of suicide as appropriate in other sorts of circumstances. Social, political, and moral contexts may be held to demand the suicide of an individual for the sake of the good of the society or the family (see the discussion of altruistic suicide earlier in this chapter). In any case, most arguments supporting the moral appropriateness of suicide require that the person engaged in such an action be rational when the action is undertaken.

Arguments opposed to the morality of suicide either assume that anyone engaged in such an action is not rational or that there are other overriding moral values that come into play. To demonstrate this last point, almost all religions oppose taking one's own life. This may be because they believe that the individual's life is not wholly his or hers alone (it belongs to God) or because scripture forbids it. Many religious traditions do accept some self-destructive acts as morally acceptable, but only under very specific conditions. These conditions vary from one tradition to another. Although it is impossible to describe in any simple way a given religious tradition's view on suicide, the following statements offer a sampling of religious positions:

Judaism

"For Judaism, human life is 'created in the image of God.' . . . The sanctity of human life prescribes that, in any situation short of self-defense or martyrdom, human life be treated as an end in itself. . . . Even individual autonomy is secondary to the sanctity of human life and therefore, a patient is not permitted to end his or her life" (Feldman & Rosner, 1984, p. 106). Notice the exceptions given here.

Christianity

The *Declaration on Euthanasia* from the Roman Catholic tradition in Christianity includes the following statement: "Intentionally causing one's own death, or suicide, is . . . equally as wrong as murder; such an action on the part of a person is to be considered as a rejection of God's sovereignty and loving plan. Furthermore, suicide is also often a refusal of love for self, the denial of the natural instinct to live, a flight from the duties of justice and charity owed to one's neighbor, to various communities, or to the whole of society" (Sacred Congregation for the Doctrine of the Faith, 1982, p. 512). This last point is reinforced by David Smith (1986, p. 64), arguing out of the Anglican tradition: "In any context suicide is a social act . . . because selfhood is so social, suicide cannot be simply a matter of private right. . . . As a child of God the Christian must relate all choices to that relationship." He also argues (in the context of suicide because of medical circumstances, but this argument might be extended to all suicidal contexts), "the great difficulty with supposed altruistic suicide, on medical grounds, is that it ignores the guilt felt by others and the desertion of them that is involved."

Islam

The *Qur'an* contains the following relevant passages: "Do not with your own hands cast yourselves into destruction" (2, 195), and "Do not destroy yourselves . . . he that does that through wickedness and injustice shall be burned in fire" (4, 29). However, Rahman (1987, p. 126) reports, "The only way a Muslim can and is expected to freely give and take life is 'in the path of Allah,' as a martyr in jihad or holy war. According to a Hadith a person who dies defending self, family, and property (by extension also the country) against aggression is also a martyr."

Hinduism

"Hinduism condemns suicide as evil when it is a direct and deliberate act with the intention voluntarily to kill oneself for self-regarding motives. Subjectively, the evil resides in the act as the product of ignorance and passion; objectively, the evil encompasses the karmic consequences of the act which impede the progress of liberation." This view is modified, however, under some circumstances: "Hinduism permits selective recourse to suicide when it is religiously motivated. . . . The whole of Hindu discipline is an exercise in progressive renunciation, and continuous with that, *suicide is the supreme act of renunciation.* For the sage, it is the death of death" (Crawford, 1995, pp. 68, 71).

Buddhism

"The standard Buddhist attitude towards suicide is that it is a futile, misguided act motivated by the desire for annihilation . . . the affirmation of nirvana cannot be a choice against life." Again, however, under some circumstances, suicide might be acceptable to Buddhists: "Bodhisattvas who sacrifice themselves are not choosing against life but displaying a readiness to lay down their lives in the service of their fellow man. They do not seek death for its own sake, but accept that death may come, so to speak, in the course of their duty" (Keown, 1995, pp. 58, 59).

Summary

In this chapter, we explored some of the many dimensions and implications of suicide and life-threatening behavior. We sought to clarify the concept of suicide and to emphasize the many elements that may enter into a completed suicide. We also sketched some common patterns in suicidal behavior, and we examined psychological, biological, and sociological explanations of such behavior. We gave special attention to the impact on someone who survives the suicide of another person, and we identified interventions that individuals and society might initiate to minimize suicidal behavior. Finally, we considered whether or not suicide could ever be considered to be a rational or morally appropriate action, listing statements on that point from five major religious traditions.

Questions for Review and Discussion

1. This chapter began with examples of two individuals who ended their own lives: Ernest Hemingway and Sylvia Plath. Using what you have learned about suicide, what similarities and differences do you see in these two actions?

2. This chapter also included the example of Mohamed Atta and the terrorists who planned and carried out the September 11 attacks on America. What do you think this example teaches us about suicide?

3. Have you ever thought about ending your life? Has anyone you know and care about reported to you thoughts about ending his or her life? What was going on in your life (or in the other person's life) that led to such thoughts and/or that helped you (or the other person) get past that point? What might you (or someone else) have done to help a person with such thoughts get past that point?

4. Have you ever known someone who ended his or her life by suicide? What was your response to that action? Think about how other people reacted to that action. How were these responses like what we learned about grief and mourning in Chapter 9? How were they different?

Suggested Readings

Introductions to the subject of suicide and suicide intervention are found in:

Evans, G., & Farberow, N. L. (Eds.). (1988). *The Encyclopedia of Suicide.*

Farberow, N. L., & Shneidman, E. S. (Eds.). (1965). *The Cry for Help.*

Hatton, C. L., & Valente, S. M. (Eds.). (1984). *Suicide: Assessment and Intervention* (2nd ed.).

Leenaars, A. A., & Wenckstern, S. (Eds.). (1991). *Suicide Prevention in the Schools.*

Leenaars, A. A., Maltsberger, J. T., & Neimeyer, R. A. (1994). *Treatment of Suicidal People.*

Lester, D. (1990b). *Understanding and Preventing Suicide: New Perspectives.*

Lester, D. (1992). *Why People Kill Themselves* (3rd ed.).

Maris, R. W. (1981). *Pathways to Suicide: A Survey of Self-Destructive Behaviors.*

Maris, R. W. (Ed.). (1988). *Understanding and Preventing Suicide.*

Plath, S. (1971). *The Bell Jar.*

Poland, S. (1989). *Suicide Intervention in the Schools.*

Shneidman, E. S. (1980/1995). *Voices of Death.*

Silverman, M. M., & Maris, R. W. (1995). *Suicide Prevention: Toward the Year 2000.*

More detailed analyses include:

Alvarez, A. (1970). *The Savage God: A Study of Suicide.*

Durkheim, E. (1897/1951). *Suicide: A Study in Sociology.*

Jamison, K. R. (1999). *Night Falls Fast: Understanding Suicide.*

Menninger, K. (1938). *Man Against Himself.*

Shneidman, E. S. (1985). *Definition of Suicide.*

Survivors and the aftermath of suicide are the focus in:

Cain, A. (Ed.). (1972). *Survivors of Suicide.*

Dunne, E. J., McIntosh, J. L., & Dunne-Maxim, K. (Eds.). (1987). *Suicide and Its Aftermath: Understanding and Counseling the Survivors.*

Hewett, J. (1980). *After Suicide.*

Smolin, A., & Guinan, J. (1993). *Healing after the Suicide of a Loved One.*

Wallace, S. E. (1973). *After Suicide.*

An important, specialized topic is considered in:

Farberow, N. L. (Ed.). (1980). *The Many Faces of Suicide: Indirect Self-Destructive Behavior.*

InfoTrac College Edition
For more information, explore the InfoTrac College Edition at **http://www.infotrac-college.com/Wadsworth**

Enter search terms: ALTRUISTIC SUICIDE, ANOMIC SUICIDE, EGOISTIC SUICIDE, FATALISTIC SUICIDE, RATIONAL SUICIDE, SUICIDE.

Chapter Eighteen

ASSISTED SUICIDE AND EUTHANASIA: INTENTIONALLY ENDING A HUMAN LIFE

In THIS CHAPTER, WE EXAMINE CONCEPTUAL and moral issues related to the intentional ending of a human life. In particular, we explore two matters of personal and social importance in today's society: *assisted suicide* and *euthanasia*. We begin with a brief vignette describing a case of assisted suicide in Oregon and a short section designed to distinguish assisted suicide and euthanasia from other modes of (intentionally) ending a human life. Then we turn to two key points central to defining and differentiating assisted suicide and euthanasia: *agency* (who acts?) and *intent* (what goals guide decision making?).

Next, we discuss the morality of assisted suicide and euthanasia, examining arguments for and against such activities. For this, we first look at several philosophical arguments. Then we turn to perspectives from five of the world's great religions. We consider religious perspectives for two reasons. First, they often play a significant role in individual judgments on these matters. Second, care providers may find themselves working with persons whose religious backgrounds differ from their own. These differences in religious beliefs can lead to quite different views about the appropriateness of intentionally ending human life and may become a source of tension between those who provide and those who receive care. Last, we discuss the role that social policy has taken in the recent past (using examples from euthanasia practices and recent legislation in the Netherlands, as well as legislation authorizing physician-assisted suicide in Oregon) and might take in the future in these matters. ■

A Case of Assisted Suicide

In March 1998, the first person assisted in dying under the Oregon "Death with Dignity Act" was an 85-year-old woman with metastatic breast cancer. This is a report on her death:

> According to published news accounts, the woman's original physician refused to participate for unspecified reasons and referred her to a second physician, who also refused, claiming the patient was "depressed." Her husband called Compassion in Dying, which found her a doctor willing to participate.
>
> Peter Goodwin, MD, medical director of Compassion in Dying, said he had two lengthy telephone conversations with the woman. He also spoke to her son and daughter on the phone. He was satisfied . . . that she was "rational, determined and steadfast."
>
> He didn't feel the woman was depressed, he said. . . .
>
> He said the woman had been doing aerobic water exercises up until two weeks before she contacted him. She told him she couldn't do them anymore, nor could she still garden, a favorite activity.
>
> She was not bedridden. She still looked after her own house, walked up and down the stairs, albeit slowly, and was not in great pain, he said.
>
> "But the quality of her life was just disappearing," Dr. Goodwin said.
>
> And he thought it prudent to move quickly before the woman lost her ability to make decisions for herself.
>
> The woman was "going downhill rapidly. . . . She could have had a stroke tomorrow and lost her opportunity to die in the way that she wanted," he said.
>
> Dr. Goodwin referred her to a doctor who was willing to help her. That doctor referred her to a specialist and a psychiatrist, all of whom determined she had met the qualifications for physician-assisted suicide under the law. . . .
>
> Dr. Goodwin said the psychiatrist met with the woman only once but that the visit had been a long one. . . .
>
> The doctor who prescribed the lethal medication . . . said, "It was an extremely moving experience for me. . ." (Gianelli, 1998, p. 39).
>
> Another report on this same case said: "The woman, who was not named, was prescribed a lethal dose of barbiturates, which she took with brandy. She died at home 30 minutes after drinking the mixture" (Josefson, 1998, p. 1037).

Situating the Issues

The issues we will explore in this chapter concern decisions made intentionally in certain specific situations to end a life. Such decisions often arise as a consequence of advances that have been made in enhancing the quality and extending the length of human lives. For example, beginning in the second half of the 20th century, modern technology has kept many individuals alive who clearly would have died in earlier times. Such persons include those unable to breathe on their own and many persons with severe brain trauma or with progressive debilitating diseases who would have died when respirators or nasogastric feeding tubes were unavailable. In addition, chemotherapy, radiation therapy, organ and tissue transplants, and many other techniques have extended the lives of many persons. This is a widely admired outcome of modern medicine.

However, these technologies have not only made possible the continuation of someone's living but sometimes have increased the depth, length, and degree of that individual's suffering. In certain instances, the life continued by these techniques has been felt by some to be demeaning and demoralizing as well as filled with suffering. When contemporary therapies are unable effectively to handle these aspects of people's dying, some have argued that death is to be preferred to continuing such a dying.

How often this issue needs to be confronted is a matter of dispute. Hospice philosophy (see Chapter 8) would argue that inadequate care is being provided when someone experiences a demeaning dying process filled with suffering. That is, hospice philosophy suggests that it is seldom necessary that anyone with a life-threatening illness should be faced with the question of whether death is to be preferred to this present existence. That may be true. However, hospice care is not (yet) available to everyone who is dying, and there are a (perhaps small) number of situations in which even hospice or palliative care is unable successfully to handle the suffering being experienced. In these situations, the question of the desirability of choosing to end a life may still arise.

One question examined in this chapter is this: "Is it ever appropriate to choose to end rather than to continue a human life?" If this question is ever answered affirmatively, then other questions arise, such as: "In what way is it appropriate to become dead?" and "Who may properly be involved in the process of someone's becoming dead?" In addressing such questions, we look for some basis on which they might appropriately be answered and we enter a path that compels us to think explicitly about the morality of intentionally ending a human life.

In the United States in recent years, questions such as these have been most closely associated with assisted suicide and euthanasia. We select these issues for discussion here because they have become matters of intense debate in our society in recent years and also because they are often associated with a degree of conceptual and moral confusion that hinders such debate (see Box 18.1). Our principal aim in this chapter is to clarify the concepts of assisted suicide and euthanasia, and to help sort out arguments made on behalf of or against such ways of deciding to end a human life.

Box 18.1 Dr. Jack Kevorkian

During the 1990s, Dr. Jack Kevorkian helped to bring to public attention a number of issues associated with assisted suicide and euthanasia. A retired pathologist, Kevorkian publicly announced in 1990 his willingness to assist individuals to end their own lives (Betzold, 1993). Later that year, Kevorkian was involved in the assisted suicide of Janet Adkins, 54, of Portland, Oregon. While asking others to join him in these activities, Kevorkian insisted that he would do what he thought right in what he viewed as matters of self-determination and choice, regardless of individual or community opposition.

The assistance that Kevorkian provided at first took the form of a "suicide machine" through which individuals could control the administration of a series of eventually lethal drugs. Later, Kevorkian simply began providing instructions through which individuals could bring about their deaths in other ways. It appears that Kevorkian took pains to ensure that he was not present when an individual undertook the action that resulted in death or, at least, that he took no active role in that action. For whatever reasons, prosecutors found it impossible to convict Kevorkian of assisted suicide or any other substantial legal wrongdoing. Subsequently, one retrospective examination of their autopsy reports (Roscoe et al., 2000) claimed that only 17 of the first 69 persons whom Kevorkian helped kill were actually terminally ill or had less than six months to live, although most had chronic, often painful life-threatening illnesses (five appeared to have no significant physical disease).

In late 1998, Kevorkian acknowledged being present at or involved in about 130 deaths (*St. Petersburg Times*, 1998). Then, Kevorkian videotaped his own direct involvement in bringing about the death of Thomas Youk, a 52-year-old man with advanced amyotrophic lateral sclerosis (ALS or Lou Gehrig's disease). A videotape from September 15, 1998, showed Youk agreeing to this act of euthanasia and signing what Kevorkian said was a consent form. Another videotape from September 17 showed Kevorkian injecting Youk with two chemicals that caused his death (Werth, 2001). On Sunday, November 22, an edited version of these videotapes was shown on the CBS television show *60 Minutes*.

On November 25, the prosecutor in Oakland County, Michigan, charged Kevorkian with first-degree murder and criminal assisted suicide. This occurred after Kevorkian challenged the prosecutor to charge him within a week. It also followed the defeat in early November by Michigan voters of a ballot referendum approving of assisted suicide. Although the prosecutor had been elected after a pledge not to waste more public funds in futile prosecutions of Kevorkian, he is reported to have regarded the public showing of the videotape as demonstrating an obvious violation of law that he could not ignore.

At trial in March 1999, Kevorkian acted as his own lawyer. After the charge of assisted suicide was withdrawn, the judge ruled that testimony of Thomas Youk's family members would be prohibited as irrelevant to the remaining charges of murder. Subsequently, Kevorkian rested his case without calling

(continues)

Box 18.1 (cont.) **Dr. Jack Kevorkian**

himself or any other witnesses for the defense. On March 26, the jury found Kevorkian guilty of second-degree murder and delivering a controlled substance.

On April 13, Kevorkian was sentenced to 10–25 years in prison for murder and 3–7 years for delivery of a controlled substance. In handing down these sentences, the judge is reported to have said to Kevorkian that "this trial was not about the political or moral correctness of euthanasia. It was about you, sir. It was about lawlessness. It was about disrespect for a society that exists because of the strength of the legal system. No one, sir, is above the law. No one." (*St. Louis Post-Dispatch*, 1999, p. A1). The sentences are to run concurrently and Kevorkian could be eligible for parole in less than seven years. The judge refused to release Kevorkian on bail while any appeal is considered. He is currently serving his sentence at the Egeler Correctional Facility in Jackson, Michigan. ■

Deciding to End a Human Life: Who Acts?

One key issue in deciding to end a human life is the matter of *agency*. Put briefly, the question is: *Who acts?* In both assisted suicide and euthanasia, at least two individuals are always involved. The difference is in the role that these individuals play in bringing about the ultimate outcome.

Assisted Suicide: Who Acts?

In all cases of assisted suicide, like all other instances of suicide, an individual ends his or her own life. The classic portrait of a suicidal act is one in which an individual obtains a lethal means and uses it to cause his or her own death. As a form of suicide, then, *assisted suicide* follows this same pattern. The difference is that now the suicide is deliberately assisted. That is, in assisted suicide the means used to end the life of one individual (whom we might call Person A) are obtained from and with the cooperation of a second individual (whom we might call Person B) who understands that Person A intends to use those means to end his or her life. In cases of assisted suicide, Person A performs the act that ends his or her life. No other individual commits this act. If a gun is used to kill the person, Person A pulls the trigger. If a lethal drug is injected, Person A injects himself or herself. (We assume here that Person A is under no coercion from someone else to engage in these actions.) No one else need even be present when this action takes place.

Euthanasia: Who Acts?

The situation is quite different when an individual is asked to act in some way (to commit or forego an action) to end the life of another person. Suppose that a person is suffering physically or emotionally and would prefer to be dead.

Dr. Jack Kervorkian burns a cease-and-desist order in April 1997 in Detroit.

That person (Person A) might call upon someone else (Person B) to act in such a way as to end Person A's life. The action of Person B is critical to what is meant by the term *euthanasia.* Euthanasia occurs when at least two people are involved and one of those persons (Person A) dies because the other person (Person B) intends that person to die and acts in such a way as to bring about that outcome.

To be more precise, euthanasia properly refers to a situation in which the intention of the second individual (Person B) who contributes to the death of the first person (Person A) embodies an attempt to end the suffering of that first person. Whether that suffering must already be present (the person is in great suffering right now) or may be expected to be present in the future is, as we note later, a matter of some dispute. What is not in dispute in all cases of euthanasia is that the person who does not die (Person B) is the principal person involved in bringing about the death.

Discussions of euthanasia frequently make use of *a distinction concerning whether the death is accomplished with or without the permission of the person who dies.* If the person who dies asked for or assented to his or her death, this is *voluntary euthanasia* (Downing, 1974; Gruman, 1973); the will of the person who dies is known. If the will of the person who dies remains unknown, then it is *non-voluntary euthanasia.* For example, the person might be unconscious or unable to make plain his or her choice for some other reason (think of a person who has had a severe stroke). Or a person such as a child or someone intellectually or emotionally disabled might be incompetent to make such a decision. If a second person somehow intentionally contributes to the death of this sort of person, it is nonvoluntary euthanasia.

A third possibility (in theory, at least) is one in which the wishes of the person are known—he or she wants to be kept alive—but someone else decides to end that life anyway. Perhaps this could be called "involuntary euthanasia." However, to act *against* someone's wishes is more like homicide than like a "good death," so one might not want to associate this possibility with the term euthanasia in any way.

Some argue that a person who is acutely suffering, by the very fact of that suffering, has diminished capacity to make difficult decisions. If that were true, one might be uncomfortable following the directions of a person in severe physical or emotional pain. Choosing to cooperate in a person's death is an irreversible decision; in the face of that irrevocability, one would want to be as certain as possible that the person's own choice was clearly and competently presented.

So far, we have carefully distinguished between assisted suicide and euthanasia by indicating who the agent is who performs (or fails to perform) an act that results in the death. However, we acknowledge that there are situations in which the usefulness of this distinction is less obvious than our discussion indicates. Consider three possibilities. First, suppose you are able to carry out an act that results in your death. Now suppose you ask someone else to provide you with the means to carry out this act and that person agrees to provide the means for you to kill yourself. That is *assisted suicide.* Second, now suppose you could perform such an action, but you ask someone else to perform it. Suppose what that person does next is done out of compassion and results in your death. That is *euthanasia.* Third, now suppose you are unable to perform the action yourself (you are paralyzed for instance). Then if someone else performs the action that produces your death, it can be less clear whether that action is an assisted suicide or an act of euthanasia. You would kill yourself if you could (but you cannot because of your paralysis); thus the other person acts in your place because of your inability to carry out the act.

What this means is perhaps best described as follows. Assisted suicide and euthanasia belong on opposite ends of a continuum. At one end of the continuum, it is obvious that you (with means provided by another person) kill yourself. At the other end of the continuum, someone else kills you. In between these will be a variety of situations that lie closer to one end or the other of the continuum. However, these situations will less easily be assigned to the category of assisted suicide or euthanasia. This lack of certainty matters most when we begin to think about the morality of certain sorts of acts. Also, this lack of certainty suggests that any attempt to reason adequately about the morality of these issues must be subtle enough to take note of the relevant differences between these various sorts of cases.

Deciding to End a Human Life: What Is Intended?

Another key issue in discussions about deciding to end a human life is *the nature of the act itself.* One helpful element in characterizing the nature of the act is the *intention* that underlies it.

Assisted Suicide: What Is Intended?

The phrase *assisted suicide* applies to a wide range of actions in which one person intentionally acts to end his or her life and secures assistance from another person in order to achieve that result. Assisted suicide occurs only when: (1) one person

(Person A) *acts intentionally to obtain assistance* in ending his or her life from a second person (Person B), (2) Person B *acts intentionally to provide the necessary assistance* to bring about the death *with full awareness of how that assistance is to be used*, and (3) Person A *intentionally uses the assistance* provided to carry out his or her own self-destruction (or what some call "self-deliverance"). The role of intent is evident in all aspects of the assistance that defines assisted suicide.

The assistance provided in an assisted suicide could be the means used to produce the death (for instance, a gun or a drug), the environment or place in which the act occurs, emotional support, or some combination of these elements. Whether or not someone needs such forms of assistance is usually related to the individual's ability to obtain the required means. Situations that are not instances of assisted suicide include ones in which a person is able on his or her own to buy a gun and use it to end his or her life or to go to a physician's office and get a prescription for a particular medication, then go to a pharmacist and get that prescription filled, and then use that medication to end his or her own life. Only if the person buying the gun or requesting the medication (explicitly or implicitly) informs the seller or the physician/pharmacist that he or she intends to use the gun or the medication to end his or her life, and the seller or health care provider *acts in concurrence with that intention*, could these situations be regarded as instances of *assisted* suicide.

When an individual asks a physician to help end his or her life—for example, by prescribing medications that only physicians can order—this marks out a special kind of assisted suicide called *physician-assisted suicide.* In view of the special professional authority accorded to physicians in our society and their access to certain means that can be used in ending a human life, physician-assisted suicide is the type of assisted suicide that has received most public attention in recent years. However, the physician in this situation does nothing to the person when the action is taken that ends the life of the person. As we noted above, this absence of participation in the lethal act in most situations clearly marks off physician-assisted suicide from cases of euthanasia. In physician-assisted suicide, the physician provides (indirectly, if giving the person a prescription) only the means (and perhaps emotional support)—as we saw in Dr. Kevorkian's early cases (see Box 18.1).

Other individuals may also provide such means. For example, a friend or relative might have access to medications or to weapons that could be used for suicidal acts and might provide them in order to help a person end his or her life. Whenever there is a mutual (explicit or implicit) understanding of a suicidal intention, the involvement of these other individuals in deciding to end a person's life constitutes an instance of assisted suicide, but not physician-assisted suicide.

Euthanasia: What Is Intended?

The intention to end a human life is also central in cases of euthanasia. There is some confusion and disagreement about what is meant by "euthanasia" (to what it refers) in many contemporary discussions. Etymologically, *euthanasia* comes from the Greek (*eu*, "good," + *thanatos*, "death") and literally means a "good death." Since few would oppose a good death for themselves or others, the real question is what might be involved in bringing about such a death, even when acting for benevolent motives. Clearly, it would not be a good death if whatever is done or not done were not guided by a beneficent or well-meaning intention. A malevolent intention would define some form of homicide.

However, this description is incomplete. Euthanasia properly refers to a situation in which the person (Person B) who contributes to the death of another person (Person A) *intends to end the suffering of that second person.* That suffering might already be present (Person A is in great suffering right now), or it might be expected to be present in the future (think of someone in the earlier stages of Lou Gehrig's disease or Alzheimer's disease, or the person in the vignette near the beginning of this chapter). Note that this understanding of euthanasia does not limit it to situations in which someone is close to death. Some people would further limit the use of the term euthanasia to these latter situations—that is, they hold that an individual must be close to death for euthanasia to be at issue. In this view, if the person were not near death, we would be discussing homicide or manslaughter, not euthanasia. This viewpoint led some to criticize the actions of Dr. Jack Kevorkian (see Box 18.1) on the grounds that some of those whom he helped end their lives had not previously been actively dying or near death.

Active versus Passive Euthanasia

Once euthanasia has come under consideration, we must next examine the means by which the ending of a suffering person's life will occur. Here some draw a distinction between active and passive euthanasia. *Actively doing something to end suffering by ending a human life* is often called *active euthanasia.* In situations of this type, one deliberately commits an act (for benevolent motives) that in itself causes the death. This definition allows little room for ambiguity.

The case is a bit more complex when we turn to *passive euthanasia.* One might speak here of "foregoing" some intervention, which seems to include *either not doing something or omitting some action that is necessary to sustain life* (Lynn, 1986). The first of these alternatives refers to *withholding* (not supplying) some intervention necessary to sustain life; the latter to *withdrawing* (taking away) some intervention that is currently in place and may be helping to sustain life. However, some have been concerned that the act of withdrawing is not passive. Acting to withdraw an intervention seems to involve doing something to take away the existing intervention. This appears to be so even if the result does not in itself end the life but only removes an obstacle that is or may be blocking the natural processes of dying leading to death.

This distinction between active and passive euthanasia is not as clear or helpful as we might like it to be. If the person who is ill is able to walk away from the care provider, that person can simply refuse any treatment offered, and is *legally* allowed to do so. Nor do we typically describe such walking away as *immoral.* If a care provider offers you a form of treatment that he or she believes is necessary to sustain your life (say, hemodialysis or chemotherapy) and you refuse it and never return to receive it, this is not an example of an illegal (or to many minds, an immoral) act. Your personal autonomy includes the right to make such a choice.

This issue may appear to be more obscure when someone is unable to walk away (because he or she is too weak or is bedridden, paralyzed, etc.). For someone who has a life-threatening illness and who is in a medical care institution—willingly or not—to refuse apparently necessary treatment to sustain his or her life raises questions for many persons about the legitimacy of that refusal. In these circumstances, in many eyes, to refuse the chemotherapy or the treatment for one's burns carries a nuance of choosing to die that is not as clear in the situation described in the previous paragraph. That is, it may appear to be a request for someone else to help one to die and is thus an instance of passive euthanasia.

To recognize what is really going on in these situations, however, once more we must understand the *intentions* of the person who refuses the treatment and those of the caregiver. The person who walks away may or may not intend to die; if he or she does have that intention, then this may be part of a *suicidal* act. The person who cannot walk away may or may not intend to die; if he or she does have this intention, the refusal of treatment may be a request for *passive euthanasia.* Simply refusing treatment, *in and of itself,* need be neither an instance of suicide nor a request for passive euthanasia. A person might refuse treatment simply because it has become too burdensome (physically, psychologically, financially, etc.). Everything hinges on the intentions of the persons involved. It is suicide or euthanasia only when the person who refuses some treatment does this *in order to die,* and, if another person is involved, only when that person also *intends for death to occur.*

Extraordinary versus Ordinary Means

Another distinction often introduced in discussions about ending a human life is that between *extraordinary and ordinary means of treatment.* The point of this distinction is to argue that there is no moral obligation to provide extraordinary means of treatment. Many have made this claim; for instance, Roman Catholic ethicists (e.g., McCormick, 1974) have long argued that care providers have no such moral obligation.

Several criteria are offered to help implement this distinction. *Ordinary means of treatment* are those that: (1) have outcomes that are predictable and well known; (2) offer no unusual risk, suffering, or burden for either the person who is being treated or others; and (3) are effective. *Extraordinary means of treatment* fail to meet one or more of these criteria. Extraordinary means may have outcomes that are not predictable or well known, as in the case of some experimental procedures. Such procedures may not have been widely used or studied, so that one cannot be certain what will happen when one embarks on their use in particular cases. Or it may be that a procedure itself puts the patient at risk or imposes undue burdens on those who would assist the patient. That is, the procedure may have a broad range of outcomes, some of which make the person worse off than he or she was before. The side effects, for instance, of a treatment might produce more suffering than the person was undergoing before the treatment began. An extraordinary means of treatment might even produce effects that are worse than the disease. Since the outcome of using such means is unpredictable, one might have little confidence that they will in fact be helpful in dealing either with the person's symptoms or disease. That is, the actual effectiveness of an extraordinary means of treatment may be uncertain, too.

If the therapy proposed for use or already in use is an extraordinary means of treatment according to the criteria listed here, then most moralists agree that there is no moral obligation to use it. Individuals may choose not to begin (withhold) the use of such a therapy, or they may choose to terminate (withdraw) its use with no moral culpability attached to that decision.

What counts as ordinary and extraordinary means cannot be determined independently of an individual person's context—and perhaps we should not expect that interventions ever could be evaluated in such an independent way. Thus, what might be ordinary treatment in one situation could be extraordinary in another. There is no list of treatments that can—purely on their own—be determined to be ordinary, and another list of treatments that can be determined to be extraordinary. Whether a specific treatment is ordinary or extraordinary must be decided in terms of a particular person's situation.

This brings the discussion back to issues associated with euthanasia. The distinction between extraordinary and ordinary means is employed in the following way. Many would hold that not to begin to use or to stop using extraordinary means of treatment is not to be engaged in decisions about euthanasia. In this view, questions about euthanasia arise only when one is trying to decide whether or not to use even ordinary means of treatment. Those who argue in favor of euthanasia will suggest that in some situations there is no moral requirement to use ordinary means of treatment. Those who argue against euthanasia will suggest that in this situation (or in all situations) morally one must use the ordinary means of treatment under discussion; otherwise, one would be intending to end a human life.

Deciding to End a Human Life: Moral Arguments

In this section, we turn to issues relating to the morality of intentionally ending a human life. Some have argued that intentionally doing something to end someone's life and intentionally not doing something to sustain that life ought to be distinguished morally. For instance, many people hold that active euthanasia is morally unacceptable. The argument is that in active euthanasia the agent (the cause) of death is a person, and it is morally unacceptable for one person to kill another (in the circumstances under consideration in this chapter). However, many of these same people argue that passive euthanasia can, under some circumstances, be morally appropriate. The argument here is that in passive euthanasia the agent (the cause) of death is a disease process; no person causes the death of another, and thus this is morally acceptable.

Not everyone accepts these claims. Some argue that in either case, another human being is involved, and whether that person commits an act to cause the death or omits an action that could prevent the death is morally irrelevant. In either case, so the argument goes, that person is involved in the occurrence of the death and *intends* that death to occur, so the two situations are morally equivalent. People who think this way believe that if passive euthanasia is morally acceptable, so too must active euthanasia be morally acceptable. They also believe that if active euthanasia is morally unacceptable, then passive euthanasia must be morally unacceptable.

Arguments in Support of Intentionally Ending a Human Life

Prevention of Suffering An argument to support the moral acceptability of assisted suicide and euthanasia is that suffering is evil. Therefore, one function of caregivers is to prevent and, if possible, end suffering. Hence, actions involving assisted suicide and euthanasia to achieve such a goal would be permissible. Again, one could take this argument to its extreme and urge that *all* suffering is evil, and therefore that one ought *always* to strive to end *any* suffering—but probably few would hold this view. From slogans supporting physical exercise as a means to health ("no pain, no gain"), to the realization that success in most valued endeavors (such as intellectual growth, emotional maturity, artistic creativity) involves some suffering, the conclusion seems to follow that some suffering can have consequences that are good. So, at least as a means to some desired good end, suffering cannot automatically be taken as something to be eliminated altogether. Thus, one is forced to evaluate particular instances of suffering rather than to issue blanket condemnations (Cassell, 1991; Nabe, 1999). This conclusion, of course, may leave us uncertain about what to do in a particular instance.

Enhancement of Liberty Another argument sometimes used to support assisted suicide and euthanasia depends on *how human liberty is valued.* Most Americans believe that liberty is good. That is, they value being free from external coercion when making decisions about themselves and their lives. In other words, many people value autonomy—a word that literally means being able to make law *(nomos)* for oneself *(auto)* (Childress, 1990). Such individuals disvalue interference from others in matters that they believe to be their own affair. This position supports the rights of individuals to decide what to do about their own suffering. On this view, if someone so disvalues the suffering that he or she is experiencing, and that individual prefers that his or her life end, that decision ought to be supported. In short, those who value autonomy must seriously consider the view that it is the suffering person's right as an autonomous agent to make that decision and others ought not to interfere with it (see Kaplan, 1999; Werth, 1999b). This is the view that Dr. Kevorkian—correctly or incorrectly—consistently stressed.

There are two difficulties with accepting this argument as definitive. One is that it presupposes that one can tell when someone is acting autonomously. However, someone who is experiencing severe pain or emotional trauma may not be completely free of coercion. The pain or emotional suffering itself may be so affecting the person that any decision made under its influence is *not*, in fact, autonomous. It is not always easy to decide about this. However, one position to guard against is the belief that such pain or trauma is *always* a coercive factor in someone's ability to make rational decisions. Even with severe suffering, it may be possible that the person is still an autonomous agent. Individuals involved in the lives of people who are experiencing severe suffering must find ways—really listening to such a person is a step in this direction—to decide what is happening in the particular person and the concrete situation.

However, even if the person is autonomous, that does not automatically decide what *others* ought to do in the face of his or her autonomy. Really difficult moral dilemmas often involve conflicts between autonomous persons. Individuals may decide autonomously that they want their lives to end, but that may come into conflict with the autonomous decisions of others. Remember that assisted suicide and euthanasia always involve (at least) two persons. One person's autonomous decision to have his or her life ended may conflict with another person's autonomous decision not to participate in that sort of event. Furthermore, a decision to engage in assisted suicide or euthanasia seldom involves only the persons who are directly associated with the particular event of this one death. Typically, these decisions have broader social effects or repercussions. So even if someone's decision to end his or her life is autonomous, the acting out of that decision will inevitably affect others, and that, too, should be taken into account.

Quality of Life Another argument relevant to this discussion depends on *the value assigned to quality of life*. This argument holds that it is not *life as such* that is good, but rather *a certain form of life*. Most Americans do not concern themselves with life as such on a purely biological level; for example, they are perfectly willing to kill bacteria, viruses, pesky mosquitoes, and so forth. Rather, this argument maintains that we are properly concerned primarily with particular forms of life. In particular, some urge that we ought to be concerned specifically with what we understand to be *human* forms of life.

In this argument, it becomes compelling to clarify what counts as human life. That is, some people hold that certain forms of life, such as those involving certain levels of suffering or lack of individual autonomy (for example, life in a permanent comatose state) are inhuman or undignified and therefore not worth living. If such situations are intolerable, then when individuals say, "I wouldn't want to live like that," the argument is that death or ending a life is to be preferred to those situations.

This argument depends on asserting that some form of life is so disvalued that it is less valuable than death. Widespread agreement about this is unlikely. For example, a powerful videotape (*Please Let Me Die*, 1974; compare Kliever, 1989; Platt, 1975; White & Engelhardt, 1975) depicts a young man who was burned over 67 percent of his body and was subjected to excruciatingly painful baths each day to prevent infection. The young man requested that his treatments be discontinued and that he be allowed to die. Some might argue that the young man and/or those around him could learn from his suffering; others have insisted that he was clearly competent and should have had the right to reject unwanted and painful interventions. Clearly, what one person counts as unbearable someone else may not.

Arguments against Intentionally Ending a Human Life

Preservation of Life One argument used to show that intentionally ending a human life is morally inappropriate is that it violates the caregiver's (and society's) *commitment to the preservation of life.* According to this argument, it is part of the caregiver's role as a provider of care to preserve life. Thus, if a caregiver deliberately behaves in such a way that the death of the person for whom he or she has been caring will result, then that caregiver has behaved immorally. That is, the person has not fulfilled in an appropriate manner his or her role as a provider of care.

This argument holds that life is good, that there is a "sanctity" to life. If so, we ought to preserve and support life whenever we can. A qualified form of this view might contend that life is valuable, but it is not the *preeminent* value. That is, it does not take precedence over *all* other values in *all* instances. As has been said, human life is sacred but not absolute in its value. If this is the view one holds, it will not be possible to decide whether or not assisted suicide and euthanasia are morally acceptable (or even desirable) in some instances merely by appealing to the sanctity of life.

Slippery Slope Arguments Another argument used against the morality of assisted suicide and euthanasia is a *slippery slope argument.* It contends that once a decision is made to end someone's life for whatever reason, then one will have moved onto a slippery slope upon which it is all too easy to slide toward ending other people's lives for other reasons. If it is too difficult to stop once one has begun to act in these ways, this argument contends that it is better not to begin at all, at least until some way of knowing where to stop has been established. However, it is not clear that the slide down this slope is inevitable. In many parts of our lives, we are able to make careful distinctions between one sort of situation and another. Why not here?

Additional Arguments Others argue against assisted suicide and euthanasia for the following reasons: medicine is at best an uncertain science. Wrong diagnoses and prognoses are made. Also, medicine moves quickly sometimes and nearly always with some degree of unpredictability. New therapies and new cures are discovered at unknown moments. So when one contemplates ending a person's life, there is always the possibility of a misdiagnosis or of the appearance of a new cure or therapy that might ease or even end that person's suffering. Furthermore, some suggest that assisted suicide and euthanasia may undermine the trust that is essential to the physician/patient relationship or that they may detract from the role of the physician as healer and preserver of life.

These arguments have *some* weight. If that were not so, probably no one would ever have thought to advance them. Whether or not these arguments are persuasive in showing that one ought never to engage in assisted suicide and euthanasia depends on *how much* weight one gives to them. Human wisdom is always imperfect; if one waits for complete certainty in any moral matter, one will seldom act at all. But not to decide is to decide. If one chooses not to engage in assisted suicide and euthanasia, one might simply allow suffering to continue. Doing so involves its own danger. If a person's suffering is allowed to continue because of moral uncertainty or unclarity, there is a risk of becoming inured or hardened to suffering.

Further, although it is true that a new therapy or cure may come along at any time, it is not certain that such a discovery will help all persons with the particular disease or condition at issue. They may have progressed too far in the course of the disease, or their condition may involve other problems that the new therapy or cure can do nothing about. Thus these issues are relevant but not necessarily decisive.

Deciding to End a Human Life: Some Religious Perspectives

For many persons, religious teachings are important sources of beliefs about the morality of intentionally ending a human life. Therefore, it may help to study some of religious teachings related to these issues.

Most religious traditions are themselves complex. For example, it is not possible to state *the* Christian view of intentionally ending a human life because there are disagreements among Christians themselves about this issue. Such disagreements can be found in almost all religious traditions. Because there is a danger of stereotyping persons and beliefs when only brief summaries of religious traditions are given, the following discussions should be understood as no more than abbreviated introductions to some of the unique beliefs in each tradition. These are some (not all) of the beliefs that might have an impact on how believers in that tradition think about the morality of euthanasia.

Judaism

Jewish teachings come from the Hebrew scriptures (what most Christians call the "Old Testament"), from oral traditions (the *Mishnah*), from commentaries on these earlier sources (the *Talmuds*), and from the decisions of rabbis throughout the centuries on specific situations. Important Jewish beliefs related to the morality of decisions to end a human life include the following: many Jews believe that God created and thus owns a person's body (Bleich, 1979). Thus, a person is caretaker of his or her body but has no right to do with it whatever he or she chooses. A second belief held by many Jews is that life is of infinite value, independent of its quality (Davis, 1994). Based on this view, the duty to preserve life is held to take precedence over almost all other human duties. Orthodox and Conservative Jews often find these to be the most significant teachings related to assisted suicide and euthanasia, and on their basis find these acts morally unacceptable.

However, many Reform Jews (who are often more oriented toward secular Western moral views) hold that autonomy and self-determination are also values of primary importance. On this basis, these Jews often assert that it is individuals who have ultimate control over their bodies. Insofar as that is so, Reform Jews may be less critical of some forms of suicide and euthanasia.

Active euthanasia seems to be universally condemned by all Jewish groups (Rosner, 1979). Support for this condemnation is often traced to a teaching from the *Mishnah* (Shabbat, 23:5):

> They do not close the eyes of a corpse on the Sabbath, nor on an ordinary day at the moment the soul goes forth. And he who closes the eyes of a corpse at the moment the soul goes forth, lo, this one sheds blood. (Neusner, 1988, p. 207)

Using this statement from the *Mishnah* as its basis, the *Babylonian Talmud* (Tract Sabbath, p. 353) argued that one must not hasten death:

> The rabbis taught: Who closes the eyes of a dying man is like a murderer, for it is the same as a candle which is about to go out. If a man lays a finger on the dying flame, it immediately becomes extinguished, but if left alone would still burn for a little time. The same can be applied to the case of an expiring man; if his eyes were not closed, he would live a little longer, and hence it is like murder. (Rodkinson, 1896, p. 353)

Moses Maimonides (1949), a 12th-century Jewish physician/philosopher regarded by many Jews as a significant voice on moral issues, used a similar image:

> One who is in a dying condition is regarded as a living person in all respects. . . . He who touches him is guilty of shedding blood. To what may he be compared? To a flickering flame, which is extinguished as soon as one touches it. Whoever closes the eyes of the dying while the soul is about to depart is shedding blood. One should wait a while; perhaps he is only in a swoon. (*The Code of Maimonides*, Book 14, The Book of Judges, Chapter 4, paragraph 5)

Thus, most Jews find only passive euthanasia to be morally acceptable, if they accept it at all.

Christianity

Christianity has three major branches: the Orthodox churches, Roman Catholicism, and Protestantism. These three branches themselves are complex. For example, there is no Protestant church as such, but rather dozens of Protestant denominations, all independent of each other. Although this complexity should always be kept in mind, Christians do share some basic beliefs, values, and practices.

Christians also share several beliefs with Judaism and Islam. Among these is the belief that since human life comes from God, it is inherently valuable, indeed sacred. However, Christians are also likely to emphasize that only God has absolute, ultimate value; human life does not. Christians identify the sacredness of this life in its bearing and manifesting the image and purpose of the Creator (Breck, 1995). Christians also locate human dignity in considering each person to be an image of God (Cohen, 1996).

Uniquely Christian features arise from several other notions. As a Trinitarian faith, ultimate reality is understood by Christianity to be irreducibly relational (Harakas, 1993). Human beings are made for community with God and with each other; as Cicely Saunders (1970, p. 116) put it: "We belong with all other men (and) we belong with God also."

This essential interpersonal component of our humanness is also said to be revealed in the life of Jesus. Compassion and love for God and for his fellow human beings were central characteristics of Jesus' way of life. Much of his ministry involved healing, reducing the suffering of others. Since Christians are called to be an image of Christ, they too are to heal and, where that is not possible, to suffer with (be compassionate toward) others.

Some Christians hold that suffering is part of God's plan for all humans, whereas others find this belief difficult to fit with Jesus' emphasis on healing others (Breck, 1995). Suffering may be redemptive (bring individuals closer to each other and to God), but Christians are not required merely to accept it. One Christian document said of physical suffering that "human and Christian prudence suggest for the majority of sick people the use of medicines capable of alleviating or suppressing pain" (Sacred Congregation for the Doctrine of the Faith, 1982, p. 514). Christianity also teaches that we need not see ourselves as alone in our suffering; "in Jesus God was identified with (our) brokenness and suffering . . . God in Christ . . . has owned suffering for himself by undergoing it . . . thus the sufferer is not alone" (Smith, 1986, p. 7).

Christianity also has an eschatological emphasis. This means that human life's "ultimate value and meaning lie outside itself, beyond the limits of earthly existence" (Breck, 1995, p. 325). Harakas (1993, p. 540) echoes this point: Christianity "does not see any of the strivings of this world as ultimate."

What this means for the issues under discussion in this chapter is that many Christians oppose any intentional killing either of oneself or of others. Staying with, providing the necessary care to alleviate suffering, being compassionate toward each other: these are the desired goals for Christians faced with their own or someone else's death.

Islam

"Islam" means submission (to the will of Allah). Important Muslim beliefs include the following: Allah alone is God, and since Allah creates everything that exists, He is therefore the owner of every life. Thus, Muslims share with many Jews and Christians the belief that God alone may decide when a person's life is to end. Since suffering is used by Allah to remind human beings of their misdeeds and to lead them closer to Allah, to interfere with a person's suffering may also interfere with Allah's plan for that person (Hamel, 1991; Larue, 1985).

A Muslim's whole (public and private) life is ideally to be governed by Islamic law *(Shari'a)*. All Muslims accept the *Qur'an* and the *sunna* (practices and teachings) of Mohammed as sources of this law (Kelsay, 1994). Although there is no clearly stated position by Islamic leaders on assisted suicide or euthanasia (Islam has no definitive hierarchy to issue such a statement), the general impression is that they would be disapproved. A *sura* (chapter) in the *Qur'an* (4:29) reads: "Do not destroy yourselves." Many commentators take this to refer not only to suicide, but also to one Muslim killing another.

A statement from a 1981 conference in Kuwait is also relevant here:

> [The] doctor is well advised to realize his limit and not transgress it. If it is scientifically certain that life cannot be restored, then it is futile to diligently [maintain] the vegetative state of the patient by heroic means. . . . It is the process of life that the doctor aims to maintain and not the process of dying. In any case, the doctor shall not take positive measures to terminate the patient's life. (*Islamic Code of Medical Ethics*, First International Conference on Islamic Medicine, 1981, p. 10)

Hinduism

Hinduism is more like a cluster of various religious traditions than a single religion. As a group of various traditions, Hinduism has no central teaching authority or hierarchy. What most Hindus share is respect for the *Vedas* (scriptures, some of which may have been written as much as 3,500 years ago). Hindus may believe in creator gods, or they may believe that all reality is founded on Brahman, an impersonal, featureless entity from which rises all that is as waves rise from the ocean.

Many Hindus believe that most individuals will be reincarnated again and again, passing through death and rebirth through many lifetimes. The cause of these rebirths lies in one's *karma*, the actions one performs. One reaps inevitably and inexorably what one sows in one's actions. Thus, some Hindus believe that illness (life-threatening illness in particular) is an effect of one's karma and must be suffered through to pay one's karmic debt (Crawford, 1995). If so, to end life before it has run its natural course may interfere with the process of working off this debt. Assisted suicide and euthanasia would interfere with the karmic process and are thus undesirable.

However, other Hindus argue that this is a misunderstanding of karma (Crawford, 1995). If ending a human life interferes with the karmic process, then extending a human life through medical intervention interferes with that process, too. However, Hindus have developed a rich medical tradition (Ayurvedic medicine), and people who follow that tradition do not believe that it is inappropriate to alleviate someone's suffering and even to heal life-threatening disease. In this view, one is not interfering with the effects of karma if one seeks or provides treatment, or even perhaps ends a life.

Hinduism also emphasizes that one ought to avoid violence whenever possible. The Hindu term for this practice is *ahimsa*. *Ahimsa* is grounded in the view that life is sacred. Mohandas Gandhi taught that ahimsa is a central feature of a Hindu view of life. He explained what is meant by this term as follows: "*Ahimsa* does not simply mean non-killing. *Himsa* means causing pain to or killing any life out of anger, or from a selfish purpose, or with the intention of injuring it. Refraining from so doing is *ahimsa*" (Quoted in Crawford, 1995, p. 115).

At first glance, the teaching on ahimsa seems to argue against assisted suicide and active euthanasia. But the intention in active euthanasia is to end suffering, not produce it. Gandhi (1980) himself used an example suggesting that intentionally ending a life might be compatible with the doctrine of ahimsa: "Should my child be attacked with rabies and there was no helpful remedy to relieve his agony, I should consider it my duty to take his life" (p. 84).

Thus, Hindu attitudes toward the intentional ending of human life are likely to be as diverse as Hinduism itself. One can locate teachings arguing against such actions and teachings supporting their use in some circumstances.

Buddhism

Buddhism differs from theistic religions in holding that there is no god who is creator of all that is. Its core doctrines include the beliefs that every action performed has consequences for the individual who performs it (karma), that one of the effects of one's actions (one's karma) is to cause one to be reincarnated again and again, and that life as we know it here is filled with suffering and so salvation lies ultimately in ending the cycle of rebirths. The Buddha also taught an eightfold path that helps one along the way to salvation. One of the precepts in this path is the rule never to kill a living creature. It is largely from this rule that Buddhist teaching on the intentional ending of human life is derived.

Because Buddhism holds that life is a basic good (in part because it is only in life—especially in a human life—that one may reach salvation), intentionally to end such a life is unacceptable (Keown, 1995). Some of the earliest scriptures of Buddhism offer teachings as to how Buddhist monks ought to live their lives. Some commentators use these teachings as a basis for Buddhist ethics in general (not only for monks) (Keown, 1995). In the *Vinaya-Pitaka* (Book of Discipline), the Buddha is reported to have said:

> Whatever monk should intentionally deprive a human being of life or should look about so as to be his knife-bringer, or should praise the beauty of death, or should incite (anyone) to death, saying, 'Hullo there, my man, of what use to you is this evil, difficult life? Death is better for you than life,' or who should deliberately and purposefully in various ways praise the beauty of death or incite (anyone) to death: he also is one who is defeated, he is not in communion. (Horner, 1949, vol. 1, pp. 125–126)

The reference to being someone's "knife-bringer" could be understood as referring either to assisted suicide or active euthanasia. A monk who engages in such activity has failed in his religious/moral responsibilities (is defeated) and is to be excommunicated.

Although individual autonomy is also an important value in Buddhist thought (Becker, 1990), it cannot override the principle that life is a basic good. Preferring death to life is never morally acceptable (Keown, 1995).

Compassion *(karuna)* is a central virtue in Buddhism (Lecso, 1986), and thus to ease the suffering of someone is appropriate. This means that when someone is near death, one may use drugs that may have the effect of suppressing respiration and even lead to death. Also, one may legitimately not start or may remove therapies that simply prolong someone's dying. These are acts of compassion. However, one must not do this intending to cause death. What is forbidden is the intentional killing of someone.

Euthanasia, Assisted Suicide, and Social Policy

Euthanasia Practices and Legislation in the Netherlands

In the Netherlands euthanasia is technically illegal, but for many years it has also been familiar in practice (De Wachter, 1989, 1992; Thomasma et al., 1998). In this context, euthanasia is defined as "the administration of drugs with the explicit intention of ending the patient's life, at the patient's explicit request" (Van der Maas et al., 1996, p. 1700). In 1984, the Royal Dutch Medical Association issued guidelines for this practice that were later endorsed by a government-appointed commission on euthanasia. The guidelines are: "(1) the patient must be a mentally competent adult; (2) the patient must request euthanasia voluntarily, consistently, and repeatedly over a reasonable time, and the request must be documented; (3) the patient must be suffering intolerably, with no prospect of relief, although the disease need not be terminal; and (4) the doctor must consult with another physician not involved in the case" (Angell, 1996, p. 1676). Physicians in the Netherlands who practice euthanasia under these guidelines have not been subject to criminal sanctions for many years. Apparently, no moral or legal distinction is drawn in the Netherlands between this form of active euthanasia and assisted suicide.

Official studies of euthanasia practices in the Netherlands were conducted in 1990 and 1995, with a third study under way as this is written. One of the 1995 studies involved interviews with 405 physicians; the other involved questionnaires mailed to physicians identified from death certificates as having attended 6,060 deaths (Van der Maas et al., 1996). Response rates were 89 percent and 77 percent, respectively (a high rate of return). Results were that "among the deaths studied, 2.3 percent of those in the interview study and 2.4 percent of those in the death-certificate study were estimated to have resulted from euthanasia, and 0.4 percent and 0.2 percent, respectively, resulted from physician-assisted suicide" (p. 1699). The authors add that by comparison with earlier studies, "euthanasia seems to have increased in incidence since 1990" (when comparable rates were 1.9 and 1.7 percent, respectively), whereas the incidence of assisted suicide is roughly stable (with comparable 1990 rates of 0.3 and 0.2 percent, respectively). One further result is that "in 0.7 percent of cases, life was ended without the explicit, concurrent request of the patient," a slight decrease of 0.1 percent from the 1990 study.

In November 2001, new legislation—"The Dutch Termination of Life on Request and Assisted Suicide (Review Procedures) Act"—went into effect. According to an official "question and answer" pamphlet on the subject (Anonymous, 2001), this legislation incorporated in the Dutch criminal code "a special ground for exemption from criminal liability," which provides that "doctors who terminate life on request or assist in a patient's suicide can no longer be prosecuted, provided they satisfy the statutory due care criteria and notify death by non-natural causes to the appropriate regional euthanasia review committee" (p. 4). In other words, active euthanasia and assisted suicide remain illegal in the Netherlands, but the new legislation provides that when a doctor has performed them essentially in the ways described earlier in this section and has reported his or her actions correctly, and when a regional review committee (composed of at least one lawyer, one physician, and an ethicist) has decided on the basis of that report that the physician has acted with due care, the Public Prosecution Service will not be informed and no further action will be taken. Only when a review committee finds that a doctor has failed to satisfy the statutory due care criteria will the case be referred to the public prosecutor for possible prosecution.

According to official documents, "the basic principle underlying the legislation is that patients have no absolute right to euthanasia and doctors no absolute duty to perform it" (p. 6). Thus, approximately two-thirds of all requests for euthanasia in the Netherlands are refused, and one hospice doctor could say that his attitude toward this legislation and the practices that it sanctions was one of "peaceful coexistence and respectful nonparticipation" (Z. Zylicz, in a discussion at the meeting of the International Work Group on Death, Dying, and Bereavement, 6/13/01).

Those who favor the Dutch policies and practices note that all citizens of the Netherlands enjoy a high standard of living, full health insurance, a home physician, and generous retirement and social services. Nevertheless, the population of the Netherlands is aging and the government recognizes that dying patients may request euthanasia for reasons of pain, degradation, and the longing to die with dignity (see Box 18.2). Advocates also draw attention to the following facts: euthanasia accounts for only a small fraction of all deaths in the Netherlands (4,751 in 1995); it is performed in less than a third of cases when a request is made; it is performed "almost entirely on those who were terminally ill; 87 percent of the patients were expected to die within a week, and another 12 percent in a month" (Angell, 1996, p. 1676); in cases when there was no explicit request, factors such as a previous discussion of the subject, present lack of competency, and/or discussions with other physicians, nurses, or family members had influenced the decision; and reporting of these cases has increased "from about 18 percent to 41 percent" from 1990 to 1995 (Van der Wal et al., 1996, p. 1707). Thus, the authors of the 1995 studies contend, "in our view, these data do not support the idea that physicians in the Netherlands are moving down a slippery slope" (Van der Maas et al., 1996, p. 1705). They add, "a

Box 18.2 A Letter concerning the Death of Fritz van der Kloot Meijburg

Dear Friends,

I want to share with you the death of my father, Fritz van der Kloot Meijburg.

On Saturday evening January 13th, 2001, my father died in his sleep. It was at his request. At last he was at peace. This was what he had hoped for: finally, to die in his sleep.

Five years ago, at the age of 85, my father was diagnosed with Amyotrophic Lateral Sclerosis (ALS). My parents had just moved to an elderly home, but for another reason: my mother being diagnosed with Alzheimers. It was a reasonable solution and it provided my parents with some degree of support. So ALS came as a surprise to my father and the family. Ever since, this disease has been slowly eating away at his physical condition.

I have known my father as a real organizer and planner, even to the extent that what had been planned or arranged in his agenda ruled his day. At times he would get annoyed if the barber would not show up to do his hair because it said so in his agenda . . . sometimes the barber didn't even know himself he had an appointment with my father! If I promised him that I would visit with him at some time during the day, he always asked me the exact time I would come and he would write that down in his agenda.

What may sound like a weakness may also be perceived as a sign of strength: ALS wasn't planned for, it was not in his agenda and therefore he closed the door to this disease. He even neglected his disease to an extent that he would try to continue life's routines the best he could regardless of his diminishing condition. Sometimes I said to him that it didn't bother me if he would decide to stay in his apartment and save his energy instead of insisting on taking me downstairs to the entry hall to say goodbye.

It came as a great shock to him that the home physician advised my father to look for a place for my mother in a nursing home. He had hoped for himself that in the elderly home he would be able to look after his wife, but instead it was wearing him out. Ever since my mother was in the nursing home, five miles down the road, he felt guilty about himself being the cause of her being there. Consequently, he set up a scheme of visiting her on a daily basis seven days a week. At first he used his electric scooter; later on he became dependent upon others to take him there.

ALS is a rude disease and is, at an earlier age, let us say with people in their fifties, known for a relatively fast kill. What happens is that over time the nerve system withers away no longer activating the muscles. This puts the muscles out of use because they are no longer activated. In the process the speech is also affected and at the end the muscles of the breathing system are affected. ALS patients fear suffocation.

But my father, as I said before, had no place for ALS. For different reasons he ignored it in a way and that kept him alive over a longer period of time.

(continued)

Box 18.2 (cont.) A Letter concerning the Death of Fritz van der Kloot Meijburg

Looking back, I admire him for the way he took the blows. For example, the physiotherapist at a certain stage in his illness telling him that the therapy was no longer required because it no longer helped to improve or stabilize his physical condition, or the first time he had to accept that he could no longer make it to the toilet on his own, etc. In 1997 he signed a euthanasia form and asked his home physician whether he would be willing to put him out of his misery if a time would come when he could bear it no longer. The physician agreed not to abandon him if that time would come. In the years after that we have been negotiating with him about life and death. I became very cunning in offering alternatives when he said it had been enough. When can one say he is truly suffering? What is unbearable? If you can no longer walk, you can compensate by using an electric wheelchair. If you can no longer make your phone calls, I can call people up for you I argued. And there was always something to look forward to: his 60th Wedding Anniversary in 2000; he and my mother would not want to miss the visit of the town mayor! A birthday of one of his grandchildren. And how about me, his son? I could not go on without him. I offered him to put him in a nice hot bath every week and did so together with a friend for almost three quarters of a year. We stepped up the frequency of our visits to him and ended up visiting him everyday. Together with my sister we challenged his determination and nurtured his ambivalence. Part of it was unconsciously.

In September, last year, he was transferred to the nursing home where my mother had been taken to five years previously. He was terribly uncomfortable about this move. But the care he required was of such a nature now that he needed nursing home assistance. I told him that there were some advantages too: now he need no longer put in all the effort to get to his wife every day. They would be together again most of the time. It was a shock to see what happened: from the day he entered the nursing home he was totally disorientated. As long as he lived in the elderly home he managed to find his way to my mother. In the nursing home he got lost every time he tried to go down to her ward. At the end we decided to bring my mother up to where he was. It was then that I finally realized my father had set one of his feet in another world, not being the world of the living. It was the first time I was able to take his "Herman, enough is enough" seriously. I all of a sudden realized that he hadn't taken any of his beer for months in a row. And he used to drink a can of beer with his dinner every day. I noticed his appetite diminished, he lost weight. It was like the illness was making up for time lost to it in an earlier phase of the process. There was a noticeable loss of speech. And I was alarmed to see how he started to say his good bye to those who visited with him, how he told me over and over again how much he appreciated me looking after his things. I was alarmed when he started to ask me every time when I visited him whether I had sorted out the "mess" on his table. It was in December that the attending nursing home physician called me and my sister in her office to share her concerns about my father's physical and mental condition.

(continues)

Box 18.2 (cont.) A Letter concerning the Death of Fritz van der Kloot Meijburg

After New Year she called again to say that my father had requested her again to put an end to his misery. Wouldn't it be possible for him to die in his sleep and couldn't she provide him with the means. And would she be so kind not to abandon him this time. She promised and told my father she would report the case to the coroner because she considered his request to die in his sleep without the risk of accidentally waking up again as a form of euthanasia. Together with my sister we also had a long talk with my father. He was of such a clear mind about what he wanted for himself that we didn't dare to challenge him again like we used to. Enough was really enough now. There was no other option but to respect what our father was sharing with us. He now had written his own death in his agenda and we knew him well enough to know we (the physician, my sister and myself) could not blot it out. He asked us whether we would promise him to look after "Mamma," his wife. We promised and that promise was such a relief to him.

In the days after, we rallied his grandchildren. They all came and sat down with him knowing the end would come soon.

Early evening on Thursday, January the 11th, he himself took three pills out of the hands of the attending physician and swallowed them with a little water. Personally, I do not think that physician has ever been thanked before in the way my father thanked her. We sat around with him for about half an hour and talked about the big and small things of family life. At a certain moment while he was dozing away he lifted his eyes and looked at me and my sister saying "Have you passed your examinations alright and did you bring your diplomas?" Yes he was ready, organized and had prepared himself well for the journey he was about to take. He died peacefully in his sleep two days later, just as he had wanted for himself.

In the middle of the night we took our mother up to see him. She was well aware what had happened and held his hand for a while, saying that although it sometimes came in disguise, the good in the person she had loved all her life had always prevailed, even to the very end.

Herman H. van der Kloot Meijburg
Voorburg, January 2001 ■

large majority of Dutch physicians consider euthanasia an exceptional but accepted part of medical practice."

Opponents of these practices and policies (such as Hendin, 1995, 1997; Hendin et al., 1997) generally describe them as rife with danger and not possessed of adequate safeguards. They seize on what they see as "the gradual extension of assisted suicide to widening groups of patients after it is legally permitted for patients designed as terminally ill" (Hendin et al., 1997, p. 1720), failures of the guidelines and problems of underreporting despite the implementation since 1991 of a notification procedure (see Van der Wal et al., 1996), and "the documentation of cases in which patients who have not given their consent have their lives ended by physicians" (p. 1721).

Because their populations, social services, and health care systems are so dissimilar, Angell (1996, p. 1677) noted that "it is virtually impossible to draw any meaningful comparisons" between the Dutch experience and practices in the United States. She added, "until recently, physician-assisted dying has been considered in the United States to be quite different" from accepted practices in end-of-life care. However, "support for decriminalizing assisted suicide has been growing, whereas support for euthanasia remains weak," perhaps because "euthanasia can be involuntary, where suicide, by definition, must be voluntary" and assisted suicide may be considered to be less liable to abuse than euthanasia.

Assisted Suicide Legislation and Practices in Oregon

Efforts to legalize some form of active euthanasia failed in both California and Washington. In 1994, however, the voters of Oregon approved by a narrow margin a "Death with Dignity Act" authorizing physician-assisted suicide. Several groups went to court to prevent the implementation of the act. In 1997, the U.S. Supreme Court ruled that although there is no "right to die" in the U.S. Constitution, states have the constitutional right to make laws that provide for physician-assisted suicide. Meanwhile, an attempt to repeal the law was placed on the ballot in Oregon in 1997, only to be rejected by a vote of 60–40 percent. The provisions of the act stipulate the conditions under which a terminally ill, adult resident of Oregon is permitted to request that a physician provide a prescription for lethal medication that an individual can use to end his or her life (Haley & Lee, 1998). The act applies to patients with a diagnosed terminal illness and a prognosis of less than six months to live. The procedures that must be followed to comply with the act include a requirement that a physician ensure that the patient is making this request voluntarily. That is accomplished by requiring that the patient make two oral requests separated by at least 15 days and sign a written request in the presence of two witnesses. The prescribing physician must also inform the patient of his or her diagnosis, prognosis, available options (such as comfort care, hospice care, and pain control), and right to withdraw the request at any time. In addition, the prescribing physician must refer the patient to a consulting physician to confirm the diagnosis and prognosis, and to determine that the patient is capable (able to make and communicate health care decisions). Psychiatric illness or depression that might impair judgment must be ruled out. Further, the prescribing physician must request (but may not require) the patient to notify his or her next-of-kin of the prescription request. Note that the act authorizes voluntary self-administration of lethal medications prescribed by a physician for the purpose of ending one's life; euthanasia or situations in which a physician or other person directly administers a medication to end another's life is specifically prohibited. Finally, although physicians and health care systems are under no obligation to participate in the Death with Dignity Act, those physicians and patients who adhere to the requirements of the act are protected from criminal prosecution, and the choice to end one's life in this way cannot affect the status of a patient's health or life insurance policies.

Those supporting the Oregon initiative argued that quality in living, personal choice or autonomy, and quality in medical decision making are the important values to be considered in this matter (Annas, 1994). Opponents generally described such practices and policies as rife with danger and not possessed of adequate safeguards, especially those that would protect vulnerable patients from coercion of various sorts (Hendin, 1995, 1997). It should be noted that the hospice community historically has not generally favored assisted suicide or euthanasia, preferring to place its emphases instead on management of distressing symptoms and opportunities for growth at the end of life (Byock, 1994; Saunders, 1995). However, in the face of a medical community and health care system that seems unable to implement appropriate methods of pain and symptom control in end-of-life care and since hospice care is not available for everyone, there may still need to be some reflection on alternatives when the admittedly most desirable conditions are not available (Haley & Lee, 1998).

In the four years since final approval of the Oregon initiative, few persons in Oregon have requested and even fewer have carried out assisted suicide (Chin et al., 1999; Hedberg et al., 2002; Oregon Health Division, 2002; Sullivan et al., 2000; Sullivan et al., 2001). In 1998, 24 prescriptions were provided, and 16 persons ingested the prescribed medications and ended their lives. In 1999, 33 persons received prescriptions and 27 used them to end their lives. In 2000, 39 persons were provided with the required prescriptions and 27 died after ingesting the medication (one of these persons had received the prescription in 1999). In 2001, 44 prescriptions for lethal doses of medication were written and 21 persons died after using the medication (including 2 persons who received prescriptions during 2000).

The 21 deaths in 2001 represented an estimated 7 of every 10,000 deaths in Oregon in that year. Overall, on the basis of these first four years experience, it appears that few persons in Oregon (less than 1/10 of 1 percent of all deaths in the state) use assisted suicide even where it is legal. Multiple concerns appear to have motivated those who completed an act of physician-assisted suicide under the Oregon initiative. These concerns have been reported to include loss of autonomy or control of bodily functions, a decreasing ability to participate in activities that made life enjoyable, a determination to control the way in which one dies, and concerns about being a burden to others. Fear of intractable physical pain does not seem to have been a central motivation in these actions.

On November, 6, 2001, the Attorney General of the United States announced that Oregon's Death with Dignity Act violated federal drug laws and authorized the government to cancel the federal license of physicians to prescribe what are called controlled substances or "scheduled drugs" if they are used to provide assistance in dying. The practical effect of that action would be to make if difficult, if not impossible, to implement the Oregon legislation. In November 2001, however, a federal district court issued a temporary injunction to halt that action, and in April 2002 the same court made the injunction permanent, ruling that the Attorney General did not have the authority to interfere with state laws governing the practice of medicine. An appeal remains possible.

Prospects for the Future

The issues discussed in this chapter are unlikely to be easily resolved or to disappear in the future. In fact, as medical technology advances, more and more people may find themselves in situations wherein they seriously question the quality of life offered by continued medical interventions, either for themselves or for others about whom they care. Also, health care providers may find themselves in situations in which those for whom they are caring ask for assistance in ending their lives (Emanuel et al., 2000). It is already clear that especially difficult challenges appear in cases involving: (1) individuals who are not regarded as competent to make any formal decision on these or other matters (such as infants, children, or the mentally ill); (2) those who once were thought to be competent but who did not then make known their wishes about conditions under which they might want to continue or end their lives (such as those in an irreversible coma or persistent vegetative state); and (3) when the issues involve assisted suicide, active euthanasia, or the removal not only of external support (for example, a respirator), but also of artificially assisted nutrition and hydration (Lynn, 1986).

It is also likely that issues related to assisted suicide and euthanasia will be presented to society as some individuals seek to have their views prevail over others in individual situations and as efforts are made to legitimize widespread practice in some form of public policy (as in euthanasia practices in the Netherlands or assisted suicide legislation in Oregon).

Whether or not American society at large adopts policies or practices that favor assisted suicide and/or euthanasia, decisions about these matters will continue to be made in individual circumstances. That is, situations will arise in which individuals cannot avoid deciding whether or not to (help) end the life of another and, if so, how. This means, also, that *someone will decide*. Some are most concerned about this latter point—who will or ought to decide whether assisted suicide and/or euthanasia are to be provided. However, although the question of identifying appropriate decision makers is significant, the grounds for making moral decisions are the most fundamental matter. In addition, questions of who will carry out these decisions (physician, family member, etc.)—whatever the grounds and whoever the decision maker may be—will need to be addressed, as will what kind of psychological or social impact such actions might create on others (Werth, 1999a).

Summary

In this chapter, we examined issues related to intentionally ending a human life, with special attention to assisted suicide and euthanasia. We sought to define these two concepts and the central ideas with which they are linked. In this process, we first focused on two key issues: the agent who takes the decisive action and the intention behind whatever action is taken. During this discussion, we explored the distinction between voluntariness and nonvoluntariness, contrasts between ending a life actively or passively, and the difference between extraordinary and ordinary means of treatment.

Then our focus shifted to arguments for and against intentionally ending a human life, arguments drawn from general moral or philosophical premises, as well as from perspectives arising from five of the world's great religions. In presenting these arguments and perspectives, we recognized that none of them was without potential objection and that easy answers to the issues addressed were unlikely for most people. However, this does not mean that no answers of any sort are available. Obviously, many people have diverse positions on various aspects of this subject. Thoughtful positions in this complex conceptual and moral arena of human life require careful and sustained reflection.

Finally, we suggested that these topics are likely to grow in importance for individual decision makers and for social policy. To that end, we looked briefly at legislation governing euthanasia practices in the Netherlands and physician-assisted suicide in Oregon. Our primary concern throughout this discussion has been to help individuals think about this subject before they are forced to confront it in their own lives.

Questions for Review and Discussion

1. In this chapter, we suggested that humans put value on such things as freedom, privacy, persons, religious traditions, life, self-respect, justice, and a good life. Which of these are most important to you? Why? Which, if any, of these would you be willing to sacrifice in order to preserve some other more important value(s)? Why? Relate your responses to these questions to the issue of deciding whether to assist someone who is incurably ill to die.

2. In this chapter, we offered a definition of euthanasia that distinguishes euthanasia from assisted suicide and homicide. What value is there in making such distinctions? What practical consequences might result from failing to make such distinctions?

3. Would you be willing to assist someone who was thinking about ending his or her life if: (a) that person was not dying (that is, any disease condition that the person had would not cause his or her death); (b) that person was suffering great emotional distress; and (c) that person was in great pain that could not be relieved? What are the values you hold that lead you to your responses to these questions?

4. In this chapter, we described several arguments to support the moral appropriateness of assisted suicide and euthanasia, and several arguments against their moral appropriateness. Which of these arguments do you find most compelling? Which are least persuasive to you? Why?

5. Would you support a law allowing physicians to undertake actions that might be thought to involve euthanasia and/or assisted suicide? Why would you support or not support such laws?

Suggested Readings

General works concerning ethical issues in death and dying include:

Battin, M. P. (1996). *The Death Debate: Ethical Issues in Suicide.*

Beauchamp, T. L., & Veatch, R. M. (1996). *Ethical Issues in Death and Dying* (2nd ed.).

Pojman, L. P. (1992). *Life and Death: Grappling with the Moral Dilemmas of Our Time.*

Reich, W. (Ed.). (1978). *Encyclopedia of Bioethics* (4 vols.).

Veatch, R. M. (1976). *Death, Dying, and the Biological Revolution: Our Last Quest for Responsibility.*

Resources specifically concerned with issues of active euthanasia and assisted suicide include:

Battin, M. P. (Ed.). (1994). *The Least Worst Death: Essays in Bioethics on the End of Life.*

Battin, M. P., Rhodes, R., & Silvers, A. (Eds.). (1998). *Physician Assisted Suicide: Expanding the Debate.*

Beauchamp, T. L. (Ed.). (1996). *Intending Death: The Ethics of Assisted Suicide and Euthanasia.*

Fox, E., Kamakahi, J. J., & Capek, S. M. (1999). *Come Lovely and Soothing Death: The Right to Die Movement in the United States.*

Haley, K., & Lee, M. (Eds.). (1998). *The Oregon Death with Dignity Act: A Guidebook for Health Care Providers.*

Hendin, H. (1997). *Seduced by Death: Doctors, Patients and the Dutch Cure.*

Humphry, D. (1992). *Final Exit: The Practicalities of Self-Deliverance and Assisted Suicide for the Dying.*

Humphry, D., & Clement, M. (1998). *Freedom to Die: People, Politics, and the Right-to-Die Movement.*

Jamison, S. (1995). *Final Acts of Love: Families, Friends, and Assisted Dying.*

Kliever, L. D. (Ed.). (1989). *Dax's Case: Essays in Medical Ethics and Human Meaning.*

McKhann, C. F. (1999). *A Time to Die: The Place for Physician Assistance.*

Thomasma, D. C., Kimbrough-Kushner, T., Kimsma, G. K., & Ciesielski-Carlucci, C. (1998). *Asking to Die: Inside the Dutch Debate about Euthanasia.*

Weir, R. F. (Ed.). (1997). *Physician-Assisted Suicide.*

Werth, J. L. (Ed.). (1999b). *Contemporary Perspectives on Rational Suicide.*

Resources that describe religious perspectives relevant to these discussions include:

Camenisch, P. F. (Ed.). (1994). *Religious Methods and Resources in Bioethics.*

Crawford, S. C. (1995). *Dilemmas of Life and Death: Hindu Ethics in a North American Context.*

First International Conference on Islamic Medicine. (1981). *Islamic Code of Medical Ethics.*

Flannery, A. (Ed.). (1982). *Vatican Council II: More Postconciliar Documents.*

Gandhi, M. (1980). *All Men Are Brothers: Autobiographical Reflections.*

Hamel, R. (1991). *Choosing Death: Active Euthanasia, Religion, and the Public Debate.*

Horner, I. B. (1949). *The Book of Discipline (Vinaya-Pitaka)*, vol. 1.

Keown, D. (1995). *Buddhism and Bioethics.*

Maimonides, M. (1949). *The Code of Maimonides (Mishneh Torah)*, Book 14, The Book of Judges. (A. M. Hershman, Trans.).

Neusner, J. (1988). *The Mishnah: A New Translation.*

Parkes, C. M., Laungani, P., & Young, B. (Eds.). (1997). *Death and Bereavement across Cultures.*

[Qur'an] Koran. (1956). Trans. N. J. Dawood.

Rodkinson, M. L. (1896). *New Edition of the Babylonian Talmud*, vol. 2.

Rosner, F., & Bleich, J. D. (Eds.). (1979). *Jewish Bioethics.*

InfoTrac College Edition
For more information, explore the InfoTrac College Edition at **http://www.infotrac-college.com/Wadsworth**

Enter search terms: ACTIVE EUTHANASIA, ASSISTED SUICIDE, EUTHANASIA, NONVOLUNTARY EUTHANASIA, PASSIVE EUTHANASIA, PHYSICIAN-ASSISTED SUICIDE, VOLUNTARY EUTHANASIA.

Chapter Nineteen

THE MEANING AND PLACE OF DEATH IN LIFE

IN THIS CHAPTER, WE EXPLORE ISSUES THAT underlie everything we have considered throughout this book. These are issues related to the human attempt to determine the meaning and place of death in life. We first draw attention to these issues with a Buddhist tale. Then, we consider a series of alternative images of the meaning of death that have been proposed by major religious and philosophical perspectives from around the world. Next, we discuss near-death experiences—their content and interpretations. Finally, we return to the basic issue that faces all human beings—the place of death in human life.

Gotami and the Buddha

The following tale is drawn from Buddhist scriptures. It occurs in various forms; the one we present here uses several sources.

> A young woman named Gotami had a son. But when he had barely begun to walk, he died. Overcome by grief, she carried the dead boy from one house to another, begging people if they had some medicine for her son. At one house, an old man told her that there was one person who could give her medicine, Gautama (the Buddha).
>
> Gotami went to the Buddha, and asked him for medicine for her dead child. He told her that he did know of such a medicine. She was to gather a little mustard seed from each house in the village that had not been touched by death. She went from house to house, but all in vain: nowhere did she find a family that had not known death.
>
> She now began to think to herself: "I thought that my son alone had been overtaken by this thing which people call death. But I was wrong. This happens to everyone" (paraphrased from Burtt, 1955, pp. 45–46). She now understood that everything that exists is impermanent and eventually passes away.
>
> After giving her son over to the funeral rites, Gotami returned to the Buddha. He asked her if she had brought the medicine he required. She told him no, that she knew now that all people die. The Buddha said to her: "All living beings resemble the flame of these lamps, one moment lighted, the next extinguished . . ." (Ballou, 1944, p. 143).

Questions Raised by Death and Some Preliminary Responses

Questions Raised by Death

To study death, dying, and bereavement is to face some of the most profound questions confronting human beings. Almost all human beings eventually come up against an inescapable fact about themselves and those persons they love: they are mortal. For many persons, as for Gotami in the above vignette, such a moment raises questions of meaning: Why are we born? What is the meaning of our having lived? What is the impact of our death on the value and significance of our life? In short, what is the relationship between life and death? Are they simple opposites? Where there is death, is there no life? (Terkel, 2001).

These questions are part of our human reality. As the Buddha told Gotami, the fact of eventual death is common to all forms of life. But human beings can think about or reflect on this fact and its implications before the event. That ability to know in advance that one will die is perhaps unique to human beings.

Some Responses to These Questions

As human beings have reflected on questions raised by death, they have responded in many different ways (for example, Becker, 1973; Grof & Halifax, 1978). The ancient Chinese Yin/Yang symbol at the beginning of this chapter provides one response to these questions. It suggests that life (represented by the light portion of the symbol—the yang) and death (represented by the dark portion of the symbol—the yin) interpenetrate each other; the Yin overlaps and intrudes into the space of the Yang and vice versa. More than this, at the very *center* of the Yin is the Yang, and again, vice versa. Thus, this symbol suggests that wherever there is life, there is death, and wherever there is death, there is life. Another response has been to attempt to understand what happens after death (Toynbee et al., 1976). This response has appeared in art and popular culture (Bertman, 1991), anthropology (Reynolds & Waugh, 1977), literature (Enright, 1983; Weir, 1980), philosophy (Carse, 1980; Choron, 1963, 1964), religion (Johnson & McGee, 1998), and theology (Gatch, 1969; Mills, 1969; Rahner, 1973). Indeed, some of the best thinking ever done by humans has focused on such issues. Socrates and Albert Camus, Paul of Tarsus and Muhammad, the writer of *Ecclesiastes* and the writer of the *Bhagavad Gita:* in the work of such people can be found examples of attempts to address the disturbing implications of death in human life.

For instance, Socrates, who is reported (Plato, 1961, p. 46; *Phaedo,* 64a) to have said that "those who really apply themselves in the right way to philosophy are directly and of their own accord preparing themselves for dying and death" argued that everything human beings do in life is finally to be evaluated by testing it against the fact of their mortality. From this perspective, everything we have considered in this book (for example, how to treat dying persons and survivors or the place of assisted suicide and euthanasia in human life, in fact all human responses to death and dying) originates from more basic questions about the meaning of mortality. For instance, to say that people should care for dying persons in one way rather than in another way finds part of its justification in beliefs about death. If one believes that death is always and everywhere to be disvalued, and if one holds that death is the greatest evil known, this belief is likely to affect how one faces and deals with dying persons. If one believes that there can be something worse than death, that too will influence how one acts in these situations.

How death is evaluated is ultimately dependent on what can reasonably be called philosophical or theological beliefs (Congdon, 1977; Momeyer, 1988). Evaluations of death are linked in perhaps inescapable ways to beliefs about the nature and the meaning of death. Probably everyone has such beliefs, although everyone may not explicitly formulate or consciously reflect on them.

Death: A Door or a Wall?

Feifel (1977a) simplified (perhaps overly so) how humans are likely to think of death when he wrote that death can be portrayed as either a door or a wall. He meant that when one looks at death, one can ask oneself what one sees. Is death simply the cessation of life? Is it the case that where death intrudes, life is irrevocably lost? If so, death is something that all will come up against, and it will mean the end of everything that one does or can know. It is a wall into which one crashes and through which one cannot pass.

However, some people believe that death is a stage along life's way. It is a river to cross, a stair to climb, a door through which to pass. If this is one's view, then death may be seen not as the irrevocable opposite to life but rather as a passage from one sort (or stage) of life to another.

Most people hold one or the other of these beliefs. Of course, these ideas and beliefs may be unconscious or not thought through clearly. But if one is (for example) afraid of death, that fear is based on some notion of the meaning of death, such as "I will never see loved ones again," or "I will never experience a sunset like that again," or "I will be punished for my sins," or "I may be reborn into a life of poverty." Since most of us have some sort of reaction to the fact of death—happiness or sadness, fear or anticipation—we also have some beliefs about its meaning.

It is also the case, however, that the evaluation one makes of death is not tied in any obvious way to whether one sees it as a door or as a wall (Nabe, 1982). One can think of death as a wall and evaluate that as good: for example, at least all suffering is over. One can see death as a door and evaluate that as evil: for example, it may bring eternal torment or a shadowy, shallow form of life. And, of course, some would see death as a wall as something evil, and death as a door as something good. The point is only that how one thinks of death philosophically is tied in some important way to how one values it.

Alternative Images of an Afterlife

At this point, we can usefully explore some of the principal religious or philosophical images that humans have employed to try to understand how death and life are related. We do so by examining responses to the questions: "Is *this life* all there is?" and "Is death the irrevocable loss of any sort of life?" Humans have tried to respond to questions of this sort in quite an astonishing array of ways (Toynbee, 1968b). Here, we will consider several of the best-known and most influential of these ways.

Greek Concepts of the Afterlife

More than 400 years before the birth of Christ, the philosopher Socrates was a well-known figure in the city-state of Athens. When he was 70 years old, some of Socrates' critics brought charges against him for not believing in the official state gods and for corrupting the youth by teaching them to challenge the beliefs of their elders. Socrates was found guilty of these charges and condemned to death.

Box 19.1 Socrates' Thoughts about the Meaning of Death

This thing that has come upon me must be a good; and those of us who think that death is an evil must needs be mistaken. . . . For the state of death is one of two things: either the dead man wholly ceases to be and loses all consciousness or . . . it is a change and a migration of the soul to another place. And if death is the absence of all consciousness, and like the sleep of one whose slumbers are unbroken by any dreams, it will be a wonderful gain. . . . For it appears that all time is nothing more than a single night. But if death is a journey to another place, and what we are told is true—that all who have died are there—what good could be greater than this? . . . What would you not give to converse with Orpheus and Musaeus and Hesiod and Homer? . . . It would be an inexpressible happiness to converse with [heroes such as these] and to live with them and to examine them.

SOURCE: Plato, 1948, pp. 47–48; *Apology*, 40b–41a.

After these actions by the jury, Socrates began to describe what death meant to him. He said he believed that humans cannot *know* what death means in terms of our continued existence. Instead, he maintained that all people are left with *beliefs* on this point. On this most pressing question, Socrates contended that we can only make a choice to believe on less than demonstrative proof.

Socrates was content not to decide finally just what death means for our continued existence. Perhaps that was in part due to the options he presented for what death might involve. (Look at what he told the jurors about this, in Box 19.1.) If death is either a permanent sleep (unconsciousness) or a form of life in which one meets old friends and can make new ones (as Socrates suggested in the passage quoted above), then death need not appear to be frightening or threatening.

But these scenarios do not exhaust the possibilities. Socrates' beloved Homer provides another description. At one point in Homer's *Odyssey*, Odysseus calls up another Greek hero (Achilles) from the afterlife in Hades. Achilles says about that life, "Don't bepraise death to me. . . . I would rather be plowman to a yeoman farmer on a small holding than lord paramount in the kingdom of the dead" (Homer, 1937, p. 125). Achilles says this because Hades is described as an unhappy place; the dead have no sense or feeling and are mere "phantoms."

Another view found in ancient Greek sources is that of the "immortality of the soul." This view appears in the writings of Plato, who sometimes represented human beings as made up of two parts, a body (earthly, mortal) and a soul (immortal). Plato went on to offer arguments intended to prove the inherent immortality of the soul. For Plato, souls are essentially immortal, deathless by their very nature. Nothing can cause a soul not to be; thus it must exist forever. Because humans (and all bodies that move "of themselves"—that is, animals) are in part souls, death must mean only the separation of the body and the soul. It does not mean the end of the soul.

Socrates accepts his death sentence and calmly drinks the fatal poison while his friends weep.

Greek thought provided one major strand of Western beliefs about the philosophical questions we are studying. Another major strand came from the Judeo-Christian tradition and its biblical scriptures.

Some Western Religious Beliefs

Many different beliefs about an afterlife are expressed in the Hebrew and Christian scriptures. Bailey (1978) found the following notions associated with an afterlife in those texts:

1. "Immortality" is sometimes associated only with divine beings (Wisdom of Ben Sirach 17:30; 1 Timothy 6:16).
2. Sometimes "deathlessness" is seen as being given by the gods to specific human beings (for example, Enoch in Genesis 5:24, and Elijah in 2 Kings 2:1–12).
3. An afterlife might be related to a phantomlike existence, a sort of "diminished life." (Compare Achilles' description of Hades noted earlier.) Some people have found this view present in Saul's consultations with a witch, who calls up Samuel from the afterworld (see 1 Samuel 28).
4. Ongoing life after death is often related to what one leaves behind at one's death, such as one's children.

Actually, the notion of the individual surviving death is only rarely encountered in the Hebrew scriptures. If there is a notion of ongoing life after death, it is found in the community and in one's specific descendants: I may die, but my community will go on. I may die, but my children and my children's children will go on. It is the community's life that is important, and it is the ongoing life of the familial line that is significant (Bowker, 1991).

In fact, it is even uncertain whether the Greek notion of a soul discussed earlier is found in the Hebrew scriptures. The Hebrew word often translated as "soul" *(nepesh)* means most simply "life." It is necessarily tied up with a body. Thus, at death, the *nepesh* ceases to exist, since it is no longer bound up with a particular body. Eichrodt (1967) reports that various images are used: at death, the *nepesh* "dies; at the same time it is . . . feasible to think of it leaving a man at death, though this does not mean that one can ask where it has gone! . . . It is described as having been taken or swept away" (p. 135). He added: "In no instance does there underlie the use of *nepes* [a] conception of an immortal *alter ego*. . . . Equally remote from the concept . . . is the signification of a numinous substance in Man who survives death" (p. 140). If this is correct, then the notion of an immortal soul is not part of the original Judaic tradition. In fact, Eichrodt (1967) holds that this idea entered Judaic thought much later, under the influence of Hellenic (Greek) culture.

None of the meanings found in the Hebrew scriptures that have been discussed so far is clearly related to another biblical image of an afterlife—the image of resurrection. This image grows out of the Judaic belief that the human being is not a combination of two different sorts of entities, a body and a soul; each of us is rather an integrated whole. To be human is not to be a soul entombed in a body; it is to be a living-body. Life in this view cannot be understood *except* as embodied. (Islam sometimes teaches this precept, too; see Muwahidi, 1989, pp. 40–41). Thus, if there is to be a life after death, it must be an embodied life. That is what *resurrection* means: it refers to the "raising up" of a human being as a living-body. This raising up would require a new action by God—namely, a re-creation of the human being.

Western religion has also often associated an afterlife with the concepts of heaven and hell. These concepts are remarkably fully developed in Islam. According to Islam, at a Last Judgment each individual's behavior while living in this world will be judged. If a person submits to Allah ("Islam" means "to submit"), rewards will be waiting after death. If a person rebels against Allah, punishments will be waiting. These rewards or punishments are often described vividly:

> For those that fear the majesty of their lord there are two gardens . . . planted with shady trees. . . . Each is watered by a flowering spring. . . . Each bears every kind of fruit. . . . They shall recline on couches lined with thick brocade . . . there shall wait on them immortal youths with bowls and ewers and a cup of purest wine. . . . And theirs shall be the dark-eyed houris, chaste as hidden pearls . . . those [who are cursed] shall dwell amongst scorching winds and seething water: in the shade of pitch-black smoke. (*Qur'an*, 1993, 55:35–56:55)

Similar concepts can be identified in Christianity, in Hinduism, and in some forms of Buddhism.

Islam has other beliefs that are of interest here. Sakr (1995) reported that for Islam there is a form of life in the grave. The soul of the person who has died is believed to visit the grave regularly in order to receive reward or punishment.

Islamic men carry a coffin in the courtyard of a mosque.

The "grave is a center of transformation, a center of molding, a center of reshaping, a center of preparation, and a place of resynthesis" (Sakr, 1995, p. 59).

Other cultures, however, have quite different beliefs.

Some African Beliefs

The continent of Africa contains many cultures, and the philosophical and theological beliefs of the people in these various cultures have not been extensively described or studied. However, some preliminary generalizations have been made (Mbiti, 1970).

In general, for many of these people, the power that makes life possible is everywhere the same—in plants, in animals, and in human beings (Opoku, 1978, 1987). So human life is part of nature, and it is a constant cyclic process of becoming (as is nature). This process does have certain distinguishing moments or turning points in it: birth, adolescence, marriage, and death. But each of these crises only marks a particular point in the process of becoming. Those in the community who are alive are in one stage; those who are the "living-dead" (that is, those who are not living as we are here) are simply in a further stage. The community contains both the living and the "living-dead." The "living-dead" are not thought of as being in another world; they are only in a different part of this world. The transition to this other part of the world is sometimes symbolized as a land journey, often including the crossing of a river, perhaps because rivers form natural boundaries between one part of the natural world and another part. This view typically does not include a notion of a heaven (a life of bliss) or of a hell (a life of torment).

The "living-dead," in this view, are quasimaterial beings. As ancestors, they are prized and respected. Their lives are ones of serenity and dignity, given over to concern for the well-being of the living members of their families and clans. Thus the family extends into this other world.

These are images drawn from a people living in close contact with nature. There is no notion of a pale, empty afterlife, as seen in Homer. Nor is there a notion of resurrection or of heaven or hell. The afterlife as it is portrayed here is a simple, natural continuation of the life we know. There *are* differences, just as living in the desert on this side of the river is different from living in the forest on the other side of the river. However, the life of the "living-dead" is not a wholly foreign existence, and it is not a threatening one.

Some African Americans share this sort of belief. Sullivan (1995) reported that for such persons the dead and the living have reciprocal functions that create a unified whole. For these persons, to "pass on" is to be involved in "movement." It is a change in form whereby one moves on to the world of the ancestors.

Hindu and Buddhist Beliefs

When Westerners think about the philosophical and theological beliefs of the people of the Indian subcontinent, perhaps the notion that most often springs to mind is *reincarnation.* (A variety of terms are associated with this idea: *transmigration of souls, metempsychosis, rebirth;* we treat these terms here as if they are interchangeable.) This is a very ancient idea, one that can sometimes be found in Western thought, too. For example, ideas like this are found in some of Plato's dialogues. However, the idea of reincarnation is certainly older than Plato's writings (the fourth century B.C.E.).

The first writings that discuss the idea of reincarnation go back at least to the seventh century B.C.E. One Hindu scripture (the *Katha Upanishad*) contains the following passage (Radhakrishnan & Moore, 1957, pp. 45–46):

> The wise one . . . is not born, nor dies.
> This one has not come from anywhere, has not become anyone.
> Unborn, constant, eternal, primeval, this one
> Is not slain when the body is slain.
> If the slayer think to slay,
> If the slain think himself slain,
> Both these understand not.
> Know thou the self *(atman)* as riding in a chariot,
> The body as the chariot. . . .
> He . . . who has not understanding,
> Who is unmindful and ever impure,
> Reaches not the goal,
> But goes on to transmigration. . . .
> He . . . who has understanding,
> Who is mindful and ever pure,
> Reaches the goal
> From which he is born no more . . .

Devout Hindus release a dead body to the sacred waters of the river Ganges in India.

This passage expresses many important characteristics of a Hindu view of the human being. Humans are essentially an unborn, undying soul *(atman)*. This soul is repeatedly incarnated in bodies (and not necessarily always in human bodies, but also in "lower" forms). What body the soul is incarnated into depends on what one has done in previous lives. "Unmindfulness," "impurity," and a lack of understanding about the nature of reality will lead to transmigration of the soul from one body or one sort of body to another. But transmigration necessarily brings with it suffering, so the goal is to end transmigration, or rebirth. Perhaps one of the clearest statements of this view is found in the *Bhagavad Gita*. It contains the teachings of the lord Krishna (a god) to a human being (Arjuna). Arjuna is agonized about the killing that occurs in war, but Krishna tells him:

> Wise men do not grieve for the dead or for the living. . . . Never was there a time when I was not, nor thou . . . nor will there ever be a time hereafter when we shall cease to be. . . . Just as a person casts off worn-out garments and puts on others that are new, even so does the embodied soul cast off worn-out bodies and take on others that are new. (Radhakrishnan, 1948, pp. 102–108)

If this is so, then what does it tell people about how to live their lives here? Krishna answers:

> Endowed with a pure understanding, firmly restraining oneself, turning away from sound and other objects of sense and casting aside attraction, and aversion. . . . Dwelling in solitude, eating but little, controlling speech, body, and mind . . .

> taking refuge in dispassion . . . casting aside self-sense, force, arrogance, desire, anger, possession, egoless, and tranquil in mind, he becomes worthy of becoming one with *Brahman*. (Radhakrishnan, 1948, p. 370)

In other words, right living can lead to an end of the rebirths and to complete peace or union with a transcendent reality.

Prashad (1989) reported that these beliefs affect Hindu actions at the time of death. What one is thinking at the moment of death sums up all of one's life experience and can determine what the next rebirth will be. One should thus die with the name of God on one's lips, because this helps to produce a favorable outcome after death.

After death, three possibilities exist: (1) the *atman* may be in one of the heavens, awaiting rebirth; (2) the *atman* is immediately reborn; or (3) the *atman* is in a state of eternal bliss with Brahman (the transcendent reality), having achieved liberation from the cycle of rebirths.

The founder of Buddhism (Siddhartha Gautama) was raised as a Hindu but eventually found its practices and beliefs unacceptable. After years of spiritual struggle, he experienced an awakening (thus becoming the Buddha—the enlightened one). As the *Buddha*, he taught that all is impermanence; nothing (not even a soul) exists in some eternal, unchanging condition. This fact produces suffering for everything that is aware of it. For human beings, "birth is suffering; sickness is suffering; death is suffering; sorrow and lamentation, pain, grief and despair are suffering; association with the unpleasant is suffering; dissociation from the pleasant is suffering; not to get what one wants is suffering" (Rahula, 1974, p. 93). As long as one fails to recognize this fact—and to confront and transcend it—one will live again and again, reincarnated into one suffering

Buddha's parinirvana (death).

body after another. In this condition of ignorance about the true, impermanent nature of all reality, death is an evil because it only leads to rebirth into another life of suffering. Ideally, by transcending desire, one can escape the wheel of rebirths, achieving *nirvana*, a state beyond desire and thus beyond suffering, a state serene and peaceful (Radhakrishnan & Moore, 1957).

In this view, the "total balance sheet of good and evil deeds performed during a given lifetime is summarized in the state of mind held by the dying person" (Becker, 1989, p. 114). This state of mind influences rebirth. If the person clings to life, energy is sent forth that becomes associated with some child in the womb.

A Common Concern in Images of an Afterlife

The various notions we have described about what happens after death range from a permanent sleep (unconsciousness) through re-creation in an embodied form (resurrection) and on to a "blowing out" or a condition of absolute stillness. Some of these pictures seem threatening: a hell involving punishment or a Hades as it is described in Homer. Some seem attractive: meeting old companions or eternal joy in a heavenly state. Some provide a sense of peace: a surcease from a constant round of suffering. Each notion is likely to affect how one lives one's life here and now, and how one evaluates death.

In the United States at the beginning of the 21st century, many persons no longer hold the typical religious beliefs of earlier times. The modern, scientific worldview has convinced many people that they are simply natural bodies. On that basis, it seems to many that when our bodies no longer function, then we simply are no more. Death means extinction.

It is not wholly clear how this view is likely to affect one's evaluation of death. In a sense, it is an unthreatening view because there is no suffering after death, although of course, death means the loss of everything one has valued and loved. If this life is seen as basically good, then its loss is likely to be held to be an unhappy event. Death may then be only feared and hated—and denied. This may be one source of death denial.

In the face of uncertainty, people seek evidence. They would like to know what death means in terms of ongoing existence. Yet Socrates seems to have been correct; we cannot *know*. We must choose some picture of what death means and make do with it. For all of us, religious and nonreligious alike, faith is the only possible route here.

Near-Death Experiences

Is faith the only possible route? Moody's (1975) book, *Life after Life*, drew attention to a set of phenomena reported by many people. Often, the phenomena were interpreted as providing evidence that there is a life after death and what that life might be like. However, these interpretations are controversial. To understand the issues involved, we look first at the general pattern of these phenomena and then at some of the competing interpretations.

What Are Near-Death Experiences?

Those whom Moody interviewed provided similar, but not identical, reports of their experiences. Typically, these persons reported out-of-body experiences in which they felt themselves to be in a peaceful and quiet state. During these experiences they often related that they were aware of their surroundings and heard themselves being pronounced clinically dead. At the same time, they frequently had unusual sensory encounters: hearing loud noises or auditory sensations, being in a dark tunnel, coming into contact with others, meeting a being of light, reviewing their own lives, and approaching a border or limit of some type. Often, people who had these experiences were hesitant to share them with others for fear of being disbelieved or ridiculed. When encouraged to share, however, they noted difficulties in communicating what appeared to them to be overwhelming, beyond words, and indescribable. They also typically reported that this experience had changed their lives, leaving them content, joyful, and no longer afraid of death.

Moody (1975) pointed out that these reports were not all identical. Still, he thought there were sufficient similarities on the main points that it was worth paying attention to the phenomena being reported. Other writers recorded similar phenomena and attempted to describe what they considered to be the key components of the "near-death experience" (NDE). For example, Ring (1980) examined a set of 102 cases, in which 60 percent reported a feeling of peace and a sense of well-being. Some in this sample reported "a sense of detachment from one's physical body" (p. 45) and a sense of "entering the darkness" (p. 53). A few described an appearance of light, with 10 percent telling of "entering the light" (p. 60). Similarly, Sabom (1982) concluded that the most common features in the cases that he examined were a sense of calm and peace, bodily separation, being dead, and "returning" to life. Other writers (such as Blackmore, 1993; Fenwick & Fenwick, 1995; Greyson, 1999; Moody, 1988) provided further portraits of NDEs or efforts to define their essential characteristics.

In an effort to bolster the so-called archetypal NDE and control for cultural bias, others set out to broaden the field of investigation. For example, some looked for reports from individuals who had experienced some type of trauma but who were not near death (Owens et al., 1990; Stevenson et al., 1989), others recorded interviews with individuals who were dying, underwent an NDE experience, recovered to communicate it to others, and then did die (Osis & Haraldsson, 1997), and still others sought NDE reports from outside North America (for example, Lorimer, 1989). Atwater (1992) and Greyson and Bush (1992) also reported near-death experiences that were distressing or frightening.

Interpreting the Meaning of Near-Death Experiences

The most common interpretative claim made by those who report having had a NDE is the assertion that they had been dead and then had returned to life. Supporters of this claim believe that NDEs provide conclusive evidence of the existence of an afterlife—into which the NDE is thought to have offered a brief glimpse. This is the view of Elisabeth Kübler-Ross in the Foreword to Moody's (1975) book.

On the contrary, some religious people might argue that beliefs about the afterlife are in principle restricted to the realm of matters of faith, not issues on which empirical evidence can be demonstrative. As Kelly (2001, p. 230) reported, "most scientific investigators of NDEs have virtually ignored this question [of whether human consciousness survives the death of the physical body], concentrating instead on less controversial activities such as describing the aftereffects of NDEs or speculating about the physiological mechanisms that might underlie them." Such scientists seem to hold such views as: survival after death is nonsensical; interpretations favoring post-death survival on grounds of NDEs are unsound and incapable of controlled replication; and NDEs most likely are artifacts of the unusual situations in which they occur, for example, arising physiologically from anoxia (being without oxygen for a time) or chemical imbalances associated with anesthesia and surgical procedures (Nuland, 1994). In short, NDEs are essentially hallucinations (Siegel, 1992).

In fact, the claim that some persons were at one time dead and are now alive to report an NDE is awkward. That is, if what it means to be dead is to be *irreversibly* without biological life, then such persons were not dead. Perhaps they were almost dead, or near dead, or their experiences occurred during a set of processes that often lead to death. For example, they might have been "clinically dead" where that phrase means they met some criteria used to decide when death has occurred. However, the relationship between meeting such medical criteria and being dead is unclear; the two need not be identical. For instance, because someone shows no external signs of consciousness does not mean that person is having no experiences. "Unconscious" in this context means little more than "not showing signs of consciousness"; it does not mean no consciousness is present.

Kelly and her colleagues (2000) drew attention to three particular features of NDEs: "enhanced mental processes at a time when physiological functioning is seriously impaired; the experience of being out of the body and viewing events going on around it as from a position above; and the awareness of remote events not accessible to the person's ordinary senses" (p. 513). None of these features on its own is conclusive in settling the dispute as to whether NDEs can offer an expectation of an afterlife or are merely hallucinations. However, Kelly (2001) concluded that their convergence suggests the survival hypothesis "may be worthy of closer, more serious consideration—both as a framework for generating empirical research and as a candidate explanation for phenomena observed—than it has so far received from researchers" (p. 246). But note this qualification: "We emphasize, however, that near-death experiences can provide only *indirect* evidence of the continuation of consciousness after death: because the persons having these experiences have lived to report them, they were therefore not dead, however close they may have been to that condition" (Kelly et al., 2000, p. 518). And Moody has said: "I am a complete skeptic regarding the possibility that science as we know it or any sort of conventionally established methodological procedures will be able to get evidence of life after death or to come to some sort of rational determination of this question" (Kastenbaum, 1995, p. 95).

None of this rules out other lines of evidence that might support beliefs about an afterlife. However, they have not been studied extensively, and when they have been studied, the evidence is at best ambiguous. Socrates' dictum seems to stand: we do not, and perhaps cannot, know what happens after death. We must take a stand—even those who are agnostic are under the same practical compulsion—on less than complete proof. This central fact of our humanness—our mortality—remains a mystery.

The Place of Death in Human Life

Now that we have considered several images of what happens after death, it is useful to ask: What conclusions can we draw from these images for the meanings of our lives as we live them in this temporal, physical world?

Afterlife Images and Life Here and Now

One might argue that what we do here in this life influences what will happen to us after death. This becomes an argument meant to persuade us to behave in one way rather than another in order to "reap benefits" in an afterlife. Certain forms of Christianity, Islam, Hinduism, and Buddhism make suggestions like this. They contend that what we do here and now has desirable or undesirable consequences (for us) after death.

But even if one holds no such ideas, one can still make ties between what happens after death and life in the world now. For instance, if death is permanent extinction, then perhaps humans ought to live life to the fullest and seek to get as much experience as they can. Or, again, if death means extinction, one might hold that this eliminates the value of everything we know and do in our lives: all is vanity. Also, death can mean an end to suffering, as Hindus and Buddhists claim; it eliminates "the heartache and the thousand natural shocks that flesh is heir to" (*Hamlet*, III, i: 62). In this sense, death might be courted, even welcomed.

Some have gone beyond this to maintain the "conviction that in the last analysis all human behavior of consequence is a response to the problem of death" (Feifel, 1977a, xiii). If that seems too bold or too broad a thesis, then at least it can be said that we humans are able to make of death an important steering force in the way we interpret its place in our lives. If so, "appreciation of finiteness can serve not only to enrich self-knowledge but to provide the impulse to propel us forward toward achievement and creativity" (Feifel, 1977a, p. 11).

Efforts to Circumvent or Transcend Death

Many people have tried to circumvent death and have gone about it in a variety of ways. Another way to say this is that people have sought to find a way to continue after they die what they have found valuable in their lives. Lifton (1979) pointed to several such forms of what he called *symbolic immortality*. The main varieties that he described are biological, social, natural, and theological immortality. That is, one's life (and the values one finds in life) might be continued through one's biological descendants. Or it could be continued in what one has created—a painting, a garden, a book—or perhaps in the lives of others one has touched—students, patients, clients, friends. Some people have sought a continuation of their lives after their own deaths in the natural world around them. In this view, one's body returns to the ground (dust to dust), wherein its components dissolve and are reorganized into new life. Other people have looked for immortality in the form of an afterlife and reunion with or absorption into the divine. Furthermore, some have favored a program of cryonics in which one's body would be frozen at the moment of death and maintained in that state until a time comes (or so they hope) when they could be thawed out and the cause of their death cured by future generations.

Attempts to circumvent death reveal a meaning for that irrevocable, unavoidable moment: it produces suffering. If anything is valued in this life, death threatens that value. It means the loss (at least for now) of persons we have loved, places we have enjoyed, music, sunrise, the feeling of material (soil, paper and ink, the bow on the strings) coming into form through our labor.

If this is the meaning we find for death, inevitably it will influence how we live and how we treat each other. It teaches us that life is precious. So we entitled this book *Death and Dying, Life and Living*. It seems that whatever meaning we find for death, to look at death leads us to realize the fragility and the value of life. Indeed, perhaps death makes possible the value of life. A life (as we know life here) that went on indefinitely might become unbearable. Why do anything today, when there are endless tomorrows in which to do it?

Ultimately, the meaning any individual finds for death will be his or her own. In this sense, each individual is alone in facing his or her own death. But there is a history—thousands of years long—and a cultural diversity among persons with whom one can enter into dialogue. Each person can enter into this dialogue in order to gain help in choosing how to live his or her own life and how to make sense of his or her own death and the deaths of those whom he or she cares for and about. Each individual can also contribute to the history of human debate about the meaning and place of death in human life. This book is but one voice in that ongoing dialogue.

Summary

In this chapter, we engaged in a reflection on the meaning and place of death in human life. We considered questions that human beings have raised about death and responses offered, on one hand, by religious and philosophical perspectives, and, on the other, by students of near-death experiences. The lesson we drew is that each person is both free and responsible to determine for himself or herself the stand that he or she will take in the face of death.

Questions for Review and Discussion

1. This chapter reviewed several notions of what happens after death. These included: (a) immortality of the soul, (b) resurrection of the body, (c) life continued in a place of bliss (heaven) or torture (hell) or exceeding boredom (the Greek Hades), (d) rebirth (transmigration or reincarnation of the soul), (e) a life much like this one only somewhere else, and (f) permanent peace and stillness (nirvana, extinction). Which of these views are you inclined toward? How might your response to this question affect how you live your life? How might it influence how you treat someone else who is dying?
2. This chapter discussed near-death experiences. What is your assessment of what such experiences can or do tell us about what happens to us after we die?

Suggested Readings

For religious perspectives on death-related issues, consult:

Badham, P., & Badham, L. (Eds.). (1987). *Death and Immortality in the Religions of the World.*

Bailey, L. (1978). *Biblical Perspectives on Death.*

Frazer, J. G. (1977). *The Fear of the Dead in Primitive Religion.*

Gatch, M. McC. (1969). *Death: Meaning and Mortality in Christian Thought and Contemporary Culture.*

Johnson, C. J., & McGee, M. G. (Eds.). (1998). *How Different Religions View Death and Afterlife.*

Mills, L. O. (Ed.). (1969). *Perspectives on Death.*

Opoku, K. A. (1978). *West African Traditional Religion.*

Radin, P. (1973). *The Road of Life and Death: A Ritual Drama of the American Indians.*

Rahner, K. (1973). *On the Theology of Death.*

Reynolds, F. E., & Waugh, E. H. (Eds.). (1977). *Religious Encounters with Death: Insights from the History and Anthropology of Religion.*

For philosophical, conceptual, and other perspectives on death-related issues, see:

Berger, A., Badham, P., Kutscher, A. H., Berger, J., Perry, M., & Beloff, J. (Eds.). (1989). *Perspectives on Death and Dying: Cross-Cultural and Multi-Disciplinary Views.*

Carse, J. P. (1980). *Death and Existence: A Conceptual History of Mortality.*

Chan, W.-T. (1963). *A Sourcebook in Chinese Philosophy.*

Choron, J. (1963). *Death and Western Thought.*

Choron, J. (1964). *Death and Modern Man.*

Congdon, H. K. (1977). *The Pursuit of Death.*

Cox, G. R., & Fundis, R. J. (Eds.). (1992). *Spiritual, Ethical and Pastoral Aspects of Death and Bereavement.*

Doka, K. J., with Morgan, J. D. (Eds.). (1993). *Death and Spirituality.*

Durkheim, E. (1915/1954). *The Elementary Forms of Religious Life.*

Frankl, V. (1984). *Man's Search for Meaning.*

Grof, S., & Halifax, J. (1978). *The Human Encounter with Death.*

Kauffman, J. (Ed.). (1995). *Awareness of Mortality.*

Mbiti, J. S. (1970). *African Religion and Philosophy.*

Momeyer, R. W. (1988). *Confronting Death.*

Radhakrishnan, S., & Moore, C. (1957). *A Sourcebook in Indian Philosophy.*

Terkel, S. (2001). *Will the Circle Be Unbroken?: Reflections on Death, Rebirth, and Hunger for a Faith.*

Toynbee, A., Koestler, A., & Others. (1976). *Life after Death.*

Toynbee, A., Mant, A. K., Smart, N., Hinton, J., Yudkin, S., Rhode, E., Heywood, R., & Price, H. H. (1968). *Man's Concern with Death.*

Issues related to near-death experiences are examined in:

Fenwick, P., & Fenwick, E. (1995). *The Truth in the Light: An Investigation of Over 300 Near-Death Experiences.*

Kellehear, A. (1996). *Experiences near Death: Beyond Medicine and Religion.*

Moody, R. A. (1975). *Life after Life.*

Moody, R. A. (1988). *The Light Beyond.*

Osis, K., & Haraldsson, E. (1997). *At the Hour of Death* (3rd ed.).

Ring, K. (1980). *Life at Death: A Scientific Investigation of the Near-Death Experience.*

Ring, K. (1984). *Heading Toward Omega: In Search of the Meaning of the Near-Death Experience.*

Sabom, M. B. (1982). *Recollections of Death: A Medical Investigation.*

Zaleski, C. (1987). *Otherworld Journeys: Accounts of Near-Death Experience in Medieval and Modern Times.*

InfoTrac College Edition
For more information, explore the InfoTrac College Edition at **http://www.infotrac-college.com/Wadsworth**

Enter search terms: IMMORTALITY OF THE SOUL, NEAR-DEATH EXPERIENCES, REINCARNATION, RESURRECTION OF THE BODY.

Part Seven

New Challenges and Opportunities

In Chapter 20, we turn to death-related experiences that only came to attention during the last two decades of the 20th century: infection by the human immunodeficiency virus (HIV) and its end state, acquired immunodeficiency syndrome (AIDS). In particular, we use our discussion of these particular life-threatening diseases to illuminate in a concentrated manner the organizing concepts that form the framework of this book: death-related encounters, attitudes, and practices; gender, cultural, and developmental differences; and task work in coping with dying and bereavement.

In selecting HIV and AIDS for discussion in Chapter 20, we do not mean to minimize the importance of other diseases or causes of death. We chose to focus attention on HIV infection and AIDS because they have not always been well understood by the general public, and because our understanding of and experiences with them have changed rapidly over the past 20 years.

HIV infection poses new death-related challenges because it involves a new disease entity. For some time before the appearance of HIV and AIDS in the United States, most communicable diseases seemed less and less significant as agents of mortality. Then HIV arrived on the world scene as a mysterious, frightening, and lethal cause of death. It also arrived with quite a rush and with great power. As the Centers for Disease Control and Prevention (1992b, p. 142) observed: "The recognition of a disease and its emergence as a leading cause of death within the same decade is without precedent." From a global standpoint, it has been noted that "twenty years after the first clinical evidence of acquired immunodeficiency syndrome was reported, AIDS has become the most devastating disease humankind has ever faced" (UNAIDS, 2001b, p. 1). Of course, despite the novel features of HIV infection and AIDS, many of their general implications for both individuals, societies, and the international community will be familiar to persons who are knowledgeable about the dynamics of previous epidemics and about elements that enter into human interactions with death.

The point we mean to emphasize here is that HIV and AIDS force human beings to struggle once again with the four sets of enduring themes we identified in Chapter 1 that can be learned about human life and living as a result of studying death, dying, and bereavement: limitation and control, vulnerability and resilience, individuality and community, and quality in living and the search for meaning. ■

Chapter Twenty

HIV INFECTION AND AIDS

In this chapter, we draw together many of the principal concerns of this book through an examination of death-related issues as they are associated with infection by the human immunodeficiency virus (HIV) and its end state, acquired immunodeficiency syndrome (AIDS). Throughout this book, we have examined task work involved in coping with death-related challenges. Here we explore coping associated with encounters, attitudes, and practices that arise from a specific disease entity: HIV infection and AIDS.

We begin with the story of a family coping with AIDS, which emphasizes the growing impact of HIV infection and AIDS on families, women, and children. Next, we offer separate introductions to AIDS and to HIV. Then, we look at coping with HIV infection and AIDS: coping by individuals, as well as coping at the community, national, and international levels. Taken as a whole, this chapter can serve readers either as a kind of illustrative summary of many issues addressed in this book (if one ends here) or it can stand on its own as an introduction to those issues (if one begins here). ■

A Family Coping with AIDS

Even though Wanda Cooksey was only 52, she was tired. She worked five nights a week from 6:00 P.M. to 6:00 A.M. at a QuickStop store. It was a grueling schedule and sometimes late at night Wanda worried about her own safety. But this was the only full-time job that she had been able to get that allowed her to earn enough to support herself and her mother, and to take care of her two granddaughters.

A friend had helped Wanda get this job after her daughter, Melonie, had died of AIDS seven months earlier. Melonie had been an attractive young woman who was enrolled in cosmetology school when she met Harry, who swept her off her feet. She had not realized until too late that Harry had had many sexual partners and had not practiced safe sex with them. About a year and a half after Melonie and Harry were married, Harry had some flu like symptoms, but they only lasted briefly and the couple didn't pay much attention to them. They were both doing well at work and both were enjoying family life. They loved their first baby, Melissa, and were eagerly awaiting the birth of their second child.

A while later Harry became weaker and began to lose weight. When he found it difficult to go to work every day, Harry went to the doctor and was diagnosed with AIDS. The clinic recommended that other members in the family be tested. Testing showed that Melonie, Melissa, and the new baby were HIV positive also.

Harry's disease progressed quickly. As he got weaker and felt himself becoming confused, he became depressed. One day, while Melonie was at work and without warning, he took his life. Melonie was devastated. It seemed that all her dreams and hopes had suddenly been shattered. She felt that she had been left alone to cope with her own illness and to care for her two young daughters. She turned to her mother for help.

Melonie's disease progressed more slowly than Harry's, perhaps because she had been in good health when she was diagnosed and because there were more treatments available now. With the help of a nutritionist and the latest drug regimens, she was able to continue to work in the beauty shop. Her mother's help with the children made this possible. Melonie did fairly well for five years, even though her T-cell counts continued to diminish on an irregular basis. During the last winter of her life, however, she contracted a severe pneumonia, developed complications, and died.

Before Melonie's death, Wanda had never worked outside the home. She owned her house and had a modest pension from her husband's company. That had been enough to support her, and Melonie's earnings had filled out her resources while Wanda, Melonie, and the two children lived together. But with Melonie's death, Wanda's financial and personal situation became much more difficult. Now, in the midst of her grief at the death of her daughter, she had to get a job to maintain herself and her granddaughters. She finally asked her own mother, Grace, to sell her house in Arkansas and come live with her to help out.

The girls were doing reasonably well at home and in school, but over the past two to three years their overall health had deteriorated. They didn't have as much strength as they should have, they missed their mother very much, and sometimes they didn't even want to eat. Wanda asked her minister for some help, and he eventually told her about a pediatric hospice program in a nearby community that might be able to offer her their services. Even with that assistance, she awaited the future with apprehension and a deepening grief.

An Introduction to AIDS

In order to understand AIDS, we need to know some facts about the early history of this disease, including its first known appearances, as well as what it means to have AIDS near the beginning of the 21st century. We address the first of these dimensions here; we discuss the second in the remainder of this chapter.

AIDS was first brought to public attention in the United States through a report on June 5, 1981, in the *Morbidity and Mortality Weekly Report*, a publication of the U.S. Centers for Disease Control (since renamed the Centers for Disease Control and Prevention, but still widely referred to as the CDC). The report (CDC, 1981a; see also Gottlieb, M. S., et al., 1981) described five young men who had been admitted to hospitals in the Los Angeles area with an unusual type of pneumonia. Prior to that time, the pneumonia in question (which is caused by a commonly occurring protozoan, *Pneumocystis carinii*) had mainly been seen in individuals with immune system deficiencies—for example, in newborns or in adults treated with immunosuppressive drugs.

Shortly thereafter, another group of young men in New York City were reported to have *Pneumocystis carinii* pneumonia and a hitherto rare form of cancer. The cancer (*Kaposi's sarcoma*) is a tumor of blood vessel tissue in the skin and/or internal organs that had previously been found in relatively benign forms and only among elderly Italian and Jewish men of Mediterranean descent (CDC, 1981b; Gottlieb, G. J., et al., 1981; Hymes et al., 1981). Between June and August of 1981, the CDC (1981c) reported 110 of these unusual cases, all involving otherwise healthy males who were homosexual. All of these men were dying quite rapidly at a relatively young age (15–52 years old) of infectious diseases that were otherwise seldom fatal in America.

As these reports continued to appear, they were supplemented by information about similar occurrences of unusual life-threatening conditions in other groups of people, such as hemophiliacs, Haitian immigrants, intravenous drug users, children in families in which one or both parents had the disease, and heterosexual partners (female or male) of persons with the disease. Three points soon became clear. First, despite their differences, it was realized that all of the reports involved *a common syndrome*—a clinical entity or recognizable pattern of manifestations arising from an underlying cause that was as yet unknown. Second, the pattern pointed to *a deficiency in the immune systems* of those experiencing this syndrome. In other words, the syndrome suggested there were problems involving the specific systems that normally defend the body against foreign invaders. When these systems do not function properly, those involved fall victim to external invaders and internal forces that normally are not troublesome for those with healthy immune systems. Third, there seemed to be no common genetic or natural basis for this syndrome, which suggested that the deficiency in the immune systems of these individuals had somehow been *acquired.* As a result, it was concluded that affected individuals had an *acquired immunodeficiency syndrome* or *AIDS.*

Because the underlying cause of AIDS remained unknown in the early years of the epidemic, the CDC could not explain why these individuals were experiencing immune dysfunction. By the early 1990s, however, the CDC (1992) had learned a great deal about this syndrome and implemented a new definition of AIDS. It was now defined as a situation in which individuals had a CD4+ T-lymphocyte (often called *T-cells* for short) count of less than 200 per microliter (a normal count is around 1,000 per microliter). Note that this definition is based on a biological or laboratory marker, rather than a clinical finding. That led to two important consequences: (1) individuals with AIDS were able to be diagnosed much earlier so that understandings of average length of survival of people with the disease changed as persons living with AIDS were seen to live much longer than had been previously expected; and (2) more cases of AIDS were identified, particularly among women and children whose disease had often gone unrecognized when clinicians interpreted AIDS primarily through clinical manifestations most often found in adult males.

Putting all of this together, we now know that AIDS is a condition in which an individual's immune system has become so dysfunctional that the person falls victim to opportunistic infections or unusual diseases and is therefore at heightened risk of dying. (Some Internet, telephone, and journal resources for ongoing information about AIDS and HIV are listed in Box 20.1.)

An Introduction to HIV

Early Indicators about the Cause of AIDS

The fact that AIDS appeared in a large number of hemophiliacs provided an important, early clue concerning the nature of the underlying cause of this syndrome. Hemophiliacs already had one life-threatening disease in the form of a blood clotting disorder that made them susceptible to internal and external bleeding problems. To combat their bleeding problems, hemophiliacs typically receive transfusions of blood or blood products. Perhaps the transfusions were themselves somehow contaminated with an unknown agent that caused AIDS?

Those who supply blood in the United States and in other industrialized countries make many efforts to ensure the purity of the blood and blood products that they collect and provide for transfusion. For example, our blood system *screens* potential donors and *filters* the blood that they donate to remove potential contaminants. But some wondered whether there were an as-yet-unidentified contaminant that was neither recognized nor removed by these procedures from donated blood and blood products. For instance, only *sterilization* of such blood and blood products would kill a microscopic virus.

Box 20.1 Some Ongoing Resources on HIV and AIDS

Telephone Numbers and Web Sites:

- AIDS Education and Training Centers, Health Resources and Services Administration: 410-955-7634; www.hab.hrsa.gov/wel.html
- American Foundation for AIDS Research: 323-857-5900; www.amfar.org
- Canadian AIDS Society: 613-230-3580; www.cdnaids.ca
- Canadian HIV/AIDS Clearinghouse (a project of the Canadian Public Health Association): 613-725-3434; in Canada, 877-999-7740; www.cpha.ca
- CDC National HIV/AIDS Hotline: 800-342-2437; 800-344-7432 (Spanish); www.cdc.gov/hiv
- Elizabeth Glaser Pediatric AIDS Foundation: 888-499-HOPE (4673); 310-314-1459; www.pedaids.org
- National AIDS Clearinghouse (a project of the National Prevention Information Network, National Center for HIV, STD, and TB Prevention): 800-458-5231; www.cdcnpin.org
- National Association on HIV Over Fifty: 816-421-5263; www.hivoverfifty.org
- National Minority AIDS Council: 202-483-6622, www.nmac.org
- National Native American AIDS Prevention Center: 510-444-2051, www.nnaapc.org
- Positive Education, Inc.: 813-831-4159; www.pos-ed.org
- UNAIDS: www.unaids.org

Journals:

- *a & u*, Art & Understanding, Inc., mailbox@aumag.org.
- *POZ*, POZ Publishing, www.poz.com.
- *POZ en Español*, POZ Publishing, GonzaloA@pox.com
- *HIV Plus*, Liberation Publications, Inc., www.hivplusmag.com
- *Journal of Acquired Immune Deficiency Syndromes and Human Retrovirology*, Lippincott-Raven Publishers, www.jaids.com
- *Journal of the International Association of Physicians in AIDS Care*, Medical Publications Corp., www.iapac.org ■

Furthermore, although AIDS had once been referred to as "Gay Related Immune Disorder" (GRID) and although other adults with this syndrome might have transmitted its causal agent to each other through sexual activity, the same could hardly apply to infants and young children. It would seem that infants with AIDS, in particular, were very likely somehow to have acquired the agent that was producing their immune disorder from their mothers before, at the time of, or shortly after their births. The obvious question thus became: What sort of causal agent could be transmitted in all of these ways—from mother to child, via direct sexual behavior, or indirectly through transfused blood and blood products?

Ultimately, the answer was that *AIDS was caused by a virus*, one that eventually came to be called the human immunodeficiency virus (HIV). Intensive research by French and American scientists identified that virus in 1983 (see Grmek, 1990). Soon scientists were also able to identify and test for antibodies manufactured by human immune systems in their fight to repel this foreign agent. Antibody testing is still often used as a screening test for HIV infection. However, it may take the immune system of a person infected with HIV several weeks or months to manufacture such antibodies. Therefore, a single antibody test may not suffice to identify antibodies to HIV in a recently-infected person. In the meantime, individuals who are unaware of their HIV status or whose bodies have not had time to develop the antibodies that would register in a test may actually be infected with the virus and capable of transmitting it to others. In fact, some first-time donors in the United States who rushed to give blood after the terrorist attacks on America on September 11, 2001, only learned when their blood was tested that they were positive for HIV, hepatitis, syphilis, or other antigens (*St. Petersburg Times*, 2001d).

HIV Transmission

Identification of the HIV had many consequences. It quickly became clear that the virus can only be transmitted from one human to another and that it is not spread through casual contact (e.g., through using a telephone, sharing eating utensils, or touching and hugging an infected person). The primary routes of transmission through which HIV is spread are: (1) having unprotected vaginal, anal, or oral sex with an infected person (and thus exchanging semen, vaginal fluid, and/or blood); (2) by sharing needles or syringes with an infected person (and thus exchanging even microscopic quantities of blood); and (3) from mother to child through blood or breast milk.

On this basis, health educators advised the public that *the most effective ways to prevent* HIV infection are: not having vaginal, anal, or oral sex with an infected person; having sex only with a mutually monogamous uninfected person who does not share needles or syringes with anyone; not injecting nonprescribed drugs (never start or get into treatment); not sharing needles or syringes for any reason (even injecting vitamins, steroids, tattooing, or body piercing); and not engaging in activities that involve exchange of blood, semen, vaginal fluids, or breast milk. Further, the risk of HIV infection can be *reduced* by: using a latex condom every time during vaginal, anal, or oral sex; not using drugs or alcohol, which can cloud a person's judgment; cleaning needles and syringes with chlorine bleach and water if more effective prevention is not available; and using barrier protection such as latex gloves when coming into contact with blood or fluids that could contain blood.

Strenuous efforts to teach people how to prevent HIV infection have not always proved successful. Many who know how the virus is transmitted are unwilling or unable to take the steps needed to prevent infection. Some decline to remain sexually abstinent, to practice safer sex techniques, and to avoid injecting drugs or sharing unsterile needles and syringes. Others wrongly believe that they will not get infected if they have unprotected sex only once with a partner whose HIV status is unknown or if they share an unsterile needle only once. But a single exposure can result in infection, even if it does not always do so. Some people even seem to believe that becoming infected is no longer life threatening, because there now are medications available to control it. This attitude ignores the drastic life changes that go along with those medications, as well as the facts that these medications have difficult and dangerous side effects, do not work for everyone, and are unlikely to work permanently. For all of these reasons, there are now an increasing number of individuals living with AIDS in the United States, and there has been no decline in the numbers of individuals who are newly infected with HIV (see Table 20.1).

HIV in the Body

The ways in which HIV operates in an infected person's body are complicated and multifaceted. In general, HIV primarily attacks a special kind of white blood cell called a helper T4 lymphocyte. These T4 cells are the ones that organize the body's immune response to a large variety of infections and disease organisms. Under normal circumstances, the T4 is precisely the type of cell that would be among the principal enemies of HIV. HIV also appears to attack macrophages, another form of white blood cells that migrate to all parts of the body to provide protection from disease. Infected macrophages may spread HIV to cells of the central nervous system (the brain and spinal cord), thereby producing dementia and other sorts of mental disorders that are often seen in AIDS.

HIV is a retrovirus whose genetic material is RNA instead of the usual DNA. When the virus enters the affected cell, it acts through an enzyme called reverse transcriptase to turn its RNA into DNA. It then integrates this new viral DNA into the chromosomes of the cell, begins to replicate or produce new copies of itself, and eventually spreads throughout the body to infect new cells. In these

Table 20.1 Estimated Number of Persons Reported to be Living with HIV Infection[a] and Living with AIDS by Age,[b] United States, reported through June 2001

	Living with HIV Infection[c]	Living with AIDS[d]
Adults and adolescents	132,878	328,901
Children <13 years old	1,627	2,617
Total	134,505	331,518

[a] Includes only persons reported with HIV infection who have not developed AIDS.
[b] Age group based on person's age as of June 30, 2001.
[c] Includes only persons reported from areas with confidential HIV reporting. Excludes 2,273 adults/adolescents and 49 children reported from areas with confidential HIV infection reporting whose area of residence is unknown or are residents of other areas.
[d] Includes 431 adults/adolescents and 6 children whose area of residence is unknown.

SOURCE: CDC, 2002.

ways, the HIV further weakens or destroys the immune system of the infected individual. If this is permitted to go on unchecked, the result is a general, overall weakening of the body's ability to function effectively, and an increasing vulnerability to the opportunistic infections and other life-threatening challenges that the body will no longer be able to resist effectively. In many cases, this means that an individual in the advanced phase of HIV infection is likely to encounter a series of infections, medical and nutritional interventions to contain these infections, and eventually, reinfections. Each of these infections represents its own relatively unpredictable assault from one or more of a variety of possible sources; each counterattack may involve a mobilization of one's remaining natural defenses along with whatever resources are available from modern medicine.

Interventions to Fight HIV Infection

With the virus identified, scientists were able to trace the HIV itself in its various strains and mutations, and to measure the so-called "viral load" in the blood of a person who was "HIV positive" (i.e., who had acquired the virus). This made possible a wide range of interventions intended to respond either to symptoms typically associated with HIV/AIDS or to the viral infection itself. These included nutritional strategies to strengthen the body's overall health, as well as prophylactic and therapeutic regimens to respond to the presence or threat of specific symptoms and opportunistic infections. In response to HIV infection itself, a series of "combination therapies" (also called HAART or "highly active anti-retroviral therapy") came into use in the mid-1990s. These therapies involved the use of several drugs in precise combinations, including reverse transcriptase inhibitors (which interrupt early stages of HIV replication) and protease inhibitors (which inhibit a part of the virus so as to prevent its replications from infecting new cells). It is important to note, however, that these combination therapies or drug cocktails are quite expensive, often have significant side effects, and are very demanding in terms of patient compliance. Typically, a large number of pills—as many as 20 or 30—must be taken per day on a very strict schedule, some with food and some on an empty stomach (Ungvarski, 1997; see Box 20.2). Failure to comply with a prescribed regimen might result in an individual's becoming immune to an entire class of drugs.

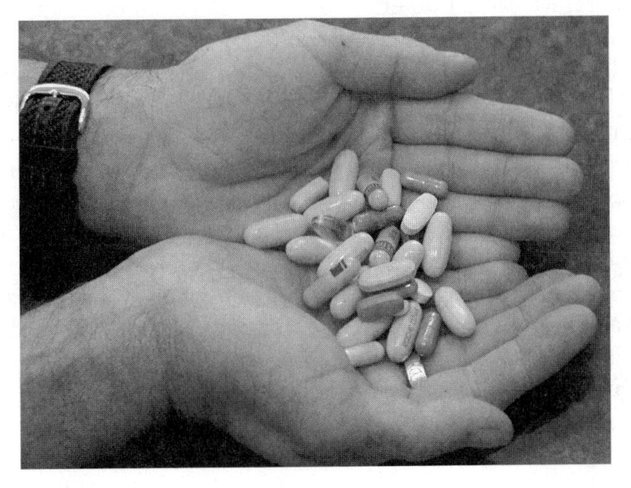

An example of the diversity and number of medications taken by one person with AIDS.

Box 20.2 A Typical Medicine Regimen for an End-Stage AIDS Patient

Daily medications:

Norvir, 100 mg	4 capsules twice a day with food (a protease inhibitor)
Fortovase, 200 mg	2 capsules twice a day with food (a protease inhibitor)
Zerit, 40 mg	1 capsule twice a day (a retroviral inhibitor)
Videx EC, 400 mg	1 capsule daily on empty stomach (a retroviral inhibitor)
Marinol, 10 mg	1 capsule twice a day (anti-nausea)
Bactrim, DS	1 tablet daily (for PCP prophylaxis; to fight infection)
Ultrase MT-20	1–2 capsules with each meal (for diarrhea)
Lopid, 600 mg	1 tablet twice a day with meals (for abnormal lipids)
Oxandrin, 2.5 mg	4 tablets twice a day (for wasting)

Weekly medications:

Zithromax, 600 mg	2 tablets once a week (for MAC prophylaxis; to fight infection)

PRN (as needed) medications:

Imodium, 2 mg	up to 8 capsules per day as needed (for diarrhea)
Compazine, 10 mg	1 tablet every 6 hours as needed (for nausea)

Totals:

Daily:	31–34 per day routinely
Weekly:	2 per week routinely
PRN:	as many as 12 in a day as needed ■

SOURCE: Based on information from LeAnn Isaly, MS, ARNP-C, ACRN, of the Pinellas Care Clinic.

Nevertheless, deaths and death rates dropped dramatically as the new combination therapies came into effect (see Table 20.2). For example, deaths associated with HIV in the United States declined by over 25 percent from 1995 to 1996 and by 70 percent from 1995 to 2000. As deaths have been reduced and the lives of many individuals have been prolonged, more and more people are living with AIDS.

However, the HIV has demonstrated its ability to mutate and eventually to become resistant to the drugs being used against it. This is a developing problem for the treatment of the disease, since by the end of 2001 it appeared that many if not most HIV infected persons had developed at least some virus strains resistant to some of the available drugs. Even when the viral load in the bloodstream of a person living with AIDS can no longer be measured, scientists have learned that the HIV has not been eradicated. It is merely in remission—it may be hiding in the body's tissues and organs, it can return in force, and there may still be a risk of transmitting this undetectable HIV. Thus, many are concerned that high expectations for these combination therapies will soon no longer be

Table 20.2 Estimated Deaths of Persons with AIDS, by Race/Ethnicity and Year of Death, 1993–2000, United States

	Year of death							
Race/ethnicity	1993	1994	1995	1996	1997	1998	1999	2000
Caucasian Americans, not Hispanic	21,803	22,828	22,189	14,665	7,310	6,016	5,234	4,532
African Americans, not Hispanic	15,543	18,024	19,115	15,936	10,316	8,803	8,576	7,781
Hispanic origin	7,780	8,976	9,215	6,992	4,116	3,368	3,166	2,780
Asian Americans and Pacific Islanders	307	410	366	293	154	124	114	90
Native Americans	134	154	195	132	93	76	73	57
Other/unknown	31	26	37	8	10	9	10	5
Total[a]	45,598	50,418	51,117	38,025	21,999	18,397	17,172	15,245

[a] Totals include estimates of persons whose race/ethnicity is unknown.
SOURCE: CDC, 2002.

met and that it may no longer be possible to postpone or prevent many additional deaths from HIV infection.

Who Becomes Infected with HIV and Dies of AIDS in the United States Today?

Even as we observe from Table 20.2 the very large declines in AIDS-related deaths that took place from 1995 to 2000 in the United States, it is important to note racial and ethnic differences in those declines. For example, AIDS-related deaths among non-Hispanic Caucasian Americans declined by nearly 80 percent during this period, but similar deaths among non-Hispanic African Americans only declined by about 59 percent and declines among the other three cultural groups noted in Table 20.2 taken together were about 70 percent. Obviously, declines were not uniform among all groups in American society.

Declines in AIDS-related deaths between 1995 and 2000 in the United States also show notable differences by sex, exposure category, and age (see Table 20.3). For example, declines of 72.9 percent among adult and adolescent males during these years are much larger than those of 55.1 percent among adult and adolescent females. Similarly, declines among men who have sex with men (78.3 percent) are far higher than those among injecting drug users, either males (67.3 percent) or females (56.5 percent). Declines among AIDS-related deaths arising from heterosexual contact are lowest of all, ranging from 49.0 percent for males and 52.5 percent for females.

Clearly, HIV infection and AIDS-related deaths are gradually, but increasingly, becoming experiences of women, persons of color, young people 18 to 25

Table 20.3 Estimated Deaths of Persons with AIDS, by Age Group, Sex, Exposure Category, and Year of Death, 1993–2000, United States

	Year of death							
	1993	1994	1995	1996	1997	1998	1999	2000
Male adult/adolescent exposure category:								
Men who have sex with men	23,956	25,534	25,044	16,854	8,666	7,048	6,230	5,439
Injecting drug use	9,325	10,454	10,844	8,551	5,346	4,476	4,119	3,551
Men who have sex with men and inject drugs	3,188	3,528	3,467	2,591	1,447	1,262	1,182	1,120
Hemophilia/coagulation disorder	357	346	330	246	136	117	100	*
Heterosexual contact	1,600	2,013	2,389	2,111	1,464	1,227	1,257	1,218
Receipt of blood transfusion, blood components, or tissue	314	304	259	217	108	83	73	*
Other/risk not reported or identified	168	143	102	66	44	28	29	187
Male subtotal	38,908	42,322	42,434	30,636	17,212	14,241	12,991	11,514
Female adult/adolescent exposure category:								
Injecting drug use	3,152	3,713	3,824	3,289	2,137	1,900	1,920	1,662
Hemophilia/coagulation disorder	17	28	31	30	20	14	17	*
Heterosexual contact	2,662	3,489	3,999	3,439	2,297	2,029	2,032	1,899
Receipt of blood transfusion, blood components, or tissue	238	224	235	170	93	75	75	*
Other/risk not reported or identified	77	56	56	32	20	15	19	95
Female subtotal	6,146	7,510	8,144	6,960	4,567	4,033	4,063	3,656
Pediatric (<13 years old) exposure category:	544	586	539	429	221	123	118	74
Total	45,598	50,418	51,117	38,025	21,999	18,307	17,112	15,245

* Data not available or included in "other" category.

SOURCE: CDC, 2002.

years of age, and even the elderly in the United States (see Box 20.3 for an example of one woman who would never have imagined she could test positive for HIV at the age of 55 in 1991).

AIDS-related deaths among children less than 13 years old in the United States declined by 86.3 percent between 1995 and 2000. In the period from 1995 to 1999, all AIDS-related deaths associated with hemophilia and coagulation disorders, together with all such deaths linked to blood transfusions, blood components, or tissue transplants, declined by 67.0 percent to represent only 0.6 percent of all such deaths. That leaves as the primary (but not exclusive) exposure categories for HIV infection and AIDS-related deaths in our society today: men who have sex with men, injecting drug users, and individuals engaged in heterosexual contact.

Box 20.3 Jane Fowler: Why Me?

Early in January 1991, shortly after returning home to Kansas City from a happy Christmas holiday, Jane Fowler found in her accumulated mail a letter that declined her application for new health insurance. The letter said that her blood test had disclosed a significant abnormality and indicated that her physician would be notified.

When she called the company, they declined on grounds of confidentiality to explain the nature of the abnormality. Then, when she visited her doctor, she was told that the insurance company claimed that she had tested positive for HIV! A second, anonymous test at a local health care facility confirmed that diagnosis.

Jane was stunned. She was 55, had lived a conventional life, did not do drugs, and had lived monogamously with her husband for 23 years until they separated in 1982. After her divorce, Jane reported that she did sleep with a few men—men who were her own age, recently divorced, and not strangers. One of these men, Jim, had been a close friend all her adult life.

Jane retreated from her diagnosis into a period of self-imposed isolation. The image of Rock Hudson pressed in on her, wasted and diminished by AIDS before his death in 1985.

But she didn't actually feel sick. She says she wouldn't have known she was infected without the insurance company's test. A journalist, Jane researched HIV and found that the initial infection is often followed by a brief period of flu-like symptoms. Sure enough, she recalled such symptoms in early 1986 and was able to confirm visits to her doctor at that time with those complaints.

After suffering from annoying skin conditions and becoming a compulsive hand washer to fight germs, by the middle of 1991 Jane retired, telling her friends that she wanted to reduce her stress and protect her health. But in fact, "I withdrew because I lacked the courage to face possible discrimination, rejection, and intolerance. I became a recluse over the next four years . . ."

At one point, Jane contacted her friend, Jim, after confirming from her diaries that they had spent a happy New Year's Eve together five years earlier and had unprotected sex that night. He denied being infected and hung up, calling back later angry that she might have discussed her disease with mutual friends and that she had given his name (and those of her other sexual partners) to the local health department. Jim never directly admitted that he was infected, acknowledged that he might have been the source of Jane's infection, or said he was sorry. He died in 1995.

Jim's death helped Jane to rethink her reactions to her illness and to overcome her isolation. She decided to acknowledge her predicament publicly and to speak about HIV to those who are not infected. Jane wanted especially to talk about HIV prevention and, in particular, to risks involving those her own

(continues)

Box 20.3 (cont.) Jane Fowler: Why Me?

age. Jane did this even though she had stage fright and did not find it easy to discuss intimate aspects of her life.

In her talks, Jane spoke about the new drug therapies that became available in 1996 and explained how the complicated dosing regimen of those drugs restricted her life. She discussed the difficult side effects of the drugs, including diarrhea, nausea, malaise, hair loss, and lipodystrophy, an accumulation of fat that made her midsection look just like it had 36 years earlier just before delivering her son—robustly pregnant.

Jane Fowler now travels and speaks extensively as co-chair of the National Association on HIV Over Fifty, based in Chicago, Illinois. ■

SOURCE: Based on Fowler, 2000.

Coping with HIV Infection and AIDS

Because HIV infection and AIDS are evolving phenomena, they demand continual changes in the ways in which we think about, understand, and respond to them. As we have noted, the virus itself is constantly changing, both in its behavior within the infected person's body and genetically over time. HIV infection has also constantly changed in terms of the groups most affected by it, at least in the industrialized nations, as we have seen. As a result, coping with HIV infection and AIDS taxes not only the resources of an infected person, but also those of local, national, and international communities.

In the remainder of this chapter we describe these different forms of coping with HIV and AIDS. Examining HIV/AIDS from these perspectives serves as a way to help organize the bewildering amount of information—and uncertainty—arising from human experiences with HIV infection and AIDS.

Coping with HIV Infection and AIDS by Individuals

As with any life-threatening situation, there are two groups of persons who are drawn into *coping with HIV infection and AIDS as individuals.* These two groups are *those who are infected themselves* and *those who are not infected but who are affected* because someone they know or love is infected. In some situations, these two groups are joined in one individual: a person who must cope with his or her own infection while also being affected by and forced to cope with the effects of an infection in another person, such as a family member or a friend. This reflects what we learned in earlier chapters: life-threatening illnesses have impacts on many individuals (not only those who are suffering from the illness) and in different ways.

Those who are infected see their lives changed dramatically in many ways: physically, emotionally, socially, economically, and spiritually. HIV infection does not result merely in minor changes, since it impacts so much of an individual's life. First, the person is confronted with his or her mortality in a way similar to all who face a life-threatening illness. When it was first recognized, HIV infection was taken to mean that death was near. Subsequently, however, it became clear that the situation is a good deal more ambiguous. Even before treatments were developed, the health of some infected persons was less impacted than that of others; not all of them moved quickly toward death. With the development of combination therapies and other interventions, the length of time between infection and death has typically lengthened, up to ten years and longer. This has led some to claim that HIV infection should be seen as a chronic, rather than an acute, disease. In turn, this has been taken by many to mean that it need not be life threatening if it is treated appropriately.

Still, the period of time after being infected is hardly a return to "normalcy." For instance, an infected individual's typical day is punctuated by the need to keep careful track of large numbers of medications. Along with the disease itself, these medications, especially after they have been used for many years, have short-term and long-term side effects, ranging from nausea, vomiting, and diarrhea to bone marrow suppression and toxic effects on the liver, kidneys, pancreas, and/or brain that result in diabetes, extremely high cholesterol, and dental problems (Sherman, 2001; see Box 20.4). Many have experienced lipid redistribution (lipodystrophy) producing an accumulation of fat around the shoulders ("buffalo hump") or midsection ("Protease paunch"). In addition, because the drugs used to treat HIV infection are themselves so toxic, it is uncertain that the infection can be controlled indefinitely. What this means is that HIV infection is still likely eventually to end in death for at least many infected persons.

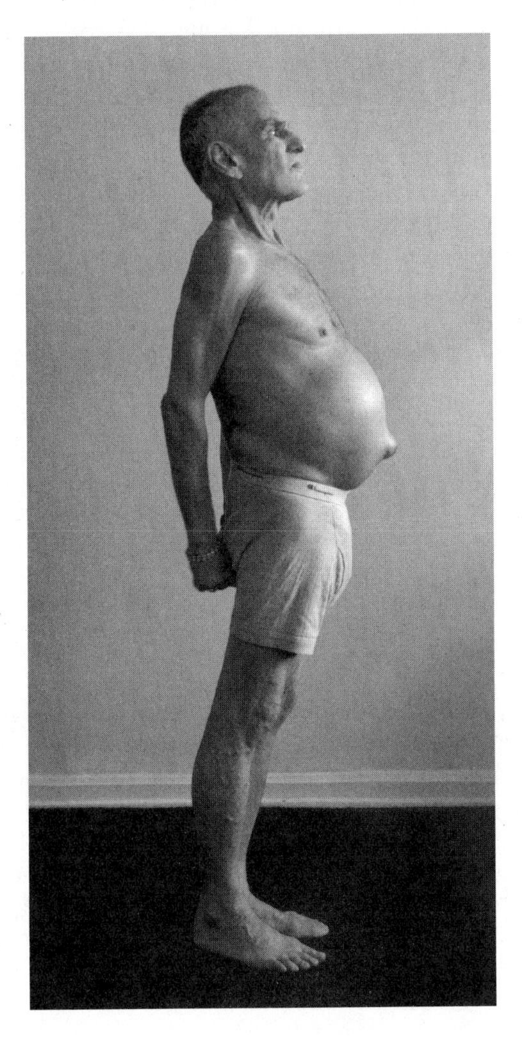

This photo of Larry Kramer illustrates one of the possible side effects that can be associated with HIV infection.

Box 20.4 Larry Kramer

Larry Kramer wrote about AIDS as early as 1981, and in 1982 he helped found the Gay Men's Health Crisis in New York, now the world's largest AIDS-service organization.

In March 1987, Kramer also founded the activist organization ACT UP (AIDS Coalition to Unleash Power). To protest the slow pace of drug research, members of ACT UP invaded the New York Stock Exchange and chained themselves to the rails. They also staged "die-ins" and political funerals, going so far as to bring the bodies of dead friends in open coffins to the gates of the White House in order to shock the government into action.

Kramer learned that he was infected with HIV in 1988. He began taking AZT pills that fall, but did not take the protease inhibitors that became available in 1996, even though they dramatically reduced AIDS-related deaths (so much so that ACT UP withered away). Kramer was fortunate that the side effects of his infection and medications were minimal for many years, and he did not experience grotesque lipodystrophy or many other complications.

Nevertheless, at the age of 65 Kramer developed end-stage liver disease. Because his liver did not process toxins from his blood, they collected in his abdomen and put pressure on his diaphragm. As a result, breathing and speaking were at times very difficult for Kramer. Doctors drew off these fluids—as much as 14 liters at a time—but they returned in a few weeks. Some experts believe "liver cirrhosis like Kramer's may soon become the leading cause of death for people with AIDS" (France, 2001, p. 44).

In December 2001, Kramer received a liver transplant, a procedure once rejected for those infected with the HIV, but with the advent of better control of the virus, now a possibility. Before his transplant, one commentator wrote, "If he survives the surgery, as most do, he will be given immune-suppressing medications to keep his body from rejecting the new tissue. This will cause his HIV to run rampant. So he will finally go on the drug cocktails he has so far avoided, hoping they will not let him down" (France, 2001, p. 46). ■

SOURCE: Based on France, 2001.

Life changes in other ways, too. Early responses of fear and ignorance all too often led to social stigma and outright discrimination (Sontag, 1989). Many ill persons were treated badly in the workplace, in schools, or in matters of housing. Health care workers who were afraid for their own safety frequently provided inadequate care. Some infected persons internalized a sense of stigma, hiding their HIV status or even isolating themselves socially. Of course, any form of discrimination, arising from others or from one's self, can interfere with the ability of an infected person to receive needed support from others. Against this, social decisions to include HIV infection under the Americans with Disabilities Act has—at least theoretically—undermined some forms of economic and residential discrimination, even if they have not been entirely eliminated. Also, many health care workers have come to realize the value of scrupulous adherence to the principles of "universal precautions" in clinical practice to minimize the possibility of accidents and contamination, not only with HIV, but also with hepatitis B and other infectious agents.

Economically, costs associated with HIV infection can be staggering for individuals. The medications associated with combination therapies alone can average $2500 a month. Persons who have the symptoms associated with AIDS typically meet monthly (at least) with a physician. At some point in the course of the infection, such persons are likely to be hospitalized—again, typically more than once. Although fortunate individuals have much of this health care covered by their insurance, insurers are reluctant to provide such coverage. In addition, many infected persons have no insurance. Loss of one's insurance is a possibility, for instance, if one is unable to work, and so is no longer covered by an employer's insurance plan. Although insurers are required by law to make available continued coverage under these circumstances, its cost is often prohibitive.

HIV infection more and more is found among poorer members of society, both in the United States and elsewhere. Medicare or Medicaid often provides care for such persons in our society, but that care is then vulnerable to the variability in those systems. Thus, whether one has one's own insurance or is being cared for under social programs, one's financial situation is likely to become more fragile once he or she is infected with HIV.

The infected person's life is impacted in other ways too. Pet ownership becomes a possible danger. (This is more evidence that living beings—human and pets—are typically more of a danger to infected persons than infected persons are to those around them.) Because house pets can carry disease agents to which human beings are vulnerable, HIV-infected persons are advised to be wary of being around and handling such animals. A long list of suggestions about the interactions of HIV-infected persons and household pets is found in the July 2001 draft of guidelines for prevention of opportunistic infections in persons infected with HIV published by the U.S. Public Health Service and Infectious Diseases Society of America (Masur et al., 2001).

This same document includes warnings about the risk to HIV-infected persons from certain foods: raw or undercooked foods, grapefruit, soft cheeses, foods from deli counters—indeed any food in which there may be some potentially untreated infectious agent or which might interact unfavorably with a medication. Water can also contain such agents, so there are warnings about exposing oneself to untreated water. Given these latter warnings, travel to developing countries is also an activity that puts HIV-infected persons at increased risk.

Although all of us are at some risk from these sorts of encounters with potential disease-causing pathogens, HIV-infected persons must pay closer attention to them. Thus, activities that noninfected persons can more or less take for granted become activities HIV-infected persons must evaluate more guardedly.

Children who have been infected with the virus also experience many of the life changes just described and some others unique to their status as children. Are they to attend school with other children or are they to be educated at home or in some special location? Since U.S. courts have ruled that being infected with HIV is not a legitimate reason to keep children out of schools, there has been a lessening of the discrimination against such children. In part, this results from the legal requirement to keep such information private. Still, as a child develops the symptoms of AIDS, it can become more and more difficult to maintain this privacy.

Many children infected with the virus live in homes of persons who are themselves infected. The parents of these children may be too ill to provide proper care for them. Thus, many of these children end up in foster care or in the homes of other family members, notably grandparents or even great-grandparents (see Caliandro & Hughes, 1998; Joslin & Harrison, 1998). When the parents of infected children die, if there is no family member who is willing or able to deal with the challenges such a child presents, there is little hope that child—now an orphan—will be adopted. Although some families have been willing to adopt these children—and two persons of the same gender have formed some of these families—many more infected children are not adopted and become subject to the difficulties associated with overworked courts and social agencies.

People who are coping with the infection of others see their lives changed, too. This is vividly noticeable in the case of persons coping with the illness and treatment of HIV-infected children. Think again about Wanda Cooksey in the vignette at the beginning of this chapter. As we showed there, HIV infection of others can be economically, emotionally, and socially challenging for the care provider.

One man comforts another at an exhibition of the AIDS quilt.

Early in the history of AIDS, many persons experienced the deaths of one after another of their friends, until they were vulnerable to "grief overload" (see Box 20.5; Nord, 1997). This experience has declined somewhat among gay men, a group most heavily affected by HIV infection in the U.S. However, it threatens to erupt again in a new generation of gay men, some of whom ignore or are unfamiliar with the experience of the

Box 20.5 A Trail of Tears in a World of AIDS

Many people . . . who are affected by HIV/AIDS realize they walk with grief daily and frequently find themselves grieving in ways not defined as "normal." They often describe their grief as delayed. They feel at a standstill as a consequence of the continual losses. They are persistently traumatized by multiple deaths, and a plethora of secondary losses: hope, dreams, ideas, future plans, loss of happiness, etc. These bereaved are additionally traumatized with each death, and confronted repeatedly with social stigma, isolation, guilt, shame, and fear. . . . We are bearing witness to the trail of tears in a world of AIDS. For many, they are grieving a recent loss, remembering past losses and anticipating still others to come. . . . People not only mourn for those who have died, but for the incalculable ways their own lives have waned by the deaths of so many, occurring so often, and for so long. . . . AIDS grief cannot follow a linear direction when there are patterns of multiple, overlapping losses, resulting in trauma and cumulative grief issues. Recovery and reorganization are stages that may never be completed in AIDS grief. Grieving may never be completed. . . . There may be such an overexposure to grief and grieving with AIDS that the traditional models of bereavement are not enough. ■

SOURCE: From Showalter, 1997, pp. 69–71.

first generation facing AIDS. This can also be a problem in those minorities that today are experiencing the onslaught of the disease—that is, African Americans and Hispanic Americans.

It is only fair to add that throughout the history of the HIV/AIDS epidemic in our society, many Americans have faced their own deaths and/or the deaths of loved ones with courage and heroism. Those who provide care, as professionals, volunteers, family members, or friends, have often set shining examples for the rest of us. In some cases, these coping efforts have been documented in various publications (for example, Garfield et al., 1995; Jones, 1994; Monette, 1995; Newman, 1995). Losses experienced by many have also had positive outcomes. For some, AIDS has helped to reinforce the value of human life. As one 11-year-old child wrote, "I often wonder how other children without AIDS learn to appreciate life. That's the best part about having AIDS." (Wiener et al., 1994, p. 13)

Coping with HIV Infection and AIDS at the Community Level

A disease that can have such powerful impacts on individuals' lives also has potentially dramatic impact on the life of formal and informal communities. *Local communities that are coping with this disease* have responded in a variety of ways. For example, at one early point in the United States AIDS was most often found in gay males, many of who had a high number of sexual partners. When that community realized the threat and was educated about harm prevention, behaviors changed dramatically. Similarly, the extreme ignorance, fear, and anger that stigmatized infected persons and those living with AIDS have declined in most parts of our society. We no longer witness the outright discrimination that excluded Ryan White (a young hemophiliac in Kokomo, Indiana, in the early 1980s who contracted HIV from contaminated blood products) and many other children from school because of exaggerated concerns that they might infect their classmates—when in fact the risk of HIV-positive children acquiring opportunistic infections from others was far greater. We might hope never again to see in America a family like the Rays in Arcadia, Florida, who in 1986 tried to send their three hemophiliac sons with HIV to school only to be threatened and have their house burned down (see Box 20.6).

Americans have often found it difficult to cope with HIV/AIDS when they are associated with injecting drug use or sexual practices of which the public at large does not understand or approve. That association has often inhibited programs that provide clean needles to addicts and other harm reduction interventions. This situation is particularly complicated in some parts of the United States (especially certain large metropolitan areas) where HIV infection is most often found among vulnerable people (including ethnic minorities) who are poor and marginalized, who experience discrimination and social exclusion, who may be missed by prevention campaigns, or who may be deprived of access to treatment for their injecting drug use.

In many American communities, the first priority in coping with HIV/AIDS has been to provide health care for sick people. Often, this has involved the development of medical and nursing expertise in addressing the challenges and complexities of a new disease entity, as well as the provision of home care, hospital, and even hospice services. As the disease evolved and new interventions were developed, requirements for care extended over time and costs increased greatly (for example, for new medications). Also, coordination between health care and social service agencies has always been a challenge.

Without a cure for HIV, communities quickly realized the importance of education in preventing infection and treating the disease. Many communities undertook campaigns to increase awareness, knowledge, and sensitivity about HIV among the general public, professionals, and groups deemed to be at high risk for infection. Other communities sent informed persons into schools, churches, health care facilities, and businesses to provide accurate information about HIV and AIDS. For example, as only one component of its many services, the AIDS Service Association of Pinellas (136 4th Street North, St. Petersburg, FL, 33701; tel. 727-895-8352; www.ASAPservices.org), a division of The Hospice of the Florida Suncoast in Pinellas County, Florida, has assembled a library of 4,000 volumes related to HIV infection, with computer and Internet access, that is open to the public and to those who might have special concerns for themselves or for those they love. Some communities have provided (often free) condoms in schools and public places. A few communities provided sterile needles to injecting drug users. Providing condoms and sterile needles is controversial, although it has been shown to be effective in reducing the spread of the disease.

Because HIV infection, as we have noted, often strains the financial resources of infected persons, many have needed to turn to their local commu-

Box 20.6 One Family with HIV/AIDS in Arcadia, Florida: Then and Now

Louise Ray and her family have a haunting history in Arcadia . . . Fifteen years ago, her boys, Ricky, Robert and Randy, were diagnosed with HIV . . . They expected support from this close-knit town. Instead they got ugly protests and death threats. . . . Someone set fire to the Rays' clapboard house. . . .

. . . when Clifford and Louise Ray learned that their three sons were HIV-positive . . . [they] informed people with the school district and tried to enroll their children in regular classes. The School Board said no.

The Rays took the School Board to federal court . . . [and] a U.S. district judge . . . ruled that the Ray children could not be excluded from regular classes. . . . The first day of school, hundreds of parents kept their children away from Memorial Elementary, where the Rays attended. . . .

Today [the Rays] see dramatic changes in the town. . . . Old friends who had signed a petition to keep the Ray boys out of school have said they wish they hadn't. . . .

Students with HIV have come through Arcadia's schools since 1987. Confidentiality laws dictate that few people in the school system can know about students who are HIV-positive . . . Some students have taken their lessons at home, but others spent at least some time in regular classes. Their secret safe, none of them reportedly was harassed.

After the Ray furor, Florida school systems were directed to beef up their HIV/AIDS education, and today Arcadia students start learning about HIV and AIDS in middle school. . . .

About four years ago, school officials were bold enough to invite a speaker who had AIDS.

They didn't get a single phone call. ■

SOURCE: Based on Buckley, 2001.

nities for assistance. For example, if infected persons become unable to work or to pay for health insurance, they may need financial assistance from a variety of public and private agencies. Some community programs help infected persons pay for health insurance or for the deductible amounts associated with that insurance. Other programs may help to pay for medications—which can cost as much as $30,000 a year—both for drugs fighting the virus infection itself and for drugs to fight the opportunistic diseases that often accompany HIV infection.

Another area in which community assistance is often needed is housing for infected persons. People living with HIV/AIDS need safe, dependable, and affordable housing. Appropriate housing for such persons improves their quality of life, encourages successful compliance with complicated medical regimens, improves access to critically needed health care opportunities, and can support the desire of family members to stay together. The response of one community to housing problems experienced by HIV-infected persons is described in Box 20.7.

Care for families and children affected by HIV infection can also take other forms. For example, both the illness itself and the financial burdens that it

Box 20.7 Doorways: An Interfaith AIDS Residence Program

In 1988, religious, business, and other community leaders in metropolitan St. Louis, Missouri, joined together to create an independent, interfaith, nonprofit corporation to meet the housing needs of people living with HIV/AIDS. Eligibility for acceptance into Doorways' programs is based on criteria such as a medically confirmed diagnosis of HIV/AIDS, limited income and a need for a place to live, and a willingness to participate in case management services and community resources.

Doorways offers four types of housing services:

- *The Residential Program* provides supervised apartments for low-income individuals and families (with rent assessed on a sliding scale) located in four apartment buildings in St. Louis neighborhoods most affected by HIV/AIDS.
- *The Own Home Program* provides rent, mortgage, and utility subsidies to individuals and families who would otherwise be unable to stay in their own homes.
- *The Clearinghouse* maintains a list of property managers and available rental units, and provides housing advocacy, placement assistance, and outreach to people living with HIV/AIDS.
- *The Supportive Housing Facility* is a licensed residential care facility—the only such facility for people living with HIV/AIDS in the state of Missouri—that provides furnished private rooms (with bath, phone, and individually controlled heating and cooling); 24-hour protective oversight; nursing care with IV infusion therapy; assistance with bathing, dressing, and other activities of daily living; laundry, housekeeping, food and nutrition services; and social and recreational services.

The Supportive Housing Facility is particularly appropriate for infected persons who are too sick to live on their own, who have problems with substance abuse or mental health, and who require supervised housing in which they can live, either indefinitely or for some period of time (for instance, until their physical, psychological, or social condition improves, or their medication program is stabilized).

Additional information about these programs can be obtained from Doorways at 4385 Maryland Avenue, St. Louis, MO, 63108; tel. 314-535-1919; www.doorwaysmo.org or info@doorwaysmo.org. ■

generates may make it impossible for parents to provide back-to-school supplies or traditional meals and presents at holidays like Thanksgiving and Christmas. A "holiday" program in many communities provides support for these important events.

Funding for community programs can come from a variety of sources. Federal grants, private donations, and grants from state and local governments all play a role. Medicare and Medicaid programs also provide some funds for

In many communities, people came together to raise public awareness about efforts that were needed to prevent HIV infection and AIDS.

these community activities. However, fund raising is a continuous, ongoing necessity for any community agency seeking to provide programs for those infected and affected by HIV. It is also important to note that fund raising for this and for many other worthwhile purposes became more difficult after the terrorist attacks on September 11, 2001, when so many charitable resources were devoted to those directly affected by the attacks.

What this discussion shows is that HIV infection and AIDS can make significant demands on communities. Some are better able to cope with those demands than others. Some simply have greater resources to be tapped; others have private or public social agencies already in place that have taken on the responsibility of dealing specifically with this disease.

We also see here, once again, a "death system" at work (see Chapter 4). Although HIV infection and AIDS are no longer an instantaneous death sentence, they are still life-threatening and life-affecting diseases. Because of the large numbers of persons who are infected—and still becoming infected—and because infected persons require continuous and expensive care, HIV and AIDS will continue to strain community resources. They demand creative, compassionate responses, and they do this in a social and political environment in which there are many barriers and competing demands.

Coping with HIV Infection and AIDS at the National Level

In considering *coping with HIV and AIDS at the national level*, we begin with reliable estimates that 134,505 persons are currently living with HIV infection in the United States, together with 331,518 who are living with AIDS (see Table

20.1). Since the beginning of the epidemic through December 2001, 457,667 people in the United States have died as a result of HIV infection and AIDS. (Additional and ongoing information about HIV/AIDS in the United States can be obtained from the CDC through its many publications and its Web site www.cdc.gov/hiv.)

In the early years of the epidemic (and perhaps still in some ways today), many members of affected communities, as well as many knowledgeable clinicians and scientists, believed that the American government and the public at large did not appreciate the scale of the disaster that had befallen the United States and was not exhibiting the political will to respond appropriately. This led one observer to title his book *And the Band Played On* (Shilts, 1987), to imply official indifference to the growing threat. Today, U.S. efforts to cope with HIV/AIDS have clearly changed, even though one could debate whether they have changed enough or in the right ways.

Still, the United States has seen many effective programs designed to educate the public about HIV and AIDS and to show what can be done to prevent infection. One early effort in this direction occurred when the Surgeon General of the United States, Dr. Everett Koop (1988), mailed to every household in the country (something never done before) a brochure, "Understanding AIDS." In addition, a major federal AIDS funding bill was named in honor of Ryan White, and Betsy Glaser founded the national Pediatric AIDS Foundation (now the Elizabeth Glaser Pediatric AIDS Foundation, 2950 31st Street, Suite 125, Santa Monica, CA 90405; tel. 310-314-1459; www.pedaids.org). Further, many legislative jurisdictions have mandated that every woman diagnosed as pregnant be offered HIV testing and counseling with subsequent treatment if she is infected.

Coping with HIV Infection and AIDS at the International Level

The Global Impact of HIV/AIDS To appreciate the worldwide impact of this disease and *coping with HIV/AIDS at the international level*, we must recognize that they have "brought about a global epidemic far more extensive than what was predicted even a decade ago" (UNAIDS, 2001a, p. 4; see also Piot et al., 2001). At the end of 2001, 40 million persons around the world were living with HIV/AIDS and 24.8 million people had died since the beginning of this pandemic (worldwide epidemic)—more than three times the population of Switzerland (see Table 20.4). In the year 2001 alone, 5 million people were newly infected with HIV and the international community experienced 3 million deaths related to HIV/AIDS. HIV and AIDS are now the leading cause of death in Africa and the fourth leading cause of death worldwide. (Additional and ongoing information about HIV and AIDS in countries around the globe can be obtained from UNAIDS, a joint project of several United Nations bodies, including the World Health Organization and the World Bank, through its many publications and its Web site www.unaids.org.)

High rates of illness and death associated with HIV/AIDS in many parts of the globe deserve attention in their own right, but it is also in their own interests for Americans to become concerned about the implications of this disease.

Table 20.4 Global Summary of the HIV/AIDS Epidemic, December 2001

	Total	Adults	Women	Children <15 Years
People newly infected with HIV in 2001	5,000,000	4,300,000	1,800,000	800,000
Number of people living with HIV/AIDS	40,000,000	37,200,000	17,600,000	2,700,000
AIDS deaths in 2001	3,000,000	2,400,000	1,100,000	580,000
Total number of AIDS deaths since the beginning of the epidemic	24,800,000	20,000,000	10,100,000	4,900,000

SOURCE: UNAIDS, 2001b

The reason for this is that when HIV and AIDS destabilize societies, they become a threat to both human and national security. This threat is compounded in areas where there already are poor employment prospects, economic insecurity, endemic poverty, political instability, mobile or displaced populations, famine, and conflict or war. Thus, in 2000 the Clinton administration formally designated AIDS as *a threat to U.S. national security* because it could "topple foreign governments, touch off ethnic wars and undo decades of work in building free-market democracies abroad" (Gellman, 2000, p. A1). A national intelligence estimate in January 2000 is reported to have identified dramatic declines in life expectancy as the strongest risk factor for "revolutionary wars, ethnic wars, genocides and disruptive regime transitions" in developing states (Gellman, 2000, p. A8). Clearly, the United States is not likely to remain untouched by the effects of HIV/AIDS around the world.

Encounters with HIV/AIDS have varied in different parts of the world (see Table 20.5). For example, the epidemic seems to have begun at different times in different regions of the world, starting as early as the late 1970s in some areas, but not until the late 1980s in other regions and still later in Eastern Europe and Central Asia. In terms of people living with HIV/AIDS, the largest numbers are found in Sub-Saharan Africa, South and Southeast Asia, and Latin America. Sub-Saharan Africa and the Caribbean have the highest adult prevalence rates of HIV infection. Numbers of people newly infected with HIV in 2001 are unusually high in Sub-Saharan Africa and South and Southeast Asia. By contrast with other regions, women are disproportionately impacted in Sub-Saharan Africa, North Africa and the Middle East, South and Southeast Asia, and the Caribbean. Also, there are clear regional differences in principal modes of transmission for adults living with HIV/AIDS: heterosexual transmission is dominant in Sub-Saharan Africa, injecting drug use in Eastern Europe and Central Asia, and men who have sex with men in Australia and New Zealand.

A United Nations special session on HIV/AIDS held on June 25–29, 2001, noted that in addition to the 25.3 million persons living with HIV/AIDS in

Table 20.5 Regional HIV/AIDS Statistics and Features, December 2001

Region	Epidemic Started	Adults and Children Living with HIV/AIDS	Adults and Children Newly Infected with HIV/AIDS	Adult Prevalence Rate[a]	Percentage of HIV-Positive Adults Who are Women	Main Mode(s) of Transmission[b] for Adults Living with HIV/AIDS
Sub-Saharan Africa	late 1970s–early 1980s	28,100,000	3,400,000	8.4%	55%	HST
North Africa and Middle East	late 1980s	440,000	80,000	0.2%	40%	HST, IDU
South and South-East Asia	late 1980s	6,100,000	800,000	0.6%	35%	HST, IDU
East Asia and Pacific	late 1980s	1,000,000	270,000	0.1%	20%	MSM, IDU, HST
Latin America	late 1970s–early 1980s	1,400,000	130,000	0.5%	30%	MSM, IDU, HST
Caribbean	late 1970s–early 1980s	420,000	60,000	2.2%	50%	HST, MSM
Eastern Europe and Central Asia	early 1990s	1,000,000	250,000	0.5%	20%	IDU
Western Europe	late 1970s–early 1980s	560,000	30,000	0.3%	25%	MSM, IDU
North America	late 1970s–early 1980s	940,000	45,000	0.6%	20%	MSM, IDU, HST
Australia and New Zealand	late 1970s–early 1980s	15,000	500	0.1%	10%	MSM
Total		40,000,000	5,000,000	1.2%	48%	

[a] The proportion of adults (ages 15–49) living with HIV/AIDS in 2001, using 2001 population numbers.
[b] HST (heterosexual transmission), IDU (transmission through injecting drug use), MSM (sexual transmission among men who have sex with men).

SOURCE: UNAIDS, 2001b.

Sub-Saharan Africa at the end of 2000, "a further 17 million had already died of AIDS—over three times the number of AIDS deaths in the rest of the world" (UNAIDS, 2001b, p. 1). In that region, 2 million more women than men are HIV positive, as are 1.1 million children under 15, and 12.1 million children had lost one or both parents to the epidemic. Adult prevalence rates in some southern Africa countries are 20 percent in Namibia and Zambia, and higher in Lesotho (24 percent), Swaziland and Zimbabwe (25 percent), and Botswana (almost 36 percent)—the worst affected country in the world even though its diamond industry has given it the highest per capita gross domestic product in Sub-Saharan Africa. The CDC (2001a, p. 436) has noted that "in the countries most affected in Africa, life expectancy has declined by 10 years and infant death rates have doubled."

Cultural Attitudes and Behaviors Many have been infected by HIV as a result of attitudes and behaviors influenced by their local cultures. Most often, this involves *sexual behavior.* In heterosexual transmission, this typically reflects: lack of access to condoms; religious, cultural, or psychological influences that work against their use; sexual coercion and violence experienced by women and girls; and situations in which females are unable to control the terms on which they have sex (all of which are found in Sub-Saharan Africa and elsewhere). Among men who have sex with men, HIV infection is facilitated in some regions (such as Latin America) by religious and cultural prohibitions against acknowledging homosexual behavior and taking appropriate precautions. In other regions (including the industrialized countries of Western Europe and North America), because "few young gay men have seen friends die of AIDS, and some mistakenly view anti-retrovirals as a cure, there is growing complacency about the HIV risk" (UNAIDS, 2001a, p. 9). In all forms of sexual transmission, multiple sexual partnerships and large sexual networks facilitate HIV infection.

In other areas, such as Central and Eastern Europe, infection rates are relatively low but climbing alarmingly, arising largely from *injecting drug use* and the difficult, large-scale social changes occurring in these countries. Here, HIV

is threatening to spread to the general population through the sexual partners of injecting drug users, growing prostitution, and high levels of sexually transmitted infections.

Coping with HIV/AIDS around the World HIV/AIDS affects communities around the world in many ways. Households lose breadwinners and care providers, children lose parents, and families are forced to apply earnings, savings, and other assets to expenditures for health care and funerals. Those who are ill or impoverished may have no one to care for them. Some who are infected or impacted by AIDS are forced to turn to commercial sex that may in turn increase their risk of transmitting or contracting HIV. Governments and businesses experience lower productivity through the loss of skilled employees to death or absenteeism, even as they face mounting costs for health care and the training of new employees. Health care, social services, and education systems become overburdened. Women are most often required to care for sick relatives or bear other family burdens, girls are removed from school to assist in that work, and teacher shortages occur. Basic food production is undermined when HIV/AIDS take the health or lives of workers with critical expertise or of unskilled workers in labor-intensive processes.

Countries have responded to the threats arising from HIV/AIDS epidemics in various ways (Buchanan & Cernada, 1998). Some have tried to turn a blind eye to the implications of HIV and AIDS. Indeed, UNAIDS has noted that "most countries in Africa—and indeed worldwide—lost valuable time because AIDS was not fully understood and its significance as a new epidemic was not grasped" (2001a, p. 19). As late as 2000, the President of South Africa, Thabo Mbeki, stunned an international AIDS conference by raising questions and theories that had long been dismissed in the global scientific community, such as whether or not HIV causes AIDS (Clifton, 2000).

However, many countries have coped by integrating HIV/AIDS into larger developmental strategies and programs, such as efforts to reduce poverty, strengthen health care and social services, and carry out campaigns of public education, risk reduction, and intervention. As the CDC (2001a, p. 437) has observed, "even countries with modest resources have demonstrated that the epidemic can be stabilized or reversed. In these countries, successful programs have included strong, high-level political leadership for HIV prevention, a national program plan, adequate funding, and strong community involvement." Efforts directed specifically at HIV/AIDS include prevention measures (such as AIDS education, condom promotion, needle exchange, and drug treatment such as oral maintenance on methadone), counseling and testing, treatment and prevention of opportunistic infections, palliative care for pain and symptom relief in ill persons, and care for orphans. Because UNAIDS (2001a, p. 11) has estimated that "conservatively nine-tenths of HIV-positive individuals worldwide do not know they are infected," it has recommended voluntary testing services on the proven premise that "finding out their infection status could expand their basket of HIV prevention options." In more prosperous countries, anti-retroviral therapies have also been used with great success to forestall death and improve quality of life, but the costs and other requirements of such interventions make them impractical for most areas of the world.

There have been regional success stories in coping with HIV/AIDS around the world. For example, Uganda is an African country that used to have the highest rates of infection in the region. But through an intensive prevention program for behavior change, condom promotion, and voluntary HIV counseling and testing, Uganda reduced the adult HIV prevalence rate from around 14 percent in the early 1990s to 8 percent in 2000. Similarly, in Australia a program for exchanging needles and syringes is slowing the increase in HIV prevalence among injecting drug users.

These achievements need to be duplicated in every part of the world, especially in countries in which the epidemic started late or remains confined to specific groups. As UNAIDS (2001a, p. 19) has noted, "once HIV has become firmly established in the general population, most new infections occur in the majority of adults who do not have a specially high number of partners. This means that prevention campaigns have to be expanded greatly, making them harder and costlier, though still very worthwhile." As the scale of the epidemic increases, the scale of the action necessary to make a difference also increases—from efforts to reduce the number of new infections to programs offering care and treatment for people living with HIV/AIDS to efforts to minimize the impact on orphans, other survivors, families, and communities.

The United Nations noted that epidemics such as HIV/AIDS bring out both the best and the worst in people: "They trigger the best when individuals group together in solidarity to combat government, community and individual denial, and to offer support and care to people living with HIV and AIDS. They bring out the worst when individuals are stigmatized and ostracized by their loved ones, their family and their communities, and discriminated against individually as well as institutionally" (UNAIDS, 2001c, p. 1).

Summary

In this chapter, we learned about HIV infection and AIDS. We paid special attention to coping with HIV/AIDS by individuals and at community, national, and international levels. We saw that the HIV/AIDS epidemic in the United States and its counterpart pandemic around the world provides a lived model that simultaneously reflects many of the patterns we have discussed throughout this book and creates new patterns of its own. It challenges us as individuals, as members of society, and as participants in a global community to look again at our beliefs, feelings, values, and behaviors associated with dying, death, and bereavement. As we do so, information must replace ignorance and reasoned judgment must replace irrational decisions in all aspects of individual behavior, interpersonal relations, public policy, the provision of care, education, and research. The reason for this is that each person who is living with HIV infection or dying with AIDS is, in the end, like all of the rest of us: most fundamentally, he or she is a person. And he or she is a person living with suffering.

In the last sentence of his novel *The Bridge of San Luis Rey*, Thornton Wilder (1927/1986, p. 148) wrote: "There is a land of the living and a land of the dead and the bridge is love, the only survival, the only meaning." As health care providers, as spiritual guides, as members of social communities, as friends, as family members, and, finally, simply as fellow human beings, we must care about and for persons with HIV infection and AIDS, and for all of those who are coping with dying, death, and bereavement. Not to do so is to risk the loss of our own best selves, our humanness. In caring for others, we care for ourselves—as individuals, as members of our own societies, and people in the worldwide community—and we become fully who we are—human beings.

Questions for Review and Discussion

1. Read once again the vignette near the beginning of this chapter. Try to imagine how HIV infection might come into your family. Think about the burdens it imposes on those who are affected as well as those who are infected. If it did come into your family, what specific issues might you have to deal with? How might you cope with such issues? What complicates these experiences when death results from HIV/AIDS? Could an experience like this help us "become fully who we are—human beings"?

2. Many (perhaps most) people in the United States report that they know how HIV is transmitted and what should be done to prevent acquiring that virus. Many Americans also report that they are not doing what is necessary to prevent transmission and acquisition of HIV. Do you know what is involved in transmission/acquisition of HIV? Are you doing what is necessary to prevent transmission/acquisition of HIV? Why or why not?

3. In your judgment, what is the most important thing that each of us as individuals should do to help individuals who are already infected with HIV and/or who have AIDS? In your judgment, what is the most important thing that society should do to help individuals who are already infected with HIV and/or who have AIDS? Are you doing such things? Is society doing such things? Why or why not?

Suggested Readings

Historical and personal accounts can be found in:

Ashe, A., & Rampersad, A. (1993). *Days of Grace: A Memoir.*

Donnelly, K. F. (1994). *Recovering from the Loss of a Loved One to AIDS.*

Fisher, M. (1994). *Sleep with the Angels: A Mother Challenges AIDS.*

Garfield, C. A., with C. Spring and D. Ober. (1995). *Sometimes My Heart Goes Numb: Love and Caring in a Time of AIDS.*

Glaser, E., & Palmer, L. (1991). *In the Absence of Angels: A Hollywood Family's Courageous Story.*

Johnson, E. "Magic," with W. Novak. (1992). *My Life.*

Jones, C. (1994). *Living Proof: Courage in the Face of AIDS.*

Louganis, G., with E. Marcus. (1995). *Breaking the Surface.*

Monette, P. (1988). *Borrowed Time: An AIDS Memoir.*

Monette, P. (1992). *Becoming a Man: Half a Life Story.*
Monette, P. (1995). *Last Watch of the Night: Essays Too Personal and Otherwise.*
Newman, L. (Ed.). (1995). *A Loving Testimony: Remembering Loved Ones Lost to AIDS.*
Ruskin, C. (1988). *The Quilt: Stories from the NAMES Project.*
Selwyn, P. A. (1998). *Surviving the Fall: The Personal Journey of an AIDS Doctor.*
Shilts, R. (1987). *And the Band Played On: Politics, People, and the AIDS Epidemic.*

For general introductions to HIV infection and AIDS, consult:

Douglas, P. H., & Pinsky, L. (1996). *The Essential AIDS Fact Book* (rev. ed.).
Frumkin, L. R., & Leonard, J. M. (1997). *Questions & Answers on AIDS* (3rd ed.).
Gifford, A. L., Lorig, K., Laurent, D., & González, V. (1997). *Living Well with HIV and AIDS.*
Koop, C. E. (1988). *Understanding AIDS.*
Pinsky, L., & Douglas, P. H. (1992). *The Essential HIV Treatment Fact Book.*

More detailed analyses are available in:

Buchanan, D., & Cernada, G. (Eds.). (1998). *Progress in Preventing AIDS?: Dogma, Dissent and Innovation—Global Perspectives.*
Doka, K. J. (1997). *AIDS, Fear, and Society: Challenging the Dreaded Disease.*
Grmek, M. D. (1990). *History of AIDS: Emergence and Origin of a Modern Pandemic.*
Hoffman, M. A. (1996). *Counseling Clients with HIV Disease: Assessment, Intervention, Prevention.*
Nord, D. A. (1997). *Multiple AIDS-Related Loss: A Handbook for Surviving a Perpetual Fall.*
Seligson, M. R., & Peterson, K. E. (Eds.). (1992). *AIDS Prevention and Treatment: Hope, Humor, and Healing.*
Sontag, S. (1989). *AIDS and Its Metaphors.*
Volberding, P. A., & Aberg, J. A. (Eds.). (1999). *The San Francisco General Hospital Handbook of HIV Management: A Guide to the Practical Management of HIV-Infected Patients.*

Special issues concerning women, children, the workplace, and other policy matters are considered in:

Boyd-Franklin, N., Steiner, G. L., & Boland, M. G. (Eds.). (1995). *Children, Families, and HIV/AIDS: Psychosocial and Therapeutic Issues.*
Hunter, N. D., & Rubenstein, W. B. (Eds.). (1992). *AIDS Agenda: Emerging Issues in Civil Rights.*
Krieger, N., & Margo, G. (Eds.). (1994). *AIDS: The Politics of Survival.*
Luna, G. C. (1997). *Youths Living with HIV: Self-Evident Truths.*
Roth, N. L., & Fuller, L. K. (1998). *Women and AIDS: Negotiating Safer Practices, Care, and Representation.*
Rubenstein, W. B., Eisenberg, R., & Gostin, L. O. (1996). *The Rights of People Who Are HIV Positive: The Authoritative ACLU Guide to the Rights of People Living with HIV Disease and AIDS.*
Terl, A. H. (1992). *AIDS and the Law: A Basic Guide for the Nonlawyer.*
Wiener, L. S., Best, A., & Pizzo, P. A. (Comps.). (1994). *Be a Friend: Children Who Live with HIV Speak.*

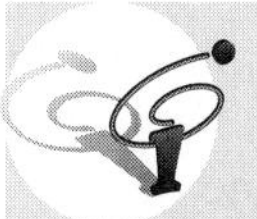

InfoTrac College Edition
For more information, explore the InfoTrac College Edition at **http://www.infotrac-college.com/Wadsworth**

Enter search terms: ACQUIRED IMMUNODEFICIENCY SYNDROME (OR ACQUIRED IMMUNE DEFICIENCY SYNDROME), AIDS, AIDS AND COMBINATION THERAPIES, HAART (HIGHLY ACTIVE ANTI-RETROVIRAL THERAPY), HIV (OR HUMAN IMMUNODEFICIENCY VIRUS), KAPOSI'S SARCOMA, LIPODYSTROPHY, PNEUMOCYSTIS CARINII, PROTEASE INHIBITORS, RETROVIRUS, REVERSE TRANSCRIPTASE INHIBITORS, RYAN WHITE PROGRAM, T-CELLS, UNIVERSAL PRECAUTIONS, VIRAL LOAD.

Epilogue

Calendar Date Gives Mom Reason to Contemplate Life

by Elizabeth Vega-Fowler

I used to think life's defining moments were dramatic, like a speeding train that hits you head on and throws you forward.

This week, however, I changed my mind.

I decided that progress in life can more often be measured in inches, not miles. All those heavenly epiphanies are really the accumulation of everyday wisdom breaking through the surface.

All this was prompted by a date on my calendar.

Somewhere in my mind June 9 registered as familiar. It took a few moments for me to realize the significance. It was the four-year anniversary of my daughter's death.

Gabrielle was born with a malignant brain tumor. In truth, she was terminally ill before birth.

She was 16 days old when she died in her father's arms.

Even today I marvel at the brevity of her life.

Her father, brothers, 8-year-old Christopher and 6-year-old Joey, and I decided that if we couldn't give her longevity, we could give her quality.

So in 16 days, she smelled flowers and tasted cotton candy. She felt the sun on her face and heard countless lullabies. Even though we knew it was only a matter of time before we had to let her go, we opened ourselves up to knowing her.

Despite her medical condition—a condition doctors said left her with only one-fourth of her brain—my daughter responded in kind.

She would look into our eyes and without a word would communicate volumes of love.

Once she took every ounce of her strength and lifted a tiny wavering hand to touch my face.

When Gabrielle died quietly at home, I thought that my life had changed forever.

Time has taught me otherwise.

My daughter's death didn't place me on a new path but rather allowed me to experience things I had missed before. In fact, everything looked the same. It just felt different.

It was this journey—continuing along every day without her—that changed me and is still changing me.

The beginning was the most arduous.

For a time, I was enraged at God. Like a town crier I shouted "Unfair" through the streets.

I cried gallons of tears. Tears I never even knew I had.

I learned grieving was not just an emotional experience. It was a physical one.

My arms throbbed with the need to hold her.

My heart really hurt from the emptiness. I had a perpetual lump in my throat for years.

Seeing the date brought another simple realization.

Instead of the torrential sorrow of years past, this June 9 brought a gentle melancholy. There is a definite sadness of what will never be—birthday parties, frilly dresses, first dates and prom.

I know that loss will always be there.

But there in the midst of it is something else—memories of a sweet little girl whose death taught me everything that was important about life.

Like the power of magnolia blossoms and unconditional love, and how the joy of knowing another human being far outweighs the void that is left when they're gone.

There is also the new knowledge that this state called grief is not a final destination but rather a continuous journey that changes me in a thousand small ways—slowly and mysteriously.

I don't know exactly where I will end up. I just know that somehow without even realizing it I found peace along the way.

SOURCE: Elizabeth Vega-Fowler, 1998. Reprinted by permission.

Appendix A

SELECTED LITERATURE FOR CHILDREN: ANNOTATED DESCRIPTIONS

Picture and Coloring Books for Preschoolers and Beginning Readers

Bartoli, J. (1975). *Nonna.* New York: Harvey House. A boy and his younger sister, with good memories of their grandmother, are permitted to participate in her funeral, burial, and the division of her property among family members so that each receives some memento of her life.

Blackburn, L. B. (1987). *Timothy Duck: The Story of the Death of a Friend.* Omaha, NE: Centering Corporation (P.O. Box 4600, Omaha, NE 68104-0600). Timothy Duck tries to understand his own reactions to the death of a friend and the ways in which the adults around her are overlooking the needs of his friend's sister. Sharing his questions and concerns with his mother and with his best friend is helpful.

Boulden, J. (1989). *Saying Goodbye.* Weaverville, CA: Boulden Publishing (P.O. Box 1186, Weaverville, CA 96093-1186). This activity book tells a story about death as a natural part of life, the feelings that are involved in saying goodbye, and the conviction that love is forever, while allowing the child-reader to draw pictures, color images, or insert thoughts on its pages.

Brown, L. K., & Brown, M. (1996). *When Dinosaurs Die: A Guide to Understanding Death.* Boston: Little, Brown. A cartoon format introduces young children to issues of death and loss.

Brown, M. W. (1958). *The Dead Bird.* Reading, MA: Addison-Wesley. Some children find a wild bird that is dead, touch its body, bury it in a simple ceremony, and return to the site each day to mourn ("until they forgot"). The moral is that sadness need not last forever; life can go on again. An early classic.

Bunting, E. (1999). *Rudi's Pond.* New York: Clarion Books. After Rudi dies, his classmates write poems and make a memorial pond that attracts a beautiful hummingbird.

Buscaglia, L. (1982). *The Fall of Freddie the Leaf: A Story of Life for All Ages.* Thorofare, NJ: Slack. Photographs of leaves on a tree in the park are accompanied by text in which one leaf (Freddie) asks another (Daniel) to explain their anticipated fall from the tree and the meaning of life. Fear of dying is compared to fear of the unknown and to natural changes in the seasons. Life itself is its own purpose and death is a kind of comfortable sleep.

Carlstrom, N. W. (1990). *Blow Me a Kiss, Miss Lilly.* New York: Harper & Row. Sara's best friend is her neighbor across the street, an old lady named Miss Lilly. When Miss Lilly is unexpectedly taken to the hospital and dies, Sara cries, looks for the light in her house, and is lonely. In spring, Sara finds happiness in Miss Lilly's garden and in her conviction that Miss Lilly is blowing her a kiss.

Carney, K. L. (1997–2001). *Barklay and Eve Activity and Coloring Book Series.* Dragonfly Publishing Company, Wethersfield, CT (277 Folly Brook Boulevard, Wethersfield, CT 06109; tel. 860-257-7635). This series of soft-cover books (24–44 pages) currently consists of seven titles: Book 1, *Together We'll Get through This!;* Book 2, *Honoring Our Loved Ones: Going to a Funeral;* Book 3, *What is the Meaning of Shiva?;* Book 4, *Our Special Garden: Understanding Cremation;* Book 5, *What IS Cancer, Anyway?;* Book 6, *Everything Changes, but Love Endures: Explaining Hospice to Children;* Book 7, *Precious Gifts: Katie Coolican's Story.* An additional book on pet loss is in preparation. Each book uses a large 8 1/2″ × 11″ format to tell a story and to offer drawings to color or blank spaces in which to draw a picture about a loss-related topic that adults often find difficult to discuss with children. In each book, two curious Portuguese water dogs learn lessons like: loss and sadness do happen; those events are not their fault; it is OK to have strong feelings as long as they are expressed in constructive ways; and "we can get through anything with the love and support of family and friends" (Book 1, p. 5). All of the books ($6.95 each, plus tax, shipping, and handling) and custom-made, 10″ replicas of Barklay and Eve in soft toy format ($16.95 each, plus tax, shipping, and handling) are available from the Web site www.barklayandeve.com. An outstanding series.

Carson, J. (1992). *You Hold Me and I'll Hold You.* New York: Orchard Books. When her Daddy's Aunt Ann dies, a little girl thinks about her parents' divorce and other losses she has experienced. During the memorial ceremony, the girl watches all the people and everything that happens. She wonders how sorry she will have to get. Being held and holding others is comforting.

Clardy, A. F. (1984). *Dusty Was My Friend: Coming to Terms with Loss.* New York: Human Sciences. Benjamin is 8 years old when his friend Dusty is killed in an automobile accident. As Benjamin struggles to understand his reactions to this tragic event, his parents give him permission to express his thoughts and feelings, mourn his loss, remember the good times he shared with Dusty, and go on with his own life.

Cohn, J. (1987). *I Had a Friend Named Peter: Talking to Children about the Death of a Friend.* New York: Morrow. The children's section of this book describes Beth's reactions when a car kills her friend, Peter, along with the helpful ways her parents and teacher respond to Beth, her classmates, and Peter's parents. An adult section tries to prepare adults to assist children in coping with death.

Connolly, M. (1997). *It Isn't Easy.* New York: Oxford University Press. When his 9-year-old brother is killed in a car accident, a little boy is sad, lonely, and angry. As he ponders many good memories of his brother, he gradually gets used to being an only child—but it isn't easy.

Curtis, C. M. (1994). *All I See Is Part of Me.* Bellevue, WA: Illumination Arts Publishing Co. (P.O. Box 1865, Bellevue, WA 98009; 888-210-8216; www.illumin.com). Through big pictures and brief text, Sister Star helps a little boy to realize that all of creation is a part of him and he is a part of all creation.

Czech, J. (2000). *The Garden Angel: A Young Child Discovers a Grandparent's Love Grows Even after Death.* Omaha, NE: Centering Corporation (P.O. Box 4600, Omaha, NE 68104-0600). After her grandpa dies, 8-year-old Camilla remembers all of his gardening activities. This year she plants the new garden herself, dresses a scarecrow with his old clothes, and spreads his old quilt behind it like wings.

Dean, A. (1991). *Meggie's Magic.* New York: Viking Penguin. After 8-year-old Meggie's illness and death, her mother, father, and sister feel sad and lonely. But one day when Meggie's sister goes to their special place, she finds it still filled with the magical qualities of the games they used to play and she realizes that Meggie's magic still remains inside each of them.

De Paola, T. (1973). *Nana Upstairs and Nana Downstairs.* New York: Putnam's. One day, Tommy is told that his beloved great-grandmother ("Nana Upstairs") is dead, but he does not believe this until he sees her empty bed. A few nights later, Tommy sees a falling star and his mother explains that it represents a kiss from Nana who is now "upstairs" in a new way. Later, an older Tommy repeats the experience and interpretation after the death of "Nana Downstairs" (his grandmother). A charming story about relationships, whose interpretations should be addressed with caution.

Dodge, N. C. (1984). *Thumpy's Story: A Story of Love and Grief Shared by Thumpy, the Bunny.* Springfield, IL: Prairie Lark Press (P.O. Box 699, Springfield, IL 62705). In picture book, coloring book, and workbook formats (in both English and Spanish), a rabbit tells a simple story about the death of his sister, Bun, and its effects on their family.

Doleski, T. (1983). *The Hurt.* Mahwah, NJ: Paulist Press. Justin is hurt by an angry insult from his friend, but he doesn't share his feelings with anyone. He takes The Hurt into his room, like a big, round, cold, hard stone, but it just gets bigger and bigger and bigger. It is ruining everything until he finally tells Daddy. As he gradually lets it go, The Hurt gets smaller and smaller until at last it goes away.

Fassler, D., & McQueen, K. (1990). *What's a Virus, Anyway? The Kids' Book about AIDS.* Burlington, VT: Waterfront Books. Just a few words or pictures on each page leaves room for coloring, drawing, and shared discussion so that parents and teachers can begin to talk about AIDS with young children.

Fassler, J. (1971). *My Grandpa Died Today.* New York: Human Sciences. Although David's grandfather has tried to prepare the boy for his impending death, when it actually happens David still needs to mourn his loss. But he does find comfort in a legacy of many good memories from his relationship with his grandfather and in the knowledge that his grandfather does not want him to be afraid to live and enjoy life.

Fox, M. (1994). *Tough Boris.* New York: Harcourt Brace & Co. Boris von der Borch is a tough, massive, scruffy, greedy, fearless, and scary pirate—just like all pirates. But when his parrot dies, Boris cries and cries—just like all pirates, and just like everyone else. A simple story with simple pictures designed to give children permission to experience and express their grief.

Gaines-Lane, G. (1995). *My Memory Book.* Gaithersburg, MD: Chi Rho Press. A good example of a workbook providing suggestions, guidelines, and space for children to draw or write out their memories of someone who has died.

Hanson, W. (1997). *The Next Place.* Minneapolis: Waldman House Press (525 North Third Street, Minneapolis, MN 55401). In a serene and comforting way, this book uses text and art to suggest how different we will find the next place we will go by contrast with the place we now inhabit.

Harris, A. (1965). *Why Did He Die?* Minneapolis: Lerner. The death of a friend's grandfather leads a mother to explain to her young son that death is something that happens when someone's body, like an engine in a car, no longer works. They discuss aging, the life cycle, memories, and quality of life.

Hazen, B. S. (1985). *Why Did Grandpa Die? A Book About Death.* New York: Golden. When Molly's much-loved Grandpa dies suddenly, Molly cannot accept that harsh fact. She feels frightened, awful, and misses Grandpa very much, but cannot cry. Only after a long time is Molly finally able to acknowledge that Grandpa will not come back, to cry, and to realize that Grandpa still is available to her through pictures, in her memories, and in stories shared with her family.

Heegaard, M. E. (1988). *When Someone Very Special Dies.* Minneapolis, MN: Woodland Press (99 Woodland Circle, Minneapolis, MN 55424; 612-926-2665). A story line about loss and death encourages children to share their thoughts and feelings through coloring and drawing.

Hesse, K. (1993). *Poppy's Chair.* New York: Scholastic. Leah visits her grandparents every summer, but this time things are different: Poppy has died. Leah remembers things she did with Poppy, but is still afraid to look at his pictures. One evening, Leah finds Gramm half asleep in Poppy's chair. They sit together, share their grief and their plans for the future, and help each other feel a little better.

Hodge, J. (1999). *Finding Grandpa Everywhere: A Young Child Discovers Memories of a Grandparent.* Omaha, NE: Centering Corporation (P.O. Box 4600, Omaha, NE 68104-0600). A little boy realizes that Grandpa is dead, not "lost" as the adults keep saying. But he consoles himself and his Grandma with this thought: Grandpa always said "to do something for someone you have to put a little of yourself into it." So memories of Grandpa and his love live on everywhere the boy looks.

Johnson, J., & Johnson, M. (1982). *Where's Jess?* Omaha, NE: Centering Corporation (P.O. Box 4600, Omaha, NE 68104-0600). A good book to use in helping young children cope with infant sibling death by explore topics like what "death" means, remembering the dead child, and the value of tears.

Jordan, M. K. (1989). *Losing Uncle Tim.* Morton Grove, IL: Albert Whitman & Co. When Uncle Tim becomes infected with HIV, develops AIDS, and dies, his nephew looks for solace through an idea they had once discussed: "Maybe Uncle Tim is like the sun, just shining somewhere else."

Kantrowitz, M. (1973). *When Violet Died.* New York: Parents' Magazine Press. After the death of their pet bird, Amy, Eva, and their friends have a funeral with poems, songs, punch, and even humor. It is sad to think that nothing lasts forever, bur then Eva recognizes that life can go on in another way through an ever-changing chain of life involving the family cat, Blanche, and her kittens.

Ladwig, T. (Illustrator.) (1997). *Psalm Twenty-Three.* Grand Rapids, MI: Eerdmans. The familiar text of this psalm, comparing God to a loving shepherd, is here accompanied by forceful and moving illustrations depicting the world of love and fear faced by an urban, African-American family.

Lanton, S. (1991). *Daddy's Chair.* Rockville, MD: Kar-Ben Copies, Inc. (800-4-KARBEN). After his father's death, Michael does not want anyone to sit in Daddy's chair so it will be ready for him when he comes back. Mommy explains what it means to be sick and die, as well as the Jewish customs involved in sitting shiva. Sharing memories of Daddy gradually enable Michael to allow the chair to be used again.

London, J. (1994). *Liplap's Wish.* San Francisco: Chronicle Books. As a rabbit named Liplap builds the winter's first snow bunny, he remembers his Grandma and misses her. He finds comfort in an old Rabbit's tale that his grandmother used to tell about how, long ago, when the First Rabbits died, they became stars in the sky who even now come out at night, watch over us, and shine forever in our hearts.

Mellonie, B., & Ingpen, R. (1983). *Lifetimes: A Beautiful Way to Explain Death to Children.* New York: Bantam. Through many examples, this book affirms that "there is a beginning and an ending for everything that is alive. In between is living. . . . So, no matter how long they are, or how short, lifetimes are really all the same. They have beginnings, and endings, and there is living in between."

Numeroff, L., & Harpham, W. (1999). *Kid's Talk: Kids Speak Out about Breast Cancer.* Dallas, TX: Susan B. Komen Breast Cancer Foundation (800-462-9273). This book uses animal drawings to depict common situations experienced by children whose mothers are diagnosed with breast cancer. Death is not directly addressed, but the book conveys children's confusion when confronted by difficult situations and offers guidelines to open communication and help parents talk to children on their level.

O'Toole, D. (1988). *Aarvy Aardvark Finds Hope.* Burnsville, NC: Compassion Books (477 Hannah Branch Road, Burnsville, NC 28714). Designed to be read aloud, this is a story about how Aarvy Aardvark comes to terms with the loss of his mother and brother. Many animals offer unhelpful advice to Aarvy; only one friend, Ralphy Rabbit, who really listens to Aarvy as the two of them share their losses, is truly helpful.

Prestine, J. S. (1993). *Someone Special Died.* Torrance, CA: Fearon Teacher Aids/Frank Schaeffer Publications (23740 Hawthorne Blvd., Torrance, CA 90505-5927). This book describes a young girl's reactions to the death of someone special. She discusses death with her mother, explains how she feels, and plans a scrapbook to remember good times shared with the person who died.

Rylant, C. (1995/1997). *Dog Heaven* and *Cat Heaven.* New York: Blue Sky Press. Vivid acrylic illustrations and charming story lines in these two books describe the delights that dogs and cats might hope to find in their own special heavens.

Schlitt, R. S. (1992). *Robert Nathaniel's Tree.* Maryville, TN: Lightbearers Publishers (P.O. Box 5895, Maryville, TN 37802-5895). A child tells about the things he likes, including getting ready for a new baby. But the baby dies, and then there is much that he does not like. Later, he likes caring for Robert Nathaniel's memorial tree and being his big brother—"even if he didn't come home."

Shriver, M. (1999). *What's Heaven?* New York: Golden Books. This book reflects the author's discussions with her 5- and 6-year-old daughters when their great-grandmother, Rose Fitzgerald Kennedy, died. It suggests that heaven is a place without hurts where your soul goes when you die.

Simon, J. (2001). *This Book Is for All Kids, but Especially My Sister Libby. Libby Died.* Austin, TX: Idea University Press. Five-year-old Jack struggled to understand the death of his young sister. This book reproduces his questions and comments, along with dramatic, colorful illustrations.

Stickney, D. (1985). *Water Bugs and Dragonflies.* New York: Pilgrim Press. This little book focuses on transformations in life as a metaphor for transformations between life and death. One key point is that the water bug that is transformed into a dragonfly is no longer able to return to the underwater colony to explain what has happened. Each individual must wait for his or her own transformation in order to appreciate what it entails.

Stull, E. G. (1964). *My Turtle Died Today.* New York: Holt, Rinehart & Winston. When a pet turtle dies, a boy and his friends bury it and talk about what all of this means. They conclude that life can go on in another way through the newborn kittens of their cat, Patty. Much of this is sound, but the book also poses two questions that need to be addressed with care: Can you get a new pet in the way that one child has a new mother? and Do you have to live—a long time—before you die?

Varley, S. (1992). *Badger's Parting Gifts.* New York: Mulberry Books. Although Badger is old and knows he must die, he is not afraid. He worries about his friends, who are sad when he dies but who find consolation in the special memories he left with each of them and in sharing those memories with others.

Viorst, J. (1971). *The Tenth Good Thing about Barney.* New York: Atheneum. When a pet cat dies, a boy tries to think of ten good things to say at the funeral. At first, he can only think of nine: Barney was brave and smart and funny and clean; he was cuddly and handsome and he only once ate a bird; it was sweet to hear him purr in my ear; and sometimes he slept on my belly and kept it warm. Out in the garden, he realizes the tenth good thing is that "Barney is in the ground and he's helping grow flowers."

Warburg, S. S. (1969). *Growing Time.* Boston: Houghton Mifflin. When his aging collie, King, dies, Jamie's father gets him a new puppy. At first, Jamie is not ready for the new dog, but after he is allowed to express his grief, he finds it possible to accept the new relationship.

Weir, A. B. (1992). *Am I Still a Big Sister?* Newtown, PA: Fallen Leaf Press (P.O. Box 942, Newtown, PA 18940). This simple story follows the concerns of a young girl through the illness, hospitalization, death, and funeral of her baby sister, and the subsequent birth of a new brother.

White Deer of Autumn (Horn, G.) (1992). *The Great Change.* Hillsboro, OR: Beyond Words Publishing, Inc. (20827 NW Cornell Road, Suite 500, Hillsboro, OR 97124-9808; 800-284-9673). In this story, a Native-American Indian grandmother explains to her 9-year-old granddaughter, Wanba, that death is not the end, but the Great Change—a part of the unbreakable Circle of Life in which our bodies become one with Mother Earth while our souls or spirits endure.

Wilhelm, H. (1985). *I'll Always Love You.* New York: Crown. A boy and his dog grow up together, but Elfie grows old and dies while the boy is still young. Afterward, family members regret that they did not tell Elfie they loved her. But the boy did so every night and he realizes that his love for her will continue even after her death. He doesn't want a new puppy right away, even though he knows that Elfie will not come back and there may come a time when he will be ready for a new pet.

Winsch, J. L. (1995). *After the Funeral.* Mahwah, NJ: Paulist Press. This book seeks to normalize reactions that people have after a death, like crying and feeling sad or scared. The text says, "everyone handles sadness in their own way." It recommends sharing feelings and affirms a hope in everlasting life.

Yeomans, E. (2000). *Lost and Found: Remembering a Sister.* Omaha, NE: Centering Corporation (P.O. Box 4600, Omaha, NE 68104-0600). A young girl recounts the confusing experiences that she and her parents have after her sister dies, but she also realizes many ways in which she still feels her sister's love. So Paige isn't "lost" forever; she is right there in their hearts and the girl knows where to find her.

Zolotow, C. (1974). *My Grandson Lew.* New York: Harper. When 6-year-old Lewis wonders why his grandfather has not visited lately, his mother says that Lewis had not been told that his grandfather had died because he had never asked. The boy says that he hadn't needed to ask; his grandfather just came. Son and mother share warm memories of someone they both miss: Lewis says, "He gave me eye hugs"; his mother concludes, "Now we will remember him together and neither of us will be so lonely as we would be if we had to remember him alone."

Storybooks and Other Texts for Primary School Readers

Alexander, S. (1983). *Nadia the Willful.* New York: Pantheon Books. Nadia's older brother dies and her father in his grief decrees that no one may speak of this death. Nadia helps her family, particularly her father, deal with their grief by willfully talking about her brother.

Arnold, C. (1987). *What We Do When Someone Dies.* New York: Franklin Watts. This book provides information about death-related feelings, concepts, and beliefs, but gives most attention to disposition of the body, funeral customs, and memorial practices.

Barreras, C. (1998). *Hope in Heaven.* Folsom, CA: Hope in Heaven (P.O. Box 874, Folsom, CA 95763; www.hopeinheaven.org). This slim booklet tries to show how one might talk about the possibility of death to a child with a life-threatening illness. It insists the child is important and is loved, and promises that no one will give up the fight, even while admitting that things do not always turn out as we might wish them to. The remainder of the text affirms God's presence and the expectation of heaven.

Barron, T. A. (2000). *Where Is Grandpa?* New York: Philomel Books. After Grandpa dies, family members share memories. When a young boy wants to know where Grandpa is now, they decide that Grandpa is in heaven and that "heaven is any place where people who love each other have shared some time together." The thought that Grandpa is way off in the Never Summer range of the Rockies that they used to look at together "as far as we can possibly see" from the tree house they built comforts the boy.

Boritzer, E. (2000). *What Is Death?* Santa Monica, CA: Veronica Lane Books (513 Wilshire Blvd. #282, Santa Monica, CA 90401; 800-651-1001). The third in a series by the same author (following *What Is God?* and *What Is Love?*), this book seeks to introduce children to the concept of death and to some of its implications, using examples of customs and beliefs from various religions and cultures.

Bouchard, D. (1997). *If Sarah Will Take Me.* Victoria, BC, & Custer, WA: Orca Book Publishers (P.O. Box 5626, Station B, Victoria, BC V8R 6S4, Canada; P.O. Box 468 Custer, WA 98240-0468). The author's lengthy poem accompanies paintings by Robb Dunfield, a ventilator-dependent quadriplegic since he was 19. The book is a testimonial to what Dunfield would do if only Sarah (his nurse and now wife) would take him to the places he remembers, and if only he had his life to live over again.

Boulden, J., & Boulden, B. (1992). *Uncle Jerry Has AIDS.* Weaverville, CA: Boulden Publishing (P.O. Box 1186, Weaverville, CA 96093-1186). An activity book allowing children at about grave level 3–4 to explore issues, attitudes, and emotions that might arise when a loved one has AIDS.

Buck, P. S. (1948). *The Big Wave.* New York: Scholastic. After a tidal wave kills his family and all the fishing people on the shore, Jiya chooses to live with his friend Kino's poor family instead of being adopted by a rich man. Years later, Jiya marries Kino's sister and decides to move back to the seaside with his new bride. Loss is universal and inevitable, but life is stronger than death.

Bunting, E. (1982). *The Happy Funeral.* New York: Harper & Row. Two young Chinese-American girls are puzzled when their mother says they will have a "happy funeral" for their grandfather. At the funeral, food is provided for the journey to the other side, paper play money is burned, people cry and give speeches, a marching band plays, and a small candy is provided after the ceremony to "sweeten the sorrow" of the mourners. In the end, the children realize that although no one was happy that their grandfather died, his good life and everyone's fond memories of him did make for a happy funeral.

Carrick, C. (1976). *The Accident.* New York: Seabury Press. Christopher's dog, Bodger, is accidentally killed when he runs in front of a truck. Christopher is angry at the driver, at his father for not getting mad at the driver, and at himself for not paying attention and allowing Bodger to wander across the road as they walked. Christopher's parents bury Bodger too quickly the next morning, before he can take part, but anger dissolves into tears when he and his father join together to erect a marker at Bodger's grave.

Chin-Yee, F. (1988). *Sam's Story: A Story for Families Surviving Sudden Infant Death Syndrome.* Available from the Canadian Foundation for the Study of Infant Deaths, 586 Eglinton Ave. E., Suite 308, Toronto, Ontario, Canada M4P 1P2; 416-488-3260. A rare book that tells a story about the confusing experiences of a child in a family that has experienced the sudden death of his infant brother.

Coburn, J. B. (1964). *Annie and the Sand Dobbies: A Story about Death for Children and Their Parents.* New York: Seabury Press. When young Danny encounters the deaths of both his toddler sister from a respiratory infection and his dog after it ran away from home and is found frozen to death, a neighbor uses imaginary characters to suggest that the deceased are safe with God.

Coerr, E. (1977). *Sadako and the Thousand Paper Cranes.* New York: Putnam's. This book is based on a true story about a Japanese girl who died of leukemia in 1955 as one of the long-term results of the atomic bombing of Hiroshima (which occurred when Sadako was 2 years old). In the hospital, a friend reminds Sadako of the legend that the crane is supposed to live for a thousand years and that good health will be granted to a person who folds 1,000 origami paper cranes. With family members and friends, they begin folding. Sadako died before the project was finished, but her classmates completed the work and children all over Japan have since contributed money to erect a statue in her memory.

Coleman, P. (1996). *Where the Balloons Go.* Omaha, NE: Centering Corporation (P.O. Box 4600, Omaha, NE 68104-0600). When Corey asks where balloons go as they fly up into the sky, Grandma suggests that perhaps their destination is a lovely Balloon Forest. Later, after Grandma becomes sick and dies, Corey wishes that his balloons could carry him up to the Balloon Forest to see Grandma, but settles for attaching a message of his love to a balloon and releasing it.

Corley, E. A. (1973). *Tell Me about Death, Tell Me about Funerals.* Santa Clara, CA: Grammatical Sciences. This book depicts a conversation between a young girl whose grandfather has recently died and her father. In ways that avoid euphemisms, they discuss guilt, abandonment, and choices about funerals, burial, cemeteries, and mausoleums. At one point, we are treated to a child's delightful misunderstanding about the "polarbears" who carry the casket.

Donnelly, E. (1981). *So Long, Grandpa.* New York: Crown. At 10, Michael witnesses his grandfather's deterioration and eventual death from cancer. We learn about Michael's reactions to these events and about the way in which his grandfather had helped to prepare Michael by taking him to an elderly friend's funeral.

Douglas, E. (1990). *Rachel and the Upside Down Heart.* Los Angeles: Price Stern Sloan. After Rachel's daddy died when she was 4 years old, she was sad and had to move from a house with a yard, green grass, and two dogs in Kentucky to a noisy apartment in New York City. Mommy said Daddy would always be in Rachel's heart, so she began to draw hearts but could only make them upside down. Later, Rachel begins to find some new friends and some of the hearts that she drew were upside up. Finally, when his father died, Rachel was able to talk to a new friend and help him with his loss.

Farrington, L. & Weil, J. C. (1993). *And Peter Said Goodbye.* Woodside, CA: Enchanté Publishing (P.O. Box 620471, Woodside, CA 94062; 800-473-2363). After his Grandpa moved to California and was killed in a car accident, Peter is left behind in the care of a neighbor while his parents go to the funeral. Only a magical character, Mrs. Murgatroyd, seems to understand. Through her enchanted paints Peter visits the funeral in a dream and finds within himself ways to accept the death and say goodbye.

Goble, P. (1993). *Beyond the Ridge.* New York: Aladdin/Simon & Schuster. At her death, while her family members prepare her body according to their custom, an elderly Plains Indian woman experiences the afterlife believed in by her people.

She makes the long climb up a difficult slope to see the Spirit World beyond the ridge.

Goldman, L. (1997). *Bart Speaks Out: An Interactive Storybook for Young Children about Suicide.* Los Angeles: Western Psychological Services. Provides words for children to use to discuss the sensitive topic of suicide.

Goodman, M. B. (1990). *Vanishing Cookies: Doing OK When a Parent Has Cancer.* Available from the Benjamin Family Foundation, 2401 Steeles Avenue West, Downsview, Ontario, Canada M3J 2P1. This book seeks to bridge the gap between adults and children by helping them share feelings when an adult is coping with cancer. Children are encouraged to ask questions and are offered information about cancer, treatments, coping with feelings, friends and school, and death. The title refers to the vanishing cookies that some children shared with their mother when they visited her in the hospital.

Graeber, C. (1982). *Mustard.* New York: Macmillan. Mustard is an elderly cat with a heart condition that needs to avoid stress. But one day Mustard runs outside and gets into a fight with another animal, leading to a heart attack and to Mustard's death. After Father buries Mustard, Alex goes along to donate the cat's dishes and some money to the animal shelter where they had gotten Mustard. Because he is preoccupied with sadness, Alex wisely declines (for now) a well-meaning offer of a new pet.

Greene, C. C. (1976). *Beat the Turtle Drum.* New York: Viking. This book describes 13-year-old Kate and 11-year-old Joss' loving, warm family. When Joss is abruptly and unexpectedly killed in a fall from a tree, the family is flooded with grief. Conveying this sense of the many dimensions of bereavement is the book's strong point.

Johnson, J., & Johnson, M. (1978). *Tell Me, Papa: A Family Book for Children's Questions about Death and Funerals.* Omaha, NE: Centering Corporation (P.O. Box 4600, Omaha, NE 68104-0600). Using the format of a discussion between children and a grandparent, this slim book provides an explanation of death, funerals, and saying goodbye.

Krementz, J. *How It Feels When a Parent Dies* (1981) and *How It Feels to Fight for Your Life* (1989). Boston: Little, Brown; paperback by Simon & Schuster, 1991. Short essays by children and adolescents (7–16 years old) describe their individual reactions to the death of a parent and to a variety of life-threatening illnesses. A photograph of its author accompanies each essay.

Lee, V. (1972). *The Magic Moth.* New York: Seabury. Maryanne, 5-year-old Mark-O's 10-year-old sister, dies as a result of an incurable heart disease. Mark-O is helped to make sense of this experience by the metaphor of a moth as it experiences a transition from one mode of life to another.

Marshall, B. (1998). *Animal Crackers: A Tender Book about Death and Funerals and Love.* Omaha, NE: Centering Corporation (P.O. Box 4600, Omaha, NE 68104-0600). A young girl describes her Nanny, who hid animal crackers all over her house for her grandchildren. After Nanny became forgetful, she went to live in a nursing home and eventually died. But the children always remember Nanny fondly through the good times they shared with her and through her "Nanny crackers."

McNamara, J. W. (1994). *My Mom Is Dying: A Child's Diary.* Minneapolis, MN: Augsburg Fortress. The illustrated diary format of this book offers an imaginary record of Kristine's conversations with God while her mother is dying. Notes from the author identify Kristine's reactions and suggest how they could provide a basis for discussions with children.

Miles, M. (1971). *Annie and the Old One.* Boston: Little, Brown. A 10-year-old Navajo girl is told it will be time for her grandmother "to go to Mother Earth" when her mother finishes weaving a rug. Annie tries to unravel the weaving in secret and to distract her mother from weaving, until the adults realize what is going on and her grandmother explains that we are all part of a natural cycle. When Annie realizes she cannot hold back time, she is ready herself to learn to weave.

Mills, L. (1991). *The Rag Coat.* Boston: Little, Brown. After Papa got sick and died, Minna couldn't start school because she had to stay home and help Mama make quilts to support the family. When she was eight Minna wanted to go to school, but she didn't have a winter coat. So she was happy when the "Quilting Mothers" volunteered to piece together a coat for her out of scraps of their old materials and had it ready for Sharing Day. At first, the children teased her about her rag coat, but not after she explained the stories behind each scrap that she had selected.

Peavy, L. (1981). *Allison's Grandfather.* New York: Chas. Scribners' Sons. While her friend Allison's grandfather is dying, Erica asks questions that we might all ask: Is he ready to die? Would she be told if her own grandfather was dying? When Allison's grandfather does die, Erica's mother is able to be there and to hold his hand, and to tell Erica about what it was like.

Pellegrino, M. W. (1999). *I Don't Have an Uncle Phil Anymore.* Washington, DC: Magination Press. Following the unexpected death of his uncle, a boy and his extended family go to New York to attend the funeral while he thinks about what this event will mean for all of them. In the end, he throws a sparkle blue ball up toward heaven and catches it as he used to do when he played with Uncle Phil.

Powell, E. S. (1990). *Geranium Morning.* Minneapolis, MN: CarolRhoda Books. Two children—Timothy, whose father died suddenly in an accident, and Frannie, whose mother is dying—struggle with strong feelings, memories, guilt ("if onlys"), and some unhelpful adult actions. In sharing their losses, the children help each other; Frannie's father and her mother (before she dies) are also helpful.

Saltzman, D. (1995). *The Jester Has Lost His Jingle.* Palos Verdes Estates, CA: The Jester Co. (P.O. Box 817, Palos Verdes Estates, CA 90274; 800-9-JESTER; www.thejester.org). This is the story of a Jester who wakens one morning to find laughter missing from his kingdom. The Jester and his helper, Pharley, search high and low to find it. Ultimately, they discover that laughter—the best tonic for anyone facing seemingly insurmountable obstacles—is buried deep inside each of us.

Schwiebert, P., & DeKlyen, C. (1999). *Tear Soup: A Recipe for Healing after Loss.* Portland, OR: Grief Watch (hardcover $19.95, plus shipping and handling, from 2116 NE 18th Avenue, Portland, OR 97212; tel. 503-284-7426; www.tearsoup.com). See Box 10.2.

Scrivani, M. (1994). *I Heard Your Mommy Died.* Omaha, NE: Centering Corporation (P.O. Box 4600, Omaha, NE 68104-0600). A slim booklet offering an empathic approach to a bereaved child, affirming what he or she may feel, do, experience, want, or need.

Simon, N. (1979). *We Remember Philip.* Chicago: Whitman. When the adult son of an elementary school teacher dies in a mountain climbing accident, Sam and other members of his class observe how Mr. Hall is affected by his grief. In time, the children persuade Mr. Hall to share with them a scrapbook and other memories of his son, and they plant a tree as a class memorial.

Smith, D. B. (1973). *A Taste of Blackberries.* New York: HarperCollins. After the death of Jamie as a result of an allergic reaction to a bee sting, his best friend (the book's unnamed narrator) reflects on this unexpected event: Did it really happen, or is it just another of Jamie's pranks? Could it have been prevented? Is it disloyal to go on eating and living when Jamie is dead? He concludes that no one could have prevented this death, "some questions just don't have answers," and life can go on.

Tiffault, B. W. (1992). *A Quilt for Elizabeth.* Omaha, NE: Centering Corporation (P.O. Box 4600, Omaha, NE 68104-0600). When Elizabeth was eight, her Daddy got sick and died. Elizabeth got angrier and angrier. One day, Grandma suggests that together they sew a patchwork quilt out of swatches of material from their old clothes. Each square of fabric has a story to tell and memories to recall as it binds the quilt and their lives together.

Vajentic, A., & Neuer, N. V. (1993). *Remembering: Explaining Organ and Tissue Donation; Loss, Grief and Hope.* Cleveland, OH: Academy Graphic Communication (1000 Brookpark Rd., Cleveland, OH 44109-5824). In two parts, this booklet offers a basic explanation of donation, together with some comments on loss and grief.

Van-Si, L., & Powers, L. (1994). *Helping Children Heal from Loss: A Keepsake Book of Special Memories.* Portland, OR: Continuing Education Press, School of Extended Studies, Portland State University. This workbook's structured format is intended to help a child work through his or her grief.

White, E. B. (1952). *Charlotte's Web.* New York: Harper. This is a classic story of friendship on two levels: that of a young girl named Fern who lives on a farm and saves Wilbur, the runt of the pig litter; and that of Charlotte, the spider, who spins fabulous webs that save an older and fatter Wilbur from the butcher's knife. In the end, Charlotte dies of natural causes, but her feats and her offspring live on.

Whitehead, R. (1971). *The Mother Tree.* New York: Seabury Press. Where do 11-year-old Tempe and her 4-year-old sister, Laura, turn for comfort in the early 1900s when their mother dies and Tempe is made to assume her mother's duties? To a temporary spiritual refuge in the large backyard tree of the book's title, and eventually to good memories of their mother that live on within them.

Appendix B

SELECTED LITERATURE FOR ADOLESCENTS: ANNOTATED DESCRIPTIONS

Literature for Middle School Readers

Arrick, F. (1980). *Tunnel Vision.* Scarsdale, NY: Bradbury. After Anthony hangs himself at 15, his family, friends, and teacher cope with feelings of bewilderment and guilt. There is no easy resolution for such feelings, but important questions are posed: What should be done in the face of serious problems? Where should one turn for help?

Bernstein, J. E. (1977). *Loss: And How to Cope with It.* New York: Clarion. This book provides knowledgeable advice for young readers about how to cope with loss through death. Topics include: what happens when someone dies; children's concepts of death; feelings in bereavement; living with survivors; handling feelings; deaths of specific sorts (for example, parents, grandparents, friends, pets); traumatic deaths (such as suicide or murder); and the legacy of survivors.

Blume, J. (1981). *Tiger Eyes.* Scarsdale, NY: Bradbury. After Davey's father is killed at the age of 34 during a holdup of his 7-Eleven store in Atlantic City, Davey (age 15), her mother, and her younger brother all react differently and are unable to help each other in their grief. They attempt a change of location to live temporarily with Davey's aunt in Los Alamos, but they eventually decide to move back to New Jersey to rebuild their lives.

Boulden, J., & Boulden, J. (1994). *The Last Goodbye I.* Weaverville, CA: Boulden Publishing (P.O. Box 1186, Weaverville, CA 96093-1186). This activity book offers exercises designed for children at about grade level 5–8 to process feelings and issues that surround death. Also available in a Spanish version.

Brisson, P. (1999). *Sky Memories.* New York: Delacorte. While her mother struggles with cancer and before she dies, Emily (age 10) and Mom develop a ritual to celebrate and commemorate their relationship. Together they gather "sky memories," mental pictures of the ever-changing sky in all its variety and wonder. The sky seems to reflect the phases of Mom's illness and the vitality of her soul.

Cleaver, V., & Cleaver, B. (1970). *Grover.* Philadelphia: Lippincott. When Grover was 11, his mother became terminally ill and took her own life, as she thought, to "spare" herself and her family the ravages of her illness. His father cannot face the facts of this death or the depth of his grief, so he tries to hold his feelings inside and convince his son it was an accident. Issues posed include: whether one must endure life no matter what suffering it holds; whether religion is a comfort; and how one should deal with grief.

Crawford, B. B., & Lazar, L. (1999). *In My World: A Journal for Young People Facing Life-Threatening Illness.* Omaha, NE: Centering Corporation (P.O. Box 4600, Omaha, NE 68104-0600). This journal format is designed to help teenagers who are coping with a life-threatening illness make a record of their lives and give expression to thoughts, feelings, and worries that they may find difficult to share with family members and friends.

Dragonwagon, C. (1990). *Winter Holding Spring.* New York: Atheneum/Simon & Schuster. At first, nothing is the same for 11-year-old Sarah and her father after her mother dies. Each is in great pain, but gradually they begin to share their experiences and their memories of Sarah's mother. Eventually, they realize together that "nothing just ends without beginning the next thing at the same time" (p. 11). Each season somehow contains its successor; life and love and grief can continue together, for winter always holds spring. And Sarah knows that "love is alive in me and always will be" (p. 31).

Farley, C. (1975). *The Garden Is Doing Fine.* New York: Atheneum. While dying of cancer, Corrie's father inquires about his beloved garden. Corrie can neither tell him that the garden is dead nor can she lie. Instead, she searches for reasons to explain why a good person like her father would die. She also tries to bargain with herself and with God to preserve her father's life. A wise neighbor helps Corrie see that even though there may be no reasons for her father's death, she and her brothers are her father's real garden. The seeds that he has planted in them will live on and she can let go without betraying him.

Fox, P. (1995). *The Eagle Kite.* New York: Orchard Books. Liam Cormac struggles to make sense of things when his father develops AIDS, moves out of their home to a rented cabin, and eventually dies. Liam is confused, puzzled by the half-truths he is told, and unable to understand his mother and his aunt's very different reactions. Eventually, Liam recalls a day when he was flying his eagle kite and he came upon his father embracing another man. He realizes his father is gay and comes to terms with this by sharing it with his father and later telling his mother what he had seen.

Frank, A. (1993). *The Diary of a Young Girl.* New York: Bantam. A young girl's classic record of her thoughts about events when she and her family had to hide from the Nazis in Amsterdam during World War II because they were Jewish.

Girard, L. W. (1991). *Alex, the Kid with AIDS.* Morton Grove, IL: Albert Whitman. Alex, the new kid in the fourth grade class, is at first treated differently and left out of some activities because he has AIDS. Gradually, Michael comes to appreciate Alex's weird sense of humor and they become friends. And their teacher realizes that Alex needs to be treated as a member of the class, not as someone odd or special.

Grollman, S. (1988). *Shira: A Legacy of Courage.* New York: Doubleday. Shira Putter died at age 9 in 1983 from a rare form of diabetes. This book tells Shira's story on the basis of her own writings and personal accounts from family members and friends in a way that celebrates courage, love, and hope in a life containing much hardship.

Heegaard, M. E. (1990). *Coping with Death and Grief.* Minneapolis, MN: Lerner Publications. This book describes change, loss, and death as natural parts of life, provides information and advice about coping with feelings, and suggests ways to help oneself and others who are grieving.

Jampolsky, G. G., & Murray, G. (Eds.). (1982). *Straight from the Siblings: Another Look at the Rainbow.* Berkeley, CA: Celestial Arts. Another book from the Center for Attitudinal Healing. Brothers and sisters of children who have a life-threatening illness write about the feelings of siblings and ways to help all of the children who are involved in such difficult situations.

Jampolsky, G. G., & Taylor, P. (Eds.). (1978). *There Is a Rainbow Behind Every Dark Cloud.* Berkeley, CA: Celestial Arts. Eleven children, 8 to 19 years old, explain what it is like to have a life-threatening illness and the choices that youngsters have in helping themselves (for example, when first told about one's illness, in going back to school, coping with feelings, and talking about death).

LeShan, E. (1976). *Learning to Say Good-by: When a Parent Dies.* New York: Macmillan. This book offers advice to bereaved children and the adults around them on a broad range of topics, including: what grief is like; the importance of honesty, trust, sharing, and funerals; fear of abandonment and guilt; accepting the loss of the deceased, maintaining a capacity for love, and meeting future changes.

Little, J. (1984). *Mama's Going to Buy You a Mockingbird.* New York: Viking Kestrel. Jeremy and his younger sister, Sarah, only learn that their father is dying from cancer by overhearing people talk about it. They experience many losses, large and small, that accompany his dying and death, often compounded by lack of information and control over their situation. Their need for support from others is clear.

Mann, P. (1977). *There Are Two Kinds of Terrible.* New York: Doubleday/Avon. Robbie's broken arm is one kind of terrible—but it ends. His mother's death seems to leave Robbie and his "cold fish" father with no conclusion. They are together, but each grieves alone until they begin to find ways to share their suffering and their memories.

Maple, M. (1992). *On the Wings of a Butterfly: A Story about Life and Death.* Seattle: Parenting Press. Lisa, a child dying of cancer, and Sonya, her caterpillar friend, share insights and experiences as Lisa approaches her death and Sonya prepares for her transformation into a Monarch butterfly.

McCaleb, J. (1998). *Our Hero, Freebird: An Organ Donor's Story.* Chattanooga, TN: Tennessee Donor Services (651 E. 4th St., Suite 402, Chattanooga, TN 37403; 423-756-5736). This spiral-bound book is a memorial to Chuck Foster, who died of an aneurysm and became an organ donor in 1996 just before he was to enter eighth grade. Words, pictures, and art from his classmates, along with letters from his transplant recipients and some of their family members, speak about Chuck and about organ donation.

Paterson, K. (1977). *Bridge to Terabithia.* New York: Crowell. Jess and Leslie have a special, secret meeting place in the woods, called Terabithia. But when Leslie is killed one day in an accidental fall, the magic of their play and friendship is disrupted. Jess mourns the loss of this special relationship, is supported by his family, and ultimately is able to initiate new relationships that will share friendship in a similar way with others.

Richter, E. (1986). *Losing Someone You Love: When a Brother or Sister Dies.* New York: Putnam's. Fifteen adolescents describe in their own words how they feel in response to a wide variety of experiences of sibling death.

Rofes, E. E. (Ed.), and the Unit at Fayerweather Street School. (1985). *The Kids' Book about Death and Dying, by and for Kids.* Boston: Little, Brown. The result of a class project, this book describes what its 11- to 14-year-old authors learned about a wide range of death-related topics, making clear what children want to know about these subjects and how they want adults to talk to them. One main lesson is that "a lot of the mystery and fear surrounding death has been brought about by ignorance and avoidance" (p. 111). Another lesson is expressed in the hope "that children can lead the way in dealing with death and dying with a healthier and happier approach" (p. 114).

Romond, J. L. (1989). *Children Facing Grief: Letters from Bereaved Brothers and Sisters.* St. Meinrad, IN: Abbey Press. In the form of letters to a friend, this book records the observations of 18 children (ages 6–15) who have each experienced the death of a brother or sister. Helpful comments from young people who have been there in grief.

Rudin, C. (1998). *Children's Books about the Holocaust: A Selective Annotated Bibliography.* Bayside, NY: The Holocaust Resource Center & Archives, Queensborough Community College, CUNY (718-225-1617). An annotated guide to this important body of literature for children from grade 4 onwards, containing lists of biography and memoirs, fiction, nonfiction, and reference works, as well as indexes by grade, title, and subject.

Shura, M. F. (1988). *The Sunday Doll.* New York: Dodd, Mead. This is a complex and richly textured story of a 13-year-old girl whose parents exclude her from something terrible involving her older sister (the suicide of a boyfriend) and who is frightened by her Aunt Harriet's life-threatening "spells" (transient ischemia attacks). Like the Amish doll without a face, Emily learns that she has her own strengths and can choose which face to present to the world.

Sternberg, E., & Sternberg, B. (1980). *If I Die and When I Do: Exploring Death with Young People.* Englewood Cliffs, NJ: Prentice-Hall. This book is the result of a nine-week middle school course on death and dying. The text mainly consists of drawings, poems, and statements by the students on various death-related topics, plus a closing chapter of 25 suggested activities.

Traisman, E. S. (1992). *Fire in My Heart, Ice in My Veins: A Journal for Teenagers Experiencing a Loss.* Omaha, NE: Centering Corporation (P.O. Box 4600, Omaha, NE 68104-0600). The aim here is to provide a print vehicle that can be used as a journal by teenagers who have experienced a loss. A line or two of text on each page and many small drawings offer age-appropriate prompts for this purpose.

Traisman, E. S., & Sieff, J. (Comps.). (1995). *Flowers for the Ones You've Known: Unedited Letters from Bereaved Teens.* Omaha, NE: Centering Corporation (P.O. Box 4600, Omaha, NE 68104-0600). In this support book for teens, unedited letters and poems written by bereaved peers are reproduced in various handwritten and print formats.

Wiener, L. S., Best, A., & Pizzo, P. A. (Comps.). (1994). *Be a Friend: Children Who Live with HIV Speak.* Morton Grove, IL: Albert Whitman. The vivid colors, drawings, and layout in this book seek to permit children living with HIV infection to speak in their own voices. The result is sometimes poignant, often charming, and always compelling. For example, one 11-year-old writes: "I often wonder how other children without AIDS learn to appreciate life. That's the best part about having AIDS" (p. 13).

Literature for High School Readers

Agee, J. (1969). *A Death in the Family.* New York: Bantam. This Pulitzer Prize-winning novel unerringly depicts the point of view of two children in Knoxville, Tennessee, in 1915 when they are told of the accidental death of their father. Agee skillfully portrays ways in which the children experience unusual events, sense strange tensions within the family, struggle to understand what has happened, and strive to work out their implications.

Barnouw, D., & Van der Stroom, G. (Eds.). (1989). *The Diary of Anne Frank: The Critical Edition.* Trans. A. J. Pomerans & B. M. Mooyaart-Doubleday. New York: Doubleday. A more sophisticated version (with commentaries) of this classic record of a young girl's life while hiding from the Nazis in occupied Holland during World War II. (See the entry earlier in this appendix under Frank, A.)

Bode, J. (1993). *Death Is Hard to Live With: Teenagers and How They Cope with Death.* New York: Delacorte. Teenagers speak frankly about how they cope with death and loss.

Boulden, J., & Boulden, J. (1994). *The Last Goodbye II.* Weaverville, CA: Boulden Publishing (P.O. Box 1186, Weaverville, CA 96093-1186). This activity book offers exercises designed for youngsters at about grade level 9–12 to process feelings and issues that surround death. Similar to *The Last Goodbye I,* but including topics like suicide and not acting in a destructive manner that are appropriate to these older readers.

Craven, M. (1973). *I Heard the Owl Call My Name.* New York: Dell. This novel describes a young Episcopal priest with a terminal illness. He is sent by his bishop to live with Native Americans in British Columbia, who believe that death will come when the owl calls someone's name. From them, the bishop hopes that the young priest will learn to face his own death.

Deaver, J. R. (1988). *Say Goodnight, Gracie.* New York: Harper & Row. When her close friend, Jimmy, is killed by a drunken driver in an automobile accident, Morgan is so disoriented by the extent of her loss that she is unable to face her feelings, attend Jimmy's funeral, or speak to his parents. Her own parents offer support and tolerate Morgan's withdrawal from the world, but it is not until a wise aunt intervenes that Morgan is able to confront her feelings in a way that leads her to more constructive coping and to decide to go on with living.

Geller, N. (1987). *The Last Teenage Suicide.* Auburn, ME: Norman Geller Publishing (P.O. Box 3217, Auburn, ME 04210). Text and pen-and-ink drawings describe the death by suicide of a high school senior, together with reactions from his family, friends, and acquaintances. The death mobilizes the community to develop a program to identify and respond to the needs of those who are potentially suicidal or hurting emotionally with the goal of making this the last teenage suicide in their community.

Greenberg, J. (1979). *A Season In-Between.* New York: Farrar. Carrie Singer, a seventh grader, copes with the diagnosis of her father's cancer in spring and his death that summer. She draws on the rabbinical teaching: turn scratches on a jewel into a beautiful design.

Gunther, J. (1949). *Death Be Not Proud: A Memoir.* New York: Harper. An early biographical account of the author's 15-year-old son and his lengthy struggle with a brain tumor.

Hughes, M. (1984). *Hunter in the Dark.* New York: Atheneum. A boy with overprotective parents sets out to face life and death on his own by confronting threats at different levels: his leukemia and the challenge of going hunting in the Canadian woods for the first time.

Klagsbrun, F. (1976). *Too Young to Die: Youth and Suicide.* New York: Houghton Mifflin; paperback edition by Pocket Books, 1977. A clear, informed, and readable introduction to the myths and realities surrounding youth suicide, with useful advice for helpers. Other books for young readers about suicide include W. Colman, *Understanding and Preventing Teen Suicide* (Chicago: Children's Press, 1990); D. B. Francis, *Suicide: A Preventable Tragedy* (New York: E. P. Dutton, 1989); S. Gardner & G. Rosenberg, *Teenage Suicide* (New York: Messner, 1985); M. O. Hyde & E. H. Forsyth, *Suicide: The Hidden Epidemic* (New York: Franklin Watts, 1986); J. Kolehmainen & S. Handwerk, *Teen Suicide: A Book for Friends, Family, and Classmates* (Minneapolis, MN: Lerner, 1986); J. M. Leder, *Dead Serious: A Book for Teenagers about Teenage Suicide* (New York: Atheneum, 1987); and J. Schleifer, *Everything You Need to Know about Teen Suicide* (rev. ed.; New York: The Rosen Publishing Group, 1991).

Langone, J. (1986). *Dead End: A Book about Suicide.* Boston: Little, Brown. This is a thoughtful book by a medical reporter who has published other books (*Death Is a Noun: A View of the End of Life,* 1972; *Vital Signs: The Way We Die in America,* 1974) for mature young readers about death in our society.

Lewis, C. S. (1976). *A Grief Observed.* New York: Bantam. The author, a celebrated British writer and lay theologian, recorded his experiences of grief on notebooks lying around the house. The published result is an unusual and extraordinary document, a direct and honest expression of one individual's grief that has helped innumerable readers by normalizing their own experiences in bereavement.

Martin, A. M. (1986). *With You and Without You.* New York: Holiday House; paperback by Scholastic. Family members (parents and four children) struggle to cope when the father is told that he will soon die as a result of an inoperable heart condition. Before his death, each member of the family tries to make the father's remaining time as good as possible; afterward, they strive to cope with their losses. One important lesson is that no one is ever completely prepared for a death; another is that each individual must cope in his or her own way.

Müller, M. (1998). *Anne Frank: The Biography.* Trans. R. & R. Kimber. New York: Metropolitan. A new exploration of the life and death of a young Jewish girl in occupied Holland during World War II.

O'Toole, D. (1995). *Facing Change: Falling Apart and Coming Together Again in the Teen Years.* Burnsville, NC: Compassion Books (477 Hannah Branch Road, Burnsville, NC 28714). This little book is intended to help adolescents understand loss, grief, and change, and to think about how they might respond to those experiences.

Pendleton, E. (Comp.). (1980). *Too Old to Cry, Too Young to Die.* Nashville: Thomas Nelson. Thirty-five teenagers describe their experiences in living with cancer, including treatments, side effects, hospitals, parents, siblings, and friends.

Scrivani, M. (1991). *When Death Walks In.* Omaha, NE: Centering Corporation (P.O. Box 4600, Omaha, NE 68104-0600). This little booklet was written to help teen readers explore the many facets of grief and how one might cope with them in productive ways.

Tolstoy, L. (1960). *The Death of Ivan Ilych and Other Stories.* New York: New American Library. The title story is an exceptional piece of world literature in which a Russian magistrate in the prime of his life is afflicted with a grave illness that becomes steadily more serious. As his health deteriorates, Ivan suddenly realizes that glib talk in college about mortality does not apply only to other people or humanity in general. He also discovers that many around him gradually withdraw and become more guarded in what they say to him; only one servant and his young son treat him with real compassion and candor.

REFERENCES

Ablon, J. (1970). The Samoan funeral in urban America. *Ethnology, 9*, 209–27.

Abrahamson, H. (1977). *The origin of death: Studies in African mythology.* New York: Arno Press.

Abts, H. W. (1997). *The living trust: The failproof way to pass along your estate to your heirs without lawyers, courts, or the probate system* (rev. ed.). Lincolnwood, IL: Contemporary Books.

Achté, K., Fagerström, R., Pentikäinen, J., & Farberow, N. L. (1990). Themes of death and violence in lullabies of different countries. *Omega,* 20, 193–204.

Achté, K. A., & Vauhkonen, M. L. (1971). Cancer and the psyche. *Omega,* 2, 46–56.

Adams, D. W., & Deveau, E. J. (1986). Helping dying adolescents: Needs and responses. In C. A. Corr & J. N. McNeil (Eds.), *Adolescence and death* (pp. 79–96). New York: Springer.

Adams, D. W., & Deveau, E. J. (1993). *Coping with childhood cancer: Where do we go from here?* (new rev. ed.). Hamilton, Ontario: Kinbridge.

Adams, D. W., & Deveau, E. J. (Eds.). (1995). *Beyond the innocence of childhood* (3 vols.). Amityville, NY: Baywood.

Ad Hoc Committee of the Harvard Medical School to Examine the Definition of Brain Death. (1968). A definition of irreversible coma. *Journal of the American Medical Association, 205,* 337–40.

Adler, B. (1979, March). You don't have to do homework in heaven! *Good Housekeeping,* p. 46.

Agee, J. (1969). *A death in the family.* New York: Bantam.

Aging with Dignity. (2001). *Next steps: Discussing and coping with serious illness.* Tallahassee, FL: Author.

Ahronheim, J., & Weber, D. (1992). *Final passages: Positive choices for the dying and their loved ones.* New York: Simon & Schuster.

Ajemian, I., & Mount, B. M. (Eds.). (1980). *The R. V. H. manual on palliative/hospice care.* New York: Arno Press.

Akner, L. F., with C. Whitney. (1993). *How to survive the loss of a parent: A guide for adults.* New York: Morrow.

Albert, P. L. (1994). Overview of the organ donation process. *Critical Care Nursing Clinics of North America, 6,* 553–56.

Albert, P. L. (1998). Direct contact between donor families and recipients: Crisis or consolation? *Journal of Transplant Coordination, 8*(3), 139–44.

Albom, M. (1997). *Tuesdays with Morrie: An old man, a young man, and life's greatest lesson.* New York: Doubleday.

Alderman, E., & Kennedy C. (1995). *The right to privacy.* New York: Knopf.

Aldrich, C. K. (1963). The dying patient's grief. *Journal of the American Medical Association,* 184, 329–31.

Alexander, G. J. (1988). *Writing a living will: Using a durable power-of-attorney.* New York: Praeger.

Alexander, I. E., & Adlerstein, A. M. (1958). Affective responses to the concept of death in a population of children and early adolescents. *Journal of Genetic Psychology, 93,* 167–77.

Allberg, W. R., & Chu, L. (1990). Understanding adolescent suicide: Correlates in a developmental perspective. *The School Counselor, 37,* 343–50.

Allen, B. G., Calhoun, L. G., Cann, A., & Tedeschi, R. G. (1993). The effect of cause of death on responses to the bereaved: Suicide compared to accident and natural causes. *Omega, 28,* 39–48.

Allen, M., & Marks, S. (1993). *Miscarriage: Women sharing from the heart.* New York: Wiley.

Alperovitz, G. (1995). *The decision to use the atomic bomb and the architecture of an American myth.* New York: Knopf.

Alvarez, A. (1970). *The savage god: A study of suicide.* New York: Random House.

American Academy of Pediatrics, Committee on Bioethics and Committee on Hospital Care. (2000b). Palliative care for children. *Pediatrics, 106,* 351–357.

American Academy of Pediatrics, Committee on Communications. (1995). Media violence. *Pediatrics, 95,* 949–51.

American Academy of Pediatrics, Task Force on Infant Positioning and SIDS. (1992). Positioning and SIDS. *Pediatrics, 89,* 1120–26.

American Academy of Pediatrics, Task Force on Infant Positioning and SIDS (1996). Positioning and sudden infant death syndrome (SIDS): Update. *Pediatrics, 98,* 1216–18.

American Academy of Pediatrics, Task Force on Infant Sleep Position and Sudden Infant Death Syndrome (2000a). Changing concepts of sudden infant death syndrome: Implications of infant sleeping environment and sleep position. *Pediatrics, 105,* 650–56.

American Cancer Society. (2001). *Cancer facts & figures 2001.* Atlanta, GA: Author.

American Psychological Association. (1993). *Violence & youth: Psychology's response.* Summary Report of the American Psychological Association Commission on Violence and Youth, vol. 1. Washington, DC: Author.

And we were sad, remember? [Film]. (1979). Northern Virginia Educational Telecommunications Association. (Available from the National Audiovisual Center, Reference Department, National Archives and Records Service, Washington, DC 20409.)

Andersen, C. (1998). *The day Diana died.* New York: William Morrow.

Anderson, R. (1968). *I never sang for my father.* New York: Dramatists Play Service.

Angel, M. D. (1987). *The orphaned adult.* New York: Human Sciences.

Angell, M. (1996). Euthanasia in the Netherlands—good news or bad? *New England Journal of Medicine, 335,* 1676–78.

Annas, G. J. (1994). Death by prescription: The Oregon initiative. *New England Journal of Medicine, 331,* 1240–43.

Annenberg Washington Program. (1993). *Communications and the Patient Self-Determination Act: Strategies for meeting the educational mandate.* Washington, DC: Author.

Anonymous. (1957). *Read-aloud nursery tales.* New York: Wonder.

Anonymous. (1998, Sept. 19). Listen. In A. Landers. *St. Louis Post-Dispatch,* p. D31.

Anonymous. (2001). *Q & A euthanasia 2001: A guide to the Dutch Termination of Life on Request and Assisted Suicide (Review Procedures) Act* (debated in the Senate of the States General on 10 April 2001). The Hague: Author.

Anthony, S. (1939). A study of the development of the concept of death [abstract]. *British Journal of Educational Psychology, 9,* 276–77.

Anthony, S. (1940). *The child's discovery of death.* New York: Harcourt Brace & Company.

Anthony, S. (1972). *The discovery of death in childhood and after.* New York: Basic Books. (Revised edition of *The child's discovery of death.*)

Antonovsky, A. (1967). Social class, life expectancy and overall mortality. *The Milbank Memorial Fund Quarterly, 45,* 31–73.

Ariès, P. (1962). *Centuries of childhood: A social history of family life.* Trans. R. Baldick. New York: Random House.

Ariès, P. (1974a). The reversal of death: Changes in attitudes toward death in Western societies. Trans. V. M. Stannard. *American Quarterly, 26,* 55–82.

Ariès, P. (1974b). *Western attitudes toward death: From the middle ages to the present.* Trans. P. M. Ranum. Baltimore: Johns Hopkins University Press.

Ariès, P. (1981). *The hour of our death.* Trans. H. Weaver. New York: Knopf.

Ariès, P. (1985). *Images of man and death.* Trans. J. Lloyd. Cambridge, MA: Harvard University Press.

Arkin, W., & Fieldhouse, R. (1985). *Nuclear battlefields.* Cambridge, MA: Ballinger.

Armstrong, A., & Donahue, M. R. (2000). *On your own: A widow's passage to emotional and financial well-being* (3rd ed.). Chicago: Dearborn Financial Publishing.

Armstrong, L., & Jenkins, S. (2000). *It's not about the bike: My journey back to life.* New York: Putnam.

Armstrong-Dailey, A., & Zarbock, S. (Eds.). (2001). *Hospice care for children.* New York: Oxford University Press.

Arvio, R. P. (1974). *The cost of dying and what you can do about it.* New York: Harper & Row.

Ashe, A., & Rampersad, A. (1993). *Days of grace: A memoir.* New York: Knopf.

Association for Children with Life-Threatening or Terminal Conditions and Their Families (ACT). (1995). *The ACT charter for children with life-threatening conditions and their families* (2nd ed.). Bristol, UK: Author.

Atkinson, T. E. (1953). *Handbook of the law of wills and other principles of succession, including intestacy and administration of decedents' estates* (2nd ed.). St. Paul, MN: West.

Atta, M. (2001, Sept. 28). "Oh God, Open All Doors for Me." *The Washington Post,* p. A18.

Attig, T. (1981). Death education as care of the dying. In R. A. Pacholski & C. A. Corr (Eds.), *New directions in death education and counseling* (pp. 168–75). Arlington, VA: Forum for Death Education and Counseling.

Attig, T. (1986). Death themes in adolescent music: The classic years. In C. A. Corr & J. N. McNeil (Eds.), *Adolescence and death* (pp. 32–56). New York: Springer.

Attig, T. (1991). The importance of conceiving of grief as an active process. *Death Studies, 15,* 385–93.

Attig, T. (1996). *How we grieve: Relearning the world.* New York: Oxford University Press.

Attig, T. (2000). *The heart of grief: Death and the search for lasting love.* New York: Oxford University Press.

Atwater, P. M. H. (1992). Is there a Hell? Surprising observations about the near-death experience. *Journal of Near-Death Studies,* 10, 149–60.

Auden, W. H. (1940). *Collected poems.* Ed. E. Mendelson. New York: Random House.

Austin, M. (1930). *The American rhythm: Studies and reexpressions of Amerindian songs* (new & enlarged ed.). Boston: Houghton Mifflin.

The Authors for the Live Organ Donor Consensus Group. (2000). Consensus Group. (2000). Consensus statement on the live organ donor. *Journal of the American Medical Association, 284,* 2919–26.

Bachman, J. G., Johnston, L. D., & O'Malley, P. M. (1986). *Monitoring the future: Questionnaire responses from the nation's high school seniors, 1986.* Ann Arbor, MI: University of Michigan.

Bachman, R. (1992). *Death and violence on the reservation: Homicide, family violence, and suicide in American Indian populations.* New York: Auburn House.

Bacon, F. (1962). Of marriage and single life. In *Francis Bacon's Essays.* New York: Dutton. (Original work published 1625.)

Bacon, J. B. (1996). Support groups for bereaved children. In C. A. Corr & D. M. Corr (Eds.), *Handbook of childhood death and bereavement* (pp. 285–304). New York: Springer.

Badham, P., & Badham, L. (Eds.). (1987). *Death and immortality in the religions of the world.* New York: Paragon House.

Bailey, L. (1978). *Biblical perspectives on death.* Philadelphia: Fortress Press.

Bailey, S. S., Bridgman, M. M., Faulkner, D., Kitahata, C. M., Marks, E., Melendez, B. B., & Mitchell, H. (1990). *Creativity and the close of life.* Branford, CT: The Connecticut Hospice.

Baker, J. E., & Sedney, M. A. (1996). How bereaved children cope with loss: An overview. In C. A. Corr & D. M. Corr (Eds.), *Handbook of childhood death and bereavement* (pp. 109–29). New York: Springer.

Baker, J. E., Sedney, M. A., & Gross, E. (1992). Psychological tasks for bereaved children. *American Journal of Orthopsychiatry,* 62, 105–16.

Balk, D. E. (1983). Adolescents' grief reactions and self-concept perceptions following sibling death: A study of 33 teenagers. *Journal of Youth and Adolescence, 12,* 137–61.

Balk, D. E. (1984). How teenagers cope with sibling death: Some implications for school counselors. *The School Counselor, 32,* 150–58.

Balk, D. E. (1990). The self-concepts of bereaved adolescents: Sibling death and its aftermath. *Journal of Adolescent Research, 5*, 112–32.

Balk, D. E. (Ed.). (1991a). Death and adolescent bereavement [Special issue]. *Journal of Adolescent Research, 6*(1).

Balk, D. E. (1991b). Death and adolescent bereavement: Current research and future directions. *Journal of Adolescent Research, 6*, 7–27.

Balk, D. E. (1991c). Sibling death, adolescent bereavement, and religion. *Death Studies, 15*, 1–20.

Balk, D. E. (1995). *Adolescent development: Early through late adolescence.* Pacific Grove, CA: Brooks/Cole.

Balk, D. E., & Corr, C. A. (2001). Bereavement during adolescence: A review of research (pp. 199–218). In M. S. Stroebe, R. O. Hansson, W. Stroebe, & H. Schut (Eds.), *Handbook of bereavement research: Consequences, coping, and care.* Washington, DC: American Psychological Association.

Balk, D. E., & Hogan, N. S. (1995). Religion, spirituality, and bereaved adolescents. In D. W. Adams & E. J. Deveau (Eds.), *Beyond the innocence of childhood: Helping children and adolescents cope with death and bereavement* (vol. 3, pp. 61–88). Amityville, NY: Baywood.

Ball, A. (1995). *Catholic book of the dead.* Huntington, IN: Our Sunday Visitor.

Ballou, R. O. (Ed.). (1944). *The Viking portable world library bible.* New York: The Viking Press.

Balmer, L. E. (1992). *Adolescent sibling bereavement: Mediating effects of family environment and personality.* Unpublished doctoral dissertation, York University, Toronto.

Bandura, A. (1980). The stormy decade: Fact or fiction? In R. E. Muuss (Ed.), *Adolescent behavior and society: A book of readings* (3rd ed., pp. 22–31). New York: Random House.

Banks, R. (1991). *The sweet hereafter.* New York: HarperCollins.

Barnard, D., Towers, A., Boston, P., & Lambrinidou, Y. (2000). *Crossing over: Narratives of palliative care.* Oxford: Oxford University Press.

Barnickol, C. A., Fuller, H., & Shinners, B. (1986). Helping bereaved adolescent parents. In C. A. Corr & J. N. McNeil (Eds.), *Adolescence and death* (pp. 132–47). New York: Springer.

Barrett, R. K. (1996). Adolescents, homicidal violence, and death. In C. A. Corr & D. E. Balk (Eds.), *Handbook of adolescent death and bereavement* (pp. 42–64). New York: Springer.

Barrett, T. W., & Scott, T. B. (1990). Suicide bereavement and recovery patterns compared with nonsuicide bereavement patterns. *Suicide and Life-Threatening Behavior,* 29, 1–15.

Basta, L., with C. Post (1996). *A graceful exit: Life and death on your own terms.* New York & London: Plenum.

Battin, M. P. (Ed.). (1994). *The least worst death: Essays in bioethics on the end of life.* New York: Oxford University Press.

Battin, M. P. (1996). *The death debate: Ethical issues in suicide.* Upper Saddle River, NJ: Prentice-Hall.

Battin, M. P., Rhodes, R., & Silvers, A. (Eds.). (1998). *Physician assisted suicide: Expanding the debate.* New York: Routledge.

Bauer, Y. (1982). *A history of the Holocaust.* New York: Franklin Watts.

Bauer, Y. (1986). Introduction. In E. Kulka, *Escape from Auschwitz* (pp. xiii–xvii). South Hadley, MA: Bergin & Garvey.

Baxter, G., Bennett, L., & Stuart, W. (1989). *Adolescents and death: Bereavement support groups for secondary school students* (2nd ed.). Etobicoke, Ontario: Canadian Centre for Death Education and Bereavement at Humber College.

Beaty, N. L. (1970). *The craft of dying.* New Haven, CT: Yale University Press.

Beauchamp, T. L. (Ed.). (1996). *Intending death: The ethics of assisted suicide and euthanasia.* Upper Saddle River, NJ: Prentice-Hall.

Beauchamp, T. L., & Veatch, R. M. (1996). *Ethical issues in death and dying* (2nd ed.). Upper Saddle River, NJ: Prentice-Hall.

Becker, C. B. (1989). Rebirth and afterlife in Buddhism. In A. Berger, P. Badham, A. H. Kutscher, J. Berger, M. Perry, & J. Beloff (Eds.), *Perspectives on death and dying: Cross-cultural and multi-disciplinary views* (pp. 108–25). Philadelphia: Charles Press.

Becker, C. B. (1990). Buddhist views of suicide and euthanasia. *Philosophy East & West, 40*, 543–56.

Becker, D., & Margolin, F. (1967). How surviving parents handled their young children's adaptations to the crisis of loss. *American Journal of Orthopsychiatry, 37*, 753–57.

Becker, E. (1973). *The denial of death.* New York: Free Press.

Bendann, E. (1930). *Death customs: An analytical study of burial rites.* New York: Knopf.

Benenson, E. (1998). Donor husband, donor father: UNOS board member Kenneth Moritsugu looks beyond tragedy to serving others. *UNOS Update* [Special Ed., Spring], p. 26.

Bengtson, V. L., Cuellar, J. B., & Ragan, P. K. (1977). Stratum contrasts and similarities in attitudes toward death. *Journal of Gerontology, 32,* 76–88.

Benjamin, B. (1965). *Social and economic factors affecting mortality.* The Hague: Mouton & Co.

Bennett, C. (1980). *Nursing home life: What it is and what it could be.* New York: Tiresias Press.

Bennett, K. M., & Bennett, G. (2001). "And there's always this great hole inside that hurts": An empirical study of bereavement in later life. *Omega, 42,* 237–51.

Benoliel, J. Q., & Crowley, D. M. (1974). The patient in pain: New concepts. In *Proceedings of the national conference on cancer nursing* (pp. 70–78). New York: American Cancer Society.

Bensinger, J. S., & Natenshon, M. A. (1991). Difficulties in recognizing adolescent health issues. In W. R. Hendee (Ed.), *The health of adolescents* (pp. 381–410). San Francisco: Jossey-Bass.

Beresford, L. (1993). *The hospice handbook: A complete guide.* Boston: Little, Brown.

Berger, A., Badham, P., Kutscher, A. H., Berger, J., Perry, M., & Beloff, J. (Eds.). (1989). *Perspectives on death and dying: Cross-cultural and multi-disciplinary views.* Philadelphia: Charles Press.

Berkovitz, I. H. (1985). The role of schools in child, adolescent, and youth suicide prevention. In M. L. Peck, N. L. Farberow, & R. E. Litman (Eds.), *Youth suicide* (pp. 170–90). New York: Springer.

Berman, A. L. (1986). Helping suicidal adolescents: Needs and responses. In C. A. Corr & J. N. McNeil (Eds.), *Adolescence and death* (pp. 151–66). New York: Springer.

Berman, A. L. (1988). Fictional depiction of suicide in television film and imitation effects. *American Journal of Psychiatry, 145,* 982–86.

Berman, A. L., & Jobes, D. (1991). *Adolescent suicide: Assessment and intervention.* Washington, DC: American Psychological Association.

Bern-Klug, M., DeViney, S., & Ekerdt, D. J. (2000). Variations in funeral-related costs of older adults and the role of preneed funeral contracts and type of disposition. *Omega, 41,* 23–38.

Bertman, S. L. (1974). Death education in the face of a taboo. In E. A. Grollman (Ed.), *Concerning death: A practical guide for the living* (pp. 333–61). Boston: Beacon.

Bertman, S. L. (1984). Children's and others' thoughts and expressions about death. In H. Wass & C. A. Corr (Eds.), *Helping children cope with death: Guidelines and resources* (2nd ed., pp. 11–31). Washington, DC: Hemisphere.

Bertman, S. L. (1991). *Facing death: Images, insights, and interventions.* Washington, DC: Hemisphere.

Bertman, S. L. (Ed.). (1999). *Grief and the healing arts: Creativity as therapy.* Amityville, NY: Baywood.

Bettelheim, B. (1977). *The uses of enchantment—The meaning and importance of fairy tales.* New York: Vintage Books.

Betzold, M. (1993). *Appointment with Doctor Death.* Troy, MI: Momentum Books.

Birren, J. E. (1964). *The psychology of aging.* Englewood Cliffs, NJ: Prentice-Hall.

Black, H. C. (1999). *Black's law dictionary* (7th ed.). St. Paul, MN: West Group.

Blackhall, L. J., Murphy, S. T., Frank, G., Michel, V., & Azen, S. (1995). Ethnicity and attitudes toward patient autonomy. *Journal of the American Medical Association, 274,* 820–25.

Blackman, S. (1997). *Graceful exits: How great beings die.* New York: Weatherhill.

Blackmore, S. (1993). *Dying to live: Science and the near-death experience.* London: Grafton.

Blane, D. (Editorial). (1995). Social determinants of health: Socioeconomic status, social class, and ethnicity. *American Journal of Public Health, 85,* 903–905.

Blank, J. W. (1998). *The death of an adult child: A book for and about bereaved parents.* Amityville, NY: Baywood.

Blauner, R. (1966). Death and social structure. *Psychiatry, 29,* 378–94.

Bleich, J. D. (1979). The obligation to heal in the Judaic tradition: A comparative analysis. In F. Rosner & J. D. Bleich (Eds.), *Jewish bioethics* (pp. 1–44). New York: Sanhedrin Press.

Bleyer, W. A. (1990). The impact of childhood cancer on the United States and the world. *CA-A Cancer Journal for Clinicians, 40,* 355–67.

Block, C. R. (1993). Lethal violence in the Chicago Latino community. In A. V. Wilson (Ed.), *Homicide: The victim/offender connection* (pp. 267–342). Cincinnati: Anderson.

Blos, P. (1941). *The adolescent personality: A study of individual behavior.* New York: D. Appleton-Century.

Blos, P. (1979). *The adolescent passage: Developmental issues.* New York: International Universities Press.

Bluebond-Langner, M. (1977). Meanings of death to children. In H. Feifel (Ed.), *New meanings of death* (pp. 47–66). New York: McGraw-Hill.

Bluebond-Langner, M. (1978). *The private worlds of dying children.* Princeton, NJ: Princeton University Press.

Bluebond-Langner, M. (1991). Living with cystic fibrosis: The well sibling's perspective. *Medical Anthropology Quarterly,* 5(2), 133–52.

Bluebond-Langner, M., Perkel, D., & Goertzel, T. (1991). Pediatric cancer patients' peer relationships: The impact of an oncology camp experience. *Journal of Psychosocial Oncology,* 9(2), 67–80.

Blume, J. (1981). *Tiger eyes.* Scarsdale, NY: Bradbury.

Boase, T. S. R. (1972). *Death in the middle ages: Mortality, judgment and remembrance.* New York: McGraw-Hill.

Bolton, C., & Camp, D. J. (1987). Funeral rituals and the facilitation of grief work. *Omega, 17,* 343–52.

Bolton, I. (1995). *My son, my son: A guide to healing after a suicide in the family* (rev. ed.). Atlanta: Bolton Press.

Borg, S., & Lasker, J. (1989). *When pregnancy fails: Families coping with miscarriage, stillbirth, and infant death* (rev. ed.). New York: Bantam.

Borkman, T. (1976). Experiential knowledge: A new concept for the analysis of self-help groups. *Social Service Review,* 50, 445–56.

Boss, P. (1999). *Ambiguous loss: Learning to live with unresolved grief.* Cambridge, MA: Harvard University Press.

Bowen, M. (1991). Family reactions to death. In F. Walsh & M. McGoldrick (Eds.), *Living beyond loss: Death in the family* (pp. 164–75). New York: Norton.

Bowker, J. (1991). *The meanings of death.* Cambridge, England: Cambridge University Press.

Bowlby, J. (1961). Processes of mourning. *International Journal of Psychoanalysis, 42,* 317–40.

Bowlby, J. (1973–82). *Attachment and loss* (3 vols.). New York: Basic Books.

Bowman, L. E. (1959). *The American funeral: A study in guilt, extravagance and sublimity.* Washington, DC: Public Affairs Press.

Boyd-Franklin, N., Steiner, G. L., & Boland, M. G. (Eds.). (1995). *Children, families, and HIV/AIDS: Psychosocial and therapeutic issues.* New York: Guilford.

Brabant, S. (1996). *Mending the torn fabric: For those who grieve and those who want to help them.* Amityville, NY: Baywood.

Brabant, S., Forsyth, C., & McFarlain, G. (1995). Life after the death of a child: Initial and long term support from others. *Omega, 31,* 67–85.

Bradach, K. M., & Jordan, J. R. (1995). Long-term effects of a family history of traumatic death on adolescent individuation. *Death Studies, 19,* 315–36.

Brady, E. M. (1979). Telling the story: Ethics and dying. *Hospital Progress, 60,* 57–62.

Bramblett, J. (1991). *When good-bye is forever: Learning to live again after the loss of a child.* New York: Ballantine.

Braun, K., Pietsch, J., & Blanchette, P. (Eds.). (2000). *Cultural issues in end-of-life decision making.* Thousand Oaks, CA: Sage.

Braza, K., & Bright, B. (1991). *Memory book: For bereaved children.* Salt Lake City, UT: Holy Cross Hospital Grief Center.

Breck, J. (1995). Euthanasia and the quality of life debate. *Christian Bioethics, 1,* 322–37.

Breed, W. (1972). Five components of a basic suicide syndrome. *Life-Threatening Behavior, 2,* 3–18.

Brennan, C. (1988, Nov. 5). Al Joyner can't escape memories of FloJo. *USA Today,* p. 5E.

Brent, S. (1978). Puns, metaphors, and misunderstandings in a two-year-old's conception of death. *Omega, 8,* 285–94.

Brent, S. B., & Speece, M. W. (1993). "Adult" conceptualization of irreversibility: Implications for the development of the concept of death. *Death Studies, 17,* 203–24.

Brodman, B. (1976). *The Mexican cult of death in myth and literature.* Gainesville: University of Florida Press.

Brokaw, T. (1998). *The greatest generation.* New York: Random House.
Brothers, J. (1990). *Widowed.* New York: Simon & Schuster.
Brown, J. A. (1990). Social work practice with the terminally ill in the Black community. In J. K. Parry (Ed.), *Social work practice with the terminally ill: A transcultural perspective* (pp. 67–82). Springfield, IL: Charles C Thomas.
Brown, J. E. (1987). *The spiritual legacy of the American Indian.* New York: Crossroad.
Brown, J. H., Henteleff, P., Barakat, S., & Rowe, C. J. (1986). Is it normal for terminally ill patients to desire death? *American Journal of Psychiatry, 143,* 208–11.
Brown, M. W. (1958). *The dead bird.* Reading, MA: Addison-Wesley.
Brown, R. A. (1975). *The law of personal property* (3rd ed., by W. B. Rauschenbush). Chicago: Callaghan.
Broyard, A. (1992). *Intoxicated by my illness, and other writings on life and death.* Comp. and Ed. A. Broyard. New York: Clarkson Potter.
Brubaker, E. (1985). Older parents' reactions to the death of adult children: Implications for practice. *Journal of Gerontological Social Work, 9,* 35–48.
Bruner, J. S. (1962). *The process of education.* Cambridge: Harvard University Press.
Bryer, K. B. (1979). The Amish way of death: A study of family support systems. *American Psychologist, 34,* 255–61.
Buchanan, D., & Cernada, G. (Eds.). (1998). *Progress in preventing AIDS? Dogma, dissent and innovation—global perspectives.* Amityville, NY: Baywood.
Buckingham, R. W. (1992). *Among friends: Hospice care for the person with AIDS.* Buffalo, NY: Prometheus.
Buckley, S. (2001, Sept. 2). Slow change of heart. *St. Petersburg Times.* pp. 1A, 8A–9A.
Buckman, R. (1988). *I don't know what to say: How to help and support someone who is dying.* Toronto: Key Porter Books.
Buckman, R. (1992). *How to break bad news: A guide for health care professionals.* Toronto: University of Toronto Press.
Bühler, C. (1968). The general structure of the human life cycle. In C. Bühler & F. Massarik (Eds.), *The course of human life: A study of goals in the humanistic perspective* (pp. 12–26). New York: Springer.
Bumiller, E. (2001, Nov. 12). Honoring lost lives from some 80 nations in memorial for world. *The New York Times,* p. B10.
Bunting, E. (1982). *The happy funeral.* New York: Harper & Row.
Bunting, E. (1999). *Rudi's Pond.* New York: Clarion Books.
Burns, S. B. (1990). *Sleeping beauty: Memorial photography in America.* Altadena, CA: Twelvetrees Press.
Burtt, E. A. (1955). *The teachings of the compassionate Buddha.* New York: New American Library.
Busch, K. G., Zagar, R., Hughes, J. R., Arbit, J., & Bussell, R. E. (1990). Adolescents who kill. *Journal of Clinical Psychology, 46,* 472–85.
Butler, C. L., & Lagoni, L. S. (1996). Children and pet loss. In C. A. Corr & D. M. Corr (Eds.), *Handbook of childhood death and bereavement* (pp. 179–200). New York: Springer.
Butler, R. N. (1963). The life review: An interpretation of reminiscence in the aged. *Psychiatry, 26,* 65–76.
Butler, R. N. (1969). Age-ism: Another form of bigotry. *The Gerontologist, 9,* 243–46.
Butler, R. N. (1975). *Why survive? Being old in America.* New York: Harper & Row.
Butler, R. N., & Lewis, M. I. (1982). *Aging and mental health* (3rd ed.). St. Louis: C. V. Mosby.
Byock, I. R. (1994). The hospice clinician's response to euthanasia/physician assisted suicide. *Hospice Journal, 9,* 1–8.
Byock, I. (1997). *Dying well: The prospect for growth at the end of life.* New York: Putnam.
Cade, S. (1963). Cancer: The patient's viewpoint and the clinician's problems. *Proceedings of the Royal Society of Medicine, 56,* 1–8.
Cain, A. (Ed.). (1972). *Survivors of suicide.* Springfield, IL: Bannerstone House.
Caine, L. (1975). *Widow.* New York: Bantam Books.
Calhoun, L. G., Abernathy, C. B., & Selby, J. W. (1986). The rules of bereavement: Are suicidal deaths different? *Journal of Community Psychology, 14,* 213–18.
Caliandro, G., & Hughes, C. (1998). The experience of being a grandmother who is the primary caregiver for her HIV-positive grandchild. *Nursing Research, 47,* 17–113.
Callanan, M., & Kelley, P. (1992). *Final gifts: Understanding the special awareness, needs, and communications of the dying.* New York: Poseidon.

Callender, C. O., Hall, L. E., Yeager, C. L., Barber, J. B., Dunston, G. M., & Pinn-Wiggins, V. W. (1991). Organ donation and blacks: A critical frontier. *New England Journal of Medicine, 325*, 442–44.

Calvin, S., & Smith, I. M. (1986). Counseling adolescents in death-related situations. In C. A. Corr & J. N. McNeil (Eds.), *Adolescence and death* (pp. 215–30). New York: Springer.

Camenisch, P. F. (Eds.). (1994). *Religious methods and resources in bioethics.* Boston: Kluwer.

Campbell, G. R. (1989). The political epidemiology of infant mortality: A health crisis among Montana American Indians. *American Indian Culture and Research Journal, 13*, 105–48.

Campbell, S., & Silverman, P. R. (1996). *Widower: When men are left alone.* Amityville, NY: Baywood.

Campos, A. P. (1990). Social work practice with Puerto Rican terminally ill clients and their families. In J. K. Parry (Ed.), *Social work practice with the terminally ill: A transcultural perspective* (pp. 129–43). Springfield, IL: Charles C. Thomas.

Camus, A. (1972). *The plague.* Trans. S. Gilbert. New York: Vintage Books. (Original work published 1947.)

Canadian Palliative Care Association. (1995). *Palliative care: Towards a consensus in standardized principles of practice* (first phase working document). Ottawa, Canada: Author (5 Blackburn Avenue, Ottawa, Ontario, Canada K1N 8A2).

Canine, J. D. (1999). *What am I going to do with myself when I die?* Stamford, CT: Appleton & Lange.

Cantor, N. L. (1987). *Legal frontiers of death and dying.* Bloomington, IN: Indiana University Press.

Cantor, N. L. (1993). *Advance directives and the pursuit of death with dignity.* Bloomington, IN: Indiana University Press.

Cantor, R. C. (1978). *And a time to live: Toward emotional well-being during the crisis of cancer.* New York: Harper & Row.

Carey, R. G. (1979). Weathering widowhood: Problems and adjustment of the widowed during the first year. *Omega, 10*, 263–74.

Carr, B. A., & Lee, E. S. (1978). Navajo tribal mortality: A life table analysis of the leading causes of death. *Social Biology, 25*, 279–87.

Carrick, C. (1976). *The accident.* New York: Seabury Press.

Carse, J. P. (1980). *Death and existence: A conceptual history of mortality.* New York: Wiley.

Carson, U. (1984). Teachable moments occasioned by "small deaths." In H. Wass & C. A. Corr (Eds.), *Childhood and death* (pp. 315–43). Washington, DC: Hemisphere.

Carter, B., & McGoldrick, M. (Eds.). (1988). *The changing family life cycle: A framework for family therapy* (2nd ed.). New York: Gardner.

Carter, J. (1998). *The virtues of aging.* New York: Library of Contemporary Thought/ Ballantine.

Cassell, E. J. (1985). *Talking with patients: Volume 1, The theory of doctor-patient communication; Volume 2, Clinical technique.* Cambridge, MA: MIT Press.

Cassell, E. J. (1991). *The nature of suffering and the goals of medicine.* New York: Oxford University Press.

Cassileth, B. R., Zupkis, R. V., Sutton-Smith, K., & March, V. (1980). Information and participation preferences among cancer patients. *Annals of Internal Medicine, 92*, 832–36.

Cate, F. H., & Gill, B. A. (1991). *The Patient Self-Determination Act: Implementation issues and opportunities.* Washington, DC: The Annenberg Washington Program.

Centers for Disease Control. (1981a). *Pneumocystis* pneumonia—Los Angeles. *Morbidity and Mortality Weekly Report, 30*, 250–52.

Centers for Disease Control. (1981b). Kaposi's sarcoma and *Pneumocystis* pneumonia among homosexual men—New York City and California. *Morbidity and Mortality Weekly Report, 30*, 305–308.

Centers for Disease Control. (1981c). Follow-up on Kaposi's sarcoma and *Pneumocystis* pneumonia. *Morbidity and Mortality Weekly Report, 30*, 409–10.

Centers for Disease Control. (1992a). 1993 revised classification system for HIV infection and expanded surveillance case definition for AIDS among adolescents and adults. *Morbidity and Mortality Weekly Report, 41*, No. RR-17.

Centers for Disease Control and Prevention. (1992b). *HIV/AIDS Surveillance Report, 4*(1).

Centers for Disease Control and Prevention. (2001a). The global HIV and AIDS epidemic, 2001. *Morbidity and Mortality Weekly Report,* 50(21), 434–439.

Centers for Disease Control and Prevention. (2001b). *HIV/AIDS Surveillance Report, 12*(2).
Centers for Disease Control and Prevention (2002). *HIV/AIDS Surveillance Report, 13*(1).
Chan, W.-T. (1963). *A sourcebook in Chinese philosophy.* Princeton, NJ: Princeton University Press.
Chance, S. (1992). *Stronger than death.* New York: Norton.
Chappell, B. J. (2001). My journey to the Dougy Center. In O. D. Weeks & C. Johnson (Eds.), *When all the friends have gone: A guide for aftercare providers* (pp. 141–54). Amityville, NY: Baywood.
Charmaz, K. (1980). *The social reality of death: Death in contemporary America.* Reading, MA: Addison-Wesley.
Chethik, N. (2001). *FatherLoss: How sons of all ages come to terms with the deaths of their dads.* New York: Hyperion.
Childers, P., & Wimmer, M. (1971). The concept of death in early childhood. *Child Development, 42,* 1299–1301.
Childress, J. F. (1990). The place of autonomy in bioethics. *Hastings Center Report, 20*(1), 12–17.
Chin, A. E., Hedberg, K., Higginson, G. K., & Fleming, D. W. (1999). Legalized physician-assisted suicide in Oregon—The first year's experience. *New England Journal of Medicine, 340,* 577–83.
Choice in Dying. (1996). *Advance directives and end-of-life decisions.* New York: Author.
Choron, J. (1963). *Death and Western thought.* New York: Collier.
Choron, J. (1964). *Death and modern man.* New York: Collier.
Christ, G. H. (2000). *Healing children's grief: Surviving a parent's death from cancer.* New York: Oxford University Press.
Clardy, A. E. (1984). *Dusty was my friend: Coming to terms with loss.* New York: Human Sciences.
Claypool, J. R. (1974). *Tracks of a fellow struggler: How to handle grief.* Waco, TX: Word Books.
Clayton, P. J. (1973). The clinical morbidity of the first year of bereavement: A review. *Comprehensive Psychiatry, 14,* 151–57.
Clayton, P. J. (1974). Mortality and morbidity in the first year of widowhood. *Archives of General Psychiatry, 30,* 747–50.
Clayton, P. J., Herjanic, M., Murphy, G. E., & Woodruff, R. A. (1974). Mourning and depression: Their similarities and differences. *Canadian Psychiatric Association Journal, 19,* 309–12.
Cleckley, M., Estes, E., & Norton, P. (Eds.). (1992). *We need not walk alone: After the death of a child* (2nd ed.). Oak Brook, IL: The Compassionate Friends.
Clifford, D., & Jordan, C. (1994). *Plan your estate* (3rd ed.). Berkeley, CA: Nolo Press.
Clifton, C. E. (2000). Mbeki fails to break the silence. *Positively Aware, The Journal of Test Positive Aware Network, 11*(5), 54–55.
Coffin, M. M. (1976). *Death in early America: The history and folklore of customs and superstitions of early medicine, burial and mourning.* Nashville: Thomas Nelson.
Cohen, C. B. (1996). Christian perspectives on assisted suicide and euthanasia: The Anglican tradition. *Journal of Law, Medicine & Ethics, 24,* 369–79.
Cohen, M. N. (1989). *Health and the rise of civilization.* New Haven, CT: Yale University Press.
Cohn, J. (1987). *I had a friend named Peter: Talking to children about the death of a friend.* New York: Morrow.
Coleman, J. C. (1978). Current contradictions in adolescent theory. *Journal of Youth and Adolescence, 7,* 1–11.
Colen, B. D. (1991). *The essential guide to a living will: How to protect your right to refuse medical treatment.* New York: Prentice Hall Press.
Collett, L., & Lester, D. (1969). The fear of death and the fear of dying. *Journal of Psychology, 72,* 179–81.
Colorado Collaboration on End-of-Life Care. (n.d.). *Five themes for caring: Spiritual care giving guide.* Denver, CO: Author.
Comstock, G. A., & Paik, H. (1991). *Television and the American child.* San Diego: Academic Press.
Congdon, H. K. (1977). *The pursuit of death.* Nashville: Abingdon.
Conger, J. J., & Peterson, A. C. (1984). *Adolescence and youth: Psychological development in a changing world* (3rd ed.). New York: Harper & Row.
Connor, S. R. (1998). *Hospice: Practice, pitfalls, and promise.* Briston, PA: Taylor & Francis.
Cook, A. S., & Dworkin, D. S. (1992). *Helping the bereaved: Therapeutic interventions for children, adolescents, and adults.* New York: Basic Books.

Cook, A. S., & Oltjenbruns, K. A. (1998). *Dying and grieving: Lifespan and family perspectives* (2nd ed.). Fort Worth, TX: Harcourt Brace.

Corace, B. (2000). End-of-life care: A personal reflection. *Innovations in end-of-life care, 2*(4), www.edc.org/lastacts.

Corless, I. B. (2001). Bereavement. In B. R. Ferrell & N. Coyle (Eds.), *Textbook of palliative nursing* (pp. 352–62). New York: Oxford University Press.

Corless, I. B., & Foster, Z. (Eds.). (1999). The hospice heritage: Celebrating our future [Special issue]. *The Hospice Journal, 14* (3/4).

Corley, E. A. (1973). *Tell me about death, tell me about funerals.* Santa Clara, CA: Grammatical Sciences.

Corr, C. A. (1978). A model syllabus for death and dying courses. *Death Education, 1*, 433–57.

Corr, C. A. (1980). Workshops on children and death. *Essence, 4*, 5–18.

Corr, C. A. (1981). Hospices, dying persons, and hope. In R. A. Pacholski & C. A. Corr (Eds.), *New directions in death education and counseling: Enhancing the quality of life in the nuclear age* (pp. 14–20). Arlington, VA: Forum for Death Education and Counseling.

Corr, C. A. (1984a). Helping with death education. In H. Wass & C. A. Corr (Eds.), *Helping children cope with death: Guidelines and resources* (2nd ed., pp. 49–73). Washington, DC: Hemisphere.

Corr, C. A. (1984b). A model syllabus for children and death courses. *Death Education, 8*, 11–28.

Corr, C. A. (1991). Should young children attend funerals? What constitutes reliable advice? *Thanatos, 16*(4), 19–21.

Corr, C. A. (1992a). A task-based approach to coping with dying. *Omega, 24*, 81–94.

Corr, C. A. (1992b). Teaching a college course on children and death: A 13-year report. *Death Studies, 16*, 343–56.

Corr, C. A. (1992c). *Someone you love is dying: How do you cope?* Houston, TX: Service Corporation International.

Corr, C. A. (1993a). Coping with dying: Lessons that we should and should not learn from the work of Elisabeth Kübler-Ross. *Death Studies, 17*, 69–83.

Corr, C. A. (1993b). The day we went to Auschwitz. *Omega, 27*, 105–13.

Corr, C. A. (1995a). Children and death: Where have we been? Where are we now? In D. W. Adams & E. J. Deveau (Eds.), *Beyond the innocence of childhood: Factors influencing children and adolescents' perceptions and attitudes toward death* (vol. 1, pp. 15–28). Amityville, NY: Baywood.

Corr, C. A. (1995b). Children's understandings of death: Striving to understand death. In K. J. Doka (Ed.), *Children mourning, mourning children* (pp. 3–16). Washington, DC: Hospice Foundation of America.

Corr, C. A. (1995c). Death education for adults. In I. B. Corless, B. B. Germino, & M. A. Pittman (Eds.), *A challenge for living: Dying, death, and bereavement* (pp. 351–65). Boston: Jones & Bartlett.

Corr, C. A. (1995d). Entering into adolescent understandings of death. In E. A. Grollman (Ed.), *Bereaved children and teens: A support guide for parents and professionals* (pp. 21–35). Boston: Beacon.

Corr, C. A. (1996). Children and questions about death. In S. Strack (Ed.), *Death and the quest for meaning: Essays in honor of Herman Feifel* (pp. 317–38). Northvale, NJ: Jason Aronson.

Corr, C. A. (1998a). Developmental perspectives on grief and mourning. In K. J. Doka & J. D. Davidson (Eds.), *Living with grief: Who we are, how we grieve* (pp. 143–59). Washington, DC: Hospice Foundation of America.

Corr, C. A. (1998b). Enhancing the concept of disenfranchised grief. *Omega, 38*, 1–20.

Corr, C. A. (2000a). Using books to help children and adolescents cope with death: Guidelines and bibliography. In K. J. Doka (Ed.), *Living with grief: Children, adolescents, and loss* (pp. 295–314). Washington, DC: Hospice Foundation of America.

Corr, C. A. (2000b). What do we know about grieving children and adolescents? In K. J. Doka (Ed.), *Living with grief: Children, adolescents, and loss* (pp. 21–32). Washington, DC: Hospice Foundation of America.

Corr, C. A. (2001a). Restructuring relationships: Four examples. *Journeys: A Newsletter to Help in Bereavement*, July 2001, pp. 1, 3.

Corr, C. A. (2001b). Some reflections on the National Donor Quilt. *For Those Who Give and Grieve, 9*(4), p. 6.

Corr, C. A. (2001c). Death-related literature for children and adolescents: Selected, annotated, and with guidelines and resources for adults. In A. Armstrong-Dailey & S. Zarbock (Eds.),

Hospice care for children (2nd ed.; pp. 378–401). New York: Oxford University Press.
Corr, C. A., & Balk, D. E. (Eds.). (1996). *Handbook of adolescent death and bereavement.* New York: Springer.
Corr, C. A., Coolican, M. B., Nile, L. G., & Noedel, N. R. (1994). What is the rationale for or against contacts between donor families and transplant recipients? *Critical Care Nursing Clinics of North America, 6,* 625–32.
Corr, C. A., & Corr, D. M. (Eds.). (1983). *Hospice care: Principles and practice.* New York: Springer.
Corr, C. A., & Corr, D. M. (Eds.). (1985a). *Hospice approaches to pediatric care.* New York: Springer.
Corr, C. A., & Corr, D. M. (1985b). Situations involving children: A challenge for the hospice movement. *Hospice Journal, 1,* 63–77.
Corr, C. A., & Corr, D. M. (1985c). Pediatric hospice care. *Pediatrics, 76,* 774–80.
Corr, C. A., & Corr, D. M. (1988). What is pediatric hospice care? Children's Health Care, 17, 4–11.
Corr, C. A., & Corr, D. M. (1992a). Adult hospice day care. *Death Studies, 16,* 155–71.
Corr, C. A., & Corr, D. M. (1992b). Children's hospice care. *Death Studies, 16,* 431–49.
Corr, C. A., & Corr, D. M. (Eds.). (1996). *Handbook of childhood death and bereavement.* New York: Springer.
Corr, C. A., & Corr, D. M. (1998). Key elements in a framework for helping grieving children and adolescents. *Illness, Crisis, and Loss, 6*(2), 142–60.
Corr, C. A., & Corr, D. M. (2000). Anticipatory mourning and coping with dying: Similarities, differences, and suggested guidelines for helpers. In T. A. Rando (Ed.), *Clinical dimensions of anticipatory mourning: Theory and practice in working with the dying, their loved ones, and their caregivers* (pp. 223–51). Champaign, IL: Research Press.
Corr, C. A., Doka, K. J., & Kastenbaum, R. (1999). Dying and its interpreters: A review of selected literature and some comments on the state of the field. *Omega, 39,* 239–259.
Corr, C. A., Fuller, H., Barnickol, C. A., & Corr, D. M. (Eds.). (1991). *Sudden infant death syndrome: Who can help and how.* New York: Springer.
Corr, C. A., & McNeil, J. N. (Eds.). (1986). *Adolescence and death.* New York: Springer.
Corr, C. A., & the Members of the Executive Committee of the National Donor Family Council. (2001). The National Donor Family Council and its Giving, Grieving, Growing(TM) program. *Progress in Transplantation.* December, 2001.
Corr, C. A., Morgan, J. D., & Wass, H. (Eds.). (1994). *Statements about death, dying, and bereavement by the International Work Group on Death, Dying, and Bereavement.* London, Ontario: King's College.
Corr, C. A., Nabe, C. M., & Corr, D. M. (1994). A task-based approach for understanding and evaluating funeral practices. *Thanatos, 19*(2), 10–15.
Corr, C. A., Nile, L. G., & the other members of the National Donor Family Council of the National Kidney Foundation. (1994). A bill of rights for donor families. *For Those Who Give and Grieve* (a quarterly newsletter for donor families published by the National Kidney Foundation), *2*(4), 4–5.
Corr, C. A., & the Staff of the Dougy Center. (1991). Support for grieving children: The Dougy Center and the hospice philosophy. *American Journal of Hospice and Palliative Care, 8*(4), 23–27.
Counts, D. R., & Counts, D. A. (Eds.). (1991). *Coping with the final tragedy: Cultural variation in dying and grieving.* Amityville, NY: Baywood.
Cousins, N. (1979). *Anatomy of an illness as perceived by the patient: Reflections on healing and regeneration.* New York: Norton.
Cousins, N. (1989). *Head first: The biology of hope.* New York: E. P. Dutton.
Cox, G. R., & Fundis, R. J. (Eds.). (1992). *Spiritual, ethical and pastoral aspects of death and bereavement.* Amityville, NY: Baywood.
Crase, D. R., & Crase, D. (1976). Helping children understand death. *Young Children, 32*(1), 21–25.
Crase, D. R., & Crase, D. (1984). Death education in the schools for older children. In H. Wass & C. A. Corr (Eds.), *Childhood and death* (pp. 345–63). Washington, DC: Hemisphere.
Craven, J., & Wald, F. S. (1975). Hospice care for dying patients. *American Journal of Nursing, 75,* 1816–22.
Craven, M. (1973). *I heard the owl call my name.* New York: Dell.
Crawford, S. C. (1995). *Dilemmas of life and death: Hindu ethics in a North American context.* Albany: State University of New York Press.

Cremation Association of North America. (2000). www.cremationassociation.org

Crenshaw, D. A. (1995). *Bereavement: Counseling the grieving throughout the life cycle.* New York: Crossroad.

Crissman, J. K. (1994). *Death and dying in central Appalachia: Changing attitudes and practices.* Urbana, IL: University of Illinois Press.

Culver, C. M., & Gert, B. (1990). Beyond the living will: Making advance directives more useful. *Omega, 21,* 253–58.

Czarnecki, J. P. (1989). *Last traces: The lost art of Auschwitz.* New York: Atheneum.

Czech, D. (1990). *Auschwitz chronicle, 1939–1945.* New York: Holt.

Dane, B. O. (1996). Children, HIV infection, and AIDS. In C. A. Corr & D. M. Corr (Eds.), *Handbook of childhood death and bereavement* (pp. 51–70). New York: Springer.

Dane, B. O., & Levine, C. (Eds.). (1994). *AIDS and the new orphans: Coping with death.* Westport, CT: Auburn House.

Danforth, L. M. (1982). *The death rituals of rural Greece.* Princeton, NJ: Princeton University Press.

Davidson, G. W. (1975). *Living with dying.* Minneapolis: Augsburg.

Davidson, G. W. (1984). *Understanding mourning: A guide for those who grieve.* Minneapolis: Augsburg.

Davidson, L., & Gould, M. S. (1989). Contagion as a risk factor for youth suicide. In Alcohol, Drug Abuse, and Mental Health Administration, *Report of the secretary's task force on youth suicide* (vol. 2, pp. 88–109). Washington, DC: U.S. Government Printing Office.

Davidson, L. E., Rosenberg, M. L., Mercy, J., & Franklin, J. (1989). An epidemiologic study of risk factors in two teenage suicide clusters. *Journal of the American Medical Association, 262,* 2687–92.

Davidson, M. N., & Devney, P. (1991). Attitudinal barriers to organ donation among Black Americans. *Transplantation Proceedings, 23,* 2531–32.

Davies, B. (1998). *Shadows in the sun: The experiences of sibling bereavement in childhood.* Washington, DC: Taylor & Francis.

Davies, B., Deveau, E., deVeber, B., Howell, D., Martinson, I., Papadatou, D., Pask, E., & Stevens, M. (1998). Experiences of mothers in five countries whose child died of cancer. *Cancer Nursing, 21*(5), 301–11.

Davies, B., & Howell, D. (1998). Special services for children. In D. Doyle, G. W. C. Hanks, & N. MacDonald (Eds.), *Oxford textbook of palliative medicine* (2nd ed., pp. 1077–84). New York: Oxford University Press.

Davies, B., Reimer, J. C., Brown, P., & Martens, N. (1995). *Fading away: The experience of transition in families with terminal illness.* Amityville, NY: Baywood.

Davies, D. (1993). Cluster suicide in rural western Canada. *Canadian Journal of Psychiatry, 38,* 515–19.

Davies, R. E. (1999). The Diana community nursing team and paediatric palliative care. *British Journal of Nursing, 8,* 506–11.

Davis, D. L. (1991). *Empty cradle, broken heart: Surviving the death of your baby.* Golden, CO: Fulcrum.

Davis, D. S. (1994). Method in Jewish bioethics. In P. F. Camenisch (Ed.), *Religious methods and resources in bioethics* (pp. 109–26). Dordrecht: Kluwer.

Dawidowicz, L. S. (1975). *The war against the Jews 1933–1945.* New York: Holt, Rinehart & Winston.

De Beauvoir, S. (1973). *A very easy death.* Trans. P. O'Brian. New York: Warner. (Original work published 1964.)

De Hennezel, M. (1998). *Intimate death: How the dying teach us to live.* Trans. C. B. Janeway. New York: Knopf.

De Wachter, M. A. M. (1989). Active euthanasia in the Netherlands. *Journal of the American Medical Association, 262,* 3315–19.

De Wachter, M. A. M. (1992). Euthanasia in the Netherlands. *Hastings Center Report, 22*(2), 23–30.

Deaton, R. L., & Berkan, W. A. (1995). *Planning and managing death issues in the schools: A handbook.* Westport, CT: Greenwood.

DeFrain, J., Ernst, L., Jakub, D., & Taylor, J. (1991). *Sudden infant death: Enduring the loss.* Lexington, MA: Lexington Books.

DeFrain, J., Martens, L., Story, J., & Stork, W. (1986). *Stillborn: The invisible death.* Lexington, MA: Lexington Books.

DeGregory, L. (2000, Oct. 29). Final wish granted. *St. Petersburg Times,* p. 5F.

Delgadillo, D., & Davis, P. (1990). *When the bough breaks.* San Diego: San Diego County Guild for Infant Survival.

Demi, A. S., & Miles, M. S. (1987). Parameters of normal grief: A Delphi study. *Death Studies, 11,* 397–412.

Demi, A. S. & Miles, M. S. (1988). Suicide bereaved parents: Emotional distress and physical health problems. *Death Studies, 12,* 297–307.

Des Pres, T. (1976). *The survivor: An anatomy of life in the death camps.* New York: Oxford University Press.

Detmer, C. M., & Lamberti, J. W. (1991). Family grief. *Death Studies, 15,* 363–74.

Deutsch, H. (1937). Absence of grief. *Psychoanalytic Quarterly, 6,* 12–22.

Devore, W. (1990). The experience of death: A Black perspective. In J. K. Parry (Ed.), *Social work practice with the terminally ill: A transcultural perspective* (pp. 47–66). Springfield, IL: Charles C Thomas.

Diamant, A. (1994, October). Special report: Media violence. *Parents Magazine,* pp. 40–41, 45.

Dickens, C. (1963). *Dombey and son.* Ed. E. Johnson. New York: Dell. (Original work published 1848.)

DiClemente, R. J., Stewart, K. E., Johnson, M. O., & Pack, R. P. (1996). Adolescents and acquired immune deficiency syndrome (AIDS): Epidemiology, prevention, and psychological responses. In C. A. Corr & D. E. Balk (Eds.), *Handbook of adolescent death and bereavement* (pp. 85–106). New York: Springer.

DiGiulio, R. C. (1989). *Beyond widowhood: From bereavement to emergence and hope.* New York: Free Press.

Disaster Mortuary Operational Response Team (DMORT). (1998). *Team member handbook.* USA: Author.

Doane, B. K., & Quigley, B. Q. (1981). Psychiatric aspects of therapeutic abortion. *Canadian Medical Association Journal, 125,* 427–32.

Doka, K. J. (1988). The awareness of mortality in midlife: Implications for later life. *Gerontology Review, 2,* 1–10.

Doka, K. J. (Ed.). (1989a). *Disenfranchised grief: Recognizing hidden sorrow.* Lexington, MA: Lexington Books.

Doka, K. J. (1989b). Disenfranchised grief. In K. J. Doka (Ed.), *Disenfranchised grief: Recognizing hidden sorrow* (pp. 3–11). Lexington, MA: Lexington Books.

Doka, K. J. (1993a). *Living with life-threatening illness: A guide for patients, families, and caregivers.* Lexington, MA: Lexington Books.

Doka, K. J. (1993b). The spiritual needs of the dying. In K. J. Doka & J. D. Morgan (Eds.), *Death and spirituality* (pp. 143–50). Amityville, NY: Baywood.

Doka, K. J. (Ed.). (1995). *Children mourning, mourning children.* Washington, DC: Hospice Foundation of America.

Doka, K. J. (1996a). The cruel paradox: Children who are living with life-threatening illnesses. In C. A. Corr & D. M. Corr (Eds.), *Handbook of childhood death and bereavement* (pp. 89–105). New York: Springer.

Doka, K. J. (Ed.). (1996b). *Living with grief after sudden loss: Suicide, homicide, accident, heart attack, stroke.* Washington, DC: Hospice Foundation of America.

Doka, K. J. (1997). *AIDS, fear, and society: Challenging the dreaded disease.* Washington, DC: Taylor & Francis.

Doka, K. J. (Ed.). (2000). *Living with grief: Children, adolescents, and loss.* Washington, DC: Hospice Foundation of America.

Doka, K. J. (Ed.). (2001). *Disenfranchised grief: New directions, strategies, and challenges for practice.* Champaign, IL: Research Press.

Doka, K. J., with Morgan, J. D. (Eds.). (1993). *Death and spirituality.* Amityville, NY: Baywood.

Donnelley, N. H. (1987). *I never know what to say.* New York: Ballantine.

Donnelly, K. F. (1982). *Recovering from the loss of a child.* New York: Macmillan.

Donnelly, K. F. (1987). *Recovering from the loss of a parent.* New York: Dodd, Mead.

Donnelly, K. F. (1988). *Recovering from the loss of a sibling.* New York: Dodd, Mead.

Donnelly, K. F. (1994). *Recovering from the loss of a loved one to AIDS.* New York: Fawcett Columbine.

Douglas, J. D. (1967). *The social meanings of suicide.* Princeton, NJ: Princeton University Press.

Douglas, M. (1970). *Natural symbols.* New York: Random House.

Douglas, P. H., & Pinsky, L. (1996). *The essential AIDS fact book* (rev. ed.). New York: Pocket Books.

Dowie, M. (1988). *"We have a donor": The bold new world of organ transplanting*. New York: St. Martin's Press.

Downing, A. B. (Ed.). (1974). *Euthanasia and the right to death: The case for voluntary euthanasia.* London: Peter Owen.

Doyle, D., Hanks, G. W. C., & MacDonald, N. (Eds.). (1998). *Oxford textbook of palliative medicine* (2nd ed.). New York: Oxford University Press.

DuBoulay, S. (1984). *Cicely Saunders: The founder of the modern hospice movement.* London: Hodder & Stoughton.

Dukeminier, J., & Johanson, S. M. (1995). *Wills, trusts, and estates* (5th ed.). Boston: Little, Brown.

Dumont, R., & Foss, D. (1972). *The American view of death: Acceptance or denial?* Cambridge, MA: Schenkman.

Dundes, A. (1989). *Little Red Riding Hood: A casebook.* Madison, WI: University of Wisconsin Press.

Dunlop, R. J., & Hockley, J. M. (1998). *Hospital-based palliative care teams: The hospital-hospice interface* (2nd ed.). Oxford: Oxford University Press.

Dunn, R. G., & Morrish-Vidners, D. (1988). The psychological and social experience of suicide survivors. *Omega, 18,* 175–215.

Dunne, E. J., McIntosh, J. L., & Dunne-Maxim, K. (Eds.). (1987). *Suicide and its aftermath: Understanding and counseling the survivors.* New York: Norton.

Dunsmore, J. C., & Quine, S. (1995). Information support and decision making needs and preferences of adolescents with cancer: Implications for health professionals. *Journal of Psychosocial Oncology, 13*(4), 39–56.

Durkheim, E. (1951). *Suicide: A study in sociology.* Trans. J. A. Spaulding & G. Simpson. Glencoe, IL: Free Press. (Original work published 1897.)

Durkheim, E. (1954). *The elementary forms of religious life.* Trans. J. W. Swaine. London: Allen & Unwin. (Original work published 1915.)

Dwyer, T., Ponsonby, A-L., Blizzard, L., Newman, N. M., & Cochrane, J. A. (1995). The contribution of changes in the prevalence of prone sleeping position to the decline in sudden infant death syndrome in Tasmania. *Journal of the American Medical Association, 273,* 783–89.

Edelman, H. (1994). *Motherless daughters: The legacy of loss.* Reading, MA: Addison-Wesley.

The Editors of *New York* magazine. (2001). *September 11, 2001: A record of tragedy, heroism, and hope.* New York: Abrams.

Egan, K. A. (1998). *A patient-family value based end-of-life care model.* Largo, FL: Hospice Institute of the Florida Suncoast.

Egan, K. A., & Labyak, M. J. (2001). Hospice care: A model for quality end-of-life care. In B. R. Ferrell & N. Coyle (Eds.), *Textbook of palliative nursing* (pp. 7–26). New York: Oxford University Press.

Egeland, J., & Sussex, J. (1985). Suicide and family loading for affective disorders. *Journal of the American Medical Association, 254,* 915–18.

Eichrodt, W. (1967). *Theology of the Old Testament,* vol. 2. Trans. J. A. Baker. Philadelphia: Westminster.

Eisenbruch, M. (1984). Cross-cultural aspects of bereavement. II: Ethnic and cultural variations in the development of bereavement practices. *Culture, Medicine & Psychiatry, 8,* 315–47.

Elias, N. (1991). On human beings and their emotions: A process-sociological essay. In M. Featherstone, M. Hepworth, & B. S. Turner (Eds.), *The body: Social process and cultural theory* (pp. 103–25). London: Sage.

Elkind, D. (1967). Egocentrism in adolescence. *Child Development, 38,* 1025–34.

Elliot, G. (1972). *The twentieth century book of the dead.* New York: Random House.

Elmer, L. (1987). *Why her, why now: A man's journey through love and death and grief.* New York: Bantam.

Emanuel, E. J., Fairclough, D. L., & Emanuel, L. L. (2000). Attitudes and desires related to euthanasia and physician-assisted suicide among terminally ill patients and their caregivers. *Journal of the American Medical Association, 284,* 2460–68.

Emerson, R. W. (1970). *The journals and miscellaneous notebooks of Ralph Waldo Emerson* (vol. 8, 1841–43). Ed. W. H. Gilman & J. E. Parsons. Cambridge, MA: Belknap Press of Harvard University Press.

Emswiler, M. A., & Emswiler, J. P. (2000). *Guiding your child through grief.* New York: Bantam.

Engel, G. L. (1961). Is grief a disease? A challenge for medical research. *Psychosomatic Medicine, 23,* 18–22.

Enright, D. J. (Ed.). (1983). *The Oxford book of death.* New York: Oxford University Press.

Erikson, E. H. (1959). Identity and the life cycle: Selected papers. *Psychological Issues, 1,* 1–171.

Erikson, E. H. (1963). *Childhood and society* (2nd ed.). New York: Norton. (Original edition published 1950.)

Erikson, E. H. (1968). *Identity: Youth and crisis.* London: Faber & Faber.

Erikson, E. H. (1982). *The life cycle completed: A review.* New York: Norton.

Erikson, E. H., & Erikson, J. M. (1981). On generativity and identity: From a conversation with Erik and Joan Erikson. *Harvard Educational Review, 51,* 249–69.

Erikson, E. H., Erikson, J. M., & Kivnick, H. (1986). *Vital involvements in old age.* New York: Norton.

Eron, L. D. (1993). *The problem of media violence and children's behavior.* New York: Guggenheim Foundation.

Esperti, R. A., & Peterson, R. L. (1991). *The handbook of estate planning* (3rd ed.). New York: McGraw-Hill.

Esperti, R. A., & Peterson, R. L. (1992). *The living trust revolution: Why America is abandoning wills and probate.* New York: Viking.

Evanisko, M. J., Beasley, C. L., Brigham, L. E. (1998). Readiness of critical care physicians and nurses to handle requests for organ donation. *American Journal of Critical Care, 7,* 4–12.

Evans, G., & Farberow, N. L. (Eds.). (1988). *The encyclopedia of suicide.* New York: Facts on File.

Evans, J. (1971). *Living with a man who is dying: A personal memoir.* New York: Taplinger.

Evans, R. P. (1993). *The Christmas box.* Salt Lake City: Steinway.

Ewald, P. W. (1994). *Evolution of infectious diseases.* New York: Oxford University Press.

Ewalt, P. L., & Perkins, L. (1979). The real experience of death among adolescents: An empirical study. *Social Casework, 60,* 547–51.

Fairchild, T. N. (Ed.). (1986). *Crisis intervention strategies for school-based helpers.* Springfield, IL: Charles C Thomas.

Fales, M. (1964). The early American way of death. *Essex Institution Historical Collection, 100*(2), 75–84.

Farberow, N. L. (Ed.). (1980). *The many faces of suicide: Indirect self-destructive behavior.* New York: McGraw-Hill.

Farberow, N. L. (1983). Relationships between suicide and depression: An overview. *Psychiatria Fennica Supplementum, 14,* 9–19.

Farberow, N. L., Gallagher-Thompson, D., Gilewski, M., & Thompson, L. (1992). Changes in grief and mental health of bereaved spouses of older suicides. *Journal of Gerontology, 47,* 357–66.

Farberow, N. L., & Moriwaki, S. Y. (1975). Self-destructive crises in the older person. *The Gerontologist, 15,* 333–37.

Farberow, N. L., & Shneidman, E. S. (Eds.). (1965). *The cry for help.* New York: McGraw-Hill.

Farrell, J. J. (1980). *Inventing the American way of death: 1830–1920.* Philadelphia: Temple University Press.

Faulkner, A. (1993). *Teaching interactive skills in health care.* London: Chapman & Hall.

Faulkner, W. (1930). *As I lay dying.* New York: Random House.

Faulkner, W. (1943). A rose for Emily. In *Collected stories of William Faulkner* (pp. 119–30). New York: Random House. (Original work published 1924.)

Feifel, H. (Ed.). (1959). *The meaning of death.* New York: McGraw-Hill.

Feifel, H. (1963). Death. In N. L. Farberow (Ed.), *Taboo topics* (pp. 8–21). New York: Atherton.

Feifel, H. (1977a). Preface and introduction: Death in contemporary America. In H. Feifel (Ed.), *New meanings of death* (pp. xiii–xiv, 4–12). New York: McGraw-Hill.

Feifel, H. (Ed.). (1977b). *New meanings of death.* New York: McGraw-Hill.

Feldman, D. M., & Rosner, F. (Eds.). (1984). *Compendium on medical ethics* (6th ed.). New York: Federation of Jewish Philanthropies of New York.

Fenwick, P., & Fenwick, E. (1995). *The truth in the light: An investigation of over 300 near-death experiences.* New York: Berkley Books.

Ferrell, B. R., & Coyle, N. (Eds.). (2001). *Textbook of palliative nursing.* New York: Oxford University Press.

Field, M. J., & Cassel, C. K. (Eds.). (1997). *Approaching death: Improving care at the end of life.* Washington, DC: National Academy Press.

Fingerhut, L. A., & Kleinman, J. C. (1989). Mortality among children and youth. *American Journal of Public Health, 79,* 899–901.

Fingerhut, L. A., Kleinman, J. C., Godfrey, E., & Rosenberg, H. (1991). Firearm mortality among children, youth, and young adults 1–34 years of age, trends and current status: United States, 1979–88. *Monthly Vital Statistics Report, 39*(11), Suppl. Hyattsville, MD: National Center for Health Statistics.

First International Conference on Islamic Medicine. (1981). Islamic Code of Medical Ethics. Reprinted in R. Hamel (Ed.), *Choosing death; Active euthanasia, religion, and the public debate* (1991; pp. 62). Philadelphia: Trinity Press International.

Fisher, M. (1994). *Sleep with the angels: A mother challenges AIDS.* Wakefield, RI: Moyer Bell.

Fitzgerald, H. (1992). *The grieving child: A parent's guide.* New York: Simon & Schuster.

Fitzgerald, H. (1994). *The mourning handbook: A complete guide for the bereaved.* New York: Simon & Schuster.

Fitzgerald, H. (1998). *Grief at school: A guide for teachers and counselors.* Washington, DC: American Hospice Foundation.

Fitzgerald, H. (1999). *Grief at work: A manual of policies and practices.* Washington, DC: American Hospice Foundation.

Fitzgerald, H. (2000). *The grieving teen: A guide for teenagers and their friends.* New York: Simon & Schuster.

Flannery, A. (Ed.). (1982). *Vatican Council II: More postconciliar documents.* Grand Rapids, MI: Eerdmans.

Fleming, S. J. (1985). Children's grief: Individual and family dynamics. In C. A. Corr & D. M. Corr (Eds.), *Hospice approaches to pediatric care* (pp. 197–218). New York: Springer.

Fleming, S. J., & Adolph, R. (1986). Helping bereaved adolescents: Needs and responses. In C. A. Corr & J. N. McNeil (Eds.), *Adolescence and death* (pp. 97–118). New York: Springer.

Fleming, S., & Balmer, L. (1996). Bereavement in adolescence. In C. A. Corr & D. E. Balk (Eds.), *Handbook of adolescent death and bereavement* (pp. 139–54). New York: Springer.

Floerchinger, D. S. (1991). Bereavement in late adolescence; Interventions on college campuses. *Journal of Adolescent Research, 6,* 146–56.

Flynn, E. P. (1992). *Your living will: Why, when, and how to write one.* New York: Citadel Press.

Fogarty, J. A. (2000). *The magical thoughts of grieving children: Treating children with complicated mourning and advice for parents.* Amityville, NY: Baywood.

Folta, J. R., & Deck, E. S. (1976). Grief, the funeral, and the friend. In V. R. Pine, A. H. Kutscher, D. Peretz, R. C. Slater, R. DeBellis, R. J. Volk, & D. J. Cherico (Eds.), *Acute grief and the funeral* (pp. 231–40). Springfield, IL: Charles C Thomas.

Forbes, H. (1927). *Gravestones of early New England and the men who made them, 1653–1800.* Boston: Houghton Mifflin.

Ford, G. (1979). Terminal care from the viewpoint of the National Health Service. In J. J. Bonica & V. Ventafridda (Eds.), *International symposium on pain of advanced cancer: Advances in pain research and therapy,* vol. 2 (pp. 653–61). New York: Raven Press.

Foster, Z., Wald, F. S., & Wald, H. J. (1978). The hospice movement: A backward glance at its first two decades. *New Physician, 27,* 21–24.

Fowler, J. P. (2000, July/August). Why me? I learned the hard way that you don't have to be young to get hit with HIV. *Modern Maturity, 43*(4), 58-63, 76.

Fox, E., Kamakahi, J. J., & Capek, S. M. (1999). *Come lovely and soothing death: The right to die movement in the United States.* New York: Twayne.

Fox, R. C., & Swazey, J. P. (1974). *The courage to fail: A social view of organ transplants and dialysis.* Chicago: University of Chicago Press.

Fox, R. C., & Swazey, J. P. (1992). *Spare parts: Organ replacement in American society.* New York: Oxford University Press.

Fox, R. W. (1985). *Reinhold Niebuhr: A biography.* New York: Pantheon.

Fox, S. S. (1988a). *Good grief: Helping groups of children when a friend dies.* Boston: The New England Association for the Education of Young Children.

Fox, S. S. (1988b, August). Helping child deal with death teaches valuable skills. *Psychiatric Times,* pp. 10–11.

France, D. (2001). The angry prophet is dying. *Newsweek* (June 11), pp. 42–46.

Francis, J. (2001, Mar. 9). Lives crowned by love. *St. Petersburg Times,* p. 1D.

Francis, V. M. (1859). *A thesis on hospital hygiene.* New York: J. F. Trow.

Frank, A. W. (1991). *At the will of the body: Reflections on illness.* Boston: Houghton Mifflin.

Frank, A. W. (1995). *The wounded storyteller: Body, illness, and ethics.* Chicago: University of Chicago Press.

Frankl, V. (1984). *Man's search for meaning.* New York: Simon & Schuster.

Frazer, J. G. (1977). *The fear of the dead in primitive religion.* New York: Arno Press.

French, S. (1975). The cemetery as cultural institution: The establishment of Mount Auburn and the "rural cemetery" movement. In D. E. Stannard (Ed.), *Death in America* (pp. 69–91). Philadelphia: University of Pennsylvania Press.

Freud, A. (1958). Adolescence. *Psychoanalytic Study of the Child, 13,* 255–68.

Freud, S. (1913/1954). Thoughts for the time on war and death. In *Collected works,* vol. 4, pp. 288–321. London: Hogarth.

Freud, S. (1959a). Mourning and melancholia. In J. Strachey (Ed. and Trans.), *The standard edition of the complete psychological works of Sigmund Freud* (vol. 14, pp. 237–58). London: Hogarth Press. (Original work published 1917.)

Freud, S. (1959b). *New introductory lectures on psycho-analysis.* In J. Strachey (Ed. and Trans.), *The standard edition of the complete psychological works of Sigmund Freud* (vol. 22, pp. 1–182). London: Hogarth Press. (Original work published 1933.)

Friedman, E. H. (1980). Systems and ceremonies: A family view of rites of passage. In E. A. Carter & M. McGoldrick (Eds.), *The family life cycle: A framework for family therapy* (pp. 429–60). New York: Gardner.

Friel, M., & Tehan, C. B. (1980). Counteracting burn-out for the hospice care-giver. *Cancer Nursing, 3,* 285–93.

Frist, W. H. (1989). *Transplant: A heart surgeon's account of the life and death dramas of the new medicine.* New York: Atlantic Monthly Press.

Frist, W. H. (1995). *Grand rounds and transplantation.* New York: Chapman & Hall.

Fristad, M. A., Cerel, J., Goldman, M., Weller, E. B., & Weller, R. A. (2001). The role of ritual in children's bereavement. *Omega, 42,* 321–39.

Frumkin, L. R., & Leonard, J. M. (1997). *Questions & answers on AIDS* (3rd ed.). Los Angeles: Health Information Press.

Fry, V. L. (1995). *Part of me died, too: Stories of creative survival among bereaved children and teenagers.* New York: Dutton Children's Books.

Fulton, R. (1961). The clergyman and the funeral director: A study in role conflict. *Social Forces, 39,* 317–23.

Fulton, R. (1978). The sacred and the secular: Attitudes of the American public toward death, funerals, and funeral directors. In R. Fulton & R. Bendiksen (Eds.), *Death and identity* (rev. ed., pp. 158–72). Bowie, MD: Charles Press.

Fulton, R. (1995). The contemporary funeral: Functional or dysfunctional? In H. Wass & R. A. Neimeyer (Eds.), *Dying: Facing the facts* (pp. 185–209). Washington, DC: Taylor & Francis.

Fulton, R. L., & Bendiksen, R. (1994). *Death and identity* (3rd ed.). Philadelphia: Charles Press.

Fulton, R., & Fulton, J. (1971). A psychosocial aspect of terminal care: Anticipatory grief. *Omega, 2,* 91–100.

Fulton, R., & Gottesman, D. J. (1980). Anticipatory grief: A psychosocial concept reconsidered. *British Journal of Psychiatry, 137,* 45–54.

Furman, E. (Ed.). (1974). *A child's parent dies: Studies in childhood bereavement.* New Haven, CT: Yale University Press.

Furman, R. A. (1973). A child's capacity for mourning. In E. J. Anthony & C. Koupernik (Eds.), *The child in his family: The impact of disease and death* (pp. 225–31). New York: Wiley.

Furth, G. M. (1988). *The secret world of drawings: Healing through art.* Boston: Sigo.

Gaes, J. (1987). *My book for kids with cansur: A child's autobiography of hope.* Aberdeen, SD: Melius & Peterson.

Gaines-Lane, G. (1995). *My memory book.* Gaithersburg, MD: Chi Rho Press.

Galinsky, N. (1999). *When a grandchild dies: What to do, what to say, how to cope.* Houston, TXL: Gal In Sky Publishing Co. (P.O. Box 70976, Houston, TX 77270).

Gallagher-Allred, C., & Amenta, M. (Eds.). (1993). Nutrition and hydration in hospice care: Needs, strategies, ethics [Special issue]. *Hospice Journal, 9*(2/3).

Gandhi, M. (1980). *All men are brothers: Autobiographical reflections.* New York: Continuum.

Gans, J. E. (1990). *America's adolescents: How healthy are they?* American Medical Association, Profiles of Adolescent Health Series. Chicago: American Medical Association.

Garber, B. (1983). Some thoughts on normal adolescents who lost a parent by death. *Journal of Youth and Adolescence, 12,* 175–83.

Garcia-Preto, N. (1986). Puerto Rican families. In M. McGoldrick, P. Hines, E. Lee, & N. Garcia-Preto, Mourning rituals: How cultures shape the experience of loss. *The Family Therapy Networker, 10*(6), 33–34.

Garfield, C. A. (1976). Foundations of psychosocial oncology: The terminal phase. In J. M. Vaeth (Ed.), *Breast cancer: Its impact on the patient, family, and community* (pp. 180–212). Basel, Switzerland: Karger.

Garfield, C. A., with C. Spring & D. Ober. (1995). *Sometimes my heart goes numb: Love and caring in a time of AIDS.* San Francisco: Jossey-Bass.

Garrison, C. Z., Lewinsohn, P. M., Marstellar, F., Langhinrichsen, J., & Lann, I. (1991). The assessment of suicidal behavior in adolescents. *Suicide and Life-Threatening Behavior, 21,* 329–44.

Gartley, W., & Bernasconi, M. (1967). The concept of death in children. *Journal of Genetic Psychology, 110,* 71–85.

Gatch, M. McC. (1969). *Death: Meaning and mortality in Christian thought and contemporary culture.* New York: Seabury Press.

Geddes, G. E. (1981). *Welcome joy: Death in Puritan New England.* Ann Arbor, MI: UMI Research Press.

Gelfand, D. E., Balcazar, H., Parzuchowski, J., & Lenox, S. (2001). Mexicans and care for the terminally ill: Family, hospice, and the church. *American Journal of Hospice & Palliative Care, 18,* 391–96.

Gellman, B. (2000, April 30). White House ranks AIDS as a threat to national security. *St. Louis Post-Dispatch,* pp. A1, A8.

Gerisch, B. (1998). "This is not death, it is something safer": A psychodynamic approach to Sylvia Plath. *Death Studies, 22,* 735–61.

Gertner, J. (2001). Are you ready for 100? *Money, 30*(4), 98–106.

Gervais, K. G. (1986). *Redefining death.* New Haven, CT: Yale University Press.

Gianelli, D. M. (1998). Praise, criticism follow Oregon's first reported assisted suicides. *American Medical News, 41*(14), 1, 39.

Gibson, P. (1994). Gay male and lesbian youth suicide. In G. Remafedi (Ed.), *Death by denial: Studies of suicide in gay and lesbian teenagers* (pp. 15–68). Boston: Alyson.

Gifford, A. L., Lorig, K., Laurent, D., & González, V. (1997). *Living well with HIV and AIDS.* Palo Alto, CA: Bull Publishing Co.

Gilbert, K. R. (1996). "We've had the same loss, why don't we have the same grief?" Loss and differential grief in families. *Death Studies, 20,* 269–83.

Gilbert, M. (1993). *Atlas of the Holocaust* (2nd rev. printing). New York: William Morrow.

Gill, D. L. (1980). *Quest: The life of Elisabeth Kübler-Ross.* New York: Harper & Row.

Gilligan, C. (1982). *In a different voice: Psychological theory and women's development.* Cambridge, MA: Harvard University Press.

Gillon, E. (1972). *Victorian cemetery sculpture.* New York: Dover.

Glaser, B., & Strauss, A. (1965). *Awareness of dying.* Chicago: Aldine.

Glaser, B., & Strauss, A. (1968). *Time for dying.* Chicago: Aldine.

Glaser, E., & Palmer, L. (1991). *In the absence of angels: A Hollywood family's courageous story.* New York: Putnam's.

Glick, I., Weiss, R., & Parkes, C. (1974). *The first year of bereavement.* New York: Wiley.

Glover, J. (1999). *Humanity: A moral history of the twentieth century.* London: Jonathan Cape.

Golan, N. (1975). Wife to widow to woman. *Social Work, 20,* 369–74.

Goldberg, S. B. (1973). Family tasks and reactions in the crisis of death. *Social Casework, 54,* 398–405.

Golden, T. R. (1996). *Swallowed by a snake: The gift of the masculine side of healing.* Kensington, MD: Golden Healing Publishing.

Goldman, A. (1998). Life threatening illnesses and symptom control in children. In D. Doyle, G. W. C. Hanks, & N. MacDonald (Eds.), *Oxford textbook of palliative medicine* (pp. 1033–43). New York: Oxford University Press.

Goldscheider, C. (1971). *Population, modernization, and social structure.* Boston: Little, Brown.

Goody, J. (1962). *Death, property, and the ancestors: A study of the mortuary customs of the LoDagaa of West Africa.* Stanford, CA: Stanford University Press.

Gordon, A. K. (1974). The psychological wisdom of the Law. In J. Riemer (Ed.), *Jewish reflections on death* (pp. 95–104). New York: Schocken.

Gordon, A. K. (1986). The tattered cloak of immortality. In C. A. Corr & J. N. McNeil (Eds.), *Adolescence and death* (pp. 16–31). New York: Springer.

Gordon, A. K., & Klass, D. (1979). *They need to know: How to teach children about death.* Englewood Cliffs, NJ: Prentice-Hall.

Gorer, G. (1965a). The pornography of death. In G. Gorer, *Death, grief, and mourning* (pp. 192–99). Garden City, NY: Doubleday.

Gorer, G. (1965b). *Death, grief, and mourning.* Garden City, NY: Doubleday.

Gortmaker, S. L., Beasley, C. L., et al. (1996). Organ donor potential and performance: Size and nature of the organ donor shortfall. *Critical Care Medicine, 24,* 432–39.

Gottfried, R. S. (1983). *The black death: Natural and human disaster in medieval Europe.* New York: Free Press.

Gottlieb, G. J., Ragaz, A., Vogel, J. V., Friedman-Kien, A., Rywkin, A. M., Weiner, E. A., & Ackerman, A. B. (1981). A preliminary communication on extensively disseminated Kaposi's sarcoma in young homosexual men. *American Journal of Dermatopathology, 3,* 111–14.

Gottlieb, M. S., Schroff, R., Schanker, H. M., Weisman, J. D., Fan, P. T., Wolf, R. A., & Saxon, A. (1981). *Pneumocystic carinii* pneumonia and mucosal candidiasis in previously healthy homosexual men: Evidence of a new acquired cellular immunodeficiency. *New England Journal of Medicine, 305,* 1425–31.

Gould, M. S., Wallenstein, S., Kleinman, M. H., O'Carroll, P., & Mercy, J. (1990). Suicide clusters: An examination of age-specific effects. *American Journal of Public Health, 80,* 211–12.

Gourevitch, P. (1998). *We wish to inform you that tomorrow we will be killed with our families: Stories from Rwanda.* New York: Farrar Straus and Giroux.

Gove, W. R. (1973). Sex, marital status, and mortality. *American Journal of Sociology, 79,* 45–67.

Graeber, C. (1982). *Mustard.* New York: Macmillan.

Graham, L. (1990). *Rebuilding the house.* New York: Viking Penguin.

Gray, R. E. (1987). Adolescent response to the death of a parent. *Journal of Youth and Adolescence, 16,* 511–25.

Gray, R. E. (1988). The role of school counselors with bereaved teenagers: With and without peer support groups. *The School Counselor, 35,* 188–93.

Green, R. (1999). *The Nicholas effect: A boy's gift to the world.* Sebastopol, CA: O'Reilly & Associates.

Greenberg, B. S., & Parker, E. B. (Eds.). (1965). *The Kennedy assassination and the American public: Social communication in crisis.* Stanford, CA: Stanford University Press.

Greenberg, M. R., Carey, G. W., & Popper, F. J. (1987). Violent death, violent states, and American youth. *Public Interest, 87,* 38–48.

Gregorian, V. (1998, Sept. 22). Track superstar Flo-Jo is found dead at 38. *St. Louis Post-Dispatch,* p. A1.

Greyson, B. (1999). Defining near-death experiences. *Mortality, 4,* 7–22.

Greyson, B., & Bush, N. E. (1992). Distressing near-death experiences. *Psychiatry, 55,* 95–110.

Grmek, M. D. (1990). *History of AIDS: Emergence and origin of a modern pandemic.* Trans. R. C. Maulitz & J. Duffin. Princeton, NJ: Princeton University Press.

Grof, S., & Halifax, J. (1978). *The human encounter with death.* New York: Dutton.

Grollman, E. A. (1967). Prologue: Explaining death to children. In E. A. Grollman (Ed.), *Explaining death to children* (pp. 3–27). Boston: Beacon Press.

Grollman, E. A. (1977). *Living when a loved one has died.* Boston: Beacon Press.

Grollman, E. A. (1980). *When your loved one is dying.* Boston: Beacon Press.

Grollman, E. A. (Ed.). (1981). *What helped me when my loved one died.* Boston: Beacon Press.

Grollman, E. A. (1990). *Talking about death: A dialogue between parent and child* (3rd ed.). Boston: Beacon Press.

Grollman, E. A. (1993). *Straight talk about death for teenagers: How to cope with losing someone you love.* Boston: Beacon Press.

Grollman, E. A. (Ed.). (1995a). *Bereaved children and teens: A support guide for parents and professionals.* Boston: Beacon Press.

Grollman, E. A. (1995b). *Caring and coping when your loved one is seriously ill.* Boston: Beacon Press.

Grove, S. (1978). I am a yellow ship. *American Journal of Nursing, 78*, 414.

Groves, B. M., Zuckerman, B., Marans, S., & Cohen, D. J. (1993). Silent victims: Children who witness violence. *Journal of the American Medical Association, 269*, 262–64.

Gruman, G. J. (1973). An historical introduction to ideas about voluntary euthanasia, with a bibliographic survey and guide for interdisciplinary studies. *Omega, 4*, 87–138.

Gubrium, J. F. (1975). *Living and dying at Murray Manor.* New York: St. Martin's Press.

Guest, J. (1976). *Ordinary people.* New York: Viking.

Guest, J. (1997). *Errands.* New York: Ballantine Books.

Gunther, J. (1949). *Death be not proud.* New York: Harper.

Gutman, I., & Berenbaum, M. (Eds.). (1994). *Anatomy of the Auschwitz death camp.* Bloomington, IN: Indiana University Press.

Guyer, B., Freedman, M. A., Strobino, D. M., & Sondik, E. W. (2000). Annual summary of vital statistics: Trends in the health of Americans during the 20th century. *Pediatrics, 106*, 1307–17.

Guyer, B., MacDorman, M. F., Martin, J. A., Peters, K. D., & Strobino, D. M. (1998). Annual summary of vital statistics—1997. *Pediatrics, 102*, 1333–49.

Guzman, B. (2001). The Hispanic population: Census 2000 brief. Washington, DC: U.S. Census Bureau.

Gyulay, J. E. (1975). The forgotten grievers. *American Journal of Nursing, 75*, 1476–79.

Habenstein, R. W., & Lamers, W. M. (1962). *The history of American funeral directing* (rev. ed.). Milwaukee: Bulfin.

Habenstein, R. W., & Lamers, W. M. (1974). *Funeral customs the world over* (rev. ed.). Milwaukee: Bulfin.

Haley, K., & Lee, M. (Eds.). (1998). *The Oregon death with dignity act: A guidebook for health care providers.* Portland, OR: The Center for Ethics in Health Care, Oregon Health Sciences University.

Hall, E. T. (1966). *The hidden dimension.* Garden City, NY: Doubleday.

Hall, G. S. (1922). *Senescence: The last half of life.* New York: D. Appleton.

Hamel, R. (Ed.). (1991). *Choosing death: Active euthanasia, religion, and the public debate.* Philadelphia: Trinity Press International.

Haney, C. A., Leimer, C., & Lowery, J. (1997). Spontaneous memorialization: Violent death and emerging mourning ritual. *Omega, 35*, 159–71.

Hanlan, A. (1979). *Autobiography of dying.* Garden City, NY: Doubleday.

Hanson, J. C., & Frantz, T. T. (Eds.). (1984). *Death and grief in the family.* Rockville, MD: Aspen Systems Corp.

Hanson, W. (1978). Grief counseling with Native Americans. *White Cloud Journal of American Indian/Alaska Native Mental Health, 1*(2), 19–21.

Harakas, S. S. (1993). An Eastern Orthodox approach to bioethics. *The Journal of Medicine and Philosophy, 18*, 531–48.

Harley, R. (1999). Foreword. In J. D. Canine, *What am I going to do with myself when I die?* (pp. vii–viii). Stamford, CT: Appleton & Lange.

Harmer, R. M. (1963). *The high cost of dying.* New York: Collier.

Harmer, R. M. (1971). Funerals, fantasy and flight. *Omega, 2*, 127–35.

Harper, B. C. (1994). *Death: The coping mechanism of the health professional* (rev. ed.). Greenville, SC: Swiger Associates.

Harper, C. D., Royer, R. H., & Humphrey, G. M. (1988). *The special needs of grieving children: A seven-week structured support group with resource section and bibliography*, vol. 1, No. 1. North Canton, OH: The Grief Support and Education Center.

Haskell, P. G. (1994). *Preface to wills, trusts, and administration* (2nd ed.). Mineola, NY: Foundation Press.

Hassl, B., & Marnocha, J. (2000). *Bereavement support group program for children* (2nd ed.). Philadelphia: Accelerated Development.

Hatton, C. L., & Valente, S. M. (Eds.). (1984). *Suicide: Assessment and intervention* (2nd ed.). Norwalk, CT: Appleton-Century-Crofts.

Hauser, M. J. (1987). Special aspects of grief after a suicide. In Dunne, E. J., McIntosh, J. L., & Dunne-Maxim, K. (Eds.), *Suicide and its aftermath: Understanding and counseling the survivors* (pp. 57–70). New York: Norton.

Havighurst, R. J. (1953). *Human development and education.* New York: Longmans, Green.

Havighurst, R. J. (1972). *Developmental tasks and education* (3rd ed.). New York: McKay.

Hazell, L. V. (2001). Disaster mortuary operational response teams (DMORT). *The Forum, 27*(6), 5, 8.

The Heart of the New Age Hospice [Videotape]. (1987). Houston: The University of Texas at Houston, Health Sciences Center.

Hedberg, K., Hopkins, D., & Southwick, K. (2002). Legalized physician-assisted suicide in Oregon, 2001. *New England Journal of Medicine, 346*, 450–52.

Heiney, S. P., Dunaway, N. C., & Webster, J. (1995). Good grieving—an intervention program for grieving children. *Oncology Nursing Forum, 22*, 649–55.

Heinz, D. (1999). *The last passage: Recovering a death of our own.* New York: Oxford University Press.

Hemingway, E. (1926). *The sun also rises.* New York: Scribner.

Hemingway, E. (1929). *A farewell to arms.* New York: Scribner.

Hemingway, E. (1940). *For whom the bell tolls.* New York: Scribner.

Hemingway, E. (1952). *The old man and the sea.* New York: Scribner.

Hendin, H. (1995). Selling death and dignity. *Hastings Center Report, 25*(3), 19–23.

Hendin, H. (1997). *Seduced by death: Doctors, patients and the Dutch Cure.* New York: W. W. Norton.

Hendin, H., Rutenfrans, C., & Zylicz, Z. (1997). Physician-assisted suicide and euthanasia in the Netherlands: Lessons from the Dutch. *Journal of the American Medical Association, 277*, 1720–22.

Hersey, J. (1948). *Hiroshima.* New York: Bantam.

Hewett, J. (1980). *After suicide.* Philadelphia: Westminster Press.

Hill, D. C., & Foster, Y. M. (1996). Postvention with early and middle adolescents. In C. A. Corr & D. E. Balk (Eds.), *Handbook of adolescent death and bereavement* (pp. 250–72). New York: Springer.

Hines, P. (1986). Afro American families. In M. McGoldrick, P. Hines, E. Lee, & N. Garcia-Preto, Mourning rituals: How cultures shape the experience of loss. *The Family Therapy Networker, 10*(6), 32–33.

Hinton, J. (1963). The physical and mental distress of the dying. *Quarterly Journal of Medicine*, New Series, *32*, 1–21.

Hinton, J. (1967). *Dying.* New York: Penguin.

Hinton, J. (1984). Coping with terminal illness. In R. Fitzpatrick, J. Hinton, S. Newman, G. Scambler, & J. Thompson (Eds.), *The experience of illness* (pp. 227–45). London: Tavistock Publications.

Hirayama, K. K. (1990). Death and dying in Japanese culture. In J. K. Parry (Ed.), *Social work practice with the terminally ill: A transcultural perspective* (pp. 159–74). Springfield, IL: Charles C Thomas.

Hodge, E. (1998). *Write through loss and grief: A guide to recovery through writing.* Bairnsdale, Victoria, Australia: BW Publications.

Hoess, R. (1959). *Commandant of Auschwitz: The autobiography of Rudolf Hoess.* Trans. C. FitzGibbon. Cleveland: World Publishing.

Hoffman, A. (1996). *Counseling clients with HIV disease: Assessment, intervention, and prevention.* New York: Guilford.

Hogan, N. S., & Balk, D. E. (1990). Adolescent reactions to sibling death: Perceptions of mothers, fathers, and teenagers. *Nursing Research, 39*, 103–106.

Hogan, N. S., & DeSantis, L. (1992). Adolescent sibling bereavement: An ongoing attachment. *Qualitative Health Research, 2*, 159–77.

Hogan, N. S., & DeSantis, L. (1994). Things that help and hinder adolescent sibling bereavement. *Western Journal of Nursing Research, 16*, 132–53.

Hogan, N. S., & Greenfield, D. B. (1991). Adolescent sibling bereavement symptomatology in a large community sample. *Journal of Adolescent Research, 6*, 97–112.

Holinger, P. C., Offer, D., Barter, J. T., & Bell, C. C. (1994). *Suicide and homicide among adolescents.* New York: Guilford.

Homer. (1937). *Odyssey.* Trans. W. H. D. Rouse. New York: New American Library.

Hopmeyer, E., & Werk, A. (1994). A comparative study of family bereavement groups. *Death Studies, 18*, 243–56.

Hoppe, S. K., & Martin, H. W. (1986). Patterns of suicide among Mexican Americans and

Anglos, 1960–1980. *Social Psychiatry, 21,* 83–88.

Horner, I. B. (Trans.). (1949). *The Book of Discipline (Vinaya-Pitaka),* vol. 1. London: Luzac & Company.

Horowitz, M. J., Weiss, D. S., Kaltreider, N., Krupnick, J., Marmar, C., Wilner, N., & DeWitt, K. (1984). Reactions to the death of a parent. *Journal of Nervous and Mental Disease, 172,* 383–92.

Hostetler, J. A. (1994). *Amish society* (4th ed.). Baltimore: Johns Hopkins University Press.

Howarth, G. (1996). *Last rites: The work of the modern funeral director.* Amityville, NY: Baywood.

Howarth, G., & Leaman, O. (Eds.). (2001). *Encyclopedia of death and dying.* New York: Routledge.

Howell, D. A. (1993). Special services for children. In D. Doyle, G. W. C. Hanks, & N. MacDonald (Eds.), *Oxford textbook of palliative medicine* (pp. 718–25). New York: Oxford University Press.

Hoyert, D. L., Arias, E., Smith, B. L., Murphy, S. L., & Kochanek, K. D. (2001). Deaths: Final data for 1999. *National Vital Statistics Reports, 49*(8). Hyattsville, MD: National Center for Health Statistics.

Hoyert, D. L., Singh, G. K., & Rosenberg, H. M. (1995). Sources of data on socioeconomic differential mortality in the United States. *Journal of Official Statistics, 11,* 233–60.

Hughes, L. (1994). *Collected poems.* New York: Knopf.

Hughes, M. (1995). *Bereavement and support: Healing in a group environment.* Washington, DC: Taylor & Francis.

Hughes, T. E., & Klein, D. (2001). *A family guide to wills, funerals, and probate: How to protect yourself and your survivors.* New York: Facts on File/Checkmark Books.

Hultkrantz, A. (1979). *The religions of the American Indians.* Trans. M. Setterwall. Berkeley: University of California Press.

Humphry, D. (1992). *Final exit: The practicalities of self-deliverance and assisted suicide for the dying.* New York: Dell.

Humphry, D., & Clement, M. (1998). *Freedom to die: People, politics, and the right-to-die movement.* New York: St. Martin's.

Hunter, N. D., & Rubenstein, W. B. (Eds.). (1992). *AIDS agenda: Emerging issues in civil rights.* New York: New Press.

Hunter, S., & Sundel, M. (Eds.). (1989). *Midlife myths: Issues, findings, and practice implications.* Newbury Park, CA: Sage.

Hurd, M., & Macdonald, M. (2001). *Beyond coping: Widows reinventing their lives.* Halifax, Nova Scotia: Pear Press.

Huston, A. C., Donnerstein, E., Fairchild, H., Feshbach, N. D., Katz, P. A., Murray, J. P., Rubinstein, E. A., Wilcox, B. L., & Zuckerman, D. (1992). *Big world, small screen: The role of television in American society.* Lincoln, NE: University of Nebraska Press.

Huxley, A. (1939). *After many a summer dies the swan.* New York: Harper & Brothers.

Hyland, L., & Morse, J. M. (1995). Orchestrating comfort: The role of funeral directors. *Death Studies, 19,* 453–74.

Hymes, K. B., Greene, J. B., Marcus, A., et al. (1981). Kaposi's sarcoma in homosexual men: A report of eight cases. *Lancet, 2,* 598–600.

Ilse, S. (1989). *Miscarriage: A shattered dream.* Wayzatta, MN: Pregnancy and Infant Loss Center. Long Lake, MN: Wintergreen Press.

Imber-Black, E. (1991). Rituals and the healing process. In F. Walsh & M. McGoldrick (Eds.), *Living beyond loss: Death in the family* (pp. 207–23). New York: Norton.

Infeld, D. L., Gordon, A. K., & Harper, B. C. (Eds.). (1995). *Hospice care and cultural diversity.* Binghamton, NY: Haworth.

Ingles, T. (1974). St. Christopher's Hospice. *Nursing Outlook, 22,* 759–63.

Ingram, P. (1992). The tragedy of Tibet. *Contemporary Review, 261,* 122–25.

Institute of Medicine. (1986). *Confronting AIDS: Directions for public health, health care, and research.* Washington, DC: National Academy Press.

Irion, P. E. (1966). *The funeral: Vestige or value?* Nashville: Abingdon.

Irion, P. E. (1968). *Cremation.* Philadelphia: Fortress Press.

Irion, P. E. (1971). *A manual and guide for those who conduct a humanist funeral service.* Baltimore: Waverly Press.

Irion, P. E. (1991). Changing patterns of ritual response to death. *Omega, 22,* 159–72.

Irish, D. P., Lundquist, K. F., & Nelson, V. J. (Eds.). (1993). *Ethnic variations in dying, death, and grief: Diversity in universality.* Washington, DC: Taylor & Francis.

Iserson, K. V. (1994). *Death to dust: What happens to dead bodies?* Tucson, AZ: Galen Press.

Iserson, K. V., & Iserson, K. Y. (1999). *Grave words: Notifying survivors about sudden, unexpected death.* Tucson, AZ: Galen Press.

Iverson, B. A. (1990). Bodies for science. *Death Studies, 14,* 577–87.

Jackson, C. O. (Ed.). (1977). *Passing: The vision of death in America.* Westport, CT: Greenwood Press.

Jackson, E. N. (1963). *For the living.* Des Moines, IA: Channel Press.

Jackson, E. N. (1966). *The Christian funeral: Its meaning, its purpose, and its modern practice.* New York: Channel Press.

Jackson, E. N. (1984). The pastoral counselor and the child encountering death. In H. Wass & C. A. Corr (Eds.), *Helping children cope with death: Guidelines and resources* (2nd ed., pp. 33–47). Washington, DC: Hemisphere.

Jackson, M. (1980). The Black experience with death: A brief analysis through Black writings. In R. A. Kalish (Ed.), *Death and dying: Views from many cultures* (pp. 92–98). Farmingdale, NY: Baywood.

Jacobs, S., Mazure, C., & Prigerson, H. (2000). Diagnostic criteria for traumatic grief. *Death Studies, 24,* 185–99.

Jacobs, S., & Prigerson, H. (2000). Psychotherapy of traumatic grief: A review of evidence for psychotherapeutic treatments. *Death Studies, 24,* 479–95.

Jacques, E. (1965). Death and the mid-life crisis. *International Journal of Psychoanalysis, 46,* 502–14.

Jamison, K. R. (1999). *Night falls fast: Understanding suicide.* New York: Alfred A. Knopf.

Jamison, S. (1995). *Final acts of love: Families, friends, and assisted dying.* New York: Tarcher/Putman.

Janoff-Bulman, R. (1992). *Shattered assumptions: Towards a new psychology of trauma.* New York: The Free Press.

Jewett, C. L. (1982). *Helping children cope with separation and loss.* Harvard, MA: Harvard Common Press.

Jimenez, S. L. M. (1982). *The other side of pregnancy: Coping with miscarriage and stillbirth.* Englewood Cliffs, NJ: Prentice-Hall.

Johnson, C. J., & McGee, M. G. (Eds.). (1998). *How different religions view death and afterlife.* Philadelphia: The Charles Press.

Johnson, C., & Weeks, O. D. (2001). How to develop a successful aftercare program. In O. D. Weeks & C. Johnson (Eds.), *When all the friends have gone: A guide for aftercare providers* (pp. 5–23). Amityville, NY: Baywood.

Johnson, E. "Magic," with W. Novak. (1992). *My life.* New York: Random House.

Johnson, J., Johnson, S. M., Cunningham, J. H., & Weinfeld, I. J. (1985). *A most important picture: A very tender manual for taking pictures of stillborn babies and infants who die.* Omaha, NE: Centering Corporation.

Johnson, S. (1987). *After a child dies: Counseling bereaved families.* New York: Springer.

Jonah, B. A. (1986). Accident risk and risk-taking behaviour among young drivers. *Accident Analysis and Prevention, 18,* 255–71.

Jones, B. (1967). *Design for death.* Indianapolis: Bobbs-Merrill.

Jones, C. (1994). *Living proof: Courage in the face of AIDS.* New York: Abbeville.

Jones, E. O. (1948). *Little Red Riding Hood.* New York: Golden Press.

Jonker, G. (1997). The many facets of Islam: Death, dying and disposal between orthodox and historical convention. In C. M. Parkes, P. Laungani, & B. Young (Eds.), *Death and bereavement across cultures* (pp. 147–65). London: Routledge.

Jonsen, A. R., & Helleghers, A. E. (1974). Conceptual foundations for an ethics of medical care. In L. R. Tancredi (Ed.), *Ethics of health care* (pp. 3–20). Washington, DC: National Academy of Science.

Josefson, D. (1998). US sees first legal case of physician assisted suicide. *British Medical Journal, 316,* 1037.

Joseph, J. (1992). *Selected poems.* Newcastle-upon-Tyne, England: Bloodaxe Books.

Joslin, D., & Harrison, R. (1998). The "hidden patient": Older relatives raising children orphaned by AIDS. *Journal of the American Medical Women's Association,* 53, 65–71, 76.

Jozefowski, J. T. (1999). *The Phoenix phenomenon: Rising from the ashes of grief.* Northvale, NJ: Jason Aronson.

Jung, C. G. (1970). The stages of life. In H. Read, M. Fordham, & G. Adler (Eds.), *The collected works of Carl G. Jung* (2nd ed., vol. 8). Princeton, NJ: Princeton University Press. (Original work published 1933.)

Jurich, A. P., & Collins, O. P. (1996). Adolescents, suicide, and death. In C. A. Corr & D. E. Balk (Eds.), *Handbook of adolescent death and bereavement* (pp. 65–84). New York: Springer.

Jury, M., & Jury, D. (1978). *Gramps: A man ages and dies.* Baltimore: Penguin.

Kail, R. V., & Cavanaugh, J. C. (2000). *Human development: A lifespan view* (2nd ed.). Belmont, CA: Wadsworth/Thomson Learning.

Kalergis, M. M. (1998). *Seen and heard: Teenagers talk about their lives.* New York: Stewart, Tabori & Chang.

Kalish, R. A. (Ed.). (1980). *Death and dying: Views from many cultures.* Farmingdale, NY: Baywood.

Kalish, R. A. (1985a). Death and dying in a social context. In R. H. Binstock & E. Shanas (Eds.), *Handbook of aging and the social sciences* (2nd ed., pp. 149–70). New York: Van Nostrand.

Kalish, R. A. (1985b). The horse on the dining-room table. In *Death, grief, and caring relationships* (2nd ed., pp. 2–4). Pacific Grove, CA: Brooks/Cole.

Kalish, R. A. (1989). Death education. In R. Kastenbaum & B. Kastenbaum (Eds.), *Encyclopedia of death* (pp. 75–79). Phoenix, AZ: Oryx Press.

Kalish, R. A., & Goldberg, H. (1978). Clergy attitudes toward funeral directors. *Death Education, 2,* 247–60.

Kalish, R. A., & Goldberg, H. (1980). Community attitudes toward funeral directors. *Omega, 10,* 335–46.

Kalish, R. A., & Johnson, A. I. (1972). Value similarities and differences in three generations of women. *Journal of Marriage and the Family, 34,* 49–54.

Kalish, R. A., & Reynolds, D. K. (1981). *Death and ethnicity: A psychocultural study.* Farmingdale, NY: Baywood. (Originally, Los Angeles: Andrus Gerontology Center, 1976.)

Kane, B. (1979). Children's concepts of death. *Journal of Genetic Psychology, 134,* 141–53.

Kaplan, K. J. (1999). Right to die versus sacredness of life [Special issue]. *Omega, 40*(1).

Kapp, M. B. (Ed.). (1994). *Patient self-determination in long-term care: Implementing the PSDA in medical decisions.* New York: Springer.

Kapust, L. R. (1982). Living with dementia: The ongoing funeral. *Social Work in Health Care,* 7(4), 79–91.

Kassis, H. (1997). Islam. In H. Coward (Ed.), *Life after death in world religions* (pp. 48–65). Maryknoll, NY: Orbis Books.

Kastenbaum, R. (1967). The mental life of dying geriatric patients. *The Gerontologist,* 7(2), Pt. 1, 97–100.

Kastenbaum, R. (1969). Death and bereavement in later life. In A. H. Kutscher (Ed.), *Death and bereavement* (pp. 28–54). Springfield, IL: Charles C Thomas.

Kastenbaum, R. (1972). On the future of death: Some images and options. *Omega, 3,* 306–18.

Kastenbaum, R. (1973, January). The kingdom where nobody dies. *Saturday Review, 56,* 33–38.

Kastenbaum, R. (1977). Death and development through the lifespan. In H. Feifel (Ed.), *New meanings of death* (pp. 17–45). New York: McGraw-Hill.

Kastenbaum, R. (1989a). Ars moriendi. In R. Kastenbaum & B. Kastenbaum (Eds.), *Encyclopedia of death* (pp. 17–19). Phoenix, AZ: Oryx Press.

Kastenbaum, R. (1989b). Cemeteries. In R. Kastenbaum & B. Kastenbaum (Eds.), *Encyclopedia of death* (pp. 41–45). Phoenix, AZ: Oryx Press.

Kastenbaum, R. (1989c). Dance of death *(danse macabre).* In R. Kastenbaum & B. Kastenbaum (Eds.), *Encyclopedia of death* (pp. 67–70). Phoenix, AZ: Oryx Press.

Kastenbaum, R. (1995). Raymond A. Moody, Jr: An *Omega* interview. *Omega, 31,* 87–98.

Kastenbaum, R. (2000). *The psychology of death* (3rd ed.). New York: Springer.

Kastenbaum, R. (2001). *Death, society, and human experience* (7th ed.). Boston: Allyn and Bacon.

Kastenbaum, R. (2002). *Macmillan encyclopedia of death and dying.* New York: Macmillan.

Kastenbaum, R., & Aisenberg, R. (1972). *The psychology of death.* New York: Springer.

Kastenbaum, R., & Thuell, S. (1995). Cookies baking, coffee brewing: Toward a contextual theory of dying. *Omega, 31,* 175–87.

Katzenbach, J. (1986). *The traveler.* New York: Putnam's.

Kaufert, J. M., & O'Neil, J. D. (1991). Cultural mediation of dying and grieving among Native Canadian patients in urban hospitals. In D. R. Counts & D. A. Counts (Eds.),

Coping with the final tragedy: Cultural variation in dying and grieving (pp. 231–51). Amityville, NY: Baywood.

Kauffman, J. (Ed.). (1995). *Awareness of mortality.* Amityville, NY: Baywood.

Kaufman, S. R. (1986). *The ageless self: Sources of meaning in late life.* Madison, WI: University of Wisconsin Press.

Kavanaugh, R. E. (1972). *Facing death.* Los Angeles: Nash.

Kay, W. J. (Ed.). (1984). *Pet loss and human bereavement.* Ames, IA: Iowa State University Press.

Kay, W. J., Cohen, S. P., Nieburg, H. A., Fudin, C. E., Grey, R. E., Kutscher, A. H., & Osman, M. M. (Eds.). (1988). *Euthanasia of the companion animal: The impact on pet owners, veterinarians, and society.* Philadelphia: Charles Press.

Keating, D. (1990). Adolescent thinking. In S. S. Feldman & G. R. Elliott (Eds.), *At the threshold: The developing adolescent* (pp. 54–89). Cambridge, MA: Harvard University Press.

Kellehear, A. (1996). *Experiences near death: Beyond medicine and religion.* New York: Oxford University Press.

Kelly, E. W. (2001). Near-death experiences with reports of meeting deceased people. *Death Studies, 25,* 229–49.

Kelly, E. W., Greyson, B., & Stevenson, I. (2000). Can experiences near death furnish evidence of life after death? *Omega, 40,* 513–19.

Kelly, O. (1975). *Make today count.* New York: Delacorte Press.

Kelly, O. (1977). Make today count. In H. Feifel (Ed.), *New meanings of death* (pp. 182–93). New York: McGraw-Hill.

Kelsay, J. (1994). Islam and medical ethics. In P. F. Camenisch (Ed.), *Religious methods and resources in bioethics* (pp. 93–107). Dordrecht: Kluwer.

Kemp, C. (1995). *Terminal illness: A guide to nursing care.* Philadelphia: Lippincott.

Keneally, T. (1982). *Schindler's list.* New York: Simon & Schuster.

Kenyon, B. L. (2001). Current research in children's conceptions of death: A critical review. *Omega, 43,* 63–91.

Keown, D. (1995). *Buddhism and bioethics.* New York: St. Martin's Press.

Kephart, W. M. (1950). Status after death. *American Sociological Review, 15,* 635–43.

Kerbel, M. R. (2000). *If it bleeds, it leads: An anatomy of television news.* Boulder, CO: Westview.

Kessler, D. (2001). *A question of intent: A great American battle with a deadly industry.* New York: PublicAffairs.

King, A. (1990). A Samoan perspective: Funeral practices, death and dying. In J. K. Parry (Ed.), *Social work practice with the terminally ill: A transcultural perspective* (pp. 175–89). Springfield, IL: Charles C Thomas.

Kirk, W. G. (1993). *Adolescent suicide: A school-based approach to assessment and intervention.* Champaign, IL: Research Press.

Kitagawa, E. M., & Hauser, P. M. (1973). *Differential mortality in the United States: A study in socioeconomic epidemiology.* Cambridge, MA: Harvard University Press.

Kitano, H. H. L. (1976). *Japanese-Americans: The evaluation of a subculture* (2nd ed.). Englewood Cliffs, NJ: Prentice-Hall.

Klagsbrun, F. (1976). *Too young to die: Youth and suicide.* New York: Houghton Mifflin.

Klass, D. (1982). Elisabeth Kübler-Ross and the tradition of the private sphere: An analysis of symbols. *Omega, 12,* 241–61.

Klass, D. (1985a). Bereaved parents and the Compassionate Friends: Affiliation and healing. *Omega, 15,* 353–73.

Klass, D. (1985b). Self-help groups: Grieving parents and community resources. In C. A. Corr & D. M. Corr (Eds.), *Hospice approaches to pediatric care* (pp. 241–60). New York: Springer.

Klass, D. (1988). *Parental grief: Solace and resolution.* New York: Springer.

Klass, D. (1999). *The spiritual lives of bereaved parents.* Philadelphia: Taylor & Francis.

Klass, D., & Hutch, R. A. (1985). Elisabeth Kübler-Ross as a religious leader. *Omega, 16,* 89–109.

Klass, D., & Shinners, B. (1983). Professional roles in a self-help group for the bereaved. *Omega, 13,* 361–75.

Klass, D., Silverman, P. R., & Nickman, S. L. (Eds.). (1996). *Continuing bonds: New understandings of grief.* Washington, DC: Taylor & Francis.

Klicker, R. L. (2000). *A student dies, a school mourns: Dealing with death and loss in the school community.* Philadelphia: Accelerated Development.

Kliever, L. D. (Ed.). (1989). *Dax's case: Essays in medical ethics and human meaning.* Dallas: Southern Methodist University.

Knapp, R. J. (1986). *Beyond endurance: When a child dies.* New York: Schocken.

Kochanek, K. D., & Hudson, B. L. (1994). Advance report of final mortality statistics, 1992. *Monthly Vital Statistics Report, 43*(6), Suppl. Hyattsville, MD: National Center for Health Statistics.

Kochanek, K. D., Smith, B. L., & Anderson, R. N. (2001). Deaths: Preliminary data for 1999. *National Vital Statistics Reports, 49*(3). Hyattsville, MD: National Center for Health Statistics.

Kohn, J. B., & Kohn, W. K. (1978). *The widower.* Boston: Beacon Press.

Koocher, G. (1973). Childhood, death, and cognitive development. *Developmental Psychology, 9,* 369–75.

Koocher, G. P. (1974). Talking with children about death. *American Journal of Orthopsychiatry, 44,* 404–11.

Koocher, G. P., & O'Malley, J. E. (1981). *The Damocles syndrome: Psychosocial consequences of surviving childhood cancer.* New York: McGraw-Hill.

Koocher, G. P., O'Malley, J. E., Foster, D., & Gogan, J. L. (1976). Death anxiety in normal children and adolescents. *Psychiatria clinica, 9,* 220–29.

Koop, C. E. (1988). *Understanding AIDS.* HHS Publication No. (CDC) HHS-88-8404, U.S. Department of Health and Human Services. Washington, DC: U.S. Government Printing Office.

Koppelman, K. L. (1994). *The fall of a sparrow: Of death and dreams and healing.* Amityville, NY: Baywood.

Kotzwinkle, W. (1975). *Swimmer in the secret sea.* New York: Avon.

Kozol, J. (1995). *Amazing grace.* New York: Crown.

Krementz, J. (1981). *How it feels when a parent dies.* New York: Knopf.

Krementz, J. (1989). *How it feels to fight for your life.* Boston: Little, Brown.

Krieger, N., & Margo, G. (Eds.). (1994). *AIDS: The politics of survival.* Amityville, NY: Baywood.

Krizek, B. (1992). Goodbye old friend: A son's farewell to Comiskey Park. *Omega, 25,* 87–93.

Krugman, P. (2001, Feb. 24). Fowl play badmouthing the economy. *St. Petersburg Times,* p. 16A.

Krumholz, H. M., Phillips, R. S., Hamel, M. B., Teno, J. M., Bellamy, P., Broste, S. K., Califf, R. M., Vidaillet, H., Davis, R. B., Muhlbaier, L. H., Connors, A. F., Lynn, J., Goldman, L., for the SUPPORT Investigators. (1988). Resuscitation preferences among patients with severe congestive heart failure: Results from the SUPPORT Project. *Circulation, 98,* 648–55.

Kübler-Ross, E. (1969). *On death and dying.* New York: Macmillan.

Kübler-Ross, E. (1983). *On children and death.* New York: Macmillan.

Kübler-Ross, E. (1997). *The wheel of life: A memoir of living and dying.* New York: Scribner.

Kübler-Ross, E., & Kessler, D. (2000). *Life lessons: Two experts on death and dying teach us about the mysteries of life and living.* New York: Scribner.

Kulka, E. (1986). *Escape from Auschwitz.* South Hadley, MA: Bergin & Garvey.

Kurtz, D. C., & Boardman, J. (1971). *Greek burial customs.* Ithaca, NY: Cornell University Press.

Kurtz, L. P. (1934). *The dance of death and the macabre spirit in European literature.* New York: Institute of French Studies.

Kushner, H. S. (1981). *When bad things happen to good people.* New York: Avon.

Lack, S. A., & Buckingham, R. W. (1978). *First American hospice: Three years of home care.* New Haven: Hospice, Inc.

Lafser, C. (1998). *An empty cradle, a full heart: Reflections for mothers and fathers after miscarriage, stillbirth, or infant death.* Chicago: Loyola Press.

Lagoni, L., Butler, C., & Hetts, S. (1994). *The human-animal bond and grief.* Philadelphia: W. B. Saunders.

LaGrand, L. E. (1980). Reducing burnout in the hospice and the death education movement. *Death Education, 4,* 61–76.

LaGrand, L. E. (1981). Loss reactions of college students: A descriptive analysis. *Death Studies, 5,* 235–47.

LaGrand, L. E. (1986). *Coping with separation and loss as a young adult: Theoretical and practical realities.* Springfield, IL: Charles C Thomas.

LaGrand, L. E. (1988). *Changing patterns of human existence: Assumptions, beliefs, and coping with the stress of change.* Springfield, IL: Charles C Thomas.

LaGrand, L. E. (1997). *After-death communication: Final farewells.* St. Paul, MN: Llewellyn.

LaGrand, L. E. (1999). *Messages and miracles: Extraordinary experiences of the bereaved.* St. Paul, MN: Llewellyn.

LaGrand, L. E. (2001). *Gifts from the unknown: Using extraordinary experiences to cope with loss and change.* St. Paul, MN: Llewellyn.

Lamb, J. M. (Ed.). (1988). *Bittersweet . . . hellogoodbye.* Belleville, IL: SHARE National Office.

Lamb, M. (2001). Sexuality. In B. R. Ferrell & N. Coyle (Eds.), *Textbook of palliative nursing* (pp. 309–15). New York: Oxford University Press.

Lamberti, J. W., & Detmer, C. M. (1993). Model of family grief assessment and treatment. *Death Studies, 17,* 55–67.

Lamers, E. P. (1986). Books for adolescents. In C. A. Corr & J. N. McNeil (Eds.), *Adolescence and death* (pp. 233–42). New York: Springer.

Lamers, E. P. (1995). Children, death, and fairy tales. *Omega, 31,* 151–67.

Lamont, C. (1954). *A humanist funeral service.* New York: Horizon Press.

Landay, D. S. (1998). *Be prepared: The complete financial, legal, and practical guide for living with a life-challenging condition.* New York: St. Martin's.

Landry, S. (1999a, June 15). He wanted you to know. *St. Petersburg Times,* p. 1D.

Landry, S. (1999b, June 22). His message transcends death. *St. Petersburg Times,* p. 3D.

Lang, A. (Ed.). (1904). *The blue fairy book.* New York: Longman's Green.

Lang, L. T. (1990). Aspects of the Cambodian death and dying process. In J. K. Parry (Ed.), *Social work practice with the terminally ill: A transcultural perspective* (pp. 205–11). Springfield, IL: Charles C Thomas.

Langbein, H. (1994). *Against all hope: Resistance in the Nazi concentration camps 1938–1945.* Trans. H. Zohn. New York: Paragon House.

Larson, D. G. (1993). *The helper's journey: Working with people facing grief, loss, and life-threatening illness.* Champaign, IL: Research Press.

Larue, G. A. (1985). *Euthanasia and religion: A survey of the attitudes of world religions to the right-to-die.* Los Angeles: The Hemlock Society.

Lattanzi, M. E. (1983). Professional stress: Adaptation, coping, and meaning. In J. C. Hanson & T. T. Frantz (Eds.), *Death and grief in the family* (pp. 95–106). Rockville, MD: Aspen Systems Corp.

Lattanzi, M. E. (1985). An approach to caring: Caregiving concerns. In C. A. Corr & D. M. Corr (Eds.), *Hospice approaches to pediatric care* (pp. 261–77). New York: Springer.

Lattanzi, M. E., & Hale, M. E. (1984). Giving grief words: Writing during bereavement. *Omega, 15,* 45–52.

Lattanzi-Licht, M. E. (1989). Bereavement services: Practice and problems. *The Hospice Journal, 5*(1), 1–28.

Lattanzi-Licht, M. E. (1996). Helping families with adolescents cope with loss. In C. A. Corr & D. E. Balk (Eds.), *Handbook of adolescent death and bereavement* (pp. 219–34). New York: Springer.

Lattanzi-Licht, M. E., Mahoney, J. J., & Miller, G. W. (1998). *The hospice choice: In pursuit of a peaceful death.* New York: Simon & Schuster.

Lazar, A., & Torney-Purta, J. (1991). The development of the subconcepts of death in young children: A short-term longitudinal study. *Child Development, 62,* 1321–33.

Lazarus, R. S., & Folkman, S. (1984). *Stress, appraisal, and coping.* New York: Springer.

Leach, C. (1981). *Letter to a younger son.* New York: Harcourt Brace Jovanovich.

Lecso, P. A. (1986). Euthanasia: A Buddhist perspective. *Journal of Religion and Health, 25,* 51–57.

Lee, E. (1986). Chinese families. In M. McGoldrick, P. Hines, E. Lee, & N. Garcia-Preto, Mourning rituals: How cultures shape the experience of loss. *The Family Therapy Networker, 10*(6), 35–36.

Lee, P. W. H., Lieh-Mak, F., Hung, B. K. M., & Luk, S. L. (1984). Death anxiety in leukemic Chinese children. *International Journal of Psychiatry in Medicine, 13,* 281–90.

Leenaars, A. A. (1990). Psychological perspectives on suicide. In D. Lester (Ed.), *Current concepts of suicide* (pp. 159–67). Philadelphia: Charles Press.

Leenaars, A. A., Maltsberger, J. T., & Neimeyer, R. A. (1994). *Treatment of suicidal people.* Washington, DC: Taylor & Francis.

Leenaars, A. A., Maris, R. W., McIntosh, J. L., & Richman, J. (Eds.). (1992). *Suicide and the older adult.* New York: Guilford.

Leenaars, A. A., & Wenckstern, S. (Eds.). (1991). *Suicide prevention in the schools.* Washington, DC: Hemisphere.

Leenaars, A. A., & Wenckstern, S. (1996). Postvention with elementary school children. In C. A. Corr & D. M. Corr (Eds.), *Handbook of childhood death and bereavement* (pp. 265–83). New York: Springer.

Leininger, M. (1988). Leininger's theory of cultural care diversity and universality. *Nursing Science Quarterly, 1,* 152–60.

Leininger, M. (1991). Transcultural nursing: The study and practice field. *Imprint, 38,* 55–69.

Leininger, M. (1995). *Transcultural nursing: Concepts, theories, and practices* (2nd ed.). New York: McGraw-Hill.

Lerner, G. (1978). *A death of one's own.* New York: Simon & Schuster.

Lerner, M. (1970). When, why, and where people die. In O. Brim, H. Freeman, S. Levine, & N. Scotch (Eds.), *The dying patient* (pp. 5–29). New York: Russell Sage Foundation.

LeShan, E. (1976). *Learning to say good-by: When a parent dies.* New York: Macmillan.

LeShan, L. (1964). The world of the patient in severe pain of long duration. *Journal of Chronic Diseases, 17,* 119–26.

Lester, D. (1990a). *Current concepts of suicide.* Philadelphia: Charles Press.

Lester, D. (1990b). *Understanding and preventing suicide: New perspectives.* Springfield, IL: Charles C Thomas.

Lester, D. (1992). *Why people kill themselves* (3rd ed.). Springfield, IL: Charles C Thomas.

Lester, D. (1993). *The cruelest death: The enigma of adolescent suicide.* Philadelphia: Charles Press.

Lester, D. (1994). Differences in the epidemiology of suicide in Asian Americans by nation of origin. *Omega, 29,* 89–93.

Lester, D. (1998). The suicide of Sylvia Plath: Current perspectives [Special issue]. *Death Studies, 22*(7).

Lester, D. (2000). The social causes of suicide: A look at Durkheim's *Le Suicide* one hundred years later. *Omega, 40,* 307–21.

Lesy, M. (1973). *Wisconsin death trip.* New York: Pantheon.

Levetown, M. (Ed.). (2000). *Compendium of pediatric palliative care.* Alexandria, VA National Hospice and Palliative Care Organization.

Levetown, M. (2001). Pediatric care: The inpatient ICU perspective. In B. R. Ferrell & N. Coyle (Eds.), *Textbook of palliative nursing* (pp. 570–83). New York: Oxford University Press.

Levi, P. (1986). *Survival in Auschwitz and The reawakening: Two memoirs.* Trans. S. Woolf. New York: Simon & Schuster.

Levine, C. (Ed.). (1993). *A death in the family: Orphans of the HIV epidemic.* New York: United Hospital Fund.

Levinson, D. J. (1978). *The seasons of a man's life.* New York: Knopf.

Levinson, D. J. (1996). *The seasons of a woman's life.* New York: Knopf.

Leviton, D. (Ed.). (1991a). *Horrendous death, health, and well-being.* Washington, DC: Hemisphere.

Leviton, D. (Ed.). (1991b). *Horrendous death and health: Toward action.* Washington, DC: Hemisphere.

Levy, J. E., & Kunitz, S. J. (1987). A suicide prevention program for Hopi youth. *Social Science and Medicine, 25,* 931–40.

Lewis, C. S. (1976). *A grief observed.* New York: Bantam Books.

Lewis, O. (1970). *A death in the Sanchez family.* New York: Random House.

Ley, D. C. H., & Corless, I. B. (1988). Spirituality and hospice care. *Death Studies, 12,* 101–10.

Liegner, L. M. (1975). St. Christopher's Hospice, 1974: Care of the dying patient. *Journal of the American Medical Association, 234,* 1047–48.

Lifton, R. J. (1964). On death and death symbolism: The Hiroshima disaster. *Psychiatry, 27,* 191–210.

Lifton, R. J. (1967). *Death in life: Survivors of Hiroshima.* New York: Random House.

Lifton, R. J. (1979). *The broken connection.* New York: Simon & Schuster.

Lifton, R. J. (1982). *Indefensible weapons: The political and psychological case against nuclearism.* New York: Basic Books.

Lifton, R. J. (1986). *The Nazi doctors: Medical killing and the psychology of genocide.* New York: Basic Books.

Lifton, R. J. (1999). *Destroying the world to save it: Aum Shinrikyō, apocalyptic violence, and the new global terrorism.* New York: Metropolitan Books/Henry Holt.

Lifton, R. J., & Mitchell, G. (1995). *Hiroshima in America: Fifty years of denial.* New York: Putnam's.

Lindemann, E. (1944). Symptomatology and management of acute grief. *American Journal of Psychiatry, 101*, 141–48.
Lindemann, E., & Greer, I. M. (1972). A study of grief: Emotional responses to suicide. In A. C. Cain (Ed.), *Survivors of suicide* (pp. 63–69). Springfield, IL: Charles C Thomas. (Reprinted from *Pastoral Psychology*, 1953, 4, 9–13.)
Linenthal, E. T. (2001). *The unfinished bombing: Oklahoma City in American memory.* New York: Oxford University Press.
Linn, E. (1986). *I know just how you feel . . . Avoiding the clichés of grief.* Incline Village, NV: Publisher's Mark.
Lipstadt, D. (1993). *Denying the Holocaust: The growing assault on truth and memory.* New York: Free Press.
Litman, R. E. (1967). Sigmund Freud on suicide. In E. S. Shneidman (Ed.), *Essays in self-destruction* (pp. 324–44). New York: Science House.
Livneh, H., Antonak, R. F., & Maron, S. (1995). Progeria: Medical aspects, psychosocial perspectives, and intervention guidelines. *Death Studies, 19*, 433–52.
Loftin, C., McDowall, D., Wiersema, B., & Cottey, T. J. (1991). Effects of restrictive licensing of handguns on homicide and suicide in the District of Columbia. *New England Journal of Medicine, 325*, 1615–20.
Lonetto, R. (1980). *Children's conceptions of death.* New York: Springer.
Lonetto, R., & Templer, D. I. (1986). *Death anxiety.* Washington, DC: Hemisphere.
Longaker, C. (1998). *Facing death and finding hope: A guide to the emotional and spiritual care of the dying.* New York: Doubleday.
Lopata, H. Z. (1996). *Current widowhood: Myths and realities.* London: Sage.
Lorimer, D. (1989). The near-death experience: Cross-cultural and multi-disciplinary dimensions. In A. Berger, P. Badham, A. H. Kutscher, J. Berger, M. Perry, & J. Beloff (Eds.), *Perspectives on death and dying: Cross-cultural and multi-disciplinary views* (pp. 256–67). Philadelphia: Charles Press.
Louganis, G., with E. Marcus. (1995). *Breaking the surface.* New York: Random House.
Luna, G. C. (1997). *Youths living with HIV: Self-evident truths.* Binghamton, NY: Haworth.
Lund, D. A. (1989). *Older bereaved spouses: Research with practical applications.* Washington, DC: Hemisphere.
Lund, D. A., Dimond, M., & Juretich, M. (1985). Bereavement support groups for the elderly: Characteristics of potential participants. *Death Studies, 9*, 309–21.
Lustig, A. (1977). *Darkness casts no shadow.* New York: Inscape.
Lynch, T. (1997). *The undertaking: Life studies from the dismal trade.* New York: Penguin.
Lynn, J. (Ed.). (1986). *By no extraordinary means: The choice to forgo life-sustaining food and water.* Bloomington, IN: Indiana University Press.
Lynn, J., & Harrold, J. (1999). *Handbook for mortals: Guidance for people facing serious illness.* New York: Oxford University Press.
Lynn, J., Schuster, J. L., & Kabcenell, A. (2000). *Improving care for the end of life: A sourcebook for health care managers and clinicians.* New York: Oxford University Press.
Lynn, K. S. (1987). *Hemingway.* New York: Simon & Schuster.
Lynn, R. J. (1992). *Introduction to estate planning in a nutshell* (4th ed.). St. Paul, MN: West.
Mace, N. L., & Rabins, P. V. (1999). *The 36-hour day: A family guide to caring for persons with Alzheimer disease, related dementing illnesses, and memory loss in later life* (3rd ed.). Baltimore: Johns Hopkins University Press.
Mack, A. (Ed.). (1974). *Death in American experience.* New York: Schocken.
MacMillan, I. (1991). *Orbit of darkness.* San Diego: Harcourt Brace Jovanovich.
MacPherson, M. (1999). *She came to live out loud: An inspiring family journey through illness, loss, and grief.* New York: Scribner.
Maddox, R. J. (1995). *Weapons for victory: The Hiroshima decision fifty years later.* Columbia, MO: University of Missouri Press.
Magee, D. (1983). *What murder leaves behind: The victim's family.* New York: Dodd, Mead.
Magee, D. S., & Ventura, J. (1999). *Everything your heirs need to know: Organizing your assets, family history, final wishes* (3rd ed.). Chicago: Dearborn Financial Publishing.
Mahoney, M. C. (1991). Fatal motor vehicle traffic accidents among Native Americans. *American Journal of Preventive Medicine, 7*, 112–16.
Maier, F. (1991). *Sweet reprieve: One couple's journey to the frontiers of medicine.* New York: Crown.

Maimonides, M. (1949). *The code of Maimonides (Mishneh Torah): Book Fourteen, The Book of Judges.* Trans. A. M. Hershman. New Haven, CT: Yale University Press.
Maizler, J. S., Solomon, J. R., & Almquist, E. (1983). Psychogenic mortality syndrome: Choosing to die by the institutionalized elderly. *Death Education, 6,* 353–64.
Males, M. (2001, Mar. 17). The untold story of guns and kids. *St. Petersburg Times,* p. 14A.
Malinowski, B. (1954). *Magic, science, and religion and other essays.* New York: Doubleday.
Maloney, R., & Wolfelt, A. D. (2001). *Caring for donor families: Before, during and after.* Fort Collins, CO: Companion Press.
Mandelbaum, D. (1959). Social uses of funeral rites. In H. Feifel (Ed.), *The meaning of death* (pp. 189–217). New York: McGraw-Hill.
Mandell, H., & Spiro, H. (Eds.). (1987). *When doctors get sick.* New York: Plenum.
Manio, E. B., & Hall, R. R. (1987). Asian family traditions and their influence in transcultural health care delivery. *Children's Health Care, 15,* 172–77.
Mann, T. C., & Greene, J. (1962). *Over their dead bodies: Yankee epitaphs and history.* Brattleboro, VT: Stephen Greene Press.
Mann, T. C., & Greene, J. (1968). *Sudden and awful: American epitaphs and the finger of God.* Brattleboro, VT: Stephen Greene Press.
Manning, D. (1979). *Don't take my grief away from me: How to walk through grief and learn to live again.* Hereford, TX: In-Sight Books.
Manning, J. A. (1995). *Manning on estate planning* (5th ed.). New York: Practising Law Institute.
Margolis, O., & Schwarz, O. (Eds.). (1975). *Grief and the meaning of the funeral.* New York: MSS Information.
Maris, R. W. (1969). *Social forces in urban suicide.* Homewood, IL: Dorsey Press.
Maris, R. W. (1981). *Pathways to suicide: A survey of self-destructive behaviors.* Baltimore: Johns Hopkins University Press.
Maris, R. W. (1985). The adolescent suicide problem. *Suicide and Life-Threatening Behavior, 15,* 91–109.
Maris, R. W. (Ed.). (1988). *Understanding and preventing suicide.* New York: Guilford.
Maris, R. W., Berman, A. L., Maltsberger, J. T., & Yufit, R. I. (Eds.). (1992). *Assessment and prediction of suicide.* New York: Guilford.
Marks, A. S., & Calder, B. J. (1982). *Attitudes toward death and funerals.* Evansville, IL: Northwestern University, Center for Marketing Sciences.
Marks, R., & Sachar, E. (1973). Undertreatment of medical inpatients with narcotic analgesics. *Annals of Internal Medicine, 78,* 173–81.
Marquis, A. (1974). *A guide to America's Indians.* Norman, OK: University of Oklahoma Press.
Marshall, J. R. (1975). The geriatric patient's fears about death. *Postgraduate Medicine, 57*(4), 144–49.
Martikainen, P., & Valkonen, T. (1996). Mortality after the death of a spouse: Rates and causes of death in a large Finnish cohort. *American Journal of Public Health, 36,* 1087–93.
Martin, B. B. (Ed.). (1989). *Pediatric hospice care: What helps.* Los Angeles: Children's Hospital of Los Angeles.
Martin, S. T. (2001, Nov. 29). Willing to kill and die, but why? *St. Petersburg Times,* pp. 1D, 3D.
Martin, T. L., & Doka, K. J. (1996). Masculine grief. In K. J. Doka (Ed.), *Living with grief after sudden loss: Suicide, homicide, accident, heart attack, stroke* (pp. 161–71). Washington, DC: Hospice Foundation of America.
Martin, T. L., & Doka, K. J. (1998). Revisiting masculine grief. In K. J. Doka & J. D. Davidson (Eds.), *Living with grief: Who we are, how we grieve* (pp. 133–42). Washington, DC: Hospice Foundation of America.
Martin, T. L., & Doka, K. J. (2000). *Men don't cry, women do: Transcending gender stereotypes of grief.* Philadelphia: Brunner/Mazel.
Martinson, I. M. (Ed.). (1976). *Home care for the dying child.* New York: Appleton-Century-Crofts.
Martinson, I. M., Davies, E. B., & McClowry, S. G. (1987). The long-term effects of sibling death on self-concept. *Journal of Pediatric Nursing, 2,* 227–35.
Maruyama, N. L. (1998). How many children do you have? *Bereavement Magazine, 12*(5), 16.
Masera, G., Spinetta, J. J., Jankovic, M., Ablin, A. R., D'Angio, G. J., Van Dongen-Melman, J., Eden, T., Martins, A. G., Mulhern, R. K., Oppenheim, D., Topf, R., & Chesler, M. A. (1999). Guidelines for assistance to terminally ill children with cancer: A report of the SIOP working committee on psychosocial issues in

pediatric oncology. *Medical and Pediatric Oncology, 32*, 44–48.
Maslow, A. (1968). *Toward a psychology of being* (2nd ed.). Princeton, NJ: Van Nostrand.
Maslow, A. (1971). *The farther reaches of human nature.* New York: Viking Penguin.
Masur, H., Kaplan, J. E., & Holmes, K. K. (2001). July, 2001: Draft/2001 USPHS/IDSA. Guidelines for the Prevention of Opportunistic Infections in Persons Infected with Human Immunodeficiency Virus, p. 49.
Matchett, W. F. (1972). Repeated hallucinatory experiences as a part of the mourning process among Hopi Indian women. *Psychiatry, 35*, 185–94.
Matse, J. (1975). Reactions to death in residential homes for the aged. *Omega, 6*, 21–32.
Matthews, W. (1897). Navaho legends. *Memoirs of the American Folk-Lore Society*, vol. 5. New York: G. E. Stechert.
Mauk, G. W., & Weber, C. (1991). Peer survivors of adolescent suicide: Perspectives on grieving and postvention. *Journal of Adolescent Research, 6*, 113–31.
Maurer, A. (1964). Adolescent attitudes toward death. *Journal of Genetic Psychology, 105*, 75–90.
Maurer, A. (1966). Maturation of the conception of death. *Journal of Medical Psychology, 39*, 35–41.
May, G. (1992). For they shall be comforted. *Shalem News, 16*(2), 3.
Mayer, R. A. (1996). *Embalming: History, theory, and practice* (2nd ed.). Norwalk, CT: Appleton & Lange.
Mbiti, J. S. (1970). *African religion and philosophy.* Garden City, NY: Doubleday Anchor.
McCaffery, M., & Beebe, A. (1989). *Pain: Clinical manual for nursing practice.* St. Louis: C. V. Mosby.
McCallum, D. E., Byrne, P., & Bruera, E. (2000). How children die in hospital. *Journal of Pain and Symptom Management, 20*, 417–23.
McClowry, S. G., Davies, E. B., May, K. A., Kulenkamp, E. J., & Martinson, I. M. (1987). The empty space phenomenon: The process of grief in the bereaved family. *Death Studies, 11*, 361–74.
McCord, C., & Freeman, H. P. (1990). Excess mortality in Harlem. *New England Journal of Medicine, 322*, 173–77.
McCormick, R. (1974). To save or let die. *Journal of the American Medical Association, 224*, 172–76.
McCown, D. E., & Davies, B. (1995). Patterns of grief in young children following the death of a sibling. *Death Studies, 19*, 41–53.
McCue, J. D. (1995). The naturalness of dying. *Journal of the American Medical Association, 273*, 1039–43.
McCue, K., & Bonn, R. (1996). *How to help children through a parent's serious illness.* New York: St. Martin's.
McGinnis, J. M., & Foege, W. H. (1993). Actual causes of death in the United States. *Journal of the American Medical Association, 270*, 2207–12.
McGoldrick, M. (1988). Women and the family life cycle. In B. Carter & M. McGoldrick (Eds.), *The changing family life cycle: A framework for family therapy* (2nd ed., pp. 29–68). New York: Gardner.
McGoldrick, M., & Gerson, R. (1985). *Genograms in family assessment.* New York: Norton.
McGoldrick, M., & Gerson, R. (1988). Genograms and the family life cycle. In B. Carter & M. McGoldrick (Eds.), *The changing family life cycle: A framework for family therapy* (2nd ed., pp. 164–89). New York: Gardner.
McGoldrick, M., Pearce, J. K., & Giordano, J. (Eds.). (1982). *Ethnicity and family therapy.* New York: Guilford.
McGoldrick, M., & Walsh, F. (1991). A time to mourn: Death and the family life cycle. In F. Walsh & M. McGoldrick (Eds.), *Living beyond loss: Death in the family* (pp. 30–49). New York: Norton.
McGrath, P. A. (1998). Pain control. In D. Doyle, G. W. C. Hanks, & N. MacDonald (Eds.), *Oxford textbook of palliative medicine* (pp. 1013–31). New York: Oxford University Press.
McGuffey, W. H. (1866). *McGuffey's new fourth eclectic reader: Instructive lessons for the young* (enlarged ed.). Cincinnati: Wilson, Hinkle & Co.
McIntosh, J. L. (1983). Suicide among Native Americans: Further tribal data and considerations. *Omega, 14*, 215–29.
McIntosh, J. L. (1985). Suicide among the elderly: Levels and trends. *American Journal of Orthopsychiatry, 56*, 288–93.
McIntosh, J. L. (1987). Research, therapy, and educational needs. In Dunne, E. J., McIntosh, J. L., & Dunne-Maxim, K. (Eds.), *Suicide and*

its aftermath: Understanding and counseling the survivors (pp. 263–77). New York: Norton.

McIntosh, J. L. (1989). Suicide: Asian-American. In R. Kastenbaum & B. Kastenbaum (Eds.), *Encyclopedia of death* (pp. 233–34). Phoenix, AZ: Oryx Press.

McIntosh, J. L. (2001). *U.S.A. suicide: 1998 official final data* (rev. March 16). Washington, DC: American Association of Suicidology.

McIntosh, J. L., & Santos, J. F. (1981a). Suicide among minority elderly: A preliminary investigation. *Suicide and Life-Threatening Behavior, 11*, 151–66.

McIntosh, J. L., & Santos, J. F. (1981b). Suicide among Native Americans: A compilation of findings. *Omega, 11*, 303–16.

McKhann, C. F. (1999). *A time to die: The place for physician assistance.* New Haven: Yale University Press.

McNeil, J. N. (1986). Talking about death: Adolescents, parents, and peers. In C. A. Corr & J. N. McNeil (Eds.), *Adolescence and death* (pp. 185–201). New York: Springer.

McNeil, J. N., Silliman, B., & Swihart, J. J. (1991). Helping adolescents cope with the death of a peer: A high school case study. *Journal of Adolescent Research, 6*, 132–45.

McNurlen, M. (1991). Guidelines for group work. In C. A. Corr, H. Fuller, C. A. Barnickol, & D. M. Corr (Eds.), *Sudden Infant Death Syndrome: Who can help and how* (pp. 180–202). New York: Springer.

Mead, M. (1973). Ritual and social crisis. In J. D. Shaughnessy (Ed.), *The roots of ritual* (pp. 87–101). Grand Rapids, MI: Eerdmans.

Medical ethics, narcotics, and addiction [Editorial]. (1963). *Journal of the American Medical Association, 185*, 962–63.

Melzack, R. (1990, February). The tragedy of needless pain. *Scientific American*, pp. 27–33.

Melzack, R., Mount, B. M., & Gordon, J. M. (1979). The Brompton mixture versus morphine solution given orally: Effects on pain. *Canadian Medical Association Journal, 120*, 435–38.

Melzack, R., Ofiesh, J. G., & Mount, B. M. (1976). The Brompton mixture: Effects on pain in cancer patients. *Canadian Medical Association Journal, 115*, 125–29.

Melzack, R., & Wall, P. D. (1991). *The challenge of pain* (3rd ed.). New York: Penguin.

Menninger, K. (1938). *Man against himself.* New York: Harcourt, Brace & World.

Meshot, C. M., & Leitner, L. M. (1993). Adolescent mourning and parental death. *Omega, 26*, 287–99.

Metzgar, M. M., & Zick, B. C. (1996). Building the foundation: Preparation before a trauma. In C. A. Corr & D. M. Corr (Eds.), *Handbook of childhood death and bereavement* (pp. 245–64). New York: Springer.

Metzger, A. M. (1979). A Q-methodological study of the Kübler-Ross stage theory. *Omega, 10*, 291–302.

Meyer-Baer, K. (1970). *Music of the spheres and the dance of death: Studies in musical iconology.* Princeton, NJ: Princeton University Press.

Michalczyk, J. J. (Ed.). (1994). *Medicine, ethics, and the Third Reich: Historical and contemporary issues.* Kansas City, MO: Sheed & Ward.

Michalek, A. M., & Mahoney, M. C. (1990). Cancer in native populations—Lessons to be learned. *Journal of Cancer Education, 5*, 243–49.

Michel, L., & Herbeck, D. (2001). *American terrorist: Timothy McVeigh and the Oklahoma City bombing.* New York: Regan Books.

Miles, M. (1971). *Annie and the old one.* Boston: Little, Brown.

Miles, M. S. (1984). Helping adults mourn the death of a child. In H. Wass & C. A. Corr (Eds.), *Childhood and death* (pp. 219–41). Washington, DC: Hemisphere.

Miles, M. S. (n.d.). *The grief of parents when a child dies.* Oak Brook, IL: The Compassionate Friends.

Miles, M. S., & Demi, A. S. (1984). Toward the development of a theory of bereavement guilt: Sources of guilt in bereaved parents. *Omega, 14*, 299–314.

Miles, M. S., & Demi, A. S. (1986). Guilt in bereaved parents. In T. A. Rando (Ed.), *Parental loss of a child* (pp. 97–118). Champaign, IL: Research Press.

Miletich, L. (2001). Defining the essence of aftercare. In O. D. Weeks & C. Johnson (Eds.), *When all the friends have gone: A guide for aftercare providers* (pp. 25–34). Amityville, NY: Baywood.

Miller, J., Engelberg, S., & Broad, W. (2001). *Germs: Biological weapons and America's secret war.* New York: Simon & Schuster.

Miller, M. (1979). *Suicide after sixty: The final alternative.* New York: Springer.

Miller, P. J., & Mike, P. B. (1995). The Medicare hospice benefit: Ten years of federal policy for the terminally ill. *Death Studies, 19,* 531–42.

Mills, L. O. (Ed.). (1969). *Perspectives on death.* Nashville: Abingdon.

Milofsky, C. (1980). *Structure and process in self-help organizations.* New Haven, CT: Yale University, Institution for Social and Policy Studies.

Mindel, C. H., Habenstein, R. W., & Wright, R. (1988). *Ethnic families in America: Patterns and variations* (3rd ed.). New York: Elsevier.

Minnich, H. C. (1936a). *Old favorites from the McGuffey readers.* New York: American Book Company.

Minnich, H. C. (1936b). *William Holmes McGuffey and his readers.* New York: American Book Company.

Minow, N. N., & LaMay, C. L. (1995). *Abandoned in the wasteland: Children, television and the First Amendment.* New York: Hill & Wang.

Mitchell, L. (1977). *The meaning of ritual.* New York: Paulist Press.

Mitford, J. (1963). *The American way of death.* New York: Simon & Schuster.

Mitford, J. (1998). *The American way of death revisited.* New York: Knopf.

Mitterand, F. (1995). Preface. In M. de Hennezel, *La mort intime: Ceux qui vont mourir nous apprennent à vivre* (pp. 9–12). Paris: 'Editions Robert Laffont.

Momeyer, R. W. (1988). *Confronting death.* Bloomington, IN: Indiana University Press.

Monat, A., & Lazarus, R. S. (Eds.). (1991). *Stress and coping: An anthology* (3rd ed.). New York: Columbia University Press.

Monette, P. (1988). *Borrowed time: An AIDS memoir.* San Diego: Harcourt Brace Jovanovich.

Monette, P. (1992). *Becoming a man: Half a life story.* San Diego: Harcourt Brace Jovanovich.

Monette, P. (1995). *Last watch of the night: Essays too personal and otherwise.* San Diego: Harcourt Brace.

Montgomery, J., & Fewer, W. (1988). *Family systems and beyond.* New York: Human Sciences Press.

Moody, H. R. (1984). Can suicide on grounds of old age be ethically justified? In M. Tallmer, E. R. Prichard, A. H. Kutscher, R. DeBellis, M. S. Hale, & I. K. Goldberg (Eds.), *The life-threatened elderly* (pp. 64–92). New York: Columbia University Press.

Moody, R. A. (1975). *Life after life.* Covington, GA: Mockingbird Books. (Reprinted New York: Bantam, 1976.)

Moody, R. A. (1988). *The light beyond.* New York: Bantam.

Moore, J. (1980). The death culture of Mexico and Mexican Americans. In R. A. Kalish (Ed.), *Death and dying: Views from many cultures* (pp. 72–91). Farmingdale, NY: Baywood.

Moos, N. L. (1995). An integrative model of grief. *Death Studies, 19,* 337–64.

Moos, R. H., & Schaefer, J. A. (1986). Life transitions and crises: A conceptual overview. In R. H. Moos & J. A. Schaefer (Eds.), *Coping with life crises: An integrated approach* (pp. 3–28). New York: Plenum.

Morgan, E., & Morgan, J. (2001). *Dealing creatively with death: A manual of death education and simple burial* (14th rev. ed.). Hinesburg, VT: Upper Access.

Moroney, R. M., & Kurtz, N. R. (1975). The evolution of long-term care institutions. In S. Sherwood (Ed.), *Long-term care: A handbook for researchers, planners, and providers* (pp. 81–121). New York: Spectrum.

Morse, S. S. (Ed.). (1993). *Emerging viruses.* New York: Oxford University Press.

Moss, F., & Halamanderis, V. (1977). *Too old, too sick, too bad: Nursing homes in America.* Germantown, MD: Aspen Systems Corp.

Moss, M. S., Lesher, E. L., & Moss, S. Z. (1986). Impact of the death of an adult child on elderly parents: Some observations. *Omega, 17,* 209–18.

Moss, M. S., & Moss, S. Z. (1983). The impact of parental death on middle-aged children. *Omega, 14,* 65–75.

Moss, M. S., & Moss, S. Z. (1984). Some aspects of the elderly widow(er)'s persistent tie with the deceased spouse. *Omega, 15,* 195–206.

Motto, J. (1980). The right to suicide: A psychiatrist's view. In M. P. Battin & D. J. Mayo (Eds.), *Suicide: The philosophical issues* (pp. 212–19). New York: St. Martin's Press.

Mount, B. M., Jones, A., & Patterson, A. (1974). Death and dying: Attitudes in a teaching hospital. *Urology, 4,* 741–47.

Munson, R. (1993). *Fan mail.* New York: Dutton.
Murphy, S. L. (2000). Deaths: Final data for 1998. *National Vital Statistics Reports, 48*(11). Hyattsville, MD: National Center for Health Statistics.
Musto, B. (1999, Jan. 19). Karen's gift. *Women's World,* p. 39.
Muwahidi, A. A. (1989). Islamic perspectives on death and dying. In A. Berger, P. Badham, A. H. Kutscher, J. Berger, M. Perry, & J. Beloff (Eds.), *Perspectives on death and dying: Cross-cultural and multi-disciplinary views* (pp. 38–54). Philadelphia: Charles Press.
Myers, E. (1986). *When parents die: A guide for adults.* New York: Viking Penguin.
Nabe, C. (1999). A caregiver's quandary: How am I to evaluate and respond to the other's suffering? *Omega, 39,* 71–91.
Nabe, C. M. (1981). Presenting biological data in a course on death and dying. *Death Education, 5,* 51–58.
Nabe, C. M. (1982). "Seeing as": Death as door or wall. In R. A. Pacholski & C. A. Corr (Eds.), *Priorities in death education and counseling* (pp. 161–69). Arlington, VA: Forum for Death Education and Counseling.
Nabe, C. M. (1987). Fragmentation and spiritual care. In C. A. Corr & R. A. Pacholski (Eds.), *Death: Completion and discovery* (pp. 281–86). Lakewood, OH: Association for Death Education and Counseling.
Nadeau, J. (1998). *Families make sense of death.* Thousand Oaks, CA: Sage.
Nader, K. O. (1996). Children's exposure to traumatic experiences. In C. A. Corr & D. M. Corr (Eds.), *Handbook of childhood death and bereavement* (pp. 201–20). New York: Springer.
Nagy, M. A. (1948). The child's theories concerning death. *Journal of Genetic Psychology, 73,* 3–27. (Reprinted with some editorial changes as "The child's view of death" in H. Feifel [Ed.], *The meaning of death* [pp. 79–98]. New York: McGraw-Hill, 1959.)
National Center for Health Statistics (NCHS). (2001). National Vital Statistics System. Unpublished tabulations.
National Hospice and Palliative Care Organization (2000). *Standards of practice for hospice programs.* Alexandria, VA: Author.
National Hospice and Palliative Care Organization (2001a). Facts and figures on hospice care in America. Alexandria, VA: Author.
National Hospice and Palliative Care Organization. (2001b). *Hospice care in nursing facilities: An educational resource for effective partnerships in end-of-life care,* 2 vols. Alexandria, VA: Author.
National Hospice and Palliative Care Organization (2001c). NHPCO facts and figures. Alexandria, VA: Author.
National Hospice and Palliative Care Organization & the Center to Advance Palliative Care in Hospitals and Health Systems. (2001). *Hospital-hospice partnerships in palliative care: Creating a continuum of service.* Alexandria, VA: National Hospice and Palliative Care Organization.
National Kidney Foundation. (1997). *National communication guidelines regarding communication among donor families, transplant candidates/recipients, and health care professionals.* New York: Author.
National Research Council. (1993). *Losing generations: Adolescents in high-risk settings.* Washington, DC: National Academy Press.
National Safety Council. (2000). *Accident facts: 2000 edition.* Itaska, IL: Author.
Neaman, J. S., & Silver, C. G. (1983). *Kind words: A thesaurus of euphemisms.* New York: Facts on File Publications.
Neimeyer, R. A. (Ed.). (1994). *Death anxiety handbook: Research, instrumentation, and application.* Washington, DC: Taylor & Francis.
Neimeyer, R. A. (1998). *Lessons of loss: A guide to coping.* New York: McGraw-Hill.
Neimeyer, R. A. (Ed.). (2001). *Meaning reconstruction and the experience of loss.* Washington, DC: American Psychological Association.
Neimeyer, R. A., & Van Brunt, D. (1995). Death anxiety. In H. Wass & R. A. Neimeyer (Eds.), *Dying: Facing the facts* (3rd ed., pp. 49–88). Washington, DC: Taylor & Francis.
Nelson, B. J., & Frantz, T. T. (1996). Family interactions of suicide survivors and survivors of non-suicidal death. *Omega, 33,* 131–46.
Neugarten, B. L. (1974). Age groups in American society and the rise of the young-old. *Annals of the American Academy of Political and Social Science, 415,* 187–98.
Neugarten, B. L., & Datan, N. (1973). Sociological perspectives on the life cycle. In P. B. Baltes & K. W. Schaie (Eds.), *Life-span developmental psychology: Personality and socialization* (pp. 53–69). New York: Academic Press.

Neusner, J. (Trans.). (1988). *The Mishnah: A new translation.* New Haven, CT: Yale University Press.

New England Primer (1962). New York: Columbia University Press. (Original work published 1727.)

Newman, B. M., & Newman, P. R. (1999). *Development through life: A psychosocial approach* (7th ed.). Belmont, CA: Wadsworth.

Newman, L. (Ed.). (1995). *A loving testimony: Remembering loved ones lost to AIDS.* Freedom, CA: Crossing Press.

Nichols, M. P. (1995). *The lost art of listening.* New York: Guilford.

Nieburg, H. A., & Fischer, A. (1982). *Pet loss.* New York: Harper & Row.

Noack, D. (1999). Controversial photo draws support from readers. *Editor and Publisher, 132*(26), 8.

Noppe, I. C., & Noppe, L. D. (1997). Evolving meanings of death during early, middle and later adolescence. *Death Studies, 21,* 253–75.

Noppe, L. D., & Noppe, I. C. (1991). Dialectical themes in adolescent conceptions of death. *Journal of Adolescent Research, 6,* 28–42.

Noppe, L. D., & Noppe, I. C. (1996). Ambiguity in adolescent understandings of death. In C. A. Corr & D. E. Balk (Eds.), *Handbook of adolescent death and bereavement* (pp. 25–41). New York: Springer.

Nord, D. A. (1997). *Multiple AIDS-related loss: A handbook for surviving a perpetual fall.* Washington, DC: Taylor & Francis.

Norlander, L., & McSteen, K. (2001). *Choices at the end of life: Finding out what your parents want before it's too late.* Minneapolis: Fairview Press.

Nouwen, H. (1972). *The wounded healer: Ministry in contemporary society.* Garden City, NY: Doubleday.

Nouwen, H., & Gaffney, W. J. (1990). *Aging: The fulfillment of life.* New York: Doubleday.

Novack, D. H., Plumer, R., Smith, R. L., Ochitill, H., Morrow, G. R., & Bennett, J. M. (1979). Changes in physicians' attitudes toward telling the cancer patient. *Journal of the American Medical Association, 241,* 897–900.

Novick, P. (1999). *The Holocaust in American life.* Boston: Houghton Mifflin.

Noyes, R., & Clancy, J. (1977). The dying role: Its relevance to improved patient care. *Psychiatry, 40,* 41–47.

Nuland, S. B. (1994). *How we die: Reflections on life's final chapter.* New York: Knopf.

Nussbaum, K. (1998). *Preparing the children: Information and ideas for families facing terminal illness and death.* Kodiak, AK: Gifts of Hope Trust.

O'Carroll, P. W. (1989). A consideration of the validity and reliability of suicide mortality data. *Suicide and Life-Threatening Behavior, 19,* 1–16.

O'Connor, M. C. (1942). *The art of dying well: The development of the ars moriendi.* New York: Columbia University Press.

O'Connor, P. (1999). Hospice vs. palliative care. *The Hospice Journal, 14,* 123–37.

O'Gorman, B., & O'Brien, T. (1990). Motor neurone disease. In C. Saunders (Eds.), *Hospice and palliative care: An interdisciplinary approach* (pp. 41–45). London: Edward Arnold.

O'Toole, D. (1995). *Facing change: Falling apart and coming together again in the teen years.* Burnsville, NC: Compassion Books.

Offer, D. (1969). *The psychological worlds of the teenager.* New York: Basic Books.

Offer, D., & Offer, J. B. (1975). *From teenage to young manhood: A psychological study.* New York: Basic Books.

Offer, D., & Sabshin, M. (1984). Adolescence: Empirical perspectives. In D. Offer & M. Sabshin (Eds.), *Normality and the life cycle: A critical integration* (pp. 76–107). New York: Basic Books.

Offer, D., Ostrov, E., & Howard, K. I. (1981). *The adolescent: A psychological self-portrait.* New York: Basic Books.

Offer, D., Ostrov, E., Howard, K. I., & Atkinson, R. (1988). *The teenage world: Adolescents' self-image in ten countries.* New York: Plenum.

Oken, D. (1961). What to tell cancer patients: A study of medical attitudes. *Journal of the American Medical Association, 175,* 1120–28.

Olson, L. M., Becker, T. M., Wiggins, C. L., Key, C. R., & Samet, J. N. (1990). Injury mortality in American Indian, Hispanic, and non-Hispanic White children in New Mexico, 1958–1982. *Social Science and Medicine, 30,* 479–86.

Oltjenbruns, K. A. (1991). Positive outcomes of adolescents' experience with grief. *Journal of Adolescent Research, 6,* 43–53.

Oltjenbruns, K. A. (1996). Death of a friend during adolescence: Issues and impacts. In C. A. Corr & D. E. Balk (Eds.), *Handbook of adolescent death and bereavement* (pp. 196–215). New York: Springer.

Opoku, K. A. (1978). *West African traditional religion.* Singapore: Far Eastern Publishers.

Opoku, K. A. (1987). Death and immortality in the African religious heritage. In P. Badham & L. Badham (Eds.), *Death and immortality in the religions of the world* (pp. 9–21). New York: Paragon House.

Orbach, I. (1988). *Children who don't want to live: Understanding and treating the suicidal child.* San Francisco: Jossey-Bass.

Oregon Health Division. (2001). Oregon's Death with Dignity Act: Three years of legalized physician-assisted suicide (Annual report 2000). http://www.ohd.hr.state.or.us/chs/pas/ar-smmry.htm

Oregon Health Division. (2002). Fourth annual report on Oregon's Death with Dignity Act. (Annual report 2001). http://www.ohd.hr.state.or.us/chs/pas/ar-summry.htm

Osgood, N. J. (1992). *Suicide in later life: Recognizing the warning signs.* New York: Lexington.

Osgood, N. J. (2000). Elderly suicide [Special issue]. *Omega, 42*(1).

Osgood, N. J., Brant, B. A., & Lipman, A. (1991). *Suicide among the elderly in long-term care facilities.* New York: Greenwood.

Osis, K., & Haraldsson, E. (1997). *At the hour of death* (3rd ed.). Norwalk, CT: Hastings House.

Osmont, K., & McFarlane, M. (1986). *Parting is not goodbye.* Portland, OR: Nobility Press.

Osterweis, M., Solomon, F., & Green, M. (Eds.). (1984). *Bereavement: Reactions, consequences, and care.* Washington, DC: National Academy Press.

Owens, J. E., Cook, E. W., & Stevenson, I. (1990). Features of "near-death experience" in relation to whether or not patients were near death. *The Lancet, 336,* 1175–77.

The Oxford English Dictionary (2nd ed., 20 vols.) (1989). Ed. J. A. Simpson & E. S. C. Weiner. Oxford Clarendon Press.

Panuthos, C., & Romeo, C. (1984). *Ended beginnings: Healing childbearing losses.* South Hadley, MA: Bergin & Garvey.

Papadatou, D. (1989). Caring for dying adolescents. *Nursing Times, 85,* 28–31.

Papadatou, D. (2000). A proposed model of health professionals' grieving process. *Omega, 41,* 59–77.

Papadatou, D., & Papadatos, C. (Eds.). (1991). *Children and death.* Washington, DC: Hemisphere.

Papalia, D. E., Olds, S. W., Camp, C. J., & Feldman, R. D. (1995). *Adult development and aging.* Boston: McGraw-Hill.

Papalia, D. E., Olds, S. W., & Feldman, R. D. (1998). *A child's world: Infancy through adolescence* (8th ed.). Boston: McGraw-Hill.

Papalia, D. E., Olds, S. W., & Feldman, R. D. (2000). *Human development* (8th ed.). Boston: McGraw-Hill.

Parkes, C. M. (1970). "Seeking" and "finding" a lost object: Evidence from recent studies of reaction to bereavement. *Social Science and Medicine, 4,* 187–201.

Parkes, C. M. (1971). The first year of bereavement: A longitudinal study of the reaction of London widows to the death of their husbands. *Psychiatry, 33,* 444–67.

Parkes, C. M. (1975a). What becomes of redundant world models? A contribution to the study of adaptation to change. *British Journal of Medical Psychology, 48,* 131–37.

Parkes, C. M. (1975b). Determinants of outcome following bereavement. *Omega, 6,* 303–23.

Parkes, C. M. (1979). Evaluation of a bereavement service. In A. DeVries & A. Carmi (Eds.), *The dying human* (pp. 389–402). Ramat Gan, Israel: Turtledove.

Parkes, C. M. (1980). Bereavement counselling: Does it work? *British Medical Journal, 281,* 3–6.

Parkes, C. M. (1981). Evaluation of a bereavement service. *Journal of Preventive Psychiatry, 1,* 179–88.

Parkes, C. M. (1987). Models of bereavement care. *Death Studies, 11,* 257–61.

Parkes, C. M. (1993). Bereavement as a psychosocial transition: Processes of adaptation to change. In M. Stroebe, W. Stroebe, & R. O. Hansson (Eds.), *Handbook of bereavement: Theory, research, and intervention* (pp. 91–101). New York: Cambridge University Press.

Parkes, C. M. (2001). *Bereavement: Studies of grief in adult life* (3rd ed.). New York: Routledge.

Parkes, C. M., & Weiss, R. (1983). *Recovery from bereavement.* New York: Basic Books.

Parkes, C. M., Laungani, P., & Young, B. (Eds.). (1997). *Death and bereavement across cultures.* New York: Routledge.

Parkes, C. M., Relf, M., & Couldrick, A. (1996). *Counseling in terminal care and bereavement.* Leicester, UK: BPS Books.

Parkes, C. M., Stevenson-Hinde, J., & Marris, P. (Eds.). (1993). *Attachment across the life cycle.* New York: Routledge.

Parks, G. (1971). *Gordon Parks: Whispers of intimate things.* New York: Viking.

Parry, J. K. (Ed.). (1990). *Social work practice with the terminally ill: A transcultural perspective.* Springfield, IL: Charles C Thomas.

Parry, J. K., & Ryan, A. S. (Eds.). (1995). *A cross-cultural look at death, dying, and religion.* Chicago: Nelson-Hall.

Parsons, T. (1951). *The social system.* New York: Free Press.

Partridge, E. (1966). *A dictionary of slang and unconventional English.* New York: Macmillan.

Pattison, E. M. (1977). *The experience of dying.* Englewood Cliffs, NJ: Prentice-Hall.

Pawelczynska, A. (1979). *Values and violence in Auschwitz: A sociological analysis.* Trans. C. S. Leach. Berkeley & Los Angeles: University of California Press.

Peabody, F. W. (1927). The care of the patient. *Journal of the American Medical Association, 88,* 877–82. (Reprinted as a monograph by Harvard University Press in the same year.)

Peck, M. L., Farberow, N. L., & Litman, R. E. (Eds.). (1985). *Youth suicide.* New York: Springer.

Pendleton, E. (Comp.). (1980). *Too old to cry, too young to die.* Nashville: Thomas Nelson.

Peppers, L. G. (1987). Grief and elective abortion: Breaking the emotional bond. *Omega, 18,* 1–12.

Peppers, L. G., & Knapp, R. J. (1980). *Motherhood and mourning: Perinatal death.* New York: Praeger.

Perls, T. T., Silver, M. H., & Lauerman, J. F. (2000). *Living to 100: Lessons in living to your maximum potential at any age.* New York: Basic Books.

Pfeffer, C. R. (1986). *The suicidal child.* New York: Guilford.

Pfeffer, C. R. (Ed.). (1989). *Suicide among youth: Perspectives on risk and prevention.* Washington, DC: American Psychiatric Press.

Piaget, J. (1998). *The equilibration of cognitive structures: The central problem of intellectual development.* Trans. T. A. Brown & K. J. Thampy. Chicago: University of Chicago Press.

Piaget, J., & Inhelder, B. (1958). *The growth of logical thinking from childhood to adolescence.* Trans. A. Parsons & S. Milgram. New York: Basic Books.

Pike, M. M., & Wheeler, S. R. (1992). *Bereavement support group guide: Guidebook for individuals and/or professionals who wish to start a bereavement, mutual, self-help group.* Covington, IN: Grief, Ltd.

Pine, V. R. (1975). *Caretaker of the dead: The American funeral director.* New York: Irvington.

Pine, V. R. (1977). A socio-historical portrait of death education. *Death Education, 1,* 57–84.

Pine, V. R. (1986). The age of maturity for death education: A socio-historical portrait of the era 1976–1985. *Death Studies, 10,* 209–31.

Pinsky, L., & Douglas, P. H. (1992). *The essential HIV treatment fact book.* New York: Pocket Books.

Piot, P., Bartos, M., Ghys, P. D., Walker, N., & Schwartlander, B. (2001). The global impact of HIV/AIDS. *Nature, 410,* 968–73.

Piper, F. (1994). The number of victims. In I. Gutman & M. Berenbaum (Eds.), *Anatomy of the Auschwitz death camp* (pp. 61–76). Bloomington, IN: Indiana University Press.

Pitch of Grief. [Videotape]. (1985). Newton, MA: Newton Cable Television Foundation and Eric Stange.

Plath, S. (1964). *Ariel.* New York: Harper & Row.

Plath, S. (1971). *The bell jar.* New York: Harper & Row.

Plato. (1948). *Euthyphro, Apology, Crito.* Trans. F. J. Church. New York: Macmillan.

Plato. (1961). *The collected dialogues of Plato including the letters.* Eds. E. Hamilton & H. Cairns. New York: Bollingen Foundation.

Platt, A. (1995). The resurgence of infectious diseases. *World Watch, 8*(4), 26–32.

Platt, M. (1975). Commentary: On asking to die. *Hastings Center Report, 5*(6), 9–12.

Please Let Me Die. [Videotape]. (1974). Galveston, TX: University of Texas Medical Branch.

Plepys, C., & Klein, R. (1995). *Health status indicators: Differentials by race and Hispanic origin* (10). Washington, DC: National Center for Health Statistics.

Plopper, B. L., & Ness, M. E. (1993). Death as portrayed to adolescents through Top 40 rock and roll music. *Adolescence, 28,* 793–807.

Podell, C. (1989). Adolescent mourning: The sudden death of a peer. *Clinical Social Work Journal, 17,* 64–78.

Poe, E. A. (1948). *The letters of Edgar Allan Poe* (2 vols.). Ed. J. W. Ostrom. Cambridge, MA: Harvard University Press.

Pojman, L. P. (1992). *Life and death: Grappling with the moral dilemmas of our time.* Boston: Jones & Bartlett.

Poland, S. (1989). *Suicide intervention in the schools.* New York: Guilford.
Polednak, A. P. (1990). Cancer mortality in a higher-income Black population in New York State: Comparison with rates in the United States as a whole. *Cancer, 66*, 1654–60.
Popovic, J. R., & Kozak, L. J. (2000). National hospital discharge survey: Annual summary, 1998. *Vital and Health Statistics, 13*(148). Hyattsville, MD: National Center for Health Statistics.
Porter, J., & Jick, H. (1980). Addiction rare in patients treated with narcotics. *New England Journal of Medicine, 302*, 123.
Pound, L. (1936). American euphemisms for dying, death, and burial: An anthology. *American Speech, 11*, 195–202.
Powell-Griner, E. (1988). Differences in infant mortality among Texas Anglos, Hispanics, and Blacks. *Social Science Quarterly, 69*, 452–67.
Prashad, J. (1989). The Hindu concept of death. In A. Berger, P. Badham, A. H. Kutscher, J. Berger, M. Perry, & J. Beloff (Eds.), *Perspectives on death and dying: Cross-cultural and multi-disciplinary views* (pp. 84–88). Philadelphia: Charles Press.
President's Commission for the Study of Ethical Problems in Medicine and Biomedical and Behavioral Research. (1981). *Defining death: A report on the medical, legal, and ethical issues in the determination of death.* Washington, DC: U.S. Government Printing Office.
President's Commission for the Study of Ethical Problems in Medicine and Biomedical and Behavioral Research. (1982). *Making health care decisions: A report on the ethical and legal implications of informed consent in the patient-practitioner relationship.* vol. 1, *Report;* vol. 3, *Studies on the foundation of informed consent.* Washington, DC: U.S. Government Printing Office.
President's Commission for the Study of Ethical Problems in Medicine and Biomedical and Behavioral Research. (1983a). *Deciding to forego life-sustaining treatment: A report on the ethical, medical, and legal issues in treatment decisions.* Washington, DC: U.S. Government Printing Office.
President's Commission for the Study of Ethical Problems in Medicine and Biomedical and Behavioral Research. (1983b). *Summing up: Final report on studies of the ethical and legal problems in medicine and biomedical and behavioral research.* Washington, DC: U.S. Government Printing Office.
Preston, R. J., & Preston, S. C. (1991). Death and grieving among northern forest hunters: An East Cree example. In D. R. Counts & D. A. Counts (Eds.), *Coping with the final tragedy: Cultural variation in dying and grieving* (pp. 135–55). Amityville, NY: Baywood.
Preston, S. H. (1976). *Mortality patterns in national populations: With special reference to recorded causes of death.* New York: Academic Press.
Preston, S. H., & Haines, M. R. (1991). *Fatal years: Child mortality in late nineteenth-century America.* Princeton, NJ: Princeton University Press.
Prestopino, D. J. (1992). *Introduction to estate planning* (3rd ed.). Dubuque, IA: Kendall/Hunt.
Prigerson, H. G., & Jacobs, S. C. (2001). Traumatic grief as a distinct disorder: A rationale, consensus criteria, and a preliminary empirical test. In M. S. Stroebe, R. O. Hansson, W. Stroebe, & H. Schut (Eds.), *Handbook of bereavement research: Consequences, coping, and care* (pp. 613–45). Washington, DC: American Psychological Association.
Prigerson, H. G., Shear, M. K., Jacobs, S. C., Reynolds, C. F., Maciejewski, P. K., Pilkonis, P. A., Wortman, C. M., Williams, J.B.W., Widiger, T. A., Davidson, J., Frank, E., Kupfer, D. J., & Zisook, S. (1999). Consensus criteria for traumatic grief: A preliminary empirical test. *British Journal of Psychiatry, 174*, 67–73.
Prottas, J. (1994). *The most useful gift: Altruism and the public policy of organ transplants.* San Francisco: Jossey-Bass.
Puckle, B. S. (1926). *Funeral customs: Their origin and development.* London: Laurie.
Purtillo, R. B. (1976). Similarities in patient response to chronic and terminal illness. *Physical Therapy, 56*, 279–84.
Quackenbush, J. (1985). The death of a pet: How it can affect pet owners. *Veterinary Clinics of North America: Small Animal Practice, 15*, 305–402.
Quindlen, A. (1994). *One true thing.* New York: Random House.

[*Qur'an.*] Koran. (1993). Trans. N. J. Dawood. London: Penguin.

Radhakrishnan, S. (1948). *The Bhagavadgita: With an introductory essay, Sanskrit text, English translation and notes.* New York: Harper & Brothers.

Radhakrishnan, S., & Moore, C. (1957). *A sourcebook in Indian philosophy.* Princeton, NJ: Princeton University Press.

Radin, P. (1973). *The road of life and death: A ritual drama of the American Indians.* Princeton, NJ: Princeton University Press.

Raether, H. C. (Ed.). (1989). *The funeral director's practice management handbook.* Englewood Cliffs, NJ: Prentice-Hall.

Rahman, F. (1987). *Health and medicine in the Islamic tradition: Change and identity.* New York: Crossroad.

Rahner, K. (1973). *On the theology of death.* Trans. C. H. Henkey. New York: Seabury Press.

Rahula, W. (1974). *What the Buddha taught.* New York: Grove Press.

Rakoff, V. M. (1974). Psychiatric aspects of death in America. In A. Mack (Ed.), *Death in American experience* (pp. 149–61). New York: Schocken Books.

Ramsey, P. (1970). *The patient as person: Explorations in medical ethics.* New Haven, CT: Yale University Press.

Randall, F., & Downie, R. S. (1999). *Palliative care ethics: A companion for all specialties* (2nd ed.). Oxford: Oxford University Press.

Rando, T. A. (1984). *Grief, dying, and death: Clinical interventions for caregivers.* Champaign, IL: Research Press.

Rando, T. A. (1985). Creating therapeutic rituals in the psychotherapy of the bereaved. *Psychotherapy, 22,* 236–40.

Rando, T. A. (Ed.). (1986a). *Parental loss of a child.* Champaign, IL: Research Press.

Rando, T. A. (1986b). Death of the adult child. In T. A. Rando (Ed.), *Parental loss of a child* (pp. 221–38). Champaign, IL: Research Press.

Rando, T. A. (Ed.). (1986c). *Loss and anticipatory grief.* Lexington, MA: Lexington Books.

Rando, T. A. (1988a). Anticipatory grief: The term is a misnomer but the phenomenon exists. *Journal of Palliative Care, 4*(1/2), 70–73.

Rando, T. A. (1988b). *How to go on living when someone you love dies.* New York: Bantam.

Rando, T. A. (1993). *Treatment of complicated mourning.* Champaign, IL: Research Press.

Rando, T. A. (1996). Complications in mourning traumatic death. In K. J. Doka (Ed.), *Living with grief after sudden loss: Suicide, homicide, accident, heart attack, stroke* (pp. 139–59). Washington, DC: Hospice Foundation of America.

Rando, T. A. (Ed.). (2000). *Clinical dimensions of anticipatory mourning: Theory and practice in working with the dying, their loved ones, and their caregivers.* Champaign, IL: Research Press.

Raphael, B. (1983). *The anatomy of bereavement.* New York: Basic Books.

Rawson, H. (1981). *A dictionary of euphemisms and other doubletalk.* New York: Crown.

Reddin, S. K. (1987). The photography of stillborn children and neonatal deaths. *Journal of Audiovisual Media in Medicine, 10*(2), 49–51.

Reder, P. (1969). *Epitaphs.* London: Michael Joseph.

Redmond, L. M. (1989). *Surviving: When someone you love was murdered.* Clearwater, FL: Psychological Consultation and Education Services.

Reece, R. D., & Ziegler, J. H. (1990). How a medical school (Wright State University) takes leave of human remains. *Death Studies, 14,* 589–600.

Reed, M. D., & Greenwald, J. Y. (1991). Survivor-victim status, attachment, and sudden death bereavement. *Suicide and Life-Threatening Behavior, 21,* 385–401.

Reed, M. L. (2000). *Grandparents cry twice: Help for bereaved grandparents.* Amityville, NY: Baywood.

Rees, W. D. (1972). The distress of dying. *British Medical Journal, 2,* 105–107.

Reich, W. (Ed.). (1978). *Encyclopedia of bioethics* (4 vols.). New York: Free Press.

Reid, J. K., & Reid, C. L (2001). A cross marks the spot: A study of roadside death memorials in Texas and Oklahoma. *Death Studies, 25,* 341–56.

Reitlinger, G. (1968). *The final solution: The attempt to exterminate the Jews of Europe 1939–1945* (2nd rev. ed.). London: Vallentine, Mitchell.

Retherford, R. D. (1975). *The changing sex differential in mortality.* Westport, CT: Greenwood Press.

Reynolds, F. E., & Waugh, E. H. (Eds.). (1977). *Religious encounters with death: Insights from the history and anthropology of religion.* State College, PA: Pennsylvania State University Press.

Reynolds, S. E. (1992). *Endings to beginnings: A grief support group for children and adolescents.* Minneapolis: HRG Press.

Rickgarn, R. L. V. (1994). *Perspectives on college student suicide.* Amityville, NY: Baywood.

Rickgarn, R. L. V. (1996). The need for postvention on college campuses: A rationale and case study findings. In C. A. Corr & D. E. Balk (Eds.), *Handbook of adolescent death and bereavement* (pp. 273–92). New York: Springer.

Ring, K. (1980). *Life at death: A scientific investigation of the near-death experience.* New York: Coward, McCann & Geoghegan.

Ring, K. (1984). *Heading toward omega: In search of the meaning of the near-death experience.* New York: Morrow.

Roberts, C. (1998). *We are our mothers' daughters.* New York: William Morrow.

Robertson, J. A. (1991). Second thoughts on living wills. *Hastings Center Report, 21*(6), 6–9.

Rochlin, G. (1967). How younger children view death and themselves. In E. A. Grollman (Ed.), *Explaining death to children* (pp. 51–85). Boston: Beacon Press.

Rodin, J., & Langer, E. J. (1977). Long-term effects of a control-relevant intervention with the institutionalized aged. *Journal of Personality and Social Psychology, 35,* 879–902.

Rodkinson, M. L. (Trans.). (1896). *New edition of the Babylonian Talmud,* vol. 2. New York: Talmud Publishing Company.

Rolcik, K. A. (1998). *Living trusts and simple ways to avoid probate: With forms* (2nd ed.). Naperville, IL: Sourcebooks.

Romanoff, B. D., & Terenzio, M. (1998). Rituals and the grieving process. *Death Studies, 22,* 697–711.

Romond, J. L. (1989). *Children facing grief: Letters from bereaved brothers and sisters.* St. Meinrad, IN: Abbey Press.

Ropp, L., Visintainer, P., Uman, J., & Treloar, D. (1992). Death in the city: An American childhood tragedy. *Journal of the American Medical Association, 267,* 2905–10.

Roscoe, L. A., Melphurs, J. E. Dragovic, L. J., & Cohen, D. (2000). Dr. Jack Kevorkian and cases of euthanasia in Oakland County, Michigan, 1990-1998. *New England Journal of Medicine, 343,* 1735–36.

Rosen, E. J. (1990). *Families facing death: Family dynamics of terminal illness.* Lexington, MA: Lexington Books.

Rosen, H. (1986). *Unspoken grief: Coping with childhood sibling loss.* Lexington, MA: Lexington Books.

Rosenberg, C. E. (1987). *The care of strangers: The rise of America's hospital system.* New York: Basic Books.

Rosenberg, T. (2000, Dec. 28). Death of dedicated Ugandan healer. *St. Petersburg Times,* p. 15A.

Rosenblatt, P. C. (1983). *Bitter, bitter tears: Nineteenth-century diarists and twentieth-century grief theories.* Minneapolis: University of Minnesota Press.

Rosenblatt, P. C. (2000). *Parent grief: Narratives of loss and relationship.* Philadelphia: Brunner/Mazel.

Rosenblatt, P. C. (2001). *Help your marriage survive the death of a child.* Philadelphia: Temple University Press.

Rosenblatt, P. C., Walsh, P. R., & Jackson, D. A. (1976). *Grief and mourning in cross-cultural perspectives.* Washington, DC: Human Relations Area Files.

Rosenthal, N. R. (1986). Death education: Developing a course of study for adolescents. In C. A. Corr & J. N. McNeil (Eds.), *Adolescence and death* (pp. 202–14). New York: Springer.

Rosenthal, T. (1973). *How could I not be among you?* New York: George Braziller.

Rosenwaike, I., & Bradshaw, B. S. (1988). The status of death statistics for the Hispanic population of the Southwest. *Social Science Quarterly, 69,* 722–36.

Rosenwaike, I., & Bradshaw, B. S. (1989). Mortality of the Spanish surname population of the Southwest: 1980. *Social Science Quarterly, 70,* 631–41.

Rosner, F. (1979). The Jewish attitude toward euthanasia. In F. Rosner & J. D. Bleich (Eds.), *Jewish bioethics* (pp. 253–65). New York: Sanhedrin Press.

Rosof, B. D. (1994). *The worst loss: How families heal from the death of a child.* New York: Henry Holt.

Ross, C. P. (1980). Mobilizing schools for suicide prevention. *Suicide and Life-Threatening Behavior, 10,* 239–43.

Ross, C. P. (1985). Teaching children the facts of life and death: Suicide prevention in the schools. In M. L. Peck, N. L. Farberow, & R. E. Litman (Eds.), *Youth suicide* (pp. 147–69). New York: Springer.

Ross, E. S. (1967). Children's books relating to death: A discussion. In E. A. Grollman (Ed.), *Explaining death to children* (pp. 249–71). Boston: Beacon Press.

Roth, N. L., & Fuller, L. K. (1998). *Women and AIDS: Negotiating safer practices, care, and representation.* Binghamton, NY: Haworth.

Roy, A. (1990). Possible biologic determinants of suicide. In D. Lester (Ed.), *Current concepts of suicide* (pp. 40–56). Philadelphia: Charles Press.

Rozovsky, F. A. (1990). *Consent to treatment: A practical guide* (2nd ed.). Boston: Little, Brown. (Also see 1994 Supplement.)

Rubel, B. (1999). *But I didn't say goodbye: For parents and professionals helping child suicide survivors.* Kendall Park, NJ: Griefwork Center, Inc.

Rubenstein, W. B., Eisenberg, R., & Gostin, L. O. (1996). *The rights of people who are HIV positive: The authoritative ACLU guide to the rights of people living with HIV disease and AIDS.* Carbondale & Edwardsville, IL: Southern Illinois University Press.

Rubin, B., Carlton, R., & Rubin, A. (1979). *L.A. in installments: Forest Lawn.* Santa Monica, CA: Hennessey & Ingalls.

Ruby, J. (1987). Portraying the dead. *Omega, 19,* 1–20.

Ruby, J. (1991). Photographs, memory, and grief. *Illness, Crisis and Loss, 1,* 1–5.

Ruby, J. (1995). *Secure the shadow: Death and photography in America.* Cambridge, MA: MIT Press.

Ruccione, K. S. (1994). Issues in survivorship. In C. L. Schwartz, W. L. Hobbie, L. S. Constine, & K. S. Ruccione (Eds.), *Survivors of childhood cancer: Assessment and management* (pp. 329–37). St. Louis: C. V. Mosby.

Rudestam, K. E. (1987). Public perceptions of suicide survivors. In E. J. Dunne, J. L. McIntosh, & K. Dunne-Maxim (Eds.), *Suicide and its aftermath: Understanding and counseling the survivors* (pp. 31–44). New York: Norton.

Rudin, C. (Comp.). (1998). *Children's books about the holocaust: A selective annotated bibliography.* Bayside, NY: The Holocaust Resource Center and Archives, Queensborough Community College.

Rudman, M. K., Gagne, K. D., & Bernstein, J. E. (1993). *Books to help children cope with separation and loss,* vol. 4. New Providence, NJ: R. R. Bowker. (Vol. 1 [1978] & vol. 2 [1984] by Bernstein alone; vol. 3 [1989] by Bernstein & Rudman.)

Ruskin, C. (1988). *The quilt: Stories from the NAMES Project.* New York: Pocket Books.

Ryan, C., & Ryan, K. M. (1979). *A private battle.* New York: Simon & Schuster.

Rynearson, E. K. (1978). Humans and pets and attachment. *British Journal of Psychiatry, 133,* 550–55.

Sabatino, C. P. (1990). *Health care powers of attorney: An introduction and sample forms.* Washington, DC: American Bar Association.

Sabom, M. B. (1982). *Recollections of death: A medical investigation.* New York: Harper & Row.

Sacred Congregation for the Doctrine of the Faith. (1982). Declaration on euthanasia. In A. Flannery (Ed.), *Vatican Council II: More Postconciliar Documents* (pp. 510–17). Grand Rapids, MI: Eerdmans.

St. Louis Post-Dispatch. (1995, Jan. 12). Breast cancer death rate drops dramatically, but not for Blacks, p. A5.

St. Louis Post-Dispatch. (1998, Sept. 4). Little change has been reported in death rates in 15 years for women in pregnancy, childbirth, p. A4.

St. Louis Post-Dispatch. (1999, April 14). Judge assails "lawlessness" of Kevorkian, gives him 10–25 years, p. A1.

St. Petersburg Times. (1998, Nov. 28). Kevorkian is charged in killing, released, pp. A1, A12.

St. Petersburg Times. (2000, Dec 6). Doctor who led Ebola battle dies, p. 2A.

St. Petersburg Times. (2001a, Feb. 7). Sick woman tested for Ebola virus, p. 14A.

St. Petersburg Times. (2001b, Feb. 23). For first time, rape found to be war crime, p. 2A.

St. Petersburg Times. (2001c, Feb. 23). Pakistan may arm subs with nukes, p. 20A.

St. Petersburg Times. (2001d, Sept. 29). Some blood donors stunned to learn they have HIV, hepatitis, p. 10A.

St. Petersburg Times. (2001e, Oct. 1). Brian Sweeney's last message, p. 10A.

St. Petersburg Times. (2001f, Oct. 6). Foreign officials seek out their own, p. 12A.

Sakr, A. H. (1995). Death and dying: An Islamic perspective. In J. K. Parry & A. S. Ryan (Eds.), *A cross-cultural look at death, dying, and religion* (pp. 47–73). Chicago: Nelson-Hall.

Salcido, R. M. (1990). Mexican-Americans: Illness, death and bereavement. In J. K. Parry (Ed.), *Social work practice with the terminally ill: A transcultural perspective* (pp. 99–112). Springfield, IL: Charles C Thomas.

Sanders, C. M. (1979). A comparison of adult bereavement in the death of a spouse, child and parent. *Omega, 10,* 303–22.

Sanders, C. M. (1989). *Grief: The mourning after.* New York: Wiley.

Sanders, C. M. (1992). *Surviving grief . . . and learning to live again.* New York: Wiley.

Saul, S. R., & Saul, S. (1973). Old people talk about death. *Omega, 4,* 27–35.

Saunders, C. M. (1967). *The management of terminal illness.* London: Hospital Medicine Publications.

Saunders, C. M. (1970). Dimensions of death. In M. A. H. Melinsky (Ed.), *Religion and medicine: A discussion* (pp. 113–16). London: Student Christian Movement Press.

Saunders, C. M. (1976). The challenge of terminal care. In T. Symington & R. L. Carter (Eds.), *Scientific foundations of oncology* (pp. 673–79). London: William Heinemann.

Saunders, C. M. (Ed.). (1990). *Hospice and palliative care: An interdisciplinary approach.* London: Edward Arnold.

Saunders, C. M. (1995). In Britain: Fewer conflicts of conscience. *Hastings Center Report, 25*(3), 41–42.

Saunders, C. M., Baines, M., & Dunlop, R. (1995). *Living with dying: A guide to palliative care* (3rd ed.). New York: Oxford University Press.

Saunders, C. M., & Kastenbaum, R. (1997). *Hospice care on the international scene.* New York: Springer.

Saunders, C. M., & Sykes, N. (Eds.). (1993). *The management of terminal malignant disease* (3rd ed.). London: Edward Arnold.

Schaefer, D., & Lyons, C. (1993). *How do we tell the children? A step-by-step guide for helping children two to teen cope when someone dies* (2nd ed.). New York: Newmarket.

Schatz, W. H. (1986). Grief of fathers. In T. A. Rando (Ed.), *Parental loss of a child* (pp. 293–302). Champaign, IL: Research Press.

Scheper-Hughes, N. (1992). *Death without weeping: The violence of everyday life in Brazil.* Berkeley: University of California Press.

Schiff, H. S. (1977). *The bereaved parent.* New York: Crown.

Schiff, H. S. (1986). *Living through mourning: Finding comfort and hope when a loved one has died.* New York: Viking Penguin.

Schilder, P., & Wechsler, D. (1934). The attitudes of children toward death. *Journal of Genetic Psychology, 45,* 406–51.

Schneider, J. M. (1980). Clinically significant differences between grief, pathological grief, and depression. *Patient Counseling and Health Education, 2,* 161–69.

Schultz, N. W., & Huet, L. M. (2000). Sensational! Violent! Popular! Death in American movies. *Omega, 42,* 137–49.

Schulz, R. (1976). Effect of control and predictability on the physical and psychological well-being of the institutionalized aged. *Journal of Personality and Social Psychology, 33,* 563–73.

Schulz, R., & Aderman, D. (1974). Clinical research and the stages of dying. *Omega, 5,* 137–44.

Schwab, R. (1990). Paternal and maternal coping with the death of a child. *Death Studies, 14,* 407–22.

Schwartz, C. L., Hobbie, W. L., Constine, L. S., & Ruccione, K. S. (Eds.). (1994). *Survivors of childhood cancer: Assessment and management.* St. Louis: C. V. Mosby.

Schwartz, M. (1999). *Morrie: In his own words.* New York: Walker & Co. (Originally published in 1996 by the same publisher as *Letting go: Morrie's reflections on living while dying.*)

Schwiebert, P. & DeKlyen, C. (1999). *Tear soup: A recipe for healing after loss.* Portland, OR: Grief Watch.

Schwiebert, P., & Kirk, P. (1986). *Still to be born: A guide for bereaved parents who are making decisions about the future.* Portland, OR: Perinatal Loss.

Scott, S. (2000). Grief reactions to the death of a divorced spouse revisited. *Omega, 41,* 207–19.

Seale, C. (1998). *Constructing death: The sociology of dying and bereavement.* Cambridge: Cambridge University Press.

Seiden, R. H. (1977). Suicide prevention: A public health/public policy approach. *Omega, 8,* 267–76.

Seligson, M. R., & Peterson, K. E. (Eds.). (1992). *AIDS prevention and treatment: Hope, humor, and healing.* Washington, DC: Hemisphere.

Selkin, J. (1983). The legacy of Emile Durkheim. *Suicide and Life-Threatening Behavior, 13,* 3–14.

Seltzer, F. (1994, April/June). Trend in mortality from violent deaths: Suicide and homicide, United States, 1960–1991. *Statistical Bulletin,* pp. 10–18.

Selwyn, P. A. (1998). *Surviving the fall: The personal journey of an AIDS doctor.* New Haven: Yale University Press.

Selye, H. (1978a, October). On the real benefits of eustress. *Psychology Today,* pp. 60–61, 63–64, 69–70.

Selye, H. (1978b). *The stress of life* (rev. ed.). New York: McGraw-Hill.

Seneca, L. A. (1932). *Seneca's letters to Lucilius* (2 vols.). Trans. E. P. Barker. Oxford: Clarendon Press.

Shakoor, B., & Chalmers, D. (1991). Co-victimization of African-American children who witness violence and the theoretical implications of its effect on their cognitive, emotional, and behavioral development. *Journal of the National Medical Association, 83,* 233–38.

Shapiro, E. R. (1994). *Grief as a family process: A developmental approach to clinical practice.* New York: Guilford.

Shaw, E. (1994). *What to do when a loved one dies: A practical and compassionate guide to dealing with death on life's terms.* Irvine, CA: Dickens Press.

Shephard, D. A. E. (1977). Principles and practice of palliative care. *Canadian Medical Association Journal, 116,* 522–26.

Sherman, D. W. (2001). Patients with Acquired Immune Deficiency Syndrome. In B. R. Ferrell & N. Coyle (Eds.), *Textbook of palliative nursing* (pp. 467–500). New York: Oxford University Press.

Shield, R. R. (1988). *Uneasy endings: Daily life in an American nursing home.* Ithaca, NY: Cornell University Press.

Shilts, R. (1987). *And the band played on: Politics, people, and the AIDS epidemic.* New York: St. Martin's Press.

Shine, T. M. (2000). *Fathers aren't supposed to die: Five brothers reunite to say good-bye.* New York: Simon & Schuster.

Shirley, V., & Mercier, J. (1983). Bereavement of older persons: Death of a pet. *The Gerontologist, 23,* 276.

Shneidman, E. S. (1971). Prevention, intervention, and postvention of suicide. *Annals of Internal Medicine, 75,* 453–58.

Shneidman, E. S. (1973a). *Deaths of man.* New York: Quadrangle.

Shneidman, E. S. (1973b). Suicide. *Encyclopedia Britannica* (14th ed.; vol. 21, pp. 383–85). Chicago: William Benton.

Shneidman, E. S. (1978). Some aspects of psychotherapy with dying persons. In C. A. Garfield (Ed.), *Psychosocial care of the dying patient* (pp. 201–18). New York: McGraw-Hill.

Shneidman, E. S. (1980/1995). *Voices of death.* New York: Harper & Row/Kodansha International.

Shneidman, E. S. (1981). *Suicide thoughts and reflections, 1960–1980.* New York: Human Sciences Press.

Shneidman, E. S. (1983). Reflections on contemporary death. In C. A. Corr, J. M. Stillion, & M. C. Ribar (Eds.), *Creativity in death education and counseling* (pp. 27–34). Lakewood, OH: Forum for Death Education and Counseling.

Shneidman, E. S. (1985). *Definition of suicide.* New York: Wiley.

Shneidman, E. S., & Farberow, N. L. (1961). *Some facts about suicide* (PHS Publication No. 852). Washington, DC: U.S. Government Printing Office.

Showalter, J. E. (1983). Foreword. In J. H. Arnold & P. B. Gemma, *A child dies: A portrait of family grief* (pp. ix–x). Rockville, MD: Aspen Systems Corp.

Showalter, S. E. (1997). Walking with grief: The trail of tears in a world of AIDS. *The American Journal of Hospice and Palliative Care, 14*(2), 68–74.

Shrock, N. M. (1835). On the signs that distinguish real from apparent death. *Transylvanian Journal of Medicine, 13,* 210–20.

Shryock, H. S., Siegel, J. S., & Associates. (1980). *The methods and materials of demography* (4th printing, rev.; 2 vols.). Washington, DC: U.S. Government Printing Office, U.S. Bureau of the Census.

Shulman, W. L. (Ed.). (2001). *Association of holocaust organizations: Directory.* Bayside, NY: The Holocaust Resource Center and Archives, Queensborough Community College.

Siegel, K., & Weinstein, L. (1983). Anticipatory grief reconsidered. *Journal of Psychosocial Oncology, 1*, 61–73.

Siegel, M. (Ed.). (1997). *The last word:* The New York Times *book of obituaries and farewells—a celebration of unusual lives.* New York: William Morrow & Co.

Siegel, R. (1982). A family-centered program of neonatal intensive care. *Health and Social Work*, 7, 50–58.

Siegel, R., Rudd, S. H., Cleveland, C., Powers, L. K., & Harmon, R. J. (1985). A hospice approach to neonatal care. In C. A. Corr & D. M. Corr (Eds.), *Hospice approaches to pediatric care* (pp. 127–52). New York: Springer.

Siegel, R. K. (1992). *Fire in the brain.* New York: Dutton.

Siggins, L. (1966). Mourning: A critical survey of the literature. *International Journal of Psychoanalysis, 47*, 14–25.

Silver, R. L., & Wortman, C. B. (1980). Coping with undesirable life events. In J. Garber & M. E. P. Seligman (Eds.), *Human helplessness: Theory and applications* (pp. 279–340). New York: Academic Press.

Silverman, E., Range, L., & Overholser, J. (1994). Bereavement from suicide as compared to other forms of bereavement. *Omega, 30*, 41–51.

Silverman, M. M., & Maris, R. W. (1995). *Suicide prevention: Toward the year 2000.* New York: Guilford.

Silverman, P. R. (1969). The widow-to-widow program: An experiment in preventive intervention. *Mental Hygiene, 53*, 333–37.

Silverman, P. R. (1974). Anticipatory grief from the perspective of widowhood. In B. Schoenberg, A. Carr, A. Kutscher, D. Peretz, & I. Goldberg (Eds.), *Anticipatory grief* (pp. 320–30). New York: Columbia University Press.

Silverman, P. R. (1978). *Mutual help groups: A guide for mental health workers.* Rockville, MD: National Institute of Mental Health.

Silverman, P. R. (1980). *Mutual help groups: Organization and development.* Newbury Park, CA: Sage.

Silverman, P. R. (1986). *Widow to widow.* New York: Springer.

Silverman, P. R. (2000). *Never too young to know: Death in children's lives.* New York: Oxford University Press.

Silverman, P. R., Nickman, S., & Worden, J. W. (1992). Detachment revisited: The child's reconstruction of a dead parent. *American Journal of Orthopsychiatry, 62*, 494–503.

Silverman, P. R., & Worden, J. W. (1992a). Children and parental death. *American Journal of Orthopsychiatry, 62*, 93–104.

Silverman, P. R., & Worden, J. W. (1992b). Children's understanding of funeral ritual. *Omega, 25*, 319–31.

Simeone, W. E. (1991). The Northern Athabaskan potlatch: The objectification of grief. In D. R. Counts & D. A. Counts (Eds.), *Coping with the final tragedy: Cultural variation in dying and grieving* (pp. 157–67). Amityville, NY: Baywood.

Siminoff, L. A., Arnold, R. M., Caplan, A. L., Virnig, B. A., & Seltzer, D. L. (1995). Public policy governing organ and tissue procurement in the United States. *Annals of Internal Medicine, 123*, 10–17.

Simon, C. (2001). *Fatherless women: How we change after we lose our dads.* New York: Wiley.

Simon, N. (1979). *We remember Philip.* Chicago: Whitman.

Simonds, W., & Rothman, B. K. (Eds.). (1992). *Centuries of solace: Expressions of maternal grief in popular literature.* Philadelphia: Temple University Press.

Simpson, M. A. (1976). Brought in dead. *Omega*, 7, 243–48.

Singh, G. K., & Yu, S. M. (1995). Infant mortality in the United States: Trends, differentials, and projections, 1950 through 2010. *American Journal of Public Health, 85*, 957–64.

Singh, G. K., Mathews, T. J., Clarke, S. C., Yannicos, T., & Smith, B. L. (1995). Annual summary of births, marriages, divorces, and deaths: United States, 1994. *Monthly Vital Statistics Report, 43*(13). Hyattsville, MD: National Center for Health Statistics.

Sklar, F., & Hartley, S. F. (1990). Close friends as survivors: Bereavement patterns in a "hidden" population. *Omega, 21*, 103–12.

Slaby, A. (1992). Creativity, depression, and suicide. *Suicide and Life-Threatening Behavior, 22*, 157–66.

Sloane, D. C. (1991). *The last great necessity: Cemeteries in American history.* Baltimore: Johns Hopkins University Press.

Smilansky, S. (1987). *On death: Helping children understand and cope.* New York: Peter Lang.

Smith, A. A. (1974). *Rachel.* Wilton, CT: Morehouse-Barlow.

Smith, D. H. (1986). *Health and medicine in the Anglican tradition: Conscience, community, and compromise*. New York: Crossroad.

Smith, D. W. E. (1995). Why do we live so long? *Omega, 31,* 143–50.

Smith, H. I. (1994). *On grieving the death of a father.* Minneapolis: Augsburg.

Smith, H. I. (1996). *Grieving the death of a friend.* Minneapolis: Augsburg.

Smith, H. I. (1999). *A decembered grief: Living with loss when others are celebrating.* Kansas City: Beacon Hill Press.

Smith, H. I., & Jeffers, S. L. (2001). *ABCs of healthy grieving: Light for a dark journey.* Shawnee Mission, KS: Shawnee Mission Medical Center Foundation.

Smith, I. (1991). Preschool children "play" out their grief. *Death Studies, 15,* 169–76.

Smith, I. (2000). *A tiny boat at sea.* Portland, OR: Author (3254 SE Salmon, Portland, OR 97214).

Smolin, A., & Guinan, J. (1993). *Healing after the suicide of a loved one.* New York: Simon & Schuster.

Society for the Right to Die. (1991). Refusal of treatment legislation: A state by state compilation of enacted and model statutes. New York: Author.

Solomon, K. (1982). Social antecedents of learned helplessness in the health care setting. *The Gerontologist, 22,* 282–87.

Sontag, S. (1978). *Illness as metaphor.* New York: Farrar, Straus & Giroux.

Sontag, S. (1989). *AIDS and its metaphors.* New York: Farrar, Straus & Giroux.

Sorlie, P. D., Backlund, E., & Keller, J. B. (1995). U.S. mortality by economic, demographic, and social characteristics: The National Longitudinal Mortality Study. *American Journal of Public Health, 85,* 949–56.

Soto, A. R., & Villa, J. (1990). Una platica: Mexican-American approaches to death and dying. In J. K. Parry (Ed.), *Social work practice with the terminally ill: A transcultural perspective* (pp. 113–27). Springfield, IL: Charles C Thomas.

Sourkes, B. M. (1995). *Armfuls of time: The psychological experience of the child with a life-threatening illness.* Pittsburgh: University of Pittsburgh Press.

Souter, S. J., & Moore, T. E. (1989). A bereavement support program for survivors of cancer deaths: A description and evaluation. *Omega, 20,* 31–43.

Speece, M. W., & Brent, S. B. (1984). Children's understanding of death: A review of three components of a death concept. *Child Development, 55,* 1671–86.

Speece, M. W., & Brent, S. B. (1996). The development of children's understanding of death. In C. A. Corr & D. M. Corr (Eds.), *Handbook of childhood death and bereavement* (pp. 29–50). New York: Springer.

Spiegel, D. (1993). *Living beyond limits: New hope and help for facing life-threatening illness.* London: Vermilion.

Spiegelman, V., & Kastenbaum, R. (1990). Pet Rest Cemetery: Is eternity running out of time? *Omega, 21,* 1–13.

Spinetta, J. J., & Deasy-Spinetta, P. (1981). *Living with childhood cancer.* St. Louis: C. V. Mosby.

Spinetta, J. J., & Maloney, L. J. (1975). Death anxiety in the out-patient leukemic child. *Pediatrics, 56,* 1034–37.

Spinetta, J. J., Rigler, D., & Karon, M. (1973). Anxiety in the dying child. *Pediatrics, 52,* 841–49.

Sprang, G., & McNeil, J. (1995). *The many faces of bereavement: The nature and treatment of natural, traumatic, and stigmatized grief.* New York: Bruner/Mazel.

Stahlman, S. D. (1996). Children and the death of a sibling. In C. A. Corr & D. M. Corr (Eds.), *Handbook of childhood death and bereavement* (pp. 149–64). New York: Springer.

Stambrook, M., & Parker, K. C. (1987). The development of the concept of death in childhood: A review of the literature. *Merrill Palmer Quarterly, 33,* 133–57.

Stannard, D. E. (Ed.). (1975). *Death in America.* Philadelphia: University of Pennsylvania Press.

Stannard, D. E. (1977). *The Puritan way of death: A study in religion, culture, and social change.* New York: Oxford University Press.

Staples, B. (1994). *Parallel time: Growing up in black and white.* New York: Pantheon.

Starr, P. (1982). *The social transformation of American medicine.* New York: Basic Books.

Staton, J., Shuy, R., & Byock, I. (2001). *A few months to live: Different paths to life's end.* Washington, DC: Georgetown University Press.

Staudacher, C. (1991). *Men and grief.* Oakland, CA: New Harbinger Publications.

Stearns, A. K. (1985). *Living through personal crisis.* New York: Ballantine.
Stearns, A. K. (1988). *Coming back: Rebuilding lives after crisis and loss.* New York: Random House.
Stedeford, A. (1978). Understanding confusional states. *British Journal of Hospital Medicine, 20,* 694–704.
Stedeford, A. (1979). Psychotherapy of the dying patient. *British Journal of Psychiatry, 135,* 7–14.
Stedeford, A. (1984). *Facing death: Patients, families and professionals.* London: William Heinemann.
Steinbach, U. (1992). Social networks, institutionalization, and mortality among elderly people in the United States. *Journal of Gerontology, 47,* S183–S190.
Stevens, M. M. (1993). Family adjustment and support. In D. Doyle, G. W. C. Hanks, & N. MacDonald (Eds.), *Oxford textbook of palliative medicine* (pp. 707–17). New York: Oxford University Press.
Stevens, M. M. (1998). Psychological adaptation of the dying child. In D. Doyle, G. W. C. Hanks, & N. MacDonald (Eds.), *Oxford textbook of palliative medicine* (2nd ed.; pp. 1046–55). New York: Oxford University Press.
Stevens, M. M., & Dunsmore, J. C. (1996a). Adolescents who are living with a life-threatening illness. In C. A. Corr & D. E. Balk (Eds.), *Handbook of adolescent death and bereavement* (pp. 107–35). New York: Springer.
Stevens, M. M., & Dunsmore, J. C. (1996b). Helping adolescents who are coping with a life-threatening illness, along with their siblings, parents, and peers. In C. A. Corr & D. E. Balk (Eds.), *Handbook of adolescent death and bereavement* (pp. 329–53). New York: Springer.
Stevens, R. (1989). *In sickness and in wealth: American hospitals in the twentieth century.* New York: Basic Books.
Stevenson, A. (1989). *Bitter fame: A life of Sylvia Plath.* Boston: Houghton Mifflin.
Stevenson, I., Cook, E. W., & McClean-Rice, N. (1989). Are persons reporting "near-death experiences" really near death? A study of medical records. *Omega, 20,* 45–54.
Stevenson, R. G. (Ed.). (2001). *What will we do? Preparing a school community to cope with crises* (2nd ed.). Amityville, NY: Baywood.
Stevenson, R. G., & Stevenson, E. P. (1996a). Adolescents and education about death, dying, and bereavement. In C. A. Corr & D. E. Balk (Eds.), *Handbook of adolescent death and bereavement* (pp. 235–49). New York: Springer.
Stevenson, R. G., & Stevenson, E. P. (Eds.). (1996b). *Teaching students about death: A comprehensive resource for educators and parents.* Philadelphia: The Charles Press.
Stewart, M. F. (1999). *Companion animal death: A practical and comprehensive guide for veterinary practice.* Woburn, MA: Butterworth-Heinemann Medical.
Stillion, J. M. (1985). *Death and the sexes: An examination of differential longevity, attitudes, behaviors, and coping skills.* Washington, DC: Hemisphere.
Stillion, J. M., & McDowell, E. E. (1996). *Suicide across the life span: Premature exits* (2nd ed.). Washington, DC: Taylor & Francis.
Stillion, J. M., McDowell, E. E., & May, J. (1989). *Suicide across the life span: Premature exits.* Washington, DC: Hemisphere.
Stinson, R., & Stinson, P. (1983). *The long dying of Baby Andrew.* Boston: Little, Brown.
Stoddard, S. (1992). *The hospice movement: A better way of caring for the dying* (rev. ed.). New York: Vintage.
Stokes, J., & Crossley, D. (1995). Camp Winston: A residential intervention for bereaved children. In S. C. Smith & M. Penells (Eds.), *Interventions with bereaved children* (pp. 172–92). London: Jessica Kingsley Publications.
Stolberg, S. G. (2001, April 7). After two centuries, Washington is losing its only public hospital. *The New York Times,* pp. A1, A13.
Storey, P. (1996). *Primer of palliative care* (2nd ed.). Glenview, IL: American Academy of Hospice and Palliative Medicine.
Strasburger, V. C. (1993). Children, adolescents, and the media: Five crucial issues. *Adolescent Medicine: State of the Art Review, 4,* 479–93.
Strickland, A. L., & DeSpelder, L. A. (1995). Communicating about death and dying. In I. B. Corless, B. B. Germino, & M. A. Pittman (Eds.), *A challenge for living: Dying, death, and bereavement* (pp. 37–51). Boston: Jones and Bartlett.
Stroebe, M. (1992). Coping with bereavement: A review of the grief work hypothesis. *Omega, 26,* 19–42.
Stroebe, M. S., Hansson, R. O., Stroebe, W., & Schut, H. (Eds.). (2001). *Handbook of bereavement research: Consequences, coping, and care.*

Washington, DC: American Psychological Association Press.

Stroebe, M., & Schut, H. (1999). The dual process model of coping with bereavement: Rationale and description. *Death Studies, 23*, 197–224.

Stroebe, M., van den Bout, J., & Schut, H. (1994). Myths and misconceptions about bereavement: The opening of a debate. *Omega, 29*, 187–203.

Stroebe, W., & Stroebe, M. S. (1987). *Bereavement and health: The psychological and physical consequences of partner loss.* Cambridge: Cambridge University Press.

Sudnow, D. (1967). *Passing on: The social organization of dying.* Englewood Cliffs, NJ: Prentice-Hall.

Sugar, M. (1968). Normal adolescent mourning. *American Journal of Psychotherapy, 22*, 258–69.

Sullivan, A. D., Hedberg, K., & Fleming, D. W. (2000). Legalized physician-assisted suicide in Oregon—The second year. *New England Journal of Medicine, 342*, 598–604.

Sullivan, A. D., Hedberg, K., & Hopkins, S. (2001). Legalized physician-assisted suicide in Oregon, 1998-2000. *New England Journal of Medicine, 344*, 605.

Sullivan, L. (1991). Violence as a public health issue. *Journal of the American Medical Association, 265*, 2778.

Sullivan, M. A. (1995). May the circle be unbroken: The African-American experience of death, dying, and spirituality. In J. K. Parry & A. S. Ryan (Eds.), *A cross-cultural look at death, dying, and religion* (pp. 160–71). Chicago: Nelson-Hall.

Sumner, L. H. (2001). Pediatric care: The hospice perspective. In B. R. Ferrell & N. Coyle (Eds.), *Textbook of palliative nursing* (pp. 556–69). New York: Oxford University Press.

The SUPPORT Principal Investigators. (1995). A controlled trial to improve care for seriously ill hospitalized patients: The Study to Understand Prognoses and Preferences for Outcomes and Risks of Treatments (SUPPORT). *Journal of the American Medical Association, 274*, 1591–98.

Supportive Care of the Dying: A Coalition for Compassionate Care. (1997). *Living and healing during life-threatening illness: Executive summary.* Portland, OR: Author.

Swenson, W. M. (1961). Attitudes toward death in an aged population. *Journal of Gerontology, 16*, 49–52.

Tagliaferre, L., & Harbaugh, G. L. (1990). *Recovery from loss: A personalized guide to the grieving process.* Deerfield Beach, FL: Health Communications.

Tanner, J. G. (1995). Death, dying, and grief in the Chinese-American culture. In J. K. Parry & A. S. Ryan (Eds.), *A cross-cultural look at death, dying, and religion* (pp. 183–92). Chicago: Nelson-Hall.

Tatelbaum, J. (1980). *The courage to grieve.* New York: Lippincott & Crowell.

Tedeschi, R. G. (1996). Support groups for bereaved adolescents. In C. A. Corr & D. E. Balk (Eds.), *Handbook of adolescent death and bereavement* (pp. 293–311). New York: Springer.

Templer, D. (1970). The construction and validation of a death anxiety scale. *Journal of General Psychology, 82*, 165–77.

Templer, D. (1971). Death anxiety as related to depression and health of retired persons. *Journal of Gerontology, 26*, 521–23.

Terkel, S. (2001). *Will the circle be unbroken?; Reflections on death, rebirth, and hunger for a faith.* New York: New Press.

Terl, A. H. (1992). *AIDS and the law: A basic guide for the nonlawyer.* Washington, DC: Taylor & Francis.

Thomasma, D. C., Kimbrough-Kushner, T., Kimsma, G. K., & Ciesielski-Carlucci, C. (1998). *Asking to die: Inside the Dutch debate about euthanasia.* Boston: Kluwer Academic Publishers.

Thompson, B. (1990). Amyotrophic lateral sclerosis: Integrating care for patients and their families. *American Journal of Hospice and Palliative Care, 7*(3), 27–32.

Thompson, J. W., & Walker, R. D. (1990). Adolescent suicide among American Indians and Alaska natives. *Psychiatric Annals, 20*, 128–33.

Thorson, J. A. (1995). *Aging in a changing society.* Belmont, CA: Wadsworth.

Thorson, J. A. (2000a). *Aging in a changing society.* Philadelphia: Brunner/Mazel.

Thorson, J. A. (Ed.). (2000b). *Perspectives on spiritual well-being and aging.* Springfield, IL: Charles C Thomas.

Thorson, J. A., Powell, F. C., & Samuel, V. T. (1998). African- and Euro-American samples differ little in scores on death anxiety. *Psychological Reports, 83*, 623–26.

Thurman, H. (1953). *Meditations of the heart.* New York: Harper & Row.

Tibbetts, E. (2000). Learning to value every moment. *Innovations in end-of-life care, 2*(4), www.edc.org/lastacts.

Tobin, D. (1999). *Peaceful dying: The step-by-step guide to preserving your dignity, your choice, and your inner peace at the end of life.* Cambridge, MA: Perseus.

Tolstoy, L. (1960). *The death of Ivan Ilych and other stories.* Trans. A. Maude. New York: New American Library. (Original work published 1884.)

Tomer, A., & Eliason, G. (1996). Toward a comprehensive model of death anxiety. *Death Studies, 20,* 343–66.

Tong, K. L., & Spicer, B. J. (1994). The Chinese palliative patient and family in North America: A cultural perspective. *Journal of Palliative Care, 10*(1), 26–28.

Toray, T., & Oltjenbruns, K. A. (1996). Children's friendships and the death of a friend. In C. A. Corr & D. M. Corr (Eds.), *Handbook of childhood death and bereavement* (pp. 165–78). New York: Springer.

Toynbee, A. (1968a). The relation between life and death, living and dying. In A. Toynbee, A. K. Mant, N. Smart, J. Hinton, S. Yudkin, E. Rhode, R. Heywood, & H. H. Price, *Man's concern with death* (pp. 259–71). New York: McGraw-Hill.

Toynbee, A. (1968b). Traditional attitudes towards death. In A. Toynbee, A. K. Mant, N. Smart, J. Hinton, S. Yudkin, E. Rhode, R. Heywood, & H. H. Price, *Man's concern with death* (pp. 59–94). New York: McGraw-Hill.

Toynbee, A., Koestler, A., & others. (1976). *Life after death.* New York: McGraw-Hill.

Toynbee, A., Mant, A. K., Smart, N., Hinton, J., Yudkin, S., Rhode, E., Heywood, R., & Price, H. H. (1968). *Man's concern with death.* New York: McGraw-Hill.

Trozzi, M., & Massimini, K. (1999). *Talking with children about loss: Words, strategies, and wisdom to help children cope with death, divorce, and other difficult times.* New York: Penguin Putnam.

Tucker, J. B. (2001). *Scourge: The once and future threat of smallpox.* New York: Atlantic Monthly Press.

Turner, R. E., & Edgley, C. (1976). Death as theatre: A dramaturgical analysis of the American funeral. *Sociology and Social Research, 60,* 377–92.

Twomey, J. (2001, May 19). Youth crime: It's not what you think. *St. Petersburg Times,* p. 14A.

Twycross, R. G. (1976). Long-term use of diamorphine in advanced cancer. In J. J. Bonica & D. Albe-Fessard (Eds.), *Advances in pain research and therapy,* vol. 1 (pp. 653–61). New York: Raven Press.

Twycross, R. G. (1979a). The Brompton cocktail. In J. J. Bonica & V. Ventafridda (Eds.), *International symposium on pain of advanced cancer: Advances in pain research and therapy,* vol. 2 (pp. 291–300). New York: Raven Press.

Twycross, R. G. (1979b). Overview of analgesia. In J. J. Bonica & V. Ventafridda (Eds.), *International symposium on pain of advanced cancer: Advances in pain research and therapy,* vol. 2 (pp. 617–33). New York: Raven Press.

Twycross, R. G. (1982). Principles and practice of pain relief in terminal cancer. *Cancer Forum, 6,* 23–33.

Twycross, R. G. (1994). *Pain relief in advanced cancer.* New York: Churchill Livingstone.

Twycross, R. G. (1995a). *Introducing palliative care.* New York: Radcliffe Medical Press.

Twycross, R. G. (1995b). *Symptom management in advanced cancer.* New York: Radcliffe Medical Press.

Twycross, R. G., & Lack, S. A. (1989). *Oral morphine in advanced cancer* (2nd ed.). Beaconsfield, England: Beaconsfield.

U.S. Bureau of the Census. (1975). *Historical statistics of the United States, colonial times to 1970, bicentennial edition* (2 parts). Washington, DC: U.S. Government Printing Office.

U.S. Bureau of the Census. (1998). *Statistical abstract of the United States, 1998* (118th ed.). Washington, DC: U.S. Government Printing Office.

U.S. Bureau of the Census. (2000). *Statistical abstract of the United States, 2000* (120th ed.). Washington, DC: U.S. Government Printing Office.

U.S. Bureau of the Census. (2001). *Statistical abstract of the United States, 2001* (121st ed.). Washington, DC: U.S. Government Printing Office.

U.S. Congress. (1986). *Indian health care.* Washington, DC: U.S. Government Printing Office.

U. S. Department of Health and Human Services, Health Care Financing Administration. (1998). Medicare and Medicaid programs; hospital conditions of participation; identification of potential organ, tissue, and eye donors and transplant hospitals' provision of transplant-related data. *Federal Register, 63*, 33856–74.

U.S. Department of Health and Human Services, Health Resources and Services Administration and Health Care Financing Administration, (2000). *Roles and training in the donation process: A resource guide.* Rockville, MD: Authors.

Uhlenberg, P. (1980). Death and the family. *Journal of Family History, 5*, 313–20.

UNAIDS. (2001a). AIDS epidemic update: December 2000.

UNAIDS. (2001b). AIDS epidemic update: December 2001.

UNAIDS. (2001c). HIV/AIDS: Global crisis—global action.

UNAIDS. (2001d). UNAIDS fact sheet: An overview of HIV/AIDS-related stigma and discrimination.

Ungvarski, P. (1997). Adherence to prescribed HIV-1 protease inhibitors in the home setting. *Journal of the Association of Nurses in AIDS Care, 8*(Supplement), 37–45.

United Network for Organ Sharing. (2001). www.unos.org.

United Network for Organ Sharing. (2002). www.unos.org.

Until We Say Goodbye. [Film]. (1980). Washington, DC: WJLA-TV.

Urofsky, M. I. (1993). *Letting go: Death, dying and the law.* New York: Charles Scribner's Sons.

Vachon, M. L. S. (1979). Staff stress in care of the terminally ill. *QRB/Quality Review Bulletin, 6*, 13–17.

Vachon, M. L. S. (1987). *Occupational stress in the care of the critically ill, the dying, and the bereaved.* Washington, DC: Hemisphere.

Valente, S. M., & Saunders, J. M. (1987). High school suicide prevention programs. *Pediatric Nursing, 13*(2), 108–112, 137.

Valente, S. M., & Sellers, J. R. (1986). Helping adolescent survivors of suicide. In C. A. Corr & J. N. McNeil (Eds.), *Adolescence and death* (pp. 167–82). New York: Springer.

Valentine, L. (1996). Professional interventions to assist adolescents who are coping with death and bereavement. In C. A. Corr & D. E. Balk (Eds.), *Handbook of adolescent death and bereavement* (pp. 312–28). New York: Springer.

Van der Maas, P. J., Van der Wal, G., Haverkate, I., de Graaff, C. L. M., Kester, J. G. C., Onwuteaka-Philipsen, B. D., van der Heide, A., Bosma, J. M., & Willems, D. L. (1996). Euthanasia, physician-assisted suicide, and other medical practices involving the end of life in the Netherlands, 1990–1995. *New England Journal of Medicine, 335*, 1699–1705.

Van der Wal, G., Van der Maas, P. J., Bosma, J. M., Onwuteaka-Philipsen, B. D., Willems, D. L., Haverkate, I., & Kostense, P. J. (1996). Evaluation of the notification procedure for physician-assisted death in the Netherlands. *New England Journal of Medicine, 335*, 1706–11.

Van der Zee, J., Dodson, O., & Billops, C. (1978). *The Harlem book of the dead.* Dobbs Ferry, NY: Morgan & Morgan.

Van Dongen, C. J. (1990). Agonizing questioning: Experiences of survivors of suicide victims. *Nursing Research, 39*, 224–29.

Van Dongen, C. J. (1991). Experiences of family members after a suicide. *Journal of Family Practice, 33*, 375–80.

Van Gennep, A. (1961). *The rites of passage.* Trans. M. B. Vizedom & G. L. Caffee. Chicago: University of Chicago Press.

Van Winkle, N. W., & May, P. A. (1986). Native American suicide in New Mexico, 1957–1979: A comparative study. *Human Organization, 45*, 296–309.

Veatch, R. M. (1975). The whole-brain-oriented concept of death: An outmoded philosophical formulation. *Journal of Thanatology, 3*(1), 13–30.

Veatch, R. M. (1976). *Death, dying, and the biological revolution: Our last quest for responsibility.* New Haven, CT: Yale University Press.

Veninga, R. (1985). *A gift of hope: How we survive our tragedies.* New York: Ballantine Books.

Ventura, S. J., Peters, K. D., Martin, J. A., & Maurer, J. D. (1997). Births and deaths: United States, 1996. *Monthly Vital Statistics Report, 46*(1), Supplement 2. Hyattsville, MD: National Center for Health Statistics.

Vernick, J., & Karon, M. (1965). Who's afraid of death on a leukemia ward? *American Journal of Diseases of Children, 109*, 393–97.

Verwoerdt, A. (1976). *Clinical geropsychiatry.* Baltimore: Williams & Wilkins.

Verwoerdt, A., Pfeiffer, E., & Wang, H. S. (1969). Sexual behavior in senescence. *Geriatrics, 24*, 137–54.

Vickers, J. L., & Carlise, C. (2000). Choices and control: Parental experiences in pediatric terminal home care. *Journal of Pediatric Oncology Nursing, 17,* 12–21.

Viorst, J. (1986). *Necessary losses.* New York: Simon & Schuster.

Volberding, P. A., & Aberg, J. A. (Eds.). (1999). *The San Francisco General Hospital handbook of HIV management: A guide to the practical management of HIV-infected patients.* Boca Raton, FL: CRC Press-Parthenon Publications.

Volkan, V. (1970). Typical findings in pathological grief. *Psychiatric Quarterly, 44,* 231–50.

Volkan, V. (1985). Complicated mourning. *Annual of Psychoanalysis, 12,* 323–48.

Waechter, E. H. (1971). Children's awareness of fatal illness. *American Journal of Nursing, 71,* 1168–72.

Waechter, E. H. (1984). Dying children: Patterns of coping. In H. Wass & C. A. Corr (Eds.), *Childhood and death* (pp. 51–68). Washington, DC: Hemisphere.

Wagner, S. (1994). *The Andrew poems.* Lubbock, TX: Texas Tech University Press.

Wall, P. D., & Melzack, R. (Eds.). (1994). *Textbook of pain* (3rd ed.). New York: Churchill Livingstone.

Wallace, S. E. (1973). *After suicide.* New York: Wiley-Interscience.

Wallis, C. L. (1954). *Stories on stone: A book of American epitaphs.* New York: Oxford University Press.

Walsh, F., & McGoldrick, M. (1988). Loss and the family life cycle. In C. J. Falicov (Ed.), *Family transitions: Continuity and change over the life cycle* (pp. 311–36). New York: Guilford.

Walsh, F., & McGoldrick, M. (1991a). Loss and the family: A systemic perspective. In F. Walsh & M. McGoldrick (Eds.), *Living beyond loss: Death in the family* (pp. 1–29). New York: Norton.

Walsh, F., & McGoldrick, M. (Eds.). (1991b). *Living beyond loss: Death in the family.* New York: Norton.

Walter, T. (1999). *On bereavement: The culture of grief.* Buckingham, UK, & Philadelphia: Open University Press.

Walton, D. N. (1979). *On defining death: An analytic study of the concept of death in philosophy and medical ethics.* Montreal: McGill-Queen's University Press.

Walton, D. N. (1982). Neocortical versus whole-brain conceptions of personal death. *Omega, 12,* 339–44.

Wass, H. (1984). Concepts of death: A developmental perspective. In H. Wass & C. A. Corr (Eds.), *Childhood and death* (pp. 3–24). Washington, DC: Hemisphere.

Wass, H. (2002). Media violence. In R. Kastenbaum (Ed.), *Macmillan encyclopedia of death and dying* (pp. xxx). New York: Macmillan.

Wass, H., & Cason, L. (1984). Fears and anxieties about death. In H. Wass & C. A. Corr (Eds.), *Childhood and death* (pp. 25–45). Washington, DC: Hemisphere.

Wass, H., & Corr, C. A. (Eds.). (1984a). *Childhood and death.* Washington, DC: Hemisphere.

Wass, H., & Corr, C. A. (Eds.). (1984b). *Helping children cope with death: Guidelines and resources* (2nd ed.). Washington, DC: Hemisphere.

Wass, H., Corr, C. A., Pacholski, R. A., & Forfar, C. S. (1985). *Death education II: An annotated resource guide.* Washington, DC: Hemisphere.

Wass, H., Corr, C. A., Pacholski, R. A., & Sanders, C. M. (1980). *Death education: An annotated resource guide.* Washington, DC: Hemisphere.

Wasserman, H., & Danforth, H. E. (1988). *The human bond: Support groups and mutual aid.* New York: Springer.

Waugh, E. (1948). *The loved one.* Boston: Little, Brown.

Webb, J. P., & Willard, W. (1975). Six American Indian patterns of suicide. In N. L. Farberow (Ed.), *Suicide in different cultures* (pp. 17–33). Baltimore: University Park Press.

Webb, M. (1997). *The good death: The new American search to reshape the end of life.* New York: Bantam.

Webb, N. B. (Ed.). (1999). *Play therapy with children in crisis: Individual, group, and family treatment* (2nd ed.). New York: Guilford.

Webb, N. B. (Ed.). (1993). *Helping bereaved children: A handbook for practitioners.* New York: Guilford.

Webster, B. D. (1989). *All of a piece: A life with multiple sclerosis.* Baltimore: Johns Hopkins University Press.

Wechsler, H., Davenport, A., Dowdall, G., Moeykens, B., & Castillo, S. (1994). Health and behavioral consequences of binge drinking in college: A national survey of students at

140 campuses. *Journal of the American Medical Association, 272*, 1672–77.

Weeks, O. D. (2001). Ritualistic downsizing and the need for aftercare. In O. D. Weeks & C. Johnson (Eds.), *When all the friends have gone: A guide for aftercare providers* (pp. 187–97). Amityville, NY: Baywood.

Weeks, O. D., & Johnson, C. (Eds.). (2001). *When all the friends have gone: A guide for aftercare providers.* Amityville, NY: Baywood.

Wehrle, P. F., & Top, F. H. (1981). *Communicable and infectious diseases* (9th ed.). St. Louis: Mosby.

Weinberg, J. (1969). Sexual expression in late life. *American Journal of Psychiatry, 126*, 713–16.

Weiner, I. B. (1985). Clinical contributions to the developmental psychology of adolescence. *Genetic, Social, and General Psychology Monographs, 111*(2), 195–203.

Weir, R. F. (Ed.). (1980). *Death in literature.* New York: Columbia University Press.

Weir, R. F. (Ed.). (1997). *Physician-assisted suicide.* Bloomington & Indianapolis: Indiana University Press.

Weisman, A. D. (1972). *On dying and denying: A psychiatric study of terminality.* New York: Behavioral Publications.

Weisman, A. D. (1977). The psychiatrist and the inexorable. In H. Feifel (Ed.), *New meanings of death* (pp. 107–22). New York: McGraw-Hill.

Weisman, A. D. (1984). *The coping capacity: On the nature of being mortal.* New York: Human Sciences Press.

Weisman, M-L. (1982). *Intensive care: A family love story.* New York: Random House.

Weizman, S. G., & Kamm, P. (1985). *About mourning: Support and guidance for the bereaved.* New York: Human Sciences Press.

Welch, K. J., & Bergen, M. B. (2000). Adolescent parent mourning reactions associated with stillbirth or neonatal death. *Omega, 40*, 435–51.

Weller, E. B., Weller, R. A., Fristad, M. A., Cain, S. E., & Bowes, J. M. (1988). Should children attend their parent's funeral? *Journal of the American Academy of Child and Adolescent Psychiatry, 27*, 559–62.

Wender, P., Ketu, S., Rosenthal, D., Schulsinger, F., Ortmann, J., & Lunde, I. (1986). Psychiatric disorders in the biological and adoptive families of adopted individuals with affective disorders. *Archives of General Psychiatry, 43*, 923–29.

Wendler, D., & Dickert, N. (2001). The consent process for cadaveric organ procurement: How does it work? How can it be improved? *Journal of the American Medical Association, 285*, 329–33.

Wentworth, H., & Flexner, S. B. (Eds.). (1967). *Dictionary of American slang* (with supplement). New York: Crowell.

Wertenbaker, L. T. (1957). *Death of a man.* New York: Random House.

Werth, J. L. (1999a). The role of the mental health professional in helping significant others of persons who are assisted in death. *Death Studies, 23*, 239–55.

Werth, J. L. (Ed.). (1999b). *Contemporary perspectives on rational suicide.* Philadelphia: Taylor & Francis.

Werth, J. L. (2001). Using the Youk-Kevorkian case to teach about euthanasia and other end-of-life issues. *Death Studies, 25*, 151–77.

Weseen, M. H. (1934). *A dictionary of American slang.* New York: Crowell.

Westberg, G. (1971). *Good grief.* Philadelphia: Fortress Press.

Westerhoff, J. H. (1978). *McGuffey and his readers: Piety, morality, and education in nineteenth-century America.* Nashville: Abingdon.

Westphal, M. (1984). *God, guilt, and death.* Bloomington, IN: Indiana University Press.

Wheeler, I. (2001). Parental bereavement: The crisis of meaning. *Death Studies, 25*, 51–66.

Wheeler, M. S., & Cheung, A. H. S. (1996). Minority attitudes toward organ donation. *Critical Care Nurse, 16*, 30–35.

White, E. B. (1952). *Charlotte's web.* New York: Harper.

White, R. B., & Engelhardt, H. T. (1975). A demand to die. *Hastings Center Report, 5*(3), 9–10, 47.

Whitfield, J. M., Siegel, R. E., Glicken, A. D., Harmon, R. J., Powers, L. K., & Goldson, E. J. (1982). The application of hospice concepts to neonatal care. *American Journal of Diseases of Children, 136*, 421–24.

Whitney, S. (1991). *Waving goodbye: An activities manual for children in grief.* Portland, OR: The Dougy Center.

Wiener, L. S., Best, A., & Pizzo, P. A. (Comps.). (1994). *Be a friend: Children who live with HIV speak.* Morton Grove, IL: Albert Whitman.

Wiesel, E. (1960). *Night.* Trans. S. Rodway. New York: Avon.

Wilcoxon, S. A. (1986). Grandparents and grandchildren: An often neglected relationship between significant others. *Journal of Counseling and Development, 65,* 289–90.

Wilder, T. (1986). *The bridge of San Luis Rey.* New York: Harper & Row. (Original work published 1927.)

Wilhelm, H. (1985). *I'll always love you.* New York: Crown.

Wilkes, E., Crowther, A. G. O., & Greaves, C. W. K. H. (1978). A different kind of day hospital—For patients with preterminal cancer and chronic disease. *British Medical Journal, 2,* 1053–56.

Wilkes, E., et al. (1980). *Report of the working group on terminal care of the standing subcommittee on cancer.* London: Her Majesty's Stationary Office.

Willans, J. H. (1980). Nutrition: Appetite in the terminally ill patient. *Nursing Times, 76,* 875–76.

Williams, P. G. (1989). *Life from death: The organ and tissue donation and transplantation source book, with forms.* Oak Park, IL: P. Gaines Co.

Williams, P. G. (1991). *The living will and the durable power of attorney for health care book, with forms* (rev. ed.). Oak Park, IL: P. Gaines Co.

Willinger, M. (1995). Sleep position and sudden infant death syndrome [Editorial]. *Journal of the American Medical Association, 273,* 818–19.

Willinger, M., James, L. S., & Catz, D. (1991). Defining the sudden infant death syndrome (SIDS): Deliberations of an expert panel convened by the National Institute of Child Health and Human Development. *Pediatric Pathology, 11,* 677–84.

Wolfe, J., Grier, H. E., Klar, N., Levin, S. B., Ellenbogen, J. M., Salem-Schatz, E., Emanuel, E. J., & Weeks, J. C. (2000a). Symptoms and suffering at the end of life in children with cancer. *New England Journal of Medicine, 342,* 326–33.

Wolfe, J., Klar, N., Grief, H. E., Duncan, J., Salem-Schatz, S., Emanuel, E. J., & Weeks, J. C. (2000b). Understanding of prognosis among parents of children who died of cancer: Impact on treatment goals and integration of palliative care. *Journal of the American Medical Association, 284,* 2469–75.

Wolfe, T. (1940). *You can't go home again.* New York: Harper & Brothers.

Wolfelt, A. D. (1996). *Healing the bereaved child: Grief gardening, growth through grief and other touchstones for caregivers.* Fort Collins, CO: Companion Press.

Wolfenstein, M. (1966). How is mourning possible? *Psychoanalytic Study of the Child, 21,* 93–123.

Wolfenstein, M., & Kliman, G. (Eds.). (1965). *Children and the death of a president.* Garden City, NY: Doubleday.

Woodson, R. (1976). The concept of hospice care in terminal disease. In J. M. Vaeth (Ed.), *Breast cancer* (pp. 161–79). Basel: Karger.

Woodward, K. (1986). Reminiscence and the life review: Prospects and retrospects. In T. R. Cole & S. A. Gadow (Eds.), *What does it mean to grow old? Reflections from the humanities* (pp. 135–61). Durham, NC: Duke University Press.

Worden, J. W. (1982). *Grief counseling and grief therapy: A handbook for the mental health practitioner.* New York: Springer.

Worden, J. W. (1991). *Grief counseling and grief therapy: A handbook for the mental health practitioner* (2nd ed.). New York: Springer.

Worden, J. W. (1996). *Children and grief: When a parent dies.* New York: Guilford.

Worden, J. W. (2001, April 22). Personal communication.

Worden, J. W. (2002). *Grief counseling and grief therapy: A handbook for the mental health practitioner* (3rd ed.). New York: Springer.

World Health Organization [WHO]. (1990). Cancer pain relief and palliative care. WHO Technical Report Series 804. Geneva, Switzerland: Author.

World Health Organization [WHO]. (1998). *Cancer pain relief and palliative care in children.* Geneva, Switzerland: Author.

Wortman, C. B., & Silver, R. C. (1989). The myth of coping with loss. *Journal of Clinical Consulting Psychology, 57,* 349–57.

Wortman, C. B., & Silver, R. C. (2001). The myths of coping with loss revisited. In M. S. Stroebe, R. O. Hansson, W. Stroebe, & H. Schut (Eds.), *Handbook of bereavement research: Consequences, coping, and care* (pp. 405–29). Washington, DC: American Psychological Association.

Wright, R. H., & Hughes, W. B. (1996). *Lay down body: Living history in African-American cemeteries.* Detroit: Visible Ink Press.

Wrobleski, A. (1984). The suicide survivors grief group. *Omega, 15,* 173–83.

Wyler, J. (1989). Grieving alone: A single mother's loss. *Issues in Comprehensive Pediatric Nursing, 12,* 299–302.

Wyschogrod, E., & Caputo, J. D. (1998). Postmodernism and the desire for God: An E-mail exchange. *Cross Currents, 48*(3), 293–310.

Yalom, I. D. (1995). *The theory and practice of group psychotherapy* (4th ed.). New York: Basic Books.

Yalom, I. D., & Vinogradov, S. (1988). Bereavement groups: Techniques and themes. *International Journal of Group Psychotherapy, 38,* 419–46.

Yeung, W. (1995). Buddhism, death, and dying. In J. K. Parry & A. S. Ryan (Eds.), *A cross-cultural look at death, dying, and religion* (pp. 74–83). Chicago: Nelson-Hall.

Yin, P., & Shine, M. (1985). Misinterpretations of increases in life expectancy in gerontology textbooks. *The Gerontologist, 25,* 78–82.

Yu, E. (1982). The low mortality rates of Chinese infants: Some plausible explanatory factors. *Social Science and Medicine, 16,* 253–65.

Yu, E.S.H. (1986). Health of the Chinese elderly in America. *Research on Aging, 8,* 84–109.

Zalaznik, P. H. (1992). *Dimensions of loss and death education* (3rd ed.). Minneapolis: Edu-Pac.

Zaleski, C. (1987). *Otherworld Journeys: Accounts of near-death experience in medieval and modern times.* New York: Oxford University Press.

Zambelli, G. C., & DeRosa, A. P. (1992). Bereavement support groups for school-age children: Theory, intervention, and case example. *American Journal of Orthopsychiatry, 62,* 484–93.

Zanger, J. (1980, February). Mount Auburn Cemetery: The silent suburb. *Landscape,* pp. 23–28.

Zerwekh, J. V. (1983). The dehydration question. *Nursing 83, 13,* 47–51.

Zerwekh, J. V. (1994). The truth-tellers: How hospice nurses help patients confront death. *American Journal of Nursing, 94,* 31–34.

Zielinski, J. M. (1975). *The Amish: A pioneer heritage.* Des Moines, IA: Wallace-Homestead Book Co.

Zielinski, J. M. (1993). *The Amish across America* (rev. ed.). Kalona, IA: Amish Heritage Publications.

Zinner, E. S. (Ed.). (1985). *Coping with death on campus.* San Francisco: Jossey-Bass.

Zinner, E. S., & Williams, M. B. (1999). *When a community weeps: Case studies in group survivorship.* Philadelphia: Brunner/Mazel.

Zipes, J. (1983). *The trials and tribulations of Little Red Riding Hood: Versions of the tale in sociocultural context.* South Hadley, MA: Bergin & Garvey.

Zisook, S., & DeVaul, R. A. (1983). Grief, unresolved grief, and depression. *Psychosomatics,* 24, 247–56.

Zisook, S., & DeVaul, R. A. (1984). Measuring acute grief. *Psychiatric Medicine, 2,* 169–76.

Zisook, S., & DeVaul, R. A. (1985). Unresolved grief. *American Journal of Psychoanalysis, 45,* 370–79.

Zittoun, R. (1990). Patient information and participation. In J. C. Holland & R. Zittoun (Eds.), *Psychosocial aspects of oncology* (pp. 27–44). Berlin: Springer-Verlag.

Zlatin, D. M. (1995). Life themes: A method to understand terminal illness. *Omega, 31,* 189–206.

Zorza, V., & Zorza, R. (1980). *A way to die.* New York: Knopf.

Zulli, A. P. (2001). The aftercare workers and support group facilitation. In O. D. Weeks & C. Johnson (Eds.), *When all the friends have gone: A guide for aftercare providers* (pp. 199–213). Amityville, NY: Baywood.

NAME INDEX

SUBJECT INDEX

Photo Credits

Chapter 1. 2: The Grief Center of Texas **4:** Copyright © Chastin Brinkley **8:** Kevin A. Corr **11:** © Bryan Lee Curtis Family/*St. Petersburg Times* **12:** © V. Jane Windsor/*St. Petersburg Times* **15:** Hospice of the Florida Suncoast

Chapter 2. 18: © Michael Grecco/Stock Boston **37:** © Michael Weisbrot/Stock Boston **40:** Stefan Verwey

Chapter 3. 44: © AP/Wide World Photos **52:** Dr. Jay Ruby **63:** North Wind Picture Archives

Chapter 4. 66: © AFP/Corbis **68:** Joyce Dopkeen/*The New York Times* **69:** U. S. Postal Service. Reprinted with permission **74:** © Bill Pugliano/Getty Images **79:** © Ira Nowinski/CORBIS **92:** © CORBIS

Chapter 5. 99: © Kathy McCoughlin/The Image Works **104:** Hospice of the Florida Suncoast **107:** © Bob Daemmrich/Stock Boston **112:** © Peter Turnley/CORBIS **115:** © Peter Menzel/Stock Boston **116:** Hospice of the Florida Suncoast **121:** Ting-Li Wang/*The New York Times* **123:** © Museum of History & Industry/CORBIS

Chapter 6. 128: © Spencer Grant **134:** Hospice of the Florida Suncoast **139:** Stefan Verwey **144:** Hospice of the Florida Suncoast **146:** Hospice of the Florida Suncoast

Chapter 7. 152: © Joel Gordon **160:** Hospice of the Florida Suncoast **164:** © Julie Stovall/From the Hip/The Image Works **165:** Hospice of the Florida Suncoast **167:** Hospice of the Florida Suncoast **170:** Hospice of the Florida Suncoast

Chapter 8. 179: United States Postal Service. Reprinted by permission **183:** Stefan Verwey **185:** Hospice of the Florida Suncoast **189:** APIS/Globe Photos **193:** Hospice of the Florida Suncoast **198:** Hospice of the Florida Suncoast **200:** Hospice of the Florida Suncoast

Chapter 9. 206: John Seakwood **209:** Hospice of the Florida Suncoast **211:** Illustration © Taylor Bills. Reprinted with permission of Grief Watch **216:** © Reuters NewMedia Inc./CORBIS **224:** © Jerry Berndt/Stock Boston **233:** Laurent Van der Stockt/Getty Images **238:** Edward Keating/*The New York Times*

Chapter 10. 243: Ron Olshwanger **247:** Illustration © Taylor Bills. Reprinted with permission of Grief Watch **250:** © AFP/CORBIS **254:** © Maggie Steber/Stock Boston **261:** Hospice of the Florida Suncoast **265:** AP/Wide World Photos

Chapter 11. 268: Vincent Laforet/*The New York Times* **271:** © AFP/CORBIS **276:** © Reuters NewMedia Inc./CORBIS **280:** © Reuters NewMedia Inc./CORBIS **282:** © Lee Snyder/The Image Works **284:** Kevin A. Corr **293:** Illustration © Taylor Bills. Reprinted with permission of Grief Watch

Chapter 12. 299: Hospice of the Florida Suncoast **307:** Courtesy of the Center for Attitudinal Healing **317:** Hospice of the Florida Suncoast **321:** Lawrence Shles **331:** Stefan Verwey **334:** Hospice of the Florida Suncoast **335:** Hospice of the Florida Suncoast

Chapter 13. 339: Courtesy of the Ad Council (U. S. Dept. of Transportation) **342:** Lawrence Shles **357:** © Mary Houtchens/Index Stock **362:** © Mark Antman/The Image Works **364:** © Michael Siluk/The Image Works **371:** © Jim Mahoney/The Image Works

Chapter 14. 373: © David H. Wells/CORBIS **386:** © Spencer Grant/Stock Boston **390:** Fred Kinghorn **398:** AP/Wide World Photos

Chapter 15. 401: © Gale Zucker **402:** © AFP/CORBIS **409:** Stefan Verwey **413:** Hospice of the Florida Suncoast

Chapter 16. 424: U. S. Postal Service. Reprinted with permission **447:** Courtesy of NW Organ Procurement **450:** Left and right, courtesy of Barbara Musto

Chapter 17. 457: © Jeremiah Barnard/Index Stock **460:** © CORBIS **461:** © UPI/CORBIS **468:** Jack Pottle 1980/Design Conceptions

Chapter 18. 484: © Fiona Hanson/Topham/The Image Works **489:** AP/Wide World Photos

Chapter 19. 518: North Wind Picture Archives **520:** © David Lees/CORBIS **522:** © Hulton/Deutsch Collection/CORBIS **523:** Remy Benali/Getty Images

Chapter 20. 532: Copyright © Friends-Together, Inc., and the 4th District American Advertising Federation **539:** Photo by Joseph Lennox-Smith **545:** © Ethan Hill **548:** © Glen Korengold/Stock Boston **553:** © Joseph Sohm/ChromoSohm Inc./CORBIS **557:** Stefan Verwey

TO THE OWNER OF THIS BOOK:

I hope that you have found *Death and Dying, Life and Living*, Fourth Edition, useful. So that this book can be improved in a future edition, would you take the time to complete this sheet and return it? Thank you.

School and address: ____

____

____

Department: ____

Instructor's name: ____

1. What I like most about this book is: ____

____

____

2. What I like least about this book is: ____

____

____

3. My general reaction to this book is: ____

____

____

4. The name of the course in which I used this book is: ____

____

5. Were all of the chapters of the book assigned for you to read? ____

   If not, which ones weren't? ____

6. In the space below, or on a separate sheet of paper, please write specific suggestions for improving this book and anything else you'd care to share about your experience in using this book.

____

____

____

OPTIONAL:

Your name:_______________________________ Date:________________

May we quote you, either in promotion for *Death and Dying, Life and Living*, Fourth Edition, or in future publishing ventures?

Yes: _________ No: _________

Sincerely yours,

Charles A. Corr

Clyde M. Nabe

Donna M. Corr

FOLD HERE

NO POSTAGE NECESSARY IF MAILED IN THE UNITED STATES

BUSINESS REPLY MAIL

FIRST CLASS PERMIT NO. 358 PACIFIC GROVE, CA

POSTAGE WILL BE PAID BY ADDRESSEE

ATTN: PSYCHOLOGY EDITOR: VICKI KNIGHT

BROOKS/COLE/THOMSON LEARNING
511 FOREST LODGE ROAD
PACIFIC GROVE, CA 93950-9968

FOLD HERE